German for Reading

German for Reading

Karl C. Sandberg
MACALESTER COLLEGE

John R. Wendel
UNIVERSITY OF ARIZONA

PRENTICE-HALL, INC., Englewood Cliffs, New Jersey

Printed in the United States of America

ISBN: 0-13-354019-7

Library of Congress Catalog Card Number: 72-2556

20 19 18 17 16 15 14 13

Prentice-Hall International, Inc., *London*
Prentice-Hall of Australia Pty. Limited, *Sydney*
Prentice-Hall of Canada, Ltd., *Toronto*
Prentice-Hall of India Private Limited, *New Delhi*
Prentice-Hall of Japan, Inc., *Tokyo*
Prentice-Hall of Southeast Asia Pte. Ltd., *Singapore*
Whitehall Books Limited, *Wellington, New Zealand*

Contents

Chapter One

Chapter Two

Chapter Three

Chapter Four

Chapter Five

Chapter Six

Chapter Seven

Chapter Eight

Chapter Nine

Chapter Ten

Chapter Eleven

Chapter Twelve

Chapter Thirteen

Chapter Fourteen

Chapter Fifteen

Chapter Sixteen

Chapter Seventeen

Chapter Eighteen

Chapter Nineteen

Chapter Twenty

Chapter Twenty-One

Chapter Twenty-Two

Chapter Twenty-Three

Chapter Twenty-Four

Appendices

To the Student

You may find it helpful at the outset to know the biases of the authors. We gladly admit them: language is the most significant and fascinating of human phenomena; for the serious scholar it is useful and necessary to read other languages than his own; for everyone it is interesting and enlightening to see how another culture expresses its perception of reality through its language; everyone can learn language; everyone who can learn his own language can learn a new language; the principles and techniques of programmed learning can significantly increase the efficiency and decrease the frustrations of language study.

We have also assumed that your study time is valuable and that if you have been introduced to this text it is because sometime you seriously wanted to learn to read German. We have therefore made use of new approaches and developments in programmed learning in order to provide you with the most systematic and direct means possible of doing so. We have likewise assumed that the students using this type of text are of mature interests, and we have consequently included passages that will introduce you directly though briefly to some of the thinkers, scholars, authors and political leaders who have given German culture its diversity and impact.

German for Reading presupposes no previous acquaintance with German and can be used with equal effectiveness by graduate students in the arts and sciences who are preparing to pass a reading knowledge examination, or by undergraduates who are beginning to deal seriously with the problems of reading. It may be used before, simultaneously with, or after an aural-oral introduction to German. Its programmed format permits it to be used either as a classroom text or by individuals working on their own. In an audio-lingual course it can be used as a complement to the audio-lingual text; in a course oriented principally toward reading, it can be used as the primary text, with the course moving at a proportionately more rapid rate.

What you may expect to get out of the course

When you finish *German for Reading* you should be able to recognize the meanings signaled by all the basic grammatical patterns of German, plus the meanings of about twelve hundred content words. You will also have developed numerous techniques of reading in a foreign language which will enable you to learn new vocabulary and derive meanings from context without depending totally on a dictionary. With some additional work to build vocabulary in special fields, you will be able to start using German as an academic tool in research or in course work in some field. You should be able, for example, to read a German newspaper or journal with fair to good comprehension or to begin the serious study of German literary texts.

What you should expect to put into the course

The above results are predictable on the basis of classroom testing and depend on your fulfilling the following conditions:

1. That you spend the 80–120 hours of study time that it has taken other students to complete the course
2. That you study and review *consistently*.
3. That you familiarize yourself with the theoretical base of the book and follow the instructions.

Format of the text

One of the basic assumptions of *German for Reading* is that among the 10,000–20,000 words that one must be able to recognize in order to read German easily (estimates differ), the first priority in order of presentation should go to the function words (those that do not have a meaning in and of themselves, e.g. **wo,** *where* or **denn,** *for*) and grammatical signals (e.g. verb endings) as opposed to the content words (the words that do express a meaning by themselves, e.g. **vergessen,** *to forget* or **Pferd,** *horse*). It is the function words and grammar structures of the language which provide the framework of context. Accordingly, this text is so organized as to make a systematic presentation of the patterns and function words of German while helping you to develop reading skills and to build a basic recognition vocabulary of content words.

Each chapter is thus composed of several sets of grammar explanations with accompanying exercises and a short reading passage. As you do these exercises, you will find that they introduce the vocabulary and structures of the reading passage while also reviewing pertinent material from previous chapters. Each exercise calls for some kind of response from you and is programmed through the left-hand column to provide you with an immediate verification of the accuracy of your response. At the end of each chapter is a progress test which enables you to determine for yourself how well you have learned the material.

The advantages of this format are numerous—you spend all of your time in active reading instead of in the mechanical process of thumbing to the end vocabulary; you are not dependent on the classroom or professor in order to establish meaning; you can thus proceed as rapidly as you want to or as slowly as you need to; and at the same time you are learning to read eminent German writers in their own words almost at the outset.

How to use the text

1. Begin each section by reading the explanations of the grammar. If the terminology used is unfamiliar to you, consult the definitions of grammatical terms in the appendices.
2. Proceed then to do the exercises following each section. They ask for

some kind of response from you, such as supplying the missing words, choosing the correct alternative, or simply stating the meaning of the German sentence. *Cover the left hand verification column with a card until you have made the response asked for.*

3. After you have made an active response to the German sentence, slide your card down on the left-hand column and verify your answer. When the instructions ask you to translate the German to English, remember that there are often several ways of translating to achieve the same meaning. Your version does not need to coincide exactly with the version in the text so long as the general meaning is the same.

   The success or failure of your efforts depends to a large extent on how well you follow this procedure. If you do not make a real effort to read the German before looking at the English, you will probably not be able to read the German passage at the end of the section.
4. Each time you meet a word that you do not recognize immediately, underline it. After you learn its meaning put a circle around it (but *do not* write the English equivalent between the lines). After you have finished the set of exercises, review the circled words, and associate them with their context.
5. Then take the progress test and see which points you need to review. Learn each block of material thoroughly before going on.
6. Study in short blocks of time. If you were to allot two hours a day to the study of German, it would be better to divide them into four periods of thirty minutes each than to spend the two hours consecutively.
7. *Review frequently!* Before each new chapter, spend five minutes or so reviewing the words you have circled in the previous chapter.

ACKNOWLEDGMENTS

The authors are indebted to many colleagues and students for advice and helpful criticism in the preparation of this text. Special thanks are due to Professor Richard Clark of Macalester College for help in conducting a testing program of a preliminary version, to Professor Otto Sorenson of Macalester for a critical reading of the manuscript, to Mrs. Barbara Heather of the University of Arizona for much help and valued assistance in the preparation of the manuscript, and to students at Macalester and the University of Arizona who generously shared their responses and offered suggestions for the revision of the preliminary text.

K.S.
J.W.

German for Reading

Chapter One

1. *Cognates—definition*
2. *Nouns—recognition, gender, and cognate patterns*
3. *Nouns—formation of the plural forms*
4. *Compound nouns*
5. *Cognates—partially similar meanings*
6. *False Cognates*

1. *Cognates—definition*

1. The task of learning German vocabulary is simplified by *true cognates*, i.e., words which have similar spellings and identical or similar meanings. From common Germanic roots come cognates such as **Sommer** and *summer*, **Wolf** and *wolf*. From other common roots come cognates such as **Echo** and *echo*, **Sphäre** and *sphere*.

2. The task is sometimes hindered by *partial cognates* (words which look alike but have both similar and divergent meanings) and *false cognates* (words with similar spellings but no related meanings).

Partial cognates:

Existenz = *existence* but also *subsistence*
Fleisch = *flesh* but also *meat* or *pulp*

False cognates:

Rock = *coat, skirt*
Kind = *child*

3. A logical first step in learning to read German is to learn how to recognize the true cognates and to become aware of the partial or false cognates.

2. *Nouns—recognition, gender, and cognate patterns*

1. All nouns in German are capitalized:

Der Mann trinkt ein Glas Bier. *The man drinks a glass of beer.*

2. German nouns, unlike English nouns, are one of three genders: masculine, feminine, or neuter. Masculine nouns are often preceded by a form of **der** (*the*) or **ein** (*a* or *an*), feminine nouns by a form of **die** or **eine,** and neuter nouns by a form of **das** or **ein.** (The case of these articles will be explained in chapter 4.)

3. A knowledge of the following consonant relationships which exist between German and English will help you to recognize or remember German-English cognates more readily:

GERMAN		ENGLISH
f,ff (medial or final)	usually corresponds to	*p*
ein Schiff		*a ship*
die Hilfe		*the help*
pf (initial, medial, or final)	usually corresponds to	*p,pp*
der Pfeffer		*the pepper*
ein Apfel		*an apple*
der Trumpf		*the trump*
b (medial or final)	usually corresponds to	*v* or *f*
das Silber		*the silver*
d	usually corresponds to	*th*
die Erde		*the earth*
ein Bruder		*a brother*
ch	usually corresponds to	*k*
die Milch		*the milk*
der Mönch		*the monk*
cht	usually corresponds to	*ght*
die Macht		*the might*
ein Licht		*a light*
g	usually corresponds to	*y* or *i*
der Weg		*the way*
eine Magd		*a maid*
k	usually corresponds to	*ch* or *c*
der Käse		*the cheese*

GERMAN		**ENGLISH**
die Klasse		*the class*
s, ss, ß (medial or final)	usually corresponds to	*t*
eine Straße		*a street*
das Wasser		*the water*
das Los		*the lot (fate)*
tz, z	usually corresponds to	*t*
eine Katze		*a cat*
das Salz		*the salt*
t	usually corresponds to	*d*
das Wort		*the word*
der Traum		*the dream*

What are the English cognates of the following German words?

	1. ein A**ff**e
1. an ape	**2.** der **Pf**e**ff**er
2. the pepper	**3.** ein **Pf**und
3. a pound	**4.** die **Pf**laume
4. the plum	**5.** ein Tro**pf**en
5. a drop	**6.** der **D**ie**b**
6. the thief	**7.** die Le**b**er
7. the liver	**8.** eine Ö**ff**nung
8. an opening	**9.** die **Pf**ei**f**e
9. the pipe	**10.** ein **D**ing
10. a thing	**11.** eine Fe**d**er
11. a feather	**12.** der Schmie**d**
12. the smith	**13.** die Mil**ch**
13. the milk	**14.** der Stor**ch**
14. the stork	**15.** ein Ku**ch**en

15. a cake	**16.** die Leu**cht**e
16. the light	**17.** die Na**cht**
17. the night	**18.** das Re**cht**
18. the right	**19.** das Le**d**er
19. leather	**20.** eine **T**o**ch**ter
20. a daughter	**21.** der **Pf**enni**g**
21. the penny	**32.** ein Au**g**e
22. an eye	**23.** der Na**g**el
23. the nail	**24.** eine **K**irche
24. a church	**25.** das **K**inn
25. the chin	**26.** ein **K**amerad
26. a comrade	**27.** der Schwei**ß**
27. the sweat	**28.** der Re**g**en
28. the rain	**29.** eine **K**ammer
29. a chamber	**30.** die Hi**tz**e
30. the heat	**31.** das **Z**inn
31. tin	**32.** das Her**z**
32. the heart	**33.** der **T**a**g**
33. the day	**34.** das Blu**t**
34. the blood	**35.** ein Ne**tz**
35. a net	**36.** die **Z**unge
36. the tongue	**37.** eine **T**ür
37. a door	

PROGRESS TEST

Give the English cognate of the following German words.

	1. eine Pfeife
1. a pipe	**2.** die Leber
2. the liver	**3.** das Ding
3. the thing	**4.** ein Kuchen
4. a cake	**5.** die Nacht
5. the night	**6.** ein Auge
6. an eye	**7.** ein Kamerad
7. a comrade	**8.** das Kinn
8. the chin	**9.** die Hitze
9. the heat	**10.** das Herz
10. the heart	**11.** der Tag
11. the day	

When you can recognize all the above consonant shifts, go on to the next section.

3. *Nouns—formation of the plural forms*

1. English usually signals the plural by means of a final *-s* (table, table*s*), a vowel change (m*a*n, m*e*n), or by a quantity word + *-s* or a vowel change (*some* chair*s*, *some* men). German usually signals the plural of nouns by the use of the definite article **die** (or a quantity word) plus

(a) the noun endings **-e, -er, -n, -en:**

der Arm	*the arm*	**die Arm*e***	*the arms*
das Kind	*the child*	**die Kind*er***	*the children*
der Staat	*the state*	**die Staat*en***	*the states*
die Frau	*the woman*	**die Frau*en***	*the women*
der Bauer	*the farmer*	**die Bauer*n***	*the farmers*

(b) an umlaut added to a medial vowel:

der Vater	*the father*	**die V*ä*ter**	*the fathers*
die Tochter	*the daughter*	**die T*ö*chter**	*the daughters*

(c) the noun endings and an umlaut:

die Hand	*the hand*	**die H*ä*nd*e***	*the hands*
der Fuß	*the foot*	**die F*ü*ß*e***	*the feet*
der Mann	*the man*	**die M*ä*nn*er***	*the men*
das Buch	*the book*	**die B*ü*ch*er***	*the books*

Notice that you must look for a *combination* of **die** (or various plural markers to be discussed later, e.g. **diese,** *these*) and one of the above:

das Mädchen	*the girl*	***die* Mädchen**	*the girls*
die Mutter	*the mother*	**die M*ü*tter**	*the mothers*

Since **Mädchen** carries an umlaut in the singular, the only way to tell the plural is by the addition of **die. Mutter,** being feminine, takes **die** as the definite article in both the singular and the plural, and the plural is therefore recognized only by the addition of the umlaut.

2. There are a few words ending in **-el** or **-en** that add neither an ending nor an umlaut. The plural of these words is signaled only by the definite article **die:**

der Onkel	*the uncle*	***die* Onkel**	*the uncles*
der Wagen	*the car*	***die* Wagen**	*the cars*

3. A few nouns taken from foreign languages form their plural by adding **-s:**

das Auto	**die Auto*s***
das Restaurant	**die Restaurant*s***

4. The ending **-(e)s** is usually the sign of the gentive (possessive) case of masculine and neuter nouns in the singular, which will be explained later.

Which of the following is the plural form? What distinguishes it from the singular?

	1. der Garten die Gärten
1. *die Gärten:* the umlaut and *die* (gardens)	**2.** die Töchter die Tochter
2. *die Töchter:* the umlaut (daughters)	**3.** der Finger die Finger
3. *die Finger: die* (fingers)	**4.** die Maus die Mäuse
4. *die Mäuse: -e* and umlaut (mice)	**5.** der Arm die Arme
5. *die Arme: -e* and *die* (arms)	**6.** der Fuß die Füße
6. *die Füße: -e*, umlaut and *die* (feet)	**7.** die Haare das Haar
7. *die Haare: -e* and *die* (hair)	**8.** das Buch die Bücher
8. *die Bücher: -er*, umlaut and *die* (books)	**9.** die Männer der Mann
9. *die Männer: -er*, umlaut and *die* (men)	**10.** die Felder das Feld
10. *die Felder: -er* and *die* (fields)	**11.** der Onkel die Onkel
11. *die Onkel: die* (uncles)	**12.** das Haus die Häuser
12. *die Häuser: -er*, umlaut and *die* (houses)	**13.** die Lippe die Lippen
13. *die Lippen: -n* (lips)	**14.** die Klassen die Klasse
14. *die Klassen: -n* (classes)	**15.** die Familien die Familie

15. *die Familien: -n* (families)	**16.** die Türen die Tür
16. *die Türen: -en* (doors)	**17.** die Radios das Radio
17. *die Radios: -s* and *die* (radios)	**18.** das Café die Cafés
18. *die Cafés: -s* and *die* (cafés)	**19.** die Minute die Minuten
19. *die Minuten: -n* (minutes)	**20.** der Satellit die Satelliten
20. *die Satelliten: -en* and *die* (satellites)	**21.** die Nacht die Nächte
21. *die Nächte: -e* and umlaut (nights)	**22.** die Schulen die Schule
22. *die Schulen: -n* (schools)	**23.** die Sofas das Sofa
23. *die Sofas: -s* and *die* (sofas)	**24.** das Licht die Lichter
24. *die Lichter: -er* and *die* (lights)	**25.** die Sonne die Sonnen
25. *die Sonnen: -n* (suns)	

PROGRESS TEST

Which of the following forms is the plural?

	1. die Töchter die Tochter
1. die Töchter	**2.** die Onkel der Onkel

2. die Onkel	**3.** die Füße der Fuß
3. die Füße	**4.** das Buch die Bücher
4. die Bücher	**5.** die Lippen die Lippe
5. die Lippen	**6.** die Studenten der Student
6. die Studenten	**7.** das Hotel die Hotels
7. die Hotels	

When you can recognize the plural forms of the above nouns, go on to the next section.

4. *Compound nouns*

1. Characteristic of German is the coining of new words from simpler German words:

krank (*sick*) + **das Haus** (*house*) = **das Krankenhaus** (*hospital*)
die Hand (*hand*) + **der Schuh** (*shoe*) = **der Handschuh** (*glove*)
das Wasser (*water*) + **der Stoff** (*stuff*) = **der Wasserstoff** (*hydrogen*)
das Volk (*people*) + **der Wagen** (*car*) = **der Volkswagen**

There is often a connective (**-(e)s-** or **-(e)n-**) between the two elements.

2. The gender of the noun is determined by the last component.

3. Plurals of compound nouns are formed from the last component:

das Krankenhaus	*the hospital*
die Krankenhäuser	*the hospitals*
die Wasserstoffbombe	*the hydrogen bomb*
die Wasserstoffbomben	*the hydrogen bombs*

Guess the meanings of the following compound nouns.

	1. der Zahn = *tooth* **der Arzt** = *doctor* **der Zahnarzt** = ________
1. dentist	**2. das Jahr** = *year* **die Zeit** = *time* **die Jahreszeit** = ________
2. season	**3. der Flug** = *flight* **der Hafen** = *harbor, port* **der Flughafen** = ________
3. airport	**4. das Schwein** = *pig, swine* **das Fleisch** = *meat* **das Schweinefleisch** = ________
4. pork	**5. die Bürger** = *townspeople, citizens* **der Meister** = *master* **der Bürgermeister** = ________
5. mayor	**6. sich rasieren** = *to shave* **der Apparat** = *apparatus* **der Rasierapparat** = ________
6. razor	**7. das Leben** = *life* **das Mittel** = *means* **das Geschäft** = *business, shop* **das Lebensmittelgeschäft** = ________
7. grocery store	**8. unter** = *under* **der Grund** = *ground* **die Bahn** = *railroad, railway* **die Untergrundbahn** = ________
8. subway	**9. das Leder** = *leather* **die Ware** = *goods* **die Produktion** = *production* **die Lederwarenproduktion** = ________
9. production of leather goods	**10. die Sonne** = *sun* **das System** = *system* **das Sonnensystem** = ________

10. solar system	**11.** **das Silber** = *silver* **der Berg** = *mountain* **das Werk** = *work(s)* **das Silberbergwerk** = ________
11. silver mine	**12.** **der Friede** = *peace* **der Hof** = *yard, court* **der Friedhof** = ________
12. cemetery	

5. *Cognates—partially similar meanings*

1. A German cognate may have meanings additional to its English counterpart:

die Seite	*side*	but also	*page* (of a book)
die Macht	*might*		*authority*
der Hund	*hound*		*dog*

2. The meanings of partial cognates must be determined from the context or from a dictionary:

	1. **Der Vater sitzt mit der kleinen Tochter auf der Bank.** = *The father is sitting on the* ________ *with his small daughter.* The German **Bank** suggests the English *bank* which normally would not make sense in this context. In German the letter **k** may often be equivalent to the English *ch*. The word is ________.
1. bench	**2.** **Es gibt Eis zum Nachtisch.** = *There is* ________ *for dessert.* The reference to dessert suggests that **Eis** would not be translated by *ice* but by ________.

2. ice cream	**3. Darf man den Brief mit einer Feder schreiben?** = *May one write the letter with a ________?* Here the context suggests that the translation of **Feder** is not *feather* but ________.
3. pen	

6. *False Cognates*

1. Many false cognates exist between German and English. Since the meaning will not always be discernible from the context, you will have to establish the meaning by means of a dictionary:

das Tier	*the animal* (not *deer*)
der Tisch	*the table* (not *dish*)
das Gift	*the poison* (not *gift*)

What is the English meaning of the italicized words?

	1. Der Mensch ist ein *Tier*. Man is an ________.
1. animal	**2.** Nimm die Ellbogen vom *Tisch*! Take your elbows off the ________!
2. table	**3.** Der Löwe ist der König der *Tiere*. The lion is the king of ________.
3. beasts	**4.** Arsen ist ein gefährliches *Gift*. Arsenic is a dangerous ________.
4. poison	**5.** Er sitzt am *Tisch* und liest die Zeitung. He is sitting at the ________ and reading the paper.
5. table	**6.** *Gift* ist kein schönes Geschenk. ________ is not a nice gift.
6. Poison	

Chapter Two

7. *Verbs—cognates*

1. All German verbs in their infinitive form end in **-en** or sometimes simply **-n:**

beginn*en*	*to begin*
wander*n*	*to wander, to hike, to walk*

There are many cognate verbs in German and English which will facilitate your learning to read.

2. Remember that infinitives may also be used as nouns simply by capitalizing the verb. The gender will always be neuter. To translate an infinitive used as a noun into English add *-ing* to the English infinitive:

beginnen	*to begin*
das Beginnen	*the beginning*
trinken	*to drink*
das Trinken	*the drinking*

Cover the left hand column with your card. Give the meaning of the German words. Move your card down to verify your rendering.

	1. bringen
1. to bring	**2.** denken
2. to think	**3.** finden

3. to find	**4.** hindern
4. to hinder	**5.** sinken
5. to sink	**6.** das Sinken
6. the sinking	**7.** schlummern
7. to slumber	**8.** kommen
8. to come	**9.** das Kommen
9. the coming	**10.** das Marschieren
10. (the) marching	**11.** marschieren
11. to march	

8. *Verbs—partial and false cognates*

1. Some partial German-English cognates are as follows:

liegen	*to lie, to be situated*
lernen	*to learn, to study*
sagen	*to say, to tell*
scheinen	*to shine, to seem, to appear*
tun	*to do, to make, to put*

2. False cognates, such as the following, need to be memorized:

bilden	*to form, to educate*
bekommen	*to receive*
handeln	*to act, to trade, to bargain*
mangeln	*to lack, to be wanting*

The following exercises prepare you to read the passage at the end of the chapter on the geography of Germany.

	1. In the verb **schieben,** you might expect the **b** to become ________ in English.
1. v: to shove (to push)	**2.** den Mann schieben

2. to push the man	**3.** **die Grenzen** = *the borders* die Grenzen verschieben
3. to shift the borders	**4.** **mehrfach** = *repeatedly* die Grenzen mehrfach verschieben
4. to shift the borders repeatedly	**5.** In the verb **suchen** you might expect the **ch** to become ________.
5. k: to seek, to look for, to try	**6.** **versuchen** = *to try, to attempt* Sie versuchen, Land zu gewinnen.
6. They try to obtain land.	**7.** **größten** = *largest* den größten Staat bilden
7. to form the largest state	**8.** spielen eine Rolle (In English one would say to ________ a role.)
8. to play	**9.** **zusammen** = *together* eine Rolle zusammen spielen
9. to play a role together	

PROGRESS TEST

Choose the answer which expresses the meaning of the italicized German word.

1. *versuchen,* Land zu gewinnen
(a) to forsake (b) to forgive (c) to seek
2. den größten Staat *bilden*
(a) to educate (b) to form (c) to construct
3. die Grenzen *verschieben*
(a) to forsake (b) to shovel (c) to shift

Answer key: **1.** (c); **2.** (b); **3.** (c).

9. *Present tense verb endings; personal pronouns*

1. The stem for the present tense is found by dropping the final **-en** or **-n** of the infinitive:

sing*en*: sing-; **wander*n*: wander-.**

2. The present tense of most German verbs is recognized by one of the following endings attached to the stem:

ich sing*e*	*I am singing, I sing, I do sing*
du sing*st*	*you are singing, you sing, you do sing*
er (sie, es) sing*t*	*he (she, it) is singing, sings, does sing*
wir sing*en*	*we are singing, we sing, we do sing*
ihr sing*t*	*you are singing, you sing, you do sing*
sie sing*en*	*they are singing, they sing, they do sing*
Sie sing*en*	*you are singing, you sing, you do sing*

Note that one German form expresses all three forms of the English present. There are no progressive (*I am singing*) or emphatic (*I do sing*) forms in German.

3. **Sie** capitalized can only be translated *you*, unless it begins a sentence. To differentiate between **sie** (*she*) and **sie** (*they*) you must look to the verb ending. To differentiate between **Sie** (*you*), **sie** (*they*), and **sie** (*she*) at the beginning of a sentence, you must look at the verb ending or the context in which **Sie** is used.

4. **Du** and **ihr** are used when addressing family, close friends, children, animals, and Deity. For polite and formal relationships **Sie** is used.

Notice that **er** and **sie** may refer either to persons or to things.

5. The conjugations of **sein** (*to be*), **haben** (*to have*) and **werden** (*to get, to become; will*) are irregular:

	sein		**haben**		**werden**	
ich	**bin**	*I am*	**habe**	*have*	**werde**	*become*
du	**bist**	*you are*	**hast**	*have*	**wirst**	*become*
er (sie, es)	**ist**	*he (she, it) is*	**hat**	*has*	**wird**	*becomes*
wir	**sind**	*we are*	**haben**	*have*	**werden**	*become*
ihr	**seid**	*you are*	**habt**	*have*	**werdet**	*become*
sie	**sind**	*they are*	**haben**	*have*	**werden**	*become*
Sie	**sind**	*you are*	**haben**	*have*	**werden**	*become*

Werden itself means *will* or *shall* only when combined with the infinitive to form the future. This point will be taken up later.

Select the correct answer. Be sure to cover the left hand column with a card. Circle any words that you do not immediately recognize.

	1. **er** singt (*he/they*)
1. he	2. **sie** singt (*she/they*)
2. she—the verb ending tells you that **sie** is 3rd person singular	3. Singen **Sie?** (*they/you*)
3. you—the capitalized **S** tells you	4. **ich** singe (*I/you*)
4. I	5. **ihr** singt (*you/we*)
5. you	6. **es** singt (*it/we*)
6. it	7. **du** singst (*you/he*)
7. you	8. **sie** singen (*she/they*)
8. they—the verb ending tells you that **sie** is 3rd person plural	9. **wir** singen (*we/it*)
9. we	

Which pronoun goes with the following verbs?

	10. ______findet **(ich/er)**
10. er	11. ______findet **(sie/du)**
11. sie	12. ______finden **(Sie/ihr)**
12. Sie	13. ______findet **(ihr/ich)**
13. ihr	14. ______finde **(ich/sie)**
14. ich	15. ______findet **(sie/wir)**
15. sie	16. ______finden **(ich/sie)**
16. sie	17. ______findet **(du/es)**
17. es	18. ______findest **(du/sie)**
18. du	19. ______finden **(er/wir)**

19. wir	

Now select the best translation according to the context.

	20. **schon** = *already* Das Wasser kocht schon. (**kocht** = *boils/is boiling*)
20. is boiling	**21.** Sie geht schon nach Hause. (**geht** = *goes/is going*)
21. is going	**22.** **heute** = *today* **wieder** = *again* Heute fliegt sie wieder nach Italien. (**fliegt** = *is flying/flies*)
22. is flying	**23.** **auch** = *too, also* Lernt er auch Deutsch? (**lernt** = *learns/is learning*)
23. is learning	**24.** **oft** = *often* Wir gehen oft ins Theater. (**gehen** = *go/are going*)
24. go	**25.** **nur** = *only* Paul tanzt nur mit Margarete. (**tanzt** = *dances/is dancing*)
25. dances	**26.** **wo** = *where* Wo wohnen Sie? (**wohnen** = *live/do . . . live*)
26. Where do you live?	**27.** **die Zeit** = *time* Hat er nur heute Zeit zu studieren? (**hat** = *have/does . . . have*)
27. Does he only have time to study today?	

Select the correct pronoun to go with the verb.

	28. _____bin (**ich**/**er**)
28. ich	**29.** _____werdet (**er**/**ihr**)

29. ihr	**30.** ______habt **(sie/ihr)**
30. ihr	**31.** ______wirst **(du/sie)**
31. du	**32.** ______ist **(ich/es)**
32. es	**33.** ______hat **(sie/ich)**
33. sie	**34.** ______seid **(ihr/er)**
34. ihr	**35.** ______werden **(sie/du)**
35. sie	

Select the correct translation.

	36. **Ich bin** hier. (*I am/you are*)
36. *I am* here.	**37.** **Wir haben** einen Hund. (*we have/they have*)
37. *We have* a dog.	**38.** **Ihr seid** dumm! (*she is/you are*)
38. *You are* stupid!	**39.** **Er hat** Hunger. (*you have/he has*)
39. *He is* hungry. (literally: *He has* hunger.)	**40.** **Ihr werdet** älter. (*I am getting/you are getting*)
40. *You are getting* older.	**41.** **Es wird** kalt. (*it is getting/they are getting*)
41. *It is getting* cold.	**42.** **Sie sind** in dem Hause. (*they are/she is*)
42. *They are* in the house.	

PROGRESS TEST

Choose either the appropriate pronoun or the correct form of the verb.

1. ______ findet
(a) du (b) Sie (c) wir (d) ihr

2. ________ lernst
(a) du (b) er (c) ich (d) ihr

3. ich ________
(a) kocht (b) koche (c) kochen (d) kochst

4. er ________
(a) werdet (b) werden (c) wird (d) wirst

5. ihr ________
(a) sind (b) sein (c) bin (d) seid

Answer key: **1.** (d); **2.** (a); **3.** (b); **4.** (c); **5.** (d).

Now read the following phrases and vocabulary drawn from the reading passage.

	43. **liegen** = *to lie, be located* Deutschland **liegt** in Europa.
43. Germany *is located* in Europe.	**44.** **wohnen** = *to live* Die Deutschen **wohnen** in Deutschland.
44. The Germans *live* in Germany.	**45.** **dieser, diese, dieses** = *this* Dieses Land, in dem die Deutschen wohnen, ist . . . (**in dem** here probably means—*in which/from which*)
45. This land *in which* the Germans live is . . .	**46.** **zwischen** = *between* Der Rio Grande ist die Grenze zwischen den USA und Mexiko. (**Grenze** = ________)
46. border, boundary	**47.** Deutschland hat **keine** natürlichen Grenzen. (**keine** = *some/no*)
47. Germany has *no* natural borders.	**48.** **fast** = *almost* Deutschland hat **fast** keine natürlichen Grenzen.
48. Germany has *almost* no natural borders. (The context tells us that the German word **fast** is not the equivalent to our English *fast*.)	**49.** **verschieden** = *different* Verschiedene Länder grenzen an Deutschland. (**grenzen an** probably means ________)
49. to border on	**50.** Deutschland ist von verschiedenen Ländern begrenzt. (**begrenzt** probably means ________)

50. bounded, or equivalent	**51.** Deutschland liegt zwischen Holland und Polen, zwischen Dänemark und der Schweiz.
51. Germany lies between Holland and Poland, between Denmark and Switzerland.	**52.** Deutschland liegt nicht in Amerika. (**Nicht** probably means—*definitely/not*)
52. Germany is not in America.	**53.** **verstehen** = *to understand* Verstehen wir Deutschland als ein Land? (**als** probably means—*as/than*)
53. Do we understand Germany *as* a country?	**54.** **schwer** = *difficult, heavy* Ist es schwer, dieses Land zu verstehen? (**schwer** in this sentence means ______)
54. Is it difficult to understand this country?	**55.** Warum verstehen wir die europäischen Länder nicht? (**Warum** is a question word which probably means—*where/why*)
55. *Why* don't we understand the European countries?	**56.** **stehen** = *to stand, to be* Deutschland steht fast inmitten aller europäischen Länder. (**inmitten** probably means—*in the middle of/outside of*)
56. Germany is almost *in the middle of* all European countries.	**57.** Warum steht Deutschland inmitten aller großen Konflikte? (This question presupposes that Germany has been in a large number of major wars: *true/false*)
57. True—Why is Germany in the midst of all big conflicts?	**58.** **Geschichte** = *history, story* Die Geschichte Deutschlands ist interessant. (**Deutschlands** means ________)
58. The history *of Germany* is interesting.	**59.** A **Volkswagen** is a car for all ________.
59. people	**60.** **Völker,** the plural of **Volk,** means ________.
60. peoples, nations	**61.** Alle Völker Europas spielen eine Rolle in der Geschichte dieses Landes. (a) **Europas** means ________. (b) **dieses Landes** means ________.

61. (a) of Europe (b) of this country	**62. viele** = *many* Viele verschiedene Nationen spielen eine Rolle in der Geschichte dieses Landes.
62. Many different nations play a role in the history of this country.	**63. wollen** = *to want* Wir wollen die Deutschen als ein Volk verstehen. (**wollen verstehen** means ________)
63. We *want to understand* the Germans as a people.	**64. das Land** = *country* **die Karte** = *map, chart, card* **die Landkarte** = ________
64. map	**65. anschauen** = *to look at* Wir wollen eine Landkarte anschauen.
65. We want to look at a map.	**66. wenn** = *when, if* Wenn wir Deutschland verstehen wollen . . . (**wenn** means here—*if/when*)
66. *If* we want to understand Germany . . .	**67. müssen** = *must, to have to* . . . müssen wir nicht nur Geschichte lernen . . .
67. . . . we must not only learn history . . .	**68. sondern** = *but (rather)* **auch** = *also* . . . sondern auch eine Landkarte anschauen.
68. . . . but also look at a map.	**69.** Rom ist eine Stadt in Italien. (**Stadt** means—*city/building*)
69. Rome is a *city* in Italy.	**70.** Römer wohnen in der Stadt Rom. (**Römer** means ________)
70. *Romans* live in the city of Rome.	**71. seit** = *since* **Seit der Römerzeit** probably means—*Since the Romans came/Since the time of the Romans*
71. Since the time of the Romans	**72. Durchgang** = *thoroughfare* (literally "*through passage*") Deutschland ist **ein Durchgangsland.**

72. Germany is *a country through which others travel* (or equivalent).	**73.** Seit der Römerzeit ist Deutschland ein Durchgangsland.
73. Since the time of the Romans Germany has been a land through which others travel.	**74.** **geteilt** = *divided* Deutschland ist ein geteiltes Land.
74. Germany is a divided country.	**75.** **der Teil** = *part* Die Bundesrepublik ist ein Teil des heutigen Deutschlands. (**Des heutigen** means — *of yesterday's/of today's/of tomorrow's*)
75. The Federal Republic is a part *of today's* Germany.	**76.** Adenauer war Kanzler der Bundesrepublik. (**Die Bundesrepublik** is also known as—**Westdeutschland/Ostdeutschland**)
76. **Westdeutschland** Adenauer was Chancellor of the Federal Republic.	**77.** **heißen** = *to be called* Der andere Teil Deutschlands heißt die Deutsche Demokratische Republik. (**Andere** probably means — *other/and*)
77. The *other* part of Germany *is called* the German Democratic Republic.	**78.** Seit 1945 ist Deutschland ein geteiltes Land.
78. Since 1945 Germany has been a divided country.	**79.** Die Bundesrepublik und die DDR, **d.h.** die Deutsche Demokratische Republik, bilden . . . (**d.h.** is equivalent to ________)
79. The Federal Republic and the GDR, *that is* (*i.e.*) the German Democratic Republic, form . . .	**80.** **größte** = *largest* Zusammen bilden die Bundesrepublik und die DDR die größte Nation Europas, außer Rußland natürlich.
80. Together the Federal Republic and the GDR form the largest nation of Europe, except for Russia naturally.	**81.** **vereinigt** = *united* Deutschland ist nicht vereinigt **wie** die Vereinigten Staaten. (**Wie** means — *how/as*)
81. Germany is not united *as* (is) the United States.	**82.** **wiedervereinigen** = *to reunite* Die **Wiedervereinigung** Deutschlands ist ein großes Problem.

82. The *reunification* of Germany is a big problem.	**83.** **größer** = *more serious, greater* Das Problem wird größer.
83. The problem is becoming more serious (greater).	**84.** **die Frage** = *the question* **ganz** = *all, entire* Die **Wiedervereinigungsfrage** steht hinter der ganzen Politik Europas.
84. The *question of reunification* lies behind all European politics.	**85.** Die **Außenpolitik** der Bundesrepublik . . . (If **Innenpolitik** means *domestic policy,* **Außenpolitik** probably means ______.)
85. The *foreign policy* of the Federal Republic . . .	**86.** Das **Wiedervereinigungsproblem** steht hinter der ganzen Außenpolitik Europas.
86. The *problem of reunification* lies behind all European foreign policy.	**87.** Kanada ist ein Nachbarland zu den Vereinigten Staaten. (**Nachbarland** means ______)
87. neighboring country	**88.** **der Raum** = *room, space, area* Deutschland ist ein umgrenzter Raum. (**umgrenzt** = *enclosed/open*)
88. Germany is an *enclosed* area.	**89.** **fest** = *firmly, solidly, permanently* Dieses Land ist kein fest umgrenzter Raum.
89. This land is not a permanently enclosed space.	**90.** Deutschland ist der größte Staat Europas, außer Rußland. (**außer** = *except/in addition to*)
90. Germany is the largest state of Europe except Russia.	

Before you go on to the next section, review all of the words you have circled.

10. Es gibt, es ist, es sind

1. Geben means *to give* but **es gibt** is used idiomatically to indicate existence. It is translated *there is* or *there are* depending on the context:

Es gibt **eine Universität in Hamburg.**	***There is*** *a university in Hamburg.*
Gibt es **viele Studenten auf der Universität?**	***Are there*** *many students at the university?*

2. Es ist (*there is*) and **es sind** (*there are*) are used in a like manner:

***Es ist* nur ein Mensch in diesem Haus.**	***There is** only one person in this house.*
***Es sind* drei Menschen in dem Volkswagen.**	***There are** three people in the Volkswagen.*

3. The past of these expressions is:

es gab	*there was, there were*
es war	*there was*
es waren	*there were*

Note also:

Ich bin es.	*It is I.*
Ist er es?	*Is it he?*
Es waren meine Kinder.	*It was* my children.

Give the meanings of the indicated phrases.

	1. sehr = *very* Sehr viele Länder umschließen Deutschland. (**umschließen** probably means ________)
1. Very many countries *surround* Germany.	**2. die** = *which* **Es gibt** neun Länder, die Deutschland umschließen. (*there is/there are*)
2. *There are* nine countries which surround Germany. (As you see, **die** can be used as a relative pronoun meaning *who* or *which*, as well as an article meaning *the*.)	**3. die Mitte** = *middle, center* **Es ist** in der geographischen Mitte Europas. (*there is/it is*)
3. *It is* in the geographical center of Europe.	**4. einmal** = *once* Einmal **gab es** viele Deutsche in der Tschechoslowakei. (*it gave/there were*)
4. *There were* once many Germans in Czechoslovakia.	**5.** Warum **ist es** ein Durchgangsland? (*is there/is it*)
5. Why *is it* a country through which others travel?	**6. da** = *since* . . . da **es** fast keine natürlichen Grenzen **gibt.** (*it gives/there are*)

6. . . . since *there are* almost no (hardly any) natural borders.	**7.** **eigentlich** = *really, actually* Gab es eigentlich **ein** Deutschland? (*a/one*)
7. Was there really *one* Germany?	**8.** **Es war** sehr schwer, diese Frage zu verstehen. (*there was/it was*)
8. *It was* very hard to understand this question.	**9.** **Es gibt** zwei Teile Deutschlands, die zusammen den größten Staat Europas bilden.
9. *There are* two parts of Germany which together form the largest state in Europe.	**10.** **das Gebiet** = *the area* **Es waren** auch romanische, slawische und magyarische Völker auf diesem Gebiet. (*there were/they were*)
10. *There were* also Romanic, Slavic, and Magyar peoples in this area.	**11.** **also** = *therefore* Also **gibt es** seit der Römerzeit romanische, slawische und magyarische Völker auf diesem Gebiet. (*there were/there have been*)
11. Therefore *there have been* Romanic, Slavic, and Magyar peoples in this area since the time of the Romans.	**12.** Er hat nur eine Landkarte Europas. (**Landkarte** probably means — *automobile/map*)
12. He has only one *map* of Europe.	**13.** Vier (4) verschiedene Länder waren **auf** der Landkarte. (*on/to*)
13. Four different countries were *on* the map.	**14.** **Es waren** nur vier Länder auf der Landkarte. (*they were/there were*)
14. *There were* only four countries on the map.	**15.** **Es gibt** viele Völker, die in Europa wohnen. (*there is/there are*)
15. *There are* many peoples which live in Europe.	**16.** **Es sind** viele Länder, die in diesem Gebiet liegen. (*there is/there are*)
16. *There are* many countries which lie (with)in this area.	**17.** Die Russen wohnen in Rußland. (**Rußland** means ________)

17. The Russians live in *Russia*.	**18.** **von** = *of* **Er ist** kein großer Freund von den Russen. (*it is/he is*)
18. *He is* not a great friend of the Russians.	**19.** Also **war es und ist es** das größte Problem der Politik Europas. (*he was and is/it was and is*)
19. Therefore *it was and is* the biggest problem of European politics.	**20.** **nennen** = *to call* Wir nennen diesen Teil Europas, Mitteleuropa.
20. We call this part of Europe, central Europe.	**21.** In der geographischen Mitte Europas, **die** wir Mitteleuropa nennen, findet man Deutschland. (*which/the*)
21. In the geographical center of Europe, *which* we call Central Europe, we find (one finds) Germany.	

PROGRESS TEST

Mark the phrases which you do not identify correctly, and then review them before going on.

1. **Es sind** nur vier Länder auf dieser Landkarte.
   (a) *they are* (b) *there are* (c) *there were*
2. **Es war** nur eine Landkarte an der Wand.
   (a) *there was* (b) *it was* (c) *it is*
3. **Gab es** eigentlich ein Deutschland?
   (a) *is there* (b) *was there* (c) *did he give*
4. **Es waren** nur vier Länder auf der Landkarte.
   (a) *they were* (b) *there were* (c) *there are*
5. **Es ist** nur eine Person in dem Volkswagen.
   (a) *it is* (b) *there is* (c) *he is*

Answer key: **1.** (b); **2.** (a); **3.** (b); **4.** (b); **5.** (b).

Die Geographie Deutschlands

Wenn wir Deutschland als ein Land verstehen wollen, müssen wir nicht nur Geschichte lernen, sondern auch eine Landkarte anschauen. Die Geographie Deutschlands kann uns sehr viel sagen. Deutschland liegt in der geographischen Mitte Europas, in dem Teil Europas, den wir Mitteleuropa nennen. Natürlich liegt nicht nur Deutschland in diesem Gebiet, sondern auch andere Länder. In dieser Zone leben also germanische, slawische, romanische und magyarische Völker. Zusammen bilden die Bundesrepublik Deutschland (d.h. Westdeutschland) und die Deutsche Demokratische Republik (d.h. Ostdeutschland) den größten Staat Europas, außer Rußland natürlich. Bevölkerung,[1] Industrie und Bruttosozialprodukt[2] sind die größten in Europa. Die Wiedervereinigungsfrage steht nicht nur hinter aller deutschen Außenpolitik, sondern auch hinter der ganzen Politik Europas.

Dieses Land, in dem die Deutschen wohnen, ist kein fest umgrenzter Raum, da es fast keine natürlichen Grenzen gibt. Wenn wir die Landkarte wieder anschauen, finden wir nur im Norden und im Süden „natürliche Grenzen". Im Norden gibt es die Nord- und die Ostsee, im Süden die Bayrischen Alpen,[3] den Bodensee[4] und den Rhein. Nach Westen und Osten liegt Deutschland offen.

Neun verschiedene Länder umschließen Deutschland: Dänemark, die Niederlande, Belgien, Luxemburg, Frankreich, die Schweiz, Österreich, die Tschechoslowakei und Polen. Es ist nicht schwer zu verstehen, warum dieses Land seit der Römerzeit inmitten aller großen Konflikte steht, warum es ein Durchgangsland ist. Die Grenzen im Osten und im Westen verschieben sich,[5] wenn Deutschland oder seine Nachbarländer versuchen, mehr Land oder Lebensraum[6] zu gewinnen. Skandinavier vom Norden, Römer vom Süden, Slawen vom Osten, Romanen[7] vom Westen und Nomadenvölker aus dem Südosten, alle diese Völker spielen eine Rolle in der Geschichte dieses Landes.

1 *population*
2 *gross national product*
3 *the Bavarian Alps*
4 *Lake Constance*
5 *change*
6 *living space*
7 *Neo-Latin peoples*

Chapter Three

11. *Word order—the basic structure of German sentences*

1. The task of reading German is greatly facilitated if one knows how to locate the verb. Generally speaking, the personal form of the verb is found in one of three places in German:

(a) immediately after the subject (normal word order)
(b) immediately preceding the subject (inverted word order)
(c) at the end of the sentence or clause (dependent word order)

2. These three basic forms of German word order are as follows:

(a) *Normal word order*
Subject and its modifiers + verb + verbal modifiers

Der alte Mann / ***geht*** **/ langsam in das Haus.**
The old man goes slowly into the house.

(b) *Inverted word order*
Any word except a conjunction or interjection + verb + subject and its modifiers + other modifiers

Wann / ***kommt*** **/ Karl / nach Hause?**
When is Karl coming home?
Gehen **/ Sie / bitte nach Hause!**
Please go home!
Den Hund / ***sehe*** **/ ich / auf der Straße.**
I see the dog in the street.

(c) *Dependent (or transposed) word order*
Subordinating conjunction or words functioning as such + subject and its modifiers + other modifiers + verb

Ich weiß, / daß / der alte Mann / in das Haus / *geht.*
I know that the old man is going into the house.
Der alte Mann, / der / in das Haus / *geht*, / ist mein Vater.
The old man going into the house is my father.
Paul weiß, / warum / ich / Deutsch / *studiere.*
Paul knows why I study German.

Notice that in English the regular word order is retained in dependent clauses. In German any dependent clause calls for dependent word order.

The following exercises introduce new vocabulary for the reading passage and give you practice in recognizing the basic patterns of German word order. Continue to circle any words which you do not immediately recognize, and identify the subject and verb of each clause.

	1. **besprechen** = *to discuss* In diesem Kapitel besprechen wir andere Länder, **wo** man Deutsch spricht. (*who/where*)
1. In this chapter we discuss other countries *where* one speaks German.	**2.** **Außer** Deutschland gibt es andere Länder . . . (*in/besides*)
2. *Besides* Germany there are other countries . . .	**3.** Außer Deutschland gibt es andere Länder, wo man die deutsche Sprache spricht.
3. Besides Germany there are other countries where one speaks the German language.	**4.** **selbst** = *self* **stehen** = *to stand* ein **selbständiges** Land = ________
4. an *independent* country	**5.** Österreich ist heute ein selbständiger und neutraler Staat.
5. Austria today is an independent and neutral state.	**6.** **Jeder** weiß, daß Österreich heute ein selbständiger und neutraler Staat ist. (*everyone/no one*)
6. *Everyone* knows that Austria today is an independent and neutral state.	**7.** **obwohl** = *although* Obwohl Österreich heute ein selbständiger und neutraler Staat ist . . .

7. Although Austria is today an independent and neutral state . . .	**8.** **hängen** = *to hang* **zusammen** = *together* **zusammenhängen** = ________
8. to hang together, i.e. to be connected	**9.** **eng** = *closely* . . . hängt Österreichs Geschichte sehr eng mit der deutschen Geschichte zusammen.
9. . . . Austria's history is connected very closely with German history. (Note that the prefix **zusammen** is separable and comes at the end of the sentence.)	**10.** **sein** = *its (his, her)* Seine Geschichte hängt sehr eng mit der deutschen Geschichte zusammen.
10. Its history is very closely connected with German history.	**11.** **umgeben** = *surrounded* Österreich ist von **nur** sechs Ländern umgeben. *(now/only)*
11. Austria is surrounded by *only* six countries.	**12.** **gemeinsam** = *common* Österreich hat gemeinsame Grenzen mit nur sechs Ländern.
12. Austria has common boundaries with only six countries.	**13.** Im Kontrast zu Deutschland ist Österreich nicht von so vielen Ländern umgeben.
13. In contrast to Germany Austria is not surrounded by so many countries	**14.** Obwohl Österreich von nur sechs Ländern umgeben ist . . .
14. Although Austria is surrounded by only six countries . . .	**15.** Im westlichen und im südlichen Teil des Landes sind Berge und Täler. (If **Berge** means *mountains*, **Täler** must mean ________.)
15. *valleys* In the western and southern part of the country are mountains and valleys.	**16.** **berühmt** = *famous* Diese Berge und Täler sind sehr berühmt.
16. These mountains and valleys are very famous.	**17.** **da** = *since* Da diese Berge und Täler so berühmt sind . . .
17. Since these mountains and valleys are so famous . . .	**18.** **besuchen** = *to visit* . . . besuchen Millionen von Menschen dieses Alpenland.

18. . . . millions of people visit this alpine country.	**19.** **bedecken** = *to cover* Da Berge und Täler Österreich bedek-ken . . .
19. Since mountains and valleys cover Austria . . . (When *ck* is divided by a hyphen, the *c* is changed to *k*.)	**20.** . . . gibt es viele Touristen, **die** das Land besuchen. *(who/the)*
20. . . . there are many tourists *who* visit the country. (Remember that **die, der, das,** etc., can be used both as articles and as relative pronouns.)	**21.** **ungefähr** = *approximately* Berge und Täler bedecken ungefähr 60% der **Oberfläche** Österreichs. *(tourist industry/surface)*
21. Mountains and valleys cover approximately 60% of the *surface* of Austria.	**22.** Ungefähr 60% der Oberfläche Österreichs ist von den berühmten Bergen und Tälern bedeckt.
22. Approximately 60% of the surface of Austria is covered by its (the) famous mountains and valleys.	**23.** **die Donau** = *the Danube* Der andere Teil ist Donauland.
23. The other part is Danube country.	**24.** In dem Donauland liegt **Wien.** *(wine/Vienna)*
24. *Vienna* is located (lies) in the Danube country.	**25.** Wien, die **Hauptstadt** Österreichs . . . (If **Haupt** means *main* or *principal,* **Hauptstadt** must mean ________.)
25. *capital* Vienna, the *capital* of Austria . . .	**26.** **die Gesamtbevölkerung** = *the entire population* **Ein Viertel** der Gesamtbevölkerung Österreichs wohnt in Wien. *(a fourth/a fifth)*
26. *A fourth* of the entire population of Austria lives in Vienna.	**27.** Hier liegt Wien, in **dem** heute ein Viertel der Gesamtbevölkerung wohnt. *(the/which)*
27. Here is Vienna, in *which* today a quarter of the entire population lives.	

PROGRESS TEST

The following sentences are intended to test your recognition of grammatical forms. Therefore, some of the vocabulary is new. Simply respond to the sentences by choosing the correct answer.

1. Seit Jahrhunderten erlebt die Schweiz auf ihrem Boden keinen Krieg mehr.
The subject of **erlebt** *is*
(a) Krieg (b) Boden (c) Jahrhunderten (d) Schweiz

2. Wir wissen, daß die Schweiz die Achtung und das Vertrauen der Welt genießt.
Schweiz *is the subject of*
(a) wissen (b) Vertrauen (c) genießt (d) Achtung

3. Ungefähr 60% der Oberfläche Österreichs ist von den berühmten Bergen und Tälern bedeckt.
The subject of **ist** *is*
(a) Bergen und Tälern (b) 60% der Oberfläche Österreichs (c) ungefähr (d) Österreichs

4. Zweimal bedrohten die Türken Zentraleuropa.
The subject of **bedrohten** *is*
(a) Türken (b) Zentraleuropa (c) zweimal

5. Hitler und der Anschluß vereinigten Deutschland und Österreich.
The subject of **vereinigten** *is*
(a) Hitler (b) Anschluß (c) Hitler und der Anschluß (d) Deutschland und Österreich

6. Wenn Deutschland versucht, mehr Lebensraum in Polen zu gewinnen, dann gibt es Krieg.
The subject of **gibt** *is*
(a) dann (b) Polen (c) es (d) Krieg

Answer key: **1.** (d); **2.** (c); **3.** (b); **4.** (a); **5.** (c); **6.** (c).

Review the words you circled in the frames as well as any points missed on this test. Then go on to the next section.

12. *Future tense—**werden***

1. Werden + infinitive tells you that the action is in future time:

Viele Menschen *werden* das Gebirgsland *besuchen.*	*Many people **will visit** the mountainous country.*
Wann *wird* er nach Österreich *fliegen?*	*When **will** he **fly** to Austria?*

2. In normal and inverted word order the infinitive is generally at the end of the clause. In dependent word order the infinitive precedes **werden:**

Du *wirst* doch den Brief bald *bekommen.*	*You **will** surely **receive** the letter soon.*
Aber vielleicht *wirst* du den Brief morgen *bekommen.*	*But perhaps you **will receive** the letter tomorrow.*
Ich weiß, daß du niemals einen Brief *bekommen wirst.*	*I know that you **will** never **receive** a letter.*

The subject of word order with modal verbs will be taken up in greater detail in other sections.

3. Remember that **werden** without the infinitive expresses the meaning *to become:*

Der Mann wird alt.	*The man is becoming (is getting) old.*

Give the tense and meaning of the verbs in the following sentences.

	1. deutschsprechend = *German speaking* Sie **werden** noch mehr von den deutschsprechenden Ländern **lesen.**
1. You *will read* still more about German speaking countries.	**2.** Wir **lernen** noch mehr über den Einfluß der deutschen Kultur.
2. We *are learning* still more about the influence of German culture.	**3.** Vielleicht **werden** wir mehr über die deutsche Kultur **lernen.** *(are learning/will learn)*
3. Perhaps we *will learn* more about German culture.	**4. etwas** = *something* Wir **werden** auch etwas über die Schweiz **sagen.**
4. We *will* also *say* something about Switzerland.	**5. möglich** = *possible* Es ist möglich, daß Sie etwas von der Habsburger Monarchie **lesen werden.**
5. It is possible that you *will read* something about the Hapsburg monarchy.	**6.** Der Großvater **wird** alt. *(is getting/will be)*
6. The grandfather *is getting* old.	

13. *Adjectives—cognates, agreement, comparison*

1. As with verbs and nouns, there are a number of cognates which will facilitate your reading knowledge of German:

alt	*old*
jung	*young*
grün	*green*
dumm	*stupid, dull*

2. For the purposes of reading it is important to be able to identify gender, number, and case. Some of the grammatical signals which help you to do so are the adjective endings, which are either strong or weak.

3. Strong adjective endings tell gender, number, and case of the noun, when no preceding word gives this information. These endings generally conform to those of the definite article:

	MASCULINE	FEMININE	NEUTER	PLURAL
Nominative	**-er**	**-e**	**-es**	**-e**
Genitive	**-en**	**-er**	**-en**	**-er**
Dative	**-em**	**-er**	**-em**	**-en**
Accusative	**-en**	**-e**	**-es**	**-e**

The concept of case will be discussed in chapter 4.

Gut*en* Wein kann man nicht überall finden. (masc. acc.)	*One cannot find good wine everywhere.*
Ein gut*er* Ruf ist köstlicher als groß*er* Reichtum. (masc. nom.)	*A good reputation is more precious than great riches.*
Alt*e* Männer sitzen auf der Treppe. (nom. pl.)	*Old men are sitting on the steps.*
Ein dumm*es* Kind hört nicht auf seine Eltern. (neuter nom.)	*A stupid child does not listen to his parents.*

4. An adjective takes a weak ending if it is preceded by any limiting article which indicates gender, number, and case. The weak endings are:

	MASCULINE	FEMININE	NEUTER	PLURAL
Nominative	**-e**	**-e**	**-e**	**-en**
Genitive	**-en**	**-en**	**-en**	**-en**
Dative	**-en**	**-en**	**-en**	**-en**
Accusative	**-en**	**-e**	**-e**	**-en**

Der alt*e* Mann und seine hübsch*e* jung*e* Frau wohnen in diesem alt*en* grau*en* Haus.	*The old man and his young and pretty wife live in this old gray house.*

5. The majority of adjective endings in German will be weak.

6. Adjectives which do not appear directly before the noun they modify will take no ending:

Der Mensch wird *alt* aber bleibt doch *dumm*.	*Man grows old but still remains stupid.*

As you respond to the following exercises, pay special attention to adjective and noun endings as indicators of number.

	1. Es gibt andere Länder Europas, wo man Deutsch spricht. (**andere Länder** = *another country/other countries*)
1. There are *other countries* in Europe where German is spoken (lit.: where one speaks German).	**2.** You can tell that **andere Länder** is plural because of ________ .
2. the umlaut and the endings	**3.** Deutschland hat eine gemeinsame Grenze mit Österreich.
3. Germany has a common border with Austria.	**4.** Österreich hat gemeinsame Grenzen mit sechs verschiedenen Ländern. (**gemeinsame Grenzen** = *common border/common borders*)
4. Austria has *common borders* with six different countries.	**5.** You can tell that **gemeinsame Grenzen** is plural because ________ .
5. **ein** is missing and because of the ending added to **Grenze**	**6.** Die Schweiz ist ein neutrales Land.
6. Switzerland is a neutral country.	**7.** **wirklich** = *really* Gibt es wirklich neutrale Länder? (**neutrale Länder** = *neutral country/neutral countries*)
7. Are there really *neutral countries?*	**8.** You know that **Länder** is plural because ________ .
8. of the umlaut and endings	

PROGRESS TEST

Tell whether the italicized nouns are singular or plural. If you miss any of the following, review the preceding exercises before continuing.

1. Alle guten *Pläne* scheitern. (**scheitern** = *to fail*)
2. *Kriege* sind nicht neutral.
3. *Die Schweiz* ist ein europäisches Paradies.

Answer key: **1.** plural: plans; **2.** plural: wars; **3.** singular: Switzerland.

14. *Adverbs*

Adverbs in German take no special ending, whereas they do in English:

Er läuft *schnell.*	*He runs quick**ly**.*
Er spricht *langsam.*	*He speaks slow**ly**.*

This section will give you practice in recognizing nine common adverbs. Continue to circle words which you do not immediately recognize.

	1. Wir wollen **noch** Frankreich besuchen. (*still/never*)
1. We *still* want to visit France.	**2.** Im Sommer bedeckt der Schnee **noch** die Alpen. (*never/still*)
2. The snow *still* covers the Alps in the summer.	**3.** **Vielleicht** schaut er die Landkarte an. (*perhaps/not*)
3. *Perhaps* he is looking at the map.	**4.** Die Landkarte hängt **noch** an der Wand. (*still/never*)
4. The map is *still* hanging on the wall.	**5.** Wenn Deutschland **wieder** vereinigt wird, . . . (*again/not ever*)
5. If Germany is *again* united . . .	**6.** **Vielleicht** ist es auf der Landkarte. (*perhaps/not*)
6. *Perhaps* it is on the map.	**7.** **Heute** lesen wir, daß die Schweiz ein europäisches Paradies ist. (*yesterday/today*)
7. *Today* we read that Switzerland is a European paradise.	**8.** Kann uns die Geographie Deutschlands **sehr** viel sagen? (*little/very*)
8. Can Germany's geography tell us *very* much?	**9.** Hier leben **also** viele Völker. (*therefore/also*)
9. *Therefore* many nations live here.	**10.** ***Also** sprach Zarathustra.* (*also/thus*)

10. ***Thus*** *spake Zarathustra.* (Title of the work by Nietzsche)	**11.** Nicht **sehr** viele Länder umschließen die Schweiz. (*little/very*)
11. Not *very* many countries surround Switzerland.	**12.** Du kennst das Land **also** nicht. (*so/also*)
12. *So* you don't know that country.	**13.** **Heute** ist Deutschland eine große Macht. (*today/tomorrow*)
13. *Today* Germany is a great power.	**14.** **erleben** = *to experience* **Auch** Belgien erlebt den Krieg. (*even/still*)
14. *Even* Belgium experiences the war.	**15.** **erobern** = *to conquer* Wenn wir versuchen, **auch** Polen zu erobern . . . (*also/still*)
15. If we try to *also* conquer Poland . . .	**16.** **Nur** Rußland hat eine größere Bevölkerungszahl. (*still/only*)
16. *Only* Russia has a larger population.	**17.** **Schon** im Jahre 955 beginnt Österreich . . . (*not yet/already*)
17. *Already* in the year 955 Austria begins . . .	**18.** **die Uhr** = *watch* Schweizer Uhren kennt **schon** jeder. (*no doubt/not at all*)
18. *No doubt* everyone has heard of Swiss watches.	**19.** Schweizer Käse kennt man **auch.** (*therefore/also*)
19. One *also* knows about Swiss cheese.	

PROGRESS TEST

Give the correct meaning of the italicized words. Mark those which you do not give correctly the first time, and review them before continuing.

1. Bedeckt der Schnee im Sommer *noch* die Alpen?
2. Hier leben *also* viele Völker.
3. Wenn wir versuchen, *auch* Polen zu erobern . . .
4. *Nur* Hitler vereinigte Deutschland und Österreich.

Answer key: **1.** still; **2.** therefore; **3.** also; **4.** only.

READING PREPARATION

This section reviews structures already studied and introduces vocabulary necessary for the reading passage. Continue to circle new or unfamiliar words.

	1. Jetzt werden wir etwas sagen über Österreichs Einfluß **auf** das politische Leben Europas. (*on/of*)
1. Now we will say something about Austria's influence *on* the political life of Europe.	**2.** **schon** = *already* Schon im Jahre 955, dem **Geburtsjahr** des Habsburger Österreichs . . . (*birthday/year of the birth*)
2. Already in the year 955, the *year of the birth* of Hapsburg Austria . . .	**3.** **ausüben** = *to exert* **auszuüben** = *to exert* . . . **beginnt** dieses Land einen großen Einfluß auf Europa auszuüben.
3. . . . this land *begins* to exert a great influence on Europe. (Notice the use of the present tense for historical narrative.)	**4.** . . . beginnt dieses Land einen großen Einfluß auf das kulturelle und politische Leben Europas auszuüben.
4. . . . this land begins to exert a great influence on the cultural and political life of Europe.	**5.** **bleiben** = *to remain* Die Habsburger bleiben fast 1000 Jahre an der Macht.
5. The Hapsburgs remain in power almost 1000 years.	**6.** **bis zum** = *until the . . .* Bis zum Jahre 1918 bleibt die Habsburger Monarchie Österreich-Ungarn an der Macht.
6. Until the year 1918 the Hapsburg monarchy of Austria-Hungary remains in power.	**7.** **und zwar** = *namely* Nur einmal sind Deutschland und Österreich vereinigt, und zwar unter Hitler (1938–45).
7. Only once were (are) Germany and Austria united, namely under Hitler (1938–45).	**8.** **die Beziehung** = *relation* Österreichs **Beziehungen** zu den ost- und südeuropäischen Ländern . . . (*singular/plural*)

8. Austria's *relations* with the East European and South European countries . . .	**9.** **einstige** = *former* Österreichs einstige **wertvolle** Beziehungen . . . (*valuable/unimportant*)
9. Austria's former *valuable* relations . . .	**10.** Der **Eiserne Vorhang** hängt zwischen der Bundesrepublik und der Deutschen Demokratischen Republik. (If **Eiserne** is *iron*, **Vorhang** is ________ .)
10. The *Iron Curtain* lies (hangs) between the Federal Republic and the German Democratic Republic.	**11.** Der Eiserne Vorhang hängt auch zwischen Österreich und den osteuropäischen Ländern.
11. The Iron Curtain lies also between Austria and the East European countries.	**12.** **abgeschnitten** = *cut off* Also sind Österreichs einstige wertvolle Beziehungen zu den ost- und südeuropäischen Ländern abgeschnitten.
12. Therefore Austria's former valuable relations with the East European and South European countries are cut off.	**13.** Diese Länder sind **durch** den Eisernen Vorhang abgeschnitten. (*by/near*)
13. These countries are cut off *by* (*means of*) the Iron Curtain.	**14.** **sollten** = *ought* Vielleicht sollten wir etwas über die Schweiz sagen.
14. Perhaps we ought to say something about Switzerland.	**15.** Vielleicht werden wir wieder etwas über Österreich sagen.
15. Perhaps we will again say something about Austria.	**16.** Da die Schweiz ein neutrales Land ist, erlebt **sie** keinen Krieg.
16. Since Switzerland is a neutral country, *it* does not experience war. (**Sie** refers here to the feminine noun **die Schweiz.**)	**17.** **der Boden** = *territory* (*floor, ground*) **auf seinem Boden** = *on its territory* Seit Jahrhunderten erlebt dieses neutrale Land keinen Krieg auf seinem Boden.
17. For centuries this neutral country has not experienced any war on its territory.	**18.** **vertrauen** = *to trust* Die Welt vertraut diesem kleinen Land.
18. The world trusts this little country.	**19.** **genießen** = *to enjoy* Dieses Land genießt das Vertrauen der Welt.

19. This country enjoys the trust of the world.	**20.** **die Achtung** = *respect* Als neutrales Land genießt die Schweiz nicht nur die Achtung, sondern auch das Vertrauen der Welt.
20. As a neutral country Switzerland enjoys not only the respect but also the trust of the world.	**21.** Dieses klassische Gebirgsland ist berühmt für seine **wunderschöne Landschaft.** (In the context of Switzerland, **wunderschöne Landschaft** must mean *extremely beautiful* ________.)
21. This classic mountainous country is famous for its *beautiful landscape*.	**22.** **ansehen** = *to consider, respect* (also: *to look at*) **das Ansehen** = *esteem* Das klassische Gebirgsland, welches viele Menschen jedes Jahr besuchen, genießt internationales Ansehen.
22. The classic mountainous country, which many people visit every year, enjoys international esteem.	**23.** **die Währung** = *currency* **das Bankwesen** = *banking institutions, banking system* Nicht nur ist die schweizerische Landschaft berühmt, sondern auch die Schweizer Währung und das Schweizer Bankwesen.
23. Not only is the Swiss landscape famous but also Swiss currency and Swiss banking institutions.	**24.** Die Schweizer Währung und das Schweizer Bankwesen genießen internationales Ansehen.
24. Swiss currency and Swiss banking institutions enjoy international esteem.	**25.** Jeder kennt doch auch Schweizer Schokolade, Schweizer Uhren und Schweizer **Käse.** (**Käse** probably means ________.)
25. Surely everyone has also heard (knows) of Swiss chocolate, Swiss watches, and Swiss *cheese*.	**26.** **vieles** = *much* **tun** = *to do* Wir können noch vieles über die Schweiz sagen, aber wir werden es nicht tun.
26. We can still say much about Switzerland, but we will not do so (literally: do it).	

Andere deutschsprechende Länder

Außer Deutschland gibt es andere Länder Europas, wo man die deutsche Sprache spricht: Österreich und die Schweiz. Österreich ist heute ein selbständiger und neutraler Staat, aber seine Geschichte hängt sehr eng mit der deutschen Geschichte zusammen. Im Kontrast zu Deutschland ist Österreich nicht von so vielen Ländern umgeben. Es hat gemeinsame Grenzen mit nur sechs Ländern: der Tschechoslowakei, Deutschland, der Schweiz, Italien, Jugoslawien und Ungarn. Im westlichen und im südlichen Teil des Landes sind die berühmten Berge und Täler, das Alpenland, das ungefähr 60% der Oberfläche Österreichs bedeckt. Das andere ist Donauland. Hier liegt Wien, Hauptstadt des Landes, in dem heute ein Viertel der Gesamtbevölkerung wohnt.

Schon im Jahre 955, dem Geburtsjahr des Habsburger Österreichs, beginnt dieses Land, einen großen Einfluß auf das kulturelle und politische Leben Europas auszuüben. Bis zum Jahre 1918 bleibt die Habsburger Monarchie Österreich-Ungarn an der Macht. Nur einmal sind Deutschland und Österreich vereinigt, und zwar unter Hitler (1938–45). Heute sind Österreichs einstige wertvolle Beziehungen zu den ost- und südeuropäischen Ländern, wie Ungarn, Rumänien und Jugoslawien, zum Teil durch den Eisernen Vorhang abgeschnitten.

Über die Schweiz können wir vieles sagen. In diesem Land spricht man nicht nur Deutsch, sondern auch Französisch, Italienisch und Romaunsch, einen romanischen Dialekt. Nur vier Länder umschließen dieses Land: Deutschland, Frankreich, Italien und Österreich. Seit Jahrhunderten erlebt dieses Land keinen Krieg mehr auf seinem Boden. Als neutrales Land genießt es die Achtung und das Vertrauen der Welt. Die Schweiz ist berühmt für ihre wunderschöne Landschaft. Hier ist das klassische Gebirgsland, welches viele Menschen jedes Jahr besuchen. Schweizer Schokolade, Schweizer Uhren und Schweizer Käse kennt doch jeder. Auch die Schweizer Währung und das Schweizer Bankwesen genießen internationales Ansehen. Wenn es ein europäisches Paradies gibt, dann ist es die Schweiz.

Chapter Four

15. *Case of the noun*

1. There are four different forms of German articles, nouns, pronouns, and adjectives. These forms are called cases.

(a) The nominative case is used for the subject and predicate noun:

***Der Wagen* fährt sehr schnell.**	***The car** goes very fast.*
Paul ist *der Mann.*	*Paul is **the man.***

(b) The genitive expresses possession or relationship. It also is used with certain prepositions and verbs, and is often translated by *of the*, by an adjective, or by *'s* (plural *s'*):

die Stimme *der Frau*	*the voice **of the woman,** the woman**'s** voice*
trotz *der Hitze*	*in spite **of the heat***
die Zivilisation *des Westens*	*Western civilization (the civilization **of the West**)*
Vater*s* Haus	*father**'s** house*

(c) The dative is the case of the indirect object. Certain verbs and prepositions also call for this case:

Ich gebe *meinem Freund* das Buch.	*I give the book **to my friend.***
Peter antwortet *dem Lehrer* nicht.	*Peter does not answer **the teacher.***
Auf *dem Haus* sitzt ein Storch.	*A stork is sitting **on top of the house.***

(d) The accusative is the case of the direct object; it is also used with certain prepositions:

Hans findet *das Hotel.*	*Hans finds **the hotel.***
Er fährt *durch die Stadt.*	*He drives **through the city.***

2. Case is shown by the endings of the article or adjectives preceding the noun, or, less frequently, by the noun itself. Familiarity with the cases of German will help you to identify the role of the noun in the sentence. Context will also give a clue as to what role a noun plays in a sentence. A knowledge of the position of the verb relative to the subject will give additional help. But the case endings are still the most direct way of identifying the nouns, especially when a direct or indirect object introduces the sentence:

Wolfgang schreibt sein*em* Freund ein*en* Brief. *Wolfgang writes his friend a letter.*
Sein*em* Freund schreibt Wolfgang ein*en* Brief.
Ein*en* Brief schreibt Wolfgang sein*em* Freund.

3. The following tables outline the endings of the definite and indefinite article of the various cases:

	MASCULINE	FEMININE	NEUTER	PLURAL
Nominative	**der**	**die**	**das**	**die**
Genitive	**des**	**der**	**des**	**der**
Dative	**dem**	**der**	**dem**	**den**
Accusative	**den**	**die**	**das**	**die**
Nominative	**ein**	**eine**	**ein**	**keine** (*not any*, or *no*)
Genitive	**eines**	**einer**	**eines**	**keiner**
Dative	**einem**	**einer**	**einem**	**keinen**
Accusative	**einen**	**eine**	**ein**	**keine**

There is no plural of **ein,** but the case endings are added to possessive adjectives as well as to **kein.**

State whether the indicated nouns are used as subjects (nominative), objects (dative or accusative), or in an expression of possession (genitive).

	1. **der Wissenschaftler** = *scientist* **Die** deutschen **Wissenschaftler** sind weltbekannt.
1. subject (nominative plural): German *scientists* are world famous.	**2.** **der Dichter** = *the poet* Wir sprechen jetzt von **den** deutschen **Dichtern** und **Wissenschaftlern.**
2. object (dative plural: **von** always takes the dative, and moreover, the noun endings are plural): We are now talking about German *poets* and *scientists.*	**3.** **Das Universum** ist groß.

3. subject (nominative): *The universe* is large.	**4. die Vorstellung** = *conception* Die Vorstellung **des Universums** war im 19. Jahrhundert ganz anders als heute.
4. genitive: In the 19th century the conception *of the universe* was completely different from the conception today.	**5. hat geändert** = *has changed* Einsteins Relativitätstheorie hat unsere Vorstellung **des Universums** geändert.
5. genitive: Einstein's theory of relativity has changed our conception *of the universe.*	**6. unwiderruflich** = *irrevocably* Einstein hat unsere Vorstellung **des Universums** unwiderruflich geändert.
6. genitive: Einstein irrevocably changed our conception *of the universe.*	**7. der Bereich** = *sphere* **der Kulturbereich** = *cultural sphere* In **dem** deutschen **Kulturbereich** sind viele Länder.
7. object (dative singular): There are many countries in *the* German *cultural sphere.*	**8. stammen aus** = *to come from* Aus **dem** deutschen **Kulturbereich** stammt auch der jüdische Religionsphilosoph Martin Buber.
8. object (**aus** always takes the dative): The Jewish religious philosopher Martin Buber also comes from *the* German *cultural area.*	**9. die Bewegung** = *movement* Der Expressionismus ist eine literarische Bewegung.
9. subject (predicate nominative): Expressionism is a *literary movement.*	**10. sowie** = *as well as* **zugleich** = *at the same time* **Der Expressionismus** ist zugleich eine künstlerische sowie eine literarische Bewegung.
10. subject (nominative): *Expressionism* is at the same time an artistic as well as a literary movement.	**11. mit** = *with* Die Mona Lisa hat nichts mit **dem Expressionismus** zu tun.
11. object (**mit** always takes the dative): The Mona Lisa has nothing to do with *Expressionism.*	**12.** In **der** deutschen **Geschichte** ist Martin Luther zugleich Politiker sowie Theologe.
12. object (dative singular): In German *history* Martin Luther is at the same time a politician as well as a theologian.	**13. verheerend** = *devastating* **verheerendster** = *most devastating* **Der Dreißigjährige Krieg** (30 Years' War) war Deutschlands verheerendster Krieg.

13. subject (nominative singular): *The Thirty Years' War* was Germany's most devastating war.	**14.** **führen** = *to lead* Luthers 95 Thesen führen zu **dem** verheerendsten **Kriege** Deutschlands. (**dem** = dative/accusative)
14. dative (**zu** always requires the dative): Luther's 95 theses lead to Germany's most devastating *war*.	**15.** **ihre Märchen** = *their tales* **Die Brüder Grimm** sind berühmt für ihre Märchen.
15. subject (nominative plural): *The Grimm brothers* are famous for their tales.	**16.** **unterhalten** = *to entertain* Die Brüder Grimm und ihre Märchen unterhalten Kinder und Erwachsene noch heute. (If **Kinder** means *children*, **Erwachsene** probably means ________.)
16. The Grimm brothers and their tales still (today) entertain children and adults.	**17.** **leisten** = *to achieve* **Die** deutsche **Kultur** leistet sehr viel auf dem Gebiet der Wissenschaft.
17. subject (nominative singular): German *culture* achieves very much in the area of science.	**18.** **gab** = *gave* **Die Bibelübersetzung** gab **den Deutschen** eine gemeinsame Sprache.
18. **die** = nominative; **den** = dative plural: *The translation of the Bible* gave *the Germans* a common language.	**19.** **vergessen** = *to forget* **Den größten** von allen vergessen wir aber nicht: Mozart.
19. object (accusative): We are not, however, forgetting *the greatest* of all: Mozart. (**Aber** in the middle of a phrase means *however*.)	**20.** Thomas Mann und Bertolt Brecht spielen **eine** große **Rolle** in **der Weltliteratur.**
20. **eine** = accusative; it is the direct object. **der** = dative; it is governed by the preposition **in**: Thomas Mann and Bertolt Brecht play *a* great *role* in *world literature*.	**21.** **rein** = *pure* Die deutsche Kultur gibt uns auch ein Beispiel **der** reinen **Humanität.**
21. genitive: German culture gives us also an example *of* pure *humanity*.	**22.** Albert Schweitzer stammt aus **dem Elsaß.**
22. object (**aus** always takes the dative): Albert Schweitzer comes from *Alsace*.	**23.** In der Zivilisation **des Westens** gibt es keine andere Kultur . . .

23. **des** is always genitive: In *western* civilization there is no other culture . . .	**24.** **hat beigetragen** = *has contributed* Es gibt keine andere Kultur, die zur (zu **der) Geschichte der Musik** soviel beigetragen hat wie die deutsche.
24. object (dative singular); genitive singular: There is no other culture which has contributed so much to *the history of music* as the German.	**25.** **der Komponist** = *the composer* Wie heißt **der** größte deutsche **Komponist?**
25. subject (nominative): What is the name of *the* greatest German *composer*?	**26.** Abraham Lincoln wurde am (an dem) 12. Februar geboren. (**wurde geboren** = ____________)
26. Abraham Lincoln *was born* on the twelfth of February.	**27.** Er ist im (in dem) Jahre 1865 gestorben. (**ist gestorben** = __________)
27. He *died* in the year 1865.	**28.** Können Sie mir den Namen **eines Dichters** nennen, der 1749 geboren wurde und 1832 gestorben ist?
28. **eines** = genitive: Can you tell me the name *of a poet* who was born in 1749 and who died in 1832?	

PROGRESS TEST

Tell in what case the indicated phrases are.

1. Der Sohn **der Frau** hat keine Schokolade mehr.
(genitive/nominative)
2. Für Amerika begann **der zweite Weltkrieg** am 7. Dezember 1941.
(nominative/genitive)
3. **der Löwe** = *lion*
Den Christen gibt er die Löwen.
(dative plural/accusative singular)
4. Er gibt jetzt dem Löwen **den unschuldigen Christen.**
(dative plural/accusative singular)
5. Die Geschichte **des Landes** ist schon alt.
(nominative/genitive)
6. Siehst du **das junge Mädchen** da drüben?
(nominative/genitive/accusative)
7. **Die Frau** gibt Paul ein Stück Schokolade.
(nominative/accusative)
8. Versteht sie **die deutsche Kultur?**
(nominative/accusative)

Answer key: **1.** genitive; **2.** nominative; **3.** dative plural: He gives the lions to the Christians. **4.** accusative singular: He is now giving the innocent Christian to the lion. **5.** genitive; **6.** accusative; **7.** nominative: The woman is giving Paul a piece of chocolate. **8.** accusative: Does she understand German culture?

When you can easily recognize all of the above vocabulary, go on to the next section.

16. *Past tense of weak verbs*

1. There are two kinds of verbs in German: strong and weak. A weak verb does not change its stem vowel in any of its past forms, whereas a strong verb does. Most German verbs are weak.

Weak: **glauben** (*to believe*) — **ich glaubte** (*I believed*)
Strong: **singen** (*to sing*) — **ich sang** (*I sang*)

2. The sign of the past tense of weak verbs is a **-t-** added to the stem:

	leben (*to live*)	**antworten** (*to answer*)	**öffnen** (*to open*)
ich	**lebte**	**antwortete**	**öffnete**
du	**lebtest**	**antwortetest**	**öffnetest**
er (sie, es)	**lebte**	**antwortete**	**öffnete**
wir	**lebten**	**antworteten**	**öffneten**
ihr	**lebtet**	**antwortetet**	**öffnetet**
sie	**lebten**	**antworteten**	**öffneten**
Sie	**lebten**	**antworteten**	**öffneten**

You will notice that an **e** may be inserted before the **-t-** when the stem ends in **-t, -d** or a succession of dissimilar consonants.

Do not confuse the **-t-** of the past tense with the **-t** which is part of the stem:

Ihr arbeit*et* zu schnell. *You work too fast.*
Ihr arbeit*etet* zu schnell. *You work**ed** too fast.*

3. Both the first and third person singular of the weak verb in the past tense end in **-e:**

ich sagte *I said*
er sagte *he said*

4. The German **-t-** added to the stem corresponds to the English **-d** in designating the past:

ich höre *I hear*
ich hörte *I heard*

5. German past tense is used primarily for literary narration and description and is translated by the English past or past progressive, depending on the context.

Als sie kamen, arbeiteten wir.	*When they came, we were working.*
Als wir in der Schule waren, arbeiteten wir immer schwer.	*When we were in school, we always worked hard.*

The purpose of this section is to enable you to distinguish the past from the present of weak verbs and to familiarize you further with the vocabulary of the reading passage. Respond to the sentences by giving the correct meaning of the indicated verbs.

	1. Zu diesem Jahrhundert **gehören** Komponisten wie Mahler und Hindemith. (*belong/belonged*)
1. Composers such as Mahler and Hindemith *belong* to this century.	2. Beethoven **gehörte** zu dem 19. Jahrhundert. (*belongs/belonged*)
2. Beethoven *belonged* to the nineteenth century.	3. **das Beispiel** = *the example* Wir **erinnerten** uns an Beispiele wie die Brüder Grimm und ihre Märchen. (*remember/remembered*)
3. We *remembered* examples such as the Grimm brothers and their fairy tales.	4. **manchmal** = *sometimes* **gern** = *like* (to do what the verb indicates) Manchmal **erinnern** wir uns auch an Kaiser, Diktatoren, Könige und Politiker, aber nicht gern. (*remember/remembered*)
4. Sometimes we also *remember* emperors, dictators, kings, and politicians, but we don't like to (lit: but not willingly).	5. **das Gebot** = *the commandment* Schweitzer **verkörpert** das Gebot: „Du sollst deinen Nächsten lieben wie dich selbst.“ (*embodies/embodied*)
5. Schweitzer *embodies* the commandment: "Thou shalt love thy neighbor as thyself."	6. **glauben** = *to believe* Manche Menschen glauben, daß auch Ghandi dieses Gebot **verkörperte.** (*embodies/embodied*)

6. Some people believe that Ghandi also *embodied* this commandment.	**7.** **was für ein** = *what kind of a* Was für eine Macht haben die Ideen von Marx und Engels über die heutige Welt?
7. What kind of power do the ideas of Marx and Engels have over today's world?	**8.** Wir wissen schon, was für eine Macht die Ideen von Marx und Engels auf unsere heutige Welt **ausüben.** (*exert/exerted*)
8. We already know what kind of power the ideas of Marx and Engels *exert* over today's world.	**9.** **Spielen** Bonhoeffer und Bultmann eine führende Rolle in der heutigen Theologie? (*do . . . play/did . . . play*)
9. *Do* Bonhoeffer and Bultmann *play* a leading role in today's theology?	**10.** Er **sagte** uns, daß Barth und Tillich schon damals eine große Rolle in der protestantischen Theologie **spielten.** (*tells/told*) (*play/played*)
10. He *told* us that Barth and Tillich already at that time *played* a great role in Protestant theology.	**11.** **trauen** = *to trust* **das Mißtrauen** = __________
11. distrust, mistrust, suspicion	**12.** **gegenseitig** = *mutual, reciprocal* Grenzen sind ein Symbol des gegenseitigen Mißtrauens.
12. Boundaries are a symbol of mutual distrust.	**13.** Die Grenzen, die uns Menschen zu oft **trennen,** sind ein Symbol des gegenseitigen Mißtrauens. (*separate/separated*)
13. The boundaries which too often *separate* men (lit: us humans) are a symbol of mutual distrust.	**14.** **der Haß** = *hate* Nicht nur die Grenzen des Mißtrauens, sondern auch die Grenzen des Hasses **trennten** die europäischen Nationen. (*separate/separated*)
14. Not only the boundaries of mistrust but also the boundaries of hate *separated* the European nations.	**15.** Man **feiert** Wunderkinder wie Mozart nicht mehr, nur Athleten. (*celebrates/celebrated*)
15. We do not *celebrate* (lit: One celebrates not . . .) child prodigies like Mozart any more, only athletes.	**16.** **welch** = *which* Welche Dichter **meinen** sie? (*do . . . mean/did . . . mean*)

16. Which poets *do* they *mean*?	**17.** **wissen** = *to know* Ich weiß, welche Philosophen ihr **meintet.** (*mean/meant*)
17. I know which philosophers you *meant*.	**18.** **schließlich** = *finally* Eine gemeinsame Sprache **führte** schließlich zu einer politischen Einheit. (*leads/led*)
18. A common language *led* finally to a political unity.	**19.** **leisten** = *to produce, accomplish* Ein großes Gebiet, wo die deutsche Kultur sehr viel **leistet,** ist die Wissenschaft. (*produces/produced*)
19. A large area in which (where) German culture *produces* a great deal is science.	**20.** Einstein **leistete** sehr viel auf dem Gebiet der Physik. (*accomplishes/accomplished*)
20. Einstein *accomplished* a great deal in the realm of physics.	**21.** sich **verbreiten** = *to spread* Der Einfluß des deutschen Expressionismus **verbreitete** sich noch weiter. (*spreads/spread*)
21. The influence of German Expressionism *spread* still further.	**22.** **vernichten** = *to destroy, to do away with* Das Vertrauen zueinander: dadurch **vernichten** wir die Grenzen. (*destroy/destroyed*)
22. Trusting in one another: by this means we *destroy* the boundaries.	**23.** Wissen Sie, ob Napoleon die Grenzen zwischen den Ländern **vernichtete,** als er Kaiser war? (*did/does away with*)
23. Do you know if Napoleon *did away with* the borders between countries when he was emperor?	**24.** **wenig** = *little* Ich **brauchte** wenig über diese berühmten Künstler zu sagen. (*need/needed*)
24. I *needed* to say little about these famous artists.	**25.** Diese Komponisten sind so berühmt, daß ich wenig über sie zu sagen **brauche.** (*need/needed*)

25. These composers are so famous that I *need* to say little about them.	**26.** **der Anfang** = *the beginning* Man **findet** die expressionistische Bewegung in Deutschland am (an dem) Anfang des 20. Jahrhunderts. (*present/past*)
26. *present:* One finds the Expressionist movement in Germany at the beginning of the twentieth century.	**27.** **Unterhalten** Grimms Märchen Kinder und Erwachsene noch heute? (*present/past*)
27. *present:* Do Grimms' fairy tales still entertain children and adults today?	**28.** Wie lange **arbeitete** Einstein an der Formel $E = mc^2$? (*present/past*)
28. *past:* How long did Einstein work on the formula $E = mc^2$?	**29.** **gründen** = *to base* Worauf **gründete** er seine Theorie? (*present/past*)
29. *past:* On what did he base his theory?	**30.** **zeigen** = *to point out* Was **zeigen** uns Jung und Freud heute? (*point out/are pointing out*)
30. What *do* Jung and Freud *point out* to us today?	**31.** Wissen Sie, daß damals ganz Europa Mozart als Wunderkind **feierte?** (*celebrates/celebrated*)
31. Do you know that at that time all of Europe *celebrated* (*was celebrating*) Mozart as a child prodigy?	**32.** **glauben** = *to believe* **unglaublich** = ________
32. *unbelievably, unbelievable.*	**33.** Unglaublich primitive Instinkte **schlummern** in uns. (*are slumbering/slumber/do slumber*)
33. any of the three: Unbelievably primitive instincts *slumber* (*are slumbering, do slumber*) within us.	**34.** **die Seele** = *the soul* Schlummerten viele primitive Instinkte auch in der griechischen Seele zur Zeit des Platons? (*slumbered/were slumbering*)
34. *Were* many primitive instincts *slumbering* also in the Greek soul at the time of Plato?	**35.** **was für** = *what* Freud und Jung zeigen uns, was für unglaublich primitive Instinkte in uns schlummern.

35. Freud and Jung show us what unbelievably primitive instincts slumber within us.	

PROGRESS TEST

Tell whether the indicated verbs are in the past or present.

1. Der Architekt Gropius **verbreitet** seinen Einfluß weiter auf andere Architekten.
2. Wissen Sie, ob auch Gandhi dieses Gebot **verkörperte?**
3. Sie **beurteilte** uns nicht.
4. Ich weiß, welche Philosophen ihr **meintet.**
5. Dadurch **vernichten** wir die Grenzen.
6. Obwohl manche sich über Schweitzers ärztliche Methoden **streiten . . .**
7. Was **zeigten** uns Planck und Hahn?

Answer key: **1.** present; **2.** past; **3.** past; **4.** past; **5.** present; **6.** present; **7.** past.

When you can easily distinguish the present from the past tense of weak verbs, go on to the next section.

17. *Past tense of* ***haben, sein,*** *and* ***werden***

The past tense forms of **haben, sein,** and **werden** are as follows:

	haben	**sein**	**werden**
ich	**hatte** (*had*)	**war** (*was*)	**wurde** (*became*)
du	**hattest**	**warst** (*were*)	**wurdest**
er (sie, es)	**hatte**	**war** (*was*)	**wurde**
wir	**hatten**	**waren** (*were*)	**wurden**
ihr	**hattet**	**wart** (*were*)	**wurdet**
sie	**hatten**	**waren** (*were*)	**wurden**
Sie	**hatten**	**waren** (*were*)	**wurden**

Give the meaning and the tense of the following verbs.

	1. Ich **habe** eine Theorie über den Einfluß von der Politik auf Künstler. (*have/had*)

1. I *have* a theory about the influence of politics on artists.	**2.** **darüber** = *about that* Ich **hatte** eine Theorie darüber. (*have had/had*)
2. I *had* a theory about that.	**3.** **der Ursprung** = *the origin* Die Astronomen **haben** zwei verschiedene Vorstellungen von dem Ursprung des Weltalls (des Universums). (*have/had*)
3. Astronomers *have* two different ideas (conceptions) of the origin of the universe.	**4.** **Hatte Hitler** viel Macht am Anfang der dreißiger Jahre? (*Does Hitler have/Did Hitler have*)
4. *Did Hitler have* much power at the beginning of the thirties?	**5.** **Wir hatten** keinen Einfluß auf ihn. (*we have/we had*)
5. *We had* no influence on him.	**6.** **Hattest du** einen Bruder? (*do you have/did you have*)
6. *Did you have* a brother?	**7.** **Hast** du eine Schwester? (*do . . . have/did . . . have*)
7. *Do* you *have* a sister?	**8.** Ich weiß, daß ihr keine Zeit **habt.** (*do . . . have/did . . . have*)
8. I know that you *do* not *have* any time.	**9.** **eigentlich** = *actually, really* Eigentlich **hattet ihr** keine Zeit. (*you have/you had*)
9. Really, *you had* no time.	**10.** **der Arzt** = *the doctor* **seit wann** = *since when, how long* Seit wann **ist** der Arzt hier? (*is/was*)
10. How long has the doctor been here? (lit.: Since when *is* the doctor here?)	**11.** **das Geld** = *the money* Seit wann **hat er** das Geld?
11. How long has he had the money? (lit.: Since when *has he* the money?	**12.** Schweitzer **stammt aus** dem Elsass. (*comes from/came from*)
12. Schweitzer *comes from* Alsace.	**13.** **Wer war** der aus dem Elsaß stammende Mann? (*who is/who was*)

13. *Who was* the man who came from Alsace? (lit.: coming out of Alsace)	**14.** **arm** = *poor* **die Armut** = __________
14. *poverty*	**15.** **vergessen** = *to forget* **die Vergessenheit** = __________
15. *oblivion* (the condition of being forgotten)	**16.** **das Los** = *the lot (fate)* **Sind Armut und Vergessenheit** das Los vieler Künstler? (*are poverty and oblivion/were poverty and oblivion*)
16. *Are poverty and oblivion* the lot (fate) of many artists?	**17.** **Es waren** eigentlich viele, die gegen Hitler waren. (*there is/there were*)
17. Actually, *there were* many who were against Hitler.	**18.** **Ihr seid** alle Politiker! (*you are/you were*)
18. *You are* all politicians!	**19.** **der Monat** = *the month* **Sie ist** schon seit zwei Monaten in Deutschland. (*she is/she has been*)
19. *She has* already *been* in Germany for two months. (Notice how *seit* and the present in German is expressed by the present perfect in English.)	**20.** **gestern** = *yesterday* **Warst du** gestern in Salzburg? (*are you/were you*)
20. *Were you* in Salzburg yesterday?	**21.** **Bist du** Christ, Jude oder Muselmann? (*are you/were you*)
21. *Are you* a Christian, Jew, or Moslem?	**22.** **Ich werde** alt. (*I am getting/I was getting*)
22. *I am getting* old.	**23.** **dick** = *fat* **Ich wurde** dick. (*I am getting/I got*)
23. *I got* fat.	**24.** **Du wirst** groß. (*you are getting/were getting*)
24. *You are getting* big.	**25.** **Du wurdest** Arzt. (*you are becoming/you became*)

25. *You became* a doctor.	**26.** Sie **wird** nicht dick, sondern dünn. (*she is becoming/she became*)
26. *She is* not *becoming* fat but thin.	**27.** **fahren** = *to travel* **Wird sie** nach Salzburg **fahren?** (*will they travel/will she travel*)
27. *Will* she *travel* to Salzburg?	**28.** **nie** = *never* Die Franzosen werden Napoleon nie vergessen.
28. The French will never forget Napoleon.	**29.** **Wurde Schweitzer** Theologe? (*does Schweitzer become/did Schweitzer become*)
29. *Did Schweitzer become* a theologian?	**30.** **Wir werden** Physiker und Politiker. (*we are becoming/we were becoming*)
30. *We are becoming* physicists and politicians..	**31.** Freud und Jung **wurden** Psychiater und Psychologen. (*become/became*)
31. Freud and Jung *became* psychiatrists and psychologists.	**32.** **Ihr werdet** Musiker. (*you are becoming/you were becoming*)
32. *You are becoming* musicians.	**33.** **Wurdet ihr** Künstler? (*are you becoming/did you become*)
33. *Did you become* artists?	**34.** **Werden sie** Wissenschaftler? (*are the becoming/were they becoming*)
34. *Are they becoming* scientists?	

PROGRESS TEST

Give the meaning of the sentence and the tense of the indicated verbs.

1. **Hatte** Hitler viel Macht am Anfang der dreißiger Jahre?
2. Ihr **wurdet** Künstler.
3. **Warst** du gestern in Salzburg?
4. Du **wurdest** Arzt.
5. **Hattest** du einen Bruder?

Now give the meaning of the indicated words.

6. Wie können wir zum Teil die Grenzen **vernichten**, die uns Menschen zu oft trennen?
(a) to forget (b) for nothing (c) to do away with (d) to enjoy

7. Gibt es eine andere Kultur, die zur Geschichte der Musik soviel **beigetragen hat** wie die deutsche?
(a) has contributed (b) has harmed (c) has defamed (d) has made famous

8. Auf dem wissenschaftlichen Gebiet **leistet** sie auch sehr viel.
(a) lasts (b) accomplishes (c) is striving (d) loses

9. Aus dem deutschen Kulturbereich **stammt** auch der jüdische Religionsphilosoph Martin Buber.
(a) criticizes (b) praises (c) remained (d) comes

10. **Eigentlich** gibt es sehr wenige große deutsche Künstler.
(a) at the present time (b) actually (c) formerly (d) however

11. Die einzige große künstlerische **Bewegung** ist der Expressionismus.
(a) movement (b) figure (c) idea (d) technique

12. Luthers 95 Thesen führen zu dem **verheerendsten** Kriege Deutschlands.
(a) most unusual (b) most devastating (c) most remembered (d) most ludicrous

13. Luthers Bibelübersetzung führte **schließlich** zu einer gemeinsamen Sprache und zu einer politischen Einheit.
(a) originally (b) unknowingly (c) tumultuously (d) finally

Answer key:
1. Did Hitler have much power at the beginning of the thirties? (past) **2.** You became artists. (past) **3.** Were you in Salzburg yesterday? (past) **4.** You became a doctor. (past) **5.** Did you have a brother? (past) **6.** (c); **7.** (a); **8.** (b); **9.** (d); **10.** (b); **11.** (a); **12.** (b); **13.** (d).

Before going on to the reading passage, review all of the words you have circled.

Deutsche Kultur

Wenn wir von deutschen Dichtern, Künstlern, Philosophen, Wissenschaftlern, Komponisten und Theologen sprechen, meinen wir nicht nur die, die aus Deutschland stammen, sondern auch die, die Deutsch als Muttersprache sprechen. Dadurch vernichten wir zum Teil die Grenzen, die uns Menschen allzuoft trennen. Wie heißen diese Menschen, die nicht nur in der deutschen Kultur, sondern oft auch in der Welt eine führende Rolle spielen?

Wenn wir von Philosophen sprechen, so erinnern wir uns an Namen wie Kant, Hegel, Marx, Engels, Schopenhauer, Nietzsche, Spengler und Karl Jaspers. Wir wissen schon, was für eine Macht die Ideen von Marx und Engels auf unsere heutige Welt ausüben.

Deutsche Dichter wie Goethe, Schiller, Kafka, Brecht und Thomas Mann spielen eine große Rolle in der Weltliteratur. Die Brüder Grimm und ihre Märchen unterhalten Kinder und Erwachsene heute immer noch.

In der Zivilisation des Westens gibt es keine andere Kultur, die soviel zur Geschichte der Musik beigetragen hat wie die deutsche. Also braucht man wenig über Namen wie Bach, Haydn, Beethoven, Schubert, Schumann, Hugo Wolf, Brahms und Wagner zu sagen. Zu diesem Jahrhundert gehören Richard Strauss, Mahler, Schönberg, Anton Webern, Hindemith, Alban Berg und Carl Orff. Wir vergessen aber nicht den größten von allen, in Salzburg geboren, als Wunderkind von ganz Europa gefeiert und in Armut und Vergessenheit gestorben: Mozart.

Auch ein großes Gebiet, wo die deutsche Kultur sehr viel leistet, ist die Wissenschaft. Astronomen, Mathematiker, Physiker und Chemiker, wie Kepler, Leibniz, Bunsen und Kirchhoff, Röntgen, Planck, Hahn und Einstein, haben unsere Vorstellung des Universums und des Atoms unwiderruflich geändert. Psychologen und Psychiater, wie Freud aus Österreich und Jung aus der Schweiz, zeigen uns, was für unglaublich primitive Instinkte in uns schlummern.

Auch ein Beispiel der reinen Humanität gibt uns die deutsche Kultur, wenn auch aus dem Elsaß stammend: Albert Schweitzer, Theologe, Musiker, und Arzt von Beruf, aber auch Philosoph, Humanist und Christ. Von den heutigen protestantischen Theologen sind Karl Barth und Paul Tillich bekannt. Dietrich Bonhoeffer und Rudolf Bultmann spielen auch eine führende Rolle in der heutigen Theologie. Der große jüdische Religionsphilosoph Martin Buber stammt auch aus dem deutschen Kulturbereich.

Man erinnert sich manchmal nicht gern an Kaiser, Könige, Diktatoren und Politiker. Wir sollten aber den Einfluß von Friedrich Barbarossa, Friedrich dem Großen und Maria Theresia, Bismarck und Hitler nicht vergessen. Obwohl Martin Luther Theologe war, dürfen wir seine Rolle in der Politik nicht übersehen. Seine 95 Thesen beginnen die Reformation, die zu dem verheerendsten Kriege Deutschlands führt, dem Dreißigjährigen Kriege. Seine Bibelübersetzung, die den Deutschen eine Bibel gab, gab ihnen auch eine gemeinsame Sprache, die schließlich zu einer politischen Einheit führte.

Chapter Five

18. *Prepositions—genitive case*

1. The case of the noun changes according to the preposition which precedes it. Some prepositions are followed by the genitive case, some by the dative, and some by the accusative:

Trotz **des schlechten Wetters bleibt er draußen.** (genitive)	***In spite of*** *the bad weather he remains outside.*
Er wohnt *bei* seiner Tante. (dative)	*He lives* ***with*** *his aunt.*
Sie läuft *durch* das Haus. (accusative)	*She runs* ***through*** *the house.*

2. The more commonly used prepositions followed by the genitive case are:

(an)statt	*instead of*
Anstatt **des Bruders kommt die Schwester.**	*The sister is coming* ***instead of*** *the brother.*
trotz	*in spite of*
Trotz **des schlechten Wetters fliegt er morgen nach New York.**	***In spite of*** *the bad weather he is flying to New York tomorrow.*
während	*during*
Während **des Tages schläft er.**	*He sleeps* ***during*** *the day.*

wegen	*on account of, because of*
***Wegen* meiner Freunde bleibe ich hier. Meiner Freunde *wegen* bleibe ich hier.**	*I am staying here* ***on account of*** *my friends.*
außerhalb	*outside of*
Er wohnte *außerhalb* der Stadt.	*He lived* ***outside of*** *the city.*
innerhalb	*inside of, within*
***Innerhalb* eines Tages wird er das Mädchen vergessen.**	***Within*** *a day he will forget the girl.*
diesseits	*on this side of*
***Diesseits* des Flusses liegt eine Fabrik.**	***On this side of*** *the river is a factory.*
jenseits	*on that side of*
***Jenseits* des Flusses ist Luftverpestung.**	***On the other side of*** *the river is air pollution.*
oberhalb	*above*
***Oberhalb* des Dorfes liegt eine einsame Kirche.**	***Above*** *the village lies a lonely church.*
unterhalb	*below*
***Unterhalb* der Kirche liegt ein verlassener Friedhof.**	***Below*** *the church lies a deserted cemetery.*
um . . . willen	*for the sake of*
***Um* seines Vaters *willen* ging er nicht ins Kino.**	***For his father's sake*** *he did not go to the movies.*

Trotz and **wegen** may also be followed by the dative case.

The following exercises give you practice in recognizing the meaning of prepositions. Choose the correct meaning of the indicated words. Remember to keep the left hand column covered until you have made a real effort to read the German.

	1. **Anstatt** eines Kanzlers hatten die Deutschen einen Diktatoren. (*because of/instead of*)
1. *Instead of* a chancellor the Germans had a dictator.	**2.** **Statt** eines Königs haben wir in den Vereinigten Staaten einen Präsidenten.

2. *Instead of* a king we in the United States have a president.	**3.** **die Angst** = *anxiety* **Trotz** der Psychologie haben wir immer noch Angst. (*in spite of/because of*)
3. *In spite of* psychology, we are still filled with anxieties.	**4.** **Trotz** unserer Humanität gibt es viel Haß in diesem Land.
4. *In spite of* our humanity, there is much hate in this country.	**5.** **Während** des Krieges blieben wir in Berlin. (*moreover/during*)
5. *During* the war we remained in Berlin.	**6.** **wird verpestet** = *is becoming polluted* **Wegen** der vielen Autos wird die **Luft** verpestet. (**die Luft** probably means ________)
6. *Because of* the many automobiles *the air* is becoming polluted.	**7.** **Während** dieses Jahrhunderts wird die Luft immer mehr verpestet.
7. *During* this century the air is becoming more and more polluted.	**8.** Sprechen die Deutschen **wegen** der Bibelübersetzung eine gemeinsame Sprache? (*in spite of/because of*)
8. Do the Germans speak a common language *because of* the translation of the Bible?	**9.** **Wegen** Hitler liegt Deutschland jetzt getrennt.
9. *Because of* Hitler Germany is now divided (lit.: now lies separated).	**10.** **Trotz** der Vorstellungen des Universums verstehen wir immer noch nicht das Warum.
10. *In spite of* the ideas about the universe, we still do not understand the "*why of it.*" (Notice that **Warum** is here used as a noun.)	**11.** **Statt** einer neuen Vorstellung des Universums hatten sie wieder ein Nichts.
11. *Instead of* a new conception of the universe they again had nothing. (i.e. their ideas again did not conform to their observations.)	**12.** Das Land liegt **außerhalb** seines Einflusses. (*within/outside of*)
12. That country lies *outside of* his influence.	**13.** **Außerhalb** dieses Semesters werden wir nicht Deutsch studieren.

13. *Outside of* this semester we will not study German.	**14.** **die Ruhe** = *peace* **Innerhalb** der Städte gibt es keine Ruhe mehr. (Being the opposite of **außerhalb, innerhalb** must mean ________.)
14. *Within* the cities there is no longer any peace. (**der Staat** = *state;* **die Stadt** = *city*)	**15.** **Innerhalb** eines Jahres müssen wir diese Arbeit zu Ende bringen.
15. *Within* a year we must bring this work to an end.	**16.** **die Kirche** = *the church* **Oberhalb** der Kirche sieht man einen Weinberg.
16. One sees a vineyard *above* the church.	**17.** **das Tal** = *valley* **Unterhalb** des Dorfes liegt das Tal.
17. *Below* the village lies the valley.	**18.** Liegt ein Wald **außerhalb** des Dorfes?
18. Does a forest lie *outside of* the village?	**19.** ***der*** **See** = *the lake* **Unterhalb** des Dorfes liegt ein See.
19. *Below* the village lies a lake. (cf. ***die*** **See** = *the sea, the ocean*)	**20.** **Jenseits** des Atlantischen Ozeans liegt Europa.
20. Europe lies *on the other side of* the Atlantic Ocean.	**21.** Europa liegt **diesseits** des heutigen Rußlands.
21. Europe lies *this side of* present-day Russia.	**22.** Wollen die Menschen **diesseits** des Meeres in Ruhe und Frieden wohnen?
22. Do the people *on this side of* the ocean want to live in peace?	**23.** **aufhören** = *to stop, desist* **Um** Himmels **willen,** hören Sie auf!
23. *For* heaven's *sake* stop it!	**24.** **Um** Inges **willen** will er nicht mehr kommen.
24. *For* Inge's *sake* he is not going to come any more. (Here **will nicht** expresses resolution, intention)	**25.** **Um** Pauls **willen** brauchen Sie nicht mehr zu kommen.
25. You do not need to come *for* Paul's *sake* any more.	**26.** **wohl** = *surely, truly* Gibt es ein **Jenseits**? Das weiß man nicht, aber es gibt wohl ein **Diesseits.** (In a discussion of religion **Jenseits** and **Diesseits** probably refer to ________.)

26. Is there a *next world*? We don't know about that, but there is truly a *present world* (*a this side*).	

PROGRESS TEST

Choose the correct meaning of the indicated words.

1. **verfolgen** = *to persecute*
   Wurde Kopernikus von der Kirche verfolgt **wegen** der neuen Vorstellung des Weltalls?
   (a) in spite of (b) during (c) because of (d) instead of
2. **die Mauer** = *wall*
   Trotz der Mauer versuchen Deutsche immer noch nach West-Berlin zu fliehen.
   (a) beneath (b) in spite of (c) because of (d) on the other side of
3. **Anstatt** des Friedens werden wir nur Krieg haben.
   (a) instead of (b) during (c) in spite of (d) because of
4. **Außerhalb** dieses Semesters werden wir nicht Deutsch studieren.
   (a) in addition to (b) because of (c) in spite of (d) outside of
5. **fliegen** = *to fly*
   Während des Sommers müssen wir nach Österreich fliegen.
   (a) ago (b) on account of (c) before (d) during
6. **der Wachtturm** = *watch tower*
   Jenseits der Grenze steht ein großer Wachtturm.
   (a) because of (b) on that side of (c) on this side of (d) in spite of

Answer key: **1.** (c); **2.** (b); **3.** (a); **4.** (d); **5.** (d); **6.** (b).

19. *Prepositions—dative case*

1. The dative case follows these prepositions:

aus	*out of, of, from* (cities or countries)
Er geht *aus* dem Hause.	*He goes **out of** the house.*
außer	*except, besides*
***Außer* ihm ist niemand da.**	*No one is there **except** him.*
bei	*near, at, in or at the house of, with*
Das Restaurant liegt *beim* (*bei dem*) Bahnhof.	*The restaurant is **near** the railway station.*
gegenüber	*opposite, across from*
Der Lehrer sitzt mir *gegenüber*.	*The teacher is sitting **opposite** me.*

mit	*with*
Sie schreibt *mit* einem Bleistift.	*She is writing **with** a pencil.*
nach	*after, to* (cities and countries)
Wir fahren nächstes Jahr *nach* Deutschland.	*We will travel **to** Germany next year.*
Wird es *nach* dem Krieg Frieden geben?	*Will there be peace **after** the war?*
seit	*since, for* (duration of time)
***Seit* der Zeit spricht er nicht mehr mit mir.**	***Since** that time he has not spoken with me any more.*
von	*from, of, by* (authorship), *about*
Der Brief kommt *von* meinem Freund.	*The letter comes **from** my friend.*
zu	*to*
Was sagte er *zu* Ihnen?	*What did he say **to** you?*

2. As you have no doubt noticed previously, several of these prepositions may be contracted with the definite article:

außerm	=	**außer dem**
beim	=	**bei dem**
vom	=	**von dem**
zum	=	**zu dem**
zur	=	**zu der**

Hans wohnt *beim* Onkel.	*Hans lives **with** his uncle.*
Paula geht *zur* Universität.	*Paula goes **to** the university.*

Choose the best meaning for the indicated words. Continue to circle unfamiliar words for review.

	1. Der Präsident kommt **aus** dem Hotel. (*of/out of*)
1. The president is coming *out of* the hotel.	**2.** **steigen** = *to climb* Hans steigt **aus** dem Auto. (*out of/away from/into*)

2. Hans climbs *out of* the automobile.	**3.** Friedrich ist **aus** Berlin. (*of/out of/from*)
3. Friedrich is *from* Berlin.	**4.** Paul wohnt **bei** seinem Onkel. (*away from/with*)
4. Paul lives *with* his uncle (*at his uncle's home*).	**5.** Emil war gestern **bei** seiner Tante. (*by/at the home of*)
5. Emil was *at his aunt's* yesterday.	**6.** Inge wohnt **bei** der Kirche. (*near/at*)
6. Inge lives *near* the church.	**7.** Potsdam liegt **bei** Berlin. (*with/at/near*)
7. Potsdam is *near* Berlin.	**8.** **dir** = *you* Hast du kein Geld **bei** dir? (*near/with/at*)
8. Don't you have any money *with* you?	**9.** **sich** = *you* Haben Sie das Buch **bei** sich? (*with/near*)
9. Do you have the book *with* you?	**10.** Fahren Sie morgen **nach** München? (*after/to*)
10. Are you going to travel *to* Munich tomorrow?	**11.** **das Essen** = *eating, the meal* **Nach** dem Essen trinken wir eine Tasse Kaffee. (*after/to*)
11. *After* eating (the meal) we drink a cup of coffee.	**12.** Was **wird aus** Deutschland? (In connection with **wird, aus** must mean: *of/out of/from*)
12. What will become *of* Germany?	**13.** Heute besteht Deutschland **aus** zwei Teilen. (*from/of/out of*)
13. Today Germany consists *of* two parts.	**14.** **gesehen** = *seen* **geteilt** = *separated, divided* **Vom** (von dem) kirchlichen Standpunkt aus gesehen, ist Deutschland geteilt.

14. Seen *from* the standpoint of the church, Germany is divided.	**15.** Deutschland war nur **von** 1871 bis 1945 ein Staat. (*of/by/from*)
15. Germany was a single state only *from* 1871 to 1945.	**16.** *Mein Kampf* ist **von** Hitler. (*by/from/of*)
16. Hitler wrote *Mein Kampf*. (lit.: *Mein Kampf* is *by* Hitler.)	**17.** **ganz** = *entirely, wholly* **das Ganze** = ________
17. the whole, the entirety	**18.** **wurde vereinigt** = *was united* Deutschland wurde **von** Bismarck zu einem Ganzen vereinigt. (*of/by/from*)
18. Germany was united *by* Bismarck into a whole.	**19.** **die Gegenüberstellung** = *the confrontation* Ist Deutschland ein Symbol für die Gegenüberstellung **von** Osten und Westen? (*by/from/of*)
19. Is Germany a symbol of the confrontation *of* East and West?	**20.** **hauptsächlich** = *essentially, largely* Zeigt Deutschland auch die Gegenüberstellung **von** dem hauptsächlich protestantischen Norden und dem hauptsächlich katholischen Süden? (*of/by/from*)
20. Does Germany also demonstrate (lit.: point, show) the confrontation *of* the largely Protestant North and the largely Catholic South?	**21.** **Außer** Deutschland sind andere Länder geteilt, zum Beispiel Irland, Vietnam und Korea. (*except/besides*)
21. *Besides* Germany other countries are divided, for example Ireland, Vietnam, and Korea.	**22.** **der Schwerpunkt** = *focal point* Geographisch und historisch gesehen, ist Deutschland ein Land **mit** vielen Schwerpunkten, Ländern und Dialekten.
22. Seen geographically and historically, Germany is a country *with* many focal points, states, and dialects.	**23.** **Seit** Luther wird Deutschland von einer gemeinsamen Sprache geeinigt. (*for/since*)
23. *Since* Luther Germany has been united by a common language.	**24.** **außerm** is the contraction of ________

24. außer dem	**25. beim** is the contraction of ________
25. bei dem	**26. vom** is the contraction of ________
26. von dem	**27. zum** is the contraction of ________
27. zu dem	**28. zur** is the contraction of ________
28. zu der	

PROGRESS TEST

Give the meanings of the indicated words. If you miss any of them, review them before continuing to the next section.

1. **bestehen** = *to consist*
   Heute besteht Irland **aus** zwei Teilen.
2. Paul wohnt **bei** seiner Tante.
3. Heute ist Deutschland ein Symbol für die Gegenüberstellung **von** Osten und Westen.
4. **Außer** Deutschland sind andere Länder geteilt, zum Beispiel Irland, Vietnam und Korea.
5. Geographisch und historisch gesehen, ist Deutschland ein Land **mit** vielen Schwerpunkten, Ländern und Dialekten.
6. **Nach** dem Essen trinken wir eine Tasse Kaffee.
7. **Seit** Luther wird Deutschland von einer gemeinsamen Sprache geeinigt.
8. Was sagt der deutsche Dramatiker Bertolt Brecht **zur** Wiedervereinigungsfrage?

Answer key: **1.** of; **2.** with, at the home of; **3.** of; **4.** besides; **5.** with; **6.** after; **7.** since; **8.** about.

20. *Prepositions—accusative case*

1. The accusative case follows these prepositions:

bis	*until, to, as far as*
Er fährt nur *bis* München.	*He is only traveling **as far as** Munich.*
durch	*through, by means of*
Reist du nicht *durch* Italien?	*Aren't you going to travel **through** Italy?*

für	*for*
Der Vater kaufte einen Ball *für* seinen Sohn.	*The father bought a ball **for** his son.*
gegen	*against, toward* (time *or* direction)
Ich habe nichts *gegen* ihn.	*I have nothing **against** him.*
Erika kommt *gegen* sechs Uhr nach Hause.	*Erika will come home **about** (**toward**) six o'clock.*
ohne	*without*
***Ohne* Wasser kann man nicht leben.**	*One cannot live **without** water.*
um	*around, at* (time)
Der Bus fährt *um* die Ecke.	*The bus drives **around** the corner.*
Kommt Anja *um* sechs?	*Is Anja coming **at** six?*
wider	*against*
Das ist *wider* meine Natur.	*That is **against** my nature.*

2. Two accusative prepositions usually follow their objects:

entlang	*along*
Den Fluß *entlang* stehen hohe Bäume.	*Tall trees stand **along** the river.*
lang	*long, for, during*
Viele Jahre *lang* war er ein armer Mensch.	***For** many years he was a poor man.*

3. Common contractions of the accusative prepositions are:

durchs = **durch das**
fürs = **für das**
ums = **um das**

Michael läuft *durchs* Haus. — *Michael runs **through** the house.*

Select the meaning of the indicated prepositions which is suggested by the context.

1. **bleiben** = *to remain*
Zwei Monate **lang** blieb Margarete auf dem Lande.
(*along/for*)

1. *For* two months Margarete remained in the country.	**2.** Die ganze Familie sitzt noch einmal **um** einen Tisch. (*around/for*)
2. The whole family is sitting once again *around* a single table.	**3.** **die Ecke** = *the corner* Nie geht er **um** die Ecke zum Postamt. (*at/for/around*)
3. He never goes *around* the corner to the post office.	**4.** **Um** drei Uhr komme ich wieder nach Hause. (*at/for*)
4. *At* three o'clock I will come home again.	**5.** **bitten** = *to ask* **höflich** = *courteously, politely* Der Räuber bat mich höflichst **um** mein Geld. (*for/at/around*)
5. The robber asked me most courteously *for* my money.	**6.** **wer** = *whoever, who* Wer nicht mit mir ist, ist **wider** mich. (Bibel) (*for/against*)
6. Whoever is not with me is *against* me.	**7.** **mag** = *can, may* Ist Gott für uns, wer mag **wider** uns sein? (Bibel) (*for/against*)
7. If God is for us, who can be *against* us?	**8.** **Graz:** a city in Austria Kommen Sie bald **wieder** nach Graz! (*against/again*)
8. Come back *again* soon to Graz!	**9.** Wann werden wir Sie **wieder** sehen?
9. When will we see you *again*?	**10.** **stürzen** = *to fall heavily* **der Sturz** = ________
10. *the fall, crash, collapse, downfall*	**11.** Deutschland blieb ein Staat **bis** 1945 und Hitlers Sturz. (*after/until/before*)
11. Germany remained a united state *until* 1945 and Hitler's downfall.	**12.** **beide** = *both* **Bis** die beiden Staaten, die Bundesrepublik und die DDR, die notwendigen Konzessionen machen . . . (*to/as far as/until*)

12. *Until* the two states, the Federal Republic and the German Democratic Republic, make the necessary concessions . . .	**13.** **Bayern** = *Bavaria* Fahren Sie nur **bis** München, die Hauptstadt Bayerns! (*until/as far as*)
13. Travel only *as far as* Munich, the capital city of Bavaria.	**14.** **dürfen** = *are permitted* Die West- und Ostberliner dürfen nur **bis an** die Mauer gehen. (*until/as far as*)
14. The residents of West and East Berlin are permitted to go only *as far as* the wall.	**15.** **reisen** = *to travel* Darf man eigentlich **durch** die ganzen Vereinigten Staaten ohne Paß reisen? (*throughout/by means of*)
15. Can one really travel *throughout* the whole United States without a passport?	**16.** Wurde Deutschland sprachlich **durch** Luther zu einem Ganzen vereinigt? (*through/by*)
16. Was Germany linguistically united *by* Luther into a whole?	**17.** **voraussehen** = *to foresee* Ist es wahr, daß **gegen** 1945 Hitlers Sturz klar vorauszusehen war? (*towards/against*)
17. Is it true that *towards* 1945 Hitler's downfall was clearly (to be) foreseen?	**18.** **die Gnade** = *mercy* **Gegen** seine Feinde zeigte er keine Gnade. (*against/towards*)
18. He showed no mercy *towards* his enemies.	**19.** Im Zweiten Weltkrieg kämpften die Engländer, Russen, Amerikaner, Franzosen und noch andere **gegen** die Deutschen. (*against/towards*)
19. In the Second World War the English, Russians, Americans, French, as well as others, fought *against* the Germans.	**20.** Das Los der Hitler-Politik: Deutsche **gegen** Deutsche. (*towards/against*)
20. The lot of Hitler's policies: Germans *against* Germans.	**21.** **das Gefängnis** = *the prison* Die Mauer in Berlin ist eine Barrikade **für** Ostdeutsche, die fliehen wollen, und ein Gefängnis **für** die Westberliner, die Bewegungsfreiheit haben wollen. (*for/four*)

21. The Berlin Wall is a barricade *for* East Germans who want to flee, and a prison *for* West Berliners who want to have freedom of movement.	**22.** **schön** = *beautiful* **die Schönheit** = ________
22. *beauty*	**23.** **einmalig** = *unique* Dresden ist berühmt **für** seine einmalige Schönheit.
23. Dresden is famous *for* its unique beauty.	**24.** **sichern** = *to secure* **Ohne** die Mauer in Berlin konnte die DDR die ökonomische Stabilität nicht sichern. (*without/with*)
24. *Without* the Berlin Wall the German Democratic Republic could not secure economic stability.	**25.** **nachts** = *in the night* Nachts **um** zwölf wollen sie die Mauer sehen. (*around/at*)
25. They want to see the Wall *at* twelve midnight.	**26.** **bedingen** = *to stipulate* Kann eine Wiedervereinigung je stattfinden, **ohne** die notwendigen Konzessionen, die eine Wiedervereinigung bedingen? (*because/without*)
26. Can a reunification ever take place *without* the necessary concessions which stipulate a reunification (i.e. which are necessary for reunification)?	**27.** Die Mauer **entlang** sieht man viele Wachttürme. (*along/long*)
27. *Along* the Wall one sees many watchtowers.	**28.** Wien, heute die Hauptstadt Österreichs, war fast fünf Jahrhunderte **lang** deutsche Hauptstadt. (*for/long*)
28. Vienna, today the capital of Austria, was *for* almost five centuries the German capital.	**29.** **Durchs** is the contraction of ________
29. **durch das**	**30.** **Fürs** is naturally the contraction of ________
30. **für das**	**31.** And **ums** can only be the contraction of ________

31. um das	

PROGRESS TEST

Choose the correct meaning for the indicated words.

1. **Bis** die Bundesrepublik und die DDR die notwendigen Konzessionen machen . . .
   (a) after (b) until (c) before (d) while
2. Wurde Deutschland sprachlich **durch** Luther zu einem Ganzen vereinigt?
   (a) in spite of (b) during (c) against (d) by
3. Ist es wahr, daß **gegen** 1945 Hitlers Sturz klar vorauszusehen war?
   (a) towards (b) away from (c) against (d) for
4. Der Räuber bat mich höflichst **um** mein Geld.
   (a) until (b) towards (c) around (d) for
5. Die Mauer in Berlin ist eine Barrikade **für** Ostdeutsche, die fliehen wollen, und ein Gefängnis **für** Westberliner, die Bewegungsfreiheit haben wollen.
   (a) until (b) with (c) for (d) towards
6. Kann eine Wiedervereinigung je stattfinden, **ohne** die notwendigen Konzessionen, die eine Wiedervereinigung bedingen?
   (a) with (b) through (c) although (d) without
7. Wer nicht mit mir ist, ist **wider** mich.
   (a) against (b) in favor of (c) with (d) without
8. Die Mauer **entlang** sieht man viele Wachttürme.
   (a) through (b) along (c) because of (d) in spite of
9. Zwei Monate **lang** blieb Margarete auf dem Land.
   (a) languishingly (b) through (c) for (d) after

Answer key: **1.** (b); **2.** (d); **3.** (a); **4.** (d); **5.** (c); **6.** (d); **7.** (a); **8.** (b); **9.** (c).

21. *Prepositions—dative/accusative*

1. Some prepositions may be followed either by the dative or by the accusative case.

2. The dative case designates a stationary relationship or a confined movement. The accusative indicates motion towards a specific goal. The translation of the preposition varies according to the English verb upon which it depends.

3. The prepositions are listed along with specific examples in both cases, first in the dative, then in the accusative:

an	*at, on, to, in*
Ich sitze *an* dem Fenster.	*I sit **at** the window.*
Ich gehe *an* das Fenster.	*I go **to** the window.*
auf	*on, upon, on top of, in, at, to*
Wir sitzen *auf* dem Sofa.	*We are sitting **on** the sofa.*
Wir setzen uns *auf* das Sofa.	*We sit down **on** the sofa.*
hinter	*behind*
Das Kind steht *hinter* dem Tisch.	*The child stands **behind** the table.*
Das Kind geht *hinter* den Tisch.	*The child goes **behind** the table.*
in	*in, into, to*
Sie bleibt *in* der Kirche.	*She remains **in** the church.*
Sie geht *in* die Kirche.	*She goes **into** the church.* *She goes **to** church.*
neben	*beside, next to*
Ihr sitzt *neben* dem neuen Studenten.	*You are sitting **next to** the new student.*
Setzt euch *neben* den neuen Studenten!	*Sit down **next to** the new student!*
über	*above, over, about, across*
Wir fliegen *über* den Bergen.	*We are flying **above** the mountains.*
Wir fliegen *über* die Berge.	*We are flying **over** the mountains (from one side to another).*
unter	*under, beneath, below, among*
Der Teufel ist *unter* den Menschen.	*The devil is **among** men.*
Eine Katze schleicht *unter* das Haus.	*A cat slinks **under** the house.*
vor	*before, in front of, ago* (time)
Du stehst *vor* dem Haus.	*You are standing **in front of** the house.*
Du gehst *vor* das Haus.	*You are going **to the front of** the house.*
zwischen	*between*
Sie sitzt *zwischen* den zwei reichsten Männern.	*She sits **between** the two richest men.*

Sie setzt sich *zwischen* die zwei reichsten Männer.	*She sits down **between** the two richest men.*

4. Some of these prepositions may be contracted as follows:

an dem	=	**am**
an das	=	**ans**
auf das	=	**aufs**
hinter das	=	**hinters**
in dem	=	**im**
in das	=	**ins**
über das	=	**übers**
unter dem	=	**unterm**
unter das	=	**unters**
vor das	=	**vors**

Er geht *vors* Haus.	*He goes **to the front of the** house.*
Wir werfen den Ball *übers* Haus.	*We throw the ball **over the** house.*
Der faule Mensch liegt *im* Bett.	*The lazy man lies **in** bed.*
Die einsame Frau sitzt *am* Fenster.	*The lonely woman sits **at the** window.*

Give the meaning of the indicated prepositions as well as of the entire sentences

	1. Hoffen die Deutschen **in** der DDR mehr auf eine Wiedervereinigung als die in der Bundesrepublik?
1. Do the Germans *in* the German Democratic Republic hope more for a reunification than those in the Federal Republic?	2. Deutschland ist immer noch geteilt, **in** den hauptsächlich protestantischen Norden und den hauptsächlich katholischen Süden.
2. Germany is still separated *into* the largely Protestant North and the largely Catholic South.	3. **ehemalig** = *former, previous* Berlin, die ehemalige Hauptstadt, liegt auch **in** zwei Teile zerschnitten.
3. Berlin, the former capital, is also cut *into* two parts.	4. Er kaufte ein Haus **neben** dem Haus seines Vaters.
4. He bought a house *next to* his father's house.	5. Nur wenige fliehen **hinter** den Eisernen Vorhang.

5. Only a few flee *behind* the Iron Curtain. (Note that the English sentence can be interpreted in two ways, the German in only one. Here the meaning is clearly to flee from a non-Iron Curtain country into an Iron Curtain country.)	**6.** **die Jungen** = *the boys* **Hinter** dem Kuhstall teilen die Jungen ihre Zigaretten.
6. The boys divide their cigarettes *behind* the (cow) barn.	**7.** Meine Freunde helfen mir **über** die Mauer.
7. My friends help me *over* the wall.	**8.** **erst** = *only* (*for the first time, not until*) Erst **unter** Bismarck wurde die preußische Hauptstadt Berlin die Hauptstadt Deutschlands.
8. Only *under* Bismarck did the Prussian capital Berlin become the capital of Germany.	**9.** **mich** = *me* Diese Klasse wird mich **unter** die Erde bringen.
9. This class will be the death of me. (lit.: will bring me *under* the earth.)	**10.** **das Bild** = *picture* **die Wand** = *wall* Das Bild hängt **an** der Wand.
10. The picture hangs *on* the wall.	**11.** Niemand klopft **an** die Türe.
11. No one is knocking *at* the door.	**12.** **die Arbeit** = *work* Gehen Sie **an** die Arbeit? (*at/on/to*)
12. Are you going *to* work?	**13.** Er ist jung **an** Jahren. (*on/to/in*)
13. He is young *in* years.	**14.** **klein** = *little* Stellen Sie die Lampe **auf** den kleinen Tisch! (*in/to/on*)
14. Place the lamp *on* the little table.	**15.** **wiederholen** = *to repeat* Können Sie das **auf** deutsch wiederholen? (*on top of/in/at*)
15. Can you repeat that *in* German?	**16.** Wir alle gehen **auf** die Universität. (*at/on/to/in*)

16. We all go *to* the university.	**17.** **Vor** dem Haus steht ein schöner Mercedes. (*before/in front of/ago*)
17. *In front of* the house is a beautiful Mercedes.	**18.** Some of the more common contractions of this group of prepositions are: **am** = ________
18. **an dem**	**19.** **Ans** is the contraction of ________
19. **an das**	**20.** Similarly **aufs** is the contraction of ________
20. **auf das**	**21.** **Ins** can only be a contraction of ________
21. **in das**	**22.** **Im** is no doubt a contraction of ________
22. **in dem**	**23.** Occasionally one sees **hintern,** a contraction of ________
23. **hinter den**	**24.** or **untern,** a contraction of ________
24. **unter den**	**25.** Keep in mind that it is always a (definite/indefinite) article which is contracted.
25. *definite*	

22. *Infinitival phrases*

The prepositions **(an)statt, ohne,** and **um** may introduce infinitival phrases having the following meanings:

(an)statt . . . zu	*instead of*
ohne . . . zu	*without*
um . . . zu	*in order to*
Anstatt **in die Bibliothek *zu* gehen, geht er ins Kino.**	***Instead of*** *going to the library he goes to the movies.*
Ohne **ein Wort *zu* sagen, starb er.**	***Without*** *saying a word, he died.*
Um **Deutsch *zu* lernen, muß man viel arbeiten.**	***In order to*** *learn German one has to study a lot.*

Choose the correct phrase or preposition as called for, and then give the English meaning of the sentence.

1. **Anstatt** nur eine Hauptstadt **zu** haben wie England und Frankreich, hat Deutschland viele.
(*in order to*/*instead of*)

---

1. *Instead of* having only one capital city, as England and France (do), Germany has many.

2. **die Gesellschaft** = *society*
einheitlich = *uniform*
Statt eine einheitliche Gesellschaft und e i n e n Staat zu haben wie Großbritannien und Frankreich . . .
(The preposition is: **statt**/**statt . . . zu**)

---

2. **statt . . . zu**
Instead of having a uniform society and *one* state as (do) Great Britain and France . . .
The separation of the letters of a word as here with **e i n e n** indicates the word is stressed. Here it also changes the meaning of the word from *a* to *one*.

3. **die Lage** = *the position*
Ohne zu verstehen, was Deutschland damals war, können wir Deutschlands heutige Lage nicht verstehen.
(*without*/*in order to*)

---

3. We can not understand Germany's current position *without* understanding what Germany was then.

4. **hinzufügen** = *to add to*
Ohne hinzuzufügen, daß die Deutschen keine einheitliche Gesellschaft hatten wie die Engländer und Franzosen . . . (The preposition is: **ohne**/**ohne . . . zu**)

---

4. **ohne . . . zu**
Without adding that the Germans did not have a uniform society as the English and the French did . . .

5. **wahrscheinlich** = *probably*
Um die heutige Lage Deutschlands besser **zu** verstehen, müssen wir wahrscheinlich wissen, was Deutschland einmal war.
(*in order to*/*instead of*)

---

5. *In order to* understand Germany's present situation one must probably know what Germany once was.

6. **kennenlernen** = *to become acquainted with, to get* (*learn*) *to know*
Robert wird nach Deutschland fahren, um die verschiedenen Stämme und Dialekte kennenzulernen.
(The preposition is: **um . . . zu**/**um**)

---

6. **um . . . zu**
Robert will travel to Germany in order to become acquainted with the different races and dialects.

7. **umgekehrt** = *vice versa*
Ohne die Mundart (den Dialekt) zu kennen, kann der Bayer den Friesen nicht verstehen, und umgekehrt.
(The preposition is: **ohne**/**ohne . . . zu**)

---

7. **ohne . . . zu** Without knowing the dialect the Bavarian cannot understand the Frisian, and vice versa.	**8.** **das Vertrauen** = *trust* Vielleicht haben wir Menschen, als Bürger verschiedener Nationen, nicht das Vertrauen zueinander . . .
8. Perhaps we people, as citizens of different countries, do not have the trust towards one another . . .	**9.** **die Not** = *need, necessity* **notwendig** = ________
9. *necessary*	**10.** **aufbauen** = *to build* . . . das notwendig ist, **um** eine Welt des Friedens auf**zu**bauen.
10. . . . that is necessary *in order to* build a world of peace.	**11.** **Um** eine Welt des Friedens auf**zu**bauen, müssen wir als Bürger Vertrauen zueinander haben.
11. As citizens we must trust one another *in order to* build a world of peace. (Lit.: *In order to* build a world of peace, we as citizens must have trust in one another.)	**12.** **hat verdorben** = *has corrupted* **Anstatt** eine neue Welt auf**zu**bauen, haben wir die alte verdorben.
12. *Instead of* building a new world we have corrupted the old one.	

READING PREPARATION

The following exercises introduce and review vocabulary for the reading passage. Continue to circle new or unfamiliar words.

	1. **wurde vereinigt** = *was united* Deutschland wurde durch Luther und Bismarck zu einem Ganzen vereinigt.
1. Germany was united into a whole (a nation) by Luther and Bismarck. (**Wurde** plus past participle forms the passive voice.)	**2.** Deutschland, durch Luther und Bismarck zu einem Ganzen vereinigt, liegt wieder geteilt.
2. Germany, united by Luther and Bismarck into a single unit, is again divided.	**3.** Deutschland, das sprachlich durch Luther und viel später politisch von Bismarck zu einem Ganzen vereinigt wurde, liegt wieder geteilt.

3. Germany, which was united into a single entity linguistically by Luther and much later politically by Bismarck, is again divided.	**4.** **sollte** = *ought* Was sollte wieder vereinigt werden?
4. What ought to be again united?	**5.** Etwas sollte wieder vereinigt werden.
5. Something ought to be again united.	**6.** Was wieder vereinigt werden sollte, ist etwas, das nur ein Mal vereint war.
6. What ought to be again united is something that was only united once.	**7.** Noch etwas teilt dieses Land.
7. Something else (lit.: still something) divides this country.	**8.** Es ist nicht einfach zu erklären, was dieses Land teilt.
8. It is not easy to explain what divides this country.	**9.** Großbritannien und Frankreich besitzen praktisch nur eine Hauptstadt.
9. Practically speaking, Great Britain and France possess only one capital.	**10.** **im Vergleich zu** = *in comparison to* **mehrere** = *several* Im Vergleich zu Großbritannien und Frankreich hat Deutschland mehrere Städte . . .
10. In comparison to Great Britain and France, Germany has several cities . . .	**11.** **galten** = past tense of **gelten** (*to serve*) Im Vergleich zu Großbritannien und Frankreich hat Deutschland mehrere Städte, die als historische Zentren der verschiedenen Länder Deutschlands galten.
11. In comparison to Great Britain and France Germany has several cities which served as historical centers of the different regions of Germany.	**12.** Heute haben die Deutschen wahrscheinlich immer noch nicht eine gemeinsame Tradition, eine einheitliche Gesellschaft und einen Staat wie die Engländer und Franzosen.
12. Today the Germans probably still do not have a common tradition, a uniform society, and *one* state as (do) the English and French.	**13.** Leipzig und Dresden sind Städte in der Ostzone.

13. Leipzig and Dresden are cities in the East Zone.	**14.** **die Messe** = *the fair* Leipzig, die älteste Messestadt Europas, und Dresden, die Hauptstadt des Königreichs Sachsen, sind jetzt in der Ostzone.
14. Leipzig, the city with the oldest trade fair of Europe, and Dresden, the capital of the kingdom of Saxony, are now in the East Zone.	**15.** Germanische Völker wohnen in Deutschland.
15. Germanic peoples live in Germany.	**16.** Deutschland ist ein Land, von germanischen Völkern bewohnt.
16. Germany is a country inhabited by Germanic peoples.	**17.** **zum Teil** = *in part* Deutschland ist ein Land, von germanischen Völkern bewohnt und zum Teil von einer gemeinsamen Sprache vereint.
17. Germany is a country inhabited by Germanic peoples and united in part by a common language.	**18.** Berlin liegt in zwei Teile zerschnitten.
18. Berlin is cut into two parts.	**19.** **ehemalig** = *former* Berlin, die ehemalige Hauptstadt, liegt auch in zwei Teile zerschnitten.
19. Berlin, the former capital, is also cut into two parts.	**20.** Berlin, die ehemalige Hauptstadt, liegt auch in zwei Teile zerschnitten, und ist ein Symbol der heutigen politischen Lage Deutschlands.
20. Berlin, the former capital, is also cut into two parts and is a symbol of the present political situation of Germany.	**21.** Die Mauer trennt jede vierte Familie Berlins.
21. The Wall separates every fourth family of Berlin.	**22.** **dauern** = *to last* **Wie lange** wird der Krieg dauern?
22. *How long* will the war last?	**23.** **je . . . desto . . .** = *the . . . the . . .* **Je länger** wir leben, **desto dümmer** werden wir.
23. *The longer* we live *the more stupid* we become.	**24.** **schwierig** = *difficult* Es wird schwierig sein . . .

24. It will be difficult . . .	**25.** Es wird schwierig sein, eine Wiedervereinigung zu schaffen.
25. It will be difficult to bring about a reunification.	**26.** **die Versöhnung** = *reconciliation* Es wird schwierig sein, eine Versöhnung, eine Wiedervereinigung zu schaffen.
26. It will be difficult to bring to pass a reconciliation, a reunification.	**27.** **bedingen** = *to be prerequisite, to stipulate* Welche Konzessionen bedingen eine Wiedervereinigung?
27. Which concessions are prerequisite to a reunification?	**28.** Wollen und können beide Staaten die notwendigen Konzessionen machen, **die** eine Wiedervereinigung bedingen? (*which/the*)
28. Do both states want to and are they able to make the necessary concessions *which* are prerequisite to a reunification?	**29.** **der Zustand** = *the situation* Je länger dieser Zustand dauert, desto schwieriger wird es sein, eine Versöhnung, eine Wiedervereinigung zu schaffen.
29. The longer this situation lasts, the more difficult it will be to bring about a reconciliation, a reunification.	**30.** **sicher** = *certain, sure* Eins ist sicher, je länger dieser Zustand dauert, desto schwieriger wird es sein, eine Versöhnung, eine Wiedervereinigung zu schaffen.
30. One thing is sure, the longer this situation lasts, the more difficult it will be to bring about a reconciliation, a reunification.	**31.** Deutschland wird **einmal** vereint sein. (*once/one day*)
31. Germany will *one day* be united.	**32.** **niemand** = *no one* Deutschland wird **einmal** vereint sein, niemand weiß, wann. (*once again/one time*)
32. Germany will *once again* be united ; no one knows when.	**33.** Wenn Deutschland einmal vereint sein wird — jeder weiß, das wird kommen, niemand weiß, wann . . .
33. When Germany is once again united — everyone knows that will come, no one knows when . . .	**34.** „Wenn Deutschland einmal vereint sein wird — jeder weiß, das wird kommen, niemand weiß, wann — wird es nicht sein durch Krieg." (Bertolt Brecht)

34. "When Germany is once again united — everyone knows that will come, no one knows when — it will not be through war."	

Review the words you have circled throughout this chapter, and then go on to the reading passage.

Deutschland gestern, heute und morgen

Das Land, das sprachlich durch Luther und viel später politisch von Bismarck zu einem Ganzen vereinigt wurde, liegt wieder geteilt. Und was wieder vereinigt werden sollte, ist etwas, das nur einmal in seiner Geschichte vereint war. Wie ist das zu verstehen? Was teilt denn dieses Land?

Historisch gesehen, war Deutschland fast nie e i n Reich. Nur von 1871 unter Bismarck bis 1945 und Hitlers Sturz war Deutschland wirklich e i n Staat. Deutschland ist, seit Luther, von einer gemeinsamen Sprache vereinigt, aber vom kirchlichen Standpunkt gesehen, ist es immer noch geteilt: in den hauptsächlich protestantischen Norden und den hauptsächlich katholischen Süden. Noch etwas teilt dieses Land: die verschiedenen Stämme und Dialekte, die heute noch existieren. Diese Dialekte sind die wahre Sprache der Germanen. Noch heute kann ein Bayer nicht die Mundart (den Dialekt) der Friesen verstehen und umgekehrt.

Hinzuzufügen ist, daß die Deutschen keine gemeinsame Tradition, keine einheitliche Gesellschaft, keinen Staat hatten, und wahrscheinlich immer noch nicht haben, wie die Engländer oder die Franzosen. Im Vergleich zu Großbritannien und Frankreich, welche praktisch nur eine Hauptstadt besitzen, London und Paris, hat Deutschland mehrere Städte, die als historische Zentren der verschiedenen Länder Deutschlands galten, zum Beispiel: die alte Kaiserstadt Frankfurt; die preußische Hauptstadt Berlin, die erst unter Bismarck die Hauptstadt Deutschlands wurde; München, die Hauptstadt Bayerns; die alte Hansestadt Hamburg; Leipzig, die älteste Messestadt Europas; und Dresden, berühmt für seine einmalige Schönheit und Hauptstadt des Königreichs Sachsen. Wien, heute die Hauptstadt Österreichs, war fast fünf Jahrhunderte lang deutsche Hauptstadt.

Das alles hilft uns vielleicht, die heutige Lage Deutschlands besser zu verstehen, nämlich, daß Deutschland wieder das ist, was es schon fast immer war: ein Land, von germanischen Völkern bewohnt und zum Teil von einer gemeinsamen Sprache vereint. Geographisch und historisch gesehen, ist es ein Land mit vielen Schwerpunkten, Ländern und Dialekten.

Das Tragische ist, daß dieses Land im Kleinen ein Symbol für ganz Europa ist: nämlich für die Gegenüberstellung von Osten und Westen, Norden und Süden. Der Eiserne Vorhang zeigt, daß wir Menschen als Bürger verschiedener Nationen nicht das Vertrauen zueinander haben, das notwendig ist, um eine Welt des Friedens aufzubauen. Der protestantische Norden und der katholische Süden zeigen, daß die christliche Welt nicht einig ist. Berlin, die ehemalige Hauptstadt, liegt auch in zwei Teile zerschnitten, als Symbol der heutigen politischen Lage Deutschlands. Die Mauer sichert der DDR die ökonomische Stabilität. Aber zugleich trennt die Mauer jede vierte Familie Berlins. Sie ist eine Barrikade für Ostdeutsche, die fliehen wollen, sie ist ein Gefängnis für Westberliner, die Bewegungsfreiheit haben wollen.

Was wird aus Deutschland? Wird die Wiedervereinigung je stattfinden? Hoffen die Deutschen in der DDR mehr darauf als die in der Bundesrepublik? Wollen und können beide Staaten die notwendigen Konzessionen machen, die eine Wiedervereinigung bedingen? Eins ist sicher, je länger dieser Zustand dauert, desto schwieriger wird es sein, eine Versöhnung, eine Wiedervereinigung zu schaffen.

Chapter Six

Review! Before beginning Chapter 6, take a few minutes to review the words and phrases you circled in the previous chapters.

23. *Personal pronouns—declension*

1. The personal pronouns introduced in Chapter 2 have the following case forms:

1st PERSON	**SINGULAR**			**PLURAL**		**SING. & PLURAL**	
Nominative	**ich**	*I*		**wir**	*we*		
Genitive	**meiner**	(*of*) *me*		**unser**	(*of*) *us*		
Dative	**mir**	(*to*) *me*		**uns**	(*to*) *us*		
Accusative	**mich**	*me*		**uns**	*us*		
2nd PERSON							
Nominative	**du**	*you*		**ihr**	*you*	**Sie**	*you*
Genitive	**deiner**	(*of*) *you*		**euer**	(*of*) *you*	**Ihrer**	(*of*) *you*
Dative	**dir**	(*to*) *you*		**euch**	(*to*) *you*	**Ihnen**	(*to*) *you*
Accusative	**dich**	*you*		**euch**	*you*	**Sie**	*you*
3rd PERSON							
Nominative	**er**	*he*	*it*	**sie**	*they*		
Genitive	**seiner**	(*of*) *him*		**ihrer**	(*of*) *them*		
Dative	**ihm**	(*to*) *him*	(*to*) *it*	**ihnen**	(*to*) *them*		
Accusative	**ihn**	*him*	*it*	**sie**	*them*		

	SINGULAR		
Nominative	**sie**	*she*	*it*
Genitive	**ihrer**	*(of) her*	
Dative	**ihr**	*(to) her*	*(to) it*
Accusative	**sie**	*her*	*it*

Nominative	**es**	*it*	*he*	*she*
Genitive	**seiner**	*(of) it*	*(an archaic form)*	
Dative	**ihm**	*(to) it*	*(to) him*	*(to) her*
Accusative	**es**	*it*	*him*	*her*

2. Notice that in German it is possible to have a masculine or feminine *it:*

Der Motor läuft nicht.	*The motor doesn't run.*
***Er* läuft nicht.**	***It** doesn't run.*
Die Maschine ist kaputt.	*The machine is broken.*
***Sie* ist kaputt.**	***It** is broken.*

3. Likewise it is possible to have a neuter *he* or *she:*

Das Männlein sagte nichts.	*The little man said nothing.*
***Es* sagte nichts.**	***He** said nothing.*
Das Mädchen ist schön.	*The girl is beautiful.*
***Es* ist schön.**	***She** is beautiful.*

This set of exercises is intended to familiarize you with the declension of the personal pronouns. Select the correct meaning and give the case of the indicated pronouns.

	1. **denken** = *to think* **gedenken** = *to remember* Gedenken Sie **meiner** nicht mehr!
1. Remember *me* no more! (genitive) (Think *of me* no more.)	**2.** Der Dramatiker gibt **mir** ganz neue Gedanken. (*of me/me*)
2. The playwright gives *me* completely new thoughts. (dative)	**3.** Für **mich** kaufst du den neuen Wagen? (*me/I*)
3. Are you buying the new car for *me*? (accusative)	**4.** **sich schämen** = *to be ashamed of* Schämt er sich **deiner**? (*of you/of her*)
4. Is he ashamed *of you*? (genitive) (Note that **sich schämen** is a reflexive verb. See section 50.)	**5.** Rudi erklärt **dir,** wie er die Barrikade stürmte. (*to you/yours*)

5. Rudi is explaining *to you* how he stormed the barricade. (dative)	**6.** Besucht er **dich** morgen? (*you/me*)
6. Is he going to visit *you* tomorrow? (accusative)	**7.** **harren** = *to wait for, expect* Karl ist in München. Karin harrt **seiner.** (*for him/for her*)
7. Karl is in Munich. Karin is waiting *for him*. (genitive)	**8.** **leisten** = *to perform, achieve, make, do* **Hilfe leisten** = *to help* Ich leiste **ihm** keine Hilfe mehr. (*her/(to) him*)
8. I do not help *him* any more. (dative)	**9.** Wir leisten **ihr** keine Hilfe mehr. (*her/him/you*)
9. We do not help *her* any more. (dative)	**10.** Erst müssen wir **ihn** umringen. (*them/him*)
10. First we must surround *him*. (accusative)	**11.** Jetzt erinnere ich mich **ihrer.** (*you/her*)
11. Now I remember *her*. (genitive)	**12.** Jetzt erinnere ich mich **Ihrer.** (*you/her*)
12. Now I remember *you*. (genitive)	**13.** **wußte** = *past of wissen, to know* Ich wußte nicht, daß es **euch** gehörte. (*to you/to us/to her*)
13. I did not know that it belonged *to you*. (dative)	**14.** Ich wußte nicht, daß das Stück Käse **ihr** gehörte. (*to you/to her*)
14. I did not know that the piece of cheese belonged *to her*. (dative)	**15.** **rasend** = *furious* Der Gedanke, daß er ihr untreu ist, macht **sie** rasend. (*she/her*)
15. The thought that he is unfaithful to her makes *her* furious. (accusative)	**16.** Der Gedanke, daß sie **ihm** untreu ist, macht ihn rasend. (*to her/to him/to you*)
16. The thought that she is unfaithful *to him* makes him furious. (dative)	**17.** **der Stoß** = *push* Das Auto läuft nicht. Geben Sie **ihm** einen kleinen Stoß, bitte. (*him/it/them*)

17. The automobile does not run. Give *it* a little push, please. (dative)	**18.** Ich kann **es** nicht finden. (*he/it*)
18. I cannot find *it*. (accusative)	**19.** Es waren **unser** fünf. (*of us/of them/of you*)
19. There were five *of us*. (genitive)	**20.** **fremd** = *foreign* Diese Mundart ist **uns** fremd. (*to you/to us/to them*)
20. This dialect is foreign *to us*. (dative)	**21.** Dieses Gefängnis kann **uns** nicht halten. (*of us/us*)
21. This prison cannot hold *us*. (accusative)	**22.** Der Gedanke, daß er **ihr** untreu ist, macht sie rasend. (*to her/to you*)
22. The thought that he is unfaithful *to her* makes her furious. (dative) (Remember that **ihr** means *you* only in the nominative.)	**23.** Der Gedanke, daß er **ihnen** untreu ist, macht sie rasend. (*to him/to them*)
23. The thought that he is unfaithful *to them* makes them furious. (dative)	**24.** **sich erbarmen** = *to have pity* Er erbarmt sich **euer.** (*on you/on us/on her*)
24. He has pity *on you*. (genitive)	**25.** **versprechen** = *to promise* Wir versprechen **euch,** nicht mehr zu kommen. (*you/her*)
25. We promise *you* not to come any more. (dative)	**26.** Sie versucht nicht mehr, **euch** zu sehen. (*you/us*)
26. She is not trying to see *you* any more. (accusative)	**27.** Wir versprechen **ihr,** nicht mehr zu kommen. (*her/you*)
27. We promise *her* not to come any more. (dative)	**28.** Ihr versprecht **ihm,** nicht mehr zu kommen! (*you/him*)
28. You promise *him* not to come any more! (dative) (**ihr** in nominative case means *you*.)	**29.** **Ihr** seid alle Dummköpfe! (*her/you*)

29. *You* are all blockheads! (nominative)	**30.** **ist bewußt** = *is aware* Obwohl sie vor ihm stehen, ist er **ihrer** nicht bewußt. (*of them/of her*)
30. Although they are standing in front of him, he is not aware *of them*. (genitive) (**stehen** indicates the plural.)	**31.** Obwohl sie vor ihm steht, ist er **ihrer** nicht bewußt. (*of them/of her*)
31. Although she is standing in front of him, he is not aware *of her*. (**steht** indicates the singular.)	**32.** Die gesamte Bevölkerung wird **Ihnen** folgen. (*you/them*)
32. The entire population will follow *you*. (dative) (Notice the capital letter — **Ihnen** — which distinguishes the 2nd person pronoun from the 3rd person pronoun.)	**33.** **dürfen** = *to be permitted, may* Ich darf mit **ihnen** sprechen. (*you/them*)
33. I may speak with *them*. (dative)	**34.** Wir verstehen **sie** schon nicht mehr. (*they/he/them*)
34. We already do not understand *them* any more. (accusative)	**35.** Uns verstehen **sie** nicht mehr. (*they/her/you*)
35. They do not understand us any more.	**36.** Es sind **Ihrer** drei. (*of her/of them/of you*)
36. There are three *of you*. (genitive) (**Ihrer** = *of you*; **ihrer** = *of them* or *of her*.)	**37.** Maria spricht nur Französisch. Wir verstehen **sie** nicht. (*them/her*)
37. Maria speaks only French. We don't understand *her*. (accusative)	**38.** **Sie** versteht uns nicht. (*they/she*)
38. *She* doesn't understand us. (nominative) (The verb ending tells you the number.)	**39.** Ich kann **Sie** nicht verstehen! (*you/her/them*)
39. I cannot understand *you*. (accusative)	

PROGRESS TEST

Choose the correct answer. Review any points you miss before going on.

1. Jetzt erinnere ich mich *ihrer*.
Depending on the context, *ihrer* could be translated:
(a) her, them (b) her, you (c) them, you (d) us, them

2. Der Gedanke, daß er *Ihnen* untreu ist, macht mich rasend.
(a) him (b) her (c) you (d) them

3. Ich wußte nicht, daß es *euch* gehörte.
(a) us (b) you (c) them (d) me

4. Karin harrt *unser*.
(a) us (b) you (c) him (d) them

5. Erst müssen wir *sie* umringen.
sie can be translated as:
(a) you, them (b) they, us (c) she, they (d) them, her

Answer key: **1.** (a); **2.** (c); **3.** (b); **4.** (a); **5.** (d).

24. *Modal auxiliary verbs—present tense*

1. The modals and their approximate meanings are:

permission:	**dürfen**	*to be permitted or allowed to, may*
ability:	**können**	*to be able to, can*
possibility:	**mögen**	*to like (to), may, to care for*
necessity:	**müssen**	*to have to, must*
obligation:	**sollen**	*to be obliged* or *supposed to, am to, shall*
intention:	**wollen**	*to want to, intend to*

2. Notice that the present tense endings of the modals follow the weak verb pattern for the plural but not for the singular:

ich darf	*I may*	**ich kann**	*I can*
du darfst		**du kannst**	
er, sie, es darf		**er, sie, es kann**	
wir dürfen		**wir können**	
ihr dürft		**ihr könnt**	
sie dürfen		**sie können**	
Sie dürfen		**Sie können**	

ich mag	*I like*	**ich muß**	*I must*
du magst		**du mußt**	
er, sie, es mag		**er, sie, es muß**	
wir mögen		**wir müssen**	
ihr mögt		**ihr müßt**	
sie mögen		**sie müssen**	
Sie mögen		**Sie müssen**	

ich soll	*I am to, I am supposed to*	**ich will**	*I want to*
du sollst		**du willst**	
er, sie, es soll		**er, sie, es will**	
wir sollen		**wir wollen**	
ihr sollt		**ihr wollt**	
sie sollen		**sie wollen**	
Sie sollen		**Sie wollen**	

3. Modal verbs are auxiliary or "helping" verbs. They are usually followed, as in English, by the infinitive form of the verb. In German, this dependent infinitive will generally be found at the end of the clause, or in dependent word order as the next to the last word:

Heinz will nächstes Jahr nach Deutschland fliegen.	*Heinz wants to fly to Germany next year.*
Will Heinz nächstes Jahr nach Deutschland fliegen?	*Does Heinz want to fly to Germany next year?*
Ich weiß, daß Heinz nächstes Jahr nach Deutschland fliegen will.	*I know that Heinz wants to fly to Germany next year.*

4. Remember that **werden (er wird)**, not **wollen (er will)**, is used in forming the future tense:

Heinz wird nächstes Jahr nach Deutschland fliegen.	*Heinz will fly to Germany next year.*

This set of exercises reviews vocabulary from previous chapters and asks you to differentiate between the various modals. Select the correct meaning of the indicated verbs.

	1. anbieten = *to offer* **Darf** ich dir ein Stück Schweizer Schokolade anbieten? (*dare/may*)
1. *May* I offer you a piece of Swiss chocolate?	**2. Dürfen** wir die Teilung Deutschlands als Symbol für die Teilung Europas nehmen? (*may/must*)

2. *May* we take the division of Germany as a symbol for the division of Europe?	**3.** **Kann** er historisch und sehr einfach erklären, was Deutschland eigentlich war? (*is able to/does intend to*)
3. *Is* he *able to* explain historically and very simply what Germany really was?	**4.** **das Mittelalter** = *the Middle Ages* **Können** Sie mir vier Künstler des deutschen Mittelalters nennen?
4. *Can* you name me four artists of the German Middle Ages?	**5.** **Darf** man sagen, daß Luther sprachlich und Bismarck politisch Deutschland zu einem Ganzen vereinigten? (*must/may*)
5. *May* one say that Luther linguistically and Bismarck politically united Germany into a whole?	**6.** Er **mag** weltbekannt sein, aber ich werde trotzdem seine Bücher nicht lesen. (*may/must*)
6. He *may* be world famous, but I will still (in spite of it) not read his books.	**7.** Seines Stils wegen **will** ich seine Bücher lesen. (*will/want to*)
7. I *want* to read his books because of his style.	**8.** Den Kaffee **mögen** wir nicht. (*may/do . . . like*)
8. We *do* not *like* the coffee.	**9.** Heute **kann** ein Bayer nicht die Mundart des Friesen verstehen, und umgekehrt. (*is . . . able to/may*)
9. Today a Bavarian *is* not *able to* understand the dialect of a Frisian, and vice versa.	**10.** Alle, die Deutsch studieren, **müssen** sehr intelligent sein. (*must/may*)
10. Everyone who studies German *must* be very intelligent.	**11.** **Muß** er wissen, welche Rolle Adenauer in der deutschen Geschichte spielte? (*does . . . have to/may*)
11. *Does* he *have to* know what role Adenauer played in German history?	**12.** Napoleon **mag** ein großer Diktator sein, aber . . . (*must/may*)
12. Napoleon *may* be a great dictator, but . . .	**13.** **verehren** = *honor, venerate, respect* . . . als großen Diktator **soll** ich ihn doch nicht verehren! (*intend to/am . . . to*)

13. . . . I *am* certainly not *to* honor him as a great dictator!	**14.** **unsere Feinde** = *our enemies* **Sollen** wir unsere Feinde lieben? (*are . . . supposed to/are . . . allowed to*)
14. *Are* we *supposed to* love our enemies?	**15.** **Müssen** Sie erklären, was dieses Land teilt? (*do . . . have to/are . . . able to*)
15. *Do* you *have to* explain what divides this country?	**16.** **Wollen** die beiden Staaten die notwendigen Konzessionen machen? (*do . . . want to/are . . . obliged to*)
16. *Do* both nations *want to* make the necessary concessions?	**17.** Er **will** die Grenze zwischen Polen und Deutschland vernichten! (*may/intends to*)
17. He *intends to* do away with the border between Poland and Germany.	**18.** Du **sollst** deinen Nächsten lieben wie dich selber. (*shalt/may*)
18. Thou *shalt* love thy neighbor as thyself.	**19.** Sie **wollen** nicht die Mona Lisa wieder anschauen? (*may/do . . . want to*)
19. You (they) *do* not *want* to look at the Mona Lisa again?	**20.** **Will** Luther eine neue Kirche gründen? (*will/does . . . want to*)
20. *Does* Luther *want to* found a new church?	**21.** **je** = *ever* **Wird** die Wiedervereinigung je stattfinden? (*will/become*)
21. *Will* the reunification ever take place?	**22.** **Wird** die christliche Welt je einig sein? (*will/does . . . want to*)
22. *Will* the Christian world ever be united?	**23.** **Will** die christliche Welt je einig sein? (*will/does . . . want to*)
23. *Does* the Christian world *want to* ever be united?	**24.** **verschieben** = *to shift* Hitler **will** die Grenzen zwischen Polen und Deutschland nicht vernichten, nur verschieben. (*wants to/will*)

24. Hitler *does* not *want to* destroy the borders between Poland and Germany, only to shift them.	**25.** Lehrt uns die Geschichte, daß wir je eine Welt des Friedens aufbauen **werden**? (*will/become*)
25. Does history teach us that we *will* ever build a world of peace?	

PROGRESS TEST

Choose the correct meaning of the indicated verbs.

1. *Willst* du Deutsch studieren?
   (a) Can you (b) Will you (c) Should you (d) Do you want to
2. *Darf* man sagen, daß seine Bücher weltbekannt sind?
   (a) May (b) Must (c) Ought (d) Will
3. Seine Bücher *mögen* weltbekannt sein, aber ich will sie nicht lesen.
   (a) must (b) should (c) may (d) like to
4. Seine Bücher *werden* weltbekannt.
   (a) are worth (b) will (c) are becoming (d) intend to
5. Sie *wird* seine Bücher nicht lesen.
   (a) is becoming (b) wants to (c) may (d) will

Answer key: **1.** (d); **2.** (a); **3.** (c); **4.** (c); **5.** (d).

25. *Modals—idiomatic meanings*

1. The dependent infinitive may be omitted if it is clear what the omitted verb is:

Darf man hier Fußball spielen? Ja, das darf man.	*May one play soccer here? Yes, one may (play).*

2. It is common practice to omit the verbs **gehen** (*to go*), **tun** (*to do*), or any other verb of motion or doing:

Hinaus will er.	*He wants to go out.*
Darfst du das?	*May you do that?*

3. Idiomatic meanings must be learned by observation and practice. Here are some of the more common idiomatic usages:
The affirmative of **dürfen** implies permission, but the negative **nicht dürfen** is translated *must not:*

Er darf hier bleiben.	*He is permitted to (may) stay here.*
Sie dürfen hier nicht rauchen.	*You must not smoke here.*

Können implies ability, possibility, permission:

Er kann gut lesen.	*He can (is able to) read well.*
Ich kann schwimmen.	*I know how to swim.*
Das kann wahr sein.	*That may be true. (It is possible that that is true.)*
Sie können heute ins Kino gehen.	*You may go to the movies today.*

Mögen expresses inclination, liking, possibility:

Ich mag das nicht tun.	*I don't care to do that.*
Er mag dieses Buch nicht.	*He doesn't like (doesn't care for) this book.*
Das mag sein.	*That may be (so).*

Müssen expresses necessity or obligation and is usually translated by *must* or *have to:*

Sie müssen jetzt nach Hause gehen.	*You must (have to) go home now.*
Ihr müßt das tun.	*You must do that. (You have to do that. You are obliged to do that.)*

Sollen implies an obligation (such as a commandment) or a conjecture (rumor):

Du sollst nicht stehlen.	*Thou shalt not steal.*
Sie soll um neun Uhr zu Hause sein.	*She is expected (told, commanded, supposed) to be home at nine o'clock.*
Herr Braun soll sehr reich sein.	*Mr. Braun is said to be very rich.*

Wollen expresses volition, intention, determination; it also translates *to claim to* and *to be about to:*

Ich will morgen sehr früh aufstehen.	*I want (intend, am determined) to get up very early tomorrow.*
Ich wollte eben gehen.	*I was just on the point of going (I was just about to go).*

The following exercises introduce new vocabulary for the reading passage and give you practice in recognizing the modal verbs. Give the best meaning for the indicated word.

	1. Wir **wollen** eine Diskussion von Nietzsches und Kafkas Ideen über Macht beginnen. (*want/will*)
1. We *want* to begin a discussion of Nietzsche's and Kafka's ideas on power.	**2.** **die Gewalt** = *force, power* Wir **werden** eine Anekdote von der Gewalt des Militärs lesen. (*will/want to*)
2. We *will* read an anecdote about the power of the military.	**3.** **erzählen** = *to tell a story* Kafka **erzählt uns eine Anekdote** von der Gewalt des Militärs.
3. Kafka *tells us an anecdote* about the power of the military.	**4.** **ergreifen** = *to seize* In dieser Anekdote kommen zwei Soldaten und **ergreifen** einen Zivilisten.
4. In this anecdote two soldiers come and *seize* a civilian.	**5.** **zu jeder Zeit** = *at any time, always* Die zwei Soldaten **können** ihn zu jeder Zeit ergreifen. (**können** expresses — *ability/desire*)
5. ability: The two soldiers *can* seize him at any time.	**6.** **sich wehren** = *to defend oneself* Er **kann** sich nicht wehren, denn sie halten ihn fest. (**kann** here expresses — *possibility/ability/permission*)
6. ability: He *can*not defend himself, for they are holding him fast.	**7.** **führen** = *to take, to lead* Die Soldaten führen ihn vor **ihren** Kapitän. (*her/their*)
7. The soldiers take him to *their* captain.	**8.** **der Herr** = *the superior* Die Soldaten führen **den Zivilisten** vor ihren Herrn. (*civilian/civilians*)
8. The soldiers take *the civilian* to their superior.	**9.** Die Soldaten **sollen** den Zivilisten vor ihren Herrn, einen Offizier, führen. (*may/are to*)

9. The soldiers *are to* take the civilian to their superior, an officer.	**10.** **bunt** = *bright, colorful* **Wie** bunt ist seine Uniform! (*why/how*)
10. *How* colorful is his uniform!	**11.** Er **mag** seine bunte Uniform. (*may/likes*)
11. He *likes* his colorful uniform.	**12.** **fragen** = *to ask* Der Zivilist fragt: „Was **wollt** ihr denn von mir, ich bin ein Zivilist." (*will/want*)
12. The civilian asks, "What do you *want* of me — I am a civilian." (**Denn** here serves merely as an intensifier.)	**13.** Der Zivilist **will** sich gegen den Offizier wehren. (*will/wants to*)
13. The civilian *wants to* defend himself against the officer.	**14.** Es **mag** sein, daß du ein Zivilist bist. (**mag** expresses — *possibility/inclination*)
14. possibility: It *may* be that you are a civilian.	**15.** **fassen** = *to seize* Das **hindert** uns nicht, dich zu fassen. (*stop/help*)
15. That does not *stop* us from seizing you.	**16.** **lächeln** = *to smile* Der Offizier lächelte und sagte: „Das **wird** uns nicht hindern, dich zu fassen." (*wants to/is . . . going to*)
16. The officer smiled and said, "That *is* not *going to* stop us from seizing you."	**17.** **denn** = *for* Wir **können** dich fassen, denn das Militär hat Gewalt über alles.
17. We *can* seize you, for the military has power over everything.	**18.** **nach** = *according to* Das Militär **mag** Gewalt über alles haben, aber es soll nicht, Kafka nach. (**mag** expresses — *possibility/inclination*)
18. possibility: The military *may* have power over everything, but it is not supposed to (have), according to Kafka.	**19.** Kafka nach **können** Zivilisten sich nicht gegen die Gewalt des Militärs wehren. (*may/can*)
19. According to Kafka, civilians *can*not defend themselves against the power of the military.	**20.** **betreffs** = *concerning* Nietzsche ist berühmt für seine Ideen betreffs des „Übermenschen".

20. Nietzsche is famous for his ideas concerning the "superman." (**Betreffs** takes the genitive case.)	**21.** **hat gemacht** = *did* Um die deutsche Geschichte besser zu verstehen, müssen wir wissen, was der Nationalsozialismus mit Nietzsches Ideen gemacht hat.
21. In order to better understand German history we must know what National Socialism did with Nietzsche's ideas.	**22.** **das Glück** = *happiness* Das Gefühl der Macht **kennen,** das ist Glück! (*to know/to be able to*)
22. *To know* the feeling of power, that is happiness!	**23.** **erhöhen** = *to increase* **die Macht** = *power* Nietzsche nach **soll** alles, was das Gefühl der Macht im Menschen erhöht, gut sein. (*is supposed to/might be*)
23. According to Nietzsche, everything which heightens the feeling of power in man *is supposed to* be good.	**24.** **die Zufriedenheit** = *contentment, satisfaction* Nietzsche **will,** daß der Mensch nicht Zufriedenheit, sondern mehr Macht sucht. (*will/desires*)
24. Nietzsche *desires* that man seek not contentment but rather greater power.	**25.** **der Widerstand** = *obstacle* Um Glück zu kennen, **muß** man nicht nur gegen Widerstände kämpfen . . . (*must/may*)
25. In order to know happiness one *must* not only fight against obstacles . . .	**26.** **überwinden** = *to overcome* . . . sondern man **muß** diese Widerstände auch überwinden.
26. . . . but one *must* also overcome these obstacles.	**27.** **wird überwunden** = *is being overcome* Glück ist ein Gefühl davon, daß ein Widerstand überwunden wird.
27. Happiness is a feeling that an obstacle is being overcome. (Note that *davon* is not translated.)	**28.** Was ist **schlecht?** (**Schlecht,** the opposite of **gut,** means __________.)

28. What is *bad?*	**29.** **schwach** = *weak* **die Schwäche** = *weakness* Alles, **was** aus der Schwäche stammt, ist schlecht. (*which/what*)
29. Everything *which* stems from weakness is bad.	**30.** **Kann** alles, was aus der Schwäche stammt, schlecht sein? (*does . . . know/can*)
30. *Can* everything which originates from weakness be bad?	**31.** **die Mißratenen** = *misfits* **die Schwachen** = *weaklings* Nietzsche hat auch etwas über den Mißratenen und Schwachen zu sagen.
31. Nietzsche also has something to say about misfits and weaklings.	**32.** **zugrunde gehen** = *to perish* Nietzsche nach **sollen** die Schwachen und Mißratenen zugrunde gehen. (*should/are expected to*)
32. According to Nietzsche, the weak and the misfits *should* perish.	**33.** **noch dazu** = *moreover* Man **soll** ihnen noch dazu helfen. (*should/is said to*)
33. Moreover, one *should* help them (in this).	**34.** **schädlich** = *damaging, dangerous, pernicious* **das Laster** = *vice, depravity* Das Christentum **soll** schädlicher als irgend ein Laster sein. (*ought to be/is said to be*)
34. Christianity *is said to be* more damaging than any vice.	**35.** Ich kann diesen deutschen **Satz** nicht lesen. (*sentence/principle*)
35. I cannot read this German *sentence*.	**36.** Kann der erste **Satz** unsrer Menschenliebe sein: Zugrunde mit den Schwachen und Mißratenen? (*principle/sentence*)
36. Can the first *principle* of our love of mankind be: The weaklings and the misfits ought to perish?	**37.** **die Tüchtigkeit** = *efficiency* **die Tugend** = *virtue* Tüchtigkeit, nicht Tugend, **will** der Grund des Glückes sein. (*wants to/claims to/will*)

37. Efficiency, not virtue, *claims to* be the foundation of happiness.	**38.** **hinführen** = *to lead to* Wo **wird** der Wille zur Macht diese Welt hinführen? (*will/becomes*)
38. Where (to what) *will* the will to power lead the world?	**39.** **der Rand** = *edge, brink, verge* **das Verderben** = *ruin* **Wird** der Wille zur Macht diese Welt an den Rand des Verderbens führen?
39. *Is* the will to power *going to* lead this world to the verge of ruin?	

PROGRESS TEST

Choose the correct meaning for the indicated words.

1. Die Soldaten *mögen* den Zivilisten nicht vor ihren Herrn, einen Offizier, führen.
(a) may not (b) do not care to (c) should not (d) will not

2. Ich *kann* mich nicht wehren, denn sie halten mich fest.
(a) will (b) can (c) must (d) am to

3. Das Militär *mag* Gewalt über alles haben, aber es sollte nicht!
(a) may (b) will (c) must (d) is thought to have

4. Das Christentum *soll* schädlicher sein als irgendein Laster.
(a) ought to be (b) desires to be (c) may be (d) is said to be

5. Die Schwachen und die Mißratenen *sollen* zugrunde gehen.
(a) must (b) may (c) should (d) want to

6. Wenn man Deutsch sprechen *will*, so *wird* man nach Deutschland gehen müssen.
(a) will, will (b) wants, becomes (c) will, becomes (d) wants, will

7. Was man will, ist nicht immer was man *soll*.
(a) shall (b) should (c) is said to be (d) claims to be

8. Was man *mag*, ist nicht immer was man *darf*.
(a) wants . . . can (b) may . . . can (c) likes . . . may do (d) cares . . . wants

Answer key: **1.** (b); **2.** (b); **3.** (a); **4.** (d); **5.** (c); **6.** (d); **7.** (b); **8.** (c).

26. *Wissen, kennen*

1. The verb **wissen** (*to know*), in the present tense, follows the conjugation pattern of the modals:

ich weiß		**wir wissen**
du weißt	**Sie wissen**	**ihr wißt**
er, sie, es weiß		**sie wissen**

Note: Do not confuse the first and third person form **weiß** with **weiß** meaning *white.*

Kennen (*to be acquainted with, to know*) takes the regular present tense verb endings:

ich kenne		**wir kennen**
du kennst	**Sie kennen**	**ihr kennt**
er, sie, es kennt		**sie kennen**

2. **Wissen** means *to know a fact:*

Weißt du, wann er kommt? *Do you know when he is coming?*

3. **Kennen** means *to be acquainted with:*

Kennen Sie Herrn Braun? *Do you know Mr. Braun?*

Remember that **können** may also be translated *to know* (*a language*):

Ich **kann** Deutsch. *I know German.*

The verbs *to speak, read,* and *write* are here understood to be included in **kann.**

The purpose of the following exercises and review sentences is to point out the differences between ***wissen, kennen,*** *and* ***können.*** *Give the correct meaning of the indicated words.*

	1. **nennen** = *to call* **Weißt** du, was Nietzsche gut nennt?
1. *Do* you *know* what Nietzsche calls good?	**2.** Natürlich **wißt** ihr, was schlecht ist.
2. Of course you *know* what is bad.	**3.** **Wissen** Sie, was schädlicher ist als irgendein Laster?
3. *Do* you *know* what is more dangerous than any vice?	**4.** Das Christentum **kennt** nur das Mitleiden der Tat mit allen Mißratenen und Schwachen.
4. Christianity *has* (*knows*) only active compassion for all misfits and weaklings.	**5.** Er **kann** sich überhaupt nicht gegen die Soldaten wehren.
5. He *cannot* defend himself at all against the soldiers.	**6.** Die Soldaten **kennen** mich nicht.

6. The soldiers *do* not *know* me (*are* not *acquainted* with me).	**7.** Das **kann** uns überhaupt nicht hindern, dich zu fassen.
7. That *cannot* hinder us at all from seizing you.	**8.** Es **kamen** zwei Soldaten und **ergriffen** mich. (Are the verbs in the present or in the past?)
8. Two soldiers *came* and *seized* me.	**9.** Das Gefühl der Macht **kennen,** das ist Gluck!
9. *To know* the feeling of power, that is happiness!	**10.** Wer **kann** das denn glauben?
10. Who *can* (*is able to*) believe that?	**11.** **Kennst** du den alten Herrn?
11. *Are* you *acquainted with* (*Do* you *know*) the old gentleman?	**12.** Das **können** sie nicht.
12. They *cannot do* that. Or: They *do* not *know* how to do that.	**13.** Ich **weiß** schon, wie weiß das Stück Papier ist.
13. I already *know* how white that piece of paper is.	

READING PREPARATION

The following is a review of German word order. Express in English the meaning of the German sentences.

	1. Alles erhöht die Macht.
1. Everything increases power.	**2.** Alles, was im Menschen die Macht erhöht, . . .
2. Everything which increases power in man . . .	**3.** Alles, was das Gefühl der Macht im Menschen erhöht, . . .
3. Everything which increases the feeling of power in man . . .	**4.** **der Wille** = *the desire* Alles, was das Gefühl der Macht, den Willen zur Macht im Menschen erhöht, . . .
4. Everything which increases the feeling of power, the desire for power (the will to power) in man . . .	**5.** Alles, was das Gefühl der Macht, den Willen zur Macht, die Macht selbst im Menschen erhöht, ist gut.

5. Everything which increases the feeling of power, the desire for power, power itself in man, is (morally) good.	**6.** Glück ist ein Gefühl.
6. Happiness is a feeling.	**7.** Glück ist ein Gefühl, daß die Macht wächst.
7. Happiness is a feeling that power is growing.	**8.** Glück ist ein Gefühl, daß die Macht wächst, daß ein Widerstand überwunden wird.
8. Happiness is a feeling that power is growing, that an obstacle is being overcome.	**9.** Was ist Glück? — Das Gefühl davon, daß die Macht wächst, — daß ein Widerstand überwunden wird.
9. What is happiness? — the feeling that power is growing, — that an obstacle is being overcome.	**10.** Tüchtigkeit ist Tugend.
10. Efficiency is virtue.	**11.** Tüchtigkeit, für Nietzsche, ist Tugend.
11. For Nietzsche efficiency is virtue.	**12.** Für Nietzsche ist Tüchtigkeit Tugend im Renaissance-Stile, *virtu*, moralinfreie Tugend.
12. For Nietzsche efficiency is virtue in the Renaissance style, *virtu**, virtue free of moral hypocrisy. (* *Virtu* may mean here any or all of the following: manliness, bravery; ability, fitness, soundness, excellence, proficiency; virtue.)	**13.** **das Mitleiden** = *pity, sympathy, compassion* (*literally: suffering with*) Das Mitleiden ist schädlicher als irgendein Laster.
13. Compassion is more damaging than any vice.	**14.** **die Tat** = *the deed* **das Mitleiden der Tat** = *the active compassion* Das Mitleiden der Tat ist schädlicher als irgendein Laster.
14. Active compassion is more harmful than any vice.	**15.** Das Mitleiden der Tat mit allen Mißratenen und Schwachen ist schädlicher als irgendein Laster.

15. Active compassion for all misfits and weaklings is more damaging than any vice.	

PROGRESS TEST

A. *Choose the correct meaning for the indicated words.*

1. Ist es *schädlich* für die Gesundheit, wenn man raucht und trinkt?
(a) beneficial (b) damaging (c) healthy (d) indifferent

2. Er *wehrte sich* vergebens gegen die Macht der Liebe.
(a) forced himself (b) fought himself (c) defended himself (d) submitted himself

3. Im Anfang war die *Tat*! (Goethe)
(a) deed (b) death (c) test (d) chaos

4. „Ach!" — spricht er — „die größte Freud' ist doch die *Zufriedenheit*!!" (Wilhelm Busch)
(a) contentment (b) joy (c) dismay (d) despair

B. *Choose the approximate meaning for the following.*

1. Tugend, nicht Krieg, ist, was den Menschen erhöht.
(a) War is beneficial to man.
(b) Virtue, not war, is what makes the man.
(c) Peace not vice is what man should exalt.
(d) Peace not war is what enhances man.

2. Das Gefühl der Macht ist erster Satz unserer Menschenliebe.
(a) The desire for power is the first principle of mankind.
(b) The first sentence we read is that the feeling of authority is part of our love for mankind.
(c) The feeling of power is the first principle of our love for our fellow human beings.
(d) The principle of love is the first step on the road to power.

Answer key: **A.** **1.** (b); **2.** (c); **3.** (a); **4.** (a).
B. **1.** (b); **2.** (c).

Review all of the words you have circled in this chapter. Then go on to the reading passage.

Franz Kafka: Hochzeitsvorbereitungen auf dem Lande.

Es kamen zwei Soldaten und ergriffen mich. Ich wehrte mich, aber sie hielten fest. Sie führten mich vor ihren Herrn, einen Offizier. Wie bunt war seine Uniform! Ich sagte: „Was wollt ihr denn von mir, ich bin ein Zivilist." Der Offizier lächelte und sagte: „Du bist ein Zivilist, doch hindert uns das nicht, dich zu fassen. Das Militär hat Gewalt über alles."

Friedrich Nietzsche: Der Antichrist.

Was ist gut? — Alles, was das Gefühl der Macht, den Willen zur Macht, die Macht selbst im Menschen erhöht.

Was ist schlecht? — Alles, was aus der Schwäche stammt.

Was ist Glück? — Das Gefühl davon, daß die Macht wächst, — daß ein Widerstand überwunden wird.

Nicht Zufriedenheit, sondern mehr Macht; nicht Friede überhaupt, sondern Krieg; nicht Tugend, sondern Tüchtigkeit (Tugend im Renaissance-Stile, *virtu*, moralinfreie Tugend).

Die Schwachen und Mißratenen sollen zugrunde gehen: erster Satz unsrer Menschenliebe. Und man soll ihnen noch dazu helfen.

Was ist schädlicher als irgendein Laster? — Das Mitleiden der Tat mit allen Mißratenen und Schwachen — das Christentum . . .

Chapter Seven

27. *Comparison of adjectives*

1. There are three basic forms of the adjective, both in German and in English:

Positive	**alt**	*old*
Comparative	**älter**	*older*
Superlative	**ältest-**	*oldest*

2. The comparative form in German is recognized by the **-er** ending, the superlative by the **-(e)st-** attached to the positive form. (*More* and *most* are not used in forming the comparative forms in German: **interessant, interessanter, interessantest-.**)

3. The following adjectives have irregular forms:

groß, größer, größt-	*big*
gut, besser, best-	*good*
hoch, höher, höchst-	*high*
nah(e), näher, nächst-	*near*
viel, mehr, meist-	*much, many*

4. Monosyllabic adjectives with stem vowels of **a, o,** or **u** generally take an umlaut. Polysyllabic adjectives never do:

warm, wärmer, wärmst-	*warm, warmer, warmest*
einfach, einfacher, einfachst-	*simple, simpler, simplest*

5. In addition to the comparative endings, adjectives will take the case endings explained earlier. Do not confuse the normal adjective ending with the comparative:

der alte Mann	*the old man*
ein alter Mann	*an old man*
etwas älter	*somewhat older*
der ältere Mann	*the older man*
ein älterer Mann	*an older man*
alle älteren Männer	*all older men*
die schönste Frau	*the most beautiful woman*
der älteste Mann	*the oldest man*
Der Mann ist am ältesten.	*The man is oldest.*

Note that there are two forms of the superlative in German.

6. Common adjective formulas are:

. . . als	**: älter als**	*older than*
(nicht) so . . . wie	**: (nicht) so alt wie**	*(not) as old as*
je . . . desto . . .	**: je älter, desto besser**	*the older, the better*
immer . . .	**: immer älter**	*older and older*
Peter ist älter als du.		*Peter is older than you.*
Grete ist nicht so alt wie Inge.		*Grete is not as old as Inge.*
Je älter der Wein, desto besser schmeckt er.		*The older the wine, the better it tastes.*
Wir werden alle immer älter.		*We are all getting older and older.*

The reading passage for this chapter is from one of Dietrich Bonhoeffer's letters from prison. In the next set of exercises you will practice recognition of the comparative forms of adjectives, review old vocabulary, and learn new vocabulary for this reading passage. Remember to circle unfamiliar words for review.

	1. Im letzten Kapitel mußten Sie einen Abschnitt (Paragraphen) aus Nietzsches *Der Antichrist* lesen.
1. In the last chapter you had to read a paragraph out of Nietzsche's *The Antichrist.*	**2.** Nietzsche wurde 1844 geboren und starb im Jahre 1900.
2. Nietzsche was born in 1844 and died in (the year) 1900.	**3.** Nietzsche nach gibt es zwei Sorten Menschen: die Starken und die Schwachen und Mißratenen.
3. According to Nietzsche there are two kinds of people: the strong and the weaklings and misfits.	**4.** Um **stärker** zu werden, muß man Widerstände überwinden.

4. In order to become *stronger,* one must overcome obstacles.	**5.** **der Durchschnittsmensch** = *the average person* War Nietzsche körperlich **stärker** oder **schwächer** als der Durchschnittsmensch?
5. Was Nietzsche physically *stronger* or *weaker* than the average person?	**6.** Was ist **schädlicher** als irgendein Laster?
6. What is *more harmful* than any vice?	**7.** Das Christentum ist **am schädlichsten.**
7. Christianity is *most harmful.*	**8.** Das **schönste** Gefühl im Leben ist, daß die Macht in einem wächst.
8. The *most beautiful* feeling in life is that power is growing in oneself.	**9.** **Das Schönste** im Leben ist das Gefühl, daß die Macht in einem wächst.
9. *The most beautiful thing* in life is the feeling that power is growing within oneself. (Notice how the adjective is used as a neuter noun.)	**10.** Sprechen wir jetzt von Dietrich Bonhoeffer.
10. Let us talk now of Dietrich Bonhoeffer.	**11.** Bonhoeffer war Christ.
11. Bonhoeffer was a Christian.	**12.** Bonhoeffer wurde am 4. Februar 1906 geboren.
12. Bonhoeffer was born on the 4th of February, 1906.	**13.** **verhaften** = *to arrest* **wurde verhaftet** = *was arrested* Im Jahre 1943 wurde er von den Nazis verhaftet.
13. In the year 1943 he was arrested by the Nazis.	**14.** **hinrichten** = *to execute* **wurde hingerichtet** = *was executed* Er wurde am 4. Februar 1906 geboren, im Jahre 1943 verhaftet und schließlich am 9. April 1945 als Widerstandskämpfer hingerichtet.
14. He was born on the 4th of February, 1906, arrested in 1943, and finally executed as a resistance fighter on April 9, 1945.	**15.** Nietzsches Werk *Der Antichrist* ist gegen das Christentum.
15. Nietzsche's work *The Antichrist* is against Christianity.	**16.** **der Brief** = *letter* Als Bonhoeffer im Gefängnis war, **schrieb** er viele Briefe über das Christentum. (*writes/wrote*)

16. When Bonhoeffer was in prison he *wrote* many letters about Christianity.	**17.** **bejahen** = *to affirm* Bonhoeffer bejaht in seinen Briefen das Christentum.
17. Bonhoeffer in his letters affirms Christianity.	**18.** Nietzsche meint, **das Beste,** was ein Mensch tun kann, ist die Macht in sich selbst erhöhen.
18. Nietzsche feels (that) *the best thing* one can do is to increase power within oneself.	**19.** **verzichten auf (etwas)** = *to renounce, abandon* (*something*) Bonhoeffer meint, **das Beste,** was man tun kann, ist völlig darauf verzichten, aus sich selbst etwas zu machen.
19. Bonhoeffer feels *the best thing* one can do is to fully abandon making something (out) of oneself (in the sense of fame, power, etc.).	**20.** **möglich** = *possible* **die Möglichkeit** = *possibility* Welche Meinung finden Sie **besser**? Gibt es **bessere** Möglichkeiten?
20. Which opinion do you find *better*? Are there *better* possibilities?	**21.** **das Verhältnis** = *the relation* Welcher, Nietzsche oder Bonhoeffer, ist **einsamer** in seinem Verhältnis zum Weltall?
21. Which one, Nietzsche or Bonhoeffer, is more lonely in his relation to the universe?	**22.** **in dem** = *in which, in whom* Der **gute** Mensch ist der Mensch, in dem die Macht wächst.
22. The *good* person is the individual in whom power is growing.	**23.** Das Christentum ist **das schädlichste** Laster.
23. Christianity is *the most harmful* vice.	**24.** **werfen** = *to throw* Bonhoeffer will, daß der Mensch sich **ganz** in die Arme Gottes wirft.
24. Bonhoeffer wants man to throw himself *completely* into the arms of God (to rely totally on God).	**25.** **so etwas** = *something like that* Nietzsche sagt, nur ein **Schwacher** tut so etwas. (*a weak person/a weaker person*)
25. Nietzsche says, only *a weak person* does something like that.	**26.** Wer ist **schwächer**? Ein Mensch, der sich in die Arme Gottes wirft, oder ein Mensch, der das nicht tut?

26. Who is *weaker*? A man who relies on God, or one who doesn't?	**27.** **sprechen** = *to speak* **besprechen** = *to discuss* **Was für** Themen bespricht Bonhoeffer in seinen Briefen?
27. *What kind of* themes does Bonhoeffer discuss in his letters?	**28.** **die Diesseitigkeit** = *this-worldliness, secular life, preoccupation with things of this world* In seinem Brief vom 21.7.1944 bespricht Bonhoeffer das Thema der Diesseitigkeit.
28. In his letter of July 21, 1944, Bonhoeffer discusses the theme of the secular life. (cf. **dieseits** = *this side*)	**29.** **bequem** = *comfortable, easygoing* Bonhoeffer meint, der bequeme Mensch lebt in platter und banaler Diesseitigkeit.
29. Bonhoeffer feels that the comfortable individual lives (in) a shallow and banal secular life.	**30.** **die Aufgeklärten** = *the enlightened* (*persons*) **die Betriebsamen** = *the busy* (*persons*) Aber auch die Aufgeklärten und Betriebsamen leben in platter und banaler Diesseitigkeit.
30. But the enlightened and the busy (persons) also live a shallow and banal life of preoccupation with things of this world.	**31.** **tief** = *profound* (*deep*) **die Zucht** = *discipline* Tiefe Diesseitigkeit ist für Bonhoeffer **voller** Zucht. (*fuller/full of*)
31. A profound secular life for Bonhoeffer is *full of* discipline (i.e. is characterized by discipline). (**Voller** is a genitive form.)	**32.** **der Tod** = *death* In seinen Briefen spricht er von dem Tod und der **Auferstehung.** (After death comes the ________)
32. *resurrection.* In his letters he speaks of death and the resurrection.	**33.** **die Erkenntnis** = *knowledge* **gegenwärtig** = *present* Die Erkenntnis des Todes und der Auferstehung ist **immer** gegenwärtig in der tiefen Diesseitigkeit.
33. The knowledge of death and resurrection is *always* (i.e. *constantly*) present in a profound secular life.	**34.** Johannes der **Täufer** und Jesus Christus waren **große** und **tiefe** Menschen. (From the context, you would know that he is talking about John the ________ .)

34. John the *Baptist* and Jesus Christ were *great* and *profound* individuals.	**35.** Wer war der **größere, tiefere** Mensch: Johannes der Täufer oder Jesus Christus?
35. Who was the *greater* and *more profound* individual: John the Baptist or Jesus Christ?	**36.** Christus war nicht **so alt wie** Johannes, aber er war doch der **größere, tiefere** von den beiden.
36. Christ was not *as old as* John but he was still the *greater, more profound* of the two.	**37.** Hier kann man nicht sagen, **je älter, desto besser.**
37. Here one cannot say *the older the better.*	**38.** Als er starb, war Bonhoeffer nicht **so alt wie** Nietzsche.
38. Bonhoeffer was not *as old as* Nietzsche when he died.	**39.** Bonhoeffer ist **jünger als** Nietzsche.
39. Bonhoeffer is *younger than* Nietzsche.	**40.** Nietzsche nach ist Krieg **besser** als Friede.
40. According to Nietzsche war is *better* than peace.	**41.** **Je stärker** der Mensch, **desto besser** ist er; **je schwächer, desto schlechter.**
41. *The stronger* the person, *the better* he is; *the weaker, the worse* (he is).	**42.** Das Gefühl der Macht in einem Menschen wird **immer stärker, je mehr** er Widerstände überwindet.
42. The feeling of power in a person becomes *stronger and stronger the more* he overcomes obstacles.	**43.** **wirken** = *to cause, to produce* **Immer schädlicher** wirkt das Christentum, je mehr es Mitleiden der Tat mit allen Mißratenen und Schwachen hat.
43. Christianity produces *more and more harm* the more it has active compassion for all misfits and weaklings.	**44.** Was ist **schädlicher als** irgendein Laster?
44. What is *more harmful than* any vice?	**45.** Mit den Jahren lernt Bonhoeffer **immer mehr** die tiefe Diesseitigkeit des Christentums kennen und verstehen.
45. With the years Bonhoeffer learns *more and more* to recognize and understand the profound preoccupation with things of this world (characteristic) of Christianity.	**46.** **Je mehr** man völlig darauf verzichtet, aus sich etwas zu machen, **desto mehr** wirft man sich Gott ganz in die Arme.
46. *The more* one fully abandons making something of oneself, *the more* one relies on God.	**47.** Darf man sagen, daß Nietzsche das Christentum **nicht so gut** versteht **wie** Bonhoeffer?

47. Can one say that Nietzsche does *not* understand Christianity *as well as* Bonhoeffer?	**48.** Für Bonhoeffer ist der wahre Mensch ein Christ. Und für Nietzsche?
48. For Bonhoeffer the true individual is a Christian. And for Nietzsche?	**49.** Das Christentum ist eine alte Religion.
49. Christianity is an old religion.	**50.** Das Christentum ist **älter als** der Islam aber nicht **so alt wie** das Judentum.
50. Christianity is *older than* Islam but not *as old as* Judaism.	**51.** Das Judentum ist **die älteste** von den drei Religionen.
51. Judaism is *the oldest* of the three religions.	

PROGRESS TEST

Choose the correct answer for the italicized words.

1. Das *schönste* Gefühl im Leben ist, daß die Macht in einem wächst.
   (a) beautiful (b) most beautiful (c) more beautiful (d) beautifully
2. *Je schwächer* man ist, *desto mehr* Schwierigkeiten wird man haben.
   (a) the more . . . the merrier (b) the weaker . . . the better (c) the stronger . . . the more (d) the weaker . . . the more
3. Bonhoeffer war *nicht so alt wie* Nietzsche.
   (a) not as old as (b) not so much older than
4. Er war ein *einfacher* Mann.
   (a) more ordinary (b) ordinary (c) very ordinary (d) most ordinary
5. Ist das Christentum *genau so schädlich wie* Nietzsche?
   (a) not as harmful as (b) just as harmful as (c) more harmful than (d) none

Answer key: **1.** (b); **2.** (d); **3.** (a); **4.** (b); **5.** (b).

28. *Comparison of adverbs*

1. The forms of the German adverb in the comparative and superlative do not differ essentially from the predicate adjective:

Die Frau singt schön.	*The woman sings beautifully.*
Die Frau singt schöner.	*The woman sings more beautifully.*
Die Frau singt am schönsten.	*The woman sings most beautifully.*

The **am** ________**-en** form is the only superlative of the adverb.

2. The same adjective formulas mentioned above apply to the adverb as well:

Der Franzose spricht schneller als der Deutsche.	*The Frenchman speaks more quickly than the German.*
Hans singt nicht so laut wie du.	*Hans does not sing so loudly as you.*
Je schöner sie singt, desto mehr schwärme ich für sie.	*The more beautifully she sings, the more I am enraptured with her.*
Er spricht immer langsamer.	*He speaks more and more slowly.*

3. The following adverbs are irregular:

bald, eher, am ehesten	*soon*
gern, lieber, am liebsten	*like (with pleasure, willingly)*

Gern and its comparative forms are translated as follows:

Ich trinke gern Wasser.	*I like to drink water.*
Ich trinke lieber Milch.	*I prefer to drink milk.*
Ich trinke am liebsten Bier.	*I like to drink beer best of all.*

This section continues to introduce vocabulary for the reading passage and gives you practice in recognizing the adverb forms. Give the meaning of the indicated words.

	1. **antworten** = *to answer, reply* **die Antwort** = *the answer, reply* Er **beantwortet** die Frage.
1. He *answers* the question.	**2.** **eine Frage stellen** = *to ask a question* **Am liebsten** stellt er ganz einfache Fragen, die schwer zu beantworten sind.
2. He *likes best* to ask very simple questions which are hard to answer.	**3.** **heilig** = *holy, saintly* Bonhoeffer will **lieber** glauben als ein Heiliger werden.
3. Bonhoeffer would *rather* believe than become a saint.	**4.** **mögen** = *to like* **mochte** = *liked* **möchte** = *would like* Bonhoeffer will **lieber** sagen: er möchte glauben lernen.

4. Bonhoeffer *prefers* to say (wants *rather* to say), he would like to learn to believe.	**5.** Er möchte **am liebsten** ein ganz einfacher Mensch sein, **der** glauben kann. (**der** = *the/who*)
5. He would like *best* to be a completely simple person *who* is able to believe (have faith). (Notice that **der** is here used as a pronoun.)	**6.** **gelebt hat** = *lived* Bonhoeffer glaubt **gern,** daß Luther in der tiefen Diesseitigkeit gelebt hat.
6. Bonhoeffer *likes to* believe that Luther lived a profound secular life.	**7.** **widersprechen** = *to contradict* Warum widersprechen sie ihm so **gern**?
7. Why do they *like* to contradict him so much?	**8.** **im allgemeinen** = *generally* Im allgemeinen möchte man **am liebsten** alles wissen; da man nicht kann, so glaubt man.
8. One would generally *like best* to know everything; since one cannot, one believes.	**9.** **der Pfarrer** = *the pastor* **das Gespräch** = *the conversation* Er erinnert sich **gern** an das Gespräch, das er vor 13 (dreizehn) Jahren mit einem jungen französischen Pfarrer hatte.
9. He *likes* to recall the conversation which he had 13 years ago with a young French minister.	**10.** Im allgemeinen wirft man sich **gern** Gott ganz in die Arme?
10. In general, does one *like* to rely completely on God?	**11.** **das Erlebnis** = *experience* **erleben** = __________
11. to experience	**12.** **die Lasziven** = *the sensualists* Die Aufgeklärten, die Betriebsamen, die Bequemen und die Lasziven **werden** die tiefe Diesseitigkeit des Lebens nicht bald erleben. (**werden** = *will/are becoming*)
12. The enlightened, the busy, the comfortable, and the sensualists *will* not soon experience a profound secular life.	**13.** **leer** = *empty* Sie werden **eher** das leere Nichts erleben.
13. They will *sooner* experience empty nothingness.	**14.** **Eher** will Bonhoeffer sich in die Arme Gottes werfen als ein Heiliger werden.

14. Bonhoeffer would *rather* rely on God than become a saint.	**15.** Bonhoeffer meint **am ehesten** zu glauben, wenn er darauf verzichtet, etwas aus sich selbst zu machen.
15. Bonhoeffer feels that he will believe *most easily* (*soonest*) when he gives up trying to make something of himself. (**Darauf** = "*therefrom*"—refers to the idea in the following phrase.)	**16.** **Eher** wird der Pfarrer ein Heiliger als ein Gläubiger.
16. The minister will *sooner* become a saint than a believer.	**17.** Das Gespräch wird **bald** zu Ende sein.
17. The conversation will *soon* be at an end.	**18.** **erst** = *not until* (*first*) **Am ehesten** können wir uns erst nächstes Jahr wiedersehen.
18. *At the earliest* we cannot see one another again until next year.	**19.** **leiden** = *to suffer, bear* **das Leiden** = ________
19. *suffering*	**20.** **nimmt** = *present of* **nehmen,** *to take* Nimmt man das Leiden Gottes in der Welt **ernst**?
20. Does one take *seriously* the suffering of God in the world?	**21.** **Ernster** kann er das Leiden Gottes in der Welt nicht nehmen.
21. He cannot take the suffering of God in the world *more seriously* (than he already does).	**22.** **Immer mehr** versteht Bonhoeffer die tiefe Diesseitigkeit des Christentums.
22. *More and more* Bonhoeffer understands the profound this-worldliness of Christianity.	**23.** Wir stellen uns **ganz einfach** die Frage, was wir mit unserem Leben eigentlich wollen.
23. We ask ourselves *very simply* the question, what do we really want from our life.	**24.** Er war ein **einfacher** Mann. (*simple/simpler*)
24. He was a *simple* man.	**25.** Er war ein **einfacherer** Mann als sein Sohn.
25. He was a *simpler* man than his son.	**26.** **wer** = *who* Wer kann es **einfacher** tun?
26. Who can do it *more simply*?	**27.** **erst** = *first, only* Man lernt glauben **erst** in der vollen Diesseitigkeit des Lebens.

27. One learns to believe *only* by living completely in this world.	

PROGRESS TEST

Choose the correct answer.

1. Bonhoeffer will *lieber* glauben als Heiliger werden.
(a) love (b) live (c) rather (d) sooner

2. Warum widerspricht er ihm so *gern?*
(a) love (b) like (c) endearingly (d) lovely

3. Er kommt *eher* als ich.
(a) later (b) more slowly (c) faster (d) sooner

4. *Einfacher* kann er es nicht erklären.
(a) more simply (b) simply (c) most simply (d) simple

5. Er singt ____________ ein altes Volkslied.
(a) das liebste (b) lieber als (c) so lieb wie (d) am liebsten

Answer key: **1.** (c); **2.** (b); **3.** (d); **4.** (a); **5.** (d).

29. *Adjectives used as nouns*

1. Adjectives used as nouns are capitalized, but they retain their adjective endings:

Der *blinde* Mann ist nicht hier.	*The blind man is not here.*
Der *Blinde* sitzt in der Ecke.	*The blind man sits in the corner.*

2. Adjectival nouns may be masculine, feminine, or neuter. If masculine or feminine, singular or plural, they refer to persons:

der Alte	*the old man*
die Alte	*the old woman*
ein Armer	*a poor man*
eine Arme	*a poor woman*
die Alten (Armen)	*the old people (poor people)*

If neuter, they refer to an abstract quality or a thing:

***Das Rote* will ich.**	*I want **the red one.***
Das ist *das Schöne* daran.	*That is **the beautiful thing** about it.*

3. Neuter adjectival nouns are commonly found after the indefinite pronouns:

allerlei	*all kinds of, all sorts of*
Sagt er *allerlei Dummes?*	*Does he say* ***all sorts of stupid things?***
alles	*all, everything*
Wir wünschen Ihnen *alles Gute!*	*We wish you* ***all the best!***
etwas	*something*
***Etwas Neues* wissen Sie doch!**	*You must know* ***something new!***
nichts	*nothing*
Sie hat *nichts Neues* gesagt.	*She (has) said* ***nothing new.***
viel	*much*
Er hat *viel Gutes* getan.	*He has done* ***much good.***
wenig	*little*
Sie hat nur *wenig Gutes* über ihn zu sagen.	*She has* ***little good*** *to say about him.*

In three instances the adjective will not be capitalized:

alles andere	*all else*
alles mögliche	*everything possible*
alles übrige	*all the rest*

Give the meaning of the indicated words.

	1. Ein **aufgeklärter** Mensch ist er nicht.
1. He is not an *enlightened* human being.	**2.** **Ein Aufgeklärter** ist er nicht.
2. He is not *an enlightened human being.*	**3.** Es gibt keinen **aufgeklärteren** Menschen auf der Welt.
3. There is no man in the world who is *more enlightened* (. . . *more enlightened* man in the world).	**4.** Er glaubt, daß er **der aufgeklärteste** Mensch auf der Welt ist.
4. He believes that he is *the most enlightened* person in the world.	**5.** In einem **betriebsamen** Menschen findet man die tiefe Diesseitigkeit nicht.
5. In a *busy* individual one does not find profound acceptance of life on this earth.	**6.** In einem **Betriebsamen** findet man die tiefe Diesseitigkeit nicht.
6. One does not find in a *busy individual* profound acceptance of life on this earth.	**7.** Auch nicht in einem **bequemen** oder **lasziven** Menschen.

7. Nor in a *comfortable* or *lascivious* person.	**8.** Auch nicht in einem **Bequemen** oder **Lasziven.**
8. Nor in a *comfortable* or *lascivious person.*	**9.** Der Pfarrer sagte, er möchte ein heiliger Mann werden.
9. The pastor said he would like to become a holy man.	**10.** Der Pfarrer sagte, er möchte ein **Heiliger** werden.
10. The pastor said he would like to become a *saint.*	**11.** . . . einen Gerechten oder einen Ungerechten . . . (If **einen Gerechten** means *a just person,* **einen Ungerechten** must mean________.)
11. *an unjust person*	**12.** . . . einen Kranken oder einen Gesunden (If **einen Kranken** means *a sick person,* **einen Gesunden** must mean ________.)
12. *a healthy person*	**13.** Kranke und gesunde, gerechte und ungerechte Menschen gibt es überall.
13. There are sick and healthy, just and unjust people everywhere.	**14.** Überall sieht man die **Kranken** und die **Gesunden,** die **Gerechten** und die **Ungerechten.**
14. One sees everywhere the *sick* and the *well,* the *just* and the *unjust* (the righteous and the unrighteous).	**15.** **Etwas anderes** als ein **Heiliger** will Bonhoeffer werden.
15. Bonhoeffer wants to become *something other* than a *saint.*	**16.** **Nichts Plattes** und **Banales** darf in dem wahren Christ sein.
16. There must be *nothing shallow* and *banal* in the true Christian.	**17.** If **Brief** is *a letter* and **Wechsel** is *exchange,* **der Briefwechsel** must mean ________.
17. *correspondence*	**18.** **enthalten** = *to contain* Enthält Bonhoeffers Briefwechsel **viel Ernstes?**
18. Does Bonhoeffer's correspondence contain *much that is serious?*	**19.** **die Zukunft** = *the future* **die Gegenwart** = *the present* **die Vergangenheit** = ________
19. *the past*	**20.** Denken Sie an **etwas Vergangenes** oder an **etwas Gegenwärtiges?**

20. Are you thinking of *something in the past* or of *something in the present?*	**21.** Der Gedanke, daß Gott tot ist, ist **nichts Neues.**
21. The thought that God is dead is *nothing new.*	**22.** Nietzsche hat **wenig Gutes** über das Christentum zu sagen.
22. Nietzsche has *little good* to say about Christianity.	**23.** **darüber** = *about it* Er hat **viel Schlechtes** darüber zu sagen.
23. He has *much that is bad* to say about it.	**24.** **Allerlei Neues** erfährt man, wenn man sich Gott ganz in die Arme wirft.
24. One experiences *all kinds of new things* when one relies completely on God.	**25.** **vergänglich** = *transitory, fleeting* **Alles Schöne** auf der Welt ist vergänglich.
25. *All that is beautiful* in the world is transitory.	**26.** **lehren** = *to teach* Kommt **wenig Gutes** aus Bonhoeffers Lehre?
26. Does *little good* come from Bonhoeffer's teachings?	**27.** Findet man **allerlei Gesundes** in Nietzsches Werken?
27. Does one find *all kinds of wholesome things* in Nietzsche's works?	**28.** **Alles mögliche** finden Sie in Nietzsches Werken.
28. You find *every possible thing in* Nietzsche's works.	

PROGRESS TEST

Find the approximate meaning of the italicized words.

1. Was ist denn überhaupt *das Schönste* im Leben?
   (a) beautiful (b) most beautiful (c) the most beautiful thing (d) most beautifully
2. Tut *ein Schwacher* so etwas?
   (a) a weak (b) a weaker (c) a weaker person (d) a weak person
3. *Die Arme* sitzt da drüben, ganz allein und einsam.
   (a) the poor woman (b) the arm (c) poor women (d) arms
4. Denken sie an *etwas Gegenwärtiges?*
   (a) nothing in the past (b) something in the future (c) much in the present (d) something in the present

5. *Alles Vergangene* kommt nie wieder.
   (a) all gone (b) all that has passed (c) everything goes (d) everything passes
6. *Allerlei Neues* erfährt man.
   (a) all new things (b) everything is new (c) all kinds of new things (d) every new thing

Answer key: **1.** (c); **2.** (d); **3.** (a); **4.** (d); **5.** (b); **6.** (c).

30. *Uses of* ***man***

1. The indefinite pronoun **man** may be translated by

(a) *one:*

Man liest in der Bibel, daß . . .	*One reads in the Bible that . . .*

(b) *people, you, we, they,* or *any of the persons,* depending on the context:

Hier spricht man kein Deutsch.	*People (they) don't speak German here.*
Man kann sie überhaupt nicht verstehen.	*We cannot understand them at all.*

(c) the passive:

Man tut das nicht.	*That is not done.*

2. Do not confuse **man** with the noun **der Mann** which is translated as *the man:*

Der Mann kommt nicht wieder.	*The man will not come back.*
Wird man geboren, so wird man sterben.	*If we are born, we will die.*

3. **Man** is declined as follows:

N	**man**	*one*
G	**eines**	*of one*
D	**einem**	*(to) one*
A	**einen**	*one*

Do not confuse **ein**-forms of **man** with the indefinite article, but note also that occasionally **einer** is used instead of **man** in the nominative:

Wenn *einer* etwas sagt, dann müssen wir aufhören.	*If one says anything, we (will) have to stop.*

These exercises continue the discussion of Bonhoeffer. Give the English meaning of the following.

	1. **schlechthin** = *simply* Man sieht, daß der Christ nicht ein *homo religiosus,* sondern ein Mensch schlechthin ist.
1. One sees that the Christian is not a *homo religiosus* but simply a human being (man).	**2.** **der Unterschied** = *contrast, difference* Der Unterschied zwischen Jesus und Johannes dem Täufer ist groß.
2. The difference between Jesus and John the Baptist is great.	**3.** **ist geworden** = *has become* Hält der **Mann** es für möglich, daß er ein Heiliger geworden ist?
3. Does the *man* consider it possible that he has become a saint?	**4.** **der Eindruck** = *the impression* **beeindrucken** = *to impress* Der Pfarrer beeindruck**te** Bonhoeffer sehr.
4. The minister impress*ed* Bonhoeffer very much.	**5.** **obwohl** = *although* Bonhoeffer widersprach dem Pfarrer, obwohl der Pfarrer ihn damals sehr beeindruckte.
5. Bonhoeffer disagreed with the pastor although the pastor impressed him very much at the time.	**6.** **der Gegensatz** = *contrast* Man liest, daß Bonhoeffer lange Zeit die Tiefe dieses Gegensatzes nicht verstanden hat.
6. One reads that for a long time Bonhoeffer did not understand the depth of this contrast. **(verstanden** = past participle of **verstehen)**	**7.** **dachte** = *thought* **könnte** = *could* Bonhoeffer dachte, ein Mensch könnte glauben lernen.
7. Bonhoeffer thought a person could learn to believe.	**8.** Viele Christen wollen ein heiliges Leben führen.
8. Many Christians want to lead a holy life.	**9.** **indem er selbst versucht** = *by (himself) trying* Man könnte glauben lernen, indem man selbst so etwas wie ein heiliges Leben zu führen versuchte.

9. One could learn to believe by trying to lead a somewhat holy life.	**10. später** = *later* **erfahren** = *to discover, experience* Was erfuhr Bonhoeffer später und was erfährt er jetzt? (The context shows that **erfuhr** is — past/present)
10. past What did Bonhoeffer discover later and what does he discover now?	**11. die Stunde** = *hour* Was erfährt er bis zur Stunde?
11. What does he discover to the present time (to the hour)?	**12.** Bonhoeffer dachte, er könnte glauben lernen . . .
12. Bonhoeffer thought he could learn to believe . . .	**13. da** = *since* . . . da er ein heiliges Leben zu führen versuchte.
13. . . . since he was trying to lead a holy life.	**14. sei es** = *be it* (subjunctive) Man soll völlig darauf verzichten, aus sich etwas zu machen, sei es einen Heiligen, einen bekehrten Sünder oder einen Kirchenmann.
14. One must deny completely any attempt to make something of oneself, be it a saint, a converted sinner or a churchman.	**15. nennen** = *to call* **sogenannt** = *so-called* **die Gestalt** = *figure, type* Ein Kirchenmann ist eine sogenannte priesterliche Gestalt.
15. A man of the Church is a so-called priestly type.	**16.** Er dachte, er könnte glauben lernen, indem er selbst ein heiliges Leben zu führen versuchte.
16. He thought he could learn to believe by himself trying to lead a holy life.	**17.** Er dachte, er könnte glauben lernen, indem er selbst so etwas wie ein heiliges Leben zu führen versuchte.
17. He thought he could learn to believe by himself trying to lead a somewhat holy life.	**18. ratlos** = *perplexed* **die Ratlosigkeit** = __________

18. *perplexity*	**19.** **der Erfolg** = *success* **der Mißerfolg** = __________
19. *failure*	**20.** **die Aufgabe** = *assignment, duty* Bonhoeffer nennt dies Diesseitigkeit, nämlich in der Fülle der Aufgaben, Fragen, Erfolge und Mißerfolge, Erfahrungen und Ratlosigkeiten leben.
20. By a secular life ("this-worldliness") Bonhoeffer means living in the fullness of life's duties, questions, successes and failures, experiences, and perplexities.	**21.** **übermütig werden** = *to become proud, arrogant* Oft kann man bei Erfolgen übermütig werden.
21. Often one can become arrogant with success.	**22.** **irre werden** = *to become confused* Oft kann man **an** Mißerfolgen irre werden. (*at/by*)
22. One can often become confused *by* failures.	**23.** **sollte** = *should* Wie sollte man bei Erfolgen übermütig oder an Mißerfolgen irre werden . . .
23. How should one become arrogant with success or become confused by failures . . .	**24.** **mitleiden** = *to suffer with* . . . wenn man im diesseitigen Leben Gottes **Leiden** mitleidet? (*sufferings/joys*)
24. . . . if in the secular life one shares God's *sufferings?*	**25.** **bekehren** = *to convert* **ein bekehrter Sünder** = *a converted*______
25. *sinner*	

PROGRESS TEST

Choose the answer which most closely approximates the indicated statement.

1. *Man sagt,* daß alles möglich ist.
   (a) the man says (b) man says (c) one says
2. Die Betriebsamen, die Aufgeklärten, die Bequemen und die Lasziven wissen genau, daß die tiefe Diesseitigkeit voller Zucht ist.
   (a) The busy, the enlightened, the comfortable, and the lascivious appreciate the secular life.

(b) They know that the secular life has many restrictions.
(c) The profound secular life embraces only those who know discipline.
(d) The busy, the enlightened, comfortable and lascivious can never know the profound secular life.

3. Bonhoeffer beeindruckte den Pfarrer, obwohl der Pfarrer ihm damals widersprach.
(a) Bonhoeffer made an impression on the minister.
(b) Bonhoeffer impressed the minister because Bonhoeffer contradicted him.
(c) Bonhoeffer contradicted the minister even though the minister impressed him very much.

4. Nietzsche nach gibt es zwei Sorten Menschen: die Starken und die Schwachen und Mißratenen.
(a) According to Nietzsche it is better to be strong than weak.
(b) After Nietzsche come two groups of people, the old, and the misfits.
(c) According to Nietzsche there are two groups of human beings, those who are strong and those who are weak and misfits.

5. Wenn man völlig darauf verzichtet, in der Fülle der Aufgaben, Fragen, Erfolge und Mißerfolge, Erfahrungen und Ratlosigkeiten zu leben, dann wird man ein Heiliger, ein Gerechter, ein bekehrter Sünder.
(a) One becomes a saint by renouncing all of life's experiences.
(b) Only by living a full life can one become a righteous person.
(c) To fully live one must experience all things.

Answer key: **1.** (c); **2.** (b); **3.** (a); **4.** (c); **5.** (a).

Briefe und Aufzeichnungen aus der Haft. Neuausgabe 1970, Seite 401/402. Chr. Kaiser Verlag, München.

Dietrich Bonhoeffer: Widerstand und Ergebung

Ich habe in den letzten Jahren mehr und mehr die tiefe Diesseitigkeit des Christentums kennen und verstehen gelernt. Nicht ein *homo religiosus*, sondern ein Mensch schlechthin ist der Christ, wie Jesus — im Unterschied wohl zu Johannes dem Täufer — Mensch war. Nicht die platte und banale Diesseitigkeit der Aufgeklärten, der Betriebsamen, der Bequemen oder der Lasziven, sondern die tiefe Diesseitigkeit, die voller Zucht ist, und in der die Erkenntnis des Todes und der Auferstehung immer gegenwärtig ist, meine ich. Ich glaube, daß Luther in dieser Diesseitigkeit gelebt hat.

Ich erinnere mich eines Gespräches, das ich vor 13 Jahren in Amerika mit einem französischen jungen Pfarrer hatte. Wir hatten uns ganz einfach die Frage gestellt, was wir mit unserem Leben eigentlich wollten. Da sagte er: ich möchte ein Heiliger werden (— und ich halte für möglich, daß er es geworden ist —); das beeindruckte mich damals sehr. Trotzdem widersprach ich ihm und sagte ungefähr: ich möchte glauben lernen. Lange Zeit habe ich die Tiefe dieses Gegensatzes nicht verstanden. Ich dachte, ich könnte glauben lernen, indem ich selbst so etwas wie ein heiliges Leben zu führen versuchte...

Später erfuhr ich und erfahre es bis zur Stunde, daß man erst in der vollen Diesseitigkeit des Lebens glauben lernt. Wenn man völlig darauf verzichtet hat, aus sich selbst etwas zu machen — sei es einen Heiligen oder einen bekehrten Sünder oder einen Kirchenmann (eine sogenannte priesterliche Gestalt!), einen Gerechten oder einen Ungerechten, einen Kranken oder einen Gesunden — und dies nenne ich Diesseitigkeit, nämlich in der Fülle der Aufgaben, Fragen, Erfolge und Mißerfolge, Erfahrungen und Ratlosigkeiten leben —, dann wirft man sich Gott ganz in die Arme, dann nimmt man nicht mehr die eigenen Leiden, sondern das Leiden Gottes in der Welt ernst, dann wacht man mit Christus in Gethsemane, und ich denke, das ist Glaube, das ist „Metanoia“[1], und so wird man ein Mensch, ein Christ (vgl.[2] Jerem.[3] 45!). Wie sollte man bei Erfolgen übermütig oder an Mißerfolgen irre werden, wenn man im diesseitigen Leben Gottes Leiden mitleidet?

---

1 metanoia—a Greek word meaning *repentance*
2 vgl. (vergleiche)—cf. (compare)
3 Jeremiah

Chapter Eight

31. *Interrogative and relative pronouns **wer** and **was***

1. Wer may be used as an interrogative pronoun (to ask questions) or as a relative pronoun (to join two clauses). It refers only to persons and is declined and translated as follows:

Nominative	**wer**	*who*
Genitive	**wessen**	*whose*
Dative	**wem**	*(to) whom*
Accusative	**wen**	*whom*

Wer ist dein Freund?	*Who is your friend?*
Wessen Buch ist das?	*Whose book is that?*
Wem geben Sie die Schokolade?	*To whom are you giving the chocolate?*
Wen sieht Jürgen?	*Whom does Jürgen see?*
Wer sieht Jürgen?	*Who sees Jürgen?*

2. Occasionally **wer** is translated as *"he who"* or *"whoever":*

Wer das sagt, ist kein Freund von mir.	*He who (whoever) says that is no friend of mine.*

3. Was may also be used as an interrogative or relative pronoun. It is not declined and refers only to things. It may be translated as *what, whatever, that, which:*

Was ist das?	*What is that?*
Was sieht Jürgen?	*What does Jürgen see?*
Ich weiß, was er sagt.	*I know what he is saying.*
Alles, was er sagt, ist die Wahrheit.	*Everything that he says is the truth.*
Das, was sie sagen, ist falsch.	*That which they are saying is false.*
Was ich sehe, (das) weiß ich.	*Whatever I see, that I know.*

4. When a form of **wer** or **was** is used in a dependent clause (a relative pronoun clause), the verb will be at the end of the clause:

Ich weiß, wer da ist.	*I know who is there.*
Paul weiß, mit wem Sie nach Deutschland fahren.	*Paul knows with whom you are travelling to Germany.*

This section contains vocabulary and phrases drawn from the previous two chapters. Give the meanings of the indicated words.

	1. **Wer** ergreift den Zivilisten?
1. *Who* is apprehending the civilian?	2. **Wer** spricht gegen das Christentum?
2. *Who* is speaking against Christianity?	3. **Wessen** Wort sollen wir ernst nehmen?
3. *Whose* word are we to take seriously?	4. **Wessen** Idee ist das?
4. *Whose* idea is that?	5. **Wem** sollen wir helfen?
5. *Whom* are we supposed to help?	6. **Wem** wirft man sich ganz in die Arme?
6. *Upon whom* does one rely completely?	7. **Wen** ergreifen die Soldaten?
7. *Whom* do the soldiers seize?	8. **Wen** führen die Soldaten vor ihren Herrn?
8. *Whom* do the soldiers take to their superior? (Literally: . . . lead before their superior.)	9. **Mit wem** spricht der Pfarrer?
9. *With whom* is the minister speaking?	10. **Wer** soll zugrunde gehen?
10. *Who* is supposed to perish?	11. **Was** soll zugrunde gehen?
11. *What* is supposed to perish?	12. In **wessen** Arme soll man sich ganz werfen?
12. *Upon whom* should one rely completely?	13. **Wer** möchte glauben lernen?
13. *Who* would like to learn to believe?	14. **Was** muß man glauben lernen?
14. *What* must one learn to believe?	15. **Wo** ist heute ein wahrer Mensch?

15. *Where* is a true person today?	**16. Wo** sollen die Schwachen und Mißratenen hingehen?
16. *Where* are the weaklings and misfits to go?	**17. Wer** die Leiden Gottes in der Welt ernst nimmt, wird ein Mensch, ein Christ.
17. *Whoever* takes the sufferings of God in the world seriously will become a human being, a Christian.	**18. Was** aus der Schwäche stammt, ist schlecht.
18. *Whatever* stems from weakness is bad.	**19. Was** ist schädlicher als irgendein Laster?
19. *What* is more harmful than any vice?	**20.** Alles, **was** aus der Schwäche stammt, ist schlecht.
20. Everything *which* stems from weakness is bad.	**21. Wer** hält mich fest?
21. *Who* is holding me fast?	**22.** Ich weiß nicht, was ihr von **ihr** wollt.
22. I do not know what you want of *her*.	

PROGRESS TEST

Select the correct translation for the indicated words.

1. Er kann sich nicht erinnern, *wer* das Gespräch begonnen hat.
(a) where (b) whose (c) what (d) who

2. *Was* aus der Schwäche stammt, ist schlecht.
(a) whatever (b) whose (c) whoever (d) where

3. *Wo* ist heute ein wahrer Mensch?
(a) who (b) where (c) what (d) to whom

4. *Wessen* Leiden sollen wir ernst nehmen?
(a) who (b) where (c) whose (d) what

5. *Wem* sollen wir helfen?
(a) when (b) whom (c) what (d) whose

6. *Wen* führen die Soldaten vor ihren Herrn?
(a) whom (b) from whom (c) when (d) what

Answer key: **1.** (d); **2.** (a); **3.** (b); **4.** (c); **5.** (b); **6.** (a).

32. *The interrogatives* **wann, warum, wie, wo, welch-,** *and* **was für ein**

1. The interrogatives below are translated as follows:

wann	*when*
warum	*why*
wie	*how*
wo	*where*
welch-	*which, what*
was für ein	*what kind (of) a*

2. All of these interrogatives except **welch-** and **was für ein** are not declined (do not have case endings):

***Wo* ist der Mann?**	***Where*** *is the man?*
***Warum* kommt er nicht?**	***Why*** *does he not come?*

3. Welch- acts as a limiting adjective and thus will take an ending which indicates the gender, number, and case of the noun it precedes:

In welchem Haus wohnt Karl?	*In which house does Karl live?*
Welche Frau hat sieben Kinder?	*Which woman has seven children?*

4. Ein of **was für ein** (plural **was für**) is declined as the indefinite article **ein. Für** does not function as a preposition in this expression:

Was für eine Frau ist sie?	*What kind of a woman is she?*
Was für Frauen sind sie?	*What kind of women are they?*

Was für ein (was für) used in exclamations are translated *what a* or *what:*

Was für ein Auto!	*What an automobile!*
Was für Leute!	*What people!*

This section contains vocabulary and phrases from previous chapters. Give the meanings of the indicated words.

	1. **Wann** war Deutschland vereinigt?
1. *When* was Germany united?	2. **Warum** sind Wien und die Donau das Tor Mitteleuropas?

2. *Why* are Vienna and the Danube the gateway to Central Europe?	3. **Warum** sind Österreichs einstige wertvolle Beziehungen zu ost- und südeuropäischen Ländern zum Teil abgeschnitten?
3. *Why* are Austria's former valuable relations with eastern and southern European countries in part cut off?	4. **blieben** = *past of* **bleiben** **Wie lange** blieben die Habsburger an der Macht?
4. *How long* did the Hapsburgs remain in power?	5. **Wo** spricht man die deutsche Sprache?
5. *Where* does one speak the German language?	6. **Wo** liegt jetzt die Grenze zwischen Deutschland und Polen?
6. *Where* is the border now between Germany and Poland?	7. **der Schweizerbund** = *the Swiss Confederation* **Wie alt** ist der Schweizerbund?
7. *How old* is the Swiss Confederation?	8. **gelten** = *to pass for, are considered* **Warum** hat Deutschland mehrere Städte, die als historische Zentren gelten?
8. *Why* does Germany have several cities which are considered to be historical centers? (Notice that **die** is here used as a relative pronoun.)	9. **Wann** wird die Wiedervereinigung Deutschlands stattfinden?
9. *When* will the reunification of Germany take place?	10. **Wer** vereinigte Deutschland und Österreich zum ersten und einzigen Male?
10. *Who* united Germany and Austria for the first and only time?	11. **Wo** ist der Bodensee?
11. *Where* is Lake Constance?	12. **Welche** neun Länder umringen Deutschland?
12. *Which* nine countries surround Germany?	13. Dürer und Grünewald sind Maler **welches** Landes?
13. Dürer and Grünewald are painters *from which* country?	14. **Welchen** Dialekt sprechen Sie?
14. *Which* dialect do you speak?	15. **Was für ein** Mann war Bismarck?

15. *What kind of a* man was Bismarck?	**16.** **herrlich** = *wonderful* **Was für** herrliche Schokolade!
16. *What* wonderful chocolate!	**17.** **der Esel** = *donkey* **Was für** dumme Esel!
17. *What* stupid fools (asses, donkeys)!	**18.** Es gibt andere Länder, **wo** man die deutsche Sprache spricht.
18. There are other countries *where* one speaks the German language.	**19.** **Wie** kann die Wiedervereinigung Deutschlands je stattfinden?
19. *How* can the reunification of Germany ever take place?	**20.** Können die beiden deutschen Staaten die notwendigen Konzessionen machen?
20. Can both German states make the necessary concessions?	**21.** Hier ist das klassische Gebirgsland, **welches** Millionen von Menschen jedes Jahr besuchen.
21. Here is the classic mountain country *which* millions of people visit every year.	**22.** **Wie** schmeckt der Schweizer Käse?
22. *How* does the Swiss cheese taste?	

PROGRESS TEST

Choose the correct translation for the indicated words.

1. *Warum* sind Österreichs einstige wertvolle Beziehungen zu ost- und südeuropäischen Ländern zum Teil abgeschnitten?
(a) when (b) how (c) why (d) where

2. *Wie* ist es möglich, daß Hitler immer noch großen Einfluß auf Europa ausüben kann?
(a) how (b) when (c) where (d) who

3. *Wo* ist Karl Marx geboren?
(a) who (b) where (c) when (d) why

4. In *welcher* deutschen Stadt sieht man das Symbol der politischen Lage des heutigen Deutschlands?
(a) that (b) why (c) when (d) which

5. *Was für* Pläne hatten die Türken?
(a) why (b) what kind of (c) when (d) who

Answer key: **1.** (c); **2.** (a); **3.** (b); **4.** (d); **5.** (b).

33. *Separable verb prefixes*

1. In German, as in English, it is possible to form new verbs and meanings by adding a prefix:

stehen	*to stand*
***be*stehen**	*to exist, to pass*
***ge*stehen**	*to confess*
***ver*stehen**	*to understand*
***auf*stehen**	*to get up*
***bei*stehen**	*to aid, to stand by*
***vor*stehen**	*to stand before, to preside over*

2. Verb prefixes are either separable or inseparable. Prefixes such as **be-, ge-,** and **ver-** in our above examples are inseparable prefixes, i.e. they are never separated from the stem. Few in number, the other common inseparable prefixes are **emp-, ent-, er-,** and **zer-.**

3. Separable prefixes, however, are numerous. Primarily, they are either adverbs or prepositions, and the meaning of the prefix is generally added to the verb. **Auf-, bei-,** and **vor-** in the above are examples of prepositions used as separable prefixes.

4. The separable prefix will always be at the end of the clause, where it may or may not be attached to the verb, depending on the word order of the clause or on the verb tense:

Normal word order, present:

Ich stehe um acht Uhr *auf.* — *I get up at 8 o'clock.*

Inverted word order, past:

Stand er um acht Uhr *auf?* — *Did he get up at 8 o'clock?*

Dependent word order, present (past):

Ich weiß, daß er um acht Uhr *auf*steht (*auf*stand). — *I know that he gets up* (*got up*) *at 8 o'clock.*

Only in the simple present and simple past tenses, in normal or inverted word order, will the prefix be separated from the rest of the verb.

5. A separable prefix verb used with a modal is found at the end of a clause and is joined with its prefix:

Darf* ich mit Ihnen zum Bahnhof *mitfahren? — ***May I ride along*** *with you to the railway station?*

Ich weiß, daß er mich nicht *ansehen will.* — *I know that he does not* ***want to look at*** *me.*

6. As has been mentioned, prepositions used as separable verb prefixes will be found at the end of the clause. Used simply as prepositions, they precede their objects:

Der Professor *sieht* die Studenten scharf *an*.	*The professor* ***looks at*** *the students sharply.*
Der Professor geht *an* die Tafel.	*The professor goes* ***to*** *the board.*

7. Two common adverbial prefixes are **hin** and **her. Hin** denotes motion away from; **her** denotes motion towards the speaker or observer. They are often used in conjunction with other prefixes:

Dieser Kurs wächst mir zum Halse heraus.	*I've had enough of this course.* Literally: *This course grows up to my throat and out.*
Das Ewig-Weibliche zieht uns hinan. (Goethe)	*The eternal feminine draws us upwards.*

Her, with an adverb or phrase of time, may indicate past time and is then translated *ago:*

Es ist schon lange her, daß ich Geld hatte.	*It was a long time ago that I had money.*

Give the infinitive form of the verbs in the following sentences.

	1. Schauen wir die Landkarte an!
1. anschauen — Let us look at the map.	**2.** Wie leidet man im diesseitigen Leben Gottes Leiden mit?
2. mitleiden — How does one suffer with God's suffering in this earthly life (How does one share in God's sufferings in this life here on earth)?	**3.** Wann löste sich die Habsburger Monarchie auf?
3. auflösen — When did the Hapsburg monarchy break up?	**4. fand** = *past of* **finden** Vor dreizehn (13) Jahren fand ein Gespräch zwischen Bonhoeffer und einem jungen französischen Pfarrer statt.
4. stattfinden — Thirteen years ago a conversation took place between Bonhoeffer and a young French pastor.	**5.** Die Geschichte Österreichs hängt sehr eng mit der deutschen Geschichte zusammen.

5. **zusammenhängen** — The history of Austria is connected very closely with German history.	6. Bauen wir eine Welt des Friedens oder des Krieges auf?
6. **aufbauen** — Are we building a world of peace or war?	7. Die Soldaten hielten den Zivilisten fest.
7. **festhalten** — The soldiers held the civilian fast.	

What are the meanings of the following sentences?

	8. **einflußreich** = *influential* **der Schriftsteller** = *writer* Sigmund Freud ist ein einflußreicher Schriftsteller.
8. Sigmund Freud is an influential writer.	9. **einer** = *one* Er ist einer **der** einflußreichsten Schriftstellern **der** modernen Zeit. (*of/the/of the*)
9. He is one of the most influential writers *of* modern times.	10. Wie Sie schon wissen, ist er der Vater **der** Psychologie und **der** Psychoanalyse. (*of/the*)
10. As you already know, he is the father *of* psychology and (*of*) psychoanalysis.	11. **dieses Kapitels** = *of this chapter* **seiner** = *of his* Am Ende dieses Kapitels **werden** Sie einen seiner Gedanken über die Liebe lesen. (*will/become*)
11. At the end of this chapter you *will* read one of his ideas about love.	12. **der Nächste** = *neighbor* Freud schreibt, daß er es sehr schwer findet, seinen Nächsten zu lieben.
12. Freud writes that he finds it very difficult to love his neighbor.	13. Heinrich Heine ist ein berühmter deutscher Dichter des 19. Jahrhunderts.
13. Heinrich Heine is a famous German poet of the 19th century.	14. Auch er findet es sehr schwer, seinen Nächsten zu lieben.

14. He too finds it very difficult to love his neighbor.	**15.** Sie werden auch lesen, was Heine über dieses Problem zu sagen hat.
15. You will also read what Heine has to say about this problem.	**16.** **folgendes** = *the following* Die Bibel sagt uns folgendes über das Problem der Nächstenliebe.
16. The Bible tells us the following about the problem of loving one's neighbor.	**17.** Du sollst den Nächsten lieben wie dich "selbst."
17. Thou shalt love thy neighbor as thyself.	**18.** Ist es möglich, den Nächsten zu lieben, wenn man sich selbst nicht liebt?
18. Is it possible to love one's neighbor, if one does not love oneself?	**19.** **fordern** = *to demand* **die Forderung** = *claim, demand, standard* Die Nächstenliebe ist eine sehr ideale Forderung.
19. The love of one's neighbor is a very ideal demand (standard).	**20.** **stolz** = *proud* **der Anspruch** = *claim* Das Christentum ist sehr stolz auf diesen Anspruch der Nächstenliebe.
20. Christianity is very proud of this claim (profession) of the love of one's neighbor.	**21.** **vorweisen** = *to show, to display* Das Christentum weist diese sogenannte Idealforderung als seinen stolzesten Anspruch vor.
21. Christianity displays this so-called ideal standard as its proudest claim.	**22.** **gewiß** = *certainly* Diese sogenannte Idealforderung ist gewiß älter als das Christentum, **das** sie als seinen stolzesten Anspruch vorweist. (*which/the*)
22. This so-called ideal standard is certainly older than Christianity, *which* displays it as its proudest claim.	**23.** **zustande bringen** = *to bring about, to accomplish* Wie bringen wir die Nächstenliebe zustande?
23. How are we to bring about the love of one's neighbor?	**24.** Wissen Sie, wie man **das** zustande bringen kann? (*which/that/the*)

24. Do you know how one can bring *that* about?	**25.** **fremd** = *strange, foreign* Wie wird es uns möglich, einen **Fremden** zu lieben?
25. How will it become possible for us to love a *stranger?*	**26.** **gleichstellen** = *to put on an equal footing* Freud stellt den Fremden seinen Freunden nicht gleich.
26. Freud does not put a stranger on an equal footing with his friends.	**27.** Er glaubt, daß es gewiß ein Unrecht an seinen Freunden ist, wenn er den Fremden ihnen gleichstellt.
27. He believes it is certainly an injustice to his friends, if he puts a stranger on the same level with them.	**28.** **nah** = *near* **zusehen** = *to look on, to take care* Wenn er näher zusieht, . . .
28. If he looks more closely . . .	**29.** **schwierig** = *difficult* **die Schwierigkeit** = *difficulty* Wenn er näher zusieht, findet er noch mehr Schwierigkeiten.
29. If he looks more closely he finds still more difficulties.	**30.** **das Gebot** = *commandment* Ein zweites Gebot heißt: Liebe deine Feinde!
30. A second commandment is: Love thine enemies!	**31.** **weisen** = *to show, to point* **abweisen** = *to turn away, to reject* Freud weist es ab, seine Feinde zu lieben.
31. Freud rejects the idea of loving his enemies. (**Es** anticipates the following phrase.)	**32.** **wahr** = *true* **der Schein** = *appearance* **wahrscheinlich** = *probable* Es ist wahrscheinlich, daß der Feind das Gebot auch abweisen wird.
32. It is probable that the enemy will also reject the commandment.	**33.** **fordern** = *to demand, to exact* **auffordern** = *to ask* (*to challenge*) Fordere den Nächsten auf, dich zu lieben wie sich selbst!
33. Ask your neighbor to love you as himself!	**34.** Wenn wir den Nächsten auffordern, uns zu lieben wie sich selbst, wird er es tun?
34. If we ask our neighbor to love us as he loves himself, will he do it?	

PROGRESS TEST

Choose the correct infinitive form of the verb in the following sentences.

1. Legt uns Liebe Pflichten auf?
(a) liegen (b) auflegen (c) legen
2. Ein Leid stößt meinem Freund zu.
(a) stoßen (b) einstoßen (c) zustoßen
3. Kommen Sie doch mit mir!
(a) kommen (b) mitkommen
4. Ich weiß, daß er mich durch keinen eigenen Wert anzieht.
(a) anziehen (b) durchanziehen (c) anziehtwissen

Now give the meaning of the indicated words.

5. Das ist ja schon eine Woche *her*.
(a) here (b) her (c) ago (d) towards the speaker
6. Er sieht *zum Fenster hinaus*.
(a) into the window (b) by the window (c) out of the window (d) toward the window

Answer key: **1.** (b); **2.** (c); **3.** (a); **4.** (a); **5.** (c); **6.** (c).

34. *Inseparable verb prefixes—meanings*

1. be- changes intransitive verbs to transitive (i.e. lets the verb take a direct object):

kommen	*to come*
bekommen	*to receive*
wohnen	*to live*
bewohnen	*to inhabit*

2. ent- (or **emp-** before **f**) denotes:
(a) the beginning of an action:

stehen	*to stand*
entstehen	*to come into existence*

(b) the meaning of "opposite":

wickeln	*to wind up*
entwickeln	*to develop* (*to unwind*)

(c) the meaning of separation:

gehen	*to go*
entgehen	*to escape*

3. **er-** denotes completion of an action or origin:

leben	*to live*
erleben	*to experience*
reichen	*to reach*
erreichen	*to attain*

4. **ge-:**

(a) shows result or completeness as shown in the past participle:

machen	*to make*
gemacht	*made*

(b) may also denote successful action:

gewinnen	*to gain*

5. **miß-** (generally an inseparable prefix) usually corresponds to English *mis-* or *dis-*. It denotes that something is amiss, false, wrong, or bad:

verstehen	*to understand*
mißverstehen	*to misunderstand*
trauen	*to trust*
mißtrauen	*to distrust*
handeln	*to act, to behave*
mißhandeln	*to abuse, to ill-treat*

6. **ver-** has several meanings:

(a) it may denote that the action of the verb miscarried:

kennen	*to know*
verkennen	*to fail to recognize*

(b) it is sometimes the equivalent of *for-:*

vergessen	*to forget*
vergeben	*to forgive*

(c) it may denote an action carried out to its logical conclusion:

hungern	*to hunger*
verhungern	*to die of hunger*

7. **zer-** denotes the destruction or damage resulting from the original verb and has the meaning of *to pieces, in pieces:*

brechen	*to break*
zerbrechen	*to break to pieces*
stören	*to disturb*
zerstören	*to destroy*

The following exercises combine practice in recognizing prefixes with introduction of more vocabulary for the reading passage. Give the meanings of the entire sentences. Remember to circle new words for review.

	1. **kennen** = *to know* **bekennen** = *to confess* **ehrlich** = *honest, honestly* Was muß Freud ehrlich bekennen?
1. What must Freud honestly confess?	**2.** **die Feindseligkeit** = *hostility* Freud muß ehrlich bekennen, der Fremde hat mehr Anspruch auf seine Feindseligkeit, sogar auf seinen Haß.
2. Freud must honestly confess that the stranger has more claim to his hostility, even to his hatred.	**3.** **zeigen** = *to point out, to show* **bezeigen** = *to show, to express* **die Rücksicht** = *consideration* Freuds Feinde bezeigen ihm keine Rücksicht.
3. Freud's enemies don't show him any consideration.	**4.** **gering** = *slight, small, inferior* Der Feind bezeigt ihm nicht die geringste Rücksicht.
4. The enemy does not show him the slightest consideration.	**5.** **gewinnen** = *to gain (over), to win* **davon** = *therefrom* Was gewinnt man davon, daß man nur seine Freunde liebt?
5. What does one gain from loving only one's friends?	**6.** **horchen** = *to listen, to overhear* **gehorchen** = *to obey* Es scheint, daß Freud dem Gebot der Nächstenliebe nicht gehorchen kann oder will.
6. It appears that Freud cannot or will not obey the commandment to love one's neighbor.	**7.** **trauen** = *to trust, to dare* **mißtrauen** = *to mistrust, to suspect* Scheint es Ihnen, daß Freud dem Gebot der Nächstenliebe mißtraut?

7. Does it appear to you that Freud mistrusts the commandment to love one's neighbor?	**8.** **brauchen** = *to use, to need* **mißbrauchen** = *to misuse, to abuse* Man kann und will sogar das Gebot der Nächstenliebe mißbrauchen.
8. One can and even wants to abuse the commandment to love one's neighbor.	**9.** **dienen** = *to serve* **verdienen** = *to earn, to deserve* Wenn ich einen anderen liebe, muß er es auf irgendeine Art verdienen.
9. If I love someone, he must deserve it (be worthy of it) in some way or other.	**10.** **die Kultur** = *culture, civilization* **die Gesellschaft** = *society* **die Kulturgesellschaft** = ___________
10. *civilized society*	**11.** **lauten** = *to read, to be as follows* **Eine der** sogenannten Idealforderungen der Kulturgesellschaft lautet: Du sollst den Nächsten lieben wie dich selbst. (*the one/one of the*)
11. *One of the* so-called ideal standards of civilized society reads: Thou shalt love thy neighbor as thyself.	**12.** Diese Idealforderung ist weltberühmt und gewiß **älter als** das Christentum. (*as old as/older than*)
12. This ideal standard is world famous and certainly *older than* Christianity.	**13.** Das Christentum aber **weist** diese Idealforderung als seinen stolzesten Anspruch **vor.**
13. Christianity, however, *displays* this ideal standard as its proudest claim.	**14.** **sicherlich** = *surely* Das Gebot ist gewiß älter als das Christentum, aber es ist sicherlich nicht sehr alt.
14. The commandment is certainly older than Christianity, but it is surely not very old.	**15.** In historischen Zeiten war das Gebot **den Menschen** noch fremd. (acc. sing./dat. plural)
15. dative plural: the adjective **fremd** requires a dative object. In historical times the commandment was still foreign *to man* (men still knew nothing of it).	**16.** Freud fragt: „Warum sollen wir das? Was soll es uns helfen?"
16. Freud asks, "Why should we do that? How is it to help us?"	**17.** **Vor allem** aber, wie bringen wir das zustande? (*for everyone/above all*)

17. *Above all,* however, how do we accomplish this?	**18.** Wie verdient man die Liebe **eines anderen** Menschen? (genitive/nominative)
18. genitive: **ein anderer Mensch** would be nominative. How does one earn the love *of another* individual?	**19.** Freud meint, daß ein Fremder seine Liebe **auf irgendeine Art** verdienen muß. (*artfully/in some way*)
19. Freud feels that a stranger must *in some way* merit his love.	**20.** **ähnlich** = *similar to, like* Wenn unser Nächster uns ähnlich ist, so können wir ihn lieben, sagt Freud.
20. Freud says, if our neighbor is similar to us, then we can love him.	**21.** **wichtig** = *important* **das Stück** = *piece, bit; here: aspect, respect* Freud meint, man verdient seine Liebe, wenn man **ihm** in wichtigen Stücken ähnlich ist. (*him/to him*)
21. Freud feels one earns his love when one is similar *to him* in important respects. (Note that **ähnlich** requires a dative object.)	**22.** **in dem einen** = *in the other* Freud meint, man verdient seine Liebe, wenn man ihm in wichtigen Stücken so ähnlich ist, daß er in dem einen sich selbst lieben kann.
22. Freud feels one is worthy of his love when one is so similar to him in important respects that he can love himself in the other.	**23.** **vollkommen** = *perfect* Freud sagt, ich kann den anderen lieben, wenn er **soviel vollkommener** ist als ich, daß ich mein Ideal von meiner eigenen Person in ihm lieben kann.
23. Freud says, I can love another if he is *so much more perfect* than I that I can love my ideal of myself (of my own person) in him.	**24.** Wir müssen den Nächsten lieben, wenn er der Sohn **unseres** Freundes ist. (*of your/of our*)
24. We must love our neighbor when he is the son *of our* friend.	**25.** Wenn er mir fremd ist, sagt Freud, wird es **mir schwer,** ihn zu lieben. (*hard for me/hard for him*)

25. If he is a stranger to me, says Freud, it is (becomes) *hard for me* to love him. (Note that **schwer** calls for a dative object.)	**26.** **ziehen** = *to pull* **anziehen** = *to attract* Wenn er mich durch keinen **eigenen Wert** anziehen kann, wird es mir schwer, ihn zu lieben. (*own worth/one word*)
26. If he cannot attract me by his *own worth*, it is difficult for me to love him.	**27.** Dieser Fremde ist nicht nur **im allgemeinen** nicht liebenswert . . . (*in general/not at all*)
27. *In general*, this stranger is not only not worthy of love . . .	**28.** . . . sondern er hat auch im allgemeinen mehr Anspruch auf meine **Feindseligkeit.** (*friendship/hostility*)
28. . . . but in general he also has more claim to my *hostility*.	**29.** **mindest:** irregular superlative form of **wenig** = *less* **wenig, weniger, wenigst-** or **wenig, minder, mindest-** Der Fremde scheint nicht die mindeste Liebe für mich zu haben.
29. *least* The stranger does not seem to have the least (trace of) love for me.	**30.** **das Bedenken** = *hesitation, reflection* **schädigen** = *to injure* Ein Fremder **hat keine Bedenken,** mich zu schädigen.
30. A stranger *does not hesitate* to injure me.	**31.** **der Nutzen** = *advantage, use* Wenn es ihm einen Nutzen bringt, hat der Fremde keine Bedenken, mich zu schädigen.
31. If it brings him an advantage, the stranger does not hesitate to injure me.	**32.** **groß** = *large, great* **die Art** = *manner* **großartig** = *grand, splendid* Das ist ein großartiges Gebot.
32. That is a splendid commandment.	**33.** **lauten** = *to sound, to read* Wie lautet jenes großartige Gebot wieder?
33. How does that splendid commandment read again?	**34.** **ja** = *indeed* **würde** = *would, were to* Ja, wenn jenes großartige Gebot lauten würde . . .

34. Indeed, if that splendid commandment were to read . . .	**35.** **widersprechen** = *to contradict, to object* Ja, wenn jenes großartige Gebot lauten würde: Liebe deinen Nächsten wie dein Nächster dich liebt, dann würde ich nicht widersprechen.
35. Indeed, if that splendid commandment were to read: Love thy neighbor as thy neighbor loves thee, then I would not object (to it).	**36.** **unfaßbar** = *incomprehensible, unintelligible* Es gibt ein zweites Gebot, das mir noch unfaßbarer scheint. **Es heißt:** Liebe deine Feinde. (*it is/it calls*)
36. There is a second commandment which appears even more incomprehensible to me. *It is:* Love thine enemies.	**37.** **eher:** from **bald, eher, ehest-** **Weil** der Nächste eher dein Feind ist, sollst du ihn lieben wie dich selbst. (*while/because*)
37. *Because* your neighbor is more apt to be your enemy, you should love him as yourself.	**38.** **der Fall** = *case, situation* Das ist ein ähnlicher Fall wie das *Credo quia absurdum*, **das** unfaßar ist. (*which/the*)
38. That is a case similar to that of *Credo quia absurdum* (I believe it, because it is absurd), *which* is incomprehensible.	**39.** **die Begründung** = *reason* Mit welchen Begründungen **wird** mein Nächster mich abweisen? (*become/will*)
39. For which reasons *will* my neighbor reject me?	**40.** **nämlich** (adj.) = *same* Wird der Nächste **genau so** antworten **wie** ich und mich mit den nämlichen Begründungen abweisen? (*exactly as/probably*)
40. Will the neighbor answer *exactly as* I and reject me for the same reasons?	**41.** **derselbe, dieselbe, dasselbe** = *the same* **das Recht** = *right; here: grounds* Ich hoffe, nicht mit demselben objektiven Recht, aber dasselbe wird **auch** er meinen. (*you/also*)
41. I hope not with the same objective grounds, but he will *also* suppose the same (i.e. will hold the same opinion).	**42.** **denn** = *for* **der Lohn** = *reward* **der Zöllner** = *publican* Denn so ihr liebet, die euch lieben, was werdet ihr für Lohn haben? Tun nicht dasselbe auch die Zöllner? (Bibel)

42. For if ye love them which love you, what reward have ye? Do not even the publicans the same?	**43.** Was halten Sie davon? (*hold/think*)
43. What do you think about that?	**44.** **die Gesinnung** = *disposition, belief* **Was für eine** Gesinnung hat der Dichter Heinrich Heine? (*what for a /what kind of a*)
44. *What kind of a* disposition does the poet Heinrich Heine have?	**45.** **friedlich** = *peaceable* Der Dichter Heine hat die **friedlichste** Gesinnung. (*peaceable/most peaceable*)
45. The poet Heine has the *most peaceable* disposition.	**46.** **bescheiden** = *modest* Der Dichter hat nur bescheidene **Wünsche**. (*wishes/witches*)
46. The poet has only modest *wishes*.	**47.** **die Hütte** = *cottage, hut* **das Strohdach** = *thatched roof (straw roof)* Er will eine bescheidene Hütte mit einem Strohdach.
47. He wants a modest cottage with a thatched roof.	**48.** **die Blume** = *flower* **das Fenster** = *window* **die Tür** = *door* Seine Wünsche sind: eine bescheidene Hütte, ein Strohdach, Blumen **vor** dem Fenster, einige schöne Bäume **vor** der Tür. (*for/in front of*)
48. His wishes are a modest cottage, a straw roof, flowers *in front of* the window, some beautiful trees *in front of* the door.	**49.** Heine will seine Feinde an den Bäumen **aufgehängt** sehen. (*hang/hung*)
49. Heine wants to see his enemies *hung* from the trees.	**50.** **etwa** = *some* Heine will etwa sechs bis sieben **seiner** Feinde an diesen Bäumen aufhängen. (*of his/his*)

50. Heine wants to hang some six or seven *of his* enemies from these trees.	**51.** **das Glück** = *fortune, happiness, (good) luck* **glücklich** = *fortunate, happy* Wenn etwa sechs bis sieben seiner Feinde an diesen Bäumen hängen, dann ist er glücklich.
51. When some six or seven of his enemies are hanging from these trees, then he will be happy.	**52.** **zufügen** = *to add to, to cause, to do to* **die Unbill** = *injustice* Seine Feinde fügten ihm allerlei Unbill im Leben zu.
52. His enemies did all kinds of wrong to him in their lifetime.	**53.** **verzeihen** = *to forgive* Heine kann seinen Feinden nicht verzeihen . . .
53. Heine cannot forgive his enemies . . .	**54.** . . . bis er sie aufgehängt sieht.
54. . . . until he sees them hung.	**55.** **der Tod** = *death* Vor ihrem Tode wird er ihnen die Unbill nicht verzeihen, die sie ihm im Leben zugefügt haben.
55. Before their death he will not forgive them the wrong they have done to him in their lifetime.	**56.** **die Freude** = *joy* Welche Freude will Heine erleben?
56. What joy does Heine want to experience?	**57.** **lassen** = *to let, to cause* **aufhängen lassen** = *to cause to be hung* **Etwa** sechs bis sieben seiner Feinde will er an den Bäumen aufhängen lassen. (*some/something*)
57. He wants *some* six or seven of his enemies hung from the trees.	**58.** Laß mich die Freude erleben, daß an diesen Bäumen etwa sechs bis sieben meiner Feinde **aufgehängt werden.** (*will hang/are hanged*)
58. Let me experience the joy that from these trees some six or seven of my enemies *are hanged.*	**59.** **rühren** = *to touch, to stir up, to move* **gerührt** = *full of emotion* Mit gerührtem Herzen werde ich ihnen alle Unbill verzeihen.

59. With a heart full of emotion I will forgive them all wrong.	**60.** **gehenkt worden sind** (passive) = *have been hanged* **früh** = *early* Ja, man muß seinen Feinden verzeihen, aber nicht früher, als bis sie gehenkt worden sind.
60. Yes, one must forgive one's enemies, but not until (earlier than) they have been hanged.	

PROGRESS TEST

Choose the correct meaning of the indicated verbs.

1. Freud kann nicht der Idee entfliehen, daß er seine Feinde hassen soll.
If **fliehen** means *to flee*, then **entfliehen** must mean ____________.
(a) to flee toward (b) to flee from (c) to fly to pieces (d) to fly away

2. Ich erwarte meinen Freund um sechs.
If **warten** means *to wait*, then **erwarten** must mean ____________.
(a) to expect (b) to wait (c) to wait on

3. Wollen wir Freuds Argument zergliedern?
If **gliedern** means *to organize, to arrange,* then **zergliedern** must mean ____________.
(a) to disorganize (b) to forget to organize (c) to analyze (d) to misorganize

4. Ich darf sein Argument nicht verwerfen.
If **werfen** means *to throw,* then **verwerfen** must mean: ____________.
(a) to throw up (b) to approve (c) to throw for (d) to condemn

And now choose the approximate meaning of the following sentences.

5. Wenn wir den Nächsten auffordern, uns zu lieben wie er sich selbst liebt, wird er es tun?
(a) Whenever we command our neighbor to love us as we love ourselves, will he do it?
(b) When we further ourselves by loving our neighbor as he himself does, won't he challenge us?
(c) If we command our neighbor to love us as he loves himself, will he do it?
(d) none

6. Mein Feind braucht nicht einmal einen Nutzen davon zu haben, um mich zu zerschlagen.
(a) My friend doesn't need an excuse to condemn me.
(b) My friend really does not need to injure me.

(c) My enemy is foolish to attack me.
(d) none

7. Wenn ich es recht überlege, habe ich unrecht.
(a) Whenever I truly lay it on him, I am uneasy.
(b) It is not right for me to give it to him.
(c) If I were truly mean, I would be wrong.
(d) I am wrong, if I truly think it over.

8. Ja, man muß seinen Feinden verzeihen, aber nicht früher als bis sie gehenkt worden sind.
(a) Yes, one must forgive one's friends, but not until they have been hanged.
(b) Yes, one must forgive one's enemies, but only after they have been hanged.
(c) Yes, one's enemies must be hanged, if they are not to be forgiven.

Answer key: **1.** (b); **2.** (a); **3.** (c); **4.** (d); **5.** (c); **6.** (d); **7.** (d); **8.** (b).

Sigmund Freud: Das Unbehagen in der Kultur

Eine der sogenannten Idealforderungen der Kulturgesellschaft . . . lautet: Du sollst den Nächsten lieben wie dich selbst; sie ist weltberühmt, gewiß älter als das Christentum, das sie als seinen stolzesten Anspruch vorweist, aber [sie ist] sicherlich nicht sehr alt; in historischen Zeiten war sie den Menschen noch fremd . . . Warum sollen wir das? Was soll es uns helfen? Vor allem aber, wie bringen wir das zustande? Wie wird es uns möglich? . . . Wenn ich einen anderen liebe, muß er es auf irgendeine Art verdienen . . . Er verdient es, wenn er mir in wichtigen Stücken so ähnlich ist, daß ich in ihm mich selbst lieben kann; er verdient es, wenn er soviel vollkommener ist als ich, daß ich mein Ideal von meiner eigenen Person in ihm lieben kann; ich muß ihn lieben, wenn er der Sohn meines Freundes ist . . . Aber wenn er mir fremd ist und mich durch keinen eigenen Wert . . . anziehen kann, wird es mir schwer, ihn zu lieben . . . Es ist ein Unrecht an [meinen Freunden], wenn ich den Fremden ihnen gleichstelle . . .

Wenn ich näher zusehe, finde ich noch mehr Schwierigkeiten. Dieser Fremde ist nicht nur im allgemeinen nicht liebenswert, ich muß ehrlich bekennen, er hat mehr Anspruch auf meine Feindseligkeit, sogar auf meinen Haß. Er scheint nicht die mindeste Liebe für mich zu haben, bezeigt mir nicht die geringste Rücksicht. Wenn es ihm einen Nutzen bringt, hat er kein Bedenken, mich zu schädigen . . . Ja, wenn jenes großartige Gebot lauten würde: Liebe deinen Nächsten wie dein Nächster dich liebt, dann würde ich nicht widersprechen. Es gibt ein zweites Gebot, das mir noch unfaßbarer scheint . . . Es heißt: Liebe deine Feinde . . .

Weil der Nächste nicht liebenswert und eher dein Feind ist, sollst du ihn lieben wie dich selbst. Ich verstehe dann, das ist ein ähnlicher Fall wie das *Credo quia absurdum.*

Es ist nun sehr wahrscheinlich, daß der Nächste, wenn er aufgefordert wird, mich so zu lieben wie sich selbst, genau so antworten wird wie ich und mich mit den nämlichen Begründungen abweisen wird. Ich hoffe, nicht mit demselben objektiven Recht, aber dasselbe wird auch er meinen.

Heinrich Heine: Gedanken und Einfälle

„Ich habe die friedlichste Gesinnung. Meine Wünsche sind: eine bescheidene Hütte, ein Strohdach, aber ein gutes Bett, gutes Essen, Milch und Butter, sehr frisch, vor dem Fenster Blumen, vor der Tür einige schöne Bäume, und wenn der liebe Gott mich ganz glücklich machen will, läßt er mich die Freude erleben, daß an diesen Bäumen etwa sechs bis sieben meiner Feinde aufgehängt werden. Mit gerührtem Herzen werde ich ihnen vor ihrem Tode alle Unbill verzeihen, die sie mir im Leben zugefügt — Ja, man muß seinen Feinden verzeihen, aber nicht früher, als bis sie gehenkt worden."

Chapter Nine

35. *Past tense of strong verbs and* **werden**

1. The past tense of a German strong verb is recognized by a vowel change in the stem:

ich singe	*I sing*	**ich sang**	*I sang*
du singst	*you sing*	**du sangst**	*you sang*
er singt	*he sings*	**er sang**	*he sang*
wir singen	*we sing*	**wir sangen**	*we sang*
ihr singt	*you sing*	**ihr sangt**	*you sang*
sie singen	*they sing*	**sie sangen**	*they sang*
Sie singen	*you sing*	**Sie sangen**	*you sang*

2. The following endings added to the stem indicate person and number:

(ich)	**-**			**(wir)**	**-en**
(du)	**-(e)st**	**(Sie)**	**-en**	**(ihr)**	**-(e)t**
(er, sie, es)	**-**			**(sie)**	**-en**

With the exception of the first and third person singular, the endings are the same as the present tense endings. Thus it is important to recognize the vowel shift:

Du verlierst das Buch.	*You lose the book.*
Du verlorst das Buch.	*You lost the book.*
Wir sehen den Mann.	*We see the man.*
Wir sahen den Mann.	*We saw the man.*

3. The verb **werden** is irregular in the past tense:

ich wurde (ward)	*I became*
du wurdest (wardst)	*etc.*
er wurde (ward)	
wir wurden	
ihr wurdet	
sie wurden	
Sie wurden	

The above alternatives in parenthesis are less common.

4. In a few cases not only the vowel changes but the following consonant as well. Below are some of the more common examples:

schneiden	(*to cut*)	**ich schneide**	**ich schnitt**
greifen	(*to grab*)	**du greifst**	**du griffst**
treffen	(*to meet, hit*)	**er trifft**	**er traf**
fallen	(*to fall*)	**sie fällt**	**sie fiel**
leiden	(*to suffer*)	**wir leiden**	**wir litten**
sitzen	(*to sit*)	**ihr sitzt**	**ihr saßt**
ziehen	(*to pull*)	**sie ziehen**	**sie zogen**
gehen	(*to go*)	**Sie gehen**	**Sie gingen**
kommen	(*to come*)	**ich komme**	**ich kam**
stehen	(*to stand*)	**du stehst**	**du standst**

5. Dictionaries and glossaries often indicate this vowel change by listing the principal parts of the verb:

singen, (singt), sang, gesungen
to sing, (sings), sang, sung

or by giving only the vowel change:

singen, (i), a, u

6. To determine the infinitive of an unknown strong verb, observe the consonants of the stem. Then either go to a list of strong verbs to find the corresponding form or to a dictionary to find the proper vowel.

The following exercises introduce the vocabulary of the reading passage, drawn from Marx's ***Das Kapital,*** *and give you practice in recognizing the past tense of strong verbs. Distinguish between the present and past tenses in the following sentences.*

1. **die Nachbarin** = *lady next door*
„Karl Marx schreibt wieder ein Buch," sagte die alte Nachbarin.

1. "Karl Marx is writing a book again," said the old lady next door.	**2.** Es heißt *Das Kapital.*
2. It is called *Capital.*	**3.** Verstehen Sie, warum er das Buch **schrieb**? (The present tense of **er schrieb** is ________.)
3. **er schreibt** Do you understand why he *wrote* the book?	**4.** Wie **hieß** das Buch wieder? (past/present)
4. past What *was the name* of the book again?	**5.** **besonders** = *especially* Wissen Sie, was Marx und besonders Engels **sahen,** als sie in England wohnten? (The present of **sahen** is ________.)
5. **sehen** Do you know what Marx and especially Engels *saw* when they lived in England?	**6.** Was sieht man heute in den Ghettos der amerikanischen Großstädte?
6. What does one see today in the ghettos of large American cities?	**7.** Wir alle wissen, **wer** Karl Marx ist. (*where/who*)
7. We all know *who* Karl Marx is.	**8.** Sie wissen auch, daß Marx ein Deutscher **war.** (*is/was*)
8. You also know that Marx *was* a German.	**9.** **die Zusammenfassung** = *summary* Sie **werden** jetzt eine Zusammenfassung von ein paar Seiten aus Marxens *Das Kapital* lesen. (**werden** = *will/become*)
9. You *will* now read a summary of several pages from Marx's *Capital.*	**10.** **die Arbeit** = *work* **die Bedingung** = *condition* Diese Zusammenfassung **spricht** von den Arbeitsbedingungen in den damaligen englischen Fabriken. (**spricht** = *talks of/talked of*)
10. This summary *talks of* working conditions in English factories of the time.	**11.** **die Gießerei** = *foundry* **das Eisen** = *iron* **die Eisengießerei** = ________

11. *iron foundry*	**12.** **neunjährig** = *nine years old* **morgens** = *in the morning* George Allinsworth, neunjährig, **fängt** um 3 Uhr morgens **an,** in einer Eisengießerei zu arbeiten. (present/past)
12. *present* of **anfangen** Nine year old George Allinsworth *begins* work at 3 a.m. in an iron foundry.	**13.** **abends** = *in the evening* **u.s.w.** = **und so weiter** = *and so forth, etc.* Am anderen Tag **fing** er 6 Uhr morgens **an** und **endete** 6 oder 7 Uhr abends u.s.w. (present/past)
13. *past* The next day he *began* work at 6 in the morning and *ended* at 6 or 7 in the evening, etc.	**14.** **daher** = *therefore, hence* Daher **blieb** er die ganze Nacht. (The infinitive of **blieb** is ________.)
14. **bleiben** Hence he *remained* the whole night.	**15.** Er **bleibt** die ganze Nacht in der Eisengießerei. (present/past)
15. He *stays* the whole night at the iron foundry.	**16.** **der Schurz** = *apron* **das Fell** = *skin, hide, fur* **das Schurzfell** = ________
16. *leather apron*	**17.** **die Flur** = *field(s), meadow(s)* Ich **schlafe** auf der Flur mit einem Schurzfell unter mir. (present/past)
17. I *sleep* in the fields with a leather apron under me.	**18.** Ich **schlief** mit einer kleinen Jacke über mir. (present/past)
18. I *slept* with a little jacket on top of me.	**19.** **bitte** = *please* **Kommen** Sie bitte **her**! (The infinitive is ________.)
19. **herkommen** *Come here,* please.	**20.** **ebenfalls** = *likewise* **der Hochofen** = *blast furnace* Bevor ich **herkam, arbeitete** ich ebenfalls in einem Hochofen. (present/past)

20. past Before I *came* here I likewise *worked* at a blast furnace.	**21.** Ich **begann** ebenfalls samstags morgens um 3 Uhr zu arbeiten. (present/past)
21. past I likewise *began* to work Saturdays at three o'clock in the morning.	**22.** **Beginnt** er auch um 3 Uhr?
22. *Does* he also *begin* at 3 o'clock?	**23.** Er geht schlafen.
23. He is going to sleep (to bed).	**24.** **wenigstens** = *at least* **Ging** er wenigstens um 12 Uhr nachts nach Hause? (The infinitive of **ging** is ________.)
24. **gehen** *Did* he *go* home at least at midnight?	**25.** **lassen** = *to let* Er **ließ** das Kind ebenfalls auf der Flur schlafen. (The infinitive of **ließ** is ________.)
25. **lassen** He likewise *let* the child sleep in the field.	**26.** **auffassen** = *to understand, to regard* **Laßt** uns nun hören, wie das Kapital selbst dieses Vierundzwanzig (24)-Stundensystem auffaßt. (present/past)
26. *Let* us now hear how capital itself regards this twenty-four hour system.	**27.** **treiben** = *to drive, to carry on* **übertreiben** = *to exaggerate* **die Übertreibung** = ________
27. *exaggeration*	**28.** **übergehen** = *to pass over, to omit* Das Kapital übergeht die Übertreibungen des Systems.
28. Capital overlooks the exaggerations (extreme forms) of the system.	**29.** Wie **faßt** das Kapital dieses Vierundzwanzig-Stundensystem **auf**?
29. How does capital *regard* this twenty-four hour system?	**30.** **brauchen** = *to use, to need* **mißbrauchen** = *to misuse, abuse* **der Mißbrauch** = ________
30. *misuse, abuse*	**31.** **schweigen** = *to be silent, to stop (speaking)* **das Schweigen** = *silence* **das Stillschweigen** = ________

31. *silence*	**32.** Das Kapital überging den Mißbrauch des Systems natürlich mit Stillschweigen.
32. Naturally, Capital overlooked the abuse of the system in silence.	**33.** **die Tagarbeit** = *work by day* **die Nachtarbeit** = ________
33. *work by night*	**34.** **der Unterschied** = *difference* Wir finden nicht, daß Tag- oder Nachtarbeit irgendeinen Unterschied in der Gesundheit der Herren Naylor und Vickers macht.
34. We do not find that work by day or by night makes any difference in the health of Messrs. Naylor and Vickers.	**35.** Wir **fanden** keinen Unterschied in der Gesundheit der beiden Herren. (present/past)
35. We *found* no difference in the health of the two gentlemen.	**36.** **die Ruhe** = *rest, quiet, peace* **die Ruheperiode** = ________
36. *period of rest*	**37.** **wechseln** = *to change, to exchange* Wahrscheinlich schlafen Leute besser, wenn sie dieselbe Ruheperiode **genießen,** als wenn sie wechselt. (present/past)
37. Probably people sleep better if they *enjoy* the same period of rest than if it varies.	**38.** **Genossen** sie immer dieselbe Ruheperiode? (The infinitive of **genossen** is ________.)
38. **genießen** *Did* they always *enjoy* the same period of rest?	**39.** Das Kapital **spricht** nur von dem System in seiner „normalen" Form. (present/past of ________)
39. present of **sprechen** Capital only *speaks* of the system in its "normal" form.	**40.** Es **sprach** nur von dem System in seiner „normalen" Form.
40. It only *spoke* of the system in its "normal" form.	**41.** **die Hitze** = *heat* Welch eine Hitze!
41. How hot it is! (lit.: What a heat!)	**42.** **der Knabe** = *boy* Die Knaben leiden unter der Hitze.
42. The boys suffer from (lit.: under) the heat.	**43.** **durchaus** = *throughout, absolutely* **durchaus nicht** = *not at all, by no means* Die Knaben leiden durchaus nicht unter der Hitze.

43. The boys do not suffer at all from the heat.	**44.** **Litt** der Knabe nicht von der Hitze? (present/past of **leiden**)
44. *Did* not the boy *suffer* from the heat? **(leiden unter** is more usual than **leiden von)**	**45.** **die Zeitung** = *newspaper* Was **lasen** sie gestern in der Zeitung? (present/past of ________)
45. past of **lesen** What *did* they *read* in the paper yesterday?	**46.** **die Schmiede** = *smithy, forge* In Marxens Buch lesen wir, daß man in der Schmiede von 12 Uhr bis 12 Uhr arbeitet.
46. In Marx's book we read that in the forge one works from 12 to 12.	**47.** **das Hammerwerk** = *foundry, iron works* **das Walzwerk** = *rolling mill* In den Hammer- und Walzwerken **arbeitete** man oft sechzehn (16) Stunden am Tag.
47. One often *worked* sixteen hours a day in the iron foundries and rolling mills.	**48.** **einzeln** = *individual* In einem Walzwerk **ist** der nominelle Arbeitstag für den einzelnen Arbeiter 11½ Stunden.
48. In a rolling mill the nominal work day for the individual worker *is* 11½ hours.	**49.** **jung** = *young* **der Junge** = ________
49. *the boy*	**50.** **mindestens** = *at least* Ein Junge **arbeitet** 4 Nächte jede Woche bis mindestens 8½ Uhr abends des nächsten Tages. (present/past)
50. A boy *works* four nights every week until at least 8:30 in the evening of the next day.	**51.** **ablösen** = *to relieve* **die Ablösung** = ________
51. *the relief*	**52.** **der Ablösungstermin** = (*work*) *shift* **manchmal** = *sometimes* Drei zwölfstündige Ablösungstermine nacheinander **arbeitete** manchmal ein Junge im Alter von 9 Jahren. (present/past)
52. Sometimes a nine year old boy *worked* three twelve hour shifts running (i.e. after another).	**53.** Er **tut** es nicht mehr lange. (present/past)

53. present tense but with future meaning He **will** not **do** it much longer.	**54.** **sterben** = *to die* Er **tat** es so lange bis er starb. (present/past)
54. He *did* it until the time he died.	**55.** Am nächsten Tag **hatten** wir um 3 Uhr morgens anzufangen. (present/past)
55. The next day we *had* to begin at three o'clock in the morning.	**56.** Ich **wohne** fünf Meilen von hier. (present/past)
56. I *live* five miles from here.	**57.** Wo **wohntet** ihr, als ihr im Walzwerk **arbeitetet**? (present/past)
57. Where *did* you *live* when you *worked* in the rolling mill?	**58.** Die Arbeit **beginnt** 6 Uhr morgens und **endet** 6 oder 7 Uhr abends. (present/past)
58. Work *begins* at 6 a.m. and *ends* at 6 or 7 p.m.	**59.** **zwanzig** = *twenty* Wie **faßte** das Kapital selbst dieses Vierundzwanzig-Stundensystem **auf**? (present/past)
59. How *did* capital itself *regard* this twenty-four hour system?	**60.** Wie **faßt** das Kapital selbst die Arbeitsbedingungen **auf**? (present/past)
60. How *does Capital* itself *regard* the working conditions?	**61.** **die Länge** = *length* **verlängern** = *to lengthen, to prolong, to extend* **die Verlängerung** = __________
61. *the lengthening, prolongation, extension*	**62.** **grausam** = *cruel* **unglaublich** = *incredible* Das Kapital **mißbraucht** das System zur grausamen und unglaublichen Verlängerung des Arbeitstages. (present/past)
62. Capital *abuses* the system by cruel and incredible extension of the working day.	**63.** Es **mißrauchte** das System zur grausamen und unglaublichen Verlängerung des Arbeitstages. (present/past)

63. It *abused* the system by cruel and incredible extension of the working day.	**64.** Es **überging** diese Verlängerung ebenfalls mit Stillschweigen. (present/past)
64. It likewise *passed over* this extension in silence.	**65.** Es **sprach** nur von dem System in seiner „normalen“ Form. (present/past)
65. It *spoke* of the system only in its "normal" form.	**66.** **die Fabrik** = *the factory* **das Fabrikat** = *the (manufactured) product* **die Fabrikation** = *the manufacture* **der Fabrikant** = ________
66. *the manufacturer*	**67.** **der Stahl** = *steel* **der Stahlfabrikant** = ________
67. *the steel manufacturer*	**68.** **die Anwendung** = *application* **anwenden** = ________
68. *to use, to employ*	**69.** Wieviele Personen **wenden** eigentlich die Stahlfabrikanten **an**? (present/past)
69. How many persons *do* the steel manufacturers actually *employ*?	**70.** Die Herren Naylor und Vickers, Stahlfabrikanten, **wendeten** manchmal zwischen 600 und 700 Personen **an.** (present/past)
70. Messrs. Naylor and Vickers, steel manufacturers, sometimes *employed* between 600 and 700 persons.	**71.** **äußern** = *to express, to utter* **das Personal** = *staff, personnel* Die 20 Knaben, die zum Nachtpersonal **gehören, äußern** sich wie folgt. (present/past)
71. The 20 boys who *belong* to the night staff *express* themselves as follows. (Notice the use of **die** as a relative pronoun.)	**72.** Was **folgte,** nachdem sie sich **äußerten**? (present/past)
72. What *happened* (*followed*) after they *expressed* themselves?	**73.** Wir **fanden** fast keinen Unterschied in der Gesundheit der Knaben. (present/past)
73. We *found* hardly any difference in the health of the boys.	**74.** Was **macht** keinen Unterschied? (present/past)

74. What *does* not *make* any difference?	**75.** **ob** = *whether* Ob sie wirklich dieselbe Ruheperiode **haben**? (present/past)
75. (I wonder) whether they really *have* the same rest period?	**76.** Wahrscheinlich **schliefen** die Leute besser, wenn sie immer dieselbe Ruheperiode **genossen,** als wenn sie **wechselte.** (present/past)
76. People probably *slept* better if they always *enjoyed* the same period of rest than if it *varied.*	**77.** **Litten** sie unter der Hitze? **Leiden** sie immer noch?
77. *Did* they *suffer* from the heat? *Do* they still *suffer*?	**78.** **kriegen** = *to get* **Kriegt** man Jungen so viel man **will** für die Arbeit in den Fabriken? (present/past)
78. *Does* one *get* as many boys as one *wants* to work (for the work) in the factories?	**79.** **verwenden** = *to use, to employ* **gering** = *small* **Verwendeten** sie eine geringere Proportion von Jungen? (present/past)
79. *Did* they *employ* a smaller proportion of lads?	**80.** **beschränken** = *to limit, to restrict* **die Beschränkung** = ________
80. *the limitation*	**81.** **wichtig** = *important* **die Wichtigkeit** = ________
81. *the importance*	**82.** Beschränkungen der Nachtarbeit **waren** von wenig Wichtigkeit oder Interesse für uns. (present/past)
82. Restrictions on (of) night work *were* of little importance or interest to (for) us.	**83.** Die Jungen **werden** immer größer. (present/past)
83. The boys *are getting* taller and taller.	**84.** Die Arbeit **wird** immer geringer. (present/past)
84. Work *is getting* less and less.	**85.** Die Temperatur **wurde** immer heißer. (present/past)

85. The temperature *became* hotter and hotter.	**86.** Es **wurde** auch Arbeit, jeden Morgen um 5 Uhr aufzustehen. (present/past)
86. It also *became* work to get up every morning at five o'clock.	**87.** Die Produktionskosten **werden** dasselbe **bleiben.** (present/future)
87. The production costs *will remain* the same.	**88.** **fähig** = *capable* **unfähig** = *incapable* Morgen **wirst** du unfähig, es länger zu tun.
88. Tomorrow you *will become* incapable of doing it any longer.	**89.** Ihr **wurdet** größer als wir. (present/past)
89. You *became* taller than we.	**90.** Ihr **werdet** manchmal drei Ablösungstermine nacheinander arbeiten, von Montag morgen bis Dienstag nacht. (present/future)
90. Sometimes you *will* work three shifts running, from Monday morning until Tuesday night.	**91.** **geschickt** = *skilled, capable* **das Haupt** = *head* Es **wird** immer schwerer, geschickte Hände und Häupter für jede Abteilung zu finden. (present/future)
91. It *is becoming* more and more difficult to find skilled hands and heads for every department.	

Be aware of the passive voice (to be discussed in a later chapter). Note the following sentence from the reading passage, first given in the present passive, then the past passive:

	92. In der Schmiede **wird** von 12 Uhr bis 12 Uhr **gearbeitet.**
92. In the forge the hours *are* from 12 to 12 (*is worked* from 12 o'clock to 12 o'clock).	**93.** **Wurde** in der Schmiede von 12 Uhr bis 12 Uhr **gearbeitet**?
93. *Were* the hours in the forge from 12 to 12 (*Did one work . . .*)?	

PROGRESS TEST

A. *Choose the correct infinitive of the following verbs:*

1. *Genossen* sie immer dieselbe Ruheperiode?
(a) genossen (b) genießen (c) genesen (d) niesen

2. *Litt* der Junge nicht unter der Hitze?
(a) leiten (b) laden (c) leiden (d) lauten

3. Er *tat* es nur bis sechs.
(a) tuten (b) tun (c) tonen (d) töten

B. *Choose the correct past tense verb form of:*

1. gehen: Ich ______ . . .
(a) gehe (b) ginge (c) ging (d) gähnte

2. stehen: du ______ . . .
(a) standst (b) stehst (c) stahlst (d) stankst

3. sehen: und ______ zur Erde.
(a) siehst (b) sagst (c) sehnte (d) sahst

C. *Choose the correct equivalent of the indicated word.*

1. Sie *kam* Freitag hierher.
(a) is coming (b) came (c) comes

2. Er *erwies* mir jede Rücksicht und Schonung.
(a) showed (b) shows (c) is going to show

3. Er *blieb* die ganze Nacht zu Hause.
(a) stayed (b) stays (c) will stay

4. Morgen *fange* ich zu arbeiten *an*.
(a) am going to begin (b) began (c) begun

5. Das Kapital *überging* die Übertreibungen des Systems.
(a) overlooks (b) overlooked (c) will overlook

6. Sie *verwendeten* einige Jungen in der Fabrik.
(a) employ (b) employed (c) will employ

7. Die Jungen *wurden* immer größer.
(a) would (b) become (c) will become (d) became

8. Die Produktionskosten *werden* immer wichtiger sein.
(a) are becoming (b) were (c) will (d) became

Answer key: A. **1.** (b); **2.** (c); **3.** (b).
B. **1.** (c); **2.** (a); **3.** (d).
C. **1.** (b); **2.** (a); **3.** (a); **4.** (a); **5.** (b); **6.** (b); **7.** (d); **8.** (c).

36. *Past tense of modals and* ***wissen***

1. The modals are conjugated as follows in the past tense:

ich durfte (*I was permitted to*)
du durftest
er durfte
wir durften
ihr durftet
sie durften
Sie durften

ich konnte (*I could, I was able to*)
du konntest
er konnte
wir konnten
ihr konntet
sie konnten
Sie konnten

mögen
ich mochte (*I liked to*)
du mochtest
er mochte
wir mochten
ihr mochtet
sie mochten
Sie mochten

müssen
ich mußte (*I had to*)
du mußtest
er mußte
wir mußten
ihr mußtet
sie mußten
Sie mußten

sollen
ich sollte (*I was supposed to*)
du solltest
er sollte
wir sollten
ihr solltet
sie sollten
Sie sollten

wollen
ich wollte (*I wanted to*)
du wolltest
er wollte
wir wollten
ihr wolltet
sie wollten
Sie wollten

2. Modals in the past may be recognized by the weak verb endings added to the stem. Note also that the umlaut in the verbs **dürfen, können, mögen, müssen** is dropped.

3. The past tense of **wissen** follows the pattern of the modals:

ich wußte (*I knew*)
du wußtest
er wußte

Sie wußten

wir wußten
ihr wußtet
sie wußten

The first fourteen sentences review the meanings of the modal verbs. Give their meanings and circle any unfamiliar words. The vocabulary is from Das Kapital.

	1. Während der sechs Monate, wo er engagiert ist, **muß** er vier Nächte jede Woche arbeiten.
1. During the six months he is employed he *must* work four nights a week.	**2.** **Muß** man manchmal drei zwölfstündige Ablösungstermine nacheinander arbeiten?
2. *Does* one sometimes *have to* work three twelve hour shifts running?	**3.** **im Alter von** = *at the age of* **Soll** ein Junge im Alter von zehn Jahren zwei Tage und zwei Nächte nacheinander arbeiten?
3. *Is* a ten year old lad supposed to work two days and two nights running?	**4.** Ihr **sollt** nicht von 6 Uhr nachmittags bis den anderen Tag 12 Uhr während einer ganzen Woche arbeiten.
4. You *are* not *to* work a whole week from six in the afternoon until twelve noon of the next day.	**5.** Ja, dies ist ein heißer Platz! Ich **mag** ihn nicht.
5. Yes, this is a hot place. I *do* not *like* it.	**6.** Wir **mögen** nicht hören, wie *Das Kapital* dieses Vierundzwanzigstundensystem auffaßt.
6. We *do* not *like* to hear how Capital regards this twenty-four hour system.	**7.** Ich **kann** wenigstens nach Hause schlafen gehen.
7. I *can* at least go home to sleep.	**8.** Wir **können** es nicht recht tun ohne die Nachtarbeit von Jungen unter achtzehn Jahren.
8. We *cannot* do it well without lads under eighteen working at night.	**9.** Jungen kriegt man so viel man **will.**
9. One is able to get as many lads as one *wants*. (We can get any number of lads.)	**10.** **einige** = *some* **fortwährend** = *always, incessantly* **Wollen** einige Hände nachts fortwährend arbeiten?

10. *Do* some hands *want to* work continually at night?	**11.** **der Wechsel** = *alternation* **Wollen** einige Hände nachts fortwährend arbeiten ohne Wechsel zwischen Tag- und Nachtzeit?
11. *Do* some hands *want to* work continually at night without alternation between day and night work?	**12.** Die Beschränkungen der Nachtarbeit **dürfen** von wenig Wichtigkeit oder Interesse für uns sein.
12. The restrictions on night work *can* be of little importance or interest to us.	**13.** **die Vermehrung** = *increase* **auf alle Fälle** = *in any case* Die Vermehrung der Produktionskosten **darf** auf alle Fälle nicht daraus resultieren.
13. In any case the increase in production costs *must* not result from it.	**14.** Hier **dürfen** sie arbeiten.
14. They *may* work here.	

Now distinguish between the present and past of the modals in the following sentences.

	15. Was **soll** ein nomineller Arbeitstag sein? (present/past)
15. What *is supposed to* be a nominal working day?	**16.** Er **sollte** arbeiten, aber er schlief lieber. (present/past)
16. He *was supposed to* work, but he preferred to sleep.	**17.** Ich weiß nicht, wann ihr anfangen **sollt.** (present/past)
17. I do not know when you *are supposed to* begin.	**18.** Ihr **solltet** in einem Hochofen arbeiten, ihr tat es aber nicht.
18. You *were to* work at a blast furnace, however, you did not do it.	**19.** **ein Dritter** = *a third* Ein Dritter, jetzt zehn Jahre, **kann** von morgens 6 Uhr bis 12 Uhr in die Nacht drei Nächte durch arbeiten.
19. A third, now ten years old, *is able to* work from six in the morning until twelve at night for three nights in a row.	**20.** Wie er arbeiten **konnte,** ohne zu schlafen, verstand er selbst nicht. (present/past)
20. He himself did not understand how he *could* work without sleeping.	**21.** Ihr **konntet** wenigstens nach Hause gehen, weil es nah war.

21. You *could* at least go home because it was near.	**22.** Er sagt, daß sie von 6 Uhr morgens bis 12 Uhr nachts während 14 Tage arbeiten **können.**
22. He says that they *can* work from six a.m. to midnight for fourteen days.	**23.** **da** = *since* Wir **mußten** viele Jungens kriegen, da wir die Produktionskosten nicht vermehren **wollten.** (present/past)
23. We *had to* get many lads since we did not want to increase the costs of production.	**24.** **ungefähr** = *approximately* Ungefähr zwanzig Knaben unter achtzehn Jahren **müssen** mit der Nachtmannschaft arbeiten. (present/past)
24. Approximately twenty boys under eighteen years of age *have to* work the night shift (with the night crew).	**25.** Er fragt, ob wir geschickte Hände und Häupter von Departments haben **müssen.** (present/past)
25. He asks if we *have to* have skilled hands and heads of departments.	**26.** **der Einwurf** = *objection* Wir **mußten** unseren Einwurf äußern. (present/past)
26. We *had to* express our objection.	**27.** Er **mochte** nicht jeden Tag siebzehn Stunden arbeiten. (present/past)
27. He *did* not *like* to work seventeen hours every day.	**28.** Er **mag** nicht jeden Tag siebzehn Stunden arbeiten. (present/past)
28. He *does* not *like* to work seventeen hours every day.	**29.** **dagegen** = *on the other hand, against that* Sie **mochten** nicht fortwährend arbeiten, aber was **konnten** sie dagegen tun? (present/past)
29. They *did* not *like* to work continually, but what *could* they do about it?	**30.** Wissen Sie, ob er das überhaupt **mag**? (present/past)
30. Do you know whether he *likes* that at all?	**31.** **der Vierte** = *the fourth* Ein Vierter **wollte** nicht drei Ablösungstermine nacheinander arbeiten. (present/past)

31. A fourth *did* not *want* to work three shifts running.	**32.** **der Fünfte** = *the fifth* **der Chef** = *boss* Weiß der Chef, daß der Fünfte das auch nicht **will**? (present/past)
32. Does the boss know that the fifth *does* not *want* to do that either?	**33.** Wir **wollen** unseren Einwurf jetzt äußern. (present/past)
33. We *want to* express our objection now.	**34.** **in Anbetracht** = *considering* In Anbetracht der geringen Proportion von Jungen, die sie verwenden **wollten . . .** (present/past)
34. Considering the small proportion of boys which they *wanted to* employ . . . (Note that **in Anbetracht** requires a genitive object.)	**35.** **übergehen** = *to pass over, overlook* Die Übertreibungen dieses Systems **darf** man **nicht** mit Stillschweigen übergehen.
35. One *must not* pass over the extreme forms of this system in silence.	**36.** In Anbetracht der Vermehrung der Produktionskosten **dürfen** wir **nicht** eine geringere Proportion von Jungen verwenden. (present/past)
36. Considering the increase in costs of production, we *must not* employ a lesser proportion of boys.	**37.** **die Ablösung** = *removal, relief, relieving guard* **die Weise** = *manner, method, way* **ablösungsweise** = __________
37. *in the manner of relief, in successive relief, in relays*	**38.** In den Walzwerken **durften** die Hände Tag und Nacht ablösungsweise arbeiten. (present/past)
38. In the rolling mills the hands *were permitted to* work day and night in relays.	**39.** **dahingegen** = *on the contrary, on the other hand* Dahingegen **durfte** alles andere Werk Tagwerk sein. (present/past)
39. On the other hand, all other work *could* be daywork.	

PROGRESS TEST

A. *Choose the most nearly correct equivalent of the indicated words.*

1. Ich *konnte* seine Idee nicht leicht verstehen.
   (a) can (b) could (c) had been able to (d) will be able to
2. Er *muß* das Buch bald zu Ende schreiben.
   (a) has to (b) had to (c) would have to (d) should
3. Sie *will* unser Problem überhaupt nicht verstehen.
   (a) will (b) wanted (c) did . . . want (d) does . . . want
4. Er *mochte* nicht jeden Tag arbeiten.
   (a) does . . . like (b) does . . . wish (c) did . . . like (d) was . . . permitted
5. Er *sollte* heute nicht zu arbeiten brauchen.
   (a) was . . . supposed to (b) is . . . supposed to (c) shall (d) ought to
6. Ihr *dürft* heute in die Stadt gehen.
   (a) will be able to (b) may (c) were permitted to (d) must

B. *Choose the most nearly correct equivalent of the following sentences or italicized words.*

1. *Er schlief auf der Flur* mit einem Schurzfell unter ihm und einer kleinen Jacke über ihm.
   (a) He slipped and fell on the floor.
   (b) He slipped out to the field.
   (c) He slept in thè field.
   (d) Sleeping in the field . . .
2. In Anbetracht der geringen Proportion von Jungen, die sie verwenden wollen . . .
   (a) Considering the large proportion of girls she wishes to fail . . .
   (b) Considering the small proportion of boys they want to employ . . .
   (c) One wants to employ as few boys as possible . . .
   (d) They want to use as many boys as possible considering the circumstances . . .
3. In den Walzwerken wollten die Hände Tag und Nacht ohne Ablösung arbeiten.
   (a) Most hands like to work day and night.
   (b) In the rolling mills the hands wished to work day and night without relief.
   (c) Not all hands who work day and night wish to work in the rolling mills.
   (d) They were not permitted to work in relays.
4. *Ungefähr* zwanzig Knaben unter 18 Jahren müssen arbeiten.
   (a) dangerous (b) not dangerous (c) approximately (d) exactly
5. Die Übertreibungen dieses Systems darf man mit Stillschweigen übergehen.
   (a) These systems let everything pass by quietly.
   (b) If one overlooks the extreme forms of this system, all is lost.
   (c) One helplessly permits these extreme forms to exist.
   (d) One can pass over the extreme forms of this system in silence.

Answer key: A. **1.** (b); **2.** (a); **3.** (d); **4.** (c); **5.** (a); **6.** (b).
B. **1.** (c); **2.** (b); **3.** (b); **4.** (c); **5.** (d).

Karl Marx: Das Kapital

„In einem Walzwerke, wo der nominelle Arbeitstag für den einzelnen Arbeiter $11\frac{1}{2}$ Stunden war, arbeitete ein Junge 4 Nächte jede Woche bis mindestens $8\frac{1}{2}$ Uhr abends des nächsten Tags und dies während der 6 Monate, wo er engagiert war." „Ein andrer arbeitete im Alter von 9 Jahren manchmal drei zwölfstündige Ablösungstermine nacheinander und im Alter von 10 Jahren zwei Tage und zwei Nächte nacheinander." „Ein Dritter, jetzt 10 Jahre, arbeitete von morgens 6 Uhr bis 12 Uhr in die Nacht drei Nächte durch und bis 9 Uhr abends während der andren Nächte." „Ein Vierter, jetzt 13 Jahre, arbeitete von 6 Uhr nachmittags bis den andren Tag 12 Uhr mittags während einer ganzen Woche, und manchmal drei Ablösungstermine nacheinander, von Montag Morgen bis Dienstag Nacht." „Ein Fünfter, jetzt 12 Jahre, arbeitete in einer Eisengießerei zu Stavely[1] von 6 Uhr morgens bis 12 Uhr nachts während 14 Tage, ist unfähig es länger zu tun." „George Allinsworth, neunjährig: „Ich kam hierhin letzten Freitag. Nächsten Tag hatten wir um 3 Uhr morgens anzufangen. Ich blieb daher die ganze Nacht hier. Wohne 5 Meilen von hier. Schlief auf der Flur mit einem Schurzfell unter mir und einer kleinen Jacke über mir. Die zwei andren Tage war ich hier um 6 Uhr morgens. Ja! dies ist ein heißer Platz! Bevor ich herkam, arbeitete ich ebenfalls während eines ganzen Jahres in einem Hochofen. Es war ein sehr großes Werk, auf dem Lande. Begann auch samstags morgens um 3 Uhr, aber ich konnte wenigstens nach Hause schlafen gehen, weil es nah war. Am andren Tage fing ich 6 Uhr morgens an und endete 6 oder 7 Uhr abends u.s.w.

Laßt uns nun hören, wie das Kapital selbst dies Vierundzwanzig-Stundensystem auffaßt. Die Übertreibungen des Systems, seinen Mißbrauch zur „grausamen und unglaublichen" Verlängerung des Arbeitstags, übergeht es natürlich mit Stillschweigen. Es spricht nur von dem System in seiner „normalen" Form.

„Die Herren Naylor und Vickers, Stahlfabrikanten, die zwischen 600 und 700 Personen anwenden, und darunter nur 10% unter 18 Jahren, und hiervon wieder nur 20 Knaben zum Nachtpersonal, äußern sich wie folgt: „Die Knaben leiden durchaus nicht von der Hitze. Die Temperatur ist wahrscheinlich 86° bis 90° . . . In den Hammer- und Walzwerken arbeiten die Hände Tag und Nacht ablösungsweise, aber dahingegen ist auch alles andre Werk Tagwerk, von 6 Uhr morgens bis 6 Uhr abends. In der Schmiede wird von

12 Uhr bis 12 Uhr gearbeitet. Einige Hände arbeiten fortwährend des Nachts ohne Wechsel zwischen Tag- und Nachtzeit . . . Wir finden nicht, daß Tag- oder Nachtarbeit irgendeinen Unterschied in der Gesundheit [der Herren Naylor and Vickers?] macht, und wahrscheinlich schlafen Leute besser, wenn sie dieselbe Ruheperiode genießen, als wenn sie wechselt . . . Ungefähr zwanzig Knaben unter 18 Jahren arbeiten mit der Nachtmannschaft . . . Wir könnten's nicht recht tun ohne die Nachtarbeit von Jungen unter 18 Jahren. Unser Einwurf ist — die Vermehrung der Produktionskosten . . . Geschickte Hände und Häupter von Departements sind schwer zu haben, aber Jungens kriegt man so viel man will . . . Natürlich, in Anbetracht der geringen Proportion von Jungen, die wir verwenden, wären Beschränkungen der Nachtarbeit von wenig Wichtigkeit oder Interesse für uns."

---

1 *Stavely = name of a town in England*

Chapter Ten

37. *Coordinating conjunctions*

1. The following words are used as coordinating conjunctions:

aber	*but, however*
denn	*for, because*
oder	*or*
sondern	*but, but rather, but on the contrary*
und	*and*

Paul ging nicht, sondern er blieb hier.	*Paul did not go but remained here.*
Er wollte es tun, aber er konnte es nicht.	*He wanted to do it, but he could not.*

2. The verb in the clauses which these conjunctions link or introduce will be found either immediately after the subject (normal word order) or immediately before the subject (inverted word order):

Normal:

Das Flugzeug fliegt nach Deutschland, und wir bleiben zurück.	*The plane flies to Germany, and we remain behind.*

Inverted:

Kommt Inge zu uns, oder bleibt sie bei Ekkehard?	*Is Inge coming to us (our place), or is she remaining at Ekkehard's?*

3. Do not confuse **denn** (*for*), which takes normal word order, with **dann** (*then*), which takes inverted word order:

Sie begannen zu essen, denn sie waren hungrig.	*They began to eat, for they were hungry.*
Klaus schrieb den Brief, dann ging er zu Bett.	*Klaus wrote the letter, then he went to bed.*

Denn may be used in the middle of the clause as an intensifier. Used thus it has a general meaning of *really* or *actually;* often it is untranslatable but shows impatience or exasperation:

Will er denn das sagen?	*Does he really want to say that?*
Wer ist denn da?	*Who* **is** *there?*

4. Several combinations of words function as conjunctions:

sowohl . . . als auch	*both . . . and*
entweder . . . oder	*either . . . or*
weder . . . noch	*neither . . . nor*
nicht nur . . . sondern auch	*not only . . . but also*
Sowohl die Jungen als auch die Alten glauben an ihn.	*Both young and old believe in him.*
Entweder du oder Max muß das tun.	*Either you or Max must do it.*
Weder sie noch ihre Kinder konnten Deutsch.	*Neither they nor their children knew German.*
Nicht nur den Mond, sondern auch die Sterne sieht man.	*One sees not only the moon but also the stars.*

Give the correct meanings of the following coordinating conjunctions.

	1. der Fabrikant = *the manufacturer, industrialist* Friedrich Engels ist am 28. November 1820 als Sohn eines Fabrikanten in Barmen (Deutschland) geboren.
1. Friedrich Engels was born November 28, 1820, as the son of an industrialist in Barmen (Germany).	**2. das Zweiggeschäft** = *branch store* In Manchester arbeitete Engels als junger Mann für ein Zweiggeschäft seines Vaters.
2. When a young man he worked for a branch of his father's business in Manchester.	**3. kennen** = *to be acquainted with, to know* **lernen** = *to learn* **kennenlernen** = ____________
3. *to become acquainted with, to get to know*	**4. der Arbeiter** = *worker* **die Frage** = *question* **die Arbeiterfrage** = *question of the working classes, labor question* In England lernt Engels die Arbeiterfrage kennen.

4. In England Engels becomes acquainted with the question of the working classes.	**5.** **das Verhältnis** = *condition* In England lernte er die Arbeiterfrage und die sozialen Verhältnisse Englands kennen.
5. In England he got acquainted with the question of the working classes and the English social conditions.	**6.** **worüber** = *about which* Hier lernte er die Arbeiterfrage und sozialen Verhältnisse in England kennen, worüber er später schrieb.
6. Here he became acquainted with the labor question and the social conditions in England about which he later wrote.	**7.** **begegnen** = *to meet* 1842 begegnete er Karl Marx zum erstenmal.
7. In 1842 he met Karl Marx for the first time.	**8.** **die Lage** = *condition, situation* Sein Buch *Die Lage der arbeitenden Klasse in England* erschien zum erstenmal im Jahre 1845.
8. His book, *The Condition of the Working Class in England,* appeared for the first time in 1845.	**9.** Lesen wir jetzt, was Engels über die Arbeiterfamilien schrieb.
9. Let us now read what Engels wrote about the workers' families.	**10.** **wohnen** = *to live, to dwell* **die Wohnverhältnisse** = *living conditions* Wir lesen jetzt, in was für Wohnverhältnissen sie damals lebten.
10. We (will) now read in what kind of conditions they lived at the time.	**11.** **folgendes** = *the following* Die Journale erzählen folgendes.
11. The newspapers tell (us) the following.	**12.** **die Wohnung** = *flat, apartment* Eine Frau lebte in einer Wohnung.
12. A woman lived in an apartment.	**13.** **sterben** = *to die* **die Verstorbene** = *the deceased* Dann erzählten die Journale folgendes von der Wohnung der Verstorbenen.
13. Then the newspapers told the following about the flat of the deceased.	**14.** **der Körper** = *body* Ein nackter Körper lag in dem Zimmer.

14. A naked body was lying in the room.	**15.** **streuen** = *to strew, to spread* Die Federn waren über den **fast** nackten Körper gestreut. (*fast/almost*)
15. The feathers were strewn over the *almost* naked body.	**16.** **die Decke** = *cover* Die Federn waren ihre einzige Decke.
16. The feathers were her only cover.	**17.** **vorhanden** = *at hand* Die Federn waren über ihren fast nackten Körper gestreut, **denn** es war keine Decke vorhanden. (*for/then*)
17. The feathers were strewn over her almost naked body, *for* there was no cover available (at hand).	**18.** **zerbeißen** = *to chew up* **das Ungeziefer** = *vermin* Ungeziefer zerbissen den Körper.
18. Vermin chewed up the body.	**19.** **abgemagert** = *emaciated* **Dann** fand er sie ganz abgemagert und von Ungeziefer zerbissen. (*then/for*)
19. *Then* he found her completely emaciated and chewed up by vermin.	**20.** **Fuß** = *foot* **der Boden** = *ground, floor* **der Fußboden** = ____________
20. *the floor*	**21.** **das Loch** = *hole* Ein Loch ist im Fußboden.
21. A hole is in the floor.	**22.** **aufreißen** = *to tear open* Man reißt ein Loch im Fußboden auf.
22. A hole is torn open in the floor.	**23.** **benutzen** = *to use, to utilize* Man benutzt das Loch im Fußboden . . .
23. The hole in the floor is used . . .	**24.** **der Abtritt** = *lavatory, water-closet* Man reißt einen Teil des Fußbodens auf und benutzt das Loch als Abtritt.
24. Part of the floor is torn up and the hole is used as a lavatory.	**25.** **war aufgerissen** = *was torn up* **wurde benutzt** = *was used* Ein Teil des Fußbodens war aufgerissen, **und** das Loch wurde als Abtritt benutzt. (*but/and/or*)

25. A part of the floor was torn open, *and* the hole was used as a lavatory.	**26. hatte . . . gewohnt** = *had lived* Sie hatte mit ihrem Mann und ihrem 19-jährigen Sohne in einem kleinen Zimmer gewohnt.
26. She had lived in a small room with her husband and her 19 year old son.	**27. sich befinden** = *to be* Was befindet sich in dem Zimmer?
27. What is in the room?	**28. die Bettstelle** = *bedstead* Befand sich eine Bettstelle **darin?** (**darin** = *in it/near it*)
28. Was there a bedstead *in it*?	**29. das Möbel** = *(piece of) furniture* **Weder** Bettstelle **noch** Möbel waren in dem Zimmer. (*either . . . or/neither . . . nor*)
29. *Neither* bedstead *nor* furniture was in the room.	**30. sonstig** = *other* Es befanden sich darin **weder** Bettstelle **noch** sonstige Möbel.
30. There was *neither* a bedstead *nor* other furniture in it.	**31. der Haufen** = *pile, heap* Der Zeitung nach lag sie tot neben ihrem Sohn auf einem Haufen Federn.
31. According to the newspaper, she lay dead next to her son on a pile of feathers.	**32. das Bettzeug** = *bedding* **das Bett(t)uch** = *sheet* Es war **weder** Decke **noch** Bettzeug **noch** Bettuch vorhanden. (*neither . . . nor/either . . . or*)
32. There was *neither* blanket *nor* bedding *nor* sheet at hand.	**33. Dann** erzählte Engels eine andere Geschichte. (*then/for*)
33. *Then* Engels told another story.	**34. das Polizeigericht** = *police court* Zwei Knaben **werden** vor das Polizeigericht **gebracht.** (*are brought/were brought*)
34. Two boys *are brought* before the police court.	**35. verzehren** = *to consume* Zwei Knaben wurden vor das Polizeigericht gebracht, **denn** sie hatten einen halbgekochten Kuhfuß gestohlen und verzehrt. (*then/for*)

35. Two boys were brought before the police court, *for* they had stolen and consumed a half-cooked cow's foot.	**36.** **der Polizeirichter** = *police magistrate* Was tat der Polizeirichter?
36. What did the police magistrate do?	**37.** **nachforschen** = *to inquire, to investigate* Der Polizeirichter mußte alles nachforschen.
37. The police magistrate had to investigate everything.	**38.** **sich veranlaßt sehen** = *to feel obliged* Der Polizeirichter sah sich veranlaßt, weiter nachzuforschen.
38. The police magistrate felt obliged to make further inquiry.	**39.** Wer, was und wo war **denn** die Mutter dieser Knaben? (*than/for/intensifier*)
39. intensifier Who, what, and where was the mother of these boys?	**40.** **die Witwe** = *widow* Sie war die Witwe eines alten Soldaten.
40. She was the widow of an old soldier.	**41.** **ergehen** = *to go, to fare* **war ergangen** = *had fared* Wie war es ihr **denn** überhaupt ergangen seit dem Tode ihres Mannes? (*for/then/intensifier*)
41. intensifier How had she really fared since the death of her husband?	**42.** **reich** = *rich* **die Reichen** = *the rich* **arm** = *poor* **die Armen** = ___________
42. *the poor*	**43.** **das Schicksal** = *fate* Das Schicksal **trifft** die Reichen und die Armen. (*strikes/runs*)
43. Fate *strikes* rich and poor (alike).	**44.** **gleich** = *same* **getroffen werden** = *to be struck, meet* **Sowohl** die Reichen **als auch** die Armen können von gleichem Schicksal getroffen werden. (*not only . . . but also/both . . . and*)

44. *Both* rich *and* poor can meet (be struck by) the same fate.	**45. Nicht nur** die Armen, **sondern auch** die Reichen werden von dem gleichen Schicksal getroffen, nämlich dem Tod. (*both . . . and/not only . . . but also*)
45. *Not only* the poor *but also* the rich are met by (meet, will meet) the same fate, namely death.	

PROGRESS TEST

When you correct this test, circle the phrases you miss and review them before continuing.

1. Die Familie wohnte in einem kleinen Zimmer, *aber* sie hatte kein Geld.
   (a) and (b) because (c) but (d) but rather
2. **hat verkaufen müssen** = *had to sell, did have to sell*
   Hat sie *denn* alles verkaufen müssen, um nur Brot zu bekommen?
   (a) for (b) or (c) but rather (d) used as an intensifier
3. **das Elend** = *misery*
   Wohnen alle Londoner Arbeiter in einem solchen Elend *oder* nur wenige?
   (a) and (b) or (c) but (d) for
4. **der Lumpen** = *rag*
   die Ecke = *corner*
   Sie schliefen nicht auf einem Bett wie wir, *sondern* auf einigen Lumpen, die in einer Ecke lagen.
   (a) but rather (b) or (c) for (d) however
5. *Entweder* lag sie tot neben ihrem Sohn auf einem Haufen Federn, *oder* wir haben es nur geträumt.
   (a) both . . . and (b) either . . . or (c) neither . . . nor (d) not only . . . but also
6. *Sowohl* die Witwe *als auch* ihre kranke Tochter wohnten in dem kleinen Zimmer.
   (a) either . . . or (b) not only . . . but also (c) both . . . and (d) neither . . . nor
7. Es befanden sich darin *weder* Bettstelle *noch* sonstige Möbel.
   (a) both . . . and (b) either . . . or (c) neither . . . nor (d) not only . . . but also
8. *Nicht nur* die Armen, *sondern auch* die Reichen werden von dem gleichen Schicksal getroffen, nämlich vom Tod.
   (a) both . . . and (b) either . . . or (c) neither . . . nor (d) not only . . . but also

Answer key: **1.** (c); **2.** (d); **3.** (b); **4.** (a); **5.** (b); **6.** (c); **7.** (c); **8.** (d).

38. *Subordinating conjunctions*

1. The following words are subordinating conjunctions which have already been used or will be introduced in this chapter:

als	*when*
bevor	*before*
bis	*until*
da	*since, because*
damit	*so that*
daß	*that*
nachdem	*after*
ob	*whether, if*
obgleich, obschon, obwohl	*although*
seit(dem)	*since (the time of)*
weil	*because*
wenn	*if, when, whenever*

2. Subordinating conjunctions introduce dependent clauses in which the verb is the last element (dependent word order):

Er sprach Russisch, *damit* ich ihn nicht verstehen konnte.	*He spoke Russian,* ***so that*** *I could not understand him.*
***Da* er kein Geld hat, kann er nicht ins Kino gehen.**	*He cannot go to the movies,* ***because*** *he has no money.*

3. **Wenn** is translated *whenever* when referring to customary or habitual action in the past or the present:

***Wenn* Paul kommt, gehen wir immer spazieren.**	***Whenever*** *Paul comes, we always go for a walk.*
***Wenn* er ging, war es immer dunkel.**	***Whenever*** *he went, it was always dark.*

Do not confuse the conjunction **wenn** (*if, whenever*) with the interrogative **wann** (*when*):

***Wann* kommt er zu uns?**	*When is he coming to visit us?*
Ich weiß, *wann* er zu uns kommt.	*I know when he is coming to visit us.*
Er weiß es, *wenn* sein Sohn die Wahrheit sagt.	*Whenever his son tells the truth, he knows it.*

4. Remember that as a subordinating conjunction **da** means *since, because,* and that as an adverb it means *there* or *then:*

Da **er es selbst *tut*, dürfen wir es auch.**	***Since*** *he himself does it, we may also.*
Da **sitzt der arme Mensch.**	***There*** *sits the poor man.*

5. When **ob** is used without an antecedent it is translated *I (we) wonder whether* or *if:*

Ob **er heute singt?**	***I wonder whether*** (*if*) *he will sing today?*

6. Do not confuse the subordinating conjunction **als** with the **als** used in comparisons or **als** meaning *as:*

Er ist *größer als* ich.	*He is* ***taller than*** *I.*
Sie will *als* Princessin zum Ball hin.	*She wants to go* ***as*** *a princess to the ball.*
Du kammst, *als* ich fort war.	*You came* ***when*** *I was out.*

Give the correct meaning of the following subordinating conjunctions.

	1. fortsetzen = *to continue* Wir wollen das Gespräch über Engels Werk fortsetzen.
1. We want to continue the discussion of Engels' work.	**2. verzehren** = *to consume* Zwei Knaben haben einen halbgekochten Kuhfuß aus dem Laden gestohlen und verzehrt.
2. Two boys stole and consumed a half-cooked cow's foot from the store.	**3. sogleich** = *immediately* Die zwei Knaben wurden vor das Polizeigericht gebracht, **weil** sie aus Hunger einen halbgekochten Kuhfuß von einem Laden gestohlen und sogleich verzehrt hatten.
3. The two boys were brought before the police court, *because* out of hunger they had stolen from a shop a half-cooked cow's foot, which they immediately consumed.	**4. der Polizeidiener** = *policeman* Der Polizeidiener kam zu der Frau.
4. The policeman came to the woman.	**5. erhalten** = *to receive* Was **erhielt** der Polizeirichter von den Polizeidienern? (*present/past*)
5. What *did* the police magistrate *receive* from the policemen?	**6. die Aufklärung** = *explanation* Der Polizeirichter **erhielt** folgende Aufklärung.

6. The police magistrate *received* the following explanation.	**7.** **hatten . . . besucht** = *had visited* Der Polizeirichter erhielt von den Polizeidienern folgende Aufklärung, **nachdem** sie die Mutter der zwei Knaben besucht hatten.
7. The police magistrate received the following explanation from the policeman *after* they had visited the mother of the two boys.	**8.** **das Hinterstübchen** = *small back room* Der Polizeidiener fand die Frau mit sechs **ihrer** Kinder in einem kleinen Hinterstübchen. (*of her/of their*)
8. The policeman found the woman with six *of her* children in a small back room.	**9.** **das Elend** = *misery* Die Witwe wohnte zusammen mit ihren neun Kindern im größten Elend, **bis** sie es nicht mehr konnte.
9. The widow lived together with her nine children in greatest misery *until* she could no longer do it.	**10.** **zusammengedrängt** = *crowded together* **Als** der Polizeidiener zu ihr kam, fand er sie mit sechs ihrer Kinder in einem kleinen Hinterstübchen zusammengedrängt, wo sie im Elend lebten.
10. *When* the policeman came to (see) her, he found her with six of her children crowded together in a little back room, where they lived in misery.	**11.** **gleich** = *directly* In einer Ecke lagen einige Lumpen, **damit** sie nicht gleich auf dem Boden schlafen mußten.
11. In a corner lay some rags *so that* they did not have to sleep directly on the floor.	**12.** **die Schürze** = *apron* In der Ecke lagen **so viel** alte Lumpen, **als** eine Frau in ihre Schürze nehmen konnte.
12. In the corner there were *as many* old rags *as* a woman could take into (carry in) her apron.	**13.** **Da** aber die Lumpen der ganzen Familie zum Bette dienten, brauchte keiner gleich auf dem Boden zu schlafen.
13. *Since* however the rags served the whole family as a bed, no one needed to sleep directly on the floor.	**14.** **schlecht** = *bad, poor* **Nachdem** der alte Soldat und spätere Polizeidiener starb, ist es seiner Frau und seinen neun Kindern sehr schlecht ergangen.
14. *After* the old soldier who later became a policeman died, his wife and nine children fared very poorly.	**15.** **Seitdem** sie eine Witwe war, war es ihr sehr schlecht ergangen.

15. *Since* she had been a widow, she had fared very poorly.	**16.** Auf dem **Herd** war ein Feuer. (*herd/hearth*)
16. In the *hearth* there was a fire.	**17. der Funke(n)** = *spark* Auf dem Herde war **kaum** ein Funken Feuer. (*scarcely/always*)
17. There was *scarcely* a spark of fire in the hearth.	**18.** Immer **wenn** er kam, war auf dem Herde kaum ein Funken Feuer.
18. *Whenever* he came, there was scarcely a spark of fire in the hearth.	**19. das Kleid** = *dress* **die Kleidung** = ____________
19. *clothing*	**20. ärmlich** = *wretched* Zur Decke hatten sie **nichts als** ihre ärmliche Kleidung.
20. For a cover they had *nothing but* (*nothing else than*) their wretched clothing.	**21. die Nahrung** = *food, nourishment* Die Witwe und ihre neun Kinder hatten keine Nahrung.
21. The widow and her nine children had no food.	**22. erhalten** = *to receive, to get* Um Nahrung zu erhalten, **hatte** sie alles **verkauft.** (*has sold/had sold*)
22. In order to get food she *had sold* everything.	**23. hat verkaufen müssen** = *had to sell* **überhaupt** = *absolutely* Sie hat überhaupt alles verkaufen müssen, **damit** ihre Familie etwas zu essen bekam.
23. She had to sell absolutely everything *so that* her family got something to eat.	**24. voriges** = *previous* Die arme Frau erzählte ihm, **daß** sie voriges Jahr ihr Bett habe verkaufen müssen, um Nahrung zu erhalten.
24. The poor woman told him *that* she had had to sell her bed the previous year in order to get food. (**Habe** is subjunctive here. Its position with the double infinitive will be explained in chapter 14.)	**25. dalassen** = *to leave* (*behind*) **hat dagelassen** = ____________

25. *has left, left*	**26.** **das Unterpfand** = *pledge* **Wenn** sie ihre Bettücher dem Viktualienhändler als Unterpfand für einige Lebensmittel daläßt, wird sie nur Lumpen haben, die zum Bette dienen.
26. *If* she leaves her sheets with the food merchant as a pledge for some food, she will only have rags serving (which will serve) as a bed.	**27.** Die Witwe hat ihre Bettücher dem Viktualienhändler als Unterpfand dagelassen.
27. The widow left her sheets with the food merchant as a pledge.	**28.** Um Nahrung zu erhalten, hatte sie alles verkauft, **bis** sie nichts mehr hatte.
28. In order to get food she had sold everything *until* she had nothing more.	**29.** **Da** sie ihre Bettücher dem Viktualienhändler als Unterpfand für einige Lebensmittel dagelassen hat, hat sie nur Lumpen, die zum Bette dienen.
29. *Since* she left her sheets with the food merchant as pledge for some food, she has only rags which serve as a bed.	**30.** **der Vorschuß** = *advance* (*cash*) Der Polizeirichter gab der Frau einen großen Vorschuß.
30. The police magistrate gave the woman a large cash advance.	**31.** **beträchtlich** = *considerable* Der Polizeirichter gibt der Frau einen beträchtlichen Vorschuß.
31. The police magistrate gives the woman a considerable cash advance.	**32.** **die Armenbüchse** = *poor box, relief fund* Der Polizeirichter gibt der Frau einen beträchtlichen Vorschuß aus der Armenbüchse.
32. The police magistrate gives the woman a considerable cash advance out of the poor box.	**33.** **Als** der Polizeirichter der Frau einen beträchtlichen Vorschuß aus der Armenbüchse gab . . .
33. *When* the police magistrate gave the woman a considerable advance out of the poor box . . .	

PROGRESS TEST

What are the meanings of the indicated words? Review the ones you miss before going on.

1. *Als* der Polizeirichter der Frau einen beträchtlichen Vorschuß aus der Armenbüchse gab . . .
   (a) although (b) after (c) because (d) when
2. Sie hatten nichts, *bis* der Polizeirichter ihnen ein Pfund aus der Armenbüchse zukommen ließ.
   (a) until (b) whether (c) if (d) because
3. *Da* sie ihre Bettücher dem Viktualienhändler als Unterpfand für einige Lebensmittel dagelassen hat . . .
   (a) so that (b) since (c) although (d) after
4. Sie hatte allmählich alles verkauft oder versetzt, *damit* sie noch essen konnte.
   (a) when (b) so that (c) if (d) because
5. *Nachdem* Herr Carter eine Totenschau über die Leiche der 45jährigen Ann Galway abhielt . . .
   (a) if (b) because (c) after (d) although
6. Wissen Sie, *ob* Engels die Londoner Arbeiter viel braver, viel ehrenwerter als sämtliche Reichen von London findet?
   (a) until (b) although (c) because (d) whether
7. *Obwohl* die obigen drei Familien in solchem Elend leben . . .
   (a) because (b) since (c) although (d) that
8. *Seitdem* die Witwe kein Geld mehr hat, muß sie in einem kleinen Hinterzimmer wohnen, worin kein einziges Stück Möbel ist.
   (a) since (b) before (c) whether (d) whenever
9. Zwei Knaben wurden vor das Polizeigericht gebracht, *weil* sie aus Hunger einen halbgekochten Kuhfuß von einem Laden gestohlen und sogleich verzehrt hatten.
   (a) while (b) because (c) although (d) if
10. Was sollen wir tun, *wenn* jeder Proletarier von gleichem Schicksal getroffen werden kann?
    (a) if (b) although (c) so that (d) until

Answer key: **1.** (d); **2.** (a); **3.** (b); **4.** (b); **5.** (c); **6.** (d); **7.** (c); **8.** (a); **9.** (b); **10.** (a).

READING PREPARATION

These exercises finish introducing the vocabulary and structures necessary to read the passage from Engels. Be sure to review new vocabulary several times before going on.

	1. **tot** = *dead* **die Toten** = *the dead* **schauen** = *to look* **die Schau** = *show, review, parade, exhibition* **die Totenschau** = ____________

1. *inquest*	**2.** **abhalten** = *to hold* Der Coroner hält eine Totenschau über die abgemagerte **Leiche** der 45 jährigen Ann Galway ab. (**Leiche** = *corpse/Leica*)
2. The coroner is holding an inquest on the emaciated *corpse* of the 45 year old Ann Galway.	**3.** **Nachdem** Herr Carter, Coroner für Surrey, eine Totenschau über die abgemagerte Leiche der 45 jährigen Ann Galway abhielt . . .
3. *After* Mr. Carter, coroner for Surrey, held an inquest on the emaciated corpse of the 45 year old Ann Galway . . .	**4.** Was für eine Aufklärung erhält der Polizeirichter von den Polizeidienern?
4. What sort of explanation does the police magistrate get from the policemen?	**5.** **rein** = *clean, pure* **reinigen** = *to cleanse, to purify, to clean* Man reinigt den Fußboden.
5. One cleans the floor.	**6.** Man reinigte die Leiche.
6. One cleansed the corpse.	**7.** **unter** = *under* **suchen** = *to seek* **untersuchen** = __________
7. *to examine, to investigate*	**8.** **der Arzt** = *doctor* Der Arzt konnte die Leiche nicht untersuchen.
8. The doctor could not examine the corpse.	**9.** **Bevor** der Arzt die Leiche untersuchen konnte, mußte man die Federn von ihr reinigen.
9. *Before* the doctor could examine the corpse one had to cleanse the feathers from it.	**10.** Der Arzt konnte die abgemagerte Leiche nicht untersuchen, **bevor** sie gereinigt war.
10. The doctor could not examine the emaciated corpse *before* it was cleaned.	**11.** **fest** = *fast* **kleben** = *to stick* **Weil** die Federn so fest an ihr klebten, konnte der Arzt die Leiche nicht sogleich untersuchen.
11. *Because* the feathers were stuck so fast to her the doctor could not immediately examine the corpse.	**12.** Wissen Sie, **ob** Engels behauptet, alle Londoner Arbeiter lebten in einem solchen Elend?

12. Do you know *if* Engels claims that all London's working class lived in such misery?	**13.** **die Ehre** = *honor* **der Wert** = *worth* **ehrenwert** = __________
13. *honorable*	**14.** Ist er ein ehrenwerter Mensch?
14. Is he an honorable person?	**15.** **sämtlich** = *all, entire* Wissen Sie, **ob** er die Londoner Arbeiter viel braver, viel ehrenwerter als sämtliche Reichen von London findet?
15. Do you know *whether* he finds London's workers much better, much more honorable than all the rich of London?	**16.** **die obigen** = *the above* **Obwohl** die obigen Familien in solchem Elend leben, kann man nicht sagen, daß sämtliche Londoner Arbeiter in solchen Verhältnissen leben.
16. *Although* the above families live in such misery, one cannot say that all London's workers live in such circumstances.	**17.** **einfallen** = *to come to mind, to occur* (*to someone*) **Obgleich** es Engels nicht einfällt, das zu behaupten, will er doch sagen, daß es den Arbeitern nicht gut geht.
17. *Although* it does not occur to Engels to claim that, he still maintains that things are not well with the workers (lit.: he still wants to say that it does not go well . . .).	**18.** **leben** = *to live* **hatten . . . gelebt** = *had lived* In welchem Zustand hatten die obigen gelebt?
18. In what conditions had the above lived?	**19.** **Ob** sie in diesem Zustand gelebt hatten?
19. (Do you know, I wonder) *whether* they had lived in this condition?	**20.** **Obschon** sie kein Geld hatten, mußten sie doch essen.
20. *Although* they had no money, they still had to eat.	**21.** **werden mit Füßen getreten** = *are trampled* Sie werden mit Füßen getreten.
21. They are trampled upon.	**22.** **ganz und gar** = *completely* Sie wird ganz und gar von der Gesellschaft mit Füßen getreten.
22. She is completely trampled upon by society.	**23.** Ich weiß wohl, **daß** zehn es besser haben, wo einer so ganz und gar von der Gesellschaft mit Füßen getreten wird.

23. I am well aware *that* ten (people) have a better life for every one who is so completely trampled upon by society.	**24.** **die Schuld** = *guilt, fault* **Kann** jeder Proletarier, ohne seine Schuld, von gleichem Schicksal **getroffen werden?** (*can meet/will meet*)
24. *Can* every proletarian without being at fault *meet* (*can be met by*) the same fate?	**25.** **die Anstrengung** = *effort, exertion, strain* Kann jeder Proletarier, trotz allen seinen Anstrengungen, von gleichem Schicksal getroffen werden?
25. Can every proletarian, in spite of all his efforts, meet the same fate?	**26.** Was sollen wir tun, **wenn** jeder Proletarier, ohne seine Schuld und trotz allen seinen Anstrengungen, von gleichem Schicksal getroffen werden kann?
26. What are we to do, *if* every proletarian can meet the same fate without being at fault and in spite of all his efforts?	**27.** In was für einer Lage befinden sich die **braven** Familien? (*good/brave*)
27. In what kind of a situation do the *good* families find themselves?	**28.** **behaupten** = *to maintain, to hold* Was **hat** Engels **behauptet**?
28. What *did* Engels *maintain*?	**29.** **fleißig** = *industrious* Aber Engels behauptet, daß Tausende von fleißigen und braven Familien sich in dieser **eines Menschen unwürdigen** Lage befinden. (*unworthy for many men/unworthy of a human being*)
29. But Engels maintains that thousands of industrious and good families find themselves in this situation which is *unworthy of a human being*. (Note that the adjective **unwürdig** takes a genitive object.)	**30.** **die Ausnahme** = *exception* **Da** jeder Proletarier, jeder ohne Ausnahme, vom gleichen Schicksal getroffen werden kann . . .
30. *Since* every proletarian, every one without exception, can meet the same fate . . .	

PROGRESS TEST

Choose the sentence which most closely corresponds to the given sentence.

1. Die arme Frau erzählte ihm, daß sie voriges Jahr ihr Bett habe verkaufen müssen, um Nahrung zu erhalten.
(a) The woman had no money to buy a bed.
(b) Last year she had money to buy a bed.
(c) In order to buy a bed she had to sell her dishes.
(d) She sold her bed to buy food.

2. Die Polizeidiener sahen sich veranlaßt, weiter nachzuforschen, denn sie wollten selber die halbgekochten Kuhfüße stehlen.
(a) The policemen feel the boys stole the cows' feet.
(b) The policemen wanted to steal the cows' feet themselves.
(c) The policemen wanted to do away with the investigation of cows' feet.
(d) The policemen wanted the investigation of stolen cows' feet under their jurisdiction.

3. Sämtliche Reichen von London befinden sich in derselben Lage wie die braven, fleißigen Proletarier.
(a) All proletarians are brave and flighty.
(b) Brave and industrious proletarians find the rich very haughty.
(c) The proletarians and the rich share a common fate.
(d) Rich and poor alike are good and industrious.

4. In dem kleinen Hinterzimmer fand man weder Bettstelle noch sonstige Möbel, aber doch einen mit Federn bedeckten Körper.
(a) Feathers were all over the room but not on the furniture.
(b) If one had a bedstead and other furniture they would not need a feather bed.
(c) Feather covered bodies are not much good for furniture.
(d) A feather covered body was the only object in the room.

Answer key: **1.** (d); **2.** (b); **3.** (c); **4.** (d).

Friedrich Engels:
Die Lage der arbeitenden Klasse in England

Bei Gelegenheit einer Totenschau, die Hr. Carter, Coroner für Surrey, über die Leiche der 45jährigen Ann Galway am 16. Nov. 1843 abhielt, erzählen die Journale folgendes von der Wohnung der Verstorbenen: Sie hatte in Nr. 3, White-Lion-Court, Bermondsey-Street, London, mit ihrem Mann und ihrem 19jährigen Sohne in einem kleinen Zimmer gewohnt, worin sich weder Bettstelle oder Bettzeug, noch sonstige Möbel befanden. Sie lag tot neben ihrem Sohn auf einem Haufen Federn, die über ihren fast nackten

Körper gestreut waren, denn es war weder Decke noch Bettuch vorhanden. Die Federn klebten so fest an ihr über den ganzen Körper, daß der Arzt die Leiche nicht untersuchen konnte, bevor sie gereinigt war, und dann fand er sie ganz abgemagert und über und über von Ungeziefer zerbissen. Ein Teil des Fußbodens im Zimmer war aufgerissen, und das Loch wurde von der Familie als Abtritt benutzt.

Montag den 15. Januar 1844 wurden zwei Knaben vor das Polizeigericht von Worship-Street, London, gebracht, weil sie aus Hunger einen halbgekochten Kuhfuß von einem Laden gestohlen und sogleich verzehrt hatten. Der Polizeirichter sah sich veranlaßt, weiter nachzuforschen, und erhielt von den Polizeidienern bald folgende Aufklärung: Die Mutter dieser Knaben war die Witwe eines alten Soldaten und späteren Polizeidieners, der es seit dem Tode ihres Mannes mit ihren neun Kindern sehr schlecht ergangen war. Sie wohnte Nr. 2, Pool's Place, Quaker-Street, Spitalfields, im größten Elende. Als der Polizeidiener zu ihr kam, fand er sie mit sechs ihrer Kinder in einem kleinen Hinterstübchen buchstäblich zusammengedrängt, ohne Möbel . . . Auf dem Herde kaum ein Funken Feuer, und in der Ecke so viel alte Lumpen, als eine Frau in ihre Schürze nehmen konnte, die aber der ganzen Familie zum Bette dienten. Zur Decke hatten sie nichts als ihre ärmliche Kleidung. Die arme Frau erzählte ihm, daß sie voriges Jahr ihr Bett habe verkaufen müssen, um Nahrung zu erhalten; ihre Bettücher habe sie dem Viktualienhändler als Unterpfand für einige Lebensmittel dagelassen, und sie habe überhaupt alles verkaufen müssen, um nur Brot zu bekommen. — Der Polizeirichter gab der Frau einen beträchtlichen Vorschuß aus der Armenbüchse . . .

Es fällt mir nicht ein, zu behaupten, alle Londoner Arbeiter lebten in einem solchen Elend, wie die obigen drei Familien; ich weiß wohl, daß Zehn es besser haben, wo Einer so ganz und gar von der Gesellschaft mit Füßen getreten wird — aber ich behaupte, daß Tausende von fleißigen und braven Familien, viel braver, viel ehrenwerter als sämtliche Reichen von London, in dieser eines Menschen unwürdigen Lage sich befinden, und daß jeder Proletarier, jeder ohne Ausnahme, ohne seine Schuld und trotz allen seinen Anstrengungen, von gleichem Schicksal getroffen werden kann.

Chapter Eleven

39. *Past tense of irregular weak verbs—conjugation*

1. The following endings and vowel changes signal the past tense of irregular weak verbs:

brennen	*to burn*	**er brannte**	*he burned*
kennen	*to know*	**er kannte**	*he knew*
nennen	*to name*	**er nannte**	*he named*
rennen	*to run*	**er rannte**	*he ran*
senden	*to send*	**er sandte (sendete)**	*he sent*
wenden	*to turn*	**er wandte (wendete)**	*he turned*
bringen	*to bring*	**er brachte**	*he brought*
denken	*to think*	**er dachte**	*he thought*

Notice that:

1 — the stem vowel changes from **e** (or **i**) to **a** in every case.

2 — the past tense of **senden** and **wenden** has two forms.

3 — the verbs **bringen** and **denken** undergo a consonant change as well as a vowel change.

2. Do not confuse **konnte** (past tense form of the verb **können** = *can, to be able to*) with **kannte** (**kennen** = *to know, to be acquainted with*).
Do not confuse **brach** (**brechen** = *to break*) with **brachte** (**bringen** = *to bring*).
Do not confuse **er kann** (*he can*) with **er kannte** (*he knew*).

3. The irregular weak verbs follow this pattern in the past tense:

kennen (*to know, to be acquainted with*)

ich kannte	*I knew*
du kanntest	
er, sie, es kannte	
wir kannten	
ihr kanntet	
sie kannten	
Sie kannten	

4. **Senden** and **wenden** may take one of two patterns:

senden (*to send*)

ich sandte	or	**sendete**
du sandtest		**sendetest**
er, sie, es sandte		**sendete**
wir sandten		**sendeten**
ihr sandtet		**sendetet**
sie sandten		**sendeten**
Sie sandten		**sendeten**

The purpose of the following exercises is to help you distinguish between the present and past tense and to introduce vocabulary from the reading passage. Give the tense and meaning of the indicated verbs.

	1. Wir **brennen** nur Kohle in unserem Ofen. (*present/past*)
1. Present: We *burn* only coal in our stove.	**2.** Sie **brannten** nur Kohle in ihrem Ofen. (*present/past*)
2. Past: They *burned* only coal in their stove.	**3.** Er **rennt** schnell. (*present/past*)
3. Present: He *runs* fast.	**4.** Er **rannte** schnell. (*present/past*)
4. Past: He *ran* fast.	**5.** **vorig** = *previous, last* Im vorigen Kapitel **sprachen** wir von Engels.
5. In the last chapter we *spoke* of Engels.	**6.** In diesem Kapitel **sprechen** wir über Bismarck.

6. In this chapter we *are going to talk* about Bismarck.	7. Bismarck **ist** 1815 **geboren** und **starb** (im Jahre) 1898.
7. Bismarck *was born* in 1815 and *died* in (the year) 1898.	**8.** Er **lebte** in einer Zeit der Demokratie und der deutschen Macht.
8. He *lived* in a time of democracy and of German power.	**9.** Als eine große historische Persönlichkeit **lebt** er immer noch.
9. He still *lives* as a great historical figure.	**10.** Er **formulierte** viele Reformen für die damaligen sozialen Verhältnisse Deutschlands.
10. He *formulated* many reforms for the then existing social conditions in Germany.	**11.** **ja** = *yes* **bejahen** = *to approve* Die Konservativen **bejahten** seinen damaligen Einfluß auf Deutschland und **bejahen** ihn heute immer noch.
11. Conservatives *approved* the influence which he had on Germany at that time and still *approve* it today.	**12.** **nicht** = *not* **vernichten** = *to destroy* Heute **betrachten** die Liberalen Bismarck als einen Vernichter ihres Landes.
12. Today the liberals *consider* Bismarck (as) a destroyer of their country.	**13.** Wie **betrachteten** die Liberalen Bismarck damals?
13. How *did* the liberals *consider* Bismarck then?	**14.** **der Schaden** = *harm* Er **bringt** dem Land nur Schaden.
14. He *brings* only harm to his country.	**15.** **unwiederbringlich** = *irreparable, irretrievable* Sie sagen, daß er dem Land unwiederbringlichen Schaden **brachte.**
15. They say that he *brought* irreparable harm to the country.	**16.** **vorbereiten** = *to prepare* Sie sagen, daß er dem Land unwiederbringlichen Schaden brachte und das Land auf die Hitlerzeit **vorbereitete.**
16. They say that he brought irreparable harm to the country and *prepared* the country for the Hitler period.	**17.** **Kennt** man den wahren Bismarck heute?

17. *Does* one *know* the real Bismarck today?	**18.** **Kann** man den wahren Bismarck **kennen?**
18. *Can* one *know* the real Bismarck?	**19.** **Konnte** man damals den wahren Bismarck **kennen?**
19. *Could* one *know* the real Bismarck then?	**20.** If **amtlich** means *official* and **das Postamt** means *the post office,* then **das Amt** must mean ________
20. *the office*	**21.** **nennen** = *to call, to name* **ernennen** = *to appoint* Oft **ernennt** ein König den politisch stärksten Mann zu einem Amt.
21. Often a king *appoints* the politically strongest man to an office.	**22.** **die Meisterschaft** = *eminent skill, mastery* Trotz Bismarcks diplomatischer Meisterschaft . . .
22. In spite of Bismarck's diplomatic skill . . .	**23.** **rufen** = *to call* **berufen** = *to appoint, to send for* Trotz Bismarcks diplomatischer Meisterschaft **berief** man ihn im Jahre 1859 nicht ins Kabinett.
23. In spite of Bismarck's diplomatic skill he *was* not *appointed* (one *did* not *appoint* him) to the cabinet in 1859.	**24.** **senden** = *to send* **hat gesandt** = *sent* (*has sent*) **der Gesandte** = *ambassador* Bismarck **als Gesandter . . .**
24. Bismarck *as an ambassador* . . .	**25.** Stattdessen **sandte** man ihn als Gesandten nach St. Petersburg.
25. Instead, he *was sent* to St. Petersburg as ambassador.	**26.** Damals **kannte man** den wahren Bismarck **nicht.**
26. At that time the real Bismarck *was not known.*	**27.** Am 23. September 1862 **ernannte** Wilhelm I. Bismarck zum Ministerpräsidenten.
27. On September 23, 1862, Wilhelm I *appointed* Bismarck Prime Minister.	**28.** **eine Rede halten** = *to give a speech* Eine Woche nach seiner Ernennung zum Ministerpräsidenten **hielt** er seine berühmte „Blood and Iron" Rede.

28. A week after his appointment to (the post of) Prime Minister he *gave* his famous "Blood and Iron" speech.	**29.** Wer heute an Bismarck **denkt,** erinnert sich an seine „Eisen und Blut" Rede.
29. Whoever *thinks* of Bismarck nowadays, remembers his "Iron and Blood" speech.	**30.** Damals **dachten** viele, daß Bismarck ein großer Ministerpräsident war.
30. At that time many *thought* that Bismarck was a great Prime Minister.	**31.** **sich zuwenden** = *to turn to* **Wenden** wir **uns** heute zu oft starken Politikern **zu,** wenn wir ein Problem haben?
31. *Do* we nowadays too often *turn* to strong politicians when we have a problem? (Note that **zuwenden** governs the dative case.)	**32.** **sich wenden an** = *to turn to* **Wendete sich** das deutsche Volk damals **an** einen starken Politiker, um Deutschlands Probleme zu lösen?
32. *Did* the German nation at that time *turn to* a strong politician in order to solve Germany's problems? (Note that the verb + **an** calls for an accusative object.)	

PROGRESS TEST

Choose the correct answer.

1. Wilhelm I. __ Bismarck zum Ministerpräsidenten.
   (a) ernennen (b) ernannte (c) ernannt (d) ernennst
2. Den wirklichen Bismarck __ man nicht kennen.
   (a) kann (b) kannte (c) kennt (d) könnt
3. Elke __ ihm seinen alten Hut.
   (a) bracht (b) bringst (c) brecht (d) brachte
4. Er __ sich um und ging zurück.
   (a) wandte (b) ranntest (c) sendet (d) kannte
5. Das Haus __ zusammen.
   (a) brachte (b) brauchte (c) brach (d) brecht

Answer key: **1.** (b); **2.** (a); **3.** (d); **4.** (a); **5.** (c).

40. *The genitive case—Review*

1. As has been noted, possession is most often expressed in German by the genitive case.

2. The genitive singular of masculine and neuter nouns is recognized by the endings **-(e)s, -en,** or **-ens.** (Nouns ending in **-mus** add nothing, however.) Remember that the preceding article, limiting adjective, or possessive adjective will end in **-es:**

Der Freund mein*es* Mann*es* wohnt in Ungarn.	*My husband's friend lives in Hungary.*
Der Wagen d*es* Student*en* ist schon sehr alt.	*The student's car is already very old.*
Der Grund sein*es* Glauben*s* ist die Liebe.	*The foundation of his faith is love.*

3. Since feminine nouns take no special endings in the singular, the reader must look to the ending of the preceding article, limiting adjective, or possessive adjective to determine the case of the noun. The genitive ending will be **-er:**

Der Sohn dies*er* Frau ist wirklich sehr schlau.	*This woman's son is truly very sly.*

4. The genitive plural of all genders is revealed by the **-er** of the preceding article, limiting adjective, or possessive adjective:

Freunde solch*er* Männer soll man meiden.	*One should avoid the friends of such men.*

5. The genitive feminine[1] ending of articles, limiting adjectives, or possessive adjectives is the same as the dative feminine[2] and genitive plural[3]. To avoid confusing them, consult the context:

[1] **Das Haus d*er* Tante ist nicht weit von hier.**	*Our aunt's house (the house of the aunt) is not far from here.*
[2] **Sie dürfen mein*er* Frau kein teures Kleid zeigen.**	*You must not show my wife an expensive dress.*
[3] **Die Geschichte d*er* Musikinstrumente ist wirklich sehr interessant.**	*The history of musical instruments is really very interesting.*

The following frames contain a review of the genitive case and other grammar points. Give the meanings of the indicated words.

	1. sollen = *should, ought to* Um den Mann Bismarck besser zu verstehen, **sollen** wir seine Ideen kennen.
1. In order to understand (the man) Bismarck better, we *should* be acquainted with his ideas.	**2. darum** = *for that reason* Darum **müssen** wir seine eigenen Reden lesen.
2. For that reason, we *must* read his own speeches.	**3.** Die Reden und Gespräche **des** Ministerpräsiden**ten** helfen uns, seine Gedanken, Philosophie und Persönlichkeit zu verstehen.
3. The speeches and conversations *of the* Prime Minister help us to understand his ideas, philosophy, and personality.	**4. vorschlagen** = *to suggest* Wenn man seine „Eisen und Blut" Rede liest, dann kann man sehen, welche Rolle er für Preußen damals vorschlug.
4. When one reads his "Iron and Blood" speech, then one can see what role he suggested for Prussia at that time.	**5.** Bismarck nach darf Deutschland nicht auf Preußen**s** Liberalismus sehen.
5. According to Bismarck, Germany must not look to Prussia'*s* liberalism.	**6.** Sondern Deutschland soll auf die Macht Preußen**s** sehen.
6. But Germany should look to Prussia'*s* power.	**7. die Rüstung** = *armor* Preußen muß seine Rüstung utilisieren.
7. Prussia must utilize its armor.	**8. Nur soll Preußen** seine Rüstung auch utilisieren. (*Only Prussia ought to/Prussia just ought to*)
8. *Prussia just ought to* utilize its armor as well.	**9. die Liebe** = *love* **die Vorliebe** = *predilection* Preußen hat die Vorliebe, eine zu große Rüstung zu tragen.
9. Prussia has a predilection for carrying too much armor.	**10. der Leib** = *body* Ein **schmaler** Leib kann weniger Rüstung tragen. (*fat/slender*)

10. A *slender* body is able to carry less armor.	**11.** Wir haben die Vorliebe, eine zu große Rüstung für unseren schmalen **Leib** zu tragen. (*body/bodies*)
11. We have a predilection for carrying too much armor for our slender bodies. Note: Were **Leib** plural, a German would consider this frame to mean that each of us has more than one body.	**12.** Die Vorliebe **der Preußen,** eine zu große Rüstung für ihren schmalen Leib zu tragen . . .
12. The predilection *of the Prussians* for wearing armor too large for their slender bodies . . .	**13.** Bayern, Württemberg, Baden mögen **dem** Liberalismus indulgieren.
13. Bavaria, Württemberg, Baden may indulge *in* liberalism.	**14.** **anweisen** = *to assign to* Keiner kann ihnen **Preußens** Rolle anweisen.
14. No one can assign to them *Prussia's* role.	**15.** Keiner **wird** ihnen Preußens Rolle anweisen.
15. No one *will* assign Prussia's role to them.	**16.** Bayern, Württemberg, Baden mögen dem Liberalismus indulgieren, darum wird ihnen doch keiner Preußens Rolle anweisen.
16. Bavaria, Württemberg, Baden may indulge in liberalism; still no one will assign Prussia's role to them for that reason.	**17.** **zusammen** = *together* **zusammenfassen** = *to gather together, to concentrate* Preußen muß seine Kraft zusammenfassen.
17. Prussia must concentrate its power.	**18.** **zusammenhalten** = *to hold together* Preußen muß seine Kraft zusammenhalten.
18. Prussia must preserve (hold together) its power.	**19.** **nachdem** = *after* Nachdem Preußen seine Kraft zusammenfaßt und zusammenhält . . .

19. After Prussia gathers together and preserves its power . . .	**20.** **das Auge** = *eye* **der Blick** = *glance, glimpse* **der Augenblick** = *moment* **Auf** welchen Augenblick muß Preußen seine Macht zusammenhalten? (*until/on top of*)
20. *Until* what moment must Prussia preserve its power?	**21.** **günstig** = *favorable* Nachdem Preußen seine Macht zusammenfaßt, muß es sie auf den günstigen Augenblick zusammenhalten.
21. After Prussia concentrates its power, it must preserve it until the favorable moment (comes).	**22.** **anwenden** = *to use* Wann muß Preußen seine Macht anwenden?
22. When must Prussia use its power?	**23.** **wird verpaßt** = *is missed* Bevor ein günstiger Augenblick noch einmal verpaßt wird, muß Preußen seine Macht anwenden.
23. Before a favorable moment is missed once again, Prussia must use its power.	**24.** **worden** = *been* Der günstige Augenblick **ist** schon einige Male **verpaßt worden.** (*has been missed/is being missed*)
24. The favorable moment *has* already *been missed* several times. (present perfect of the passive voice)	**25.** **entscheiden** = *to decide, to determine* Die Wiener Verträge entschieden die Grenzen **des damaligen Preußens.**
25. The treaties of Vienna determined the boundaries *of the Prussia of that time.*	**26.** Oft **entscheiden** Verträge die Grenzen eines Staates.
26. Treaties often *determine* the boundaries of a nation.	**27.** **werden entschieden** = *are determined* Preußens Grenzen werden nicht durch Verträge entschieden.
27. Prussia's boundaries are not determined by treaties. (**Werden entschieden** is the passive voice, to be discussed in chapter 20)	**28.** **der Beschluß** = *decision* Preußens Grenzen werden nicht durch Reden und Majoritätsbeschlüsse entschieden.
28. Prussia's boundaries are not determined by speeches and majority decisions.	**29.** **Trotz der** Reden und Majoritätsbeschlüsse **werden** die großen Fragen der Zeit nur durch Eisen und Blut **entschieden.** (*determined/decided*)

29. *In spite of the* speeches and majority decisions, the great questions of the time *are* only *decided* through iron and blood.	**30.** **der Fehler** = *mistake* Das **ist** der große Fehler von 1848 bis 1849 **gewesen.** (*has been/was*)
30. That *was* the great mistake of 1848/1849.	**31.** **das Staatsleben** = *political life* Die Grenzen, notwendig zu einem **gesunden** Staatsleben, werden nicht durch Reden und Majoritätsbeschlüsse entschieden. (*unhealthy/healthy*)
31. The boundaries necessary for a *healthy* political life are not decided through speeches and majority decisions.	**32.** Preußens Grenzen sind zu einem gesunden Staatsleben nicht günstig.
32. Prussia's borders are not favorable for a healthy political life.	**33.** Preußens Grenzen nach den Wiener Verträgen waren zu einem gesunden Staatsleben nicht günstig.
33. Prussia's borders after the treaties of Vienna were not favorable for a healthy political life.	**34.** Nicht durch Reden und Majoritätsbeschlüsse werden die großen Fragen der Zeit entschieden, sondern durch Eisen und Blut.
34. The great questions of the time are not decided by speeches and majority decisions but by iron and blood.	**35.** **die Maßregel** = *measure* Wir müssen viele Maßregeln **treffen.** (*hit/take*)
35. We must *take* many measures.	**36.** **haben getroffen** = *have taken* Wir haben viele Maßregeln getroffen.
36. We have taken many measures.	**37.** **das Heil** = *good* Sozialistisch sind viele Maßregeln, **die** wir zum großen Heil des Landes getroffen haben. (*the/which*)
37. Socialistic are many measures *which* we have taken for the great good of the country.	**38.** **sich angewöhnen** = *to become accustomed to, to get in the habit of* Der Staat gewöhnt sich **den Sozialismus** an.
38. The state is becoming accustomed to *socialism.* **(sich angewöhnen** takes an accusative object)	**39.** Der Staat muß sich **etwas mehr** Sozialismus angewöhnen.

39. The state must become accustomed to *a little more* socialism.	**40.** Etwas mehr Sozialismus wird sich der Staat bei unserem Reiche **überhaupt** angewöhnen müssen. (*really/overhead*)
40. The state will *really* have to become accustomed to a little more socialism in our empire.	**41.** **wiederherstellen** = *to restore* Man stellt die Freiheit wieder her.
41. Freedom is restored.	**42.** **der Bauernstand** = *the peasant class* Man stellt dem Bauernstande die Freiheit wieder her.
42. Freedom is restored to the peasant class.	**43.** Sozialistisch war Herstellung **der** Freiheit **des** Bauernstandes.
43. The restoration *of the* freedom *of the* peasant class was socialistic.	**44.** **das Eisen** = *iron* **die Bahn** = *path, road* **die Eisenbahn** = __________
44. *the railroad*	**45.** **zugunsten** = *in favor of* Wird jede Expropriation zugunsten **der** Eisenbahn gemacht?
45. Is every expropriation done in favor *of the* railroad?	**46.** Sozialistisch ist jede Expropriation zugunsten **der** Eisenbahn.
46. Every expropriation in favor *of the* railroad is socialistic.	**47.** **zusammenlegen** = *to put or place together* **die Zusammenlegung** = __________
47. *the consolidation*	**48.** **der Grund** = *land* **das Stück** = *piece* **die Grundstücke** = __________
48. *plots of land, real estate*	**49.** **die Kommassation** = *consolidation of plots of land;* strictly speaking: reallocation of land (to the peasants) Die Kommassation ist die **Zusammenlegung der Grundstücke.**
49. *Kommassation* is the *consolidation of plots of land.*	**50.** **der Grad** = *degree, grade, rank* **im höchsten Grade** = __________ Sozialistisch im höchsten Grade ist zum Beispiel die Kommassation.

50. *Kommassation,* for example, is socialistic *in the highest degree.*	**51.** In vielen Provinzen ist die Kommassation Gesetz.
51. In many provinces *Kommassation* is the law.	**52.** Der Sozialismus will Grundstücke **dem** einen nehmen und **dem** anderen geben.
52. Socialism wants to take land *from* one person and give it *to the* other.	**53.** Sozialistisch ist die Zusammenlegung der Grundstücke, **die** dem einen genommen werden und dem anderen gegeben.
53. The consolidation of plots of land *which* are taken from one person and given to the other is socialistic.	**54.** **bewirtschaften** = *to manage* (a farm) Der andere kann das Land besser bewirtschaften.
54. The other person can manage the land better.	**55.** **bequem** = *easy, comfortable* **bloß** = *merely* Der Sozialismus gibt **dem anderen** das Land, bloß weil der andere es bequemer bewirtschaften kann.
55. Socialism gives the land *to another* merely because the other can manage it more easily.	**56.** Bloß weil **ein anderer** das Land bequemer bewirtschaften kann, gibt der Sozialismus einem anderen das Land.
56. Socialism gives another the land merely because *another* is able to manage the land more easily.	**57.** **vollständig** = *complete* **vervollständigen** = __________
57. *to complete*	**58.** Ich **könnte** das Register noch weiter vervollständigen. (Does the context suggest that **könnte** means *could* or *was able to*?)
58. I *could* complete the list still further. (**könnte** is a subjunctive form of **können**)	**59.** **erschrecken** = *to frighten* Viele wollen manche mit dem Wort „Sozialismus" erschrecken. (The subject is: **viele/manche**)
59. *viele* Many (people) want to frighten some (people) with the word "socialism."	**60.** **jemand** = *someone* Will man jemand mit dem Wort „Sozialismus" erschrecken?
60. Do people want to frighten someone with the word "socialism"?	**61.** **einflößen** = *to fill, to instill* Kann man jemand Schrecken einflößen mit dem Wort „Sozialismus"?

61. Is it possible to fill anyone with fright with the word "socialism"?	**62.** **das Gespenst** = *ghost, something to fear* Ist für manche das Wort „Sozialismus" ein Gespenst?
62. Is for some people the word "socialism" something to fear?	**63.** **zitieren** = *to call up* (also *to quote*) Zitiert man Gespenster, wenn man das Wort „Sozialismus" **benützt**? (*uses/used*)
63. Does one call up ghosts when one *uses* the word "socialism"?	**64.** Bismarck könnte das Register noch weiter vervollständigen.
64. Bismarck could complete the list still further.	**65.** Aber wenn man glaubt, mit dem Worte „Sozialismus" jemand Schrecken **einflößen zu können** oder Gespenster zu zitieren . . .
65. But if one believes *one can fill* someone with fright or call up ghosts with the word "socialism" . . .	**66.** **überwinden** = *to overcome* **habe überwunden** = __________
66. *have overcome*	**67.** **längst** = *long ago* Ich habe diesen Standpunkt längst überwunden.
67. I overcame this point of view long ago.	**68.** **die Wassergesetzgebung** = *the laws governing the use of water* **die Reichsgesetzgebung** = __________
68. *legislation governing the state*	**69.** **durchaus** = *completely* Diese **Überwindung** ist für die Reichsgesetzgebung durchaus notwendig.
69. This *overcoming* is absolutely necessary for state legislation.	**70.** So stehen Sie auf einem Standpunkt, den ich längst ganz überwunden habe.
70. Thus you hold a point of view which I completely overcame long ago.	**71.** Sie stehen auf einem Standpunkt, dessen Überwindung für die ganze Reichsgesetzgebung durchaus notwendig ist.
71. You hold a point of view, the overcoming of which is absolutely necessary for the whole state legislation.	**72.** **fähig** = *capable, able* Er ist nicht mehr fähig, das Land zu regieren.

72. He is no longer able to rule the country.	**73.** **leider** = *unfortunately* Leider **bringt** ein politisch starker Mann keinen fähigen Nachfolger in das Amt.
73. Unfortunately a politically strong man *does* not *bring* an able successor into office.	**74.** Leider **brachte** Bismarck keinen fähigen Menschen in das Amt.
74. Unfortunately Bismarck *did* not *bring* an able man into office.	**75.** **niederschlagen** = *to strike down* Diktatoren und Tyrannen schlagen alle Opposition nieder.
75. Dictators and tyrants strike down all opposition.	**76.** **der Erfolg** = *success* **zusammenbrechen** = *to break down* (intransitive) Die Opposition gegen Diktatoren, Tyrannen und erfolgreiche Politiker **bricht** fast immer schnell **zusammen.**
76. The opposition against dictators, tyrants, and successful politicians almost always *breaks down* quickly.	**77.** **zum Teil** = *to a degree* Die Opposition gegen Bismarck **brach** zum Teil **zusammen.**
77. To a degree, the opposition against Bismarck *broke down.*	**78.** Aber Bismarck **konnte** die Macht der katholischen Kirche und der Sozialisten nicht brechen.
78. But Bismarck *could* not break the power of the Catholic Church and the socialists.	

PROGRESS TEST

Can you identify the case of nouns, adjectives, and pronouns? Review those points that you miss before going on.

1. Das Auto **meiner Tante** ist toll.
(a) genitive singular (b) genitive plural

2. Das Auto **meiner Tanten** ist kaputt.
(a) genitive singular (b) genitive plural

3. Er ist am Ende **seiner Kraft.**
(a) genitive (b) dative

4. Keiner wird **der alten Frau** die Wahrheit sagen.
(a) nominative (b) genitive singular (c) genitive plural (d) dative

5. Was war **der große Fehler** der Zeit?
(a) nominative singular (b) genitive singular (c) genitive plural (d) accusative singular

6. Sozialistisch ist jede Expropriation zugunsten **der Eisenbahnen.**
(a) nominative singular (b) genitive singular (c) genitive plural (d) dative plural

7. Die Grundstücke werden **den anderen** gegeben.
(a) accusative singular (b) dative plural

8. Bismarck hat **den Standpunkt** längst überwunden.
(a) accusative singular (b) dative plural

9. Der Soldat **der Arbeit** kann nicht mehr.
(a) genitive singular (b) dative singular (c) genitive plural (d) nominative singular

10. Den guten Willen **der Arbeiter** soll man nicht verachten.
(a) genitive singular (b) dative singular (c) nominative plural (d) genitive plural

11. Was ist die Rolle ____ für Bismarck?
(a) der Sozialismus (b) dem Sozialismus (c) des Sozialismus (d) die Sozialisten

12. Sozialistisch war Herstellung ____ des Bauernstandes.
(a) des Freiheit (b) der Freiheit (c) die Freiheit (d) den Freiheit

13. Der Sozialismus gibt ____ das Land.
(a) die anderen (b) der andere (c) den anderen (d) des anderen

14. Ganz Deutschland sieht auf Preußens Liberalismus, nicht auf seine Kraft.
(a) Part of Germany likes Prussia's power.
(b) Part of Germany likes Prussia's liberalism.
(c) both of above
(d) none of above

15. Sozialistisch ist, wenn dem einen sein Grundstück genommen werden kann, weil es ein anderer schlechter bewirtschaften kann.
(a) Socialism means to give land to those who deserve it.
(b) Socialism gives land to those who cannot farm well.
(c) Socialism takes land from one individual and gives it to a good farmer.
(d) none

Answer key: **1.** (a); **2.** (b); **3.** (a); **4.** (d); **5.** (a); **6.** (c); **7.** (b); **8.** (a); **9.** (a); **10.** (d); **11.** (c); **12.** (b); **13.** (c); **14.** (d); **15.** (b).

Otto von Bismarck:
Aus Erklärungen in der Budgetkommission.

Wir haben zu heißes Blut, wir haben die Vorliebe, eine zu große Rüstung für unsern schmalen Leib zu tragen; nur sollen wir sie auch utilisieren. Nicht auf Preußens Liberalismus sieht Deutschland, sondern auf seine Macht; Bayern, Württemberg, Baden mögen dem Liberalismus indulgieren, darum wird ihnen doch keiner Preußens Rolle anweisen; Preußen muß seine Kraft zusammenfassen und zusammenhalten auf den günstigen Augenblick, der schon einige Male verpaßt ist; Preußens Grenzen nach den Wiener Verträgen sind zu einem gesunden Staatsleben nicht günstig; nicht durch Reden und Majoritätsbeschlüsse werden die großen Fragen der Zeit entschieden — das ist der große Fehler von 1848 bis 1849 gewesen — sondern durch Eisen und Blut . . .

Berlin, 30. September 1862

Aus einer Reichstagsrede

. . . Sozialistisch sind viele Maßregeln, die wir getroffen haben, die wir zum großen Heile des Landes getroffen haben, und etwas mehr Sozialismus wird sich der Staat bei unserem Reiche überhaupt angewöhnen müssen. . . . Sozialistisch war Herstellung der Freiheit des Bauernstandes; sozialistisch ist jede Expropriation zugunsten der Eisenbahnen; sozialistisch im höchsten Grade ist zum Beispiel die Kommassation, die Zusammenlegung der Grundstücke, die dem einen genommen werden — in vielen Provinzen ist das Gesetz — und dem anderen gegeben, bloß weil der andere sie bequemer bewirtschaften kann. . . . Das ist alles sozialistisch. Ich könnte das Register noch weiter vervollständigen; aber wenn Sie glauben, mit dem Worte „Sozialismus" jemand Schrecken einflößen zu können oder Gespenster zu zitieren, so stehen Sie auf einem Standpunkte, den ich längst überwunden habe und dessen Überwindung für die ganze Reichsgesetzgebung durchaus notwendig ist . . .

Berlin, 12. Juni 1882

Chapter Twelve

41. *Relative pronouns* **der** *and* **welcher**—*declension and usage*

1. The relative pronouns **der, die, das** are declined as follows:

	M	F	N	Pl	
N	**der**	**die**	**das**	**die**	*who, which, that*
G	**dessen**	**deren**	**dessen**	**deren**	*whose*
D	**dem**	**der**	**dem**	**denen**	(*to*) *whom, which, that*
A	**den**	**die**	**das**	**die**	*whom, which, that*

2. **Dessen, deren,** and **denen** are used as relative pronouns or demonstratives. **Der, die, das, den, dem** can be used as relative pronouns, definite articles, or demonstratives. (For demonstratives, see chapter 15.)

3. The relative pronouns **der, die, das** are quite easy to distinguish from the definite article because they introduce a relative clause which is set off by commas. The definite articles are almost always followed by a noun or an adjective plus noun to which they refer, in this case **Mann:**

***Der* Mann, *der* gestern hier war, ist mein Vater.**	***The*** *man* ***who*** *was here yesterday is my father.*

4. A relative pronoun agrees in gender and number with the noun to which it refers; its case is dependent upon its use in the clause:

Der Hund, *den* ich sehe, sitzt auf einem Stuhl.	*The dog **which** I see is sitting on a chair.*
Ich sehe den Hund, *der* auf einem Stuhl sitzt.	*I see the dog **which** is sitting on a chair.*

5. Relative clauses are dependent and therefore show dependent word order, i.e. the verb is to be found at the end of the clause:

Die Frau, mit *der* ich vor zwei Tagen in die Stadt *ging*, ist . . .	*The woman with **whom I went** to town two days ago is . . .*

The reading passage for this chapter is typical of a kind of scholarly German prose and its long and involved sentences. The following exercises give you practice in identifying the relative clauses. Give the correct meaning of the indicated words.

	1. Der Mann, **dem** er hilft, ist sein alter Vater. (*whom/the*)
1. The man *whom* he is helping is his old father.	**2.** Der Mann, **den** er vorige Woche sah, ist mein Bruder. (*the/whom/him*)
2. The man *whom* he saw last week is my brother.	**3.** Siehst du das Mädchen, mit **dem** er ins Kino geht? (*the/whom/it*)
3. Do you see the girl with *whom* he is going to the movies?	**4.** Das Mädchen, **das** jetzt ins Kino geht, ist ihre Schwester. (*the/who*)
4. The girl *who* is now going to the movies is her sister.	**5.** Das Mädchen, mit **dessen** Vater er ins Kino ging, ist eine gute Freundin von mir. (*those/whose*)
5. The girl with *whose* father he is going to the movies is a good friend of mine.	**6.** Die Frau, zu **der** der alte Mann geht, ist unsere Tante. (*whom/of the/the*)
6. The woman to *whom* the old man is going (*whom* the old man is going to visit) is our aunt.	**7.** **die Eltern** = *the parents* Eure Eltern, mit **denen** ihr immer ins Kino geht, sind nicht mehr so jung. (*those/whom/the*)

7. Your parents, with *whom* you always go to the movies, are not so young any more.	**8.** Er sieht ihre Eltern, **deren** Auto der Mercedes ist. (*whose/their*)
8. He sees her parents, who own the Mercedes (*whose* car the Mercedes is).	**9.** **haben gelesen** = *have read* Wir haben einige Gedanken aus Bismarcks Reden und Gesprächen gelesen.
9. We have read a few thoughts from Bismarck's speeches and conversations.	**10.** **haben besprochen** = *have discussed* Bismarcks Ideen, **die** wir besprochen haben, handeln von der Außen- und Innenpolitik. (*the/who/which*)
10. Bismarck's ideas *which* we have discussed deal with foreign and domestic affairs.	**11.** Wir wissen, **daß** viele Bismarck als Politiker kritisiert haben. (*the/that/which*)
11. We know *that* many (people) have criticized Bismarck the politician.	**12.** **das Erbe** = *legacy* Was war Bismarcks politisches Erbe?
12. What was Bismarck's political legacy?	**13.** **beurteilen** = *to evaluate* Max Weber, **der** als Sozialökonom und Soziologe weltbekannt ist, hat einmal Bismarcks politisches Erbe beurteilt.
13. Max Weber, *who* is world-famous as a social economist and sociologist, once evaluated Bismarck's political legacy.	**14.** **erziehen** = *to educate* ohne eine politische Erziehung = ________
14. without a political education.	**15.** **alle und jede** = *any kind of, all and every* **Die** Nation war ohne alle und jede politische Erziehung. (*the/who/which*)
15. *The* nation had absolutely no political education (was without any kind of political education).	**16.** Die Nation, **die** er hinterließ, war ohne alle und jede politische Erziehung. (*which/who*)
16. The nation *which* he left behind had absolutely no political education.	**17.** **erreichen** = *to achieve* **hatte erreicht** = *had achieved* Die Nation hatte ein hohes Niveau **der** politischen Erziehung erreicht. (*of/whose*)

17. The nation had achieved a high level *of* political education. (**Der** is here used as a genitive definite article.)	**18.** **vorher** = *previously* Die Nation hatte **zwanzig Jahre vorher** ein hohes Niveau der politischen Erziehung erreicht.
18. *Twenty years previously,* the nation had achieved a high level of political education.	**19.** **die Hinsicht** = *respect, regard* In dieser Hinsicht hatte **die** Nation vorher ein hohes Niveau erreicht. (*which/the/who*)
19. In this respect *the* nation had previously achieved a high level.	**20.** **bereits** = *already* Die Nation stand tief unter dem Niveau, **das** sie in dieser Hinsicht zwanzig Jahre vorher bereits erreicht hatte. (*who/which*)
20. The nation stood far below the level *which* in this respect it had achieved twenty years previously.	**21.** **sorgen** = *to be anxious, to take care* **besorgen** = *to take care of, to manage, to conduct* **Der** große Staatsmann besorgte für sie die Politik. (*who/which/the*)
21. *The* great statesman managed the political affairs for them.	**22.** **gewohnt** = *accustomed* Und vor allem **war** die Nation **gewohnt . . .** (*was accustomed/had accustomed*)
22. And above all the nation *was accustomed . . .*	**23.** **werde besorgen** = *would manage* Und vor allem war die Nation gewohnt, **daß** der große Staatsmann für sie die Politik schon besorgen werde. (*that/which/who*)
23. And above all the nation was accustomed (to the fact) *that* the great statesman would, no doubt, manage the political affairs for it. (**Werde** is a subjunctive form of the verb **werden.**)	**24.** **gefährlich** = *dangerous* Der große Staatsmann, **dessen** Politik so gefährlich ist für eine demokratische Nation . . . (*whose/of/that*)
24. The great statesman, *whose* political ideas are so dangerous for a democratic nation . . .	**25.** **die Spitze** = *top, point* Die Nation, an **deren** Spitze ein großer Staatsmann steht . . .
25. The nation at *whose* head (at the top *of which*) a great statesman stands . . .	**26.** An **ihrer** Spitze wird der große Staatsmann für sie die Politik schon besorgen. (*its/yours*)

26. At *its* head the great statesman will, no doubt, manage the political affairs for it (the nation).	**27.** **die Zügel** = *reins* Nach Bismarck nahmen Politiker ohne alle und jede Qualifikation die Zügel **der** Regierung in die Hand. (*of the/whose/that*)
27. After Bismarck politicians without any kind of qualification took the reins *of the* government into their hands.	**28.** **ergehen** = *to happen, to befall* **etwas über sich ergehen lassen** = *to bear something patiently* Die Nation läßt alles über sich ergehen.
28. The nation bears everything patiently (accepts patiently everything that happens to it).	**29.** Die Nation **ließ** fatalistisch **alles über sich ergehen.**
29. The nation fatalistically *bore everything patiently.*	**30.** **sich gewöhnen** = *to accustom oneself* **hatte sich gewöhnt** = *had accustomed itself* Die Nation, **die** sich daran gewöhnt hatte, alles über sich ergehen zu lassen . . .
30. The nation *that* had accustomed itself to bearing everything patiently . . .	**31.** **das Gefühl** = *state of mind* (also: *feeling, sentiment*) das monarchische Gefühl
31. the monarchical state of mind, sentiment in favor of the monarchy	**32.** **nutzen** = *to be of use* **benutzen** = *to use, to utilize* **die Benutzung** = ________
32. use, utilization	**33.** **mißbrauchen** = *to misuse* **mißbräuchlich** = *improper, wrong* **die mißbräuchliche Benutzung** des monarchischen Gefühls
33. *the improper use* of the monarchical state of mind	**34.** **die Folge** = *result, consequence* **als Folge** = *as a consequence* Als Folge **der** mißräuchlichen Benutzung **des** monarchischen Gefühls, ließ die Nation alles über sich ergehen. (*of the/whose/which*)
34. As a consequence *of the* improper use *of the* monarchical state of mind, the nation put up with everything.	**35.** **der Sessel** = *armchair, seat* Was für einen Sessel hat er?

35. What kind of a chair does he have?	**36.** **sich niederlassen** = *to settle down* Sie ließen sich auf Bismarcks Sessel nieder.
36. They settled down in Bismarck's seat.	**37.** **diejenigen** = *those* Diejenigen, **die** sich auf Bismarcks Sessel niederließen, nahmen die Zügel der Regierung in die Hand. (*those/who/they*)
37. Those *who* settled down in Bismarck's seat took the reins of the government in hand.	**38.** **leer** = *empty* **leerlassen** = *to leave empty* **leergelassen** = *vacated* Die Qualifikationen **derjenigen,** die sich auf Bismarcks leergelassenen Sessel niederließen . . . (*of those/to those*)
38. The qualifications *of those* who settled down in Bismarck's vacated seat . . .	**39.** **die Unbefangenheit** = *ease* . . . und mit Unbefangenheit die Zügel der Regierung in die Hand nahmen . . .
39. . . . and took the reins of the government into their hands with ease . . .	**40.** **nunmehr** = *now* Die Unbefangenheit, mit **der** sie nunmehr die Zügel der Regierung in die Hand nahmen . . . (*who/which/the*)
40. The ease with *which* they now took the reins of government into their hands . . .	**41.** **schwer** = *hard, heavy, great* **schwerst-** = __________
41. *hardest, heaviest, greatest*	**42.** **der Schaden** = *harm, damage* Wo liegt der schwerste Schaden?
42. Where is (lies) the greatest harm?	**43.** **an diesem Punkt** = *at this point, here* Der schwerste Schaden liegt an diesem Punkt.
43. The greatest harm is at this point.	**44.** **bei weitem** = *by far* An diesem Punkt lag **der** bei weitem schwerste Schaden. (*the/whose/it*)

44. Here lay by far *the* greatest harm.	**45.** Die Tradition, **die** Bismarck hinterließ, war überhaupt keine politische Tradition. (*the/which/it*)
45. The tradition *which* Bismarck left behind was not a political tradition at all.	**46.** **selbst** = *self* **stehen** = *to stand* **selbständig** = ________
46. *independent*	**47.** **innerlich** = *within* **innerlich selbständig** = ________
47. *independent from within, i.e. independent*	**48.** **der Kopf** = *head* Ein Diktator wünscht keine innerlich selbständigen Köpfe um sich zu haben.
48. A dictator does not wish to have independent heads (men) around him.	**49.** **tragen** = *to carry, to wear* **ertragen** = *to suffer, to tolerate* Ein Diktator erträgt keine innerlich selbständigen Köpfe.
49. A dictator does not put up with independent men.	**50.** **ziehen** = *to pull* **heranziehen** = *to draw upon* Er zieht auch keine innerlich selbständigen Köpfe heran.
50. Neither does he draw upon independent men.	**51.** **hatte herangezogen** = *had drawn upon* **hatte ertragen** = *nad tolerated* Der Diktator, **dem** die eigenen Ideen heilig waren, hatte innerlich selbständige Köpfe weder herangezogen noch ertragen. (*its/the/to whom*)
51. The dictator, *to whom* his own ideas were sacred, had neither drawn upon nor tolerated independent men (around him).	**52.** **vollends** = *entirely, in every way* Innerlich selbständige Köpfe und vollends Charaktere hatte er weder herangezogen, noch auch nur ertragen.
52. Spiritually independent men and in every way men of character he had neither drawn upon nor even tolerated.	**53.** **schätzen** = *to esteem, to value* Selbständige Köpfe und vollends Charaktere, **deren** innerliche Qualitäten Bismarck nicht schätzte . . . (*its/of the/whose*)

53. Independent men, and men of character *whose* spiritual qualities Bismarck did not esteem . . .	**54.** **der Stern** = *star* **der Unstern** = *unlucky star* der Unstern **der** Nation (*the/of the/whose*)
54. the unlucky star *of the* nation	**55.** **wollen** = *to want, to will* **hatte gewollt** = *had wanted, had willed* Der Unstern der Nation hatte dies gewollt.
55. The unlucky star of the nation had willed this.	**56.** **bescheiden** = *modest, moderate* Bismarcks Sohn hatte **wahrlich** bescheidene staatsmännische Qualitäten. (*wrongly/truly*)
56. Bismarck's son had *truly* modest qualities of statesmanship.	**57.** **überschätzen** = *to overestimate* Bismarck überschätzte die wahrlich bescheidenen staatsmännischen Qualitäten **des** eigenen Sohnes. (*of his/whose/that*)
57. Bismarck overestimated the truly modest qualities of statesmanship *of his* own son.	**58.** **erstaunen** = *to be astonished* **erstaunlich** = ________
58. *astonishing, amazing, marvellous*	**59.** Bismarck überschätzte **erstaunlich** die wahrlich bescheidenen staatsmännischen Qualitäten des eigenen Sohnes.
59. Bismarck overestimated *to a surprising degree* the truly modest qualities of statesmanship of his own son.	**60.** **besitzen** = *to have, to own* Bismarck besaß einen Sohn, **dessen** wahrlich bescheidene staatsmännische Qualitäten er erstaunlich überschätzte. (*whose/its/of the*)
60. Bismarck had a son *whose* truly modest qualities of statesmanship he overestimated to a surprising degree.	**61.** **rasend** = *mad, furious* Ist er **denn** rasend? (intensifier/*for*)
61. intensifier Is he mad?	**62.** **der Argwohn** = *suspicion* Bismarck hatte einen rasenden Argwohn auf alle Persönlichkeiten . . .
62. Bismarck had a mad (uncontrollable) suspicion of all individuals . . .	**63.** **denken** = *to think* **denkbar** = *thinkable, possible* Das ist **überhaupt** nicht denkbar!

63. That is not *at all* possible!	**64.** **folgen** = *to follow, to obey* **nachfolgen** = *to follow, to succeed* **der Nachfolger** = ________
64. *successor*	**65.** **der Verdacht** = *suspicion* Bismarck hatte alle denkbaren Nachfolger in Verdacht.
65. Bismarck was suspicious of all possible successors.	**66.** Denkbare Nachfolger waren Bismarck verdächtig.
66. Possible successors were suspect to Bismarck.	**67.** **irgendwie** = *in any way* Der rasende Argwohn auf alle Persönlichkeiten, **die** Bismarck irgendwie als denkbare Nachfolger verdächtig waren . . . (*the/they/who*)
67. The mad suspicion of all individuals *who* were in any way suspect to Bismarck as possible successors . . .	**68.** **überdies** = *besides* Und der Unstern der Nation hatte überdies gewollt . . .
68. And the unlucky star of the nation had wished besides . . .	**69.** **neben** = *in addition, besides* . . . daß Bismarck neben seinem rasenden Argwohn auf alle Persönlichkeiten . . .
69. . . . that Bismarck in addition to his mad suspicion of all individuals . . .	**70.** **. . . die** ihm irgendwie als denkbare Nachfolger verdächtig waren . . . (*what/that/who*)
70. . . . *who* were in any way suspect to him as possible successors . . .	**71.** **. . . auch noch** einen Sohn besaß . . .
71. . . . *also* possessed a son . . .	**72.** **. . . dessen** wahrlich bescheidene staatsmännische Qualitäten er erstaunlich überschätzte. (*of his/whose/of that*)
72. . . . *whose* truly modest qualities of statesmanship he overestimated to a surprising degree.	

Since there is much new vocabulary in this section, review and learn the new words carefully before continuing.

PROGRESS TEST

Choose the answers that describe the italicized word. There are two correct answers for each question.

1. Bismarck hinterließ eine Nation, *die* ohne alle und jede politische Erziehung war.
(a) singular (b) plural (c) nominative (d) accusative

2. Der Unstern der Nation, *der* dies gewollt hat . . .
(a) nominative (b) genitive (c) singular (d) plural

3. Die staatsmännischen Qualitäten des eigenen Sohnes, *die* Bismarck überschätzte . . .
(a) singular (b) plural (c) nominative (d) accusative

4. Die Spitze der Nation, an *der* der große Staatsmann für sie die Politik schon besorgen werde . . .
(a) nominative (b) genitive (c) dative (d) singular (e) plural

5. Er hinterließ eine Nation, *deren* Parlament völlig machtlos war.
(a) singular (b) plural (c) dative (d) genitive

6. Er hinterließ Probleme, *deren* Lösung nicht so einfach war.
(a) singular (b) plural (c) genitive (d) nominative (e) dative

7. Bismarcks Sessel, auf *den* sie sich niederließen . . .
(a) singular (b) plural (c) dative (d) accusative

8. Das monarchische Gefühl, *dem* man alles verdanken kann . . .
(a) singular (b) plural (c) dative (d) accusative (e) genitive

Answer key: **1.** (a, c); **2.** (a, c); **3.** (b, d); **4.** (c, d); **5.** (a, d); **6.** (b, c); **7.** (a, d); **8.** (a, c).

42. *Welcher, welche, welches as relative pronouns*

1. **Welcher, welche,** and **welches** may be used as relative pronouns. Each may variously mean *who, which,* or *that*. They are declined as follows:

	M	F	N	Pl
N	**welcher**	**welche**	**welches**	**welche**
G	**dessen**	**deren**	**dessen**	**deren**
D	**welchem**	**welcher**	**welchem**	**welchen**
A	**welchen**	**welche**	**welches**	**welche**

2. There is no genitive form of the relatives **welcher, welche, welches.** Therefore, the genitive forms of the relative **der** are used.

3. The meanings and usage of **welcher, welche,** and **welches** as relative pronouns are the same as for the relatives **der, die, das.** They may refer either to persons or things:

Der Mann, *welcher* eben hier war . . .	*The man* ***who*** *was just here . . .*
Das Auto, *welches* wir gesehen haben . . .	*The automobile* ***which*** *we saw . . .*

4. You have already encountered forms of **welch-** (*which/what*) in previous chapters. The interrogative **welch-,** commonly called a **der** word, will be explained in chapter 15. It acts as an adjective and precedes the noun it modifies:

Welches **Haus ist es?**	***Which*** *house is it?*
Welcher **Bruder wohnt da?**	***Which*** *brother lives there?*

The following sentences include vocabulary and phrases you have already encountered. Give the meanings of the indicated words as you read them.

	1. Max Weber, **welcher** als Soziologe und Sozialökonom weltbekannt ist . . . (*which/who*)
1. Max Weber, *who* is world-famous as a sociologist and social economist . . .	**2.** **herrschen** = *to rule, to govern* **beherrschen** = *to rule, to govern* Das monarchische Gefühl, mit **welchem** ein starker Staatsmann eine Nation beherrschen kann . . . (*whom/which*)
2. The monarchical state of mind with *which* a strong statesman is able to rule a nation . . .	**3.** Diejenigen, **welche** sich nunmehr auf Bismarcks leergelassenen Sessel niederließen . . . (*which/who*)
3. Those *who* now settled on Bismarck's vacated seat . . .	**4.** . . . und mit erstaunlicher Unbefangenheit die Zügel der Regierung in die Hand nahmen . . .
4. . . . and with astonishing ease took the reins of the government into their hands . . .	**5.** Die Nation lag tief unter dem Niveau, **welches** sie zwanzig Jahre vorher bereits erreicht hatte. (*which/whom*)
5. The nation lay far below the level *which* it had already achieved twenty years previously.	**6.** **regieren** = *to rule* **die Regierung** = ________

6. the government	**7.** Die Zügel, mit **welchen** Bismarck nunmehr die Regierung in die Hand nahm . . . (*whom/which*)
7. The reins with *which* Bismarck now took the government into his hands . . .	**8.** Alle Persönlichkeiten, **welche** Bismarck irgendwie als denkbare Nachfolger verdächtig waren . . . (*what/which/who*)
8. All the individuals *who* were in any way suspect to Bismarck as possible successors . . .	**9.** **die Firma** = *business, establishment, firm* **unter der Firma** = *under the style of, under the leadership of* Die Firma der „monarchischen Regierung", unter **welcher** die Nation nunmehr alles über sich ergehen läßt . . .
9. The leadership of the "monarchical government", under *which* the nation patiently bears everything . . .	**10.** **hegen** = *to cherish, to entertain* (*a feeling*) Als Folge der mißbräuchlichen Benutzung des Gefühls, **welches** die Nation für die Monarchie hegte . . . (*whom/which*)
10. As a consequence of the misuse (improper use) of the sentiment *which* the nation felt towards the monarchy . . .	**11.** **wirken** = *to effect, to influence* Das politische Erbe Bismarcks, **welches** weiter auf die deutsche Nation wirkte . . . (*which/who*)
11. Bismarck's political heritage, *which* further influenced the German nation . . .	**12.** Die politische Tradition, **welche** der große Staatsmann hinterließ . . . (*dative/accusative*)
12. accusative The political tradition *which* the great statesman left behind (bequeathed) . . .	**13.** Die politische Qualifikation, mit **welcher** er das Land irgendwie regieren wollte . . . (*nominative/dative*)
13. dative The political qualification with *which* he somehow wanted to govern the country . . .	**14.** Der große Staatsmann, von **welchem** das Volk alles erwartete . . . (*dative/nominative*)
14. dative The great statesman, from *whom* the people expected everything . . .	**15.** Neben seinem rasenden Argwohn auf alle Persönlichkeiten, **welche** ihm irgendwie als denkbare Nachfolger verdächtig waren . . . (*which/whom*)

15. Besides his uncontrollable distrust of all individuals *whom* he in any way suspected to be possible successors . . .	**16.** **Welchen** Staatsmann meinen Sie? (*interrogative/relative*)
16. interrogative *Which* statesman do you mean?	**17.** Ist der Unstern, **welchen** Weber meint, Bismarck? (*relative/interrogative*)
17. relative Is Bismarck the unlucky star *which* Weber means?	**18.** Das monarchische Gefühl, **welches** der Diktator irgendwie mißbrauchte . . . (*relative/interrogative*)
18. relative The monarchical sentiment, *which* the dictator somehow misused . . .	**19.** **Welches** Gefühl mißbraucht jeder Diktator? (*relative/interrogative*)
19. interrogative *Which* feeling does every dictator misuse?	**20.** Die Nation, **welche** Weber meint, ist Deutschland. (*relative/interrogative*)
20. relative The nation *which* Weber refers to is Germany.	**21.** **Welche** politische Tradition herrscht nunmehr in den Vereinigten Staaten? (*interrogative/relative*)
21. interrogative *Which* political tradition rules at the present time in the United States?	**22.** Die Firma der monarchischen Regierung, unter **welcher** die Nation leidet . . . (*whom/which*)
22. The leadership of the monarchical government under *which* the nation suffers . . .	**23.** Der große Staatsmann, von **welchem** das Volk alles erwartete . . . (*dative/nominative*)
23. dative The great statesman, from *whom* the people expected everything . . .	

PROGRESS TEST

A. *Give the meaning of the indicated word.*

1. Bismarck, *dessen* Parlament völlig machtlos war . . .
(a) who (b) of that (c) which (d) whose

2. Die Nation, an *deren* Spitze ein Diktator saß . . .
(a) which (b) whose (c) that (d) whom

3. Dagegen hinterließ er ein Parlament, mit *welchem* man unzufrieden war.
(a) which (b) what (c) whom (d) that

4. Der schwerste Schaden, *welchen* der große Staatsmann hinterließ . . .
(a) whom (b) what (c) to which (d) that

B. *Choose all the answers that describe the italicized word.*

1. Innerlich selbständige Köpfe und vollends Charaktere, *welche* Bismarck weder herangezogen noch auch nur ertragen hatte . . .
(a) feminine (b) plural (c) singular (d) nominative (e) accusative

2. Die Firma der monarchischen Regierung, unter *welcher* die Nation fatalistisch über sich ergehen ließ . . .
(a) feminine (b) singular (c) plural (d) nominative (e) dative

3. Der politische Wille einer Nation, ohne *welchen* ein Volk völlig machtlos ist . . .
(a) singular (b) plural (c) dative (d) accusative

4. Alle Persönlichkeiten, *welchen* er verdächtig war . . .
(a) singular (b) plural (c) dative (d) accusative

Answer key: A. **1.** (d); **2.** (b); **3.** (a); **4.** (d)
B. **1.** (b, e); **2.** (a, b, e); **3.** (a, d); **4.** (b, c).

43. *Wer, was, and wo used as relatives*

1. Wer appears in indefinite relative clauses and is translated *he who* or *whoever* (see also chapter 8). It does not have an antecedent:

Wer **kein Geld hat, darf nicht mit.**	***Whoever*** *has no money may not go along.*

2. Was is used similarly when no antecedent exists and is translated *whatever:*

Was **nicht gut ist, ist schlecht.**	***Whatever*** *is not good is bad.*

3. After the following neuter antecedents **was** may be translated as *that,* or it may be left untranslated:

Alles, was **er sagt . . .**	*All (that) he says . . .*
Nichts, was **er sagt . . .**	*Nothing (that) he says . . .*
Vieles, was **er sagt . . .**	*Much (that) he says . . .*
Etwas, was **er sagt . . .**	*Something (that) he says . . .*
Manches, was **er sagt . . .**	*Many a thing (that) he says . . .*
Einiges, was **er sagt . . .**	*Some things (that) he says . . .*
Ich gab ihm ***das Beste, was*** **ich hatte.**	*I gave him the best (that) I had.*

4. When **was** sums up or derives a conclusion from another clause, translate it as *a fact which* or *a thing that:*

Er hielt es aus, *was* ich eigentlich nicht verstehen kann.	*He endured it,* ***a fact which*** *I really cannot understand.*

5. **Was** when referring to the thought of a previous clause is best translated *which:*

Wir fahren morgen nach München, *was* uns sehr erfreut.	*We will travel to Munich tomorrow,* ***which*** *makes us very happy.*

6. **Wo** used as a relative is translated *in which, where,* or *when:*

Ich kannte die Straße nicht, *wo* wir uns trafen.	*I did not know the street* ***where (in which)*** *we met.*
Zu der Zeit, *wo* ich in Berlin wohnte . . .	*At the time* ***when*** *I lived in Berlin . . .*

As you read the following sentences give the meanings of the indicated words.

	1. **hinnehmen** = *to accept* **Wer** das Böse ohne Widerspruch hinnimmt, arbeitet in Wirklichkeit mit ihm zusammen. (Martin Luther King) (*who/where/whoever*)
1. *Whoever* accepts evil without protest, in reality is working together with it.	**2.** **Wer** seine Zeit recht sehen will, soll sie von Ferne betrachten. (Ortega y Gasset) (*he who/who/where*)
2. He *who* wants to see his age in the right perspective (accurately), should look at it (view it) from a distance.	**3.** **Was** er immer sagt, ich kann es nicht glauben. (*what/whatever*)
3. *Whatever* he says, I cannot believe it. (**Immer** is used as an intensifier.)	**4.** **Was** das Gefühl der Macht erhöht, ist gut. (*what/whatever*)
4. *Whatever* increases (heightens) the feeling of power is good.	**5.** **hatte gemacht** = *had made* Und Gott sah an alles, **was** er gemacht hatte; und siehe da, es war sehr gut. (Bibel) (*what/that*)

5. And God looked at everything *that* he had created (made) and behold, it was very good.	**6.** Einiges, **was** der Unstern der Nation gewollt hatte, ging in Erfüllung. (*whatever/that*)
6. Some of the things *that* the unlucky star of the nation had willed came true (were fulfilled).	**7.** **beschließen** = *to decide, to resolve* Die Nation ließ fatalistisch über sich ergehen, **was** man über sie beschloß. (*that which/what*)
7. The nation fatalistically accepted *that which* was decided (one decided) for it.	**8.** Bismarck hinterließ ein völlig machtloses Parlament, **was** Max Weber richtig verstand. (*what/that/a fact which*)
8. Bismarck left behind a completely powerless parliament, *a fact which* Max Weber accurately understood.	**9.** Bismarcks politisches Erbe war eine Nation ohne alle und jede politische Erziehung, **was** für Deutschland kein Glück war. (*what/a fact which*)
9. Bismarck's political heritage was a nation without any kind of political education, *a fact which* was unfortunate for Germany.	**10.** **der Sinn** = *meaning, sense* **Sinn haben** = *to make sense* Zwei Soldaten kamen und ergriffen den Zivilisten, **was** für Kafka keinen Sinn hatte.
10. Two soldiers came and seized the civilian, *which* to Kafka did not make sense.	**11.** Die Schwachen und Mißratenen sollen zugrunde gehen, **was** heute undenkbar ist. (*which/what*)
11. The weaklings and misfits are to perish, *which* today is unthinkable.	**12.** Ich kenne das Haus nicht mehr, **wo** wir uns zum erstenmal sahen. (*where/who*)
12. I no longer know the house *where* we saw each other for the first time.	**13.** Das ist die Stadt, **wo** er immer noch wohnt. (*in which/who*)
13. That is the city *in which* he is still living.	

PROGRESS TEST

Now test yourself with the following exercises.

1. **die Wolke** = *cloud*
Wer viel verspricht, und hält nicht, der ist wie Wolken und Wind ohne Regen. (Die Sprüche Salomos 25, 14)
(a) where (b) he who (c) when (d) which

2. *Was* das Gefühl der Macht erhöht, ist gut.
(a) that (b) where (c) whatever (d) who

3. Nichts, *was* Gott machte, war böse.
(a) that (b) whatever (c) who (d) where

4. Bismarcks Sohn hatte nur bescheidene staatsmännische Qualitäten, *was* Bismarck nicht wußte.
(a) what (b) that (c) whom (d) a fact that

5. Ich kenne das Haus nicht mehr, *wo* wir uns zum erstenmal sahen.
(a) where (b) why (c) who (d) which

6. Einiges, *was* der Unstern gewollt hatte . . .
(a) who (b) which (c) what (d) whom

Answer key: **1.** (b); **2.** (c); **3.** (a); **4.** (d); **5.** (a); **6.** (b).

44. *Da- and wo- compounds*

1. **Wo-** (**wor-** before a vowel) compounds are contractions of **wo** (*where*) and a preposition. They refer only to things and may be used as interrogatives in direct questions or as relatives:

Womit **schreiben Sie?**	***What*** *are you writing* ***with?***
Der Bleistift, *womit* (*mit dem, mit welchem*) ich schreibe, ist meiner.	*The pencil* ***with which*** *I am writing is mine.*

2. When used interrogatively **wo(r)-** is best translated *what*. When used as a relative it means *which* and should then follow the preposition when you are translating:

Wovon **spricht er?**	***What*** *is he talking* ***about?***
Das Buch, *wovon* er spricht, ist schon ausverkauft.	*The book* ***of which*** *he speaks is already sold out.*

3. **Da-** (**dar-** before a vowel) compounds are contractions of **da** (*there*) and a preposition. These contractions refer to prepositions plus nouns or pronouns of any gender as long as they are things or ideas:

Der Mensch besteht aus Fleisch und Bein.	*Man consists of flesh and bone.*
Er besteht *daraus*.	*He consists **of that**.*
Karl-Heinz steht vor dem Haus.	*Karl-Heinz is standing in front of the house.*
Er steht *davor*.	*He is standing **in front of** (**before**) **it**.*
Sehen Sie meine Bücher? Was halten Sie *davon?*	*Do you see my books? What do you think **of them?***

Note: **da(r)-** can be translated as *it, that,* or *them.*

4. A **da(r)-** compound may refer to a dependent clause which follows it. In this case the compound may or may not be translated:

Er glaubt fest *daran*, daß der Mensch auch einen Geist besitzt.	*He believes firmly* (***in the fact***, ***in the following***) *that man also possesses a spirit.*

5. **Damit** may be either a subordinating conjunction (*so that*) or a **da-** compound (*with that, with it, with them*):

Geben Sie mir den Ball, *damit* ich ihn werfen kann!	*Give me the ball **so that** I can throw it!*
***Damit* kann ich spielen.**	*I can play **with that**.*

Give the meaning of the indicated words.

	1. **Woran** war die Nation gewöhnt? (*to what/to whom*)
1. *What* was the nation accustomed *to*?	**2.** Eine Nation, **daran** gewöhnt, unter der Firma der „monarchischen Regierung" fatalistisch über sich ergehen zu lassen . . . (*to that/need not be translated*)
2. need not be translated A nation, accustomed to fatalistically letting everything happen under the leadership of the "monarchical government" . . .	**3.** Eine politische Tradition **dagegen** hinterließ Bismarck überhaupt nicht. (*on the other hand/against it*)

3. *On the other hand,* Bismarck did not leave behind a political tradition at all.	**4.** **Woraus** besteht eine politische Tradition? (*of whom/of what*)
4. *What* does a political tradition consist *of*?	**5.** Die Firma der „monarchischen Regierung", **worunter** die Nation damals litt . . . (*under whom/under which*)
5. The leadership of the "monarchichal government" *under which* the nation then suffered . . .	**6.** **Darunter** darf man nicht mehr leiden. (*from that/under that*)
6. One must not suffer *from that* any more. (Remember that **nicht dürfen** means *must not.*)	**7.** Die erstaunliche Unbefangenheit, **womit** Bismarcks Nachfolger die Zügel der Regierung in die Hand nahmen . . . (*with what/with which*)
7. The astonishing ease *with which* Bismarck's successors took the reins of government into their hands . . .	**8.** Das Volk hatte nichts **dagegen,** daß man über sie beschloß, was man wollte. (*on the other hand/against the fact that*)
8. The people had nothing *against the fact that* whatever was wanted was decided for them. (lit.: . . . the fact that one decided for them whatever one wanted.)	**9.** Wollen wir **damit** anfangen? (*with that/so that*)
9. Do we want to begin *with that*?	**10.** **entfernen** = *to remove* Bismarck entfernte alle innerlich selbständigen Köpfe, **damit** er allein regieren konnte. (*with that/so that*)
10. Bismarck removed all the spiritually independent men, *so that* he could govern alone.	**11.** **die Gewalt** = *power, force, might* **gewaltig** = *enormous, powerful, mighty* **das gewaltige Prestige** = _________
11. *the enormous prestige*	**12.** **das Ergebnis** = *result* **Was** war das Ergebnis Bismarcks gewaltigen Prestiges? (*whatever/that/what*)
12. *What* was the result of Bismarck's enormous prestige?	**13.** **gegenüber** = *opposite* (*to*), *in relation to, opposed* (*to*) **demgegenüber** = *as opposed to that, on the other hand* Demgegenüber hinterließ Bismarck ein völlig machtloses Parlament.

13. On the other hand, Bismarck left behind a completely powerless parliament.	**14.** **rein** = *purely* (*pure*) Ein völlig machtloses Parlament war das rein negative Ergebnis **seines** gewaltigen Prestiges. (*of his/of its*)
14. A completely powerless parliament was the purely negative result *of his* enormous prestige.	**15.** **nun** = *well!, then* (also: *now*) (**nun,** an interjection, need not be translated in this example) Demgegenüber nun als ein rein negatives Ergebnis seines gewaltigen Prestiges hinterließ Bismarck ein völlig machtloses Parlament.
15. On the other hand, Bismarck left behind as a purely negative result of his enormous prestige a completely powerless parliament.	

PROGRESS TEST

Choose the correct meaning of the italicized words. If you miss any, review the grammar point in question before going on.

1. *Womit* regiert ein Diktator?
   (a) to whom (b) to where (c) with what (d) who
2. Die Regierung, *worunter* die Nation damals litt . . .
   (a) under them (b) under that (c) under this (d) under which
3. Wollen wir *damit* anfangen?
   (a) so that (b) with which (c) with whom (d) with that
4. *Daran* kann man sehen, daß er ein innerlich selbständiger Kopf ist.
   (a) in the following (b) by that (c) towards what (d) to that
5. Sie tun das, *damit* sie ihm nicht irgendwie als denkbare Nachfolger verdächtig werden.
   (a) with that (b) so that (c) therewith (d) in the following
6. Er besteht *darauf*, daß sein Sohn die Regierung übernehmen wird.
   (**bestehen auf** = *to insist*)
   (a) on top of it (b) thereupon (c) need not be translated (d) thereby

Answer key: **1.** (c); **2.** (d); **3.** (d); **4.** (b); **5.** (b); **6.** (c).

Max Weber: „Die Erbschaft Bismarcks" in: *Gesammelte Politische Schriften.* Verlag J. C. B. Mohr (Paul Siebeck), Tübingen, 1958.

Max Weber: Die Erbschaft Bismarcks

Was war infolgedessen . . . BISMARCKS politisches Erbe? Er hinterließ eine Nation ohne alle und jede politische Erziehung, tief unter dem Niveau, welches sie in dieser Hinsicht zwanzig Jahre vorher bereits erreicht hatte. Und vor allem [hinterließ er] eine Nation ohne allen und jeden politischen Willen, gewohnt, daß der große Staatsmann an ihrer Spitze für sie die Politik schon besorgen werde. Und ferner, als Folge der mißbräuchlichen Benutzung des monarchischen Gefühls . . . [hinterließ er] eine Nation, [die] daran gewöhnt [war], unter der Firma der „monarchischen Regierung" fatalistisch [alles] über sich ergehen zu lassen, was man über sie beschloß, ohne Kritik an der politischen Qualifikation derjenigen, welche sich nunmehr auf BISMARCKS leergelassenen Sessel niederließen und mit erstaunlicher Unbefangenheit die Zügel der Regierung in die Hand nahmen. An diesem Punkt lag der bei weitem schwerste Schaden. Eine politische Tradition dagegen hinterließ der große Staatsmann überhaupt nicht. Innerlich selbständige Köpfe und vollends Charaktere hatte er weder herangezogen, noch auch nur ertragen. Und der Unstern der Nation hatte überdies gewollt, daß er [Bismarck] neben seinem rasenden Argwohn auf alle Persönlichkeiten, die ihm irgendwie als denkbare Nachfolger verdächtig waren, auch noch einen Sohn besaß, dessen wahrlich bescheidene staatsmännische Qualitäten er erstaunlich überschätzte. Demgegenüber nun als ein rein negatives Ergebnis seines gewaltigen Prestiges [hinterließ er]: ein völlig machtloses Parlament.

Chapter Thirteen

45. *Past participles—recognition*

1. The past participle is generally recognized by a **ge-** prefix and an **-(e)t** or **-en** suffix attached to the stem. Weak verb past participles end in **-(e)t:**

antworten	— **geantwort*et***	*to answer*	— *answer**ed***
rauchen	— **gerauch*t***	*to smoke*	— *smok**ed***

Strong verb past participles end in **-en.** In addition, the stem vowel will generally change:

singen	— **ges*ung*en**	*to sing*	— *sung*
sterben	— **gest*o*rb*en***	*to die*	— *died*
schlafen	— **geschl*a*f*en***	*to sleep*	— *slept*

2. Haben, sein, and **werden** have the following past participles:

gehabt (*had*), **gewesen** (*been*), **geworden** (*become*)

3. Irregular weak verb past participles are recognized by a **ge-** prefix, a **-t** suffix, and also a stem vowel change:

brennen	— **gebr*a*nn*t***	*to burn*	— *burned*
kennen	— **gek*a*nn*t***	*to know*	— *known*

4. The **ge-** prefix of separable prefix verbs is found between the separable prefix and the stem:

aussehen	— **aus*ge*sehen**	*to appear*	— *appeared*
einsetzen	— **ein*ge*setzt**	*to put in*	— *put in*

5. Inseparable prefix verbs take no **ge-** prefix; however, they do take an **-(e)t** or **-en** suffix:

verbinden	— **verbunden**	*to unite*	— *united*
zerstören	— **zerstört**	*to destroy*	— *destroyed*

6. Verbs ending in **-ieren** also take no **ge-** prefix. The suffix will always be **-t:**

studieren	— **studier*t***	*to study*	— *studied*
organisieren	— **organisier*t***	*to organize*	— *organized*

7. Remember that **ge-** may also be an inseparable prefix. Therefore, not all verbs with a **ge-** prefix will be past participles:

gehören	— **gehört**	*to belong*	— *belonged*
gelingen	— **gelungen**	*to succeed*	— *succeeded*
geschehen	— **geschehen**	*to happen*	— *happened*

The purpose of this exercise is to familiarize you with the forms of the past participle.

	1. **wagen** = *to dare* **gewagt** = ________
1. dared	**2.** **zweifeln** = *to doubt* **gezweifelt** = ________
2. doubted	**3.** **schreien** = *to cry* **geschrieen** = ________
3. cried	**4.** **ziehen** = *to pull* **gezogen** = ________
4. pulled	**5.** **wenden** = *to turn* **gewandt (gewendet)** = ________
5. turned	**6.** **denken** = *to think* **gedacht** = ________

6. thought	**7. schwanken** = *to sway* **geschwankt** = ________
7. swayed	**8. bringen** = *to bring* **gebracht** = ________
8. brought	**9. schaffen** = *to create* **geschaffen** = ________
9. created	**10. rasieren** = *to shave* **rasiert** = ________
10. shaved	**11. telefonieren** = *to telephone* **telefoniert** = ________
11. telephoned	**12. ausbrechen** = *to break out* **ausgebrochen** = ________
12. broken out	**13. ausrotten** = *to exterminate* **ausgerottet** = ________
13. exterminated	**14. genießen** = *to enjoy* **genossen** = ________
14. enjoyed	**15. sich entscheiden** = *to decide* **entschieden** = ________
15. decided	**16. telegrafieren** = *to send a telegram* **telegrafiert** = ________
16. sent a telegram	**17. beleidigen** = *to insult* **beleidigt** = ________
17. insulted	**18. abändern** = *to alter* **abgeändert** = ________
18. altered	

46. *The present perfect tense—recognition, meaning, and word order*

1. The present tense of **haben** or **sein** plus the past participle identifies the present perfect tense:

Ich *habe* das gestern *gesagt.*	*I* ***said*** *that yesterday.*
Georg *ist* bei uns *geblieben.*	*George* **has remained (remained)** *with us.*

2. The meaning of the present perfect tense may be expressed in one of two ways, depending on the context:

Ich *habe* vier Jahre lang *studiert.*	*I* ***attended the university*** *for four years.* (event ended in the past)
Ihr *seid* aber groß *geworden!*	*You* ***have gotten*** *tall!* (action began in the past and its effects are related to the present)
Sie *haben* mich schon oft *besucht.*	*You* ***have*** *often* ***visited*** *me.* (intermittent action in the past continuing up to the present)

However, if the past continues *unchanged* into the present, with the prospect of continuing into the future, then the present tense is required in German, usually adding **seit** (*since*) and/or **schon** (*already*), **erst** (*only*), or similar expressions:

Er *raucht* schon lange.	*He* ***has been smoking*** **(*has smoked*)** *for a long time* (with the prospect of continuing).
Er *raucht* erst seit letzten Sonntag.	*He* ***has*** *only* ***been smoking*** *since last Sunday.*

3. Whereas English uses only the verb *to have* as an auxiliary, German calls for the verb **sein** when the verb is intransitive and shows motion, or a change of position or condition. **Sein** and **bleiben** also take **sein** as an auxiliary:

Wie weit *ist* er *gefahren?*	*How far* ***did*** *he* ***drive?***
Marie *ist* gestern in die Stadt *geritten.*	*Marie* ***rode*** *into town yesterday.*
Er *ist* vor einer Woche *gestorben.*	*He* ***died*** *a week ago.*
Wie lange *sind* Sie da *geblieben?*	*How long* ***did*** *you* ***stay*** *there?*

4. The past participle is generally found at the end of the clause. If the word order is normal or inverted, the past participle will be the final word of the clause:

Der Mann mit dem schwarzen Bart *hat* sein Brot *gegessen.*	*The man with the black beard* ***ate*** *his bread.*
Bist* du gestern in die Stadt *gegangen?	***Did*** *you* ***go*** *to town yesterday?*

A past participle may, however, be the first word of a clause for purposes of contrast:

Er *hat* das nicht *gesagt*.	*He **did** not **say** that.*
***Gesagt hat* er das nicht, aber *gedacht hat* er es bestimmt.**	*He **did** not **say** that, but he certainly **thought** it.*

If the word order is dependent, **haben** or **sein** will be the final element in the clause, and the past participle will immediately precede the auxiliary:

Ich weiß, wie lange du *geschlafen hast*.	*I know how long you **slept**.*
Daß ihr groß *geworden seid*, sehe ich schon.	*I can see that you **have gotten** tall.*

5. Occasionally the past participle of the inseparable prefix verb will be the same as a form from another tense:

Past: **Wir waren traurig, als wir unsere Bücher *verloren*.**	*We were sad when we **lost** our books.*
Present perfect: **Wir *haben* unsere Bücher *verloren*.**	*We **lost (have lost)** our books.*
Present: **Klaus, der die Frage *beantwortet*, ist mein Freund.**	*Klaus, who **is answering** the question, is my friend.*
Present perfect: ***Hat* Klaus die Frage *beantwortet?***	***Has** Klaus **answered** the question?*

6. The inseparable prefix **ge-** may be mistaken for the **ge-** of the past participle if word order is forgotten or the auxiliary is overlooked:

Present: **Ich weiß, daß das Buch mir *gehört*.**	*I know that the book **belongs** to me.*
Present perfect: **Er *hat* das Auto auf der Straße *gehört*.**	*He **heard** the car in the street.*

7. The past participle of a verb ending in **-ieren** may be mistaken for a similar present tense form. The presence or absence of an auxiliary will indicate the tense:

Was *hat* er auf der Universität *studiert?*	*What **did** he **study** at the university?*
Wissen Sie, ob er Deutsch *studiert?*	*Do you know if he **is studying** German?*

The purpose of these frames is to help you to recognize the present perfect tense as well as to introduce you to the reading passage.

	1. Im letzten Kapitel **haben** wir **gelesen,** was Weber über Bismarck sagte. (*read/have read*)

1. In the last chapter we *read* what Weber said about Bismarck.	**2.** Sie **haben** sicher einmal von Oswald Spengler **gehört.** (*have heard/heard*)
2. You *have* certainly *heard* of Oswald Spengler at some time or another.	**3.** Oswald Spengler **hat** von 1880 bis 1936 **gelebt.** (*has lived/lived*)
3. Oswald Spengler *lived* from 1880 to 1936.	**4.** **das Land** = *country* **der Morgen** = *morning* **das Morgenland** = *the orient, the East* **der Abend** = *evening* **das Abendland** = _________
4. *the occident, the West*	**5.** **der Untergang** = *(down) fall, decline* Das größte Werk, das er **geschrieben hat,** heißt *Der Untergang des Abendlandes.* (*wrote/has written*)
5. The greatest work that he *wrote* is called *The Decline of the West.*	**6.** **behaupten** = *to claim* Was **behauptet** Spengler in diesem Werk?
6. What *does* Spengler *claim* in this work?	**7.** **erleben** = *to experience* Unsere westliche Zivilisation erlebt jetzt einen Untergang.
7. Our western civilization is now experiencing a decline.	**8.** In diesem Werk **hat** Spengler **behauptet,** daß unsere westliche Zivilisation jetzt den Untergang erlebt. (*claimed/claims*)
8. In this work Spengler *claimed* that our western civilization is now experiencing its decline.	**9.** **erreichen** = *to reach* Unsere Kultur, unsere Zivilisation **hat** jetzt ihren Winter **erreicht.** (*reaches/has reached*)
9. Our culture, our civilization *has* now *reached* its winter.	**10.** **erscheinen** = *to appear* *Der Untergang des Abendlandes* **ist** zwischen den Jahren 1918 und 1922 **erschienen.**
10. *The Decline of the West appeared* between 1918 and 1922.	**11.** Spengler **hat** andere Bücher **geschrieben.**
11. Spengler *wrote* other books.	**12.** **die Entscheidung** = *decision* Eins heißt *Jahre der Entscheidung.*

12. One is called *Years of Decision.*	**13.** **der Gedanke** = *thought* Hier sind einige Gedanken **daraus.** (*of that/from it*)
13. Here are some ideas *from it.*	**14.** **das Tier** = *animal* **rauben** = *to rob* **das Raubtier** = _________
14. *wild animal, beast of prey*	**15.** **der Abschnitt** = *section* In einem Abschnitt seines Buches behauptet Spengler, daß der Mensch ein Raubtier ist.
15. In one section of his book Spengler claims that man is a beast of prey.	**16.** **ob** = *if* Er fragt nicht, ob der Mensch immer ein Raubtier **gewesen ist.**
16. He does not ask if man *has* always *been* a beast of prey.	**17.** **geschehen** = *to happen* Wenn ein Unglück **geschieht,** sagt Spengler . . .
17. Whenever an accident *happens,* says Spengler . . .	**18.** **die Tugend** = *virtue* **der Tugendbold** = *paragon of virtue* (ironical) . . . so laufen alle Tugendbolde und Sozialethiker auf der Straße zusammen.
18. . . . then all the paragons of virtue and social moralists congregate in the street.	**19.** **genießen** = *to enjoy* Sie genießen etwas auf der Straße, meint Spengler.
19. Spengler feels that they enjoy something in the street.	**20.** Die Tugendbolde und Sozialethiker genießen **dasselbe** auf der Straße . . . (*the same thing/themselves*)
20. The paragons of virtue and the social moralists enjoy in the street *the same thing* . . .	**21.** **das Blatt** = *leaf, leaflet, paper, magazine* . . . was sie im Film und in den illustrierten Blättern **genossen haben.**
21. . . . as (what) they *have enjoyed* in the movies and in the magazines.	**22.** Warum laufen sie auf der Straße zusammen, wenn ein Unglück **geschehen ist?**
22. Why do they run and gather in the street when an accident *has happened*?	**23.** **erregen** = *to excite, stir up, to stimulate* Weiß man, was ihre Nerven **erregt hat**?

23. Does one know what *stirred* them up (literally: excited their nerves)?	**24.** Spengler will sagen, daß diese Tugendbolde und Sozialethiker nur Raubtiere sind . . .
24. Spengler wishes to say that these paragons of virtue and social moralists are only beasts of prey . . .	**25.** **sich erregen** = *are stirred up* . . . und nur **darum** erregen sich ihre Nerven. (*around that/for that reason*)
25. . . . and only *for that reason* are their their nerves stirred up.	**26.** **beleidigen** = *to offend, to insult* Spengler fragt: Wenn ich den Menschen ein Raubtier nenne, wen **habe** ich damit **beleidigt,** den Menschen — oder das Tier?
26. Spengler asks: When I call man a beast of prey, whom *do* I *insult* by doing so, men—or animals?	**27.** **die Schlacht** = *battle* **die Schlächterei** = *slaughter* Er meint, daß die Tugendbolde und Sozialethiker nichts gegen die Schlächtereien der Bolschewisten **gehabt haben.**
27. He feels that the paragons of virtue and the social moralists *had* nothing against (didn't object to) the Bolshevist slaughters.	**28.** **die Tatsache** = *fact* **die Urtatsache** = *original fact* Er behauptet auch, daß der Kampf die Urtatsache des Lebens ist.
28. He also claims that struggle is the original fact of life.	**29.** Der Kampf ist die Urtatsache des Lebens, ist das Leben selbst.
29. Struggle is the original fact of life, is life itself.	**30.** **die Lust** = *joy, pleasure* Er sagt, daß der Pazifist die Lust daran nicht ganz **ausgerottet hat.** (*has rotted out/has extinguished*)
30. He says that the pacifist *has* not quite *extinguished* his enjoyment of it.	**31.** **gelingen** = *to succeed* Das gelingt den Pazifisten nicht.
31. The pacifists do not succeed in that. (Note the use of the dative with the impersonal verb.)	**32.** **der Jammer** = *misery* **jämmerlich** = *miserable, wretched* Es gelingt dem jämmerlichsten Pazifisten nicht . . .
32. The most wretched pacifist does not succeed . . .	**33.** Es **ist** auch dem jämmerlichsten Pazifisten nicht **gelungen,** die Lust an dem Kampf in seiner Seele ganz auszurotten, sagt Spengler.

33. Spengler says, not even the most wretched pacifist *has succeeded* in completely extinguishing the enjoyment of struggle in his soul.	

PROGRESS TEST

Give the meaning of the italicized verbs.

1. Weiß Helene, wie das Buch heißt, das Spengler *geschrieben hat?*
(a) has scribbled (b) wrote (c) writes (d) is writing

2. Das Werk *ist* im Jahre 1922 *erschienen.*
(a) has appeared (b) is shining (c) appeared (d) is appearing

3. Wissen Sie, wie lange sie schon auf der Straße *laufen?*
(a) have laughed (b) have been running (c) are running (d) are laughing

4. Wem *hat* Klaus das Buch *gebracht?*
(a) did bring (b) has broken (c) needed (d) did break

5. Vor wie langer Zeit *ist* Spengler *gestorben?*
(a) is dying (b) did die (c) is dead (d) has died

Answer key: **1.** (b); **2.** (c); **3.** (b); **4.** (a); **5.** (b).

47. *The past perfect tense—recognition and meaning*

1. The past perfect tense is formed by the past tense of **haben** or **sein** plus the past participle. As in English, it expresses an action or describes a situation which took place before another given or implied action or situation in the past:

Ich *hatte* fünf Jahre lang *studiert*, als . . .	*I **had attended** the university for five years when . . .*
Sie *hatte* schon lange Zigarren *geraucht*.	*She **had smoked** cigars for a long time.*
Wir *waren* noch nie in Österreich *gewesen*.	*We **had** never **been** in Austria.* (**noch** intensifies **nie**)
Wart* ihr aber groß *geworden!	***Had** you ever **gotten** tall!*
Hatten* sie es *gehabt?	***Had** they **had** it?*
Waren* Sie vorher mit dem Zug *gefahren?	***Had** you **travelled** by train before?*

2. Uses of the auxiliary and word order are the same as for the present perfect tense.

3. The German past tense used with **seit** and/or **schon** is translated by the English past perfect progressive:

Er *rauchte schon seit* zwei Jahren, als er plötzlich Krebs bekam.	*He **had been smoking for** two years when he suddenly got cancer.*

These frames will help you recognize the past perfect tense.

	1. Die Tugendbolde und Sozialethiker **haben** alle anderen **gehaßt.**
1. The paragons of virtue and social moralists *hated* all others.	**2.** **der Angriff** = *attack* Die Tugendbolde und Sozialethiker **hatten** andere wegen der Angriffe **gehaßt.**
2. The paragons of virtue and social moralists *had hated* others because of attacks.	**3.** **vermeiden** = *to avoid* Sie **hatten** selbst die Angriffe weislich **vermieden.**
3. They themselves *had* prudently *avoided* (making) attacks.	**4.** Sie **können** es nicht **vermeiden,** ein Buch über Kriege zu lesen.
4. They *can*not *avoid* reading a book about wars.	**5.** **schwach** = *weak* Sie **waren** zu schwach **gewesen,** um ein Buch über Kriege zu lesen.
5. They *had been* too weak to read a book about wars.	**6.** **wagen** = *to dare* Sie **hatten** es nicht mehr **gewagt,** auf der Straße zusammenzulaufen.
6. They *had* no longer *dared* to gather in the street any more.	**7.** Was **war** er immer wieder **geworden**?
7. What *had* he *become* again and again?	**8.** **die Trümmer** = *fragments, ruins* Die Städte liegen in Trümmern.
8. The cities are in ruins.	**9.** **altgeworden** = (*had*) *become old, ancient* Die Städte altgewordener Kulturen **waren** in Trümmer **gesunken.**
9. The cities of ancient cultures *had sunk* into ruins.	**10.** **edel** = *noble* **Ist** der Mensch schon immer edel **gewesen?** (*was/has been*)
10. *Has* man always *been* noble?	**11.** **das Geschöpf** = *creature* **Waren** die großen Raubtiere edle Geschöpfe **gewesen?**

11. *Had* the great beasts of prey *been* noble creatures?	**12.** **entrüsten** = *to provoke* **sich entrüsten** = *to become indignant* **entrüstet** = ________
12. *indignant*	**13.** Die Tugendbolde und Sozialethiker **sind entrüstet.** (*are indignant/have grown indignant*)
13. The paragons of virtue and social moralists *are indignant.*	**14.** **morden** = *to murder* Ein Lustmörder ist jemand, **der** aus sexueller Lust mordet. (*the/who*)
14. A *Lustmörder* is someone *who* murders because of sexual desire.	**15.** **hinrichten** = *to execute* Wenn der Staat einen Lustmörder **hingerichtet hatte . . .**
15. Whenever the state *had executed* a sex murderer . . .	**16.** Die Sozialethiker **waren** immer entrüstet **gewesen,** wenn der Staat einen Lustmörder **hingerichtet hatte.**
16. The social moralists *had* always *been* indignant whenever the state *had executed* a sex murderer.	**17.** **fahren** = *to drive, to travel* **erfahren** = *to experience, to find out about, to hear about* Was **haben** sie **erfahren**?
17. What *did* they *find out*?	**18.** **heimlich** = *secretly* Was **haben** sie heimlich **genossen**?
18. What *did* they secretly *enjoy*?	**19.** **gegen** = *against, toward* **der Gegner** = *opponent* Aber sie **hatten** es heimlich **genossen,** wenn sie den Mord an einem politischen Gegner erfuhren.
19. But they *had* secretly *enjoyed* it whenever they heard of the murder of a political opponent.	**20.** Auch dem jämmerlichsten Pazifisten **war** es nicht **gelungen,** die Lust daran in seiner Seele ganz auszurotten.
20. Even the most pitiable pacifist *had* not *succeeded* in completely extinguishing the enjoyment of it in his soul.	

PROGRESS TEST

A. *Choose the correct meaning of the italicized words.*

1. Der Mensch *ist* immer ein Raubtier *gewesen.*
(a) has been (b) had been (c) is becoming (d) is
2. Was *war* aus Karl *geworden?*
(a) had become (b) was becoming (c) did become (d) became
3. Seine ganze Familie *ist* nach Europa *gefahren.*
(a) is travelling (b) travelled (c) had travelled (d) is to travel
4. Alle Pazifisten *sind entrüstet.*
(a) have run away (b) are arming (c) are indignant (d) have prepared

B. *And now choose the infinitive for the indicated verb.*

1. Sie haben alle anderen *gehaßt.*
(a) haben (b) heißen (c) haßten (d) hassen
2. Es war ihnen nicht *gelungen.*
(a) gelangen (b) gelungen (c) gelingen (d) geliehen
3. Vor wie langer Zeit ist er *gestorben?*
(a) sterben (b) starben (c) streben (d) gestorben
4. Wann ist Spenglers Buch *erschienen?*
(a) erschienen (b) erschien (c) erscheinen (d) scheinen

Answer key: A. **1.** (a); **2.** (a); **3.** (b); **4.** (c);
B. **1.** (d); **2.** (c); **3.** (a); **4.** (c).

48. *Modals—past participle, conjugation in the present perfect and past perfect tenses*

1. The past participles of the modals are as follows:

dürfen	**gedurft**
können	**gekonnt**
mögen	**gemocht**
müssen	**gemußt**
sollen	**gesollt**
wollen	**gewollt**

Note the disappearance of the umlaut and also the change of the **-g** of **mögen** to the **-ch** of **gemocht.**

2. All modals are conjugated with the auxiliary **haben** in the present perfect and past perfect tenses. They follow the same rules of word order as previously outlined:

Er ***hat*** **das** ***gedurft.***	*He* ***was permitted*** *(to do) that.*
Vater wußte, daß er das immer ***gewollt hatte.***	*Father knew that he* ***had*** *always* ***wanted*** *(to do) that.*

3. More often modals are used with another verb, resulting in the so-called *double infinitive construction* which will be explained in chapter 14:

Georg ***hat*** **sein Auto** ***verkaufen müssen.***	*George* ***had to sell*** *his car.*

The purpose of these exercises is to familiarize you with the past participle forms of the modal auxiliaries. **Sollen** *and* **müssen** *are not represented as they are rarely used in this manner.*

	1. **Haben** sie das wirklich **gewollt**? (*did want/had wanted*)
1. *Did* they really *want* that?	**2.** Alle Sozialethiker **hatten** das **gewollt.** (*have wanted/had wanted*)
2. All the social moralists *had wanted* that.	**3.** Ihr **habt** es nicht mehr **gekonnt.** (*could/had been able to*)
3. You *could* not do it any more.	**4.** Daß ihr es **gekonnt hattet,** wußte ich gar nicht. (*was able/had been able*)
4. I didn't know that you *had been able* (to do) that.	**5.** Er **hatte** alle Gegner des Pazifismus nicht **gemocht,** aber . . . (*has . . . liked/had . . . liked*)
5. He *had* not *liked* all the opponents of pacifism, but . . .	**6.** **Hat** er das immer noch **gemocht**? (*does like/did like*)
6. *Did* he still *like* that?	**7.** Ich **hatte** das nicht **gedurft,** aber du **hast** es doch **gedurft.**
7. I *had* not *been allowed* (to do) that, but you *were* (*allowed*).	

READING PREPARATION

Give the meaning of the following sentences.

	1. **zurückkehren** = *to return* Wir werden **jetzt** zu dem zurückkehren, was Spengler über Tugendbolde und Sozialethiker schrieb. (*now/never*)

1. We will *now* return to what Spengler wrote about paragons of virtue and social moralists.	**2.** Spengler **wird** es immer wieder sagen: Der Mensch ist ein Raubtier. (*will/become*)
2. Spengler *will* say it again and again: Man is a beast of prey.	**3.** **gelangen** = *to reach, to attain* Aber der Sozialethiker will zur Macht gelangen.
3. But the social moralist wants to attain power.	**4.** **darüber hinaus** = *above and beyond that* Der Mensch ist ein Raubtier. Der Sozialethiker **will** darüber hinaus gelangen.
4. Man is a beast of prey. The social moralist *wants to* rise above and beyond that.	**5.** **der Zahn** = *tooth* All die Tugendbolde und Sozialethiker haben Zähne.
5. All paragons of virtue and social moralists have teeth.	**6.** **ausbrechen** = *to break out* All die Tugendbolde und Sozialethiker haben **ausgebrochene** Zähne. (*broken/break out*)
6. All paragons of virtue and social moralists have *broken* teeth.	**7.** All die Tugendbolde und Sozialethiker, **die** darüber hinaus sein oder gelangen wollen . . .
7. All the paragons of virtue and social moralists *who* want to be above that or get past that . . .	**8.** . . . sind nur Raubtiere mit **ausgebrochenen** Zähnen.
8. . . . are merely beasts of prey with *broken* teeth.	**9.** Welche Leute sind nur Raubtiere mit ausgebrochenen Zähnen?
9. Which people are merely beasts of prey with broken teeth?	**10.** All die Tugendbolde und Sozialethiker, **die** darüber hinaus sein oder gelangen wollen, sind nur Raubtiere mit ausgebrochenen Zähnen.
10. All the paragons of virtue and social moralists *who* claim to be beyond that or want to rise above it, are simply beasts of prey with broken teeth.	**11.** **ansehen** = *to look at* Seht **sie** doch an! (*she/them*)
11. Look at *them*! (**Seht . . . an!** is the imperative form of **ihr** (you).)	**12.** Warum laufen die Tugendbolde und Sozialethiker auf der Straße zusammen, wenn ein Unglück **geschehen ist**?

12. Why do the paragons of virtue and social moralists gather on the street when an accident *has occurred*?	**13.** **das Geschrei** = *shouting, screams* Sie laufen auf der Straße zusammen, um **ihre** Nerven an dem Blut und Geschrei zu erregen. (*her/their*)
13. They run together in the street in order to excite *their* nerves with the blood and the screams.	**14.** Was tun sie, wenn sie auch das nicht mehr **wagen** können? (*dare/are able*)
14. What do they do when they cannot *dare* to do that any more?	**15.** **vollkommen** = *perfect* Die großen Raubtiere sind vollkommene Geschöpfe.
15. The great beasts of prey are perfect creatures.	**16.** **die Art** = *way, manner* Die großen Raubtiere sind edle Geschöpfe in vollkommenster Art.
16. The great beasts of prey are noble creatures in the most perfect way.	**17.** **schwach** = *weak* **die Schwäche** = __________
17. *weakness*	**18.** Ist der Mensch nur aus Schwäche moralisch?
18. Is man moral only out of weakness?	**19.** **lügen** = *to lie* **verlogen** = *lying, untruthful* **die Verlogenheit** = __________
19. *untruthfulness, lying*	**20.** Sind die großen Raubtiere ohne die Verlogenheit menschlicher Moral aus Schwäche?
20. Are the great beasts of prey without the hypocrisy of human morality (that results) from weakness?	**21.** Die Sozialethiker und Tugendbolde sind entrüstet, wenn ein Lustmörder hingerichtet **wird.** (*will/is*)
21. The social moralists and paragons of virtue are indignant when a sex murderer *is* executed.	**22.** **Was für ein** politischer Gegner ist er?
22. *What kind of* a political opponent is he?	**23.** Sind sie entrüstet, wenn sie den Mord an einem politischen Gegner erfahren?

23. Are they indignant when they hear about the murder of a political opponent?	**24.** Sie sind nicht entrüstet, sie genießen es heimlich, wenn sie den Mord an einem politischen Gegner erfahren.
24. They are not indignant, they secretly enjoy it, when they hear about the murder of a political opponent.	**25.** **mögen** = *to like* **möchten** = *would like* Was möchte theoretisch auch der jämmerlichste Pazifist?
25. What would theoretically even the most pitiable pacifist like?	**26.** **der Kampf** = *battle* **kämpfen** = *to fight* **bekämpfen** = ________
26. *to combat, to fight against*	**27.** **vernichten** = *to annihilate, to exterminate* Möchte er alle Gegner **des** Pazifismus bekämpfen und vernichten? (*the/of*)
27. Would he like to fight against and exterminate all the opponents *of* pacifism?	**28.** **wenig** = *little* **minder** = *less* **mindest** = *least* **zum mindesten** = ________
28. *at least*	**29.** Zum mindesten möchte der Pazifist alle Gegner des Pazifismus bekämpfen und vernichten.
29. The pacifist would at least like to fight against and exterminate all the opponents of pacifism.	**30.** *Vom* ***Sinn*** *der Geschichte* (*sin/meaning*)
30. *Of the Meaning of History*	**31.** Man weiß wenig von den Ereignissen der Zukunft.
31. One knows little of the events of the future.	**32.** Deshalb kann man nur glauben.
32. Therefore one can only believe.	**33.** **so wenig . . . so sicher** = *as little as . . . nonetheless certain* So wenig man von der Zukunft weiß, so sicher ist es, daß . . .
33. As little as one knows of the future, it is nonetheless certain . . .	**34.** So wenig man von den Ereignissen der Zukunft weiß, so sicher ist es, daß . . .

34. As little as one knows of the events of the future, it is nonetheless certain that . . .	**35.** . . . die bewegenden Mächte der Zukunft keine anderen sind **als die** der Vergangenheit. (*as the/than those*)
35. . . . the moving powers of the future are none other *than those* of the past.	**36.** Was sind die bewegenden Mächte der Zukunft und der Vergangenheit?
36. What are the moving forces of the future and the past?	**37.** **besitzen** = *to possess, to own* **der Besitz** = *possession* Die bewegenden Mächte sind **die:** der Wille des Stärkeren, die gesunden Instinkte, die Rasse, der Wille zu Besitz. (*the/these*)
37. The moving forces are *these:* the will of the stronger man, healthy instincts, race, the will to possession.	**38.** **wirken** = *to work, to effect, to act* **die Wirkung** = *action, effect* **wirkungslos** = __________
38. *ineffectual, futile*	**39.** **darüber hin** = *over that* (*them*), *above that* (*above them*) Und darüber hin schwanken wirkungslos die Träume . . .
39. And over them (i.e. over these moving forces) those dreams sway ineffectually . . .	**40.** Und darüber hin schwanken wirkungslos die Träume, die immer Träume bleiben **werden . . .** (*will/become*)
40. And above them those dreams waver ineffectually which *will* always remain dreams . . .	**41.** Und darüber hin schwanken wirkungslos die Träume, die immer Träume bleiben werden: Gerechtigkeit, Glück und Friede.
41. And above the moving forces of the future and the past, those dreams waver ineffectually which will always remain dreams: justice, happiness, and peace.	**42.** *Vom Schicksal*
42. *Of Fate*	**43.** Nur wenige Genies **haben** die Welt **bewegt.**
43. Only a few geniuses *have moved* (changed) the world.	**44.** **der Zufall** = *fate, chance* Der Zufall **hat** sie an ihren Platz **gestellt.**
44. Chance *put* them in the right place at the right time (literally: at their place).	**45.** **gering** = *small, low, unimportant* Meist **waren es** viel geringere Personen, die der Zufall an ihren Platz stellte.

45. Usually *they were* much less important people whom chance put in the right place.	**46.** *Von der* ***Seele*** *des Menschen* (*soul/seal*)
46. *Of the Soul of Man*	**47. zweifeln an** + dative = *to doubt* Die Seele des Menschen zweifelt an allem.
47. The soul of man doubts everything.	**48.** Der **Jüngling** weiß alles. (*teacher/youth*)
48. *Youth* knows everything.	**49. der Greis** = *der alte Mann* Der Greis weiß nichts.
49. The old man knows nothing.	**50. wissen** = *to know* **die Gewißheit** = *certainty* **Erst** der Greis kommt zur Gewißheit, daß er nichts weiß. (*first/only*)
50. It is *only* the old man who becomes certain (lit.: Only the old man comes to a certainty) that he knows nothing.	**51. die Ehe** = *marriage* *Von der Ehe*
51. *Of Marriage*	**52.** Dieser Mann und diese Frau **haben** eine glückliche Ehe **gehabt.**
52. This man and this woman *have had* a happy marriage.	**53.** Was ist eine Ehe, in der Kinder nicht gewünscht oder nicht vermißt **werden**? (*will/are/become*)
53. What is a marriage in which children *are* not desired or missed?	**54. der Junggeselle** = *bachelor* **Sie** ist ein Konkubinat eines männlichen und weiblichen Junggesellen. (*she/it*)
54. *It* is a concubinage of a male and a female bachelor.	**55. das Ziel** = *goal* *Von dem Ziel*
55. *Of Goals*	**56.** Ein Ziel ist eine Ende.
56. A goal is an end.	**57. die Leere** = *emptiness* Der schöpferische Mensch kennt und fürchtet die Leere.

57. The creative individual knows and fears emptiness.	**58.** **vollenden** = *to complete* **die Vollendung** = *completion* Die Leere folgt auf die Vollendung eines Werkes.
58. Emptiness follows the completion of a work.	**59.** **deshalb** = *therefore* Soll deshalb jeder wirklich schöpferische Mensch fürchten, ein Ziel zu haben?
59. Should therefore every really creative person be afraid of having a goal?	

PROGRESS TEST

Choose the correct meaning. Before continuing, review the points you miss.

1. Sie laufen auf der Straße zusammen, *denn sie sind zu schwach,* Raubtiere mit ausgebrochenen Zähnen zu sehen.
(a) For they are too weak.
(b) Because they want to watch.
(c) Then they are to attack.
(d) Than those that are clean.

2. Denn die großen Tiere sind edle Geschöpfe *in vollkommenster Art* und ohne die Verlogenheit menschlicher Moral aus Schwäche.
(a) Perfectly artful.
(b) In a welcome form.
(c) In the most popular manner.
(d) In the most perfect way.

3. Die jämmerlichsten Pazifisten haben nichts gegen die Schlächtereien der Bolschewisten, denn *sie genießen es heimlich,* wenn sie den Mord an einem politischen Gegner erfahren.
(a) They soon learn of it.
(b) They reject it openly.
(c) They secretly enjoy it.
(d) They find it intolerable.

4. Man beleidigt den Menschen, wenn man die Raubtiere Menschen nennt.
(a) To call man an animal is an insult to all.
(b) To call beasts of prey humans is an insult to the animal.
(c) To call beasts of prey humans is an insult to humans.
(d) To call animals beasts of prey is an insult to them.

5. Die Urtatsache des Lebens ist, daß man die Angriffe anderer weislich vermeiden soll.
(a) The life of a hermit is what one should always avoid.
(b) It is a wise person who avoids the attacks of others.

(c) The basic fact of life is that one should defend onself wisely against another's fury.
(d) The attacks of others should not deter one from seeking the basic facts about life.

6. Die bewegenden Mächte der Zukunft sind genau wie die der Vergangenheit.
(a) Past and future governments will be the same.
(b) The past and the present determine the future.
(c) The moving forces of the past are the same as those of the present.
(d) The future and the past are governed by the same powers.

Answer key: **1.** (a); **2.** (d); **3.** (c); **4.** (c); **5.** (b); **6.** (d).

From *Jahre der Entscheidung. Erster Teil. Deutschland und die weltgeschichtliche Entwicklung.* C. H. Beck'sche Verlagsbuchhandlung, München, 1933.

Oswald Spengler: Jahre der Entscheidung

Der Mensch ist ein Raubtier. Ich werde es immer wieder sagen. All die Tugendbolde und Sozialethiker, die darüber hinaus sein oder gelangen wollen, sind nur Raubtiere mit ausgebrochenen Zähnen, die andere wegen der Angriffe hassen, die sie selbst weislich vermeiden. Seht sie doch an: sie sind zu schwach, um ein Buch über Kriege zu lesen, aber sie laufen auf der Straße zusammen, wenn ein Unglück geschehen ist, um ihre Nerven an dem Blut und Geschrei zu erregen, und wenn sie auch das nicht mehr wagen können, dann genießen sie es im Film und in den illustrierten Blättern. Wenn ich den Menschen ein Raubtier nenne, wen habe ich damit beleidigt, den Menschen — oder das Tier? Denn die großen Raubtiere sind edle Geschöpfe vollkommenster Art und ohne die Verlogenheit menschlicher Moral aus Schwäche.

Sie schreien: Nie wieder Krieg! — aber sie wollen den Klassenkampf. Sie sind entrüstet, wenn ein Lustmörder hingerichtet wird, aber sie genießen es heimlich, wenn sie den Mord an einem politischen Gegner erfahren. Was haben sie je gegen die Schlächtereien der Bolschewisten einzuwenden gehabt? Nein, der Kampf ist die Urtatsache des Lebens, ist das Leben selbst, und es gelingt auch dem jämmerlichsten Pazifisten nicht, die Lust daran in seiner Seele ganz auszurotten. Zum mindesten theoretisch möchte er alle Gegner des Pazifismus bekämpfen und vernichten.

From *Gedanken.* C. H. Beck'sche Verlagsbuchhandlung, München, 1941.

Vom Sinn der Geschichte

So wenig man von den Ereignissen der Zukunft weiß . . . so sicher ist es, daß die bewegenden Mächte der Zukunft keine anderen sind als die der Vergangenheit: der Wille des Stärkeren, die gesunden Instinkte, die Rasse, der Wille zu Besitz und Macht. Und darüber hin schwanken wirkungslos die Träume, die immer Träume bleiben werden: Gerechtigkeit, Glück und Friede.

Vom Schicksal

Unter den weltbewegenden Personen sind nur sehr wenige Genies, und nur wenige der Genies haben die Welt bewegt: meist waren es viel geringere Personen, die der Zufall an ihren Platz stellte.

Von der Seele des Menschen

Der Jüngling weiß alles. Der Mann zweifelt an allem. Erst der Greis kommt zur Gewißheit, daß er nichts weiß.

Von der Ehe

Eine Ehe, in der Kinder nicht gewünscht oder nicht vermißt werden, ist ein Konkubinat eines männlichen und weiblichen Junggesellen.

Von dem Ziel

Ein Ziel ist ein Ende . . . Jeder wirklich schöpferische Mensch kennt und fürchtet die Leere, die auf die Vollendung eines Werkes folgt.

Chapter Fourteen

49. *Double infinitive construction*

1. The double infinitive construction consists of the infinitive of a modal or other helping verb plus an infinitive expressing the action of the sentence. It occurs in the present perfect, past perfect, or future tense. It occurs when another verb is dependent upon a modal in one of these tenses:

Ihr *habt* es *tun können.*	*You have been able to do it.*
Hatte* er in die Stadt *fahren dürfen?	*Had he been allowed to drive to the city?*
Wer *wird* morgen *gehen müssen?*	*Who will have to go tomorrow?*

2. In the present perfect and past perfect tenses the meaning of the second infinitive is usually expressed in English by the simple past or a past participle:

Er *hat* den Film *sehen wollen.*	*He wanted (has wanted) to see the movie.*

Remember that the present perfect tense is often translated by the English past tense:

Er *hat tanzen wollen.*	*He wanted to dance.*

In this example the **hat wollen** was translated as *wanted,* to which the dependent infinitive was appended.

3. The double infinitive construction is usually the last element in the sentence, no matter what the word order:

Normal word order:

Ihr *habt* das *sagen dürfen.* — *You were allowed (have been allowed) to say that.*

Inverted word order:

Haben* sie das *singen können? — *Were they able (Have they been able) to sing that?*

Dependent word order:

Karin weiß, daß Jörg das *wird tun müssen.* — *Karin knows that Jörg will have to do that.*

4. The verb **lassen** is also commonly used in double infinitive constructions. It has the following meanings:

(a) *to let (to permit, to allow)*

Blaubart *hat* seine Bräute nicht *weglaufen lassen.* — *Bluebeard did not let his brides run away.*

(b) *to leave*

Helmut *hatte* seinen Mantel bei mir *hängen lassen.* — *Helmut had left his coat hanging at my house.*

(c) *to have something done, to cause, to make*

Der König *wird* den Koch die Suppe *bringen lassen.* — *The king will have the cook bring the soup.*

5. Several other verbs appear in double infinitive constructions, among which are:

brauchen	*to need*
heißen	*to order, to bid*
helfen	*to help*
hören	*to hear*
sehen	*to see*

Er *hatte* nicht *zu gehen brauchen.* (Note that **brauchen** requires the use of **zu.**) — *He had not needed to go.*

Er *hat* seine Sekretärin ins Büro *kommen heißen.* — *He had his secretary come into his office.*

Sie *hatte* ihn *kommen hören.* — *She had heard him come* (or *coming*).

Hat* der Alte die fliegende Untertasse wirklich *vorbeisausen sehen? — *Did the old man really see the flying saucer whiz by?*

The purpose of the following exercises is to give you practice in distinguishing the various tenses of the double infinitive construction. Give the meaning of the underlined verbs.

	1. **die Brücke** = *bridge* Sie **hat** ihn über die Brücke **kommen sehen.**
1. She *saw* him *come* over the bridge.	2. Sie **hatte** ihn über die Brücke **kommen sehen.**
2. She *had seen* him *come* over the bridge.	3. Sie **wird** ihn über die Brücke **kommen sehen.**
3. She *will see* him *come* over the bridge.	4. **Hat** Hans Sauerkraut nicht mehr **essen wollen**?
4. *Did*n't Hans *want to eat* any more sauerkraut?	5. **Hatte** er Sauerkraut nicht mehr **essen wollen?**
5. *Had*n't he *wanted to eat* sauerkraut any more?	6. **Wird** er Sauerkraut nicht mehr **essen wollen**?
6. *Won't* he *want to eat* sauerkraut any more?	7. **Hat** Ekkehardt den Brief **lesen dürfen**?
7. *Was* Ekkehardt *allowed to read* the letter?	8. **Hatte** er den Brief nicht **zu lesen brauchen?**
8. *Had* he not *needed to read* the letter?	9. **Wird** er den Brief nicht **zu lesen brauchen?**
9. *Will* he not *need to read* the letter?	10. Ich weiß, daß Inge **hat schwimmen können.**
10. I know that Inge *was able to swim.*	11. Ich weiß, daß Inge damals **hatte schwimmen dürfen.**
11. I know that at the time Inge *had been allowed to swim.*	12. Ich weiß, daß Inge am Montag **wird schwimmen wollen.**
12. I know that on Monday Inge *will want to swim.*	13. Der Polizist **hat** mich **gehen heißen.**
13. The policeman *ordered* me *to go.*	14. Ich **werde** den Soldaten nicht **gehen heißen.**
14. I *will* not *order* the soldier *to go.*	15. **der Anzug** = *suit* Er **hat** sich einen neuen Anzug **machen lassen.**

15. He *had* a new suit *made*.	**16.** Rudi **hat** das Mädchen **warten lassen.**
16. Rudi *made* the girl *wait* (*kept* the girl *waiting*).	**17.** **eilig** = *in a hurry* Sie hatte es eilig, darum **hat** sie alles **stehen-** und **liegenlassen.**
17. She was in a hurry; therefore she *left* everything just as it was (*standing* and *lying*). (Note that here the two infinitives are joined together.)	**18.** Sie **hat** den Jungen nicht näher **kommen lassen.**
18. She *did* not *let* the boy *come* any closer.	

PROGRESS TEST

Choose the correct meaning.

1. Was hatte sie den Mann essen sehen?
   (a) What did she see eating the man?
   (b) What had seen it eating the man?
   (c) What had she seen the man eating?
   (d) What had seen the man eating it?
2. Wird Ingeborg Franz das wirklich sagen hören?
   (a) Is Ingeborg really heard saying that to Franz?
   (b) Will Ingeborg truly hear Franz say that?
   (c) Will Franz truly say that Ingeborg should hear that?
   (d) Is Franz really heard by Ingeborg to say that?
3. Peter hatte nicht dafür zu sorgen brauchen.
   (a) Peter has no need to trouble himself about that.
   (b) Peter didn't care about that.
   (c) Peter needed to care not only for that.
   (d) Peter had not needed to take care of that.
4. *Choose the correct verb form:*
   (a) Wir haben den Mann singen gehört.
   (b) Wir hatten gehört den Mann singend.
   (c) Wir haben den Mann singen hören.
   (d) Wir hatten den Mann gesungen gehört.
5. *Choose the correct word order:*
   (a) Werden Sie ihn morgen kommen sehen?
   (b) Sehen Sie ihn morgen kommen werden?
   (c) Sie ihn morgen werden kommen sehen.
   (d) Morgen kommen Sie ihn werden sehen.

Answer key: **1.** (c); **2.** (b); **3.** (d); **4.** (c); **5.** (a).

50. *Reflexive verbs and pronouns*

1. A verb is said to be reflexive when its subject and object are the same person(s) or thing(s). You have previously met a few reflexive verbs and have become aware of some of their functions. The specific meanings which may be expressed by the reflexive are:

(a) an action done by the subject to itself

Ich wasche *mich*.	*I wash myself. (I am washing.)*
Hast du *dich* gleich angezogen?	*Did you get dressed immediately? (Did you dress yourself immediately?)*

(b) a reciprocal action

Wir werden *uns* wiedersehen.	*We will see one another again.*
Sie geben *sich* die Hände.	*They (you) shake hands.*

(c) a passive sense, often translated by the English passive

Das Problem *hat sich gelöst*.	*The problem was solved.*
Das Buch *liest sich* leicht.	*The book is easily read.*

Note that the reflexive pronoun may often be omitted in translation.

2. Sich lassen plus infinitive has the passive meaning *can be* plus past participle:

Es *läßt sich* nicht *tun*.	*It cannot be done.*
Das Buch *ließ sich* nicht gleich *finden*.	*The book could not be found immediately.*

3. The reflexive pronoun can also be used in an infinitival clause to refer to a preceding object:

Er rät mir, *mich* zu beeilen.	*He is advising me to hurry up.*
Ich bat ihn, *sich* daran zu erinnern.	*I asked him to remember it.*

4. German uses the personal pronouns as reflexives in the first and second person singular and plural. The third person form as well as that of the formal **Sie** is **sich.** The genitive forms will be covered later:

	Singular		Plural	
Dative	**mir**	*myself*	**uns**	*ourselves*
Accusative	**mich**		**uns**	
Dative	**dir**	*yourself*	**euch**	*yourselves*
Accusative	**dich**		**euch**	
Dative	**sich**	*himself, herself, itself, oneself*	**sich**	*themselves, each other, one another*
Accusative	**sich**		**sich**	

	Formal	
Dative	**sich**	*yourself, yourselves*
Accusative	**sich**	

5. Occasionally the addition of the reflexive pronoun changes the meaning of a verb:

denken	*to think*
sich denken (dative)	*to imagine*
erinnern	*to remind*
sich erinnern	*to remember*
setzen	*to set* (something)
sich setzen	*to sit down*

6. The reciprocal pronoun **einander** is translated *one another* or *each other:*

Wir sehen *einander* später. — *We will see each other later.*

Give the meanings of the underlined reflexive verbs and pronouns.

	1. **sich beugen** = *to bend, to bow* Der Einzelne muß **sich** der Zukunft gegenüber **beugen.**
1. The individual must *bow* to the future.	**2.** **sich unterhalten** = *to talk, to discuss* Wir **haben uns** über dieses und jenes **unterhalten.**
2. We *talked* about this and that.	**3.** Das **machte sich** leicht.

3. That *was* easy.	**4.** Das Lied **läßt sich** nicht gleich **singen.**
4. The song *can*not *be sung* immediately.	**5.** **Setzen** Sie **sich hin!**
5. *Sit down.*	**6.** **der Wald** = *forest* **Sahen** sie **sich** im Wald?
6. *Did* they *see each other* in the woods?	**7.** Die Lösung dieses Problems **wird sich** nicht gleich **finden.**
7. The solution of this problem *will* not *be found* immediately.	**8.** **durchsetzen** = *to enforce* Dieses Gesetz **wird sich** einfach nicht **durchsetzen lassen.**
8. This law *will* simply not *be able to be enforced.*	**9.** Haben sie **einander** sehen dürfen?
9. Were they allowed to see *each other?*	**10.** Wir werden **einander** wohl wiedersehen, nicht wahr?
10. We will see *each other* again, won't we? ("isn't that true?")	

51. *The intensive pronouns* **selbst** *and* **selber**

1. The intensive pronouns **selbst** and **selber** are often used with reflexive pronouns to emphasize their meanings. When they follow immediately after a noun or personal pronoun they are translated:

Er wäscht sich *selbst* (*selber*).	*He washes himself.*
Er *selbst* (*selber*) fliegt nach Deutschland.	*He himself will fly to Germany.*
Sie ist die Güte *selbst*.	*She is goodness itself.*

2. When **selbst** precedes the object, it is translated *even:*

***Selbst* Einstein hatte seine Fehler.**	*Even Einstein had his weaknesses.*

Select the correct answer or else give the meaning of the indicated words.

	1. Wir haben **uns selber** nicht mehr daran erinnern können. (*ourselves/themselves*)

1. We *ourselves* were not able to remember it.	**2.** Sie **selber** hat dem Mann helfen wollen. (*herself*/*themselves*)
2. She *herself* wanted to help the man.	**3.** Das Kind hat **sich selbst** ausziehen sollen. (*itself*/*himself*)
3. The child was supposed to get undressed by *himself* (undress *himself*).	**4.** **Selbst** er interessiert sich dafür. (*himself*/*even*)
4. *Even* he is interested in it.	**5.** Könnt ihr **euch selbst** hinlegen? (*herself*/*yourselves*)
5. Can you lie down by *yourselves*?	**6.** Schämst du **dich selber** nicht? (*yourself*/*yourselves*)
6. Aren't you *yourself* ashamed?	**7.** **Selbst** ihr habt euch schämen müssen. (*yourselves*/*even*)
7. *Even* you had to be ashamed.	**8.** Sie freuen **sich selbst** über die Nachricht. (*herself*/*themselves*)
8. They *themselves* are happy about the news.	

PROGRESS TEST

Choose the correct meaning of the indicated words.

1. Konrad zog **euch** die Schuhe aus.
(a) their (b) his (c) your (d) none

2. Das läßt **sich** nicht mehr tun.
(a) himself (b) yourself (c) herself (d) none

3. **Selbst** der Mensch ist ein Raubtier.
(a) even (b) himself (c) itself (d) none

4. Wolfgang **setzte sich hin.**
(a) set it down (b) is sitting down (c) sat down (d) none

5. Ich **erinnerte mich** an Liese.
(a) remembered (b) reminded (c) reminded myself (d) none

6. Wir waschen **einander** die Hände.
(a) our own (b) another's (c) one another's (d) none

7. Das Kind will **sich selber** waschen.
(a) even itself (b) yourself (c) themselves (d) none

Answer key: **1.** (c); **2.** (d); **3.** (a); **4.** (c); **5.** (a); **6.** (c); **7.** (d).

52. *Special uses of the dative*

1. Certain verbs take only the dative case where one might expect the accusative:

Bitte, *helfen* Sie mir!	*Please, help me!*
Paul *dankte* ihm dafür.	*Paul thanked him for it.*
Er *antwortete* dem jungen Mann.	*He answered the young man.*

2. Certain adjectives call for the dative case and generally follow the word they govern:

Inge ist mir *böse*.	*Inge is mad at me.*
Ich blieb ihm *treu*.	*I remained true to him.*
Das Buch ist mir zu *schwer*.	*The book is too difficult for me.*

Choose the correct answer, or give the meaning of the following.

	1. Der Polizist folgte **dem Dieb.** (*dative singular/accusative singular*)
1. *dative singular:* **folgen** requires a dative object. The policeman followed *the thief.*	**2.** **angenehm** = *pleasing, pleasant* Es ist **ihm** angenehm, die deutsche Sprache zu hören. (*for him/to him*)
2. It pleases him (It is pleasing *to him*) to hear the German language.	**3.** Jetzt besprechen wir den Inhalt eines Gedichtes von Erich Kästner.
3. Now we will discuss the contents of a poem by Erich Kästner.	**4.** **Machen** Sie **sich** nachher Ihre eigenen Gedanken darüber.
4. Draw your own conclusions (*make* your own thoughts) about it afterwards.	**5.** **betrachten** = *to look at* Kästner betrachtet das Führerproblem genetisch.
5. Kästner looks at the "leader problem" according to its origins (genetically).	**6.** Gott schuf die Welt in sechs Tagen.

6. God created the world in six days.	**7.** **fehlen** = *to lack* Am ersten Wochenende meinte Gott, **der Welt** fehlte nichts. (*nominative/dative*)
7. *dative:* **fehlen** requires a dative object. On the first weekend, God thought the world lacked nothing (nothing was lacking *to the world*).	**8.** **reiben** = *to rub* Da **rieb** er sich die Hände. (*present/past*)
8. *past* Then he *rubbed* his hands.	**9.** **sich vergnügen** = *to enjoy oneself* **vergnügt** = *pleased* Gott war vergnügt, als er die Welt **besah.** (*inspected/had inspected*)
9. God was pleased when he *inspected* the world.	**10.** **gefallen** = *to please* Die Welt, wie er sie schuf, gefiel ihm sehr gut. (**Ihm** tells that **gefallen** takes a ________ object.)
10. *dative* The world, as he created it, pleased him very well.	**11.** Er rieb sich vergnügt die Hände.
11. Pleased, he rubbed his hands.	**12.** **der Mut** = *courage* **der Übermut** = *pride, excessive pride* Hatte Gott eine **Art** von Übermut, nachdem er die Welt schuf? (*art/kind*)
12. Did God have a *kind* of excessive pride after he created the world?	**13.** Eine Art von Übermut **packte** ihn. (*packed/seized*)
13. A sort of excessive pride *seized* him.	**14.** **die Liebe** = *love* **lieb** = *lovable, dear* Die Welt war **ihm** sehr lieb, und er blickte stolz darauf. (**Lieb** appears to govern the ________ case.)
14. *dative* The world was very dear *to him,* and he looked at it proudly.	**15.** Was sah er denn überhaupt?

15. What did he actually see? (**Denn** here serves as an intensifier)	**16.** **die Tuberkulose** = *tuberculosis* **die Tuberkel** (pl. **Tuberkeln**) = *tubercle* (small granular tumor formed in the lungs or other organs in consumption) Er sah Tuberkeln, Standard Oil und **Waffen.** (*weapons/waffles*)
16. He saw tuberculosis (tubercles), Standard Oil, and *weapons.*	**17.** **schwer** = *hard, difficult* **die Beschwerde** = *complaint* (also: *hardship*) Was **aber** jetzt aus Deutschland kam, war eine Beschwerde. (*but/however*)
17. What now came out of Germany, *however*, was a complaint.	**18.** Es fehlte **den Deutschen** etwas. (*masculine accusative/dative plural*)
18. *dative plural* The Germans lacked something (something was lacking *to the Germans*).	**19.** **schaffen** = *to create, to provide* **erschaffen** = *to create* Die Beschwerde lautete so: „Du hast vergessen, uns einen Führer zu erschaffen."
19. The complaint ran thus: "You forgot to create a leader for us."	**20.** **versäumen** = *to neglect* Gott versäumte, **ihnen** einen Führer zu erschaffen.
20. God neglected to create a leader *for them.*	**21.** **bestürzen** = *to dismay* **bestürzt** = ________
21. *dismayed* (past participle)	**22.** Gott war bestürzt, als er hörte, daß er versäumt hatte, **den Deutschen** einen Führer zu erschaffen.
22. God was dismayed when he heard that he had forgotten to create a leader *for the Germans.*	**23.** **halt** = *just* (dialect) Er schrieb **ihnen** zurück: „Mein liebes deutsches Volk, es muß halt ohne Führer gehen."
23. He wrote back *to them:* "My dear German people, you will just have to go without a leader."	**24.** **mit Ohne** = *without a leader* Nun standen die Deutsche mit Ohne da.

24. Now the Germans stood there without a leader.	**25.** **der Freund** = *friend* **freundlich** = *friendly, kind* **freundlichst** = ________
25. *most friendly, most kindly*	**26.** **überlassen** = *to leave to, to relinquish to* Die Deutschen waren **der Weltgeschichte** freundlichst überlassen. (*nominative/dative*)
26. *dative* The Germans were most kindly left *to world history.*	**27.** Nun **standen** sie mit Ohne da, der Weltgeschichte freundlichst überlassen. (*stand/stood*)
27. There they now *stood* leaderless, most kindly left to the mercy of world history.	**28.** **fassen** = *to grasp, to comprehend* Das kann man überhaupt nicht fassen!
28. That is impossible to grasp!	**29.** **geschehen** = *to happen* Was seitdem **geschah,** ist nicht zu fassen.
29. What *has happened* since then, is incomprehensible (is not to be grasped).	**30.** **weisen** = *to show* **hinweisen** = *to point to, to point out* **der Hinweis** = ________
30. *reference, hint*	**31.** Können Sie mir einen Hinweis geben?
31. Can you give me a hint?	**32.** Das ist aber ein wertvoller Hinweis!
32. That is certainly a valuable reference!	**33.** Alles, was seitdem geschah, ist ohne diesen Hinweis nicht zu fassen.
33. All that has happened since then is incomprehensible without this reference.	

READING PREPARATION

Select the correct answer or else give the meaning of the sentence. This section is to prepare you for the reading selection.

	1. **wohl** = *probably* (used as an intensifier) Sie alle kennen wohl den Namen Adolf Hitler.

1. You probably all know the name Adolf Hitler.	**2.** **der Herr** = *gentleman, lord, master* **herrschen** = *to rule* Er ist nur einer von den Männern, die über Deutschland **geherrscht haben.**
2. He is only one of the men who *have ruled* Germany.	**3.** **hervorbringen** = *to produce, to bring forth* Deutschland hat viele verschiedene **Führer** hervorgebracht. (*singular/plural*)
3. *plural* Germany has produced many different leaders.	**4.** Aber **keiner** war wie Hitler, und wahrscheinlich wird es keinen mehr wie ihn geben. (*none/no/not a*)
4. But *none* of them was like Hitler, and there probably will not be another one like him.	**5.** Wir werden es **wenigstens** hoffen.
5. We will *at least* hope so.	**6.** Alan Bullock, der Hitlers Biograph ist, **hat** Hitler den größten Demagogen der Weltgeschichte **genannt.** (*has called/had called*)
6. Alan Bullock, who is Hitler's biographer, *has called* Hitler the greatest demagogue in world history.	**7.** **der Auszug** = *excerpt* In diesem Kapitel werden wir einen Auszug aus Hitlers *Mein Kampf* lesen.
7. In this chapter we will read an excerpt from Hitler's *Mein Kampf.*	**8.** **mischen** = *to mix* **die Mischung** = *mixture* **die Rasse** = *race* **die Rassenmischung** = ________
8. *racial mixture, miscegenation*	**9.** **zunächst** = *first of all* Zunächst werden Sie von **den Gefahren** der Rassenmischung lesen. (singular/plural)
9. *plural* First of all, you will read about *the dangers* of miscegenation.	**10.** **das Volk** = *people, nation* **völkisch** = ________
10. *national, having to do with the people, proceeding from the people* (The Nazi use of the word implied "racial.")	**11.** Der nächste Auszug **handelt** vom völkischen Staat und der Rassenhygiene. (*handles/deals*)

11. The next excerpt *deals* with the national state and with eugenics.	**12. das heißt** = *that is* Das heißt, wer darf und wer soll Kinder haben, und **welche** Rolle spielt der Staat dabei? (*that/what*)
12. That is, who may and who should have children, and *what* role does the state play in this?	**13. der Mensch** = *man* **das Recht** = *right, justice, law* **das Menschenrecht** = ________
13. *right of man, human right, human law*	**14. verletzen** = *to injure, to violate* Wir **werden** das heilige Menschenrecht nie **verletzen.**
14. We *will* never *violate* the sacred right of man.	**15.** Wir **haben** das heilige Menschenrecht nicht **verletzen können.**
15. We *have* not *been able to violate* the sacred right of man.	**16.** Wir **hatten** das heiligste Menschenrecht nicht zu **verletzen brauchen.**
16. We *had* not *needed to violate* the most sacred right of man.	**17. die Verpflichtung** = *obligation, duty* Hitler **hat** auch **sagen lassen,** daß das heiligste Menschenrecht zugleich die heiligste Verpflichtung ist.
17. Hitler also *let* it *be said* that the most sacred human right is at the same time the most sacred obligation.	**18. erhalten** = *to preserve* (also: *to keep, to receive*) Er behauptete, daß das Blut rein erhalten **bleiben soll.**
18. He claimed that blood *should be* kept pure.	**19. zeugen** = *to produce* (also: *to procreate*) Was soll jeder gesunde Mensch zeugen?
19. What is every healthy person supposed to produce?	**20. berufen** = *to call upon, to appoint* Der Staat **hat** jeden gesunden Menschen **berufen lassen . . .**
20. The state *caused* every healthy person *to be called upon . . .*	**21. das Ebenbild** = *image* Der Staat **hat** jeden gesunden Menschen **berufen lassen,** Ebenbilder des Herrn zu zeugen.
21. The state *had* every healthy person *called upon* to produce children in the image of the Lord (to produce images of the Lord).	**22. heißen** = *to order, to command* Der völkische Staat **hieß** alle gesunden Menschen Ebenbilder des Herrn **zeugen.**

22. The national state *ordered* all healthy people *to produce* children in the image of the Lord.	**23.** **die Geburt** = *birth* **die Mißgeburt** = *monstrosity, freak* (also: *abortion*) Mißgeburten zwischen Mensch und Affe **soll** der Staat nicht **leben lassen.**
23. The state *should* not *permit* monstrosities (freaks) *to live* which are halfway between man and ape.	**24.** **die Rasse** = *race* **die Schande** = *defilement* (also: *disgrace, shame*) **die Rassenschande** = ________
24. *racial defilement*	**25.** **die Ehe** = *marriage* Der völkische Staat sah die Ehe anders als wir sie sehen.
25. The national state looked upon marriage differently than we do.	**26.** **heben** = *to lift* **herausheben** = *to raise from* Der völkische Staat **wird** die Ehe aus einer dauernden Rassenschande **herausheben müssen.**
26. The national state *will have to raise* marriage from a continuous defilement of the race.	**27.** Der Staat **hat** die Ehe aus dem Niveau einer dauernden Rassenschande **herauszuheben.**
27. The state *has* (the duty) *to raise* marriage from the level of a continuous racial defilement.	**28.** **Dürfen** wir Mißgeburten zwischen Mensch und Affe **leben lassen**?
28. *May we let* monstrosities *live* which are halfway between man and ape?	**29.** **die Linie** = *the line* **in erster Linie** = *above all, first of all* Dürfen sie in erster Linie Mißgeburten leben lassen?
29. May they above all let monstrosities live?	**30.** **erreichen** = *to accomplish* Was hoffte Hitler zu erreichen?
30. What did Hitler hope to accomplish?	**31.** **bewahren** = *to preserve, to keep* **die Bewahrung** = ________
31. *preservation*	**32.** Was soll man immer bewahren?
32. What is one always supposed to preserve?	**33.** **das Wesen** = *nature, essence, being* Das Wesen des Menschen ist immer noch **unerklärt.** (*explained/unexplained*)

33. Man's nature is still *unexplained.*	**34. das Menschentum** = *mankind* Was hoffte Hitler durch die Bewahrung des besten Menschentums zu erreichen?
34. What did Hitler hope to accomplish by the preservation of mankind at its best (of the best mankind)?	**35.** Was **erhalten** wir durch die Bewahrung des besten Menschentums?
35. What *do* we *receive* by the preservation of mankind at its best?	**36. entwickeln** = *to develop, to unfold, to evolve* **die Entwicklung** = ________
36. *development, evolution*	**37.** Hoffte Hitler, uns eine edlere Entwicklung zu geben?
37. Did Hitler hope to give us a nobler development?	**38. möglich** = *possible* **die Möglichkeit** = ________
38. *possibility*	**39.** Hoffte er, uns die Möglichkeit einer edleren Entwicklung zu geben?
39. Did he hope to give us the possibility of a nobler development?	**40.** Durch die Bewahrung des besten Menschentums will Hitler die Möglichkeit einer edleren Entwicklung **dieser** Wesen geben. (*of these/to these*)
40. By the preservation of the best in mankind, Hitler wants to make possible a nobler development *of these* beings.	**41.** Was will der völkische Staat **der Ehe** geben? (*of marriage/to marriage*)
41. What does the national state want to give *to marriage*?	**42. die Weihe** = *sanctification, consecration, ordination* Der Staat will der Ehe die Weihe **dieser** Institution geben. (*of this/to this*)
42. The state wants to give to marriage the sanctification *of this* institution.	**43.** Die Ehe ist berufen, Ebenbilder des Herrn zu zeugen und nicht Mißgeburten zwischen Mensch und Affe.
43. Marriage is intended (called upon) to produce children who are images of God and not misbegotten crosses between man and ape.	**44.** Ein völkischer Staat wird die Ehe aus dem Niveau **einer** dauernden Rassenschande herauszuheben haben. (*of a/to a*)

44. A national state will have to raise marriage from the level *of a* continuous racial defilement.	**45.** . . . um **ihr** (der Ehe) die Weihe einer Institution zu geben, die berufen ist, Ebenbilder des Herrn zu zeugen. (*to her/to it*)
45. . . . in order to give *to it* (marriage) the sanctification of an institution which is intended to produce images of the Lord.	**46.** **allgemein** = *all, general* Die Rasse ist der Mittelpunkt des allgemeinen Lebens.
46. Race is the center of all life.	**47.** Der völkische Staat hat die Rasse in den Mittelpunkt des allgemeinen Lebens zu setzen.
47. The national state must put race in the center of all life.	**48.** Das Kind ist das **kostbarste** Gut eines Volkes. (*precious/most precious*)
48. The child is the *most precious* treasure of a people.	**49.** Was ist eine Schande?
49. What is a disgrace?	**50.** **bei eigener/eigenen** = *having* Es gibt nur eine Schande: bei eigener Krankheit und eigenen Mängeln **dennoch** Kinder in die Welt zu setzen. (*in spite of/still*)
50. There is only one disgrace: having sickness and defects, and *still* bringing children into the world.	**51.** Wie wird der Mensch **sich schänden**?
51. How will man *defile himself*?	**52.** Man schändet sich, wenn man bei eigener Krankheit und eigenen Mängeln dennoch Kinder in die Welt setzt.
52. People defile themselves when, being afflicted with sickness and defects, they still bring children into the world.	**53.** Was ist die höchste Ehre?
53. What is the highest honor?	**54.** Darauf zu verzichten, bei eigener Krankheit und eigenen Mängeln Kinder in die Welt zu setzen.
54. Having sickness and defects, to refuse to bring children into the world.	**55.** **werfen** = *to throw* **verwerfen** = *to reject* (i.e. *to throw out*) Was müssen wir immer verwerfen?

55. What must we always reject?	**56.** **verwerflich** = *reprehensible* Was ist verwerflich?
56. What is reprehensible (i.e. to be rejected)?	**57.** **gelten** = *to be considered, to be valued* Was muß als verwerflich gelten?
57. What must be considered as reprehensible?	**58.** **vorenthalten** = *to withhold* Es gilt als verwerflich, gesunde Kinder der Nation vorzuenthalten.
58. It is considered reprehensible to withhold healthy children from the state.	**59.** Man **hat** dem Staat gesunde Kinder nicht **vorenthalten dürfen.**
59. One *was* not *allowed to withhold* healthy children from the state.	**60.** **auftreten** = *to act, to appear* Wie muß der Staat auftreten?
60. How must the state act?	**61.** **bewahren** = *to preserve* **der Wahrer** = *guardian* (*protector*) Der Staat muß dabei als Wahrer einer tausendjährigen Zukunft auftreten.
61. The state must act as the guardian of a millenial (thousand-year) future.	**62.** **eigen** = *own* **suchen** = *to seek* **die Eigensucht** = *selfishness* Die Eigensucht des einzelnen gilt als nichts.
62. The selfishness of the individual is esteemed as nothing (has no value).	**63.** Der Zukunft gegenüber darf der Wunsch und die Eigensucht des einzelnen als nichts gelten.
63. With regard to the future, the wishes and the selfishness of the individual must be considered worthless.	**64.** Der Zukunft gegenüber erscheinen der Wunsch und die Eigensucht des einzelnen als nichts.
64. With regard to the future, the desire and the selfishness of the individual appear as nothing.	**65.** Der Zukunft gegenüber haben sie **sich** zu **beugen.**
65. They must *submit themselves* to the future.	**66.** **Fassen wir** jetzt **zusammen,** was Hitler schreibt.
66. *Let us* now *sum up* what Hitler writes.	**67.** Die Ehe ist berufen, Ebenbilder des Herrn zu zeugen, und nicht Mißgeburten zwischen Mensch und Affe.

67. Marriage is called upon (i.e. it is the calling of marriage) to produce children in the image of the Lord, and not misbegotten crosses between man and ape.	**68.** Es gibt nur eine Schande: bei eigener Krankheit und eigenen Mängeln dennoch Kinder in die Welt zu setzen.
68. There is only one disgrace: having sickness and defects and still bringing children into the world.	**69.** Gesunde Kinder muß man aber der Nation nicht vorenthalten.
69. One must, however, not withhold healthy children from the nation.	

PROGRESS TEST

Choose the closest approximation to the given sentences.

1. Die Zeugung von Mißgeburten zwischen Mensch und Affe ist die Aufgabe jedes völkischen Staates.
(a) The state should promote the production of freaks.
(b) Crosses between men and apes appear as monsters to the state.
(c) The state should do away with monsters which are a cross between men and apes.
(d) none

2. Gesunde Kinder der Nation vorzuenthalten, ist wie der Versuch, ein Auto zu fahren mit zu wenig Benzin.
(a) The healthy children of the nation are like a car without fuel.
(b) To release healthy children of the nation is like driving a car without fuel.
(c) Withholding healthy children from the nation is detrimental to the nation.
(d) none

3. Durch die Bewahrung des besten Menschentums wird die Möglichkeit einer edleren Entwicklung aller Wesen gegeben.
(a) One furthers the best in humanity by giving to all beings a noble birthright.
(b) For the noble development of all beings one will first need to make such a dream possible.
(c) All beings need help in becoming more noble specimens of the human race.
(d) The possibility of a more noble development is given to all beings by preserving the best of mankind.

4. Dem Staat gegenüber erscheinen der Wunsch und die Eigensucht des einzelnen als nichts.
(a) There is no future when one opposes the state.
(b) The state appears to respect the wishes and desires of none other than its own people.
(c) The state does not respect the wishes and desires of the people.
(d) The wishes and desires of the people do not oppose the state.

Answer key: **1.** (a); **2.** (c); **3.** (d); **4.** (c).

From : *Mein Kampf.*

Adolf Hitler: Gefahren der Rassenmischung

Es gibt nur ein heiligstes Menschenrecht, und dieses Recht ist zugleich die heiligste Verpflichtung, nämlich: dafür zu sorgen, daß das Blut rein erhalten bleibt, um durch die Bewahrung des besten Menschentums die Möglichkeit einer edleren Entwicklung dieser Wesen zu geben.

Ein völkischer Staat wird damit in erster Linie die Ehe aus dem Niveau einer dauernden Rassenschande herauszuheben haben, um ihr die Weihe jener Institution zu geben, die berufen ist, Ebenbilder des Herrn zu zeugen und nicht Mißgeburten zwischen Mensch und Affe.

Völkischer Staat und Rassenhygiene

Er [der völkische Staat] hat die Rasse in den Mittelpunkt des allgemeinen Lebens zu setzen. Er hat für ihre Reinerhaltung zu sorgen. Er hat das Kind zum kostbarsten Gut eines Volkes zu erklären. Er muß dafür Sorge tragen, daß nur, wer gesund ist, Kinder zeugt; daß es nur eine Schande gibt: bei eigener Krankheit und eigenen Mängeln dennoch Kinder in die Welt zu setzen, doch eine höchste Ehre: darauf zu verzichten. Umgekehrt aber muß es als verwerflich gelten: gesunde Kinder der Nation vorzuenthalten. Der Staat muß dabei als Wahrer einer tausendjährigen Zukunft auftreten, der gegenüber der Wunsch und die Eigensucht des einzelnen als nichts erscheinen und sich zu beugen haben.

From *Bei Durchsicht meiner Bücher.* Atrium Verlag, Zürich.

Erich Kästner: Das Führerproblem, genetisch betrachtet

Als Gott am ersten Wochenende
die Welt besah, und siehe, sie war gut,
da rieb er sich vergnügt die Hände.
Ihn packte eine Art von Übermut.

Er blickte stolz auf seine Erde
und sah Tuberkeln, Standard Oil und Waffen.
Da kam aus Deutschland die Beschwerde:
„Du hast versäumt, uns Führer zu erschaffen!“

Gott war bestürzt. Man kann's verstehn.
„Mein liebes deutsches Volk," schrieb er zurück,
„es muß halt ohne Führer gehn.
Die Schöpfung ist vorbei. Grüß Gott. Viel Glück."

Nun standen wir mit Ohne da,
der Weltgeschichte freundlichst überlassen.
Und: Alles, was seitdem geschah,
ist ohne diesen Hinweis nicht zu fassen.

Chapter Fifteen

53. *Der words*

1. The following words are declined according to the pattern of the definite article and are therefore called **der** words:

dieser	*this*
jener	*that*
jeder (pl.: **alle**)	*each, every* (pl.: *all*)
mancher	*many a* (pl.: *some*)
solcher	*such (a)*
welcher	*which, what*

Be sure to distinguish between **jeder** and **jener:**

***Jeder* Mensch will so etwas tun.**	***Every*** *person wants to do something like that.*
***Jener* Mensch wird das aber nicht tun.**	***That*** *person, however, will not do that.*

2. Using **dieser** as an example, the **der** words are declined as follows:

	M	F	N	Pl
N	**dies*er***	**dies*e***	**dies*es* (dies)**	**dies*e***
G	**dies*es***	**dies*er***	**dies*es***	**dies*er***
D	**dies*em***	**dies*er***	**dies*em***	**dies*en***
A	**dies*en***	**dies*e***	**dies*es* (dies)**	**dies*e***

3. These endings identify gender, number, and case of the nouns which follow:

Dies*er* Mann und jen*e* Frau sind verheiratet.	*This man and that woman are married.*
Welch*es* Kind sahst du auf dem Tisch?	*Which child did you see on the table?*

4. These words may be used as pronouns. The endings will be the same as the **der** words:

***Welche* gehen heute?**	*Which are going today?*
***Jeder* kennt das Lied.**	*Everyone knows the song.*
***Dieser* kommt nicht.**	*This one (person) is not coming.*

Dieser and **jener** as pronouns are often used to express *the latter* **(dieser)** and *the former* **(jener)**:

Herr Braun hat einen Volkswagen und einen Mercedes: *jener* ist billig, *dieser* ist teuer.	*Mr. Braun has a Volkswagen and a Mercedes:* ***the former*** *is inexpensive, the* ***latter*** *is expensive.*

The following exercises will introduce you to Albert Schweitzer as well as drill the meanings of the **der** *words.*

	1. Sicher kennen Sie alle den Namen Albert Schweitzer.
1. Surely you all know the name Albert Schweitzer.	**2.** **Manche** Menschen kennen den Namen Albert Schweitzer. (*those/some*)
2. *Some* people know the name Albert Schweitzer.	**3.** **Solch** ein Name ist der ganzen Welt bekannt. (*such/which*)
3. *Such* a name is known to the whole world.	**4.** Jeder sollte **diesen** Mann und sein Leben kennen. (*this/those*)
4. Everyone should know *this* man and his life.	**5.** Nicht **jeder** kennt den Theologen, Musiker und Missionsarzt.
5. Not *everyone* knows the theologian, musician, and missionary doctor.	**6.** **Jener** Mensch ist der ganzen Welt bekannt. (*every/that*)

6. *That* man is known to the whole world.	**7.** **die Vorstellung** = *idea, conception* (also: *performance*) **Welche** Vorstellung hat man von ihm? (*what/whose*)
7. *What* idea does one have of him?	**8.** **Jeder,** der den Namen kennt, hat irgendeine Vorstellung von ihm. (*that person/every person*)
8. *Every person* who knows the name has some kind of a conception of him.	**9.** **Dieser** Mensch hat jahrelang als Missionsarzt gearbeitet.
9. *This* man worked for years as a missionary doctor.	**10.** **das Gebiet** = *area, field* Auf **welchen** anderen Gebieten hat er gearbeitet? (*that/what*)
10. In what other areas did he work?	**11.** **tätig sein** = *to be active* Er war ein Meister auf **jedem** Gebiet, auf welchem er tätig war. (*that/every*)
11. He was a master in *every* area in which he was active.	**12.** **Manche** können das nicht. (*some/which*)
12. *Some* people are unable to do that.	**13.** Im französischen Kongogebiet, nämlich in Lambarene, war er Missionsarzt.
13. In the French Congo, specifically in Lambarene, he was a missionary doctor.	**14.** **der Urwald** = *jungle* In **jenem** Urwald arbeitete er als Missionsarzt. (*every/that*)
14. In *that* jungle he worked as a missionary doctor.	**15.** Sind **solche** Menschen wie Schweitzer sehr leicht auf der Welt zu finden? (*such/which*)
15. Are *such* people as Schweitzer very easy to find in the world?	**16.** Wieviele findet man heute in den Urwäldern?
16. How many does one find in the jungles today?	

PROGRESS TEST

Give the meaning and/or use of the italicized **der** *words.*

1. *Solche* Menschen wollen wir überhaupt nicht fressen!
   (a) so many (b) such (c) nominative (d) accusative
2. Dort ist ein Mann zusammen mit seiner Tante. *Diese* ist jünger als *jener*.
   (a) the latter, the former (b) this, that (c) nominative, nominative (d) accusative, genitive
3. *Die Kinder mancher Mütter* sind nicht zu ertragen.
   (a) some children's mothers (b) some mothers' children (c) children and mothers (d) the child of many a mother
4. *Jeder* Mensch hat seinen Vogel!
   (a) no (b) every (c) nominative (d) genitive plural
5. Mit *welchem* Elefanten will Hannibal die Alpen überschreiten?
   (a) which (b) whose (c) singular (d) plural (e) dative (f) accusative

Answer key: **1.** (b, d); **2.** (a, c); **3.** (b); **4.** (b, c); **5.** (a, c, e).

54. *Der as a demonstrative pronoun*

1. Der, die, das when used with nouns are definite articles and mean *the*. As demonstrative pronouns they may be used to replace a noun or a personal pronoun and are then best translated *he, she, it, that, they,* or one of their objective forms:

***Der* hat kein Geld.**	***He** has no money.*
***Der* verschenkte ich mein Herz.**	*I gave my heart **to her**.*

The use of the demonstrative pronoun indicates special emphasis (like the emphasis indicated by stressed pronunciation in English).

2. Der, die, das are declined as follows when used as demonstrative pronouns:

	M	F	N
N	**der** (*he, it*)	**die** (*she, it*)	**das** (*it, that*)
G	**dessen** (*his, its*)	**deren** (*hers, its*)	**dessen** (*its, of it*)
D	**dem** (*to him, him, it*)	**der** (*to her, her, it*)	**dem** (*to it, it*)
A	**den** (*him, it*)	**die** (*her, it*)	**das** (*it, that*)

Plural

N	**die** (*they, those*)
G	**deren** (*their*) or: **derer** (*of those*)
D	**denen** (*to them, them, to those, those*)
A	**die** (*them, those*)

3. With the exception of the second genitive plural form **derer,** the demonstrative **der** has the same forms as those of the relative **der:**

Die Frau, *die* eben hier war . . .	*The woman **who** was just here . . .*
Diese Frau, *die* hat nie Geld!	*This woman, **she** never has any money!*
Der Mann, *den* Sie gesehen hatten . . .	*The man **whom** you had seen . . .*
***Den* haben Sie nicht sehen können!**	*You could not have seen **him!***
Die Frauen, *deren* Kinder gestern hier waren . . .	*The women **whose** children were here yesterday . . .*
Er ist ein Freund *derer,* die ihm helfen.	*He is a friend **of those** who help him.*

4. Generally, the demonstratives **dessen** and **deren** are used as a substitute for the possessive adjectives **sein** (*his*) and **ihr** (*her/their*) to avoid ambiguity and are then translated *the latter:*

Maria, Inge und *deren* Freund gehen ins Kino.	*Maria, Inge, and **the latter**'s friend are going to the movies.*
Er schickte seinen Freund und *dessen* Frau in die Kirche.	*He sent his friend and **the latter**'s wife to church.*

Derer usually precedes a relative clause:

Die Frauen *derer, die* nicht hier sind . . .	*The wives **of those who** are not here . . .*

5. Unlike the definite article, the demonstrative pronoun **der** does not generally modify a noun:

***Der Mann* sah mich nicht.**	***The man** did not see me.*
***Der* sah mich nicht.**	***He** did not see me.*

6. Unlike the relative pronoun, the demonstrative pronoun **der** does not affect word order:

Das Mädchen, mit *dem* du heute sprachst, ist meine Freundin.	*The girl with **whom** you spoke today is my girlfriend.*
Es war einmal ein Bauer, *der* hatte einen Sohn.	*There was once a farmer; **he** had a son.*

Respond to the following sentences by choosing the correct alternative or by giving the correct meaning.

	1. Wir werden jetzt lesen, was Schweitzer in dem Urwald erlebte.
1. We are now going to read what Schweitzer experienced in the jungle.	**2.** **berichten** = *to report, to tell* In welchem Buch, **das** er damals schrieb, berichtet Schweitzer uns davon? (*it/that*)
2. In which book *that* he wrote at the time does Schweitzer tell us about it?	**3.** **der Erlebnisbericht** = *report of experiences* Der Erlebnisbericht, **der** damals sehr bekannt wurde . . . (*he/which*)
3. The report of his experiences, *which* became very well known at the time . . .	**4.** Der Erlebnisbericht, **den** er damals schrieb, heißt *Zwischen Wasser und Urwald.* (*that/him/it*)
4. The report of his experiences *that* he wrote at the time is called *Between Water and Jungle.*	**5.** **der Auszug** = *excerpt* In diesem Kapitel **werden** Sie einen Auszug davon lesen. (*become/will*)
5. In this chapter you *will* read an excerpt from it.	**6.** **beschreiben** = *to describe* Was beschreibt Schweitzer in diesem Auszug?
6. What does Schweitzer describe in this excerpt?	**7.** Er berichtet uns von einer Operation im Urwald.
7. He tells us about an operation in the jungle.	**8.** Was für Operationen sind **es?** (*it/they*)
8. What kind of operations are *they*?	**9.** **häufig** = *frequent* **Am häufigsten** hat er es mit Brüchen (Hernien) zu tun.
9. *Most frequently* he has to deal with hernias.	**10.** **dringlich** = *urgent* Diese Operationen sind sehr dringlich.
10. These operations are very urgent.	**11.** **unternehmen** = *to undertake* An Operationen unternimmt man im Urwald nur **die, die** dringlich sind. (. . . *which, those* . . ./. . . *those which* . . .)

11. In the jungle one undertakes only *those* operations *which* are urgent.	**12.** Nur die, die dringlich sind und versprechen sicheren **Erfolg** zu haben, unternimmt man im Urwald. (*success/failure*)
12. Only those which are urgent and promise certain *success* does one undertake in the jungle.	**13.** **behaftet mit** = *afflicted with, subject to* Die Neger Zentralafrikas sind oft mit Brüchen behaftet.
13. The Negroes of Central Africa are often afflicted with hernias.	**14.** Die Neger Zentralafrikas, mit **deren** Brüchen Schweitzer zu tun hat . . . (*whose/those*)
14. The Negroes of Central Africa, with *whose* hernias Schweitzer has to deal . . .	**15.** Im Gegensatz zu den Weißen sind die Neger Zentralafrikas **damit** behaftet. (*to them/so that*)
15. In contrast to the whites, the blacks of Central Africa are much more subject *to them.*	**16.** **Diese** haben sehr viele, **jene** haben wenige. (*these . . . those/the latter . . . the former*)
16. *The latter* have very many, *the former have* few.	**17.** **eingeklemmt** = *strangulated* (also: *pinched*) Die Neger Zentralafrikas sind viel mehr mit eingeklemmten Brüchen behaftet als die Weißen.
17. The Negroes of Central Africa are much more afflicted with strangulated hernias than the whites.	**18.** Eingeklemmte Brüche (inkarzerierte Hernien) sind bei **jenen** viel häufiger als bei **diesen.** (*the former . . . the latter/those . . . these*)
18. Strangulated (incarcerated) hernias are much more frequent with *the former* than with *the latter.*	**19.** **durch** = *through* **der Gang** = *passage* **der Durchgang** = ________
19. passage-way	**20.** **der Darm** = *intestines* Der Darm ist **undurchgänglich.**
20. The intestines are *impassable* (blocked).	**21.** In dem eingeklemmten Bruch wird der Darm undurchgänglich.
21. In strangulated hernias the intestines become impassable.	**22.** **leer** = *empty* **entleeren** = *to empty* Ein undurchgänglicher Darm kann sich nicht mehr entleeren.

22. Blocked intestines cannot move (empty themselves) any more.	**23.** Ein Mann, **dessen** Darm undurchgänglich ist, und **der** sich also nicht mehr entleeren kann . . . (*whose . . . which/which . . . he*)
23. A man *whose* intestines are blocked, and *which* therefore cannot move . . .	**24.** **treiben** = *to drive, to push* **auftreiben** = *to distend, to cause to swell up* Die Gase treiben den Darm auf.
24. The gases distend the intestines.	**25.** **wird aufgetrieben** = *is distended, is bloated* Was wird durch die Gase aufgetrieben?
25. What is distended by the gases?	**26.** **bilden** = *to form* **sich bilden** = *to form (itself)* Er (der Darm) wird durch die sich bildenden Gase aufgetrieben.
26. They (the intestines) are bloated by the gases forming (in them).	**27.** Ein Darm, **der** sich nicht mehr entleeren kann, wird durch **die** sich bildenden Gase aufgetrieben. (*which . . . the/the . . . who*)
27. Intestines *which* cannot discharge themselves any more are bloated by *the* gases forming in them.	**28.** **der Schmerz** = *pain* Jene **Auftreibung** führt zu furchtbaren Schmerzen. (*swelling/deflation*)
28. That *swelling* leads to terrible pains.	**29.** **herrühren** = *to come from, to originate* Von dieser Auftreibung rühren die furchtbaren Schmerzen her.
29. The terrible pains come from this swelling.	**30.** **grausig** = *gruesome* Der Tod ist grausig.
30. Death is gruesome.	**31.** In Afrika ist dieses grausige Sterben **etwas Gewöhnliches.** (*something unusual/something quite usual*)
31. In Africa this gruesome death is something quite usual.	**32.** Von einer inkarzerierten Hernie zu sterben ist doch etwas Grausiges.
32. To die of a strangulated hernia is, after all, something gruesome.	**33.** **sich wälzen** = *to roll (oneself) around* Ein Mann **wälzt** sich im Sande. (*present/past*)

33. *present* A man *is rolling* around in the sand.	**34.** **heulen** = *to cry, to howl* **heulend** = *howling* Der Mann **wälzte** sich heulend im Sande. (*present/past*)
34. *past* The man *was rolling* around in the sand howling.	**35.** **die Hütte** = *hut* **Tagelang** wälzte sich der Mann heulend im Sande der Hütte. (*for days/long days*)
35. *For days* the man was rolling around howling in the sand of the hut.	**36.** Schon als Knabe war der Neger **dabei,** wenn ein Mann sich tagelang heulend im Sand der Hütte wälzte. (*present/next to that*)
36. Already as a boy the Negro was *present* whenever a man was rolling around howling in the sand of the hut.	**37.** **erlösen** = *to save* Er heulte, bis der Tod als **Erlöser** kam.
37. He howled until death came as a *savior*.	**38.** **Der** wälzte sich tagelang heulend im Sande der Hütte. (*he/who/the*)
38. For days *he* rolled around howling in the sand of the hut.	**39.** So etwas ist grausig zu hören und zu sehen.
39. Something like that (such a thing) is gruesome to hear and to see.	**40.** **anflehen** = *to implore* Ein Mann, **dessen** Bruch eingeklemmt ist, fleht jemand an, ihm zu helfen. (*whose/those*)
40. A man *whose* hernia is strangulated implores someone to help him.	**41.** **sein** = *his* **die Seinen** = *his loved ones, his family* Er fleht die Seinen an.
41. He implores his loved ones.	**42.** Um was fleht er die Seinen an?
42. What does he beg of his loved ones?	**43.** Die Seinen fleht **er** an, ihn ins Kanoe zu legen und zu mir zu führen.
43. *He* implores his loved ones to lay him in the canoe and to take (lead) him to me.	**44.** **kaum** = *scarcely* Kaum fühlt also ein Mann, daß sein Bruch eingeklemmt ist . . .

44. Therefore, scarcely does a man feel that his hernia is strangulated . . .	**45.** . . . so fleht er die Seinen an, ihn zu Schweitzer zu führen.
45. . . . so he implores his loved ones to take him to Schweitzer.	**46.** Bei Frauen sind Hernien **viel seltener** als bei Männern. (*much more salty/much more seldom*)
46. Hernias are found *much more seldom* in women than in men.	

PROGRESS TEST

Choose the correct meaning for the italicized words.

1. *Der* gibt er das Buch bestimmt nicht!
   (a) he (b) who (c) to her (d) to those
2. *Der* kommt heute bestimmt nicht mehr!
   (a) he (b) who (c) her (d) to them
3. *Die* wollen wir überhaupt nicht mehr retten.
   (a) whom (b) they (c) her (d) she
4. *Die* hat überhaupt kein Geld mehr.
   (a) who (b) they (c) her (d) she
5. Es war einmal ein Kind, *das* hatte keinen Vater und keine Mutter mehr.
   (a) who (b) whom (c) it (d) the
6. *Denen* werde ich nicht helfen!
   (a) whom (b) them (c) whose (d) these
7. *Dessen* Sohn ist ein Lump!
   (a) his (b) her (c) of it (d) the
8. *Dem* verschenke ich nicht meine Tochter.
   (a) them (b) to him (c) whom (d) who
9. Hans, Fritz und *dessen* Freundin gehen ins Kino.
   (a) the former's (b) the latter's (c) whose (d) those
10. Der Mann, mit *dessen* Frau du bekannt bist, ist kein ehrlicher Kerl.
    (a) his (b) those (c) whose (d) the latter's

Answer key: **1.** (c); **2.** (a); **3.** (c); **4.** (d); **5.** (c); **6.** (b); **7.** (a); **8.** (b); **9.** (b); **10.** (c).

55. *Other demonstratives*

1. Dies, das, and **es** are translated as *this, that,* and *it* when introducing singular predicate subjects, and *these, those,* and *they* when introducing plural predicate subjects:

Das **ist mein Auto.**	***That*** *is my car.*
Es **ist kein großes Haus.**	***It*** *is not a large house.*
Dies **sind meine Kinder.**	***These*** *are my children.*
Das **sind nicht meine Freunde.**	***Those*** *are not my friends.*
Es **sind seine Kinder, nicht meine.**	***They*** *are his children, not mine.*

2. **Derselbe** (*the same*) and **derjenige** (*that, the one; pl. those*) decline both components: **der-** is declined like the definite article, **selb-** and **jenig-** like weak adjectives:

Er hat *denselben* Professor wie ich.	*He has* ***the same*** *professor as I.*
***Diejenigen*, die dies nicht verstehen, müssen mehr arbeiten.**	***Those*** *who do not understand this must study more.*

This section continues to introduce new reading vocabulary and gives you practice in recognizing the demonstratives. Respond to the exercises as indicated.

	1. Schweitzer fragt, wie er seine Gefühle **beschreiben** kann . . . (*write/describe*)
1. Schweitzer asks, how can he *describe* his feelings . . .	2. **arm** = *poor* **ein Armer** = *a poor (unfortunate) person* . . . wenn solch ein Armer **gebracht wird.** (*is brought/will bring*)
2. . . . when such an unfortunate person *is brought*.	3. Schweitzer ist ja **der einzige . . .** (*the only one/one of many*)
3. Schweitzer is *the only one* . . . (**ja** is an intensifier)	4. Er ist ja der einzige, **der** hier helfen kann, auf hunderte von Kilometern . . . (*he/who*)
4. He is the only one, for hundreds of kilometers, *who* can help here . . .	5. **retten** = *to save* Schweitzer redet nicht **davon,** daß er den Armen retten kann. (*about that*/not necessary to translate)
5. (not necessary to translate) Schweitzer does not mention that he can save the poor man.	6. **der Fall** = *condition* (also: *case*) Wenn es **derselbe** Fall ist, können wir ihn retten.
6. If it is *the same* condition, we can save him.	7. **Dasselbe** kann er auch sagen. (*himself/the same*)

7. He also can say *the same.*	**8.** **Der** kann das auch sagen. (*he/that*)
8. *He* can say that, too.	**9.** **Diejenigen, die** nach ihm kommen, sind zu retten. (*those who/all who*)
9. *Those who* come after him can be saved.	**10.** **Denjenigen, die** krank sind, soll man helfen. (*those who/him who*)
10. One should help *those who* are sick.	**11.** **quälen** = *to torture, to worry* **qualvoll, qualenreich** = *painful, excruciating, agonizing* **die Qual** = __________
11. *pain, torment, pang, agony*	**12.** **die Gnade** = *privilege* (also: *mercy, grace*) Was empfindet Schweitzer als die große, immer neue Gnade?
12. What does Schweitzer consider the great, ever new privilege to be?	**13.** Er darf die Tage **der** Qual von einem nehmen.
13. He can save someone from days *of* pain.	**14.** Das ist es, was er als die große, immer neue Gnade empfindet.
14. That is what he feels the great, ever new privilege to be.	**15.** Aber **sterben** müssen wir alle. (*strive/die*)
15. But we must all *die.*	**16.** **furchtbar** = *terrible* Der Schmerz ist ein **furchtbarerer** Herr als der Tod.
16. Pain is a *more terrible* lord of mankind than death is.	**17.** **jammern** = *to lament, to moan* **jammernd** = *moaning* Er sieht einen **jammernden** Menschen vor sich.
17. Before him he sees a person *moaning.*	**18.** **die Stirne** = *forehead* Schweitzer legt dem jammernden Menschen die Hand auf die Stirne.

18. Schweitzer puts his hand on the forehead of the moaning person.	**19.** **sei ruhig** = *don't be afraid* (lit.: *be calm, quiet, still*) Er sagt ihm: „Sei ruhig."
19. He tells him: "Don't be afraid." (**Sei** is an imperative form of **sein.**)	**20.** In einer Stunde **wirst** du **schlafen . . .**
20. In one hour you *will be asleep* . . .	**21.** . . . und wenn du wieder **erwachst,** ist kein Schmerz mehr.
21. . . . and when you *awake* again, there will be no more pain.	**22.** Die Operation ist **vorüber.** (*under/over*)
22. The operation is *over.*	**23.** **wachen** = *to wake, to watch over* **aufwachen** = *to wake up* **das Aufwachen** = ____________
23. *the awakening*	**24.** **überwachen** = *to supervise, to look after* Schweitzer überwacht das **Aufwachen** des Patienten.
24. Schweitzer supervises the *awakening* of the patient.	**25.** Unter der dunklen **Schlafbaracke** überwacht er das Aufwachen des Patienten. (*dormitory/dressing room*)
25. In the dark *dormitory* he supervises the awakening of the patient.	**26.** **sich besinnen** = *to think of, to recollect* **die Besinnung** = *reflection, consciousness* **bei Besinnung** = ____________
26. *conscious*	**27.** Der Patient ist jetzt bei Besinnung.
27. The patient is now conscious.	**28.** Kaum ist er bei Besinnung, so schaut er erstaunt umher.
28. Hardly is he conscious when he looks around with astonishment.	**29.** Der Patient wiederholt fort und fort . . .
29. The patient repeats over and over . . .	**30.** Er ist der Freund **derer, die** fort und fort wiederholen . . . (*they who/of those who*)
30. He is the friend *of those who* repeat over and over . . .	**31.** **weh** = *hurt, pain* **weh haben** = *to hurt* Ich habe ja nicht mehr weh!

31. It doesn't hurt any more!	**32.** **die meine** = *mine* (singular) Da der Patient nicht mehr weh hat, sucht seine Hand die meine.
32. Since the patient doesn't have any more pain, his hand searches for mine.	**33.** Seine Hand will die meine nicht mehr loslassen.
33. His hand does not want to let go of mine any more.	**34.** Schweitzer **fängt an** zu erzählen.
34. Schweitzer *begins* to tell (the story).	**35.** **sitzen** = *to sit* **dabei** = *there, nearby* **dabeisitzen** = ___________
35. *to sit there, to sit nearby*	**36.** Dann fängt Schweitzer an, dem Patienten und **denen, die** dabeisitzen, zu erzählen . . . (*they who/those who*)
36. Then Schweitzer begins to tell the patient and *those who* are sitting nearby . . .	**37.** **gebieten** = *to command* . . . daß es der Herr Jesus ist, **der** dem Doktor und seiner Frau geboten hat . . .
37. . . . that it is the Lord Jesus *who* has commanded the doctor and his wife . . .	**38.** . . . hier an den Ogowe zu kommen.
38. . . . to come here to the Ogowe (a river in Equatorial Africa).	**39.** **Diejenigen,** die dabeisitzen, sind Freunde des Patienten.
39. *Those* who are sitting nearby are friends of the patient.	**40.** Wer sind jene Menschen, die uns **Mittel** geben, unsere Krankheiten zu heilen? (**Mittel** probably means: *middle/means*)
40. *means* Who are those people who give us the *means* to heal our sicknesses?	**41.** **geboren** = *born* **eingeboren** = *inherent, innate* **die Eingeborenen** = *natives* Die Eingeborenen leiden viel unter Krankheiten.
41. The natives suffer much from diseases.	**42.** Woher wissen die Europäer, daß die Eingeborenen so viel unter Krankheiten leiden?
42. How (from where) do the Europeans know that the natives suffer so much from diseases?	**43.** **der Kaffee** = *coffee* **der Strauch** = *bush, shrub* **der Kaffeestrauch** = ___________

43. the coffee bush	**44.** Durch die Kaffeesträucher hindurch scheint die afrikanische Sonne in die dunkle Hütte.
44. The African sun shines through the coffee bushes into the dark hut.	**45.** **Dies** sind meine Kaffeesträucher, jene sind deine. (*this/these*)
45. *These* are my coffee bushes, those are yours.	**46.** **Das** sind seine Freunde. (*that/those*)
46. *Those* are his friends.	**47.** Wer gibt uns die Mittel, um hier für die Kranken zu leben?
47. Who gives us the means to live here to cure the sick (in order to live for the sick)?	**48.** Wer sind **jene** Menschen, wo wohnen sie? (*that/those*)
48. Who are *those* people, where do they live?	**49.** **geben** = *to give* **gebend** = *giving* Die gebenden Freunde sind in Europa.
49. The friends who give (the means) are in Europe.	**50.** Wenn nur die gebenden Freunde in Europa dabei sein **könnten!** (**könnten** probably means: *can/could*)
50. If only the friends in Europe who give (the means) *could* be here with us!	**51.** Wir aber, Schwarz und Weiß, sitzen **untereinander** und erleben es: „Ihr aber seid alle Brüder." (*under one another/side by side*)
51. But we, black and white, sit *side by side* and experience the meaning of the words: "And all ye are brethren."	**52.** Ach, könnten die gebenden Freunde in Europa in einer solchen Stunde dabei sein!
52. Oh, if only the friends in Europe who contributed could be here in such a moment!	**53.** **verdienen** = *to earn, to deserve* **Der** verdient Macht.
53. *He* deserves power.	**54.** **rechtfertigen** = *to justify* **Der** rechtfertigt seine Macht.
54. *He* justifies his power.	**55.** **der Tag** = *day* Er rechtfertigt seine Macht **täglich.**

55. He justifies his power *daily.*	**56.** Nur **der** verdient Macht, **der** sie täglich rechtfertigt. Dag Hammarsjköld
56. Only *he* deserves power *who* justifies it daily.	

PROGRESS TEST

A. *Give the meaning of the italicized words.*

1. *Es sind* seine zwei Freunde.
(a) there are (b) he is (c) they are (d) that is

2. Er ist der Held *derselben* Frauen wie ich.
(a) of the same (b) the same (c) to the same (d) those

3. *Diejenigen,* die das nicht glauben, können zum Teufel gehen.
(a) she (b) they (c) the same (d) those

4. *Das sind* dumme Esel.
(a) that is (b) those are (c) it is (d) who are

B. *Choose the answers describing the italicized words.*

1. Er hilft *denselben* Professoren wie ich.
(a) dative (b) accusative (c) singular (d) plural

2. *Derjenige,* der nicht helfen kann, ist kein Freund von uns.
(a) nominative (b) dative (c) genitive (d) singular (e) plural

C. *Choose the closest approximate meaning for the given sentence.*

1. Am häufigsten unternimmt man Operationen, die nicht dringlich sind und sicheren Erfolg versprechen.
(a) All operations are pressing and those which promise certain success are most frequently unsuccessful.
(b) Operations which are not urgent and which promise certain success are most frequently performed.
(c) The most frequent operations are those which are both urgent and promise the most success.
(d) Most frequently one undertakes only urgent operations and does not promise certain success.

2. Ein undurchgänglicher Darm verspricht furchtbare Schmerzen *und den Tod als Erlöser.*
(a) and deadly sickness.
(b) and previous to death.
(c) and the fate of the losers.
(d) and death as a savior.

3. Daß eingeklemmte Brüche bei Frauen viel seltener sind als bei Männern, zeigt, daß die Gleichheit der Geschlechter nur ein Mythus ist.
(a) Men and women are not equal.
(b) Men and women are equal.
(c) Men never have the advantage over women.
(d) It is seldom that men and women suffer from the myth of equality.

4. Die Eingeborenen leiden unter Krankheiten.
(a) Those born into this society carry burdens.
(b) The laborers clean the hospital.
(c) The natives suffer from sicknesses.
(d) The first born are susceptible to sicknesses.

5. Die große, immer neue Gnade ist, daß man die Qual von einem nehmen darf.
(a) One is permitted to undertake new sufferings.
(b) All suffering is by the grace of God.
(c) One receives ever new grace by taking away one's pain.
(d) Removing one's pain is the great, ever new privilege.

Answer key: A. **1.** (c); **2.** (a); **3.** (d); **4.** (b).
B. **1.** (a, d); **2.** (a, d).
C. **1.** (b); **2.** (d); **3.** (a); **4.** (c); **5.** (d).

From *Zwischen Wasser und Urwald.* Paul Haupt Verlag, Bern, 1922.

Albert Schweitzer: Zwischen Wasser und Urwald

An Operationen unternimmt man im Urwald natürlich nur die, die dringlich sind und sicheren Erfolg versprechen. Am häufigsten habe ich es mit Brüchen (Hernien) zu tun. Die Neger Zentralafrikas sind viel mehr mit Brüchen behaftet als die Weißen. Woher dies kommt, wissen wir nicht. Eingeklemmte Brüche (Inkarzerierte Hernien) sind bei ihnen also auch viel häufiger als bei den Weißen. In dem eingeklemmten Bruch wird der Darm undurchgänglich. Er kann sich also nicht mehr entleeren und wird durch die sich bildenden Gase aufgetrieben. Von dieser Auftreibung rühren die furchtbaren Schmerzen her . . . . In Afrika ist dieses grausige Sterben . . . etwas Gewöhnliches. Schon als Knabe war der Neger dabei, wenn ein Mann sich tagelang heulend im Sande der Hütte wälzte, bis der Tod als Erlöser kam. Kaum fühlt also ein Mann, daß sein Bruch eingeklemmt ist — Hernien bei Frauen sind viel seltener als bei Männern — so fleht er die Seinen an, ihn ins Kanoe zu legen und zu mir zu führen.

Wie meine Gefühle beschreiben, wenn solch ein Armer gebracht wird! Ich bin ja der einzige, der hier helfen kann, auf hunderte von Kilometern . . . Ich rede nicht davon, daß ich ihm das Leben retten kann. Sterben müssen wir alle. Aber daß ich die Tage der Qual von ihm nehmen darf, das ist es, was ich als die große, immer neue Gnade empfinde. Der Schmerz ist ein furchtbarerer Herr als der Tod.

So lege ich dem jammernden Menschen die Hand auf die Stirne und sage ihm: „Sei ruhig. In einer Stunde wirst du schlafen, und wenn du wieder erwachst, ist kein Schmerz mehr . . . "

Die Operation ist vorüber. Unter der dunklen Schlafbaracke überwache ich das Aufwachen des Patienten. Kaum ist er bei Besinnung, so schaut er erstaunt umher und wiederholt fort und fort: „Ich habe ja nicht mehr weh, ich habe ja nicht mehr weh!" . . . Seine Hand sucht die meine und will sie nicht mehr loslassen. Dann fange ich an, ihm und denen, die dabeisitzen, zu erzählen, daß es der Herr Jesus ist, der dem Doktor und seiner Frau geboten hat, hier an den Ogowe zu kommen und daß weiße Menschen in Europa uns die Mittel geben, um hier für die Kranken zu leben. Nun muß ich auf die Fragen, wer jene Menschen sind, wo sie wohnen, woher sie wissen, daß die Eingeborenen so viel unter Krankheiten leiden, Antwort geben. Durch die Kaffeesträucher hindurch scheint die afrikanische Sonne in die dunkle Hütte. Wir aber, Schwarz und Weiß, sitzen untereinander und erleben es: „Ihr aber seid alle Brüder." Ach, könnten die gebenden Freunde in Europa in einer solchen Stunde dabei sein! . . .

Chapter Sixteen

56. *Possessive adjectives*

1. The following words function as possessive adjectives when they qualify a noun. Their personal endings follow the **ein/kein** pattern (see chapter 4) and thus indicate gender, number, and case of the noun which follows:

		SINGULAR	FORMAL	PLURAL
1st person:		**mein** (*my*)		**unser** (*our*)
2nd person:		**dein** (*your*)	**Ihr** (*your:* sing. and plur.)	**euer** (*your*)
3rd person:	(M)	**sein** (*his, its*)		**ihr** (*their*)
	(F)	**ihr** (*her, its*)		
	(N)	**sein** (*its*)		

Meine **Eltern sind nicht zu Hause.**	***My*** *parents are not at home.*
Das ist *ihr* Buch.	*That is* ***her (their)*** *book.*
Eu(e)re **Freunde kommen heute nicht wieder.**	***Your*** *friends will not come again today.*
Ihre **Bücher liegen auf dem Tisch.**	***Her (your****: sing. or plur.,* ***their)*** *books are lying on the table.*

2. Ihr when beginning a sentence may have one of six different meanings. As a personal pronoun it could mean *you* or (*to*) *her*; as a possessive adjective it could mean *her, its, your,* or *their*. **Ihr** when capitalized within a sentence will always mean *your* (formal), but it may be either singular or plural. In all of these instances the context (e.g. verb ending) will give a clue to the correct meaning:

Ihr **seid aber nicht nett zu mir.**	***You*** *are not nice to me.*
Ihr **werde ich gar nicht helfen.**	*I will not help* ***her*** *at all.*

***Ihr* Buch liegt auf dem Tisch.** — *__Her (your, their)__ book is lying on the table.*
Läuft denn die Maschine noch? Nein! *Ihr* Motor ist kaputt! — *Does the machine still run? No! __Its__ motor is broken!*

Within the sentence uncapitalized **ihr** may have one of five different meanings. As a personal pronoun it could mean *you* or (*to*) *her*; as a possessive adjective it could mean *her, their, its*:

Habt *ihr* kein Deutsch studiert? — *Haven't __you__ studied German?*
Ich werde *ihr* gar nicht helfen. — *I will not help __her__ at all.*
Ist *ihr* Deutsch gräßlich? — *Is __her__ (__their__) German terrible?*
Die Maschine läuft nicht. Wissen Sie, ob *ihr* Motor kaputt ist? — *The machine doesn't run. Do you know if __its__ motor is broken?*

3. The possessive adjective **sein** generally has one of two meanings, *his* or *its*. However, it may be translated *her*. Context will indicate the correct equivalent:

Peter hat *seine* Schuhe verloren. — *Peter lost __his__ shoes.*
Der Stuhl steht in der Ecke. *Seine* Beine wurden neulich renoviert. — *The chair is standing in the corner. __Its__ legs were recently refinished.*
Das Mädchen verlor *seine* Schuhe. — *The girl lost __her__ shoes.*

4. **Unser** and **euer** may drop the **-e** of the stem or the **-e** of the inflectional ending: **unsre, eures, unserm** (or **unsrem**).

5. The idea *of mine, of yours,* etc. is expressed in German by the preposition **von** plus the personal pronoun:

Er ist ein guter Freund *von mir*. — *He is a good friend __of mine__.*

6. When ownership is clear, the definite article is often substituted for the possessive adjective, particularly when referring to clothing or parts of the body. Frequently, a dative of the appropriate reflexive pronoun is added:

Paul steckt *die* Hand in *die* Tasche. — *Paul puts __his__ hand in __his__ pocket.*
Du ziehst *dir die* Schuhe an. — *You are putting on __your__ shoes.*

In this section you are introduced to the vocabulary of the reading passage as well as drilled on the uses of the possessive adjectives. Continue to circle words that you do not know and review them before going on to the next section.

1. der Abschnitt = *section*
In diesem Abschnitt lesen wir das letzte Kapitel aus Erich Maria Remarques *Im Westen nichts Neues*.

1. In this section we will read the last chapter of Erich Maria Remarque's *All Quiet on the Western Front.*	**2.** Das Buch war **sein** erstes Werk und machte Remarque weltberühmt. (*his/to be*)
2. The book was *his* first work and made Remarque world famous.	**3.** **erscheinen** = *to appear* Das Buch erschien zum ersten Male im Jahre 1929 und machte **dessen** Autor weltberühmt. (*his/its*)
3. The book appeared for the first time in 1929 and made *its* author world famous.	**4.** **die Auflage** = *edition* Damals erreichte das Buch eine Auflage von sechs Millionen.
4. At that time the book reached an edition of six million copies.	**5.** Das Werk des 32 jährigen Autors **wurde** 1930 verfilmt. (*was/became*)
5. The work (the novel) of the 32 year old author *was* made into a film in 1930.	**6.** Bei der Berliner Premiere **ließ** Goebbels Mäuse laufen. (past of—*lesen/lassen*)
6. *lassen* At the premiere in Berlin Goebbels had some mice released.	**7.** **treiben** = *to drive* Er tat das, **um** das „pazifistische" Publikum auf die Stühle **zu** treiben.
7. He did that *in order to* make the pacifistic audience jump on their chairs (drive the pacifistic audience onto their chairs).	**8.** **heroisieren** = *to glamorize* **entheroisieren** = *to deglamorize* Das Buch entheroisiert den Krieg; **deshalb** ließ Goebbels Mäuse laufen. (*therefore/half of that*)
8. The book "deglamorizes" war (takes heroism out of war); *therefore* the mice were released by Goebbels.	**9.** **die Seite** = *side* **einseitig** = *onesided* **die Einseitigkeit** = __________
9. *one-sidedness*	**10.** Remarque schreibt mit bitterem Sarkasmus und Zynismus, aber auch mit **bewußter** Einseitigkeit. (*conscious/unconscious*)
10. Remarque writes with bitter sarcasm and cynicism, but also with *conscious* one-sidedness.	**11.** **zeigen** = *to demonstrate* Er will die **Sinnlosigkeit** des Krieges zeigen. (*sinlessness/senselessness*)

11. He wants to demonstrate the *senselessness* of war.	**12.** **schildern** = *to describe* Das Buch schildert die **Erlebnisse** eines jungen Mannes in dem Großen Krieg. (*experiences/memories*)
12. The book describes the *experiences* of a young man in the Great War.	**13.** Was er erlebt und gedacht hat, **wird** uns geschildert. (*is/will*)
13. What he experienced and thought *is* described to us.	**14.** **die Ruhe** = *rest* In dem letzten Kapitel des Buches hat er **vierzehn Tage Ruhe . . .**
14. In the last chapter of the book he has *a fourteen day leave* . . .	**15.** **schlucken** = *to swallow* . . . weil er etwas Gas **geschluckt hat.**
15. . . . because he *swallowed* some gas.	**16.** **enttäuschen** = *to disappoint* **die Enttäuschung** = _________
16. *disappointment*	**17.** Hier spricht er von den Hoffnungen und Enttäuschungen der Soldaten.
17. Here he speaks of the hopes and disappointments of the soldiers.	**18.** Er ist der letzte von den sieben Mann aus **seiner** Klasse hier. (*its/his*)
18. He is the last of the seven of *his* class (at school) here.	**19.** **die Waffe** = *weapon* **die Stille** = *quiet, stillness* **der Stand** = *position, condition, state* **der Waffenstillstand** = _________
19. *armistice*	**20.** **Jeder** spricht von Frieden und Waffenstillstand. (*that one/everyone*)
20. *Everyone* speaks of peace and armistice.	**21.** Da sind unsere Feinde. **Ihr** Waffenstillstand bedeutet eigentlich nichts. (*your/its/their*)
21. There are our enemies. *Their* armistice actually means nothing.	**22.** **Das** ist wirklich eine Enttäuschung! (*the/that*)
22. *That* is really a disappointment!	**23.** **Ihre** Enttäuschung ist groß, denn sie haben keine Zeit mehr. (*your/their*)

23. *Their* disappointment is great for they don't have any more time.	**24.** **zusammenbrechen** = *to break down* Wenn Friede und Waffenstillstand wieder eine Enttäuschung sind, dann *werden* die Soldaten zusammenbrechen. (*will/become*)
24. If peace and armistice are again a disappointment, then the soldiers *will* break down.	**25.** Sie werden zusammenbrechen, denn **Ihre** Hoffnungen sind zu stark. (*her/their/your*)
25. You will break down, for *your* hopes are too high.	**26.** **fortschaffen** = *to get rid of, to dismiss, to take away* Die Hoffnungen lassen sich nicht mehr fortschaffen.
26. The hopes can no longer be dismissed (or *taken away*, lit.: do not let themselves be dismissed).	**27.** Die Hoffnungen **haben** sich nicht mehr **fortschaffen lassen.**
27. The hopes *could* no longer *be dismissed.*	**28.** Gibt es wieder eine Enttäuschung, werdet **ihr** zusammenbrechen. (*her/you/its*)
28. If there is a disappointment again, *you* will break down.	**29.** Die Hoffnungen **haben** sich nicht mehr **fortschaffen lassen,** ohne zu explodieren.
29. Hope *could* no longer *be taken away* without exploding.	**30.** **stocken** = *to stop, to cease, to come to a standstill* Hier stocken **seine** Gedanken. (*his/her/its*)
30. Here *his* thoughts come to a standstill.	**31.** **weiter** = *further* **bringen** = *to bring* **weiterbringen** = __________
31. *to carry further, to help along*	**32.** Hier stocken meine Gedanken und sind nicht weiterzubringen.
32. Here my thoughts stop and cannot be carried further.	**33.** **warten** = *to wait* **erwarten** = *to wait, to expect* **Selbst** er hat so etwas nicht erwartet. (*himself/even*)
33. *Even* he did not expect such a thing.	**34.** Was erwartet **ihr?** (*you/her/their*)

34. What do *you* expect?	**35.** Was erwartet **mich?**
35. What awaits *me*?	**36.** Was erwartet **euch?**
36. What awaits *you*?	**37.** Was erwartet **sie?** (*she/they*)
37. What does *she* expect? (Also: What awaits *her*? What awaits *them*?)	**38.** Wo stocken **Ihre** Gedanken? (*her/your*)
38. Where do *your* thoughts stop?	**39.** **das Leben** = *life* **die Gier** = *lust, inordinate desire* (also: *greediness*) **die Lebensgier** = __________
39. *desire to live, lust for life*	**40.** Der Soldat, **der** Lebensgier hat — ist er ein guter oder ein schlechter Soldat? (*the/who/he*)
40. The soldier *who* has a lust for life—is he a good or a bad soldier?	**41.** **das Ziel** = *goal* Was für Ziele hat **jener** Mensch? (*this/that/every*)
41. What goals does *that* person have?	**42.** Aber **es sind** keine Ziele. (*it is/those are*)
42. But *those are* no goals.	**43.** **sich retten** = *to save oneself* Er hat sich im letzten Moment gerettet.
43. He saved himself at the last minute.	**44.** **retten** = *to save* **die Rettung** = *rescue* **der Rausch** = *intoxication, ecstacy* Der Rausch der Rettung, **den** jeder Soldat hat . . . (*whom/which/the*)
44. The intoxication of escape from death *which* every soldier has . . .	**45.** **hinziehen** = *to attract* Der Rausch der Rettung zieht ihn hin.
45. The ecstacy of rescue attracts him.	**46.** **die Übermacht** = *superior force* Der Rausch der Rettung zieht ihn mit Übermacht hin.

46. He is overwhelmingly drawn towards the intoxicating idea of rescue.	**47.** Was mich mit Übermacht hinzieht und erwartet, sind Gefühle.
47. Feelings are what overwhelmingly draw me and await me.	**48.** **die Heimat** = *native place, native country, homeland, home* **das Gefühl** = *feeling* **das Heimatgefühl** = ________
48. *love (feeling) for one's home*	**49.** Es ist Lebensgier, es ist Heimatgefühl, was mich mit Übermacht hinzieht.
49. It is lust for life, it is the love for my home, which overwhelmingly attracts me.	**50.** Lebensgier und der Rausch der Rettung sind keine Ziele, **selbst** das Heimatgefühl ist kein Ziel. (*himself/itself/even*)
50. Desire for life and the ecstacy of escape are not goals, *even* the love for one's home isn't really a goal.	**51.** **fesseln** = *to fetter* **entfesseln** = *to unfetter, to loose, to release* Unsere Erlebnisse **hatten** einen Sturm **entfesselt.** (*have loosed/had loosed*)
51. Our experiences *had loosed* a storm.	**52.** Unsere Erlebnisse, **die** haben einen Sturm entfesselt! (*they/who/which*)
52. Our experiences, *they* have released a storm!	**53.** **zurecht** = *in the right place, in good order* **finden** = *to find* **sich zurechtfinden** = ________
53. *to find one's way*	**54.** Wir finden **uns** nicht mehr auf dieser Welt zurecht.
54. We can no longer find *our* way in this world.	**55.** Die Stärke und der Schmerz unserer Erlebnisse haben einen Sturm entfesselt, und wir **werden** uns nicht mehr **zurechtfinden können.**
55. The strength and pain of our experiences have released a storm, and we *will* not *be able to orientate* ourselves any longer.	**56.** **die Wurzel** = *root* **wurzellos** = *rootless, without a root* Wenn wir jetzt zurückkehren, sind wir müde, **zerfallen,** ausgebrannt, wurzellos und ohne Hoffnung. (*in ruins/in good spirits*)

56. If we now return, we will be tired, *in ruins*, burnt out, rootless and without hope.	**57. das Geschlecht** = *generation* Das neue Geschlecht kann den Krieg nicht verstehen.
57. The new generation cannot understand the war.	**58.** Das alte Geschlecht kann **ihn** nicht vergessen. (*it/them*)
58. The old generation cannot forget *it*.	**59. verbringen** = *to spend, to pass* (*time*) Er wird das Jahr mit uns verbringen.
59. He will spend the year with us.	**60. gemein** = *common* **gemeinsam** = *in common, together* Er hat das Jahr gemeinsam mit uns verbracht.
60. He spent the year together with us.	**61. zwar** = *indeed, I admit* Das neue Geschlecht, **das** zwar die Jahre hier gemeinsam mit uns verbrachte . . . (*the/which/it*)
61. The new generation *which* indeed spent years here together with us . . .	**62. der Beruf** = *profession* Was für einen Beruf hat der Mann?
62. What kind of a profession does the man have?	**63.** Selbst **der** weiß es nicht! (*he/who/the*)
63. Even *he* doesn't know (it)!	**64.** Vor uns wächst ein Geschlecht, **das** Bett und Beruf hatte . . . (*the/which/it*)
64. Before us a generation is growing up *which* had a bed and a profession . . .	**65.** . . . und jetzt zurückgeht in seine alten Positionen.
65. . . . and now returns to its old positions.	**66.** Es geht in seine alten Positionen zurück, in **denen** es den Krieg vergessen wird. (*which/whose/those*)
66. It will go back into its old positions, in *which* it will forget the war.	**67. ähnlich** = *similar to* Hinter uns wächst ein Geschlecht, ähnlich uns **früher . . .** (*early/earlier/earliest*)

67. A generation is growing up after us, as we were *earlier* . . .	**68.** Es wächst hinter uns ein Geschlecht, ähnlich uns früher, **das** wird uns fremd sein. (*relative pronoun/demonstrative pronoun*)
68. *demonstrative:* the word order tells you so, i.e. **wird** follows immediately after **das** which is the subject. A generation is growing up after us, as we were previously, and *they* will be strangers to us.	**69.** Ein Geschlecht, **das** uns fremd sein wird, wächst hinter uns. (*relative/demonstrative*)
69. *relative:* **wird** is at the end of the clause. A generation *which* will be like strangers to us is growing up after us.	**70.** **bei** = *by, at* **die Seite** = *side* **schieben** = *to push* **beiseiteschieben** = __________
70. *to push aside*	**71.** **Das** Geschlecht wird uns beseiteschieben.
71. *That* generation will push us aside. (**Das** when stressed is translated *that.*)	**72.** Ein Geschlecht wächst hinter uns, ähnlich uns früher, **das** wird uns fremd sein und uns beiseiteschieben. (*who/which/it*)
72. A generation is growing up after us, similar to us as we used to be; and *they* (*it*) will be strangers to us and push us aside.	**73.** **überflüssig** = *superfluous* Wir sind überflüssig für uns **selbst.** (*even/ourselves*)
73. We are superfluous to *ourselves.*	**74.** Er wurde **ihr** überflüssig. (*you/for her/their*)
74. He became superfluous *for her.*	**75.** **sich anpassen** = *to adapt oneself* **Einige** passen sich an. (*own/some*)
75. *Some* adapt themselves.	**76.** Einige **haben** sich **angepaßt.**
76. Some *have adapted* themselves.	**77.** **sich fügen** = *to submit, to subordinate oneself* Einige werden sich anpassen, andere sich fügen, aber wir werden **wachsen.**

77. Some will adapt themselves, others will subordinate themselves, but we will *grow*.	**78.** Andere werden sich fügen, und viele werden **ratlos** sein. (*ruthless/perplexed*)
78. Others will subordinate themselves, and many will be *perplexed*.	**79.** **zerrinnen** = *to melt away, to vanish* Die Jahre werden zerrinnen.
79. The years will go by (melt away).	**80.** **schließlich** = *finally* Die Jahre werden zerrinnen, und schließlich werden wir zugrunde gehen.
80. The years will go by, and finally we will perish.	**81.** Ist es das Los der Menschen, daß die Jahre zerrinnen werden, und daß **sie** schließlich zugrunde gehen werden? (*she/they*)
81. Is it the fate of human beings that the years will go by and that *they* will finally perish?	

PROGRESS TEST

Choose the correct answer for the italicized word.

1. Gibt es wieder eine Enttäuschung, werdet *ihr* zusammenbrechen.
(a) you (b) her (c) its (d) your

2. Das Mädchen bleibt stehen, *seine* Gedanken stocken.
(a) their (b) her (c) its (d) to be

3. Ich weiß nicht, ob *Ihre* Probleme sich lösen werden.
(a) you (b) her (c) their (d) your

4. Ich hatte einen Wagen, aber schließlich lief *sein* Motor nicht mehr.
(a) its (b) his (c) to be (d) her

5. Kehrt ihr zu *ihr* zurück?
(a) you (b) your (c) her (d) their

6. Ich bin der letzte Mann aus __________ (*my*) Klasse.
(a) meiner (b) unserer (c) seiner (d) ihrer

7. ____ (*our*) Hoffnungen sind zu stark.
(a) eure (b) ihre (c) Ihre (d) unsere

8. In ____ (*your*) kleinen Garten sitze ich den ganzen Tag in der Sonne.
(a) ihrem (b) unsrem (c) deinem (d) seinem

Answer key: **1.** (a); **2.** (b); **3.** (d); **4.** (a); **5.** (c); **6.** (a); **7.** (d); **8.** (c).

57. *Possessives used as predicate adjectives or as pronouns*

1. When possessives appear in the predicate, they may either be adjectives or pronouns:

Das Buch ist *mein.*	*That book is **mine.*** (adj.)
Sein Haus ist größer als *unsres* (*das unsere, das unsrige*).	*His house is larger than **ours.*** (pronoun)

2. If the possessive is used *adjectivally*, it will have no ending; **ihr (Ihr),** however, is always inflected:

Dieses alte Auto ist *sein.*	*This old automobile is **his.***
Das Auto ist *Ihres.*	*That automobile is **yours.***

3. The possessive used *as a pronoun* will take an ending. Note the possibilities when the definite article is added to the possessive pronouns. Though rare, these variants do occur from time to time:

Ich schicke meiner Schwester einen Ring. Was schickst du *deiner* (*der deinen, der deinigen*)?	*I am sending my sister a ring. What are you sending **yours?***
Mein Vater ist in Deutschland. *Eurer* (*der eure, der eurige*) ist in der Schweiz.	*My father is in Germany. **Yours** is in Switzerland.*

The following frames test your knowledge of possessives used as adjectives and as pronouns. You will continue to be introduced to the vocabulary of the reading passage.

	1. **schmecken** = *to taste* Unser Bier schmeckt nicht so gut wie **deins.** (*your/yours*)
1. Our beer doesn't taste as good as *yours.*	**2.** **das Fahrrad** = *bicycle* Das Fahrrad ist **ihres.** (*her/hers*)
2. The bicycle is *hers.*	**3.** **Das meinige** steht auf der Straße. (*mine/my*)
3. *Mine* is standing on the street.	**4.** **Das seinige** ist kaputt.

4. *His* is broken.	**5.** **Die ihre** habe ich nicht mehr.
5. I do not have *hers* (*theirs*) any more.	**6.** Das Messer gehört Macki, die Pistole ist **mein.**
6. The knife belongs to Macki, the pistol is *mine.*	**7.** Es ist **unseres.** (*our/ours*)
7. It is *ours.*	**8.** Es ist **das unsere.** (*our/the our/ours*)
8. It is *ours.*	**9.** **Die Meinen** werden mich lieben. (*mine/those who belong to me*)
9. *Those who belong to me* will love me.	**10.** Er lief auf **die Seinen** zu.
10. He ran towards *his loved ones.*	**11.** Im Frühling summen die Bienen im Garten.
11. In Spring the bees hum in the garden.	**12.** Die Bienen, die im Garten summen, sind doch **eure.** (*your/yours*)
12. The bees that are humming in the garden are *yours.*	**13.** **Eure** Bienen habe ich lange nicht mehr gesehen. (*your/yours*)
13. I haven't seen *your* bees for a long time.	**14.** Ihre Bienen wohnen in **Bienenstöcken.**
14. Your (her, their) bees live in *beehives.*	**15.** Und jetzt kehren wir zurück zu *Im Westen nichts Neues.*
15. And now let us return to *All Quiet on the Western Front.*	**16.** **schwer** = *heavy* **der Mut** = *courage, spirit, heart* **die Schwermut** = *melancholy, depression, sadness* Ihm liegt eine große Schwermut auf dem Herzen.
16. His heart is filled with great sadness. (Great sadness lies on his heart.)	**17.** **stürzen** = *to fall* **bestürzen** = *to confound, to dismay* **die Bestürzung** = __________
17. *dismay, consternation, confusion*	**18.** Alles, was er denkt, ist nur Schwermut und Bestürzung.

18. His thoughts are full of melancholy and dismay.	**19.** **der Staub** = *dust* **stäuben** = *to fly off or about like dust* **fort** = *away, gone* **fortstäuben** = *to fly away like dust* Schwermut und Bestürzung stäuben fort.
19. Melancholy and confusion fly away like dust.	**20.** Schwermut und Bestürzung stäuben fort, wenn ich unter den **Pappeln** stehe. (*poplars/poppies*)
20. Melancholy and confusion fly away like dust when I stand under the *poplars*.	**21.** Aber vielleicht ist auch alles dieses, was ich denke, nur Schwermut und Bestürzung, **die** fortstäubt . . . (*which/they*)
21. *which*: the word order of **fortstäubt** tells you that it is a relative pronoun; were it a demonstrative, the verb would be **stäubt fort.** But perhaps all this that I am thinking is only melancholy and confusion *which* will fly away like dust . . .	**22.** **lauschen** = *to listen* . . . wenn ich wieder unter den Pappeln stehe und dem Rauschen **ihrer** Blätter lausche. (*of their/of her/of its*)
22. . . . when I again stand under the poplars and listen to the rustle *of their* leaves.	**23.** **der Vogel** = *bird* Lauscht er auch dem Singen **der** Vögel? (*the/of the*)
23. *of the*, as **der Vögel** can only be genitive plural. Is he also listening to the singing *of the* birds?	**24.** **weich** = *soft* Das Weiche macht unser Blut unruhig.
24. The softness makes our blood restless.	**25.** Das Weiche, das unser Blut unruhig machte, kann nicht fort sein.
25. The softness that made our blood restless cannot be gone.	**26.** **bestürzen** = *to dismay, to confound* **bestürzend** = *dismaying, confounding* **das Bestürzende** = ________
26. *the dismaying thing* (*the thing that fills us with dismay*)	**27.** **das Bestürzende** = *the dismaying thing* **das Kommende** = ________
27. *the coming thing* (*the thing that is coming*)	**28.** Das Bestürzende, das Kommende macht unser Blut weich.

28. The dismaying thing, the coming thing turns our blood to water ("makes our blood soft").	**29.** **das Gesicht** = *face* Das Ungewisse, die tausend Gesichter der Zukunft, **das** kann nicht untergehen. (*which/that*)
29. The uncertain, the thousand faces of the future, *that* cannot perish.	**30.** **die Ahnung** = *idea, notion, thought, presentiment* Die Ahnung der Frauen **hat** sein Blut unruhig **gemacht.**
30. The thought of women *made* his blood restless.	**31.** Es kann nicht sein, daß es fort ist, die Melodie aus Träumen und Büchern, das Rauschen der Pappeln und die Ahnung der Frauen.
31. It cannot be that it is gone, the melody from dreams and books, the rustling of the poplars and the thought of women.	**32.** **die Trommel** = *drum* **das Feuer** = *fire* **das Trommelfeuer** = *ceaseless bombardment* Ist das alles im Trommelfeuer untergegangen?
32. Has all that perished in the ceaseless bombardment?	**33.** **der Zweifel** = *doubt* **verzweifeln** = *to despair* **die Verzweiflung** = ________
33. *despair*	**34.** **die Mannschaft** = *troops* Es kann nicht sein, daß all das untergegangen ist in Trommelfeuer, Verzweiflung und **Mannschaftsbordells.** (**Mannschaftsbordells** probably means = ________)
34. It can't be that all that has perished in the bombing, despair, and *troop brothels.*	**35.** **leuchten** = *to shine* Wie leuchten die Bäume!
35. How the trees shine!	**36.** **bunt** = *multicolored, colorful* Es ist **Herbst,** die Bäume leuchten bunt und golden. (*harvest/autumn*)
36. It is *autumn,* the trees are shining with various colors and gold.	**37.** **die Eberesche** = *mountain ash, rowan (tree)* Die Ebereschen tragen jetzt rote **Beeren.** (*beer/berries*)

37. The mountain ash now have red *berries.*	**38.** **das Laub** = *foliage* Die Beeren der Ebereschen stehen rot im Laub.
38. The berries of the mountain ash are (lit.: stand) red among the foliage.	**39.** **laufen** = *to run* **zulaufen** = *to run towards* Die Beeren stehen rot im Laub, Landstraßen laufen weiß auf den Horizont zu.
39. The berries are red among the foliage, the highways run, white, towards the horizon.	**40.** **der Friede** = *peace* **das Gerücht** = *rumor* Die Kantinen summen wie Bienenstöcke von **Friedensgerüchten.**
40. The canteens hum like beehives with *rumors of peace.*	**41.** Friedensgerüchte, **wie Bienen,** summen überall.
41. Rumors of peace are humming everywhere, *like bees.*	**42.** **gegen** = *against, towards* **entgegen** = *against, towards* **sehen** = *to see* **entgegensehen** = __________
42. *to look forward to, to await*	**43.** Ich stehe auf und bin sehr **ruhig.** (*calm/restless*)
43. I get up and am very *calm.*	**44.** **mögen** = *let,* implying concession. **Mögen** die Monate und Jahre kommen, sie können mir nichts mehr nehmen.
44. Let the months and years come. They cannot take anything more from me. (*Even though* the months and years *may* come, *yet* they cannot take anything more from me.)	**45.** Ich kann **den Monaten** und **Jahren** ohne Furcht entgegensehen. (*dative plural/masculine singular*)
45. *dative plural:* the verb takes a dative object. I can look forward *to the months* and *years* without fear.	**46.** Ich bin so allein und so ohne **Erwartung,** daß ich ihnen entgegensehen kann ohne Furcht. (*expectation/surprise*)
46. I am so alone and so without *expectation* that I can look forward to them without fear.	**47.** **tragen** = *to carry* Das Leben **trägt** mich durch diese Jahre.

47. Life *carries* me through these years.	**48.** **das Auge** = *eye* Das Leben, das mich durch diese Jahre **trug,** ist noch in meinen Händen und Augen.
48. Life, which *carried* me through these years, is still in my hands and eyes.	**49.** **überwinden** = *to overcome* Ob ich das Leben **überwunden habe,** weiß ich selbst nicht.
49. I don't know myself whether I *have overcome* life.	**50.** Aber **so lange** das Leben da ist, wird es sich seinen Weg suchen . . .
50. But *as long as* life is there, it will seek its own way . . .	**51.** **mag dieses** = *whether that* . . . mag dieses, **das** in mir „Ich" sagt, wollen oder nicht.
51. . . . whether that *which* in me says "I" wishes it or not.	**52.** Er **fiel** im Oktober 1918; der Tag war ruhig und still.
52. He *fell* in October 1918. The day was calm and peaceful.	**53.** **das Heer** = *army* **der Bericht** = *report* **der Heeresbericht** = ________
53. *army communiqué*	**54.** **melden** = *to report* Der Heeresbericht lautet: Im Westen ist nichts Neues zu melden.
54. The army communiqué reads: There is nothing new to be reported from the West.	**55.** **sich beschränken** = *to restrict oneself* Der Heeresbericht beschränkt sich nur auf den Satz, im Westen **sei** nichts Neues zu melden.
55. The army communiqué is restricted to the sentence that there *is* nothing new to be reported from the Western front. (**sei** = subjunctive form of **sein**)	**56.** **vornübergesunken** = *sunk forwards* Er war vornübergesunken und lag **wie schlafend** an der Erde.
56. He had fallen forwards and was lying on the ground *as if sleeping*.	**57.** **drehen** = *to turn* **umdrehen** = *to turn over, to turn around* Man **drehte** ihn **um.**
57. past They *turned* him *over*.	**58.** **die Qual** = *pain, torment, suffering* **sich quälen** = *to suffer* Er **hat sich** nicht lange **gequält.**

58. He *did* not *suffer* long.	**59.** Als man ihn umdrehte, sah man, daß er **sich** nicht lange **gequält haben konnte.**
59. When they turned him over, they saw that he *could* not *have suffered* for a long time.	**60.** **das Gesicht** = *face* Von seinem Gesicht sah man, daß er sich nicht lange gequält haben konnte.
60. From his face one saw that he could not have suffered for a long time.	**61.** **gefaßt** = *calm, composed* Sein Gesicht hatte einen so gefaßten **Ausdruck . . .** (*expression/impression*)
61. His face had such a calm *expression* . . .	**62.** Er war zufrieden **damit.** (*so that/with that*)
62. He was satisfied *with that.*	**63.** **als wäre** = *as if . . . were* Sein Gesicht hatte einen so gefaßten Ausdruck, als wäre er beinahe zufrieden damit, daß es so **gekommen war.** (*was happening/had happened*)
63. His face had such a calm expression, as if he were almost satisfied that it *had happened* thus. (**wäre** = subjunctive form of **sein**)	

PROGRESS TEST

A. *Check your knowledge of the meaning of the possessives used as predicate adjectives or as pronouns.*

1. Die Bienenstöcke sind doch nicht *dein*!
   (a) your (b) yours (c) your loved ones
2. Die Pappeln, worunter wir jetzt so ruhig und allein stehen, sind *die deinen.*
   (a) your (b) yours (c) your loved ones
3. *Das eurige* läßt sich nicht sehen.
   (a) our (b) your (c) yours (d) ours
4. Mit *dem ihren* können wir nicht ins Kino fahren.
   (a) it (b) your family (c) his family (d) hers
5. *Die Ihren* werden mich lieben.
   (a) your (b) your loved ones (c) she (d) they

B. *And now check your knowledge of the vocabulary.*

1. Gemeinsam verbrachten wir die Jahre, überflüßig für uns selbst, bis wir ratlos wurden.
   (a) Through the years we had only the best of feelings for one another.
   (b) Once we were separated, our lives lost their meaning.
   (c) We became restless with the years because we had seen the futility of our lives.
   (d) We eventually became helpless because of long years of feeling superfluous.
2. Wenn der Waffenstillstand nicht kommt, werde ich zusammenbrechen.
   (a) The armistice brings to many a desire to go home.
   (b) One of the disappointments which must be accepted is that of the armistice.
   (c) The lack of an armistice breeds disappointment.
   (d) Armistice and disappointment are inevitable.
3. Wenn unsere Erlebnisse eine Revolution entfesselt hätten, wären wir zerfallen, ausgebrannt und gestorben.
   (a) All revolutions come from those dissatisfied with life.
   (b) Whenever we had a revolution we likewise buoyed up our spirits.
   (c) If a revolution had taken place we would not have lived through it.
   (d) A revolution would not have taken place, had it not been for our decadence.
4. Hinter uns ist ein Geschlecht, das uns überholen wird.
   (a) The new generation will fail.
   (b) Soon there will be a generation to replace us.
   (c) Another species will soon overtake the human race.
   (d) Behind us is a decadent generation.
5. Den Jahren und Monaten sehen sie entgegen, nicht ohne Furcht und Verzweiflung.
   (a) Despair and fear will gradually be dispelled.
   (b) Months and years will pass away without fear and despair.
   (c) You see fear and despair not only in the here and now but also in the years and months to follow.
   (d) They look to the future with fear and despair.

Answer key: A. **1.** (b); **2.** (b); **3.** (c); **4.** (d); **5.** (b).
B. **1.** (d); **2.** (c); **3.** (c); **4.** (b); **5.** (d).

From *Im Westen nichts Neues*. Verlag Kiepenheuer & Witsch, Köln, 1964.

Erich Maria Remarque: Im Westen nichts Neues

Es ist Herbst. Von den alten Leuten sind nicht mehr viele da. Ich bin der letzte von den sieben Mann aus unserer Klasse hier.

Jeder spricht von Frieden und Waffenstillstand. Alle warten. Wenn es wieder eine Enttäuschung wird, dann werden sie zusammenbrechen, die Hoffnungen sind zu stark, sie lassen sich nicht mehr fortschaffen, ohne zu explodieren. Gibt es keinen Frieden, dann gibt es Revolution.

Ich habe vierzehn Tage Ruhe, weil ich etwas Gas geschluckt habe. In einem kleinen Garten sitze ich den ganzen Tag in der Sonne. Der Waffenstillstand kommt bald, ich glaube es jetzt auch. Dann werden wir nach Hause fahren.

Hier stocken meine Gedanken und sind nicht weiterzubringen. Was mich mit Übermacht hinzieht und erwartet, sind Gefühle. Es ist Lebensgier, es ist Heimatgefühl, es ist das Blut, es ist der Rausch der Rettung. Aber es sind keine Ziele.

Wären[1] wir 1916 heimgekommen, wir hätten[2] aus dem Schmerz und der Stärke unserer Erlebnisse einen Sturm entfesselt. Wenn wir jetzt zurückkehren, sind wir müde, zerfallen, ausgebrannt, wurzellos und ohne Hoffnung. Wir werden uns nicht mehr zurechtfinden können.

Man wird uns auch nicht verstehen — denn vor uns wächst ein Geschlecht, das zwar die Jahre hier gemeinsam mit uns verbrachte, das aber Bett und Beruf hatte und jetzt zurückgeht in seine alten Positionen, in denen es den Krieg vergessen wird, — und hinter uns wächst ein Geschlecht, ähnlich uns früher, das wird uns fremd sein und uns beiseiteschieben. Wir sind überflüssig für uns selbst, wir werden wachsen, einige werden sich anpassen, andere sich fügen, und viele werden ratlos sein; — die Jahre werden zerrinnen, und schließlich werden wir zugrunde gehen.

Aber vielleicht ist auch alles dieses, was ich denke, nur Schwermut und Bestürzung, die fortstäubt, wenn ich wieder unter den Pappeln stehe und dem Rauschen ihrer Blätter lausche. Es kann nicht sein, daß es fort ist, das Weiche, das unser Blut unruhig machte, das Ungewisse, Bestürzende, Kommende, die tausend Gesichter der Zukunft, die Melodie aus Träumen und Büchern, das Rauschen und die Ahnung der Frauen, es kann nicht sein, daß es untergegangen ist in Trommelfeuer, Verzweiflung und Mannschaftsbordells.

Die Bäume hier leuchten bunt und golden, die Beeren der Ebereschen[3] stehen rot im Laub, Landstraßen laufen weiß auf den Horizont zu, und die Kantinen summen wie Bienenstöcke von Friedensgerüchten.

Ich stehe auf.

Ich bin sehr ruhig. Mögen die Monate und Jahre kommen, sie nehmen mir nichts mehr, sie können mir nichts mehr nehmen. Ich bin so allein und so ohne Erwartung, daß ich ihnen entgegensehen kann ohne Furcht. Das Leben, das mich durch diese Jahre trug, ist noch in meinen Händen und Augen. Ob ich es überwunden habe, weiß ich nicht. Aber so lange es da ist, wird es sich seinen Weg suchen, mag dieses, das in mir „Ich" sagt, wollen oder nicht.

* * *

Er fiel im Oktober 1918, an einem Tage, der so ruhig und still war an der ganzen Front, daß der Heeresbericht sich nur auf den Satz beschränkte, im Westen sei nichts Neues zu melden.

Er war vornübergesunken und lag wie schlafend an der Erde. Als man ihn umdrehte, sah man, daß er sich nicht lange gequält haben konnte; — sein Gesicht hatte einen so gefaßten Ausdruck, als wäre er beinahe zufrieden damit, daß es so gekommen war.

---

1 *wären (subjunctive form) = had*

2 *hätte (subjunctive form) = would have*

3 *die Eberesche = mountain ash, rowan (tree)*

Chapter Seventeen

58. *Indefinite pronouns and adjectives*

1. The most common indefinite pronouns and adjectives are as follows:

man	*one*
einer	*one*
keiner	*nobody, no one, none*
jemand	*somebody, someone; anybody, anyone*
irgend jemand	*anyone*
jemand anders	*someone else*
sonst jemand	*someone else*
niemand	*nobody, no one*
niemand anders	*no one else*
sonst niemand	*no one else*
jedermann	*everybody, everyone*
jeder	*everybody, everyone*
all(e)	*all*
alles	*everything*
alles mögliche	*everything possible*
alles übrige	*all the rest*
alles andere	*all else*
viel	*much*
viele	*many*
vieles	*many things*
wenig	*little* (in quantity)
wenige	*few*
nichts	*nothing*
irgend	*any, some (or other)* [rarely used alone]
irgendein (adj.)	*some (or other), any*
irgendeiner	*someone* (emphatic)

etwas	*something, some* (meaning: *just a little*)
irgend etwas	*something (or other), anything*
etwas anderes	*something else, anything other*
nichts anderes	*nothing else*
ein paar	*a few, several*
ein Paar (n.)	*a pair, two, a couple*
mehrere	*several* (in the sense of *more*)
verschiedene	*several* (in the sense of *different*)
einige	*some, a few*
etliche	*some, several, a few*
ander-	*other*
mancher	*many a* (person)
manches	*a great deal*
manche	*some* (people)
allerlei	*all sorts of*
ein bißchen	*a little*
beides	*both things*
beide	*both*

Give the meanings of the italicized words.

	1. Vielleicht kennen Sie den Namen Karl Jaspers.
1. Perhaps you are acquainted with the name Karl Jaspers.	2. Er ist **einer** von den großen deutschen Philosophen unseres Jahrhunderts.
2. He is *one* of the great German philosophers of our century.	3. **versäumen** = *to neglect, to fail, to miss* **Keiner** soll die Gelegenheit versäumen, **etwas** aus seinen Schriften zu lesen.
3. *No one* should neglect the opportunity to read *something* from his writings.	4. In diesem Kapitel werden Sie einen Auszug lesen aus seinem werk: *Die Atombombe und die Zukunft des Menschen.*
4. In this chapter you will read an extract from his *The Atom Bomb and the Future of Man.*	5. **besprechen** = *to discuss* Wir werden jetzt **einige** Gedanken daraus besprechen.
5. We are now going to discuss *some* thoughts from it.	6. **abschaffen** = *to abolish, to scrap* **Jeder** will, daß die Atombomben abgeschafft werden.
6. *Everybody* wants atom bombs to be abolished.	7. Oder ist **irgend jemand** dagegen?

7. Or is there *anyone* against that?	8. **erklären** = *to declare* **bereit** = *ready* Will **jedermann** sich dazu bereit erklären?
8. Is *everyone* willing to declare himself ready to (do) that?	9. **Alle** Denkenden wollen es, und **alle** Staaten erklären sich bereit.
9. *All* thinking people wish it, and *all* states declare themselves ready.	10. **wagen** = *to dare* **anwenden** = *to use, to employ* **Niemand** wird es wagen, die Atombomben anzuwenden.
10. *No one* will dare to use atom bombs.	11. **die Waffe** = *weapon* Wird **jemand anders** es wagen, diese Atomwaffen anzuwenden?
11. Will *someone else* dare to employ these atomic weapons?	12. Darf **sonst jemand** außer den Russen und den Amerikanern Atomwaffen besitzen?
12. May *anyone else* except the Russians and the Americans possess atomic weapons?	13. **Niemand anders** wird so verrückt sein, Atomwaffen besitzen zu wollen.
13. *No one else* will be so mad as to want to possess atomic weapons (*will they*).	14. **treffen** = *to strike* Wenn eine Waffe **beide** Gegner trifft . . . (If **gegen** means *against*, **Gegner** must mean ________)
14. *opponent* If a weapon strikes *both* opponents . . .	15. . . . wird **jemand** diese Waffe anwenden wollen?
15. . . . will *anyone* want to employ this weapon?	16. **Viele** glauben, daß ein Atomkrieg unmöglich geworden ist.
16. *Many* believe that an atomic war has become impossible.	17. Gibt es **irgendeinen,** der nicht glaubt, daß ein Atomkrieg stattfinden wird?
17. Is there *anyone* who does not believe that an atomic war will take place?	18. **verhältnismäßig** = *relatively* Wollen Sie sagen, daß nur verhältnismäßig **wenige** einen Krieg wollen?
18. Do you mean to say that only a relatively *few* want to have a war?	19. **Etliche** glauben, daß jeder Krieg unmöglich geworden ist.

19. *A few* believe that any (every) war has become impossible.	**20.** **Manche** glauben, daß keine Großmacht mehr wagen wird, einen Krieg zu beginnen.
20. *Some* believe that no great power will dare any more to begin a war.	**21.** **vernichten** = *to destroy, to annihilate* **die Vernichtung** = ________
21. *annihilation, destruction*	**22.** **könnte** = *could* Heute will **mancher** nicht glauben, daß es je einen Vernichtungskrieg geben könnte.
22. *Many a person* today does not want to believe that there could ever be a war of annihilation.	**23.** **das Zeitalter** = *age* Ist unser Zeitalter **irgend etwas anderes** als das Zeitalter der Kriege?
23. Is our age *anything else* than the age of war (wars)?	**24.** **Beides** können wir nicht auf einmal haben: Krieg und Frieden.
24. War and peace: we cannot have *both* at once.	**25.** **Vieles** wird gesagt.
25. *Much is* (*many things* are) said.	**26.** Es wird **viel** gesagt.
26. *Much* is said.	**27.** **Manches** wird gesagt, aber nichts wird getan.
27. A great deal is said, but nothing is done.	**28.** **herstellen** = *to manufacture* Kann man **nichts anderes** tun, als nur zuschauen, wie Atomwaffen hergestellt werden?
28. Can one do *nothing else* than only watch how atomic weapons are manufactured?	**29.** **Alles** können die großen Nationen nicht tun.
29. The great nations cannot do *everything*.	**30.** Wir müssen **alles mögliche** tun.
30. We must do *everything possible*.	**31.** Es kann nur **wenig** gesagt werden.
31. Only a *little* can be said.	**32.** **Alles übrige** muß man eben erfahren.

32. One will just have to experience *all the rest.*	**33.** **fortlaufen** = *to run away, to continue on* **fortlaufend** = *continuous* Wir müssen **irgendeine** Kontrolle für die fortlaufende Produktion der Atombomben finden.
33. We must find *some* (kind of) control for the continuous production of atomic bombs.	**34.** **Verschiedene** Nationen wollen keinen Krieg, **verschiedene** scheinen doch den Krieg zu wollen.
34. *Several different* nations do not want any wars; *several,* however, seem to want war.	**35.** **Mehrere** haben sich neutrale Länder genannt.
35. *Several* have proclaimed (named) themselves neutral countries.	**36.** **Ein paar** scheinen überhaupt kein Interesse daran zu haben.
36. *A few* seem to have no interest at all in that.	**37.** **reden** = *to talk* **Allerlei** wird geredet.
37. *All sorts of things* are talked about.	**38.** Ist **ein bißchen** Krieg besser als gar keiner?
38. Is *a little* (bit of) war better than none at all?	**39.** **Alles andere** muß man einfach in die Hände Gottes legen.
39. *Everything else* one must simply place into the hands of God.	**40.** **entstehen** = *to originate, to arise, to break out* Für **andere** ist es unmöglich, daß je ein Vernichtungskrieg wird entstehen können.
40. For *others* it is impossible that a war of annihilation will ever be able to break out.	

PROGRESS TEST

Choose the correct meaning for the indicated word.

1. Ist *jemand* gegen die Abschaffung der Atomwaffen?
   (a) all the rest (b) everyone (c) anyone (d) someone else
2. *Jeder* will, daß die Großmächte nicht in einen Krieg geraten.
   (a) many (b) everyone (c) several (d) some
3. *Irgendeiner* muß doch eingreifen!
   (a) a considerable number (b) several (c) a few (d) someone
4. *Alles übrige* müssen Sie tun.
   (a) all the rest (b) everything possible (c) all sorts of things (d) anything

5. *Allerlei* wird geglaubt.
(a) all the rest (b) everything (c) all sorts of things (d) anything

6. *Etliche* wollen nicht, daß sie denken sollen.
(a) some (b) many (c) all the rest (d) something

7. Es ist *sonst niemand* da.
(a) something (b) no one else (c) nothing (d) someone

8. *Verschiedene* können das nicht verstehen.
(a) all of them (b) someone else (c) many (d) several different people

Answer key: **1.** (c); **2.** (b); **3.** (d); **4.** (a); **5.** (c); **6.** (a); **7.** (b); **8.** (d).

59. *Special uses of the genitive*

1. The genitive is used to express indefinite time:

eines Tages	*one day*
eines Morgens	*one morning*
eines Abends	*one evening*
morgens	*in the morning*
abends	*in the evening*
nachts	*at night*
etc.	

2. *On my* (*your, his,* etc.) *account* is expressed by the possessive adjectives in combination with the preposition **wegen:**

meinetwegen, deinetwegen, seinetwegen, etc.

Note the **-et-** insertion between the possessive adjective and **wegen.**

3. Similarly *for my* (*your, his,* etc.) *sake* is expressed by a combination of the possessive adjective with **um . . . willen:**

um meinetwillen, um deinetwillen, um seinetwillen, etc.

Give the meaning of the indicated phrases.

	1. **einkaufen** = *to shop* **Vormittags** gehen wir immer einkaufen. (*in the morning/in the afternoon*)
1. We always go shopping *in the morning*.	**2.** **Eines Tages** müssen wir aufhören, Kriege zu führen. (*one day/one of these days*)

2. *One of these days* we must stop having wars.	**3. Euretwegen** ist er nicht gekommen.
3. He did not come *because of you.*	**4. Ihretwegen** dürfen wir nicht ins Kino gehen.
4. *Because of them* (*her, you*) we cannot go to the movies.	**5. Um ihretwillen** müssen sie das Rauchen aufgeben.
5. They have to give up smoking *for their* (*her*) *sake.*	**6. Meinetwegen** können Sie nach Hause gehen.
6. As far as I'm concerned you can go home.	

READING PREPARATION

The following frames are to prepare you for the reading passage.

	1. gültig = *valid* **die Gültigkeit** = *validity* Was Karl Jaspers damals in den fünfziger Jahren über die Atombombe zu sagen hatte, hat immer noch Gültigkeit.
1. What Karl Jaspers had to say in the fifties about the atomic bomb is still valid (today).	**2.** Alle Denkenden wollen, daß die Atomwaffen **abgeschafft werden.** (*will abolish/be abolished*)
2. All thinking people want atomic weapons to *be abolished.*	**3.** Alle Staaten erklären sich bereit.
3. All states declare themselves ready.	**4. abschaffen** = *to abolish* **die Abschaffung** = _________
4. *the abolition.*	**5. zuverlässig** = *reliable* Wir wollen **aber** eine zuverlässige Abschaffung. (*but/however*)
5. We want, *however,* a reliable abolition.	**6.** Aber die Abschaffung ist nur zuverlässig, wenn **zugleich** eine Kontrolle stattfindet.

6. But abolition is only reliable if *at the same time* a control is established (takes place).	**7.** **die Gegenseite** = *opposite side, reverse* **die Gegenseitigkeit** = *reciprocity* **gegenseitig** = *mutual, reciprocal* Eine Abschaffung ist nur zuverlässig, wenn zugleich eine gegenseitige Kontrolle stattfindet.
7. An abolition is only reliable if at the same time mutual controls are established.	**8.** Ein zweiter Gedanke ist . . .
8. A second thought is . . .	**9.** **. . . auch wenn** die Atombomben nicht abgeschafft sind . . . (*also when/even if*)
9. . . . *even if* atom bombs are not abolished . . .	**10.** . . . wird niemand es wagen, **sie** anzuwenden. (*her/them*)
10. . . . no one will dare to use *them*.	**11.** **herstellen** = *to produce* **die Herstellung** = ________
11. *production*	**12.** **das Gift** = *poison* **das Gas** = *gas* die Herstellung der Giftgase
12. the production of poison gases	**13.** **die Masse** = *mass, bulk* **massenhaft** = *wholesale, enormous* **Trotz** massenhafter Herstellung der Giftgase . . .
13. *In spite of* wholesale production of poison gases . . .	**14.** **setzen** = *to set* **einsetzen** = *to employ* Hitler **hat** die Giftgase in seiner Katastrophe nicht **eingesetzt.**
14. Hitler *did* not *employ* poison gases in his catastrophe.	**15.** Trotz massenhafter Herstellung der Giftgase hat Hitler diese **auch** in seiner Katastrophe nicht eingesetzt. (*also/even*)
15. In spite of wholesale production of poison gases Hitler did not employ these *even* in his catastrophe.	**16.** **anwenden** = *to use, employ* **anwendbar** = *usable, employable* Die Waffe ist **unanwendbar** geworden.

16. The weapon has become *unusable.*	**17.** Wenn eine Waffe **notwendig** beide Gegner vernichtend trifft . . . (*necessarily/unnecessarily*)
17. If a weapon *necessarily* annihilates (annihilatingly strikes) both opponents . . .	**18.** . . . ist **sie** unanwendbar geworden.
18. . . . *it* becomes (has become) unusable.	**19.** **Weil** der Atomkrieg unmöglich geworden ist, ist jeder Krieg unmöglich geworden. (*because/while*)
19. *Because* atomic war has become impossible, every war has become impossible.	**20.** **einsetzen** = *to employ* **der Einsatz** = ________
20. *the employment, use*	**21.** **drohen** = *to threaten* . . . der Einsatz der Atombombe droht . . .
21. . . . the use of the atomic bomb threatens . . .	**22.** **irgend** = *any, some* (*or other*) **wann** = *when* **irgendwann** = *at some time* (*or other*) In einem Weltkrieg droht irgendwann der Einsatz der Atombombe.
22. In a world war the use of the atomic bomb threatens at some time or other.	**23.** **der Staat** = *state* **die Ordnung** = *order* **die Staatsordnung** = ________
23. *political system, political order*	**24.** **der Sinn** = *meaning* der Sinn der Staatsordnung
24. the meaning of political order	**25.** **um** = *over, about* ein Weltkrieg um **den Sinn der Staatsordnung**
25. a world war over *political ideology* (i.e. *the meaning of political order*)	**26.** In einem Weltkrieg um den Sinn der Staatsordnung **droht** irgendwann **doch** der Einsatz der Atombombe.
26. In a world war over political ideology the use of the atomic bomb *does threaten* at some time or other. (**Doch** is used here as an intensifier.)	**27.** **auf Leben und Tod** = *to the death* Denn da in einem Weltkrieg um den Sinn der Staatsordnung auf Leben und Tod . . .

27. For since in a world war to the death over political ideology . . .	**28.** Denn da in einem Weltkrieg um den Sinn der Staatsordnung auf Leben und Tod irgendwann doch der Einsatz der Atombombe droht . . .
28. For since in a world war to the death over political ideology the use of the atomic bomb does threaten at some time or other . . .	**29.** . . . wird **keine** Großmacht **mehr** wagen, den Krieg zu beginnen.
29. . . . no great power will dare *any longer* to begin the war.	**30.** **würde** = *would become* **Weil** der Krieg für alle der Vernichtungskrieg würde, kann er nicht mehr entstehen.
30. *Because* the war would become for all a war of annihilation, it cannot happen any more.	**31.** **retten** = *to deliver, to save, to rescue* **der Retter** = *deliverer, rescuer, savior* **die totale Rettung** = ________
31. *the total deliverance*	**32.** **bedrohen** = *to threaten* **die totale Bedrohung** = ________
32. *the total threat*	**33.** **zeugen** = *to beget, to produce* **erzeugen** = *to breed, to generate, to produce* Die totale Bedrohung erzeugt die totale Rettung.
33. Total threat produces total deliverance.	**34.** Der Vernichtungskrieg kann nicht mehr entstehen, denn die totale Bedrohung erzeugt die totale Rettung.
34. The war of annihilation cannot arise any more since (for) total threat produces total deliverance.	**35.** **die Not** = *distress* (*need, necessity*) **die Notsituation** = ________
35. *the state of distress*	**36.** **das Dasein** = *life, presence, existence* **gestalten** = *to shape, form* **die Gestaltung** = *the shaping, form* **die Daseinsgestaltung** = ________
36. *the shaping of life, the form of existence*	**37.** **erzwingen** = *to determine necessarily, to force* Die Notsituation erzwingt die Daseinsgestaltung.

37. The state of distress necessarily determines the form of existence.	**38.** **äußer** = *outer* (*external*) **äußerst** = *utmost* Die äußerste Notsituation erzwingt die Formen **politischer** Daseinsgestaltung.
38. The most extreme state of distress necessarily determines the shaping *of political* forms of existence.	**39.** Diese Formen, zusammen mit der Atombombe, machen auch den Krieg **überhaupt** unmöglich.
39. These forms, together with the atom bomb, also make war *completely* impossible.	**40.** Die äußerste Notsituation erzwingt die Formen politischer Daseinsgestaltung, die mit der Atombombe auch den Krieg überhaupt unmöglich machen.
40. The most extreme state of distress produces forms of political existence which (together) with the atomic bomb also make war completely impossible.	**41.** **entwickeln** = *to develop, to unfold* **die Entwicklung** = ________
41. *the development*	**42.** **wäre** = *would be* (subjunctive form of **sein**) Es wäre die **glücklichste** Entwicklung.
42. It would be the *most fortunate* development.	**43.** **liegen** = *to lie* **läge** (subjunctive) = *would lie* Das Zeitalter der Kriege läge hinter uns.
43. The age of war would be (lie) behind us.	**44.** **bewegen** = *to stir, to set in motion* Neue, ganz andere Probleme **würden** uns bewegen.
44. New, completely different problems *would* stir us.	**45.** **bleiben** = *to remain* **ausbleiben** = *to stay away, to be absent* **das Ausbleiben** = ________
45. *absence, failure* (*to appear*)	**46.** Was würde durch das Ausbleiben der Kriege entstehen?
46. What would arise because of the absence of wars?	**47.** Neue, ganz andere schwere Probleme, **die** durch das Ausbleiben der Kriege entstehen, würden uns bewegen. (*who*/*which*)
47. New, completely different and difficult problems *which* arise because of the absence of war would stir us.	**48.** **geschehen** = *to happen* Was **aber** geschieht wirklich?

48. What, *however,* really happens?	**49.** **gestehen** = *to confess* **zugestehen** = *to concede, admit* **zugestanden** = *conceded, admitted* Was **wird** nicht **zugestanden?**
49. What *is* not *conceded*?	**50.** Was aber geschieht **wirklich,** da die gegenseitige Kontrolle nicht zugestanden wird?
50. What, however, *really* happens, since mutual control is not conceded?	**51.** **Weil** die gegenseitige Kontrolle nicht zugestanden wird, findet eine fortlaufende Produktion der Atombomben statt.
51. *Because* mutual control is not conceded, a continual production of atom bombs takes place.	**52.** **ständig** = *continually* Und trotz der Atombombe gibt es ständig Kriege.
52. And in spite of the atom bomb there are wars continually.	**53.** **die Wüste** = *desert* **verwüsten** = *to devastate* Sie sind aber **verwüstende** Kriege.
53. They are, however, *devastating* wars.	**54.** **messen** = *to measure* **gemessen** = *measured* **Gemessen** am Weltkrieg . . .
54. *Compared* to a world war . . .	**55.** **zwar** = *it is true, indeed* Gemessen am Weltkrieg sind es zwar kleine lokale Kriege . . .
55. Compared to a world war they are small local wars, it is true . . .	**56.** **jedoch** = *yet, however* . . . hier jedoch sind sie furchtbar verwüstende Kriege.
56. . . . here, however, they are terribly devastating wars.	**57.** Gemessen am Weltkrieg sind es **zwar** kleine lokale Kriege, hier jedoch furchtbar verwüstende Kriege.
57. Compared to a world war they are *indeed* small local wars; here, however, they are terribly devastating wars.	**58.** **der Satz** = *the sentence* Statt des Satzes: es wird keine Kriege geben . . .
58. Instead of the sentence: there will be no wars . . .	**59.** **vielmehr** = *rather* **. . . muß es vielmehr heißen:** es kann heute Kriege geben ohne Atombombe.

59. . . . *it really ought to read* (it must rather mean): today there can be wars without the atomic bomb.	**60.** **das Vorrecht** = *privilege* Ist es nur ein Vorrecht der kleinen Nationen, Krieg zu **führen?** (*lead/wage*)
60. Is it the privilege of only the small nations to *wage* war?	**61.** **der Schreck(en)** = *terror, fright* **schrecklich** = *frightful, dreadful* **Sollte** es ein schreckliches Vorrecht der Kleinen **werden,** Krieg zu führen?
61. *Should* it *become* a frightful privilege of the small nations to wage war?	**62.** **die Gewalt** = *power, force* **der Akt** = *act* **der Gewaltakt** = ________
62. *the act of power, act of force*	**63.** **vollziehen** = *to execute, to accomplish* Sie vollziehen schreckliche Gewaltakte.
63. They execute terrible acts of power.	**64.** **der Zustand** = *state, condition* Sie vollziehen Gewaltakte, **um** ihren Zustand **zu ändern.**
64. They carry out acts of power *in order to change* their condition.	**65.** **ob** = *over, above* **siegen** = *to win, to be victorious* **obsiegen** = *to triumph over, to conquer* Sie wollen mit schrecklicher Gewalt obsiegen.
65. They want to conquer with terrible force.	**66.** **das Verfahren** = *procedure, method, system* Es ist ein altes Verfahren.
66. It is an old procedure.	**67.** Sie bedrohen ihre kleinen Gegner, um **nach** alten Verfahren obzusiegen.
67. They threaten their small opponents in order, *according to* old procedures, to conquer them with force.	**68.** **die Gefahr** = *danger* **irgendeine** Gefahr des Weltkrieges
68. *any* danger of world war	**69.** **wirken auf** = *to have an effect on* Irgendeine Gefahr des Weltkrieges wirkt auf uns.

69. Any danger of world war has an effect on us.	**70.** **schüchtern** = *shy* **einschüchtern** = *to intimidate* **einschüchternd** = *intimidating* Die Gefahr des Weltkrieges **wirkt einschüchternd auf** die Großen.
70. The danger of world war *intimidates* the great (nations).	**71.** **der Vertrag** = *treaty* (*agreement, contract*) Die Kleinen brechen Verträge.
71. The small (nations) break treaties.	**72.** **die Gewalt** = *power, force* **gewaltsam** = *forcible, violent* **Verschiedene** kleine Nationen brechen gewaltsam Verträge.
72. *Various* small nations forcibly break treaties.	**73.** Wenn die Kleinen gewaltsam Verträge brechen, wagen die Großen nicht . . .
73. Whenever the small nations forcibly break treaties, the great nations do not dare . . .	**74.** **achten** = *to respect, to pay attention* **die Achtung** = ________
74. *respect, attention*	**75.** **schaffen** = *to create, to make, to do* **verschaffen** = *to gain* **Irgendetwas** muß Achtung verschaffen.
75. *Something* must gain respect.	**76.** Kann man durch Gewalt Achtung verschaffen?
76. Can one gain respect through force?	**77.** **das Recht** = *privilege, right* Das Recht, durch Gewalt gebrochen . . .
77. Rights violated by force . . .	**78.** Das durch Gewalt gebrochene Recht . . .
78. Rights violated by force . . .	**79.** Die Großen wagen nicht, dem gebrochenen Recht Achtung zu verschaffen.
79. The great nations do not dare to gain respect for violated rights.	**80.** Die Großen wagen nicht, dem durch Gewalt gebrochenen Recht durch Gewalt Achtung zu verschaffen.
80. The great nations do not dare to procure respect by force for rights violated by force.	**81.** Wenn die Kleinen gewaltsam Verträge brechen, wagen die Großen nicht, dem durch Gewalt gebrochenen Recht durch Gewalt Achtung zu verschaffen.

81. When small nations break treaties forcibly, great nations do not dare to gain respect by force for rights broken by force.	**82.** **eins** = *one* **einig** = *in agreement, agreed* Unter den großen Staaten is **keiner** einig.
82. Among the great states *no one* is in agreement.	**83.** **verteidigen** = *to defend* **die Verteidigung** = __________
83. *defense*	**84.** Die Großen sind nicht einig in der Verteidigung **des** Rechts und **der** Verträge.
84. The great nations are not in agreement about the defense *of* rights and treaties.	**85.** Aber dies Vorrecht der souveränen Kleinen, Kriege zu führen, ist nur möglich, weil die Großen nicht einig sind in der Verteidigung des Rechts und der Verträge.
85. But this privilege of the small sovereign nations to wage wars is possible only because the great nations are not in agreement concerning the defense of rights and treaties.	**86.** **nutzen** = *to make use of, to utilize* **ausnutzen** = *to exploit* Die großen Mächte nutzen die Kleinen aus.
86. The great powers exploit the small.	**87.** Die Großen nutzen **vielmehr** die Akte der Kleinen aus. (*rather/much more*)
87. *Rather* the great powers exploit the acts of the small.	**88.** **behaupten** = *to maintain, to hold* Die Großmächte wollen ihre **eigenen** Machtpositionen behaupten.
88. The great powers want to maintain their *own* positions of power.	**89.** **weiter** = *farther* **erweitern** = *to enlarge, to extend* Die Großen wollen ihre eigenen Machtpositionen **gegeneinander** erweitern oder behaupten.
89. The great nations want to enlarge or to maintain their own positions of power *towards one another*.	**90.** Sie nutzen vielmehr die Akte der Kleinen aus, um die eigenen Machtpositionen gegeneinander zu erweitern oder zu behaupten.
90. They use rather the acts of the small in order to enlarge or to maintain their own positions of power towards one another.	**91.** **lähmen** = *to lame, to paralyse* **gelähmt** = *lame, paralysed* **Je** mächtiger die Staaten, **desto** mehr scheinen sie gelähmt.

91. *The* more powerful the states, *the* more they seem (to be) paralysed.	**92.** **vorläufig** = *for the present, for the time being* Die mächtigen Staaten scheinen vorläufig gelähmt.
92. The powerful states appear for the time being (to be) paralysed.	**93.** Je mächtiger die Staaten **durch** die Bombe sind, desto mehr scheinen sie vorläufig gelähmt . . .
93. The more powerful the states are *because of* the bomb, the more they appear at the present to be paralysed . . .	**94.** **. . . während** die Kleinen ihre Gewaltakte vollziehen.
94. . . . *while* the small states carry out their acts of aggression (force).	**95.** Was ist nun weiter möglich?
95. What is now further possible?	**96.** **die Mühe** = *trouble, pains* **sich die Mühe geben** = *to take pains* **sich bemühen** = __________
96. *to take trouble, to take pains, to strive*	**97.** Die großen Staaten bemühen sich . . .
97. The great nations strive . . .	**98.** **der Kampf** = *the fight, struggle* **kämpfen** = *fight, struggle* **kämpfend** = __________
98. *fighting, struggling*	**99.** Die Großen bemühen sich, die kämpfenden Kleinen zum Frieden zu bringen.
99. The great nations strive to bring the little nations who are fighting to a peaceful settlement (i.e. to peace).	**100.** **hinter** = *behind* **der Gedanke** = *thought* **der Hintergedanke** = __________
100. *ulterior motive*	**101.** Die Großen bemühen sich, die kämpfenden Kleinen zum Frieden zu bringen, aber nicht ohne Hintergedanken.
101. The great nations strive to bring the little nations who are fighting to a peaceful settlement, but (the former are) not without ulterior motives.	**102.** **dulden** = *to endure, to tolerate,to put up with* **die Duldung** = __________
102. *endurance, tolerance*	**103.** **der Schutz** = *protection, defense* Die kleinen Staaten kämpfen unter der Duldung und dem Schutz der Großen.

103. The small states fight under the toleration and protection of the great.	**104.** **teilweis(e)** = *in part* Unter **ihrem** teilweisen Schutz kämpfen die kleinen Nationen.
104. The small nations fight under *their* partial protection.	**105.** Während die Kleinen unter der Duldung und unter dem teilweisen Schutz der Großen kämpfen . . .
105. While the small nations fight under the toleration and under the partial protection of the great nations . . .	**106.** **geraten** = *to fall into* . . . so geraten die Großen in die **Gefahr** des Weltkrieges. (*safety/danger*)
106. . . . the great nations fall into the *danger* of world war.	**107.** **tragen** = *to carry* **austragen** = *to carry out, to carry on, fight out* Die Gefahr des Weltkrieges, der **zwischen** den Großmächten auszutragen ist . . .
107. The danger of a world war which has to be fought out *between* the great powers . . .	**108.** Die Gefahr des zwischen ihnen **auszutragenden** Weltkriegs . . .
108. The danger of a world war *to be carried on* between them . . .	**109.** So geraten sie ständig selber in die Gefahr des zwischen ihnen auszutragenden Weltkriegs.
109. So they themselves fall continuously into the danger of a world war to be fought out between themselves.	**110.** So geraten die Großen, während die Kleinen unter ihrer Duldung und ihrem teilweisen Schutz kämpfen, ständig selber in die Gefahr des zwischen ihnen auszutragenden Weltkriegs.
110. Thus the great nations themselves fall continually into danger of a world war which they will have to wage against each other while the small nations fight under the toleration and the partial protection of the great ones.	**111.** **gemein** = *common* **gemeinsam** = (*in*) *common* Keine gemeinsame Ordnung hält die Großen zusammen.
111. No common order holds the great nations together.	**112.** **bewußt** = *known* **sein** = *to be* **das Bewußtsein** = *consciousness* Kein Bewußtsein **gemeinsamer** Ordnung hält sie zusammen.

112. No consciousness *of a common* order holds them together. (Notice the genitive use of **gemeinsamer.**)	**113.** **hinaus** = *out, away from* **schieben** = *to shove, to push* **hinausschieben** = *to postpone, to put off* **das Hinausschieben** = ________
113. *postponement*	**114.** Es ist **wie** ein Hinausschieben des Weltkriegs.
114. It is *like* a postponement of world war.	**115.** Es ist, da kein Bewußtsein gemeinsamer Ordnung zusammenhält, **immer nur** wie ein Hinausschieben des Weltkriegs.
115. It is *always* like a postponement of world war, since no common order holds (them) together.	**116.** **die Welt** = *world* **der Brand** = *burning, combustion, conflagration* **der Weltbrand** = ________
116. *world conflagration*	**117.** **bergen** = *to conceal, to harbor* Jeder Krieg birgt in sich die Gefahr des **Weltbrandes.**
117. Every war harbors in itself the danger of *world conflagration.*	**118.** **der Schleier** = *veil, (smoke) screen* **verschleiern** = *to veil, to disguise* **verschleiert** = *veiled, disguised, in disguise* Jeder kleine Krieg ist verschleiert ein Krieg zwischen den Großmächten.
118. Every small war is, in disguise, a war between the great powers.	**119.** Da jeder kleine Krieg verschleiert schon ein Krieg zwischen den Großmächten ist . . .
119. Since every small war is already a disguised war between the great powers . . .	**120.** . . . birgt jeder in sich die Gefahr des Weltbrandes.
120. . . . each harbors in itself the danger of world conflagration.	

PROGRESS TEST

Choose the correct meaning for the following sentences.

1. Trotz massenhafter Herstellung der Atomwaffen wird der Krieg unmöglich gemacht, denn jeder Staat hat Angst, Kriege zu führen.

(a) War will exist in spite of the massive production of atomic weapons.

(b) Because of the production of atomic weapons all nations fear war.
(c) War is impossible because of the tremendous production of atomic weapons.
(d) War is impossible in spite of massive production of atomic weapons, because every nation is afraid to make war.

2. Es gibt ständig Kriege, die furchtbar verwüstend sind, denn das ist das Vorrecht der Kleinen.
(a) No one has the right to wage war.
(b) Standing wars are the most devastating because little people will always win.
(c) It is the privilege of small nations to wage war continually.
(d) The privilege of war should only be given to small countries.

3. So geraten die Großen, während die Kleinen unter ihrer Duldung und ihrem Schutz kämpfen, ständig selber in die Gefahr des zwischen ihnen auszutragenden Weltkriegs.
(a) Great nations cause small nations to become embroiled in fighting wars.
(b) The danger of having small nations fight wars is that the large nations who support them may become caught up.
(c) Large and small nations are continually fighting a war which may bring them both to their knees if they are not careful.
(d) World war is only a possibility if the large nations do not get caught up in the affairs of the small.

4. Wenn die äußerste Notsituation die Formen politischer Daseinsgestaltung erzwingt, ist es die glücklichste Entwicklung.
(a) Forms of political success are a rare achievement.
(b) If forms of political distress bring about extreme forms of government, it is a most unlucky development.
(c) We are most fortunate if extreme state of distress determines the forms of political existence.
(d) Forms of political existence luckily develop from extremely small situations.

Answer key: **1.** (d); **2.** (c); **3.** (b); **4.** (c).

Before proceeding to the reading passage, review the vocabulary which you have circled. Repetition in learning a language is not a vice.

From *Die Atombombe und die Zukunft des Menschen;*
R. Piper & Co. Verlag, München, 1957.

Karl Jaspers: Was soll politisch geschehen?

Alle Denkenden wollen, daß die Atomwaffen abgeschafft werden. Alle Staaten erklären sich bereit. Aber die Abschaffung ist nur zuverlässig, wenn zugleich die gegenseitige Kontrolle stattfindet.

Der zweite Gedanke ist: Auch wenn die Atombomben nicht abgeschafft sind, wird niemand es wagen, sie anzuwenden. Hitler hat trotz massenhafter Herstellung der Giftgase diese auch in seiner Katastrophe nicht eingesetzt. Wenn eine Waffe notwendig beide Gegner vernichtend trifft, ist sie unanwendbar geworden.

Der dritte Gedanke ist: Weil der Atomkrieg unmöglich geworden ist, ist jeder Krieg unmöglich geworden. Denn da in einem Weltkrieg um den Sinn der Staatsordnung auf Leben und Tod irgendwann doch der Einsatz der Atombombe droht, wird keine Großmacht mehr wagen, überhaupt den Krieg zu beginnen. Weil es für alle der Vernichtungskrieg würde, kann er nicht mehr entstehen. Die totale Bedrohung erzeugt die totale Rettung. Die äußerste Notsituation erzwingt die Formen politischer Daseinsgestaltung, die mit der Atombombe auch den Krieg überhaupt unmöglich machen. Es wäre die glücklichste Entwicklung. Das Zeitalter der Kriege läge hinter uns. Neue, ganz andere schwere Probleme, die durch das Ausbleiben der Kriege entstehen, würden uns bewegen.

Was aber geschieht wirklich?

Weil die gegenseitige Kontrolle nicht zugestanden wird, findet eine fortlaufende Produktion der Atombomben statt.

Und trotz der Atombombe gibt es ständig Kriege. Gemessen am Weltkrieg sind es zwar kleine lokale, hier jedoch furchtbar verwüstende Kriege. Statt des Satzes: es wird keine Kriege geben, weil es Atombomben gibt, muß es vielmehr heißen: es kann heute Kriege geben ohne Atombombe. Sollte es ein schreckliches Vorrecht der Kleinen werden, Krieg zu führen? Sie vollziehen Gewaltakte, um ihren Zustand zu ändern. Sie bedrohen ihre kleinen Gegner, um nach alten Verfahren mit Gewalt obzusiegen. Sie bedrohen die Großen durch die Gefahr des Weltkrieges. Diese Gefahr wirkt einschüchternd. Wenn die Kleinen gewaltsam Verträge brechen, wagen die Großen nicht, dem durch Gewalt gebrochenen Recht durch Gewalt Achtung zu verschaffen. Aber dies Vorrecht der souveränen Kleinen ist nur möglich, weil die Großen nicht einig sind in der Verteidigung des Rechts und der Verträge. Sie nutzen vielmehr die Akte der Kleinen aus, um die eigenen Machtpositionen gegeneinander zu erweitern oder zu behaupten . . . Je mächtiger die Staaten durch die Bombe sind, desto mehr scheinen sie vorläufig gelähmt, während die Kleinen ihre Gewaltakte vollziehen.

Was ist nun weiter möglich? Die Großen bemühen sich, die kämpfenden Kleinen zum Frieden zu bringen, aber nicht ohne Hintergedanken. Sie ergreifen Partei und sind fast immer Partei gegeneinander. So geraten sie, während die Kleinen unter ihrer Duldung und unter ihrem teilweisen Schutz kämpfen, ständig selber in die Gefahr des zwischen ihnen auszutragenden Weltkriegs. Es ist, da kein Bewußtsein gemeinsamer Ordnung zusammenhält, immer nur wie ein Hinausschieben des Weltkriegs. Da jeder kleine Krieg verschleiert schon ein Krieg zwischen den Großmächten ist, birgt jeder in sich die Gefahr des Weltbrandes.

Chapter Eighteen

60. *Modified participial constructions*

1. In German as well as in English, present and past participles may be used as adjectives. They will take the appropriate adjective ending:

der *singende* Mann	*the* ***singing*** *man*
der *entsetzte* Mann	*the* ***horrified*** *man*

Remember that the present participle in German is formed by adding a **-d** (cf. English *-ing*) to the infinitive.

2. Participial constructions may be modified by

(a) an adverb:

der *laut* singende Mann	*the loudly singing man*

(b) a prepositional phrase:

der *zum Tode* entsetzte Mann	*the man (who was) terrified to death*

(c) another prepositional phrase modifying the participle:

Der *von dem Hund* zum Tode entsetzte Mann . . .	*The man (who was) terrified to death by the dog . . .*

(d) another present participle:

Der von dem *heranlaufenden* Hund zum Tode entsetzte Mann . . .	*The man (who was) terrified to death by the approaching dog . . .*

(e) another adverb modifying the present participle:

Der von dem *blitzschnell* heranlaufenden Hund zum Tode entsetzte Mann . . .	*The man (who was) terrified to death by the dog that was rapidly approaching ("as fast as lightning") . . .*

3. The steps taken above outline a general formula for getting to the meaning of these constructions:

(1) Find the noun with which the initial article or other **der** or **ein** word agrees in gender, number, and case:

Der . . . *Mann*

(2) Translate the adjective before the noun, in this case a past participle, and any modifiers of the adjective, such as an adverb or a prepositional phrase:

Der . . . *zum Tode entsetzte* Mann

It will often be necessary to break down the modified participial construction into a series of participial constructions as has been done here.

(3) Translate the next prepositional phrase and its modifiers:

Der *von dem blitzschnell heranlaufenden Hund* zum Tode entsetzte Mann

4. To summarize: Go from the beginning of the phrase to the end and work backwards, using relative clauses, where feasible, to reduce the extended modifiers:

Der (1) / von dem blitzschnell (5) heranlaufenden Hund (4) / zum Tode (3) / entsetzte Mann (2)

5. If a genitive object follows a noun ending a modified participial construction, the genitive object should be translated first before working back:

Die (1) / von so vielen Wissenschaftlern (5) / beachtete (4) / Arbeit (2) / *Einsteins* (3) . . .

The (1) / work (2) / of Einstein (3) / held in high esteem (4) / by so many scientists (5) . . .

6. One or more unmodified adjectives may precede the main noun. If so, they should be translated before working back:

Der von Ford erfundene und von den Deutschen weiterentwickelte *billige* Wagen des Volkes . . .	*The inexpensive car of the people, invented by Ford and further developed by the Germans . . .*

Note that with this sentence **von Ford erfundene und von den Deutschen weiterentwickelte** is one phrase. The double use of **von** indicates this as well as the time sequence in the phrase itself: *Ford invents, Germans develop further.*

Translate the following phrases into English, using natural English word order.

	1. das Auto
1. the automobile	**2. treffen** = *to hit, strike* **getroffen** = *struck* das getroffene Auto
2. the automobile which has been struck	**3. der Blitz** = *lightning* das **von dem Blitz** getroffene Auto
3. the automobile struck *by lightning*	**4. aussuchen** = *to search out, to select* **ausgesucht** = *sought out* das von dem Blitz **ausgesuchte und** getroffene Auto
4. the automobile *sought out and* struck by lightning	**5.** das **schnell** von dem Blitz ausgesuchte und getroffene Auto
5. the automobile which was *quickly* sought out and struck by lightning	**6.** das schnell von dem Blitz ausgesuchte und getroffene Auto **des jungen Studenten**
6. the automobile *of the young student* which was quickly sought out and struck by lightning	**7. die Hexe** = *witch* die tanzende Hexe
7. the dancing witch	**8.** die **zu der Musik** tanzende Hexe
8. the witch dancing *to the music*	**9. schlecht** = *badly* die **schlecht** zu der Musik tanzende Hexe
9. the witch who is dancing *badly* to the music	**10. abscheulich** = *abominable* die schlecht zu der Musik tanzende, **abscheuliche** Hexe
10. the *abominable* witch who is dancing badly to the music	**11.** die schlecht zu der Musik tanzende, abscheuliche Hexe **des alten Mannes**

11. *the old man's* abominable witch who is dancing badly to the music	**12.** eine Sprache
12. a language	**13.** **bestehen** = *to exist, to last* **bestehend** = *existing* eine **bestehende** Sprache
13. an *existing* language	**14.** eine **über den Dialekten** bestehende Sprache
14. a language which exists *over and above dialects*	**15.** Die Sprache, **die Luther schuf,** ist eine über den Dialekten bestehende Sprache.
15. The language *which Luther created* is a language which exists over and above the dialects.	**16.** **anstrengen** = *to strain* **die Anstrengung** = __________
16. *strain, exertion, effort*	**17.** alle Anstrengungen
17. all efforts	**18.** **unternehmen** = *to undertake* **unternommen** = *undertaken* alle **unternommenen** Anstrengungen
18. all efforts *which were made* (*undertaken*)	**19.** alle **von der Philosophie** unternommenen Anstrengungen
19. all efforts which were made *by philosophy*	**20.** zwischen dem Norden und dem Süden
20. between the North and the South	**21.** **begrenzen** = *to limit, to bound, to restrict* **begrenzt** = *limited, bounded, restricted* Zwischen dem Norden und dem **begrenzten** Süden . . .
21. Between the North and the South *which is bounded* . . .	**22.** Zwischen dem **skandinavischen** Norden und dem **vom Mittelmeer** begrenzten Süden . . .
22. Between the *Scandinavian* North and the South bounded *by the Mediterranean Sea* . . .	**23.** . . . zwischen dem kontinentalen Osten und dem Westen . . .
23. . . . between the continental East and the West . . .	**24.** **reichen** = *to reach* **reichend** = *reaching* . . . zwischen dem kontinentalen Osten und dem . . . **reichenden** Westen . . .

24. . . . between the continental East and the West *which reaches* . . .	**25.** . . . zwischen dem kontinentalen Osten und dem **an den Atlantischen Ozean** reichenden Westen . . .
25. . . . between the continental East and the West which stretches *to the Atlantic Ocean* . . .	**26.** Die Zone liegt zwischen dem skandinavischen Norden und dem vom Mittelmeer begrenzten Süden, dem kontinentalen Osten und dem an den Atlantischen Ozean reichenden Westen.
26. The zone lies between the Scandinavian North and the South which is bounded by the Mediterranean Sea, between the continental East and the West which stretches to the Atlantic Ocean.	**27.** **triefen** = *to drip, to trickle* **triefend** = *dripping, trickling* der Triefende
27. the dripping man (Note that the subject is a present participle used as an adjectival noun.)	**28.** der **von Schweiß** Triefende
28. the man dripping *with sweat*	**29.** der **wegen der Sonne** von Schweiß Triefende
29. the man who is dripping with sweat *because of the sun*	**30.** **untergehen** = *to go down, to go under* **untergehend** = *going down, going under* der wegen der **untergehenden** Sonne von Schweiß Triefende
30. the man who is dripping with sweat because of the sun *which is going down*	**31.** der wegen der **heißen** untergehenden Sonne von Schweiß Triefende
31. the man who is dripping with sweat because of the *hot* sun which is going down	**32.** **fürchten** = *to fear* **gefürchtet** = *feared* **die Gefürchtete** = __________
32. the feared woman (Here the subject is a past participle used as an adjectival noun.)	**33.** die **von den Kindern** Gefürchtete
33. the woman feared *by the children*	**34.** die von den Kindern und **Eltern** Gefürchtete (*friends/parents*)
34. the woman feared by the children and *parents*	**35.** die von den Kindern und **deren** Eltern Gefürchtete (*their/those*)

35. the woman feared by the children and *their* parents	**36.** **zugleich** = *at the same time, together with* die von den Kindern und deren Eltern **zugleich** Gefürchtete
36. the woman feared by the children *together with their* parents (Note that **zugleich** is tied to **Eltern,** not to **Gefürchtete.**)	

PROGRESS TEST

Choose the correct meaning of the following sentences.

1. Der schnell vom Realisten zum Idealisten umgewandelte Mensch . . .
   (a) The man changed from an idealist to a realist.
   (b) The realist quickly changed into an idealist.
   (c) The man was both a realist and an idealist.
   (d) To change from a realist to an idealist is no great trick.

2. Der wegen des Wetters etwas verspätete, mit Schifahrern überfüllte Zug aus Garmisch . . .
   (a) Because the weather was fair the train to Garmisch was somewhat ahead of schedule.
   (b) The train from Garmisch was full of skiers because the weather was bad.
   (c) The train from Garmisch, which was bursting with skiers, arrived somewhat late because of the weather.
   (d) The train to Garmisch was full of skiers because the weather promised to be great for skiing.

3. Die durch die Luft von Sibirien zum Mittelmeer dahergeflogene Maschine der reichen Dame sturzte in Italien ab.
   (a) The airplane which belonged to the rich woman from Italy flew from Siberia to the Mediterranean.
   (b) An airplane which flies from the Mediterranean to Siberia can be expected to cause air pollution in Italy.
   (c) The rich woman's airplane which had flown from Siberia to the Mediterranean crashed in Italy.
   (d) The rich woman flies machines produced in Italy to Siberia.

4. Der von Max und Moritz durch ein lautes: „Meck, meck, meck!!“ herbeigerufene, zur Tür heraussausende und ins Wasser stürzende Schneider, der sich Böck benannte, schrie, daß er ertrinke.
   (a) The tailor raced out the door to save the teasing boys who had fallen into the water and were crying for help.
   (b) The boys cried out that they were drowning in order to tease Böck, the tailor, which in turn caused him to throw them into the water.
   (c) The tailor gave Max and Moritz the name of Böck, meaning goat, because they continually bleated at him, but then they threw him into the water.
   (d) The tailor raced out the door and fell into the water because Max and Moritz intimated that he was an old goat.

Answer key: **1.** (b); **2.** (c); **3.** (c); **4.** (d).

61. *Absolute participial constructions*

1. The present participle may be used as follows in literary German:

Leise vor sich *hinpfeifend*, sah er das hübsche Mädchen an.	***Whistling*** *softly to himself, he looked at the pretty girl.*

2. Past participles are similarly used:

Zum Tode *betrübt*, ging er die Straße entlang.	***Grieved*** *to death, he walked along the street.*

Notice that in German the participles end the phrase, while in English they begin the phrase.

Give the meanings of the participial phrases.

	1. Laut **singend,** saß er inmitten der Straße.
1. *Singing* loudly he sat in the middle of the street.	**2.** **stoßen** = *to bump* Vor Freude **tanzend,** stieß er gegen den Elefanten.
2. *Dancing* for joy he bumped into the elephant.	**3.** **zurück** = *back(wards)* **ziehen** = *to pull, to draw, to drag* **sich zurückziehen** = ________
3. *to withdraw*	**4.** **das Gespenst** = *ghost, spectre* Vor dem Gespenst **sich fürchtend,** zog er sich schnell zurück.
4. *Frightened* of the spectre he quickly withdrew.	**5.** **begnadigt** = *pardoned, mercy extended* Zum Leben **begnadigt,** mußte er ein neues Leben anfangen.
5. *Allowed* to live, he had to begin a new life.	**6.** Von allen **gehaßt,** ging sie allein durch die Stadt.
6. *Hated* by all she went alone through the city.	**7.** In Salzburg **geboren,** als Wunderkind von ganz Europa **gefeiert** und in Armut und Vergessenheit **gestorben:** Mozart.

7. *Born* in Salzburg, *celebrated* as a child prodigy by all of Europe, and *dying* in poverty and oblivion: Mozart.	**8.** **hinüberführen auf** = *to lead into* Das andere ist Donauland, hügelig oder flach, auf Ungarns Ebenen **hinüberführend.**
8. The other is Danube country, hilly or flat, *leading* into Hungary's plains.	**9.** Aus dem Elsaß **stammend:** Albert Schweitzer.
9. *Originating* from Alsace: Albert Schweitzer.	

PROGRESS TEST

1. Zum Tode betrübt, saß der junge Mann auf der Bank und dachte an seine Geliebte.
   The word which means *grieved* is
   (a) dachte (b) betrübt (c) saß (d) Geliebte
2. Von Maikäfern geplagt, sauste Onkel Fritz aus dem Bett und haute und trampelte alles tot.
   The word which means *tormented* is
   (a) geplagt (b) sauste (c) trampelte (d) haute
3. Wieder aus der Pfütze steigend, muß Peter laut weinen und schreien und schnell nach Hause sausen.
   The word which means *climbing* is
   (a) sausen (b) weinen (c) schreien (d) steigend

Answer key: **1.** (b); **2.** (a); **3.** (d).

READING PREPARATION

In this section all of the structures and vocabulary for the reading passage are introduced and drilled. Continue to circle all words that you do not immediately recognize. Review them thoroughly before going on to the passage itself.

	1. Sie wissen **schon** etwas über Albert Schweitzer. (*already/beautiful*)
1. You *already* know something about Albert Schweitzer.	**2.** Über seine Arbeit als Arzt im Urwald **haben** Sie schon etwas **gelesen.** (*have read/had read*)
2. You *have* already *read* something about his work as a doctor in the jungle.	**3.** Jetzt **werden** Sie etwas aus seinen philosophischen Schriften **lesen.** (*will read/is read*)

3. Now you *will read* something from his philosophical writings.	**4.** **die Ansprache** = *speech* Er hat einmal eine Ansprache gehalten über das Thema: Das Problem **des** Ethischen. (*before/of the*)
4. He once gave a speech on the theme: The problem *of the* ethical.	**5.** **der Begriff** = *concept* In dieser Ansprache **bespricht** er den Begriff . . . (*speaks/discusses*)
5. In this speech he *discusses* the concept . . .	**6.** **die Ehre** = *honor* **die Furcht** = *fear* **die Ehrfurcht** = *awe, deep respect, reverence* Ehrfurcht **vor** dem Leben (*from/for*)
6. reverence *for* life	**7.** Von Schweitzers Begriff „Ehrfurcht vor dem Leben“ **haben** Sie sicher schon **gehört.** (*have belonged/have heard*)
7. You certainly *have heard* of Schweitzer's concept "reverence for life."	**8.** **Folgendes** ist unsere Situation in der Welt, sagt Schweitzer:
8. Schweitzer says that our situation in the world is *as follows:*	**9.** „Ich bin Leben, das leben will, inmitten von Leben, das leben will.“
9. "I am life which wants to live, in the midst of life which wants to live."	**10.** **der Friede** = *peace* **befriedigen** = *to satisfy* **befriedigend** = ________
10. *gratifying, satisfying*	**11.** **Ist** uns eine befriedigende Erkenntnis der Welt **gegeben?** (*is given/has given*)
11. *Is* a satisfying knowledge of the world *given* to us?	**12.** Eine vollständige und befriedigende Erkenntnis der Welt ist **uns** nicht gegeben. (*us/ourselves*)
12. A complete and satisfying knowledge of the world is not given to *us.*	**13.** **feststellen** = *to fix, to establish, to observe* **die Feststellung** = ________

13. *ascertainment, observation*	**14.** **beschränken** = *to limit* Wir müssen *uns* auf die Feststellung beschränken . . . (*them/ourselves*)
14. We must limit *ourselves* to the observation . . .	**15.** Wir müssen uns auf die **einfache** Feststellung beschränken . . . (*simple/complex*)
15. We must limit ourselves to the *simple* observation . . .	**16.** Was ist diese einfache Feststellung, **worauf** wir uns beschränken müssen? (*on which/to which*)
16. What is this simple observation *to which* we must limit ourselves?	**17.** **gleich** = *like, equal, similar* Diese Feststellung ist, daß alles Leben in der Welt uns gleich ist.
17. This observation is that all life in the world is similar to ourselves.	**18.** **geheim** = *secret, private* **das Geheimnis** = *secret, mystery* Alles Leben ist **Geheimnis.**
18. All life is a *mystery*.	**19.** Alles in der Welt ist Leben gleich **uns selber** und alles ist Geheimnis.
19. Everything in the world is life similar to *ourselves* and everything is a mystery.	**20.** **das Bewußtsein** = *consciousness* Verstehen wir, was das Bewußtsein **eines** Menschen ist?
20. Do we understand what the consciousness *of an* individual is?	**21.** **die Gegebenheit** = *reality, (given) fact, factor* **der Grund** = *ground, basis, reason* **die Grundgegebenheit** = *fundamental factor* Die Grundgegebenheit **unseres** Bewußtseins ist . . .
21. The fundamental factor *of our* consciousness is . . .	**22.** **unmittelbar** = *immediate, direct* Die unmittelbare Grundgegebenheit unseres Bewußtseins ist: Ich bin Leben, das leben will, inmitten von Leben, das leben will.
22. The immediate fundamental factor of our consciousness is: I am life that wants to live, in the midst of life that wants to live.	**23.** **zurück** = *back* **leiten** = *to lead, to direct* **zurückleiten** = ________

23. *to lead back, to return*	**24.** **jedesmal** = *every time* Was ist die unmittelbare Grundgegebenheit unseres Bewußtseins, auf die wir jedesmal wieder **zurückgeleitet werden?** (*will lead back/are led back*)
24. What is the immediate fundamental factor of our consciousness to which we *are led back* again every time?	**25.** **verstehen** = *to understand* **das Verständnis** = *understanding, comprehension, appreciation* Das Verständnis **unserer selbst . . .** (*of themselves/of ourselves*)
25. The understanding *of ourselves* . . .	**26.** **dringen** = *to press (forward)* **vordringen** = *to advance, to press forward, to make headway* Wollen wir zu einem Verständnis unserer selbst und **unserer** Situation in der Welt vordringen? (*dative/genitive*)
26. *genitive:* Do we want to press forward to an understanding of ourselves and *of our* situation in the world?	**27.** Die unmittelbare Grundgegebenheit unseres Bewußtseins, auf die wir jedesmal wieder zurückgeleitet werden, wenn wir zu einem Verständnis unserer selbst und unserer Situation in der Welt vordringen wollen, ist . . .
27. The immediate fundamental factor of our consciousness, to which we are led back again every time when we want to press forward to an understanding of ourselves and our situation in the world, is . . .	**28.** . . . daß ich Leben bin, **das** leben will, inmitten von Leben, **das** leben will. (*which/the*)
28. . . . that I am life, *which* wants to live, in the midst of life, *which* wants to live.	**29.** **ja** = *yes* **bejahen** = *to affirm, to say yes to* **Da** Schweitzer „Wille zum Leben" ist, bejaht er sein Leben. (*there/since*)
29. *Since* Schweitzer is "will-to-live" (will to life), he affirms his life.	**30.** **sagen** = *to say* **besagen** = *to mean, to say* Was will er **damit** besagen? (*with that/by that*)
30. What does he mean (want to say) *by that*?	**31.** Das will nicht **einfach** besagen . . . (*simple/simply*)

31. That does not *simply* mean . . .	**32.** **fortsetzen** = *to continue* Will Schweitzer sein Leben einfach **nur** fortsetzen?
32. Does Schweitzer want simply *only* to continue his life?	**33.** **das Sein** = *being* **das Dasein** = *existence* Will er sein Dasein einfach nur fortsetzen?
33. Does he simply want just to continue his existence?	**34.** **Wert legen auf** = *to attach great importance to, to set great store by* Legt er Wert darauf, sein Dasein nur **fortzusetzen?** (*thereupon to continue/to continuing*)
34. Does he attach great importance just *to continuing* his existence? **Darauf** anticipates the following phrase.	**35.** **empfinden** = *to feel* Was empfindet Schweitzer als **höchstes** Geheimnis?
35. What does Schweitzer feel is the *greatest* mystery?	**36.** **die Pflicht** = *duty* **verpflichten** = *to oblige, to obligate* **die Verpflichtung** = ________
36. *obligation, duty*	**37.** **Welche** Verpflichtung empfindet Schweitzer?
37. *What* (which) obligation does Schweitzer feel?	**38.** **gleich** = *alike, equal(ly)* **achten** = *to esteem* **gleichachten** = *to esteem alike* **Welchen** Willen zum Leben achtet Schweitzer gleich?
38. *Which* will-to-live does Schweitzer esteem to be equal to his own?	**39.** **jeglich** = *every* Jeglichen Willen zum Leben achtet er **dem seinen** gleich. (*his/its*)
39. He esteems every will-to-live to be equal to *his* (own).	**40.** **um** = *around* **die Welt** = *the world* **die Umwelt** = *environment, the world around us* Schweitzer empfindet die Verpflichtung, jeglichen Willen zum Leben in **seiner** Umwelt dem seinen gleichzuachten.

40. Schweitzer feels the obligation to esteem every will-to-live in *his* environment as equal to his own.	**41.** **gebieten** = *to tell, to order, to command* Was **gebietet** die Grundidee des Guten? (*present/past*)
41. *present:* What *does* the fundamental idea of the good *tell* (us to do)?	**42.** **erhalten** = *to preserve, to maintain* Man soll das Leben erhalten und **fördern.** (*promote/negate*)
42. One should preserve and *promote* life.	**43.** Die Grundidee des Guten gebietet, das Leben zu erhalten und zu fördern.
43. The fundamental idea of the good tells us to preserve and to promote life.	**44.** **steigern** = *to raise, to heighten* Man soll das Leben **nicht nur** erhalten und fördern, **sondern auch** zu seinem höchsten Wert steigern.
44. One should *not only* preserve and promote life, *but also* raise it to its highest value.	**45.** Das Böse steigert nicht das Leben zu seinem höchsten Wert.
45. Evil does not raise life to its highest value.	**46.** Die Grundidee des Guten **besteht** also **darin,** daß sie uns gebietet . . . (*consists of/stands in*)
46. Therefore the fundamental idea of the good *consists of* commanding us . . .	**47.** . . . das Leben zu erhalten, zu fördern und zu seinem höchsten Wert zu steigern.
47. . . . to preserve life, to promote it, and to raise it to its highest value.	**48.** **bedeuten** = *to mean, to signify* Was bedeutet das Böse für Schweitzer?
48. What does evil signify for Schweitzer?	**49.** **entwickeln** = *to develop* **die Entwicklung** = *development* Das Böse bedeutet: Leben vernichten, schädigen, an **seiner** Entwicklung hindern. (*his/its*)
49. Evil means: to destroy, injure, and to hinder life in *its* development.	**50.** Das Böse **hat** das Leben **vernichten, schädigen,** an seiner Entwicklung **hindern wollen.**
50. Evil *has wanted to destroy, injure,* and *hinder* life in its development.	**51.** Religion und Philosophie **haben** das Prinzip der Liebe **entdeckt.**
51. Religion and philosophy *have discovered* (*discovered*) the principle of love.	**52.** **ist entdeckt worden** = *has been discovered, was discovered* Das Prinzip der Liebe ist **durch** Religion und Philosophie entdeckt worden.

52. The principle of love was discovered *by* religion and philosophy.	**53.** Das Prinzip dieser *veneratio vitae* entspricht **dem** der Liebe. (*to that/to which/the*)
53. The principle of this *veneratio vitae* (veneration of life) corresponds *to that* of love.	**54.** Wonach **forschten** Religion und Philosophie? (*present/past*)
54. *past:* What *did* religion and philosophy *search* for?	**55.** Religion und Philosophie forschten **nach** dem Grundbegriff des Guten. (*for/without*)
55. Religion and philosophy searched *for* the fundamental idea of the good.	**56.** Das Prinzip der Liebe **ist** durch Religion und Philosophie **entdeckt worden,** als sie nach dem Grundbegriff des Guten forschten.
56. The principle of love *was discovered* by religion and philosophy as they searched for the fundamental concept of the good.	**57.** Ist der Begriff Ehrfurcht vor dem Leben **lebendiger oder weniger lebendig** als der Begriff Liebe?
57. Is the concept "reverence for life" *more alive or less alive* than the concept "love"?	**58.** Schweitzer meint, der Begriff Ehrfurcht vor dem Leben sei allgemeiner und **deshalb** weniger lebendig als der Begriff Liebe.
58. Schweitzer feels that the concept "reverence for life" is more general and *therefore* less alive than the concept "love."	**59.** **bergen** = *to contain* (also: *to shelter, to conceal*) Birgt der Begriff Ehrfurcht vor dem Leben die gleichen Kräfte in **sich** wie der Begriff Liebe? (*himself/themselves/itself*)
59. Does the concept "reverence for life" contain the same powers in *itself* as does the concept "love"?	**60.** Obwohl der Begriff Ehrfurcht vor dem Leben allgemeiner und deshalb weniger lebendig, als der Begriff Liebe ist schreibt Schweitzer . . .
60. Although the concept "reverence for life" is more general and therefore less vital than the concept "love", Schweitzer writes . . .	**61.** . . . so birgt **er** doch die gleichen Kräfte in sich. (*he/it*)
61. . . . *it* still contains the same powers.	**62.** **ziehen** = *to draw, to pull, to drag* **sich beziehen** = *to relate, to refer* **die Beziehung** = __________

62. *relation, reference, relationship*	**63.** **treten** = *to step, to enter* Wie können wir mit der Welt in geistige Beziehung treten?
63. How can we enter into a spiritual relationship with the world?	**64.** Schweitzer antwortet: „Durch die Ehrfurcht vor dem Leben treten wir mit der Welt in geistige Beziehung."
64. Schweitzer answers: "Through reverence for life we enter into spiritual relationship with the world."	**65.** Bonhoeffer spricht von einer anderen geistigen Beziehung zur Welt.
65. Bonhoeffer speaks of another spiritual relationship with the world.	**66.** Diesseitigkeit ist für ihn, in der Fülle der Aufgaben, Fragen, Erfolge und Mißerfolge, Erfahrungen und Ratlosigkeiten leben.
66. For him life in this world is to live in the fullness of tasks, questions, successes and failures, experiences and perplexities.	**67.** **bauen** = *to build* **erbauen** = *to erect, to build, to edify* Die Philosophie **hat** großartige Systeme **erbaut.** (*has erected/had erected*)
67. Philosophy *has erected* grandiose systems.	**68.** **vergeblich** = (*in*) *vain, futile* All die großartigen Systeme, die die Philosophie erbaut hat, **sind** vergeblich **geblieben.** (*have remained/are remaining*)
68. All the grandiose systems which philosophy has erected *have remained* futile.	**69.** **Um** uns in Beziehung mit dem Absoluten **zu** setzen, hat die Philosophie großartige Systeme erbaut, die vergeblich geblieben sind.
69. *In order to* relate us to (place ourselves into a relationship with) the absolute, philosophy has erected grandiose systems, which have remained futile.	**70.** **vorstellen** = *to represent* **die Vorstellung** = __________
70. *representation, conception, idea*	**71.** **bezeichnen** = *to denote, to stand for* Das Absolute bezeichnet eine abstrakte Vorstellung.
71. The absolute stands for an abstract idea.	**72.** **greifen** = *to grasp* **begreifen** = *to understand* **das Begreifen** = __________

72. *the understanding*	**73.** **entziehen** = *to take away, to withdraw* **sich entziehen** = *to avoid, to escape* Das Absolute entzieht sich dem lebendigen Begreifen.
73. The absolute escapes human (living) understanding. (Note that **entziehen** takes a dative object.)	**74.** Kann das Absolute **eine so** abstrakte Vorstellung bezeichnen, daß es sich dem lebendigen Begreifen entzieht? (*a so/such a*)
74. Can the absolute stand for *such an* abstract idea that it escapes human understanding?	**75.** Was **ist** uns nicht **beschieden?** (*is given/has given*)
75. What *is* not *given* to us?	**76.** **der Schöpfer** = *Creator* **der Wille** = *will* **der Schöpferwille** = ________
76. *the will of the Creator*	**77.** Es ist uns nicht beschieden, dem Schöpferwillen zu dienen. (**dienen** takes the *dative/accusative*)
77. *dative* It is not given to us to serve the Creator's will.	**78.** **gründen** = *to found, to ground* **ergründen** = *to fathom, to explore* Der Schöpferwille ist unendlich und **unergründlich.**
78. The will of the Creator is infinite and *unfathomable.*	**79.** **ruhen** = *to rest, to repose* **beruhen** = *to rest, to be based on* Alles **Sein** beruht auf dem unendlichen und unergründlichen Schöpferwillen. (*being/to be*)
79. All *being* rests upon the unending and unfathomable will of the Creator.	**80.** **die Absicht** = *intention* Was sind die Absichten des unendlichen und unergründlichen Schöpferwillens?
80. What are the intentions of the infinite and unfathomable will of the Creator?	**81.** **um** = *of, about* Ein klares Wissen um sein Wesen und seine Absichten ist uns nicht beschieden.
81. A clear knowledge of its nature and intentions is not given to us.	**82.** **Müssen** wir, um dem Schöpferwillen zu dienen, im klaren Wissen um sein Wesen und seine Absichten sein?

82. In order to serve the Creator's will, *do* we *have* to have clear knowledge of its essence and intentions?	**83.** Dem Schöpferwillen, auf dem alles Sein beruht, kann man nicht im klaren Wissen um sein Wesen und seine Absichten dienen.
83. All being rests on the Creator's will. One is not able to serve this will with a clear knowledge of its nature and its intentions.	**84.** **das Verhältnis** = *relationship* Wie treten wir in ein geistiges Verhältnis **zu** dem Schöpferwillen? (*to/with*)
84. How do we enter into a spiritual relationship *with* the Creator's will?	**85.** **wirken** = *to work, to effect, to act* **einwirken** = *to influence, to act upon* **die Einwirkung** = ________
85. *influence*	**86.** **Wenn** wir uns bewußt bleiben, unter der Einwirkung des Lebensgeheimnisses zu stehen . . . (*if/whenever/when*)
86. *If* we remain conscious of being under the influence of the mystery of life . . .	**87.** . . . treten wir in ein geistiges Verhältnis zu dem Schöpferwillen.
87. . . . we enter into a spiritual relationship with the Creator's will.	**88.** **hingeben** = *to give to, to sacrifice, to devote* **Wenn** wir uns an alle lebendigen Wesen hingeben . . .
88. *If* we sacrifice ourselves to all living creatures . . .	**89.** . . . haben wir die Gelegenheit und die Möglichkeit, **ihnen** zu helfen. (*them/you*)
89. . . . we have the opportunity and the possibility to help *them*.	**90.** **die Tat** = *deed* **tätig** = *active*(*ly*) Wenn wir uns tätig hingeben an alle lebendigen Wesen, **denen** zu helfen wir die Gelegenheit und die Möglichkeit haben . . . (*whom/those*)
90. If we devote ourselves actively to all living creatures *whom* we have the opportunity and the possibility to help . . .	**91.** **bedeuten** = *to mean, to signify* **die Bedeutung** = *meaning, significance* **Was für eine** Bedeutung kann diese Ethik haben? (*what a/what kind of*)
91. *What kind of* significance can this ethic have?	**92.** Wozu verpflichtet uns diese Ethik?

92. What does this ethic obligate us to (do)?	**93.** **die Gesellschaft** = *society* Diese Ethik verpflichtet uns **zum Dienst an der** menschlichen Gesellschaft.
93. This ethic obligates us *to serve* human society.	**94.** **einzig** = *nur* Eine Ethik, **die** uns einzig zum Dienst am Menschen und der menschlichen Gesellschaft verpflichtet, kann diese Bedeutung nicht haben.
94. An ethic *which* only obligates us to serve man and human society cannot have this meaning.	**95.** **fassen** = *to grasp, to hold* **umfassen** = *to embrace, to comprise* **umfassend** = ________
95. *extensive, comprehensive*	**96.** **aufmerken** = *to note, to give heed to* **aufmerksam** = *attentive* **die Aufmerksamkeit** = ________
96. *attention, attentiveness*	**97.** **wahrhaft** = *truly* Nur eine umfassende Ethik setzt uns wahrhaft in ein inneres Verhältnis zum Universum und dem Willen **dessen, der** sich in ihm manifestiert. (*of him who/those which*)
97. Only a comprehensive ethic puts us truly into an inner relationship with the universe and the will *of him who* manifests himself in it.	**98.** **legen** = *to lay* **auferlegen** = *to impose upon* Was **wird** eine umfassende Ethik uns **auferlegen?**
98. What *will* a comprehensive ethic *impose* upon us?	**99.** **zuwenden** = *to turn to* Wir sollen unsere tätige Aufmerksamkeit allen **Lebewesen** zuwenden. (*singular/plural*)
99. *plural* We should turn our active attention to all *living beings*.	**100.** Nur eine umfassende Ethik, **die** uns auferlegt, unsere tätige Aufmerksamkeit allen Lebewesen zuzuwenden . . . (*who/which*)
100. Only a comprehensive ethic *which* requires us to turn our active attention to all living beings . . .	**101.** . . . setzt uns wahrhaft in ein inneres Verhältnis zum Universum und dem Willen, **der** sich in ihm manifestiert. (*who/which*)

101. . . . truly places us in an inner relationship to the universe and the will *which* manifests itself in it.	

PROGRESS TEST

Choose the correct meaning of the indicated words.

1. Wir müssen uns auf die **Feststellung** beschränken, daß alles in der Welt gleich uns selber und alles Leben Geheimnis ist.
   (a) indication (b) observation (c) understanding (d) knowledge
2. Ich lege nicht Wert darauf, mein Dasein **fortzusetzen.**
   (a) to continue (b) to progress (c) to follow through (d) to examine
3. Ich bejahe mein Leben, was nicht einfach **besagen** will, daß ich Wert darauf lege, mein Dasein fortzusetzen.
   (a) to be said (b) mean (c) approve (d) feel
4. Was **gebietet** die Grundidee des Guten?
   (a) does command (b) does demand (c) does offer (d) does try
5. Sie gebietet, das Leben **zu erhalten.**
   (a) to receive (b) to get (c) to hold (d) to preserve
6. Sie gebietet, das Leben zu erhalten, zu fördern und zu seinem höchsten Wert **zu steigern.**
   (a) to stagger (b) to climb (c) to raise (d) to push
7. Wir treten in ein geistiges Verhältnis zu dem Schöpferwillen, wenn wir uns **bewußt** bleiben, unter der Einwirkung des Lebensgeheimnisses zu stehen.
   (a) thoroughly (b) unaware (c) apparent (d) conscious
8. Eine Ethik, die uns einzig zum Dienst am Menschen und der menschlichen Gesellschaft verpflichtet, kann diese **Bedeutung** nicht haben.
   (a) revelation (b) difference (c) meaning (d) understanding
9. Nur eine umfassende Ethik setzt uns **wahrhaft** in ein inneres Verhältnis zum Universum.
   (a) firmly (b) finally (c) thoroughly (d) truly
10. Alle von der Philosophie unternommenen **Anstrengungen** sind vergeblich geblieben.
    (a) efforts (b) findings (c) struggles (d) duties
11. Das Absolute **bezeichnet** eine so abstrakte Vorstellung . . .
    (a) explains (b) stands for (c) draws (d) follows
12. Das Absolute bezeichnet eine so abstrakte Vorstellung, daß es sich dem lebendigen Begreifen **entzieht.**
    (a) explains (b) despairs (c) escapes (d) develops

Answer key: **1.** (b); **2.** (a); **3.** (b); **4.** (a); **5.** (d); **6.** (c); **7.** (d); **8.** (c); **9.** (d); **10.** (a); **11.** (b); **12.** (c).

Albert Schweitzer: Die Ehrfurcht vor dem Leben

Eine vollständige und befriedigende Erkenntnis der Welt ist uns nicht gegeben. Wir müssen uns auf die einfache Feststellung beschränken, daß alles in ihr [der Welt] Leben gleich uns selber und alles Leben Geheimnis ist . . .

Die unmittelbare Grundgegebenheit unseres Bewußtseins, auf die wir jedesmal wieder zurückgeleitet werden, wenn wir zu einem Verständnis unserer selbst und unserer Situation in der Welt vordringen wollen, ist: *Ich bin Leben, das leben will, inmitten von Leben, das leben will.*

Da ich Wille zum Leben bin, bejahe ich mein Leben — was nicht einfach besagen will, daß ich Wert darauf lege, mein Dasein fortzusetzen, sondern daß ich es als höchstes Geheimnis empfinde.

Wenn ich über das Leben nachdenke, empfinde ich die Verpflichtung, jeglichen Willen zum Leben in meiner Umwelt dem meinen gleichzuachten.

Die Grundidee des Guten besteht also darin, daß sie gebietet, das Leben zu erhalten, zu fördern und zu seinem höchsten Wert zu steigern; und das Böse bedeutet: Leben vernichten, schädigen, an seiner Entwicklung hindern.

Das Prinzip dieser *veneratio vitae* [*reverence for life*] entspricht dem der Liebe, wie es durch Religion und Philosophie entdeckt worden ist, als sie nach dem Grundbegriff des Guten forschten.

Der Begriff *Ehrfurcht vor dem Leben* ist allgemeiner und deshalb weniger lebendig als der Begriff Liebe. Aber er birgt die gleichen Kräfte in sich.

* * *

Durch die Ehrfurcht vor dem Leben treten wir mit der Welt in geistige Beziehung. Alle von der Philosophie unternommenen Anstrengungen, all die großartigen Systeme, die sie erbaut hat, um uns in Beziehung mit dem Absoluten zu setzen, sind vergeblich geblieben.

Das Absolute bezeichnet eine so abstrakte Vorstellung, daß es sich dem lebendigen Begreifen entzieht. Es ist uns nicht beschieden, dem unendlichen und unergründlichen Schöpferwillen, auf dem alles Sein beruht, im klaren Wissen um sein Wesen und seine Absichten zu dienen. Aber wir treten in ein geistiges Verhältnis zu ihm, wenn wir uns bewußt bleiben, unter der Einwirkung des Lebensgeheimnisses zu stehen, und uns tätig hingeben an alle lebendigen Wesen, denen zu helfen wir die Gelegenheit und die Möglichkeit haben.

Eine Ethik, die uns einzig zum Dienst am Menschen und der menschlichen Gesellschaft verpflichtet, kann diese Bedeutung nicht haben. Nur eine umfassende Ethik, die uns auferlegt, unsere tätige Aufmerksamkeit allen Lebewesen zuzuwenden, setzt uns wahrhaft in ein inneres Verhältnis zum Universum und dem Willen, der sich in ihm manifestiert.

Chapter Nineteen

62. *The future tense—conjugation, word order, modals*

1. As you have already learned, the future tense in German is formed by the present tense of **werden** plus an infinitive:

ich *werde gehen*	*I will go*
du *wirst gehen*	*you will go*
er (sie, es) *wird gehen*	*he (she, it) will go*
wir *werden gehen*	*we will go*
ihr *werdet gehen*	*you will go*
sie *werden gehen*	*they will go*
Sie *werden gehen*	*you will go*

Note that the verb **wollen** is not used to form the future tense:

Ich *will gehen* means *I want to go.*

2. The infinitive will be the last word in the clause in normal and inverted word order. Dependent word order requires some form of **werden** to be last with the infinitive immediately preceding:

Du *wirst* ihn *besuchen.*	*You will visit him.*
Wann *werdet* ihr nach Frankreich *fliegen?*	*When will you fly to France?*
Ich weiß nicht, ob er mir einen Brief *schreiben wird.*	*I don't know whether he will write me a letter.*

3. Modals when used with another verb in the future tense will appear in infinitive form at the end of the clause (even in dependent clauses) in the so-called double infinitive construction. When deciphering the meaning of the double infinitive, go to the modal first, then to the preceding verb:

Du wirst ihn besuchen müssen.	*You will have to visit him.*
Wann werdet ihr nach Frankreich fliegen wollen?	*When will you want to fly to France?*
Ich weiß nicht, ob er mir einen Brief wird schreiben dürfen.	*I don't know whether he will be allowed to write me a letter.*

4. The future tense in German is used in essentially the same way as in English. If an adverb is used which expresses futurity, German prefers the present tense:

Morgen fährt er nach Rußland.	*Tomorrow he will travel to Russia.*

Used with an adverb like **schon** or **wohl,** meaning *probably*, the future may express probability in the present:

Sie wird das wohl verstehen.	*She probably (doubtless) understands that.*

In the following sentences, give the meanings of the indicated verbs.

	1. Sie **werden** bald nach Österreich **fliegen.**
1. They *will* soon *fly* to Austria.	**2.** Ich glaube nicht, daß du bald nach Österreich **fliegen wirst.**
2. I do not believe that you *will* soon *fly* to Austria.	**3.** Wissen Sie, daß sie bald nach Österreich **wird fliegen dürfen?**
3. Do you know that she *will* soon *be permitted to fly* to Austria?	**4.** **das Zeug** = *stuff* Ihr **werdet** das Zeug nicht **essen.**
4. You *will* not *eat* that stuff.	**5.** Du weißt, daß er das Zeug nicht **essen wird.**
5. You know that he *will* not *eat* that stuff.	**6.** Ich weiß nicht, ob ich das Zeug **werde essen können.**
6. I do not know whether I *will be able to eat* that stuff.	**7.** Wann **werdet** ihr nach Österreich **fliegen dürfen?**
7. When *will* you *be permitted to fly* to Austria?	**8.** Wie **wirst** du das Zeug **essen können?**
8. How *will* you *be able to eat* that stuff?	**9.** Alle Menschen **werden** immer älter.

9. All people *become* older and older.	**10.** Wir **werden** alle nicht **kommen.**
10. None of us will come.	**11.** Er **will** überhaupt nicht **kommen.**
11. He *does* not *want to come* at all.	**12.** Er **wird** das wohl **tun können.**
12. He *is* probably *able to do* that.	**13.** Er **wird** dick, denn er trinkt zuviel deutsches Bier.
13. He *is getting* fat, for he drinks too much German beer.	**14.** **Wird** Marie nächstes Jahr einen Mercedes **kaufen?**
14. *Will* Marie *buy* a Mercedes next year?	**15.** Paul **will** nicht zuviel deutsches Bier **trinken,** sonst **wird** er dick.
15. Paul *does* not *want to drink* too much German beer, otherwise he *will get* fat.	**16.** Marie **wird** wohl den Mercedes **nicht kaufen wollen.**
16. Marie probably *doesn't want to buy* the Mercedes.	**17.** Was **wird** aus dem kleinen Jungen?
17. What *will become* of the little boy?	

63. *The future perfect tense—conjugation, word order*

1. The future perfect, as rare in German as it is in English, is conjugated with the present tense of **werden** plus the perfect infinitive. (The perfect infinitive consists of a past participle and the infinitive **haben** or **sein.**)

2. The future perfect is conjugated as follows:

ich werde gegangen sein	*I will have gone*
du wirst gegangen sein	etc.
er (sie, es) wird gegangen sein	
wir werden gegangen sein	
ihr werdet gegangen sein	
sie werden gegangen sein	
Sie werden gegangen sein	

ich werde gesagt haben	*I will have said*
du wirst gesagt haben	etc.
er (sie, es) wird gesagt haben	
wir werden gesagt haben	
ihr werdet gesagt haben	
sie werden gesagt haben	
Sie werden gesagt haben	

3. The perfect infinitive will be found at the end of the clause or immediately preceding **werden** in dependent word order:

normal

Er wird bis übermorgen das Buch *gelesen haben.*	*He will have read the book by the day after tomorrow.*

inverted

Wird er mit ihr darüber *gesprochen haben?*	*Will he have spoken with her about it?*

dependent

Ich weiß, daß du ihm einen Brief *geschrieben haben* wirst.	*I know that you will have written him a letter.*

4. Used with **schon, wohl, doch,** or **wahrscheinlich,** the future perfect may express probability of a completed action in the past:

Karl wird wohl seine Arbeit beendet haben.	*Karl probably has finished his work.*

The following sentence variations are based on lines taken from German children's rhymes. Give the meanings of the indicated verbs.

	1. holen = *to fetch, to get* Der Storch **hat** sich drei Brote **geholt.**
1. The stork *got* three (loaves of) bread for itself.	**2.** Der Storch **hatte** sich drei Brote **geholt.**
2. The stork *had gotten* three loaves of bread for itself.	**3.** Der Storch **wird** sich drei Brote **holen.**
3. The stork *will get* itself three loaves of bread.	**4.** Der Storch **wird** sich drei Brote **geholt haben.**

4. The stork *will have fetched* three loaves of bread for itself.	**5.** **der Henker** = *the hangman* **ausschicken** = *to send out* Der Herr **hat** den Henker **ausgeschickt.**
5. The lord (master) *sent out* the hangman.	**6.** Der Herr **hatte** den Henker **ausgeschickt.**
6. The lord *had sent out* the hangman.	**7.** Der Herr **wird** den Henker **ausschicken.**
7. The lord *will send out* the hangman.	**8.** Der Herr **wird** den Henker wohl **ausgeschickt haben.**
8. The master probably *sent out* (*will have sent out*) the hangman.	**9.** Alle Vögel **sind** schon da **gewesen.**
9. All the birds *have* already *been* there.	**10.** Alle Vögel **waren** schon da **gewesen.**
10. All the birds *had* already *been* there.	**11.** Alle Vögel **werden** schon da **sein.**
11. All the birds *are* probably already there (*will* probably already *be* there).	**12.** Alle Vögel **werden** schon da **gewesen sein.**
12. All the birds *were* probably already there (*will have been* there).	**13.** So **sind** die Reiter auf ihren stolzen Pferden **geritten.**
13. Thus (in this manner) the riders *rode* on their proud horses.	**14.** So **waren** die Reiter auf ihren stolzen Pferden **geritten.**
14. Thus the riders *had ridden* on their proud horses.	**15.** So **werden** die Reiter auf ihren stolzen Pferden **reiten.**
15. In this manner the riders *will ride* on their proud horses.	**16.** So **werden** die Reiter auf ihren stolzen Pferden **geritten sein.**
16. In this manner the riders *will have ridden* on their proud horses.	

PROGRESS TEST

Choose the future form of the verb from the following possibilities.

1. __________ Marianne dieses Jahr nach Marienbad __________?
(a) will . . . fliegen (b) wird . . . getragen worden sein (c) würde . . . gehen (d) wird . . . fahren

2. Ob Erich die Zeitung ________?
(a) wird gelesen worden sein (b) darf gelesen werden (c) wird lesen dürfen (d) will lesen werden
3. Glauben Sie, daß es heute Regen ________?
(a) geben wird (b) gegeben wird (c) muß gegeben werden (d) gegeben haben will
4. ________ ihr bestimmt nach Ungarn ________?
(a) Werdet . . . gereist (b) Will . . . reisen (c) Werdet . . . reisen wollen (d) Wird . . . gereist worden sein
5. Berlin ________ wohl die größte Stadt Deutschlands ________.
(a) wird . . . gewesen sein (b) wird . . . gesungen müssen (c) wird . . . sein (d) will . . . sein

Answer key: **1.** (d); **2.** (c); **3.** (a); **4.** (c); **5.** (c).

READING PREPARATION

The following frames are to prepare you for the reading passage.

	1. Sie **haben** wohl von Wernher von Braun **gehört.**
1. You *have* surely *heard* of Wernher von Braun.	**2. die Fahrt** = *trip, journey, voyage* Vielleicht wissen manche von Ihnen, daß er ein Buch schrieb, welches betitelt ist: *Erste Fahrt zum Mond.*
2. Perhaps some of you know that he wrote a book which is entitled: *First Men to the Moon* (*First Trip to the Moon*).	**3. das Lesestück** = *reading passage* Aus dem Vorwort nehmen wir das Lesestück für dieses Kapitel.
3. From the foreword we are taking the reading passage for this chapter.	**4. etliche** = *some* Im Vorwort beantwortet von Braun etliche Fragen, die an ihn gestellt sind.
4. In the foreword von Braun answers some questions which are put to him.	**5. lauten** = *to read* Eine Frage lautet: „Warum glauben Sie, daß andere Welten **bewohnt** sind?“ (*inhabitable/inhabited*)
5. One question reads: "Why do you believe that other worlds are *inhabited*?"	**6. der Beweis** = *proof, evidence* **Was für** Beweise hat man, daß andere Welten bewohnt sind? (*what/what for*)

6. *What* proof (evidences) does one have that other worlds are inhabited?	**7.** **sparen** = *to save, to spare, to be sparing* **spärlich** = *scanty, frugal* Beweise sind **noch etwas** spärlich. (*still somewhat/never*)
7. Proofs are *still somewhat* scanty.	**8.** **vorhanden** = *at hand, existing* **das Vorhandensein** = __________
8. *existence, presence*	**9.** Beweise für das Vorhandensein von **Leben** auf anderen Welten sind noch etwas spärlich. (*love/life*)
9. Proofs for the existence of *life* on other worlds are still somewhat scanty.	**10.** **annehmen** = *to assume, to accept* **die Annahme** = __________
10. *assumption, acceptance*	**11.** **die Ruhe** = *rest* **beruhen** = *to rest* Worauf beruht denn die Annahme **seiner** Existenz?
11. Upon what, then, rests the assumption of *its* existence?	**12.** Die Annahme beruht **entweder** auf Glauben **oder** auf wissenschaftlicher Extrapolation. (*either . . . or/neither . . . nor*)
12. The assumption rests *either* on belief *or* on scientific extrapolation.	**13.** **verbinden** = *to tie, to unite, to join, to bind up* **die Verbindung** = __________
13. *union, binding* (*up*), *combination*	**14.** Diese Annahme kann auch auf einer Verbindung von beiden beruhen.
14. This assumption can also rest on a combination of both.	**15.** **Deshalb** beruht die Annahme seiner Existenz entweder auf Glauben oder auf wissenschaftlicher Extrapolation oder auf einer Verbindung von beiden.
15. *Therefore* the assumption of its existence rests either on faith or on scientific extrapolation or on a combination of both.	**16.** **fassen** = *to hold, to grasp, to take* **auffassen** = *to understand, comprehend* **die Auffassung** = __________
16. *comprehension, interpretation, conception*	**17.** Welche Auffassung von dem Vorhandensein von Leben . . .

17. What conception of the presence of life . . .	**18.** Welche Auffassung von dem Vorhandensein von Leben auf anderen Welten hatten die meisten Physiker gegen Ende des 19. Jahrhunderts?
18. What conception of the presence of life on other worlds did most physicists have toward the end of the 19th century?	**19.** Es war eine materialistische Auffassung.
19. It was a materialistic conception.	**20.** **die Gewalt** = *power, force* **gewaltig** = ________
20. *powerful, mighty, big*	**21.** **die Uhr** = *clock* Das Universum war ein gewaltiges **Uhrwerk.** (*clock that works/clockwork*)
21. The universe was a gigantic *clockwork*.	**22.** **betrachten** = *to consider* Die meisten Physiker betrachteten das Universum als eine Art gewaltig**en** Uhrwerk**s.** (The case is ________)
22. genitive Most of the physicists considered the universe to be a sort of giant clockwork.	**23.** **ziemlich** = *pretty, moderate(ly), fairly* Die Physiker glaubten den Mechanismus ziemlich gut zu verstehen. (The gender of **Mechanismus** is ________.)
23. masculine: **den** tells you the word is *masculine singular accusative.* The physicists believed (to be able) to understand the mechanism fairly well.	**24.** Das Uhrwerk, **dessen** Mechanismus sie ziemlich gut zu verstehen glaubten . . .
24. The clockwork *whose* mechanism they believed to understand fairly well . . .	**25.** **gestehen** = *to confess* **zugestehen** = *to concede, to admit* Sie **wollten** dem Schöpfer nur zugestehen . . .
25. They *were* only *willing* to concede to the creator . . . (Note that **zugestehen** takes a dative object.)	**26.** **die Aufgabe** = *task* Dem Schöpfer wollten sie als einzige Aufgabe **nur noch** zugestehen . . .
26. The only task that they were *still* willing to concede to the Creator . . .	**27.** **aufziehen** = *to wind up* Der Schöpfer **hat** das Uhrwerk **gebaut** und **aufgezogen.**

27. The Creator *built* and *wound up* the clockwork.	**28.** **konnte** = *could* (indicative mood) **könnte** = *could* (subjunctive mood) Der Schöpfer **könnte** dieses Uhrwerk **gebaut** und **aufgezogen haben.**
28. The Creator *could have built* and *wound up* this clockwork.	**29.** **wandeln** = *to change* Die Physik hat sich **gründlich** gewandelt. (*finally/thoroughly*)
29. Physics has *thoroughly* changed (itself).	**30.** **die Strecke** = *stretch, distance, section* **auf der Strecke bleiben** = *to remain by the* ________
30. *wayside*	**31.** Manch **ehrwürdiges** Prinzip blieb auf der Strecke. (*respectable/early*)
31. Many *respectable* principles (many a respectable principle) remained by the wayside.	**32.** Manch ehrwürdiges Prinzip blieb auf der Strecke, als die Relativitätstheorie zeigte . . .
32. Many respectable principles remained by the wayside when the theory of relativity showed . . .	**33.** **Raum** und Zeit besitzen keinen absoluten Wert. (*room/space*)
33. *Space* and time do not possess an absolute value.	**34.** **das Maß** = *dimension, measure* Die Maße von Raum und Zeit besitzen keinen absoluten Wert.
34. The dimensions of space and time possess no absolute values.	**35.** **die Grundlage** = *foundation* Die Grundlagen unserer physikalischen **Vorstellungen,** die Maße von Raum und Zeit, besitzen keinen absoluten Wert. (*introductions/ideas*)
35. The foundations of our physical *ideas*, the dimensions of space and time, have no absolute values.	**36.** **nachweisen** = *to point out, to prove* Manch ehrwürdiges Prinzip blieb auf der Strecke, **als** die Quantentheorie nachwies, . . . (*as/when*)
36. Many respectable principles remained by the wayside, *when* the quantum theory proved . . .	**37.** . . . daß die Grundlagen unserer physikalischen Vorstellungen, die Maße von Raum und Zeit, keinen absoluten Wert besitzen.

37. . . . that the foundations of our physical ideas, the dimensions of space and time, have no absolute values.	**38.** **bauen** = *to build* **der Stein** = *stone* die **Bausteine** der Welt
38. the *building blocks* (*stones*) of the world	**39.** **winzig** = *tiny* die **winzigen** Bausteine der Welt
39. the *tiny* building blocks of the world	**40.** **sich bewegen** = *to move, to agitate* Wie bewegen sich die winzigen Bausteine der Welt?
40. How do the tiny building blocks of the world move?	**41.** **gleichmäßig** = *uniform, similar, equal* Die winzigen Bausteine bewegen sich nicht **gleichmäßig . . .**
41. The tiny building blocks do not move *uniformly* . . .	**42.** Sie bewegen sich nicht gleichmäßig, sondern sie machen **Sprünge.** (*sounds/jumps*)
42. They do not move uniformly, rather they move erratically (make *jumps*).	**43.** **führen** = *to lead, to conduct, to guide* **vollführen** = *to execute, to carry out* Sie vollführen Sprünge.
43. They move erratically ("execute jumps").	**44.** Als die Quantentheorie nachwies, daß die winzigen Bausteine der Welt Sprünge vollführen . . .
44. When the quantum theory showed that the tiny building blocks of the world move erratically . . .	**45.** Man **spaltet** das Atom. (*splits/fuses*)
45. One *splits* the atom.	**46.** **wurde gespalten** = *was split* Als das Atom gespalten wurde . . .
46. When the atom was split . . .	**47.** Das **unteilbare** Atom wurde gespalten. (*divisible/indivisible*)
47. The *indivisible* atom was split.	**48.** **angeblich** = *alleged(ly)* das **angeblich** unteilbare Atom
48. the *allegedly* indivisible atom	**49.** Manch ehrwürdiges Prinzip blieb auf der Strecke, als das angeblich unteilbare Atom **doch** gespalten wurde.

49. Many venerable principles remained by the wayside when the allegedly indivisible atom was *indeed* split.	**50.** **bevorzugen** = *to favor* **der Bevorzugte** = ________
50. *the favored one*	**51.** Nur **wenige** Bevorzugte können mathematische Erklärungen verstehen.
51. Only *a few* favored ones can understand mathematical explanations.	**52.** Die **schwerverständlichen** mathematischen Erklärungen, die nur wenige Bevorzugte verstehen können . . .
52. The mathematical explanations *which are difficult to understand* and which only a few favored ones can understand . . .	**53.** Die schwerverständlichen mathematischen Erklärungen, **deren** innere Schönheit nur wenige Bevorzugte verstehen können . . .
53. The mathematical explanations which are hard to understand, *whose* inner beauty only a few favored ones can comprehend . . .	**54.** **weichen** = *to give way, to yield* Die schönen mechanischen Modelle **wichen . . .** (*present/past*)
54. *past* The beautiful mechanical models *gave way to* . . .	**55.** **allmählich** = *gradual(ly)* Die schönen mechanischen Modelle wichen **allmählich** schwerverständlichen mathematischen Erklärungen.
55. The beautiful mechanical models gave way *gradually* to mathematical explanations which were hard to understand.	**56.** **vereinfachen** = *to simplify* **vereinfacht** = *simplified* Die schönen vereinfachten mechanischen Modelle . . .
56. The beautiful simplified mechanical models . . .	**57.** **allzusehr** = *all too much, much too* Die schönen, allzusehr vereinfachten mechanischen Modelle . . .
57. The beautiful, much too simplified mechanical models . . .	**58.** Die schönen, allzusehr vereinfachten mechanischen Modelle wichen allmählich schwerverständlichen mathematischen Erklärungen. (The verb **weichen** takes a *dative/accusative object.*)
58. *dative* The beautiful, much too simplified mechanical models gave way gradually to mathematical explanations which are difficult to understand.	**59.** **darstellen** = *to represent* Diese Modelle **sollten** das Uhrwerk des Universums darstellen.

59. These models *were meant* to represent the clockwork of the universe.	**60.** Die schönen, allzusehr vereinfachten mechanischen Modelle, **die** das Uhrwerk des Universums darstellen sollten . . .
60. The beautiful, much too simplified mechanical models *which* were meant to represent the clockwork of the universe . . .	**61.** **zeitgenössisch** = *contemporary* Wie **sahen** die zeitgenössischen Physiker das Universum **an**?
61. How did the contemporary physicists *look at* the universe?	**62.** Die zeitgenössischen Physiker sahen das Universum nicht mehr als gigantisches Uhrwerk an, sondern **eher** als einen großen Gedanken, eine göttliche Idee. (*rather/before*)
62. The contemporary physicists no longer looked at the universe as a gigantic clockwork but *rather* as a great thought, a divine (godly) idea.	**63.** **d.h.** = **das heißt** = *that is* = *i.e.* Für Wernher von Braun ist Leben das Element des göttlichen Genius in dieser göttlichen Idee, **d.h.** in dem Universum.
63. For Wernher von Braun life is the element of divine genius in this divine idea, *i.e.* in the universe.	**64.** **das Haupt** = *chief* (also: *head*) **das Ziel** = *objective, goal* **das Hauptziel** = _________
64. *main objective*	**65.** Das Leben ist Gottes Hauptziel im Kosmos.
65. Life is God's main objective in the cosmos.	**66.** **weit** = *full* (also: *extensive, far, far reaching, broad*) **weitest** = *fullest* Das Leben ist im weitesten **Sinne** Gottes Hauptziel im Kosmos. (*sin/meaning*)
66. Life in its fullest *meaning* is God's main objective in the cosmos.	**67.** **der Tropfen** = *drop* Kein Tropfen Wasser ist **völlig** steril auf der Erde.
67. No drop of water on earth is *completely* sterile.	**68.** **die Krume** = *crumb, speck* Keine Krume Boden **enthält** keine lebenden Organismen. (*holds out/contains*)

68. There is no speck of ground which does not *contain* living organisms.	**69.** **waren** = *were* (indicative) **wären** = *were, would be* (subjunctive) **enthielten** = *contained* (indicative) **enthielten** = *would contain* (subjunctive) Men findet auf der Erde keinen Tropfen Wasser und keine Krume Boden, die völlig steril wären und keine lebenden Organismen enthielten.
69. On earth one does not find one drop of water and not one speck of ground which would be completely sterile and which would not contain any living organisms.	**70.** Von Braun weiß auch, daß **es** viele Millionen von Welten **gibt,** worauf es Leben geben könnte.
70. Von Braun knows also that *there are* millions and millions (many millions) of worlds on which there could be life.	**71.** **unbelebt** = *lifeless* Andere Welten sind unbelebt.
71. Other worlds are lifeless.	**72.** **offen** = *open* **die Sicht** = *view, sight* **offensichtlich** = *apparent* **Es sind** aber noch mehr Planeten, die offensichtlich unbelebt sind.
72. *There are,* however, still other planets which are apparently lifeless.	**73.** Das Leben ist das Hauptziel Gottes im Kosmos.
73. Life is the main objective of God in the cosmos.	**74.** **die Öde** = *wasteland* (also: *bleakness, dreariness*) Hier ist eine Öde.
74. Here is a wasteland.	**75.** **scheinbar** = *apparent* Wir haben **aber** eine scheinbare Öde. (*but/however*)
75. We have, *however,* an apparent wasteland.	**76.** **vertragen** = *to bear, to tolerate* **sich vertragen** = *to agree* Wie verträgt sich diese scheinbare Öde mit dem Glauben, daß das Leben das Hauptziel Gottes im Kosmos ist?

76. How does this apparent wasteland agree with the belief that life is the main objective of God in the cosmos?	**77.** **das Fach** = *line (of study), subject, speciality* **der Fachmann** = *specialist* **die Rationalisierung** = *rationalizing* **der Rationalisierungsfachmann** = ________
77. *the rationalizing specialist*	**78.** Von Braun will den Kosmos nicht mit den Augen eines Rationalisierungsfachmannes betrachten.
78. Von Braun does not want to consider the cosmos with the eyes of a rationalizing specialist.	**79.** **der Überfluß** = *superabundance, excess* (also: *abundance, plenty*) Der Überfluß **gehört** zum Wesen der Natur. (*belongs/belonged*)
79. Superabundance *belongs* to the essence of nature	**80.** **verschwenden** = *to squander, to waste* **verschwenderisch** = *wasteful* Verschwenderischer Überfluß gehört zum Wesen der Natur.
80. Wasteful excess belongs to the essence of nature.	**81.** **seit jeher** = *from time immemorial* Von Braun antwortet: „Verschwenderischer Überfluß gehört seit jeher zum Wesen der Natur."
81. Von Braun answers: "From time immemorial wasteful excess belongs to the essence of nature."	**82.** **der Same(n)** = *seed, sperm* **das Korn** = *grain* **das Samenkorn** = *grain of seed* Man braucht nur die Samenkörner zu betrachten.
82. One needs only to consider the grains of seed.	**83.** **herum** = *around* **liegen** = *to lie* **liegend** = *lying* **herumliegend** = ________
83. *lying around*	**84.** Man braucht nur die herumliegenden Samenkörner zu betrachten.
84. One needs only to consider the seeds which are lying around.	**85.** Man braucht **sich** nur **umzusehen . . .**

85. One needs only *to look around . . .*	**86.** **nutzen** = *to make use of, to utilize* **genutzt** = *used, utilized* **ungenutzt** = ________
86. *unused, unutilized*	**87.** Man braucht sich nur umzusehen und die Millionen ungenutzt herumliegenden Samenkörner zu betrachten.
87. One only needs to look around and to observe the millions of grains of seed which are lying around unutilized.	**88.** Seit jeher gehören diese ungenutzt herumliegenden Samenkörner zum Wesen der Natur.
88. Since time immemorial these unused grains of seed which are lying around have belonged to the essence of nature.	**89.** **wachsen** = *to grow* **heranwachsen** = *to grow up* Alle Samenkörner können zu einer Blume oder einem Baum heranwachsen.
89. All seeds can grow up into a flower or a tree.	**90.** **fähig** = *capable, qualified, able* **die Fähigkeit** = ________
90. *capacity, ability*	**91.** Alle Samenkörner besitzen die Fähigkeit, zu einer schönen Blume oder einem gewaltigen Baum heranzuwachsen.
91. All seeds possess the capacity to grow up into a beautiful flower or a mighty tree.	**92.** Wieviele Samenkörner **werden** dieses Potential **nutzen?**
92. How many seeds *will use* this potential?	**93.** **der Bruchteil** = *fraction* Nur ein winziger Bruchteil erhält die **Gelegenheit,** dieses Potential zu nutzen. (*necessity/opportunity*)
93. Only a tiny fraction has (receives) the *opportunity* to use this potential.	**94.** **jemals** = *ever* Nur ein winziger Bruchteil der Samenkörner erhält jemals die Gelegenheit, ihr Potential zu nutzen.
94. Only a tiny fraction of seeds ever get the opportunity to utilize their potential.	**95.** Für von Braun ist Leben eine göttliche, universale Idee.
95. For von Braun life is a divine universal idea.	**96.** **teilen** = *to share, to divide* **verteilen** = *to distribute* Was verteilt Gott über das ganze Universum?

96. What does God distribute throughout the whole universe?	**97.** **die Saat** = *seed* Gott verteilt seine Saat über das ganze Weltall. (**Das Weltall** probably means ________.)
97. *the universe* God distributes his seed throughout the whole universe.	**98.** Von Braun ist sicher, daß Gott seine Saat über das ganze Weltall **verteilt hat.**
98. Von Braun is positive that God *has distributed* his seed throughout the entire universe.	**99.** **Worauf** aber fällt die Saat?
99. *Upon what,* however, does the seed fall?	**100.** **der Boden** = *ground* Viel Saat fällt auf **unfruchtbaren** Boden. (*fruitful/barren*)
100. Much of the seed falls on *barren* ground.	**101.** Aber Gott weiß, daß viel Saat auf unfruchtbaren Boden fällt.
101. But God knows that much of the seed falls on barren ground.	**102.** **genug** = *enough* **genügend** = *sufficient* Gott hat genügend Zeit . . .
102. God has sufficient time . . .	**103.** Er hat genügend Zeit, auf die Ergebnisse zu warten.
103. He has sufficient time to wait for the results.	

PROGRESS TEST

After reviewing the items you have circled choose the meaning of the indicated words.

1. Die **Annahme,** daß andere Welten bewohnt sind, beruht entweder auf Glauben oder auf wissenschaftlicher Extrapolation.
   (a) judgement (b) accusation (c) assumption (d) investigation
2. Sie wollten nur **zugestehen,** daß der Schöpfer dieses Uhrwerk gebaut und aufgezogen hatte.
   (a) to stand (b) to envision (c) to deny (d) to concede
3. Manch ehrwürdiges Prinzip blieb auf der Strecke, da in den letzten fünfzig Jahren die Physik sich gründlich **wandelte.**
   (a) wandered (b) changed (c) started over (d) passed itself
4. Die **Grundlagen unserer physikalischen Vorstellungen** besitzen keinen absoluten Wert.
   (a) dimensions of our physical life (b) foundations of our physical ideas (c) beginnings of our physical worlds (d) furthering of our physical nature

5. Die winzigen Bausteine der Welt bewegen sich nicht gleichmäßig, sondern **vollführen Sprünge.**
(a) spring up (b) full of springs (c) move erratically (d) spring fully

6. Die vereinfachten mechanischen Modelle **wichen** allmählich schwerverständlichen mathematischen Erklärungen.
(a) gave way (b) followed (c) weakened (d) caused

7. Nur wenige **Bevorzugte** können diese innere Schönheit verstehen.
(a) undisputed ones (b) favored ones (c) extraordinary ones (d) predestined ones

8. Was **enthielt** jede Krume Boden?
(a) did hold out (b) did contain (c) did discover (d) did uncover

Answer key: **1.** (c); **2.** (d); **3.** (b); **4.** (b); **5.** (c); **6.** (a); **7.** (b); **8.** (b).

Wernher von Braun: Erste Fahrt zum Mond

Frage: Warum glauben Sie, daß andere Welten bewohnt sind?

Antwort: Beweise für das Vorhandensein von Leben auf anderen Welten sind noch etwas spärlich. Deshalb beruht die Annahme seiner Existenz entweder auf Glauben oder auf wissenschaftlicher Extrapolation oder auf einer Verbindung von beiden.

Gegen Ende des 19. Jahrhunderts hatten die meisten Physiker eine materialistische Auffassung: sie betrachteten das Universum als eine Art gewaltigen Uhrwerks, dessen Mechanismus sie ziemlich gut zu verstehen glaubten. Dem Schöpfer wollten sie als einzige Aufgabe nur noch zugestehen, daß er dieses Uhrwerk gebaut und aufgezogen haben könnte.

In den letzten fünfzig Jahren hat sich die Physik gründlich gewandelt. Manch ehrwürdiges Prinzip blieb auf der Strecke, als die Relativitätstheorie zeigte, daß die Grundlagen unserer physikalischen Vorstellungen, die Maße von Raum und Zeit, keinen absoluten Wert besitzen; als die Quantentheorie nachwies, daß die winzigen Bausteine der Welt sich nicht gleichmäßig bewegen, sondern Sprünge vollführen; und als das angeblich unteilbare Atom doch gespalten wurde. Die schönen, allzusehr vereinfachten mechanischen Modelle, die das Uhrwerk des Universums darstellen sollten, wichen allmählich schwerverständlichen mathematischen Erklärungen, deren innere Schönheit nur wenige Bevorzugte verstehen können. Aber die Folge war, daß die zeitgenössischen Physiker das Universum nicht mehr als gigantisches Uhrwerk ansahen, sondern eher als einen großen Gedanken, eine göttliche Idee.

Für mich ist Leben das Element des göttlichen Genius in dieser göttlichen Idee. Es ist im weitesten Sinne Gottes Hauptziel im Kosmos. Man findet auf der Erde keinen Tropfen Wasser und keine Krume Boden, die völlig steril wären und keine lebenden Organismen enthielten.

Von Braun goes on to say that the universe with its many millions of suns is made up of the same elements as our own earth. Those suns probably also have planetary systems as does our own in which at least one planet could support life. Then von Braun asks how one can reconcile this apparent absence of life, comparatively speaking, with the belief that life in the cosmos is God's chief objective. He answers his own question by pointing out that from the beginning of time an excess of waste is part of the essence of nature. Only a tiny fraction of the seeds on this earth have the opportunity to make use of their potential.

Verträgt sich diese scheinbare Öde mit dem Glauben, daß das Leben das Hauptziel Gottes im Kosmos ist?

Ich denke, wir sollten den Kosmos nicht mit den Augen eines Rationalisierungsfachmannes betrachten. Verschwenderischer Überfluß gehört seit jeher zum Wesen der Natur. Man braucht sich nur umzusehen und die Millionen ungenutzt herumliegenden Samenkörner zu betrachten. Alle besitzen die Fähigkeit, zu einer schönen Blume oder einem gewaltigen Baum heranzuwachsen, aber nur ein winziger Bruchteil erhält jemals die Gelegenheit, dieses Potential zu nutzen.

Leben ist eine göttliche, universale Idee. Ich bin sicher, daß Gott seine Saat über das ganze Weltall verteilt hat. Aber er weiß, daß viel auf unfruchtbaren Boden fällt, und er hat genügend Zeit, auf die Ergebnisse zu warten.

Chapter Twenty

64. *Passive voice*

1. You were briefly introduced to the passive voice in chapter 3 and have met it periodically in your reading. In the active voice, the subject performs the action; in the passive voice, it receives the action:

active:	*I hit the man.*
passive:	*The man was hit by me.*

2. The present tense of the passive in German is formed by the present tense of **werden** plus the past participle of the main verb:

ich werde geschlagen	*I am (being) hit*
du wirst geschlagen	etc.
er (sie, es) wird geschlagen	
wir werden geschlagen	
ihr werdet geschlagen	
sie werden geschlagen	
Sie werden geschlagen	

Note: Remember that the future tense of the active voice is formed by **werden** plus the infinitive. Do not confuse the two verb forms:

Future active:

Ich werde ihn sehen.	*I will see him.*

Passive present:

Ich werde von ihm gesehen.	*I am (being) seen by him.*

3. A synopsis of the verb **geschlagen** (*to be hit*) in the six passive tenses is as follows:

Present:	**ich werde geschlagen**	*I am (being) hit*
Past:	**ich wurde geschlagen**	*I was (being) hit*
Pres. perf.:	**ich bin geschlagen worden**	*I have been hit, was hit*
Past perf.:	**ich war geschlagen worden**	*I had been hit*
Future:	**ich werde geschlagen werden**	*I will be hit*
Fut. perf.:	**ich werde geschlagen worden sein**	*I will have been hit*

Note: 1. **Worden** (translated *been*) is a shortened form of the past participle **geworden.**
2. Some form of the verb **sein,** the auxiliary of **werden,** appears in the perfect tenses. **Sein** is translated by a form of *have*.
3. The infinitive form of **werden** in the future passive is translated *be*.

4. Von (*by*), **durch** (*by means of*), and **mit** (*with, by*) are the prepositions which express agency or instrument:

Das Buch wurde *von* Hemingway geschrieben. (past)	*The book was written by Hemingway.*
Die Stadt ist *von* Rußland *durch* die Armee geschützt worden. (present perfect)	*The city was protected by Russia by means of the army.*
War das Brot *mit* einem Messer geschnitten worden? (past perfect)	*Had the bread been cut with a knife?*

5. As usual, the participles and infinitives will occupy the final position in the clause except in dependent word order:

Das Lied wird *gesungen werden.*	*The song will be sung.*
Sie weiß, daß das Lied *gesungen werden* wird.	*She knows that the song will be sung.*

These exercises are based on phrases and vocabulary drawn from a passage by Jung concerning flying saucers. Give the meaning expressed by the verbs in these sentences.

1. beobachten = *to observe*
Tag und Nacht **werden** Objekte von uns **beobachtet.**

1. Night and day objects *are observed* by us.	**2.** Tag und Nacht **werden** wir Objekte **beobachten.**
2. Night and day we *will observe* objects.	**3.** Tag und Nacht **wurden** Objekte von uns **beobachtet.**
3. Night and day objects *were observed* by us.	**4.** Tag und Nacht **sind** Objekte von uns **beobachtet worden.**
4. Night and day objects *have been observed* by us.	**5.** Tag und Nacht **waren** Objekte von uns **beobachtet worden.**
5. Night and day objects *had been observed* by us.	**6.** Tag und Nacht **werden** Objekte von uns **beobachtet werden.**
6. Night and day objects *will be observed* by us.	**7.** Tag und Nacht **werden** wir Objekte **beobachten.**
7. Night and day we *will observe* objects.	**8.** Tag und Nacht **werden** Objekte von uns **beobachtet werden.**
8. Night and day objects *will be observed by* us.	**9.** Tag und Nacht **werden** Objekte von uns **beobachtet worden sein.**
9. Night and day objects *will have been observed* by us.	**10.** **feurig** = *fierily* **strahlend** = *shining* Feurig strahlende Körper **werden** von ihnen **gesehen.**
10. Fierily shining bodies *are seen* by them.	**11.** Sie **werden** feurig strahlende Körper **sehen.**
11. They *will see* fierily shining bodies.	**12.** Feurig strahlende Körper **wurden** von ihnen **gesehen.**
12. Fierily shining bodies *were seen* by them.	**13.** Feurig strahlende Körper **sind** von ihnen **gesehen worden.**
13. Fierily shining bodies *have been seen* by them.	**14.** Feurig strahlende Körper **waren** von ihnen **gesehen worden.**
14. Fierily shining bodies *had been seen* by them.	**15.** Feurig strahlende Körper **werden** von ihnen **gesehen werden.**
15. Fierily shining bodies *will be seen* by them.	**16.** Sie **werden** feurig strahlende Körper **sehen.**

16. They *will see* fierily shining bodies.	**17.** Feurig strahlende Körper **werden** von ihnen **gesehen werden.**
17. Fierily shining bodies *will be seen* by them.	**18.** Feurig strahlende Körper **werden** von ihnen **gesehen worden sein.**
18. Fierily shining bodies *will have been seen* by them.	**19.** **der Gedanke** = *thought* **bewußt** = *conscious* Der Gedanke **wird** nicht bewußt **gedacht.**
19. The thought *is* not consciously *thought.*	**20.** Man **wird** den Gedanken nicht bewußt **denken.**
20. One *will* not consciously *think* the thought.	**21.** Der Gedanke **wurde** nicht bewußt **gedacht.**
21. The thought *was* not consciously *thought.*	**22.** Der Gedanke **ist** nicht bewußt **gedacht worden.**
22. The thought *has* not *been* consciously *thought.*	**23.** Der Gedanke **war** nicht bewußt **gedacht worden.**
23. The thought *had* not *been* consciously *thought.*	**24.** Der Gedanke **wird** nicht bewußt **gedacht werden.**
24. The thought *will* not *be* consciously *thought.*	**25.** Man **wird** den Gedanken nicht bewußt **denken.**
25. One *will* not consciously *think* the thought.	**26.** Der Gedanke **wird** nicht bewußt **gedacht werden.**
26. The thought *will* not *be* consciously *thought.*	**27.** Der Gedanke **wird** nicht bewußt **gedacht worden sein.**
27. The thought *will* not *have been* consciously *thought.*	

PROGRESS TEST

Choose the correct verb form for the indicated verb.

1. The book *will have been read.*
   - (a) wird gelesen
   - (b) wird gelesen worden sein
   - (c) wird gelesen werden
   - (d) wird gelesen sein müssen

2. The test *was passed.*
   (a) wird bestanden (b) war bestanden worden
   (c) wurde bestanden (d) hatte bestanden
3. The orchestra *is being conducted* by Toscanini.
   (a) ist geleitet worden (b) wird geleitet werden
   (c) hat geleitet werden müssen (d) wird geleitet
4. Stravinsky's violin concerto *had been played* by Jascha Heifitz.
   (a) war gespielt worden (b) mußte gespielt werden
   (c) wird gespielt werden (d) ist gespielt worden
5. Letters *have been sent* every day.
   (a) sind geschickt (b) waren geschickt worden
   (c) sind geschickt worden (d) werden geschickt werden
6. Dinner *will be served.*
   (a) will serviert werden (b) wird servieren
   (c) wird serviert werden (d) wird serviert worden sein

Answer key: **1.** (b); **2.** (c); **3.** (d); **4.** (a); **5.** (c); **6.** (c).

65. *Use of modals in the passive*

1. There are no passive forms of the modals themselves, but modals may be used in the passive voice:

Present:	**Der Brief muß geschrieben werden.**	*The letter must be written.*
Past:	**Der Brief mußte geschrieben werden.**	*The letter had to be written.*
Pres. perf.:	**Der Brief hat geschrieben werden müssen.**	*The letter has had to be written, had to be written.*
Past perf.:	**Der Brief hatte geschrieben werden müssen.**	*The letter had had to be written.*
Future:	**Der Brief wird geschrieben werden müssen.**	*The letter will have to be written.*

Note that the verb **werden** in its infinitive form is again translated *be.*

2. Look to the end of the clause to find the modal verb:

Das Lied hatte gesungen werden müssen. *The song had had to be sung.*

3. Because of the double infinitives in the present perfect, past perfect, and future tenses, the personal form of the verb will precede the participial construction in dependent word order:

Er glaubt, daß der Wagen von den Pferden hat gezogen werden können.	*He believes that the wagon could have been pulled by the horses.*

Give the meaning of the following verb tenses.

	1. Das Brot **wird** mit einem Messer **geschnitten.**
1. The (loaf of *or* piece of) bread *is cut* with a knife.	2. Das Brot **soll** mit einem Messer **geschnitten werden.**
2. The bread *is supposed to be cut* with a knife.	3. Das Brot **sollte** mit einem Messer **geschnitten werden.**
3. The bread *should be cut* with a knife.	4. Das Brot **mußte** mit einem Messer **geschnitten werden.**
4. The bread *had to be cut* with a knife.	5. **Hat** das Brot mit einem Messer **geschnitten werden müssen?**
5. *Did* the bread *have to be cut* with a knife?	6. Das Brot **ist** mit einem Messer **geschnitten worden.**
6. The bread *has been cut* (*was cut*) with a knife.	7. Ich weiß, daß das Brot mit einem Messer **hatte geschnitten werden müssen.**
7. I know that the bread *had had to be cut* with a knife.	8. **Kann** das Brot mit einem Messer **geschnitten werden?**
8. *Can* the bread *be cut* with a knife?	9. **Wird** das Brot mit einem Messer **geschnitten werden müssen?**
9. *Will* the bread *have to be cut* with a knife?	10. Das Buch **muß** von ihm **gefunden werden.**
10. The book *must be found* by him.	11. Das Buch **mußte** von ihm **gefunden werden.**
11. The book *had to be found* by him.	12. Das Buch **wurde** von ihm **gefunden.**
12. The book *was found* by him.	13. Ich weiß, daß das Buch von ihm **hat gefunden werden können.**
13. I know that the book *could have been found* by him.	14. Das Buch **war** von ihm **gefunden worden.**

14. The book *had been found* by him.	**15. Wird** das Buch von ihm **gefunden werden können?**
15. *Will* the book *be able to be found* by him? (i.e. Will he be able to find the book?)	**16. Darf** das Buch von ihm **gefunden werden?**
16. *May* the book *be found* by him?	**17.** Inge weiß, daß das Buch von ihm nicht **hat gefunden werden sollen.**
17. Inge knows that the book *was* not *supposed to be found* by him.	

PROGRESS TEST

Choose the correct form for the indicated verb.

1. The chair *was supposed to be brought* yesterday.
(a) wird gebracht werden sollen (b) sollte gebracht geworden sein
(c) sollte gebracht werden (d) ist gebracht worden

2. The book *will have to be begun.*
(a) wird begonnen worden sein (b) will begonnen worden müssen
(c) wird begonnen werden müssen (d) soll begonnen werden müssen

3. The door *had not been able to be closed.*
(a) hatte nicht geschlossen werden können (b) hat nicht geschlossen werden können
(c) konnte nicht geschlossen werden (d) hatte nicht schließen können

4. That *must not be sung.*
(a) durfte nicht gesungen werden (b) darf nicht gesungen werden
(c) hat nicht gesungen werden dürfen (d) mußte nicht gesungen werden

5. The hotel *had to be sold.*
(a) hatte verkauft werden müssen (b) wird verkauft haben
(c) hat verkauft werden müssen (d) muß verkauft werden

Answer key: **1.** (c); **2.** (c); **3.** (a); **4.** (b); **5.** (c).

66. *The impersonal passive*

1. Constructions such as the following, formed from intransitive verbs, are examples of the impersonal passive. The pronoun **es** is either used or understood:

Es wurde gesungen.	*There was singing.*
Mir wird gesagt . . .	*I am told . . .* [lit. (*It*) *is said to me.*]
Heute abend wird getanzt.	*There is a dance this evening. There will be dancing this evening.* (Note the future meaning of the passive present in this example.)
Ihm wurde nicht geantwortet.	*He was not answered.*

Give the meaning of the following passive constructions.

	1. **wider** = *against* **sprechen** = *to speak* Dem Professor **wurde** nie **widersprochen.**
1. The professor *was* never *contradicted.*	2. **bestimmt** = *certainly* Dir **wird** bestimmt nicht **geglaubt!**
2. You *will* certainly not *be believed* (*are . . . believed*). Note future meaning.	3. Es **ist** bis spät in die Nacht **getanzt** und **gesungen worden.**
3. *Singing* and *dancing went on* until late into the night (There *was singing* and *dancing . . .*).	4. Ihm **war** zu seinem Geburtstag **gratuliert worden.**
4. He *had been congratulated* on his birthday.	5. Es **wird** bestimmt dem alten Mann **geholfen werden müssen.**
5. The old man *will* certainly *have to be helped.*	6. Meine Herren, es **wird** hier nicht **geraucht!**
6. Gentlemen, smoking is not permitted (there *is* no *smoking* here).	

67. *Constructions translated by an English passive*

1. The passive is rather cumbersome in German and is often replaced by the following substitutes:

(a) **man** plus the active voice:

Hier trinkt man kein Wasser.	*Water is not drunk here.*
Man darf das nicht lesen.	*That must not be read.*

(b) a form of the verb **sein,** followed by **zu** or **nicht zu:**

Wie ist das zu machen?	*How is that to be done?*
Er ist nicht zu verstehen.	*He cannot be understood.*

(c) **sich lassen** plus a dependent infinitive:

Das läßt sich machen.	*That can be done.*
Die große dicke Zigarre läßt sich bestimmt nicht rauchen.	*That big, fat cigar certainly cannot be smoked.*

Give the meaning of the following sentences.

	1. Man **hat** ihm nicht **geantwortet.**
1. He *was* not *answered.*	**2.** Man **kann** ihn nicht **sehen.**
2. He *cannot be seen.*	**3.** Wo **ist** das Buch **zu finden?**
3. Where *can* the book *be found?*	**4.** **überzeugen** = *to convince* Ich sehe, daß du nicht **zu überzeugen bist.**
4. I see that you *cannot be convinced.*	**5.** **das Lied** = *song* Können Sie mir zeigen, wie dieses Lied **zu singen ist?**
5. Can you show me how this song *is to be sung?*	**6.** Das **läßt sich** einfach nicht **glauben!**
6. That simply *cannot be believed!*	**7.** Das **ließ sich** überhaupt nicht **verstehen.**
7. That *could not be understood* at all.	**8.** Sein neues Lied **läßt sich** bestimmt **singen.**
8. His new song *can* certainly *be sung.*	

68. *The apparent or statal passive*

1. The apparent passive is conjugated with a form of **sein** plus a past participle. The participle acts only as an adjective.

2. Contrast the apparent passive with the true passive, which you have just learned:

PRESENT:

Die Tür ist geschlossen.	*The door is closed.*
Die Tür wird geschlossen.	*The door is being closed.*

PAST:

Die Tür war geschlossen.	*The door was closed.*
Die Tür wurde geschlossen.	*The door was being closed.*

FUTURE:

Die Tür wird geschlossen sein.	*The door will be closed.*
Die Tür wird geschlossen werden.	*The door will be closed.*

The apparent passive describes the result of a previous action. The true passive describes an action taking place at the time the verb indicates.

3. The true passive is often used to describe a customary occurrence:

Die Tür wird um acht Uhr geöffnet.	*The door is opened* (regularly) *at eight o'clock.*

The apparent passive only tells that the door is open:

Die Tür ist um acht Uhr geöffnet.	*The door is open at eight o'clock.*

Give the meaning of the following sentences.

	1. Das Licht **ist** um 10 Uhr **ausgemacht.**
1. The light *is off* at 10 o'clock.	2. Das Licht **wird** immer um 10 Uhr **ausgemacht.**
2. The light *is* always *turned off* at 10 o'clock.	3. **beenden** = *to finish* Die Arbeit **war beendet.**
3. The work *was finished.*	4. Die Arbeit **wurde** um 10 Uhr **beendet.**
4. The work *was finished* at 10 o'clock.	5. **übermorgen** = *the day after tomorrow* Das Hotel **wird** übermorgen bestimmt **verkauft sein.**

5. The hotel *will* certainly *be sold* (by) the day after tomorrow (i.e. the transaction will be completed or have taken place).	**6.** Das Hotel **wird** übermorgen bestimmt **verkauft werden.**
6. The hotel *will* certainly *be sold* the day after tomorrow (i.e. the transaction will be taking place on that day).	

PROGRESS TEST

Give the meaning of the sentence.

1. Dem Lehrer wird nicht gehorcht.
- (a) The teacher does not obey.
- (b) The teacher will not obey.
- (c) The teacher will not be obeyed.
- (d) The teacher is not obeyed.

2. Es wurde bis spät in die Nacht geplaudert.
- (a) We talked late into the night.
- (b) We often talk late in the night.
- (c) We will talk late into the night.
- (d) Late that night we talked.

3. Man tut das eigentlich nicht.
- (a) That just is not done.
- (b) The man just does not do it.
- (c) We will just not do it.
- (d) He really had not done it.

4. Else hat sich ihr Haar machen lassen.
- (a) Else let her hair fall out.
- (b) Else has made her own hair.
- (c) Else herself did her hair.
- (d) Else had her hair done.

5. Das Haus war aus Steinen gebaut.
- (a) The house was being built of stones.
- (b) The house had been built of stones.
- (c) The house was built of stones.
- (d) The house had to be built of stone.

Answer key: **1.** (d); **2.** (a); **3.** (a); **4.** (d); **5.** (c).

READING PREPARATION

Continue to circle all new or unfamiliar words. Review them two or three times before going on to the reading passage.

	1. **veröffentlichen** = *to publish* Im Jahre 1958 **wurde** ein Buch von dem berühmten Psychologen und Psychiater C. G. Jung (1875–1961) **veröffentlicht.**
1. In 1958 a book *was published* by the famous psychologist and psychiatrist C. G. Jung (1875–1961).	**2.** Der Titel lautet: *Ein moderner Mythus, von Dingen, die am Himmel gesehen werden.*
2. The title reads: *A Modern Myth, of Things Which are Seen in the Sky.* (The English title is: *Flying Saucers, A Modern Myth of Things Seen in the Skies.*)	**3.** **untersuchen** = *to investigate* In diesem Buch **will** er nicht die Ufos als physikalische Realität untersuchen.
3. In this book he *does* not *want* to investigate UFO's as physical realities.	**4.** **sich zuwenden** = *to turn to* Er will sich **lieber** der Frage nach der psychischen Natur des Phänomens zuwenden.
4. He wants *rather* to turn to the question of the psychic aspects of the phenomenon.	**5.** **zugeben** = *to admit* Er gibt zu, daß etwas **gesehen wird.**
5. He admits that something *is seen.*	**6.** Einige Fragen **können gestellt werden.**
6. Some questions *can be asked.*	**7.** Zum Beispiel, „Was **wird** am Himmel **gesehen?"**
7. For example: "What *is seen* in the skies?"	**8.** **Wenn** nichts da ist, warum wird etwas gesehen?
8. *If* nothing is there, why is something seen?	**9.** **deuten** = *to signify, to interpret, to indicate* Deutet dies auf eine Änderung in der menschlichen Psyche?
9. Does this signify a change in the human psyche?	**10.** **die Folge** = *consequence* Was sind die psychischen Folgen davon, die möglich sind?
10. What are psychic consequences which are possible?	**11.** Und jetzt **wenden wir uns** dem Text zu.

11. And now *let us turn* to the text.	**12.** **beobachten** = *to observe* **die Beobachtung** = ________
12. *the observation*	**13.** **deuten** = *to mean, to interpret* **die Deutung** = ________
13. *meaning, explanation, interpretation*	**14.** die Beobachtung und Deutung der Ufos
14. the observation and interpretation of UFO's	**15.** **Anlaß geben** = *to give rise to* Wozu **haben** die Beobachtung und Deutung der Ufos **Anlaß gegeben?**
15. What *have* the observation and interpretation of UFO's *given rise to?*	**16.** **bilden** = *to form* Sie haben zu einer richtigen Legenden bildung Anlaß gegeben.
16. They have given rise to veritable formation of a legend.	**17.** **all-** = *all* **bereit** = *ready* **allbereits** = ________
17. *already*	**18.** Die Beobachtung und Deutung der Ufos haben allbereits zu einer richtigen Legendenbildung Anlaß gegeben.
18. The observation and interpretation of UFO's have already led to a veritable formation of a legend.	**19.** **die Reihe** = *the series* Es gibt heute eine Reihe von Büchern **darüber.**
19. Today there is a series of books *on it.*	**20.** Es gibt **heute auch schon** eine Reihe von Büchern über diesen Gegenstand. (*already/beautiful*)
20. There is *already* a series of books on this subject.	**21.** **ganz abgesehen** = *quite apart* Ganz abgesehen von den Tausenden von **Zeitungs**notizen und -artikeln . . . (**Zeitung** = *magazine/newspaper*)
21. Quite apart from the thousands of *newspaper* reports and articles . . .	**22.** **der Schwindel** = *humbug, swindle* **Zum Teil** sind diese Bücher Schwindel.
22. *In part* these books are humbug.	**23.** **der Ernst** = *earnestness, severity* **ernsthaft** = *serious, grave* Zum Teil sind die Zeitungsnotizen und -artikel und Bücher ernsthaft.

23. In part the newspaper reports and articles and books are serious.	**24.** Es gibt heute auch schon eine Reihe von Büchern über diesen Gegenstand — prò et contra, zum Teil Schwindel, zum Teil ernsthaft.
24. There is now a whole literature on the subject—pro and con, some of it humbug, some of it serious.	**25.** **beeindrucken** = *to impress* Die Ufos selber **lassen sich** nicht **beeindrucken** von all den Büchern und den Tausenden von Zeitungsnotizen und -artikeln.
25. The UFO's themselves *are* not *impressed* by all the books and the thousands of newspaper reports and articles.	**26.** Das Phänomen selber **scheint sich** davon nicht beeindrucken zu lassen. (*appears/shines*)
26. The phenomenon itself *appears* not to be impressed by it.	**27.** **dartun** = *to show, to prove* Wie die neuesten Beobachtungen dartun . . .
27. As the latest observations show (prove)...	**28.** Wie die neuesten Beobachtungen dartun, scheint sich das Phänomen selber **davon** nicht beeindrucken zu lassen.
28. As the latest observations show, the phenomenon appears not to be impressed *by it*.	**29.** **vorderhand** = *for the time being, for the present* Das Phänomen scheint vorderhand weiter zu gehen.
29. The phenomenon appears for the time being to continue (to go its way undeterred).	**30.** **Was** es immer sein mag, eines steht fest.
30. *Whatever* it may be, one thing is certain.	**31.** Das Phänomen **ist** zu einem lebendigen Mythus **geworden.**
31. The phenomenon *has become* a living myth.	**32.** **die Sage** = *legend* Das Phänomen ist auch schon eine Sage.
32. The phenomenon is already a legend.	**33.** **stehen** = *to stand* **entstehen** = *to begin* (also: *to originate, to grow out of*) Eine Sage **ist entstanden.**
33. A legend *has begun.*	**34.** **bilden** = *to form* Eine Sage **ist gebildet worden.**

34. A legend *has been formed.*	**35.** **die Gelegenheit** = *opportunity* Wir haben hier eine Gelegenheit zu sehen, wie eine Sage entsteht.
35. We have here an opportunity to see how a legend begins.	**36.** **erzählen** = *to tell* **die Erzählung** = *tale* Eine **Wundererzählung** bildet sich.
36. A *miraculous tale* takes shape (forms itself).	**37.** **schwer** = *difficult* **schwierig** = *difficult* In einer schwierigen und dunkeln Zeit **der** Menschheit bildet sich eine Wundererzählung.
37. In a difficult and dark time *for* (of) humanity a miraculous tale takes shape.	**38.** **eingreifen** = *to intervene* (also: *to interfere*) **der Eingriff** = __________
38. *the intervention*	**39.** **versuchsweise** = *by way of experiment* ein versuchsweiser Eingriff
39. an intervention by way of experiment	**40.** Eine Wundererzählung bildet sich von einem versuchsweisen Eingriff „himmlischer" Mächte.
40. A miraculous tale of an experimental intervention of "heavenly" powers takes shape.	**41.** **nah** = *near* **näher** = *nearer* **annähern** = *to approach* **die Annäherung** = __________
41. *the approach*	**42.** **die Erde** = *earth* **irdisch** = *terrestrial* **außer** = *outside of* **außerirdisch** = __________
42. *extra-terrestrial*	**43.** eine Annäherung außerirdischer „himmlischer" Mächte
43. an approach of extra-terrestrial "heavenly" powers	**44.** Eine Wundererzählung von einem versuchsweisen Eingriff oder wenigstens einer Annäherung außerirdischer „himmlischer" Mächte **wird gebildet werden.**

44. A miraculous tale of an experimental intervention or at least an approach by extra-terrestrial or "heavenly" powers *will be formed.*	**45.** **sich anschicken** = *to prepare* (*to set about, to get ready*) Die menschliche **Phantasie** schickt sich an . . .
45. Human *imagination* is preparing . . .	**46.** **der Weltraum** = *space* **die Fahrt** = *journey, travel* **die Weltraumfahrt** = __________
46. *space travel*	**47.** Die menschliche Phantasie schickt sich an, die Möglichkeit der Weltraumfahrt zu diskutieren.
47. Human imagination is getting ready to discuss the possibility of space travel.	**48.** **das Gestirn** = *star, constellation* Die menschliche Phantasie schickt sich an, die Möglichkeit der Invasion anderer **Gestirne** zu diskutieren.
48. Human imagination is preparing to discuss the possibility of invasion of other *stars.*	**49.** **zugleich** = *at the same time* Zugleich leben wir in einer Zeit, **da** die menschliche Phantasie sich anschickt, . . . (*because/in which*)
49. At the same time we live in a time *in which* human imagination is preparing . . .	**50.** . . . die Möglichkeit der Weltraumfahrt und des Besuches oder sogar der Invasion anderer Gestirne allen Ernstes zu diskutieren.
50. . . . to discuss seriously (in all earnestness) the possibility of space travel and of visiting or even invading other stars.	**51.** **diesseits** = *this side of* **jenseits** = *that side of* **unsererseits** = *for our part, as for us* Wir unsererseits wollen zum Mond oder Mars.
51. We for our part want to visit the moon or Mars.	**52.** **ihrerseits** = *for their part, for her part* Und **ihrerseits** wollen die Bewohner anderer Planeten zu uns. (*for their part/for her part*)
52. And *for their part* the inhabitants of other planets want to visit us.	**53.** **der Stern** = *star* **der Fixstern** = *fixed star* Wollen ihrerseits die Bewohner anderer Planeten unseres Systems **oder sogar** von Planeten der Fixsternsphäre zu uns?

53. For their part, do the inhabitants of other planets of our system *or even* of planets of fixed stars (of the fixed star sphere) wish (to visit) us?	**54.** **bewußt** = *conscious* Unsere **Weltraumaspiration** ist uns bewußt.
54. We are conscious of our *space aspirations.*	**55.** Die außerirdische Tendenz ist mythologische Konjektur.
55. The extra-terrestrial tendency is mythological conjecture.	**56.** **entsprechen** = *to correspond to* **entsprechend** = *corresponding* Die entsprechende außerirdische Tendenz aber ist mythologische Konjektur, d.h. Projektion.
56. The corresponding extra-terrestrial tendency, however, is mythological conjecture, i.e. projection.	**57.** Unsere Weltraumaspiration ist uns bewußt, die entsprechende außerirdische Tendenz aber ist mythologische Konjektur, d.h. Projektion.
57. We are conscious of our space aspiration; the corresponding extra-terrestrial tendency, however, is mythological conjecture, i.e. projection.	**58.** **vermuten** = *to suppose, to suspect* Was **könnte** man unschwer vermuten?
58. What *could* one easily suppose?	**59.** Was **wird** unschwer **vermutet worden sein?**
59. What *will have been* easily *supposed?*	**60.** Weiß er, was unschwer **hätte vermutet werden können?**
60. Does he know what *could have* easily *been supposed?*	**61.** **eng** = *small, narrow* Man könnte unschwer vermuten, daß es der Menschheit auf der Erde zu eng **wird.**
61. One could easily suppose that the earth *is becoming* too small for mankind.	**62.** **fangen** = *to catch* **hat gefangen** = *has caught* **das Gefängnis** = *prison* Ist die Erde ein Gefängnis für die Menschheit?
62. Is the earth a prison for mankind?	**63.** **mögen** = *to like* **möchte** = *would like* (subjunctive) Möchte die Menschheit **ihrem Gefängnis** entfliehen? (**Entfliehen** takes a ________ object.)

63. dative Would mankind like to flee *from its prison?*	**64.** **drohen** = *to threaten* Was droht **der** Menschheit, daß sie der Erde, ihrem Gefängnis, entfliehen möchte? (**Drohen** takes a _________ object.)
64. dative What threatens mankind that it would like to escape from the earth, its prison?	**65.** Nicht **bloß** die Wasserstoffbombe droht... (*blossom/only*)
65. Not *only* does the hydrogen bomb threaten . . .	**66.** **die Bevölkerungszahl** = *the population figure* Was geben uns die Bevölkerungszahlen?
66. What do the population figures give us?	**67.** Was **ist** uns durch die Bevölkerungszahlen **gegeben worden?**
67. What *has been given* to us by the population figures?	**68.** **schwellen** = *to swell* **anschwellen** = *to swell* (*up*) **das Anschwellen** = *the swelling up* Was gibt uns das Anschwellen der Bevölkerungszahlen?
68. What does the increase (swelling) in the population figures give us?	**69.** **die Lawine** = *avalanche* **-artig** = *like, resembling* (suffix) **lawinenartig** = _________
69. *resembling an avalanche*	**70.** Was gibt uns das lawinenartige Anschwellen der Bevölkerungszahlen?
70. What does the avalanche-like increase in the population figures give us?	**71.** **sorgen** = *to worry, take care* **besorgen** = *to take care of, look after* **besorgt** = *anxious, solicitous* **die Besorgnis** = _________
71. *anxiety, fear, concern*	**72.** Das lawinenartige Anschwellen der Bevölkerungszahlen gibt Anlaß **zu** ernstlicher Besorgnis.
72. The prodigious increase in the population figures gives cause *for* serious concern.	**73.** Nicht bloß die Wasserstoffbombe droht, sondern — tiefer noch — das lawinenartige Anschwellen der Bevölkerungszahlen, **das** Anlaß zu ernstlicher Besorgnis gibt.

73. Not only the hydrogen bomb threatens, but, what is even profounder, the prodigious increase in the population figures threatens, *which* gives cause for serious concern.	**74.** **eng** = *narrow, small* **verengern** = _________
74. *to narrow, to shrink*	**75.** **tatsächlich** = *in fact, as a matter of fact* Tatsächlich **verengert sich** der Wohn- und Lebensraum der Menschheit.
75. Man's living space (the dwelling and living space of humanity) *is,* in fact, *shrinking.*	**76.** **das Maß** = *degree, extent* **In welchem** Maße verengert sich tatsächlich der Wohn- und Lebensraum der Menschheit?
76. *To what* degree is man's living space, in fact, shrinking?	**77.** **nehmen** = *to take* **zunehmen** = *to increase, to grow* **zunehmend** = *increasing, growing* In zunehmendem Maße verengert sich tatsächlich der Wohn- und Lebensraum der Menschheit.
77. Man's living space, in fact, is shrinking to an (ever) increasing degree.	**78.** **überschreiten** = *to overstep, to exceed* **Ist** das Optimum für eine Reihe von Völkern schon **überschritten?**
78. *Is* the optimum for many nations (a series of peoples) already *exceeded?*	**79.** **geraum** = *roomy, spacious, ample* **geraume Zeit** = *long time* **für geraume Zeit** = _________
79. *for a long time, for some time*	**80.** Für eine Reihe von Völkern **ist** das Optimum **schon** für geraume Zeit **überschritten.**
80. For many nations the optimum *has (already) been exceeded* for some time.	**81.** Tatsächlich verengert sich der Wohn- und Lebensraum der Menschheit in zunehmendem Maße, und für eine Reihe von Völkern ist das Optimum schon für geraume Zeit überschritten.
81. Man's living space, in fact, is shrinking to an ever increasing extent, and for many nations the optimum has long been exceeded.	**82.** **rücken** = *to move, to shift* **zusammenrücken** = *to move nearer* das Zusammenrücken wachsender Bevölkerungen

82. the moving nearer (to one another) of expanding (growing) populations	**83.** Die Katastrophengefahr wächst proportional dem Zusammenrücken wachsender Bevölkerungen.
83. The danger of catastrophe grows in proportion to the degree that the expanding populations come in closer contact.	**84.** **eng** = *narrow, tight, close, confined* **die Enge** = ________
84. *closeness, narrowness, tightness*	**85.** **zeugen** = *to beget, to produce* **erzeugen** = *to procreate, to breed, to generate, to produce* Enge erzeugt Angst.
85. Closeness (congestion) breeds fear.	**86.** **der Bereich** = *sphere* (also: *scope, range, province*) Angst sucht Hilfe im außerirdischen Bereich.
86. Fear seeks help from extra-terrestrial sources (in the extra-terrestrial sphere).	**87.** Enge erzeugt Angst, **welche** Hilfe im außerirdischen Bereich sucht.
87. Cramped conditions create fear *which* (in turn) seeks help from extra-terrestrial sources.	**88.** **gewähren** = *to grant, to guarantee, to provide* Die Erde gewährt die Hilfe nicht.
88. The earth grants no help.	**89.** **Da** die Erde sie nicht gewährt . . . (*there/since*)
89. *Since* the earth does not grant it . . .	**90.** Enge erzeugt Angst, welche Hilfe im außerirdischen Bereich sucht, da die Erde sie nicht gewährt.
90. Congestion creates fear, which seeks help from extra-terrestrial sources, since the earth does not grant it.	

PROGRESS TEST

Choose the approximate meaning of the following items.

1. Die Beobachtung und Deutung der Ufos hat allbereits zu Tausenden von Zeitungsnotizen und -artikeln Anlaß gegeben.
  (a) Thousands of articles in newspapers give rise to a rash of UFO sightings.
  (b) The meaning of UFO's has been thoroughly explained in the newspapers.
  (c) Thousands of newspaper articles help give the public an understanding of UFO's.
  (d) The observation of UFO's has already led to thousands of newspaper articles.

2. Eine Legende von einem versuchsweisen Eingriff oder wenigstens einer Annäherung außerirdischer „himmlischer Mächte" wird sich bilden.
  (a) Experimental intervention of heavenly powers gives rise to the legend that they are at least trying to invade the earth.
  (b) No heavenly powers are invading the earth, just observing it.
  (c) A legend about supernatural powers invading or at least experimenting with the earth is being developed right now.
  (d) Experimental intervention or at least an approach by extraterrestrial powers will be part of a miraculous tale to be formed.

3. In einer Zeit zugleich, da die menschliche Phantasie *sich anschickt,* die Möglichkeit einer Weltraumfahrt zu diskutieren.
  (a) is sending itself (b) is getting ready (c) is imagining (d) is finding itself

4. Die Erde gewährt keine Hilfe vor der Katastrophenangst.
  (a) Fear of catastrophe is not relieved by the earth.
  (b) Fear is a product of the earth's inability to give help.
  (c) The earth grants help only to those who are not afraid of catastrophic danger.
  (d) Danger and fear thereof are all that the earth can grant an individual.

5. Das Zusammenrücken wachsender Bevölkerungen wird zu einer Katastrophe führen.
  (a) The expanding population leads to row upon row of people.
  (b) The pressing together of people makes stringent sanitation measures necessary.
  (c) Overpopulation of the earth could lead to increased anxiety.
  (d) Population pressures will lead to disaster.

6. Unsere Weltraumaspiration ist uns bewußt; man könnte unschwer vermuten, daß die entsprechende außerirdische Tendenz genau so bewußt ist.
  (a) Our space aspirations may well be the same as those of extra-terrestrial beings.
  (b) One could easily feel that all space travel will come to naught.
  (c) The tendency to ascribe our space aspirations to those of other planets is unconscious speculation.
  (d) Conscious speculation about inhabitants of other worlds and their space aspirations leads to a greater desire on our part to travel in space.

Answer key: **1.** (d); **2.** (d); **3.** (b); **4.** (a); **5.** (b); **6.** (a).

C. G. Jung: Ein moderner Mythus

Die Beobachtung und Deutung der Ufos [haben] allbereits zu einer richtigen Legendenbildung Anlaß gegeben. Ganz abgesehen von den Tausenden von Zeitungsnotizen und -artikeln gibt es heute auch schon eine Reihe von Büchern über diesen Gegenstand — pro et contra, zum Teil Schwindel, zum Teil ernsthaft. Das Phänomen selber scheint sich, wie die neuesten Beobachtungen dartun, davon nicht beeindrucken zu lassen. Es scheint vorderhand weiter zu gehen. Was es immer sein mag, eines steht fest: es ist zu einem *lebendigen Mythus* geworden. Wir haben hier eine Gelegenheit zu sehen, wie eine Sage entsteht, und wie in einer schwierigen und dunkeln Zeit der Menschheit eine Wundererzählung von einem versuchsweisen Eingriff oder wenigstens einer Annäherung außerirdischer „himmlischer" Mächte sich bildet; in einer Zeit zugleich, da die menschliche Phantasie sich anschickt, die Möglichkeit der Weltraumfahrt und des Besuches oder sogar der Invasion anderer Gestirne allen Ernstes zu diskutieren. Wir unsererseits wollen zum Mond oder Mars, und ihrerseits wollen die Bewohner anderer Planeten unseres Systems oder sogar von Planeten der Fixsternsphäre zu uns. Unsere Weltraumaspiration ist uns bewußt, die entsprechende außerirdische Tendenz aber ist mythologische Konjektur, d.h. Projektion . . . Man könnte unschwer vermuten, daß es der Menschheit auf der Erde zu eng wird, und daß sie ihrem Gefängnis entfliehen möchte, wo nicht bloß die Wassertoffbombe droht, sondern — tiefer noch — das lawinenartige Anschwellen der Bevölkerungszahlen, das Anlaß zu ernstlicher Besorgnis gibt.

* * *

Tatsächlich verengert sich der Wohn- und Lebensraum der Menschheit in zunehmendem Maße, und für eine Reihe von Völkern ist das Optimum schon für geraume Zeit überschritten. Die Katastrophengefahr wächst proportional dem Zusammenrücken wachsender Bevölkerungen. Enge erzeugt Angst, welche Hilfe im außerirdischen Bereich sucht, da die Erde sie nicht gewährt.

Chapter Twenty-One

69. *The subjunctive—definition of the subjunctive mood and the formation of the present tense form*

1. All verb conjugations which have been presented up to this point have been in the indicative mood, that is, the mood of reality:

ACTIVE VOICE:

Ich *habe* ihn *gesehen*.	*I* ***saw*** (***have seen***) *him.*

PASSIVE VOICE:

Er *ist* von mir *gesehen worden*.	*He* ***was*** (***has been***) ***seen*** *by me.*

2. The subjunctive is the mood of unreality, of doubt. The conjugation of the subjunctive and indicative are identical in the present tense for the **ich, wir,** and **sie (Sie)** forms (except for the modals and **wissen**). The subjunctive is distinguished from the indicative in the other persons by the following endings or marks:

WEAK VERBS		STRONG VERBS	
INDICATIVE	**SUBJUNCTIVE**	**INDICATIVE**	**SUBJUNCTIVE**
ich sage	**ich sage**	**ich gebe**	**ich gebe**
wir sagen	**wir sagen**	**wir geben**	**wir geben**
sie sagen	**sie sagen**	**sie geben**	**sie geben**
Sie sagen	**Sie sagen**	**Sie geben**	**Sie geben**

WEAK VERBS		STRONG VERBS	
INDICATIVE	SUBJUNCTIVE	INDICATIVE	SUBJUNCTIVE
du sagst	**du sag*est***	**du gibst**	**du g*ebest***
er sagt	**er sag*e***	**er gibt**	**er g*ebe***
ihr sagt	**ihr sag*et***	**ihr gebt**	**ihr geb*et***

IRREGULAR WEAK VERBS	
INDICATIVE	SUBJUNCTIVE
ich kenne	**ich kenne**
wir kennen	**wir kennen**
sie kennen	**sie kennen**
Sie kennen	**Sie kennen**
du kennst	**du kenn*est***
er kennt	**er kenn*e***
ihr kennt	**ihr kenn*et***

3. Since most subjunctive forms have disappeared from English, both the German subjunctive and indicative forms are translated by the English indicative or by verb forms with *would* as an auxiliary:

Er sagt, seine Freundin *habe* einen guten Aufbau.	*He says his girlfriend* ***has*** *a good figure.*
Wenn er nicht so ein richtiger Windbeutel *gewesen wäre*, *hätte* er längst *heiraten können*.	*If he* ***had*** *not* ***been*** *such a real windbag, he* ***could have married*** *long ago.*
Sie *wäre* verrückt, wenn sie mit ihm *ausginge*.	*She* ***would be*** *crazy, if she* ***went out*** *with him.*

4. Subjunctive forms are used in:

(a) expressions contrary to fact (see chapter 22)
(b) indirect discourse (see chapter 23)
(c) wishes, commands, expressions of doubt or conjecture, and polite requests (see chapters 22 through 24)

Decide whether the verb is in the indicative or subjunctive form. Do not worry about the meaning of the verb. It will be explained in the subsequent chapter.

	1. Er **glaubt** mir nicht.
1. indicative He *doesn't believe* me.	**2.** Er sagte, er **glaube (glaubte).**

2. subjunctive He said he *believed.*	**3.** Der König **lebe** lange!
3. subjunctive Long *live* the king! (*May* the king *live* long!)	**4.** Der König **lebt** immer noch.
4. indicative The king *is* still *living.*	**5.** Luzie fragte Charlie noch einmal, ob er einen Dummkopf **kenne (kennte).**
5. subjunctive Lucy asked Charlie once again whether he **knew** a blockhead.	**6.** Sie **kennt** einen Dummkopf.
6. indicative She *knows* a blockhead.	**7.** **Seht** ihr Wendelin an?
7. indicative *Are* you *looking* at Wendelin?	**8.** Er verdient, daß ihr ihn nicht mehr **ansehet (ansähet).**
8. subjunctive He deserves that you don't *look at* him any more.	**9.** Was **sprichst** du da?
9. indicative What *are* you *saying?*	**10.** Bianca glaubte, du **sprechest (sprächest)** mit Max.
10. subjunctive Bianca believed you *spoke* (*were speaking*) with Max.	

70. *Past subjunctive—the formation of the past tense form of strong, weak, and irregular verbs*

1. In the past tense of strong verbs and irregular weak verbs, the subjunctive is distinguished from the indicative by the verb endings, vowel change, and when possible by an umlaut. If the vowel of a strong verb is **a, o,** or **u,** it will take the umlaut. The past subjunctive stem vowel of irregular weak verbs does not change from that of the present:

		SUBJUNCTIVE
INDICATIVE		**STRONG VERBS**
ich	**g*a*b**	**g*ä*b*e***
du	**g*a*bst**	**g*ä*b*est***
er, sie, es	**g*a*b**	**g*ä*b*e***
wir	**g*a*ben**	**g*ä*ben**
ihr	**g*a*bt**	**g*ä*b*et***
sie	**g*a*ben**	**g*ä*ben**
Sie	**g*a*ben**	**g*ä*ben**

IRREGULAR WEAK VERBS

INDICATIVE		**SUBJUNCTIVE**
ich	**k*a*nn*te***	**k*e*nn*te***
du	**k*a*nn*test***	**k*e*nn*test***
er, sie, es	**k*a*nn*te***	**k*e*nn*te***
wir	**k*a*nn*ten***	**k*e*nn*ten***
ihr	**k*a*nn*tet***	**k*e*nn*tet***
sie	**k*a*nn*ten***	**k*e*nn*ten***
Sie	**k*a*nn*ten***	**k*e*nn*ten***

2. In the past tense of regular weak verbs, the two moods are identical:

WEAK VERBS

INDICATIVE		**SUBJUNCTIVE**
ich	**sag*te***	**sag*te***
du	**sag*test***	**sag*test***
er, sie, es	**sag*te***	**sag*te***
wir	**sag*ten***	**sag*ten***
ihr	**sag*tet***	**sag*tet***
sie	**sag*ten***	**sag*ten***
Sie	**sag*ten***	**sag*ten***

Decide whether the verb is in the indicative or subjunctive form. Again, observe the translation, but do not fret about the meaning of the verb.

	1. Er sagte, wir **sähen** ihn später.
1. subjunctive He said we *would see* him later.	**2.** Wir **sahen** ihn später.

2. indicative We *saw* him later.	**3.** Wenn er mir nur **schriebe!**
3. subjunctive If only he *would write* me a letter!	**4.** Er **schrieb,** sie sei (wäre) ein Dummkopf.
4. indicative He *wrote* she was a blockhead. (**Sei** and **wäre** are, of course, subjunctive forms.)	**5.** Du **sprachst** nicht mehr darüber.
5. indicative You *didn't say* any more about it.	**6.** Wenn du nur zu mir **sprächest!**
6. subjunctive If you *would* only *speak* to me!	**7.** Ihr **nanntet** ihn einen Dummkopf? Armer Charlie!
7. indicative You *called* him a blockhead? Poor Charlie!	**8.** Linus sagte, ihr **nenntet (nennet)** Charlie immer einen Dummkopf.
8. subjunctive Linus said you always *called* Charlie a blockhead.	**9.** Ich **empfand** nur Sympathie für ihn.
9. indicative I *felt* only sympathy for him.	**10.** Ob ich Sympathie für ihn **empfände?**
10. subjunctive *Would* I *feel* sympathy for him?	

71. *The present and past tense forms of the modals and the verbs* ***wissen, haben, sein,*** *and* ***werden***

1. The present and past subjunctive of the modals and **wissen** follow patterns similar to the strong verbs and the irregular weak verbs:

PRESENT TENSE

	INDICATIVE	SUBJUNCTIVE	INDICATIVE	SUBJUNCTIVE	INDICATIVE	SUBJUNCTIVE
ich	**darf**	**dürfe**	**kann**	**könne**	**mag**	**möge**
du	**darfst**	**dürfest**	**kannst**	**könnest**	**magst**	**mögest**
er	**darf**	**dürfe**	**kann**	**könne**	**mag**	**möge**

PRESENT TENSE

	INDICATIVE	SUBJUNCTIVE	INDICATIVE	SUBJUNCTIVE	INDICATIVE	SUBJUNCTIVE
wir	dürfen	dürfen	können	können	mögen	mögen
ihr	dürft	dürfet	könnt	könnet	mögt	möget
sie	dürfen	dürfen	können	können	mögen	mögen
Sie	dürfen	dürfen	können	können	mögen	mögen
ich	muß	müsse	soll	solle	will	wolle
du	mußt	müssest	sollst	sollest	willst	wollest
er	muß	müsse	soll	solle	will	wolle
wir	müssen	müssen	sollen	sollen	wollen	wollen
ihr	müßt	müsset	sollt	sollet	wollt	wollet
sie	müssen	müssen	sollen	sollen	wollen	wollen
Sie	müssen	müssen	sollen	sollen	wollen	wollen

	INDICATIVE	SUBJUNCTIVE
ich	weiß	wisse
du	weißt	wissest
er	weiß	wisse
wir	wissen	wissen
ihr	wißt	wisset
sie	wissen	wissen
Sie	wissen	wissen

PAST TENSE

	INDICATIVE	SUBJUNCTIVE	INDICATIVE	SUBJUNCTIVE	INDICATIVE	SUBJUNCTIVE
ich	durfte	dürfte	konnte	könnte	mochte	möchte
du	durftest	dürftest	konntest	könntest	mochtest	möchtest
er	durfte	dürfte	konnte	könnte	mochte	möchte
wir	durften	dürften	konnten	könnten	mochten	möchten
ihr	durftet	dürftet	konntet	könntet	mochtet	möchtet
sie	durften	dürften	konnten	könnten	mochten	möchten
Sie	durften	dürften	konnten	könnten	mochten	möchten
ich	mußte	müßte	sollte	sollte	wollte	wollte
du	mußtest	müßtest	solltest	solltest	wolltest	wolltest
er	mußte	müßte	sollte	sollte	wollte	wollte
wir	mußten	müßten	sollten	sollten	wollten	wollten

	PAST TENSE					
	INDICATIVE	**SUBJUNCTIVE**	**INDICATIVE**	**SUBJUNCTIVE**	**INDICATIVE**	**SUBJUNCTIVE**
ihr	**mußtet**	**müßtet**	**solltet**	**solltet**	**wolltet**	**wolltet**
sie	**mußten**	**müßten**	**sollten**	**sollten**	**wollten**	**wollten**
Sie	**mußten**	**müßten**	**sollten**	**sollten**	**wollten**	**wollten**
ich	**wußte**	**wüßte**				
du	**wußtest**	**wüßtest**				
er	**wußte**	**wüßte**				
wir	**wußten**	**wüßten**				
ihr	**wußtet**	**wüßtet**				
sie	**wußten**	**wüßten**				
Sie	**wußten**	**wüßten**				

Note that the past subjunctive of **sollen** and **wollen** takes no umlaut.

2. The present and past subjunctive of **haben** and **sein** are irregular:

	PRESENT		PAST		PRESENT		PAST	
	INDICATIVE	**SUBJUNCT.**	**INDICATIVE**	**SUBJUNCT.**	**INDICATIVE**	**SUBJUNCT.**	**INDICATIVE**	**SUBJUNCT.**
ich	**habe**	**habe**	**hatte**	**hätte**	**bin**	**sei**	**war**	**wäre**
du	**hast**	**habest**	**hattest**	**hättest**	**bist**	**sei(e)st**	**warst**	**wär(e)st**
er	**hat**	**habe**	**hatte**	**hätte**	**ist**	**sei**	**war**	**wäre**
wir	**haben**	**haben**	**hatten**	**hätten**	**sind**	**seien**	**waren**	**wären**
ihr	**habt**	**habet**	**hattet**	**hättet**	**seid**	**sei(e)t**	**wart**	**wär(e)t**
sie	**haben**	**haben**	**hatten**	**hätten**	**sind**	**seien**	**waren**	**wären**
Sie	**haben**	**haben**	**hatten**	**hätten**	**sind**	**seien**	**waren**	**wären**

3. The present and past subjunctive of **werden** follow a pattern similar to strong verbs:

	PRESENT		PAST	
	INDICATIVE	**SUBJUNCT.**	**INDICATIVE**	**SUBJUNCT.**
ich	**werde**	**werde**	**wurde**	**würde**
du	**wirst**	**werdest**	**wurdest**	**würdest**
er	**wird**	**werde**	**wurde**	**würde**
wir	**werden**	**werden**	**wurden**	**würden**
ihr	**werdet**	**werdet**	**wurdet**	**würdet**
sie	**werden**	**werden**	**wurden**	**würden**
Sie	**werden**	**werden**	**wurden**	**würden**

Give both the mood and the tense of the indicated verbs.

	1. ihr **könnet**
1. present subjunctive	2. ihr **könnt**
2. present indicative	3. ihr **könntet**
3. past subjunctive	4. ihr **konntet**
4. past indicative	5. wir **möchten**
5. past subjunctive	6. wir **mögen**
6. present indicative or present subjunctive	7. ihr **sollt**
7. present indicative	8. er **solle**
8. present subjunctive	9. er **sollte**
9. past indicative or past subjunctive	10. er **müßte**
10. past subjunctive	11. er **mußte**
11. past indicative	12. er **muß**
12. present indicative	13. er **müsse**
13. present subjunctive	14. er **habe**
14. present subjunctive	15. du **habest**
15. present subjunctive	16. du **hast**
16. present indicative	17. ihr **seid**
17. present indicative	18. ihr **seiet**
18. present subjunctive	19. er **wäre**
19. past subjunctive	20. sie **wüßte**
20. past subjunctive	21. sie **wußte**
21. past indicative	22. sie **weiß**

22. present indicative	**23.** sie **wisse**
23. present subjunctive	**24.** ihr **wißt**
24. present indicative	**25.** ihr **wisset**
25. present subjunctive	**26.** ihr **wußtet**
26. past indicative	**27.** ihr **wüßtet**
27. past subjunctive	

72. *The subjunctive—formation of the compound tenses*

1. The compound tenses of the subjunctive are formed by changing the auxiliary verbs to the corresponding subjunctive forms:

PRESENT PERFECT

INDICATIVE	**SUBJUNCTIVE**
ich *habe* gesagt etc.	**ich *habe* gesagt** etc.
ich *bin* gegangen etc.	**ich *sei* gegangen** etc.

PAST PERFECT

INDICATIVE	**SUBJUNCTIVE**
ich *hatte* gesagt etc.	**ich *hätte* gesagt** etc.
ich *war* gegangen etc.	**ich *wäre* gegangen** etc.

FUTURE

INDICATIVE	**SUBJUNCTIVE**
ich *werde* sagen (gehen) etc.	**ich *werde* sagen (gehen)** etc.

FUTURE PERFECT

INDICATIVE	**SUBJUNCTIVE**
ich *werde* gesagt haben etc.	**ich *werde* gesagt haben** etc.
ich *werde* gegangen sein etc.	**ich *werde* gegangen sein** etc.

Give the mood and tense of the following. Again, do not disquiet yourself about the meaning of the sentences. For the moment, concentrate on the verb forms.

	1. Caruso gab zu, er **habe** das Lied **gesungen.**
1. present perfect subjunctive Caruso admitted he *had sung* the song.	**2.** Er sagte, er **hätte** das Lied **gesungen.**
2. past perfect subjunctive He said he *had sung* the song.	**3.** Caruso erklärte, daß er das Lied **singen werde.**
3. Future subjunctive Caruso stated that he *would sing* the song.	**4.** Er erklärte, er **werde** morgen in der Oper die schönste Arie schon **gesungen haben,** bevor der König ankäme (ankomme).
4. Future perfect subjunctive He explained that he *would* already *have sung* the most beautiful aria in the opera tomorrow by the time (before) the King arrived.	**5.** Ich **bin** in die Stadt **gegangen.**
5. Present perfect indicative I *went* to town.	**6.** Ich **wäre** in die Stadt **gegangen,** wenn . . .
6. Past perfect subjunctive I *would have gone* to town if . . .	**7.** Hilde sagte, daß sie in die Stadt **gehen werde.**
7. Future subjunctive Hilde said she *would go* to town.	**8.** Sie **wird** wohl in die Stadt **gegangen sein,** nicht wahr?
8. Future perfect indicative She probably *went* to town, didn't she? (Note here the verb is expressing past probability.)	**9.** Er fragte, ob sie es **gewesen wäre.**
9. past perfect subjunctive He asked if it *had been* she.	**10.** Sie fragte, ob er es **gehabt hätte.**
10. past perfect subjunctive She asked whether he *had had* it.	**11.** Ob sie krank **geworden wäre,** wenn . . . ?
11. past perfect subjunctive I wonder whether she *would have become* sick if . . .	**12.** Ob es morgen **regnen wird.**
12. future indicative I wonder whether it will rain tomorrow.	

PROGRESS TEST

Choose the subjunctive form from the given possibilities. See if you can give the tense as well.

1. glauben
(a) er glaubt (b) du glaubst (c) sie glaube (d) ihr glaubt

2. wissen
(a) er wüßte (b) ich wußte (c) ihr wißt (d) sie wußten

3. sprechen
(a) ich sprach (b) wir sprächen (c) ihr sprecht (d) sie spricht

4. wollen
(a) er will (b) du willst (c) ihr wollt (d) ihr wolltet

5. mögen
(a) ich mag (b) er mochte (c) ihr mögt (d) wir möchten

6. sein
(a) ich war (b) er wird gewesen sein (c) wir seien gewesen (d) ihr seid gewesen

7. haben
(a) du hättest gehabt (b) er hat gehabt (c) sie hatte (d) ihr hattet gehabt

8. werden
(a) du bist geworden (b) ich wurde (c) er werde (d) ihr wart geworden

9. grüßen
(a) du grüßt (b) er wird grüßen (c) sie werde grüßen (d) ihr habt gegrüßt

10. lieben
(a) er liebt (b) sie hatte geliebt (c) sie liebten (d) du wirst geliebt haben

Answer key: **1.** (c, present); **2.** (a, past); **3.** (b, past); **4.** (d, past); **5.** (d, past); **6.** (c, present perfect); **7.** (a, past perfect); **8.** (c, present); **9.** (c, future); **10.** (c, past).

READING PREPARATION

Remember that vocabulary building requires frequent review of new words in context. When you finish this set of exercises, go back over the words you have circled, and then go to the reading passage.

	1. Wir lesen jetzt, was Heinrich Heine über Immanuel Kant zu sagen hat.
1. We are now going to read what Heinrich Heine has to say about Immanuel Kant.	**2.** Heine schreibt, daß die Lebensgeschichte des Immanuel Kant schwer zu **beschreiben** ist . . . (*write/describe*)

2. Heine writes that the life history of Immanuel Kant is difficult to *describe* . . .	**3.** . . . denn Kant hatte **weder** Leben **noch** Geschichte.
3. . . . for Kant had *neither* a life *nor* a history.	**4.** **der Hagestolz** = *bachelor* **das Hagestolzenleben** = ________
4. *life of a bachelor*	**5.** **geordnet** = *ordered* Er lebte ein mechanisch geordnetes, **fast** abstraktes Hagestolzenleben.
5. He lived a mechanically ordered, *almost* abstract life of a bachelor.	**6.** **die Gasse** = (narrow) *street* **das Gäßchen** = *lane* Er lebte in einem Gäßchen in Königsberg.
6. He lived in a lane in Königsberg.	**7.** **abgelegen** = *remote* In einem stillen, abgelegenen Gäßchen zu Königsberg lebte der große Philosoph.
7. The great philosopher lived in a quiet, remote lane in Königsberg.	**8.** **Damals** war Königsberg eine alte Stadt an der nordöstlichen Grenze Deutschlands.
8. *At the time* Königsberg was an old city on the northeast border of Germany.	**9.** **ziemlich** = *fairly* Heute ist Königsberg eine ziemlich abgelegene Stadt in Rußland.
9. Today Königsberg is a fairly remote city in Russia.	**10.** **verwalten** = *to administrate* **die Verwaltung** = *administration* Das heißt, der Teil Preußens, in **dem** Königsberg liegt, ist jetzt unter russischer Verwaltung. (*the/whom/which*)
10. That is, the part of Prussia in *which* Königsberg is located is now under Russian administration.	**11.** **dort** = *there* **dortig** = *in that town, of that place* Die Uhr **der** dortigen Kathedrale ist sehr groß. (*of the/whose*)
11. The clock *of the* cathedral in that city is very large.	**12.** **die Leidenschaft** = *passion* **leidenschaftlich** = *full of passion* **leidenschaftslos** = ________

12. *dispassionate*	**13.** **die Regel** = *rule* **regelmäßig** = *regular(ly)* Kants Leben war genau so leidenschaftslos und regelmäßig wie das Leben dieser Uhr.
13. Kant's life was as dispassionate and regular as the life of this clock.	**14.** **vollbringen** = *accomplish* Die große Uhr der dortigen Kathedrale **vollbrachte** ihr Tagewerk leidenschaftslos und regelmäßig.
14. The large clock of the cathedral in that city *accomplished* its daily work dispassionately and regularly.	**15.** **äußeres** = *exterior* **Leidenschaftsloser** und **regelmäßiger** wie ihr Landsmann Immanuel Kant vollbrachte diese Uhr ihr äußeres Tagewerk nicht.
15. This clock did not accomplish its exterior work *more dispassionately* and *more regularly* than its compatriot Immanuel Kant. (Normally one would expect **als** rather than **wie** in the above sentence.)	**16.** Was mußte Kant **immer** tun?
16. What did Kant *always* have to do?	**17.** **spazieren** = *to take a walk* **gehen** = *to go* **spazierengehen** = ________
17. *to go for a walk*	**18.** **das Kolleg** = *course of lectures* **Kollegien lesen** = *to give lectures* Kant hat unglaublich schwierige Kollegien gelesen.
18. Kant gave unbelievably difficult lectures.	**19.** Aufstehen, Kaffeetrinken, Schreiben, Kollegienlesen, Essen, Spazierengehen, alles hatte seine **bestimmte** Zeit.
19. Getting up, drinking coffee, writing, giving lectures, eating, going for a walk, everything had its *specific* time.	**20.** Es war immer **halb vier,** wenn Kant aus seinem Haus trat. (*3:30/4:30*)
20. It was always *3:30* (half of four) when Kant stepped out of his house.	**21.** Die Nachbarn wußten **genau,** daß es halb vier war. (*precisely/probably*)

21. The neighbors knew *precisely* that it was 3:30.	**22.** **die Glocke** = *bell* Die Nachbarn wußten genau, daß die Glocke halb vier **sei,** wenn Kant aus seiner Haustüre trat. (*was/had*)
22. The neighbors knew exactly that it *was* 3:30 ("that the bell was 3:30") when Kant stepped out of the door of his house.	**23.** **der Leib** = *body* **der Rock** = *coat* (for men), *skirt* **der Leibrock** = *dress coat* Er trug **fast immer** einen grauen Leibrock . . .
23. He *almost always* wore a gray dress coat . . .	**24.** **das Rohr** = *cane* (also: *reed, tube, pipe*) **das Röhrchen** = (small) *cane* . . . in der Hand das spanische Röhrchen.
24. . . . in his hand the Spanish cane.	**25.** Wenn Kant in seinem grauen Leibrock, das spanische Röhrchen in der Hand, aus seiner Haustüre trat . . .
25. Whenever Kant stepped from the door of his house (wearing) his gray dress coat (and carrying) the Spanish cane in his hand . . .	**26.** **die Linde** = *linden tree* **die Allee** = *drive, avenue* **die Lindenallee** = __________
26. *linden drive, linden avenue*	**27.** **wandeln** = *to walk* . . . und **nach** der kleinen Lindenallee wandelte . . . (*after/toward*)
27. . . . and walked *toward* the small linden drive . . .	**28.** Die Nachbarn wußten genau, daß die Glocke halb vier sei, wenn Kant nach der kleinen Lindenallee wandelte.
28. The neighbors knew precisely that it was 3:30 whenever Kant walked to the small linden avenue.	**29.** **der Gang** = *walk* **Seinetwegen** nennt man diese Lindenallee den Philosophengang.
29. *Because of him* one calls this linden avenue the philosopher's walk.	**30.** **Noch jetzt** nennt man seinetwegen diese Lindenallee den Philosophengang.
30. Because of him one *even now* calls this linden drive the philosopher's walk.	**31.** **auf und ab** = *back and forth* **Achtmal** spazierte Kant auf dem Philosophengang auf und ab. (*eight times/slowly*)

31. Kant walked *eight times* back and forth on the philosopher's walk.	**32.** In jeder **Jahreszeit** spazierte er achtmal dort auf und ab.
32. There he walked eight times back and forth, in every *season.*	**33.** **trübe** = *gloomy* Wenn das Wetter trübe war, wandelte sein Diener hinter ihm.
33. Whenever the weather was gloomy, his servant walked behind him.	**34.** **verkündigen** = *to forecast* Wenn das Wetter trübe war oder die grauen **Wolken** einen Regen verkündigten . . . (**Wolken** probably means __________.)
34. Whenever the weather was gloomy or the gray *clouds* forecast rain . . .	**35.** **drein** = **darein** = *along* . . . sah man seinen Diener **immer** hinter ihm drein wandeln.
35. . . . one *always* saw his servant walking along behind him.	**36.** **die Angst** = *anxiety, dread* **ängstlich** = __________
36. *anxious, uneasy, distressed, nervous, timid*	**37.** **besorgt** = *anxious* Der Diener, der Lampe hieß, wandelte ängstlich besorgt hinter ihm drein.
37. The servant, whose name was Lampe, walked anxiously along behind him.	**38.** Der Diener trug einen langen **Regenschirm** unter dem Arm, wenn das Wetter trübe war . . .
38. The servant carried a long *umbrella* under his arm, whenever the weather was gloomy . . .	**39.** . . . oder wenn die grauen Wolken einen Regen verkündigten.
39. . . . or whenever the gray clouds forecast rain.	**40.** **vorsehen** = *to provide for* **die Vorsehung** = __________
40. *providence*	**41.** Wenn der Diener ängstlich besorgt hinter ihm drein wandelte, **sah** er **aus wie** ein Bild der Vorsehung.
41. Whenever the servant walked anxiously along behind him, he *looked like* a picture of providence.	**42.** Der Diener, mit einem langen Regenschirm unter dem Arm, sah aus wie ein Bild der Vorsehung.
42. The servant, with a long umbrella under his arm, looked like a picture of providence.	**43.** **zermalmen** = *to crush* **zermalmend** = *crushing* Kant hatte **weltzermalmende** Gedanken.

43. Kant had *world-crushing* ideas.	**44.** **sonderbar** = *strange, singular* **Sonderbarer** Kontrast zwischen dem äußeren Leben des Mannes . . . (*a strange/a stranger*)
44. *A strange* contrast between the external life of the man . . .	**45.** **zerstören** = *to destroy, to demolish* **zerstörend** = *destructive* . . . und seinen zerstörenden, weltzermalmenden Gedanken!
45. . . . and his destructive, world-crushing thoughts!	**46.** **grauenhaft** = *dreadful* **die Scheu** = *respect, shyness* Die Bürger **haben** eine grauenhafte Scheu **empfunden.** (*felt/found*)
46. The citizens *felt* a dreadful respect.	**47.** **ahnen** = *to sense* Wahrlich, **hätten** die Bürger von Königsberg die ganze Bedeutung dieses Gedankens **geahnt . . .** (*have sensed/had sensed*)
47. Truly, *had* the citizens of Königsberg *sensed* the full meaning of this thought . . .	**48.** **. . . hätten** sie vor jenem Manne eine weit grauenhaftere Scheu **empfunden . . .** (*would have felt/will feel*)
48. . . . they *would have felt* in the presence of that man (before that man) a far more dreadful respect . . .	**49.** **der Scharfrichter** = *executioner* . . . als vor einem Scharfrichter, der nur Menschen **hinrichtet.** (*saves/executes*)
49. . . . than in the presence of an executioner, who only *executes* people.	**50.** Wenn Kant zur **bestimmten** Stunde vorbeiwandelte . . . (*appointed/unappointed*)
50. Whenever Kant walked by at the appointed hour (at a *certain* hour) . . .	**51.** **grüßen** = *to greet* . . . grüßten sie freundlich . . .
51. . . . they greeted him in a friendly way . . .	**52.** **richten** = *to set* . . . und richteten **etwa** nach ihm ihre Taschenuhr. (*perhaps/never*)
52. . . . and *perhaps* set their pocket watch(es) according to him.	

PROGRESS TEST

Choose the sentence which most closely approximates the meaning of the given sentence.

1. Ein fast abstraktes Hagestolzenleben in einer stillen, abgelegenen Uhr lebte leidenschaftslos und regelmäßig Kants alter Diener.
- (a) Kant, together with his servant, lived on a small quiet street. His life was less passionate than it was monotonous.
- (b) Old philosophers and their servants always live dispassionate and monotonous lives.
- (c) Kant's servant lived a quiet life in a remote clock.
- (d) A clock could not be more dispassionate and monotonous than that old bachelor Kant.

2. Seinetwegen nennt man die kleine Lindenallee den Philosophengang.
- (a) Groups of philosophers wandered through the linden alley.
- (b) He is responsible for the fact that philosophers live on Linden Street.
- (c) The linden drive and the philosopher's walk are one and the same.
- (d) Linden Street is now called Kant Street.

3. Ein Scharfrichter hat weniger Bedeutung als die zerstörenden, weltzermalmenden Gedanken, die Kants Nachbarn damals nicht ahnten.
- (a) Kant and his neighbors thought devastating thoughts.
- (b) Kant's thoughts meant nothing to his neighbors nor to the judge.
- (c) An executioner has more importance than the thoughts which Kant's neighbors thought.
- (d) The destructive thoughts which Kant's neighbors did not sense have more meaning than an executioner.

4. In jeder Jahreszeit wandelte der alte, ängstliche Lampe hinter dem mit einem langen Regenschirm unter dem Arm spazierenden Philosophen.
- (a) Old Lampe was afraid to offer an umbrella to the philosopher.
- (b) The walking philosopher was followed by a man named Lampe.
- (c) In every season of the year an umbrella accompanied by a frightened servant followed the philosopher.
- (d) The philosopher took an umbrella and an old lamp with him whenever he took a walk.

Answer key: **1.** (c); **2.** (c); **3.** (d); **4.** (b).

READING PREPARATION

Kant's most influential work was his lengthy **Kritik der reinen Vernunft** *(Critique of Pure Reason). The spirit of his life and work is expressed in a short work* **Beantwortung der Frage: Was ist Aufklärung?**, *from which the following vocabulary is extracted.*

	1. **die Aufklärung** = *enlightenment, the Age of Enlightenment* Was ist Aufklärung?
1. What is enlightenment?	**2.** Diese Frage hat Kant **einmal** versucht zu beantworten.
2. Kant *once* tried to answer this question.	**3.** **der Wahlspruch** = *motto* Für Kant ist der Wahlspruch der Aufklärung: *Sapere aude!*
3. For Kant the motto of the Age of Enlightenment is: *Sapere aude* (Dare to know)!	**4.** **verstehen** = *to understand* **der Verstand** = _________
4. *the faculty of reason, understanding*	**5.** **sich bedienen** = *to make use of* Man sollte sich seines **eigenen** Verstandes bedienen.
5. One should make use of one's *own* reason. (Notice that **sich bedienen** takes a genitive object.)	**6.** **der Mut** = *courage* Habe Mut, sagt Kant, dich deines eigenen Verstandes zu bedienen!
6. Kant says to have the courage to use your own understanding.	**7.** Das ist **also** der Wahlspruch der Aufklärung.
7. That is *therefore* the motto of the Age of Enlightenment.	**8.** **unmündig** = *immature* **die Unmündigkeit** = _________
8. *immaturity*	**9.** **verschulden** = *to be the cause of* **selbstverschuldet** = *self-imposed* Die Unmündigkeit ist oft selbstverschuldet.
9. Immaturity is often self-imposed.	**10.** Die Unmündigkeit eines Menschen kann **entweder** selbstverschuldet sein **oder** nicht.
10. The immaturity of a person can be *either* self-imposed *or* not.	**11.** **der Eingang** = *entrance* **der Ausgang** = _________
11. *exit*	**12.** Aufklärung ist der Ausgang des Menschen aus seiner **selbstverschuldeten** Unmündigkeit.

12. Enlightenment is the exit of a person out of his own *self-imposed* immaturity.	**13.** **das Vermögen** = *ability* **das Unvermögen** = ________
13. *inability*	**14.** Unmündigkeit ist das Unvermögen, mich **meines eigenen** Verstandes zu bedienen.
14. Immaturity is the inability to make use *of my own* understanding.	**15.** **die Leitung** = *guidance, direction* Unmündigkeit ist das Unvermögen eines Menschen, sich seines Verstandes ohne die Leitung eines anderen zu bedienen.
15. Immaturity is the inability of a person to make use of his reasoning powers without the guidance of another.	**16.** Warum ist diese Unmündigkeit selbstverschuldet?
16. Why is this immaturity self-imposed?	**17.** **die Ursache** = *cause, reason* Die Ursache der Unmündigkeit liegt nicht am **Mangel** des Verstandes, . . . (*mangel/lack*)
17. The reason for this immaturity lies not in the *lack* of understanding . . .	**18.** **sich entschließen** = *to decide, to resolve* **die Entschließung** = *resolution, determination* . . . sondern die Ursache liegt am Mangel der Entschließung und des Mutes, . . .
18. . . . rather the cause lies in the lack of determination and courage . . .	**19.** . . . sich des Verstandes ohne Leitung eines andern zu bedienen.
19. . . . to make use of one's understanding without the direction of another (person).	**20.** **derselben** = *for it, of it* Selbstverschuldet ist diese Unmündigkeit, **wenn** die Ursache derselben . . .
20. This immaturity is self-imposed *whenever* the reason for it . . .	**21.** . . . nicht am Mangel des Verstandes, sondern der **Entschließung** und des Mutes liegt.
21. . . . lies not in the lack of understanding but rather in the lack of *resolution* and courage.	**22.** **seiner** = *of it* **sich seiner zu bedienen** = *to make use of it* Die Ursache der Unmündigkeit liegt nicht am Mangel des Verstandes, sondern der Entschließung und des Mutes, sich seiner ohne Leitung eines andern zu bedienen.

22. The cause of immaturity lies not in the lack of understanding but rather in the lack of resolution and courage to use it without the direction of another.	**23.** **faul** = *lazy* **feige** = *cowardly* **Faulheit und Feigheit** = ________
23. *laziness and cowardliness*	**24.** Faulheit und Feigheit sind Ursachen . . .
24. Laziness and cowardliness are the reasons . . .	**25.** **zeitlebens** = *for life* . . . warum ein so großer Teil der Menschen gerne zeitlebens unmündig bleiben.
25. . . . why such a large number of people like to remain immature all their lives.	**26.** **der Vormund** = *guardian* Andere **werden** ihre Vormünder.
26. Others *become* their guardians.	**27.** **sich aufwerfen** = *to set oneself up* Es wird anderen **leicht,** sich zu Vormündern aufzuwerfen. (*light/easy*)
27. It becomes *easy* for others to set themselves up as guardians. (Note that **leicht** requires a dative object.)	**28.** Faulheit und Feigheit sind die Ursachen, warum es anderen so leicht wird, sich zu **deren** Vormündern aufzuwerfen. (*their/her*)
28. Laziness and cowardliness are the reasons why it becomes so easy for others to set themselves up as *their* guardians.	**29.** Faulheit und Feigheit sind die Ursachen, warum ein so großer Teil der Menschen **gerne** zeitlebens unmündig bleiben . . .
29. Laziness and cowardliness are the reasons why such a great number of people *like* to remain immature for life . . .	**30.** . . . und warum es anderen so leicht wird, sich zu **deren** Vormündern aufzuwerfen.
30. . . . and why it becomes so easy for others to set themselves up as *their* guardians.	**31.** Es ist so **bequem,** unmündig zu sein. (*comfortable/uncomfortable*)
31. It is so *comfortable* to be immature.	**32.** Habe ich ein Buch, das für mich Verstand hat . . .
32. If I have a book which supplies me understanding ("has understanding for me") . . . (Note that **wenn** is understood in the sentence and that its place is taken by the verb.)	**33.** **die Seele** = *soul* **sorgen für** = *to care for, to look after* **der Seelsorger** = ________

33. *the pastor*	**34.** Habe ich einen Seelsorger, der für mich **Gewissen** hat . . . (*knowledge/conscience*)
34. If I have a pastor who supplies me a *conscience* . . .	**35.** **beurteilen** = *to judge* Habe ich einen Arzt, **der** für mich die Diät beurteilt . . . (*who/which/the*)
35. If I have a doctor *who* judges a diet for me . . .	**36.** Habe ich ein Buch, das für mich Verstand hat, einen Seelsorger, der für mich Gewissen hat, einen Arzt, der für mich die Diät beurteilt, usw. . . .
36. If I have a book which supplies me understanding, a pastor who supplies me a conscience, a doctor who judges a diet for me, etc. . . .	**37.** **die Mühe** = *trouble, pains* **sich bemühen** = __________
37. *to take trouble, to take pains*	**38.** **. . . so** brauche ich mich ja nicht selbst zu bemühen. (*so/then*)
38. . . . *then* I do not need to take the trouble myself.	**39.** **nötig** = *necessary* Ich habe nicht nötig zu denken.
39. It is not necessary for me to think.	**40.** **bezahlen** = *to pay* Wenn ich nur bezahlen kann, habe ich nicht nötig zu denken.
40. When I can simply pay, it is not necessary for me to think.	**41.** **verdrießlich** = *annoying, vexing* Das Denken ist mir verdrießlich.
41. Thinking is annoying for me. (Note that **verdrießlich** calls for a dative object.)	**42.** **das Geschäft** = *business* Andere werden das verdrießliche Geschäft **übernehmen.** (*overcome/take over*)
42. Others will *take over* this (the) vexing business.	**43.** **schon** = *no doubt, surely* Andere werden das verdrießliche Geschäft **schon** für mich übernehmen.
43. Others will *surely* take over this vexing business for me.	

PROGRESS TEST

Choose the correct meaning for the indicated words.

1. Aufklärung is der **Ausgang** des Menschen aus seiner selbstverschuldeten Unmündigkeit.
   (a) beginning (b) end (c) exit (d) entrance
2. Das **Unvermögen,** sich seines eigenen Verstandes zu bedienen, ist Unmündigkeit.
   (a) inability (b) possibility (c) capability (d) misapplication
3. Dieser **Mangel** des Verstandes ist selbstverschuldet.
   (a) mangling (b) achievement (c) wretchedness (d) lack
4. Die Ursache liegt am Mangel der **Entschließung** und des Mutes.
   (a) opening (b) resolution (c) unlocking (d) disentanglement
5. Der **Wahlspruch** der Aufklärung ist *sapere aude!*
   (a) motto (b) findings (c) decision (d) resolution
6. Faulheit und **Feigheit** sind die Ursachen, warum so viele Menschen unmündig sind.
   (a) laziness (b) anxiety (c) fear (d) cowardliness
7. Ist es wirklich **bequem,** unmündig zu sein?
   (a) worthwhile (b) comfortable (c) easy (d) difficult
8. Ein **Seelsorger** hat Gewissen für mich.
   (a) pastor (b) seeker of souls (c) doctor (d) seeker of truth
9. Die meisten Menschen wollen **zeitlebens** unmündig bleiben.
   (a) lively (b) all their lives (c) live and let live (d) time to live
10. Er ist der **Vormund** dessen, der seine Diät nicht selbst beurteilen will.
    (a) finder (b) helper (c) guardian (d) preserver

Answer key: **1.** (c); **2.** (a); **3.** (d); **4.** (b); **5.** (a); **6.** (d); **7.** (b); **8.** (a); **9.** (b); **10.** (c).

Before proceeding to the reading passage review all the words which you circled.

Heinrich Heine: Zur Geschichte der Religion und Philosophie in Deutschland

Die Lebensgeschichte des Immanuel Kant ist schwer zu beschreiben. Denn er hatte weder Leben noch Geschichte. Er lebte ein mechanisch geordnetes, fast abstraktes Hagestolzenleben in einem stillen, abgelegenen Gäßchen zu Königsberg, einer alten Stadt an der nordöstlichen Grenze Deutschlands. Ich glaube nicht, daß die große Uhr der dortigen Kathedrale leidenschaftsloser und regelmäßiger ihr äußeres Tagewerk vollbrachte wie ihr Landsmann Immanuel Kant. Aufstehen, Kaffeetrinken, Schreiben, Kollegienlesen, Essen, Spazierengehn, alles hatte seine bestimmte Zeit, und die Nachbarn wußten ganz genau, daß die Glocke halb vier sei, wenn Immanuel Kant in seinem grauen Leibrock, das spanische Röhrchen in der Hand, aus seiner Haustüre trat und nach der kleinen Lindenallee wandelte, die man seinetwegen noch jetzt den Philosophengang nennt. Achtmal spazierte er dort auf und ab, in jeder Jahreszeit, und wenn das Wetter trübe war oder die grauen Wolken einen Regen verkündigten, sah man seinen Diener, den alten Lampe, ängstlich besorgt hinter ihm drein wandeln, mit einem langen Regenschirm unter dem Arm, wie ein Bild der Vorsehung.

Sonderbarer Kontrast zwischen dem äußeren Leben des Mannes und seinen zerstörenden, weltzermalmenden Gedanken! Wahrlich, hätten die Bürger von Königsberg die ganze Bedeutung dieses Gedankens geahnt, sie würden vor jenem Manne eine weit grauenhaftere Scheu empfunden haben als vor einem Scharfrichter, vor einem Scharfrichter, der nur Menschen hinrichtet — aber die guten Leute sahen in ihm nichts anderes als einen Professor der Philosophie, und wenn er zur bestimmten Stunde vorbeiwandelte, grüßten sie freundlich und richteten etwa nach ihm ihre Taschenuhr.

Immanuel Kant: „Beantwortung der Frage: Was ist Aufklärung?"

Aufklärung ist der Ausgang des Menschen aus seiner selbstverschuldeten Unmündigkeit. Unmündigkeit ist das Unvermögen, sich seines Verstandes ohne Leitung eines anderen zu bedienen. *Selbstverschuldet* ist diese Unmündigkeit, wenn die Ursache derselben nicht am Mangel des Verstandes, sondern der Entschließung und des Mutes liegt, sich seiner ohne Leitung eines andern zu bedienen. *Sapere aude* [*Dare to know*]*!* Habe Mut, dich deines *eigenen* Verstandes zu bedienen! ist also der Wahlspruch der Aufklärung.

Faulheit und Feigheit sind die Ursachen, warum ein so großer Teil der Menschen . . . gerne zeitlebens unmündig bleiben; und warum es Anderen so leicht wird, sich zu deren Vormündern aufzuwerfen. Es ist so bequem, unmündig zu sein. Habe ich ein Buch, das für mich Verstand hat, einen Seelsorger, der für mich Gewissen hat, einen Arzt, der für mich die Diät beurteilt, u.s.w., so brauche ich mich ja nicht selbst zu bemühen. Ich habe nicht nötig zu denken, wenn ich nur bezahlen kann; andere werden das verdrießliche Geschäft schon für mich übernehmen.

Chapter Twenty-Two

73. *The Conditional—present time*

1. The following forms express a wish, a request, or a conditional or contrary-to-fact meaning with reference to present time:

(a) past subjunctive

Wenn ich nur ein Vogel *wäre!*	*If I only **were** a bird!*
***Hätten* Sie vielleicht ein Zimmer mit Bad?**	***Would** you perhaps **have** a room with bath?*
Wenn ich Geld *hätte*, so *flöge* ich nach Deutschland.	*If I **had** the money I **would fly** to Germany.*
***Wäre* er nicht so dumm, so würde er das hübsche Ding heiraten.**	*If he **were** not so stupid, he would marry the pretty young thing.*

Note that **wenn** (*if*) may be omitted in German. The verb then takes its position in the sentence.

Würde* er doch *bestraft!	*If he **were** only **punished!***

The above is in the passive subjunctive. It is rarely used.

(b) past subjunctive of **werden** plus infinitive

Sie *würde singen*, wenn sie eine Stimme hätte.	*She **would sing** if she had a voice.*
Würdest* du gerne eine Tasse Kaffee *trinken?	***Would** you likw **to drink** a cup of coffee?*
Ich *würde* gerne zusammen mit Ihnen *gehen.*	***I would** gladly **go** with you.*

Do not confuse this conditional form with the future, which is formed by the present indicative of **werden** plus the infinitive:

Ich *werde singen*, wenn ich meine Stimme wieder habe.	***I will sing** when I have my voice back again.*

Give the meaning of the indicated verbs.

	1. Wenn Sie das Buch nur **schreiben würden!** (*will write/would write/are writing*)
1. If you *would* only *write* the book!	**2.** Ich **werde** ein Buch **schreiben.** (*will write/would write/am writing*)
2. I *will write* a book.	**3.** Das Buch **wird** von mir **geschrieben.** (*will write/would write/is being written*)
3. The book *is being written* by me.	**4.** Wenn das doch besser **erklärt würde!**
4. If that *were* only *explained* better!	**5.** **das Lied** = *song* Ich wußte, daß Fischer-Dieskau das Lied **singen würde.**
5. I knew that Fischer-Dieskau *would sing* the song.	**6.** Ich weiß, daß er das Lied **singen wird.**
6. I know that he *will sing* the song.	**7.** Das Lied **wurde** von ihm **gesungen.**
7. The song *was sung* by him.	**8.** Wenn das Lied nur von Fischer-Dieskau **gesungen würde!**
8. If only that song *were being sung* by Fischer-Dieskau.	**9.** **Ginget** ihr gerne nach Rußland?
9. *Would* you like *to go* to Russia?	**10.** Wenn er nur Zeit **hätte!** (*did have/had/would have*)
10. If he only *had* time!	**11.** Wann **hatte** er Zeit? (*had/did have/would have*)
11. When *did* he *have* time?	**12.** **Hätten** Sie noch etwas für mich? (*have/had/would have*)
12. *Would* you still *have* something for me?	**13.** Wenn Ingeborg nur nicht so hübsch **wäre!** (*was/were*)
13. If only Ingeborg *were* not so pretty!	**14.** Wann **war** Ingeborg zu Hause? (*were/was*)

14. When *was* Ingeborg at home?	**15.** Wenn sie das Lied **sänge,** wäre es eine Katastrophe. (*sang/were to sing*)
15. If she *were to sing* the song, it would be a catastrophe.	**16.** **gescheit** = *clever, shrewd* Wenn er Philosophie **studierte,** so **wäre** er ein gescheiter Mensch. (*studied . . . were/were to study . . . would be*)
16. If he *were to study* philosophy, he *would be* a clever man.	**17.** **verrückt** = *crazy* Wenn wir dieser Musik länger **zuhören, werden** wir verrückt. (*listen to . . . will go/were to listen . . . would become*)
17. If we *listen to* this music any longer, we *will go* crazy.	**18.** Dieses Buch **wird geschrieben,** wenn wir Zeit **haben.** (*will write . . . would have/will be written . . . have*)
18. This book *will be written* if we *have* time.	**19.** **Sängen** Sie das Lied, wenn Sie **wüßten,** daß es dafür kein Geld gibt? (*sing . . . know/sang . . . knew/would sing . . . knew*)
19. *Would* you *sing* that song if you *knew* that you would not receive any money?	**20.** **als ob, als wenn** = *as if* Er sieht aus, als ob er Hunger **hätte.**
20. He looks as if he *were* hungry. (**Als ob** and **als wenn** are subordinating conjunctions and are used primarily with the subjunctive.)	**21.** **die Nachtigall** = *nightingale* Sie singt, als **wäre** sie eine Nachtigall.
21. She sings as if she *were* a nightingale. (**Als ob** and **als wenn** frequently drop the **ob** or **wenn.** The verb then moves into the place of the missing **ob** or **wenn.**)	**22.** Wenn es nur **regnen würde!**
22. If it *would* only *rain!*	**23.** Wenn es morgen nur **regnete!**
23. If it *would* only *rain* tomorrow!	**24.** Wenn das Bild nur von Van Gogh **gemalt wäre!**

24. If that picture *were* only *painted* by Van Gogh!	**25.** Sie spricht, als **wäre** sie aus Deutschland.
25. She speaks as if she *were* from Germany.	

PROGRESS TEST

Choose the equivalent of the indicated words.

1. Maria erzählt diese Geschichte, als **wäre** sie betrunken.
   (a) would have (b) were (c) was (d) would be
2. Sie sah ihn an, als **würde** sie ihn gleich zerreißen.
   (a) was (b) would (c) will (d) became
3. Klaus **wird** bestimmt von Michael **geschlagen werden.**
   (a) will be hit (b) becomes hit (c) would be hit (d) is being hit
4. Wenn ich Geld **hätte,** so **kaufte** ich mir einen ganz neuen Mercedes.
   (a) would have . . . bought (b) had . . . buy (c) will have . . . bought (d) had . . . would buy
5. Ach, **wärest** du nur hier!
   (a) was (b) were (c) would be (d) could be
6. Wenn man heute doch **tanzen würde!**
   (a) was dancing (b) would dance (c) were dancing (d) will be dancing

Answer key: **1.** (b); **2.** (b); **3.** (a); **4.** (d); **5.** (b); **6.** (c).

74. *The Conditional—past time*

The following forms express a wish, or a conditional or contrary-to-fact meaning with reference to past time:

(a) past perfect subjunctive

Wenn sie nur Deutsch *gesprochen hätten!*	*If only they **had spoken** German!*
Sie *wären* damals nach Berlin *geflogen*, wenn sie das nötige Geld dazu *gehabt hätten.*	*They **would have flown** to Berlin then, if they **had had** the necessary money.*
Heinz sieht aus, als ob er getadelt *worden wäre.*	*Heinz looks as if he **had been scolded.***

Note again the passive subjunctive.

(b) past subjunctive of **werden** plus the perfect infinitive

Wenn ich die Antwort gewußt hätte, dann *würde* ich sie *gegeben haben*.	*If I had known the answer, I **would have given** it.*
Hättest du Zeit gehabt, *würdest* du bestimmt zu mir *gekommen sein*.	*If you had had time, you certainly **would have come** to my house.*

Give the meaning of the indicated phrases.

	1. Er **würde** das **gesagt haben . . .** (*will have said/would have said/would be said*)
1. He *would have said* that . . .	**2.** **wahrscheinlich** = *probably* Er **wird** das wahrscheinlich **gesagt haben.**
2. He probably *said* that. (Remember that future perfect used with **schon, wohl, doch,** or **wahrscheinlich** indicates past meaning.)	**3.** Das **wurde** bestimmt nicht **gesagt!** (*would say/would have said/was said*)
3. That certainly *was* not *said!*	**4.** Das **wäre** bestimmt nicht **gesagt worden!** (*would have been said/were to be said/was said*)
4. That *would* certainly not *have been said!*	**5.** Ich **würde** ein Buch **gekauft haben . . .** (*would have bought/would buy/will have bought*)
5. I *would have bought* a book . . .	**6.** Er **wird** wohl das Buch **gekauft haben.** (*would have bought/bought/would buy*)
6. He probably *bought* the book.	**7.** Das Buch **wurde** von ihm **gekauft.** (*would buy/would have bought/was bought*)
7. The book *was bought* by him.	**8.** **wünschen** = *to wish* Er wünscht, er **hätte** nicht so viel **getrunken.** (*had drunk/drunk/could have drunk*)

8. He wishes that he *had* not *drunk* so much.	**9.** Ich wußte, daß er zuviel **getrunken hatte.** (*had drunk/drunk/has drunk*)
9. I knew that he *had drunk* too much.	**10.** **Wäret** ihr nur zu Hause **geblieben!** (*had remained/were to remain*)
10. If you *had* only *remained* at home!	**11.** **Wäre** das Buch **gekauft worden . . .** (*had been bought/would have been bought/were to be bought*)
11. *Had* the book *been bought* . . .	**12.** Ihr **wart** noch nicht in die Stadt **gegangen,** als er anrief. (*had gone/were going/were gone*)
12. You *had* not yet *gone* into the city when he called.	**13.** **Hättest** du lieber in München **gewohnt?** (*would have lived/had lived*)
13. *Would* you rather *have lived* in Munich?	**14.** **Hatten** sie früher schon einmal in München **gewohnt?** (*would have lived/had lived*)
14. *Had* they ever *lived* in Munich before?	**15.** **Wären** Sie nur nach Skandinavien **gefahren!** (*were to travel/had travelled*)
15. If you *had* only *travelled* to Scandinavia!	**16.** **Waren** Sie schon jemals in Skandinavien **gewesen?** (*would have been/had been*)
16. *Had* you ever *been* to Scandinavia before (already)?	**17.** Ich wünsche, ich **hätte** ihn nicht **kennengelernt.**
17. I wish I *had* not *made* his *acquaintance*.	**18.** **nett** = *nice* Es **wäre** nett **gewesen,** wenn du meinen Geburtstag nicht **vergessen hättest.**
18. It *would have been* nice, *had* you not *forgotten* my birthday.	**19.** Wenn ich nur Arzt **gewesen wäre!**
19. If I *had* only *been* a doctor!	**20.** **Hätte** mein Freund ein Auto **gehabt,** so er es mir **gegeben** hätte.
20. If my friend *had had* an automobile, he *would have given* it to me.	**21.** **das Pferd** = *horse* **der Sumpf** = *swamp* **Wäre** er nicht auf dem Pferd **geritten,** so **wäre** er nicht in den Sumpf **gefallen.**

21. If he *had* not *ridden* the horse, he *would* not *have fallen* into the swamp.	**22.** Auch wenn du mir tausend Mark **gegeben hättest, hätte** ich die Arbeit nicht **getan.**
22. Even if you *had given* me a thousand marks, I *would* not *have done* the work.	**23.** Er sah aus, als **hätte** er ein Gespenst **gesehen.**
23. He looked as if he *had seen* a ghost.	**24.** Sie sprach, als wenn sie gerade vom Lande **gekommen wäre.**
24. She spoke as if she *had* just *come* from the country.	**25.** Wir **hätten** der Musik länger **zugehört** aber dann **wären** wir vielleicht verrückt **geworden.**
25. We *would have listened to* the music longer but then we perhaps *would have gone* crazy.	**26.** Es **wurde** immer an dem Buch fleißig **gearbeitet.**
26. We always worked on the book industriously. (The book *was* always *worked* on industriously).	**27.** **Hätte** ich mich **gezeigt,** so **wäre** ich **gesehen worden.** (*would be seen/would have been seen*)
27. Had I shown myself, I *would have been seen.*	

PROGRESS TEST

Choose the equivalent of the indicated verbs.

1. Er sagte, Maria hat an dem Abend gesungen, als ob sie betrunken **gewesen wäre.**
(a) was being (b) had been (c) would have been (d) were becoming

2. Penthesilea hatte Achilles angesehen, als **hätte** sie ihn am liebsten **zerrissen.**
(a) would have torn to pieces (b) would tear to pieces (c) were to tear to pieces (d) were to be torn to pieces

3. Wenn Klaus von Dieter **geschlagen worden wäre . . .**
(a) was hit (b) had been hit (c) were to be hit (d) had hit

4. Wenn ich Geld **gehabt hätte,** so **hätte** ich das Schiff **gekauft.**
(a) have had . . . had bought (b) would have . . . would have bought (c) had . . . would buy (d) had had . . . would have bought

5. Inge **wird** Ekkehardt wohl **geheiratet haben.**
(a) would have married (b) married (c) had married (d) is to be married

Answer key: **1.** (b); **2.** (a); **3.** (b); **4.** (d); **5.** (b).

READING PREPARATION

The following frames will introduce you to the reading passage. Continue to circle all words you do not understand.

	1. **berühmt** = *famous* In diesem Kapitel **werden** Sie einen Auszug aus dem berühmtesten deutschen Buch **lesen.**
1. In this chapter you *will read* an extract from the most famous of all German books.	**2.** Das Buch heißt natürlich *Faust.*
2. Naturally, the title of the book is *Faust.*	**3.** Der Autor ist Johann Wolfgang von Goethe, 1749 geboren, 1832 gestorben.
3. Johann Wolfgang von Goethe is the author, born 1749, died 1832.	**4.** Ungefähr sechzig Jahre lang **hat** Goethe an diesem Werk **gearbeitet.**
4. Goethe *worked* on this book (work) for approximately sixty years.	**5.** **der Held** = *hero* **der Gelehrte** = *scholar* Der Held, Faust, ist ein Gelehrter, der alles **wissen will.**
5. The hero, Faust, is a scholar who *wants to know* everything.	**6.** Sie kennen solche Menschen, nicht wahr?
6. You know such people, do you not?	**7.** **Ob** er alles gelernt hat, was zu wissen ist? — Um das herauszufinden, müssen Sie das Werk selber lesen. (*up/whether*)
7. I wonder *whether* he learned everything there is to know. You must read the work for yourself to find that out.	**8.** In einem berühmten Monolog erfahren wir, was Faust schon erreicht hat und was er noch erreichen will.
8. In a famous monologue we learn what Faust has already achieved and what he still wants to achieve.	**9.** **die Juristerei** = *jurisprudence* Faust hat Philosophie, Juristerei und Medizin studiert.
9. Faust has studied philosophy, jurisprudence and medicine.	**10.** **leider** = *unfortunately* Leider hatte er auch Theologie studiert.
10. Unfortunately he had also studied theology.	**11.** Er **hätte** lieber nicht Theologie **studiert.** (*would have studied/had studied*)

11. He *would* rather not *have studied* theology.	**12.** **durchaus** = *thoroughly* Am Anfang seines Monologs sagt er: „Habe **nun,** ach! Philosophie, Juristerei und Medizin, und leider auch Theologie durchaus studiert." (*now/none*)
12. At the beginning of his monologue he says, "Oh! I have *now* made a thorough study of philosophy, jurisprudence, medicine, and unfortunately also theology."	**13.** Faust hat Philosophie, Juristerei, Medizin und, wie er sagt, leider auch Theologie durchaus studiert.
13. Faust has made a thorough study of philosophy, jurisprudence, medicine, and, as he says, unfortunately also theology.	**14.** **sich bemühen** = *to take trouble, to take pains, to strive* **das Bemühen** = __________
14. *trouble, pains, effort*	**15.** Er hat sie durchaus studiert, mit heißem Bemühn (Bemühen).
15. He has studied them thoroughly with fervent (hot) effort.	**16.** **obwohl** = *although* Obwohl er mit heißem Bemühn studiert hat . . .
16. Although he has taken great pains to study . . .	**17.** **das Tor** = *gate* **der Tor** = *fool* . . . steht er da und ist nur ein armer **Tor.**
17. . . . there he stands and is just a poor *fool.*	**18.** **zuvor** = *previously* Er ist nur so **klug** als wie zuvor. (*stupid/wise*)
18. He is only as *wise* as he was previously.	**19.** Was er studiert hat, hat ihm nicht geholfen.
19. What he studied did not help him.	**20.** „Da steh' ich nun, ich armer Tor, und bin so klug als wie zuvor", sagt er.
20. "Now here I stand as a poor fool, and am only as wise as I was previously," he says.	**21.** **der Magister** = *Master* (of Arts) Obwohl er Magister und **gar** Doktor heißt . . . (*even/therefore*)
21. Notwithstanding he is a Master and *even* a Doctor . . .	**22.** . . . und obwohl er schon zehn Jahre **unterrichtet hat . . .** (*has taught/has practiced*)

22. . . . and although he *has* already *taught* for ten years . . .	**23.** . . . sieht er, daß wir nichts wissen können.
23. . . . he sees that we cannot know anything.	**24.** **die Schule** = *school* **der Schüler** = ________ (*pupil/schools*)
24. *pupil*	**25.** **ziehen** = *to pull* **herumziehen** = *to pull about* die Schüler **an der Nase** herumziehen (*by the nose/on the nose*)
25. to pull the pupils about *by the nose*	**26.** Er **zieht** schon zehn Jahre seine Schüler an der Nase **herum.**
26. He *has* already *pulled* his pupils *about* by the nose for ten years.	**27.** **herauf** = *up* **herab** = *down* Nicht nur herum zieht er seine Schüler an der Nase, sondern auch herauf und herab.
27. Not only does he pull his pupils about by the nose but he also pulls them up and down.	**28.** **quer** = *across* **krumm** = *crooked, curved* **quer und krumm** = *to and fro, all around* Herauf, herab und quer und krumm, zieht er seine Schüler an der Nase herum.
28. Up and down, to and fro, he pulls his pupils around by the nose.	**29.** Man kann Magister oder gar Doktor heißen und **trotzdem** nichts wissen.
29. One can be called a Master or even a Doctor and *still* (*in spite of that*) know nothing.	**30.** **verbrennen** = *to consume by fire, to burn up* Das Nichts-wissen-können verbrennt Faust das Herz.
30. This being able to know nothing consumes Faust's heart.	**31.** **schier** = *nearly, almost* Das **will** mir schier das Herz verbrennen, daß wir nichts wissen können.
31. The fact that we are not able to know anything *is about to* nearly consume my heart.	**32.** **Würde** es schier unser Herz verbrennen, wenn wir nichts wissen **könnten?**
32. *Would* it nearly consume our hearts if we *were* not *able* to know anything?	**33.** **schreiben** = *to write* **der Schreiber** = ________

33. *writer, scribe*	**34.** **der Pfarrer** = *parson, parish priest* **der Pfaffe** = *priest, member of the clergy* (now usually a contemptuous expression for **Pfarrer**) Faust ist klüger als alle die Schreiber und Pfaffen.
34. Faust is wiser than all the clerks and priests.	**35.** **der Laffe** = *fop, dandy* Faust sagt, daß er zwar **gescheiter** sei als alle die Laffen, Doktoren, Magister, Schreiber und Pfaffen . . . (*wise/wiser*)
35. Faust says that he is indeed *wiser* than all the fops, doctors, masters, clerks, and priests.	**36.** Die Laffen und Pfaffen, die Schreiber, Magister und Doktoren sind nicht zwar gescheiter als Faust, aber sie verdienen mehr Geld.
36. The fops and parsons, the scribes, masters and doctors are certainly not wiser than Faust, but they earn more money.	**37.** **zweifeln** = *to doubt* **der Zweifel** = *doubt* Faust hat **weder** Skrupel **noch** Zweifel.
37. Faust has *neither* scruples *nor* doubts.	**38.** **plagen** = *to plague, to trouble* Keine Skrupel noch Zweifel plagen ihn.
38. No scruples or doubts plague him.	**39.** Wenn Skrupel oder Zweifel ihn **geplagt hätten,** wie **hätte** er seine Schüler an der Nase **herumziehen können?**
39. If scruples or doubts *had plagued* him, how *could* he *have pulled* his pupils about by the nose?	**40.** Er fürchtet sich weder vor Hölle noch Teufel. (If **Hölle** means *hell* then **Teufel** must mean __________.)
40. *devil* He fears neither hell nor devil.	**41.** **reißen** = *to tear* **entreißen** = *to wrest from, to tear from or to snatch away* Alle Freude ist ihm auch entrissen.
41. All joy is also wrested from him.	**42.** Dafür ist mir auch alle Freud' entrissen.
42. In return (for that), all joy is also wrested from me.	**43.** **sich einbilden** = *to imagine* Faust bildet sich nicht ein, daß er etwas weiß.

43. Faust does not imagine that he knows anything.	**44.** **was Rechts** = **etwas Rechtes** = *something worthwhile, something to be proud of* Faust bildet sich nicht ein, was Rechts zu wissen.
44. Faust does not imagine that he knows anything worthwhile.	**45.** Er bildet sich nicht ein, er könnte **was** lehren . . .
45. He does not imagine that he could teach *anything* . . .	**46.** **bekehren** = *to convert* . . . die Menschen zu bessern und zu bekehren.
46. . . . to improve and to convert people.	**47.** Was **müßte** man **tun,** um die Menschen zu bessern und zu bekehren?
47. What *would* one *have to do* in order to improve and to convert people?	**48.** **Nicht nur** weiß Faust, daß wir nichts wissen können, **sondern** er hat **auch** kein Geld.
48. *Not only* does Faust know that we can know nothing, but in addition he has no money.	**49.** **das Gut** = *property, possessions, goods* Auch hat er **weder** Gut **noch** Geld.
49. He also has *neither* possessions *nor* money.	**50.** **ehren** = *to honor* **die Ehre** = __________
50. *honor*	**51.** **herrlich** = *splendid* **die Herrlichkeit** = __________
51. *splendor*	**52.** Auch hab' ich weder Gut noch Geld, noch Ehr' und Herrlichkeit der Welt. (The apostrophe on **hab'** and **Ehr'** replaces the letter ____)
52. **e** I have in addition neither possessions nor wealth, nor worldly honor and splendor.	**53.** Es **möchte** kein Hund so länger leben, meint Faust. (*would like/may*)
53. Faust feels that not even a dog *would like* to live as he.	**54.** **drum** = **darum** = *for that reason* Drum will Faust **Magie** studieren. (*magi/magic*)
54. For that reason Faust wants to study *magic.*	**55.** **sich ergeben** = *to take to, to surrender to* Drum hat er sich der Magie ergeben.

55. For that reason he has taken to magic.	**56.** **die Kraft** = *power* **der Mund** = *mouth* **Kraft und Mund** = *power and speech* Durch **Geistes** Kraft und Mund . . . (*spirit's/ghost's*)
56. Through the *spirit's* power and speech . . .	**57.** **erkennen** = *to discern* . . . will er erkennen, was die Welt **im Innersten** zusammenhält. (*in its innermost being/in its extremities*)
57. . . . he wants to discern what holds the world together *in its innermost being.*	**58.** **das Geheimnis** = *secret* Er will die Geheimnisse der Welt erkennen.
58. He wants to discern the secrets of the world.	**59.** **sauer** = *bitter, sour* Er will nicht mehr mit saurem Schweiß sagen, was er nicht weiß.
59. He no longer wants to say with bitter sweat what he does not know.	**60.** **die Wirkenskraft** = *actuating force* Er will die Wirkenskraft der Welt **schauen.** (*to know/to see*)
60. He wants *to see* the actuating force of the world.	**61.** Nicht nur die Wirkenskraft, sondern auch **die Samen** der Welt will er schauen. (*the same/the seeds*)
61. He wants to see not only the actuating force but also *the seeds* of the world.	**62.** **kramen** = *to rummage* (*around*) Faust will nicht mehr in Worten kramen.
62. Faust does not want to rummage around in words any longer.	**63.** **sich ausdrücken** = *to express oneself* So drückt er sich aus: „Drum hab' ich mich der Magie ergeben . . .
63. Thus he expresses himself: "For this reason I have turned to magic . . .	**64.** **kund** = *known, manifest* . . . ob mir durch Geistes Kraft und Mund nicht manch Geheimnis **würde kund . . .**
64. . . . (to learn) whether or not by means of the power and speech of the spirit many a secret *would become manifest* to me . . .	**65.** . . . daß ich nicht mehr mit saurem Schweiß zu sagen brauche, was ich nicht weiß . . .
65. . . . so that I no longer need to say with bitter sweat what I do not know . . .	**66.** . . . daß ich erkenne, was die Welt im Innersten zusammenhält . . .

66. . . . that I may discern what holds the world together in its innermost being . . .	**67.** . . . schau' alle Wirkenskraft und Samen . . .
67. . . . see all the actuating forces and seeds . . .	**68.** **tu'** = **tue** = *do* . . . und tu' nicht mehr in Worten kramen."
68. . . . and no longer rummage around in words."	**69.** Durch Magie lernte Faust die Welt nicht kennen.
69. Faust did not come to know the world through magic.	**70.** **die Droge** = *drug* Heute ergeben sich manche nicht nur der Magie, um die Welt zu erkennen, sondern auch den Drogen.
70. Today some turn not only to magic but also to drugs in order to understand the world.	**71.** **leicht** = *easy* Wenn es nur so leicht **wäre,** die Welt zu erkennen!
71. If it *were* only that easy to understand the world!	**72.** Die große Frage ist, ob durch Geistes Kraft und durch Magie manch Geheimnis kund **wird.** (*becomes/will become*)
72. The great question is whether by means of the power of the spirit and magic many a secret *will become* known.	**73.** **kundmachen** = *to make known* Oder **werden** alle Geheimnisse nur durch sauren Schweiß **kundgemacht?**
73. Or *are* all secrets only *made known* through bitter sweat?	**74.** In der Bibel **steht es geschrieben:** (*it stands written/it is written*)
74. *It is written* in the Bible:	**75.** **das Angesicht** = *face* **Im** Schweiße deines Angesichts sollst du dein Brot essen. 1. Mose 3, 19
75. *By the* sweat of thy brow shalt thou eat bread.	

PROGRESS TEST

Choose the closest English approximation for the following sentences.

1. *Es will mir schier das Herz verbrennen, wenn ich daran denke, daß ich mit heißem Bemühn studiert habe und doch nur so klug bin als wie zuvor.*
   (a) My heart is continually burning because I thought only of studying.
   (b) No matter how hard one studies, one never becomes any smarter.
   (c) If I thought I could become smarter, my heart would burn with joy.
   (d) Because I studied industriously, I became even smarter.
2. *Entrissen ist mir alle Freud', denn ich bin zwar gescheiter als die Laffen, Pfaffen und Teufel.*
   (a) Freud does not believe he is certainly smarter than fops, priests, and devils.
   (b) Cleverness leads to a loss of joy.
   (c) I am bereft of joy because of devils, priests, and fops.
   (d) I revel in my cleverness.
3. *Die Ehre und Herrlichkeit der Welt werden nur durch die Magie kundgemacht.*
   (a) Honor and glory are revealed only to those who practice magic.
   (b) Magic reveals only a loss of wordly honor and glory.
   (c) Magic is the only true honor and glory of the world.
   (d) Only magic can give honor and glory to the world.
4. *„Leider erkenne ich", sagt Faust, „was die Welt im Innersten zusammenhält."*
   (a) Faust delights in his knowledge of the world's inner workings.
   (b) Faust rues his knowledge of the natural world.
   (c) Fortunately Faust knows what holds the world together.
   (d) Unfortunately Faust is holding the world together.
5. *Mich plagt weder Hölle noch Teufel, denn ich habe weder Skrupel noch Zweifel.*
   (a) The lack of scruples and doubts makes one a free man.
   (b) One plays with neither scruples nor doubts, with neither hell nor the devils.
   (c) Pursued by hell and the devils, I had neither doubts nor scruples.
   (d) Doubts and scruples lack the immediacy of hell and the devil.

Answer key: **1.** (b); **2.** (b); **3.** (a); **4.** (b); **5.** (a).

Before going on to the reading passage, review the vocabulary items you have circled.

Johann Wolfgang von Goethe: Faust

FAUST. Habe nun, ach! Philosophie,
Juristerei und Medizin,
Und leider auch Theologie

Durchaus studiert, mit heißem Bemühn.
Da steh' ich nun, ich armer Tor,
Und bin so klug als wie zuvor!
Heiße Magister, heiße Doktor gar,
Und ziehe schon an die zehen Jahr'
Herauf, herab und quer und krumm
Meine Schüler an der Nase herum —
Und sehe, daß wir nichts wissen können!
Das will mir schier das Herz verbrennen.
Zwar bin ich gescheiter als alle die Laffen,
Doktoren, Magister, Schreiber und Pfaffen;
Mich plagen keine Skrupel noch Zweifel,
Fürchte mich weder vor Hölle noch Teufel —
Dafür ist mir auch alle Freud' entrissen,
Bilde mir nicht ein, was Rechts zu wissen,
Bilde mir nicht ein, ich könnte was lehren,
Die Menschen zu bessern und zu bekehren.
Auch hab' ich weder Gut noch Geld,
Noch Ehr' und Herrlichkeit der Welt;
Es möchte kein Hund so länger leben!
Drum hab' ich mich der Magie ergeben,
Ob mir durch Geistes Kraft und Mund
Nicht manch Geheimnis würde kund;
Daß ich nicht mehr mit sauerm Schweiß
Zu sagen brauche, was ich nicht weiß;
Daß ich erkenne, was die Welt
Im Innersten zusammenhält,
Schau' alle Wirkenskraft und Samen,
Und tu' nicht mehr in Worten kramen.

(354–385)

Chaper Twenty-Three

75. *Conditional statements with the modals*

1. The following forms incorporating modal auxiliaries express a wish, a request, or a conditional or contrary-to-fact meaning:

(a) The past subjunctive of the modal and generally an additional infinitive is used to refer to present time

Könnte* ich nur *schwimmen!	*If I **could** only **swim!***
***Dürfte* ich bitte da vorbei?**	***Might** I **get** past there, please?*
Wenn er *wollte*, *könnte* er eine Fahrkarte *kaufen*.	*If he **wished**, he **could buy** a ticket.*
***Möchten* Sie noch ein Stück Kuchen?**	***Would** you **like** another piece of cake?*
Wenn ihr nur das *müßtet!*	*If you only **had** to do that* (and nothing else)!
Wer *sollte* das *tun*, wenn wir es nicht täten?	*Who **would have to*** (ought, should) ***do** it, if we did not do it?*

(b) The past perfect subjunctive of the modal is used to express past time. More often the double infinitive appears.

***Hätte* sie es *gedurft*, so hätte sie die Zigarre geraucht.**	*If she **had been permitted**, she would have smoked the cigar.*
Wenn ich nur *hätte schwimmen können!*	*If only I **had been able to swim!***
Hans *hätte* ihr Singen nicht *gemocht*, wenn sie eine häßliche Figur gehabt hätte.	*Hans **would** not **have liked** her singing if she had had an ugly figure.*
Hätten* sie mich nur nicht *besuchen müssen!	*If only they **hadn't had to visit** me!*

2. The following table outlines an approach to knowing the approximate meanings of double infinitive constructions in the subjunctive. The pronoun and verb are used for illustrative purposes only. They could of course be replaced by any subject or verb:

er hätte es tun dürfen	*he could, would, or should have been allowed to do it.*
er hätte es tun können	*he could have done it*
er hätte es tun mögen	*he would, could, or should have liked to do it*
er hätte es tun müssen	*he would have been obliged to do it*
er hätte es tun sollen	*he should have done it*
er hätte es tun wollen	*he would, could, or should have wanted to do it*

The following frames will review the meanings of the modals in the present and past indicative and also give you examples of conditional statements in which modals are used. Give the meaning of the indicated verbs as well as the meaning of the sentence.

	1. Georg **kann** gut **schwimmen.**
1. George *can swim* well.	**2.** Georg **konnte** gut **schwimmen.**
2. George *was able to* (*could*) *swim* well.	**3.** **faul** = *lazy* **Könnte** Georg gut **schwimmen,** wenn er nicht so faul wäre?
3. *Could* George *swim* well, if he were not so lazy?	**4.** Georg **hätte** gut **schwimmen können,** aber er war zu faul.
4. George *could have swum* well, but he was too lazy.	**5.** Wenn Georg es **gekonnt hätte,** wäre er nicht ertrunken.
5. If George *had been able to* (do) it, he would not have drowned.	**6.** Hier **darfst** du nicht **rauchen.**
6. You *must* not *smoke* here.	**7.** Hier **durftest** du **rauchen.**
7. You *were permitted to smoke* here.	**8.** **Dürfte ich hier rauchen?**
8. *Might* (*may*) I *smoke* here?	**9.** Hier **hättest** du **rauchen dürfen.**
9. You *would have been permitted to smoke* here.	**10.** Hier **hättest** du nicht **rauchen dürfen.**

10. You would not *have been allowed to smoke* here.	**11.** Wenn wir das Buch **lesen müssen,** werden wir es tun.
11. If we *have to read* the book, we will do it.	**12.** **Mußten** wir das Buch **lesen?**
12. *Did* we *have to read* the book?	**13.** **Müßten** wir das Buch **lesen,** um die Vorlesung zu verstehen?
13. *Would* we *have to read* the book in order to understand the lecture?	**14.** Wenn wir das Buch **hätten lesen müssen,** hätten wir es getan.
14. If we *had had to read* the book, we would have done it.	**15.** Wenn wir es nicht **gemußt hätten,** hätten wir das Buch nicht gelesen.
15. We would not have read the book if we *hadn't had to.*	**16.** **Tun wir es!** = *Let's do it!* (imperative form) Wenn ihr in die Berge **fahren wollt,** dann tun wir es doch!
16. If you *wish to drive* to the mountains, then let's do it!	**17.** **Wolltet** ihr in die Berge **fahren?**
17. *Did* you *want to drive* to the mountains?	**18.** **Würdet** ihr in die Berge **fahren wollen,** wenn wir Zeit hätten?
18. *Would* you *want to drive* to the mountains if we had the time?	**19.** **Hättet** ihr in die Berge **fahren wollen,** dann hätten wir euch mitgenommen.
19. If you *had wanted to drive* to the mountains, we would have taken you along.	**20.** **Hättet** ihr es **gewollt,** so wären wir in die Berge gefahren.
20. If you *had wanted to,* we would have driven to the mountains.	**21.** Er **mag** dich.
21. He *likes* you.	**22.** Er **mochte** das nicht.
22. He *did* not *like* that.	**23.** Sobald sie da ist, **möchte** er **abfahren.**
23. As soon as she is there, he *would like to leave.*	**24.** Er **hätte** das **tun mögen,** wenn sie da gewesen wäre.
24. He *would have liked to do* it, had she been there.	**25.** Er **hätte** es **gemocht,** wenn sie da gewesen wäre.
25. He *would have liked* it if she had been there.	**26.** Wenn er es **hätte tun mögen,** wäre sie froh gewesen.

26. If he *had wanted to do* it, she would have been glad.	**27.** Ich **soll** jetzt nach Hause **gehen.**
27. I *am supposed to go* home now.	**28.** **müde** = *tired* Ich **sollte** vor einer Stunde nach Hause **gehen,** aber ich war zu müde.
28. I *was supposed to go* home an hour ago, but I was too tired.	**29.** Ich **sollte** jetzt eigentlich nach Hause **gehen,** aber ich mag nicht.
29. I really *ought to go* home now but I don't feel like it.	**30.** Ich weiß, ich **hätte** nach Hause **gehen sollen.**
30. I know I *should have gone* home.	

And now check yourself with the following frames. If you have trouble getting the meaning, review the previous chapter and the meanings of the modals.

	1. Ich **müßte** ein Fisch sein, um da schwimmen zu können.
1. I *would have* to be a fish to be able to swim there.	**2.** Wenn Sie Lust **hätten, könnten** wir ins Kino gehen.
2. If you wished (*had* the desire) we *could* go to the movies.	**3.** **Dürfte** ich noch ein Glas Wasser haben, bitte?
3. *Might* I (*Could* I) have another glass of water, please?	**4.** **wollte** = *wish* Ich wollte, es **regnete** morgen.
4. I wish it *would rain* tomorrow.	**5.** Wenn ich **schlafen könnte,** so **täte** ich es auch.
5. If I *could sleep,* I *would do* it.	**6.** Wenn dir **dürften, gingen** wir ins Kino.
6. If we *were permitted,* we *would go* to the movies.	**7.** Wir **würden** die ganze Stadt **sehen können,** wenn die Luft nicht so verpestet wäre.

7. We *would be able to see* the whole city if the air were not so polluted.	**8.** **verzweifeln** = *to despair* **der Narr** = *fool* Wenn weise Männer nicht **irrten, müßten** die Narren verzweifeln. (Goethe)
8. If wise men *did* not *err*, fools *would have to* despair.	**9.** **übertreten** = *to break* (a law) Wenn man alle Gesetze **studieren sollte,** so **hätte** man gar keine Zeit, sie zu übertreten. (Goethe)
9. If one *were to study* all the laws, one *would* not *have* any time to break them.	

PROGRESS TEST

Give the meaning of the indicated verbs.

1. Ich wünschte, ich **könnte** Wienerschnitzel statt Sauerkraut **essen.**
(a) can eat (b) could eat (c) would eat (d) would have been able to eat

2. Er **hätte** das schon **sagen dürfen,** denn wir haben hier Pressefreiheit.
(a) had to be permitted to say (b) must be permitted to say (c) was permitted to say (d) would have been permitted to

3. Wenn ich ihn nur nicht **hätte küssen müssen!**
(a) had been obliged to kiss (b) would have to kiss (c) had been able to kiss (d) were supposed to kiss

4. Wenn du **wolltest,** könnten wir spazierengehen.
(a) wish (b) wished (c) will (d) want

5. **Müßte** ich mit euch spazierengehen, wäre ich lieber tot.
(a) have to (b) must (c) had to (d) were to

6. **Möchten** Sie gerne spazierengehen?
(a) could (b) would like (c) may (d) can

Answer key: **1.** (b); **2.** (d); **3.** (a); **4.** (b); **5.** (c); **6.** (b).

76. *Indirect discourse—definition, meaning*

1. Indirect discourse reports what someone else has said or thought without using his exact words. Usually subjunctive verb forms are used:

Fritz sagte: „Ich habe keine Zeit."	*Fritz said, "I have no time."*
Fritz sagte, er *habe* (*hätte*) keine Zeit.	*Fritz said he* **had** *no time.*
Edelgard fragte: „Ist Jürgen zu Hause?"	*Edelgard asked, "Is Jürgen at home?"*
Edelgard fragte, ob Jürgen zu Hause *sei* (*wäre*).	*Edelgard asked if Jürgen* **were** *at home.*

2. The following subjunctive forms express indirect discourse in the active voice:

Ilse antwortete, daß sie jetzt *gehe* (*ginge*).	*Ilse answered that she* **was leaving (would leave)** *now.*
Hans sagte, Ilse *sei* (*wäre*) schon weg*gegangen*.	*Hans said that Ilse* **had** *already* **gone** *away.*
Erich gab zu, er *habe* (*hätte*) gestern *geraucht*.	*Erich admitted he* **had smoked** *yesterday.*
Anna sagte, daß sie *singen werde* (*würde*).	*Anna said that she* **would sing.**
Maria glaubte, sie *werde* (*würde*) das Buch bis morgen fertig*gelesen haben*.	*Maria believed she* **would have read** *the book through by tomorrow.*

Notice that in indirect discourse the subjunctive is used to express things the reporter will not vouch for, whereas the indicative is used to express what he considers to be indeed true:

Franz sagte, er *komme* [*käme*] morgen.	*Franz said he* **would come** *tomorrow.*
Franz sagte, er *kommt* morgen.	*Franz said he* **is coming** *tomorrow.*

3. The following subjunctive forms express indirect discourse in the passive voice:

Ludwig fragte, ob der Brief jetzt von Maria *geschrieben werde* (*würde*).	*Ludwig asked whether the letter* **were being written** *by Maria now.*
Sie sagte, der Brief *sei* (*wäre*) schon *geschrieben*.	*She said the letter* **was** *already* **written.**
Du antwortetest, du *seiest* (*wärest*) von ihm *geschlagen worden*.	*You answered that you* **had been beaten** *by him.*
Sie glaubten, das Haus *werde* (*würde*) bald von Bomben *getroffen werden*.	*They believed the house* **would** *soon* **be hit** *by bombs.*
Sie sagten, das Flugzeug *werde* (*würde*) in zwei Stunden durch das Feuer ganz *zerstört* (*worden*) *sein*.	*They said the airplane* **would be (would have been)** *completely* **destroyed** *by the fire in two hours.*

The following frames introduce you to indirect discourse. Choose the correct meaning of the indicated verb.

	1. Er meinte, der Rolls Royce **sei** der beste Wagen.
1. He felt the Rolls Royce *was* the best car.	**2.** Er meinte, der Rolls Royce **wäre** der beste Wagen. (*is/was*)
2. He felt the Rolls Royce *was* the best car. (There is some doubt that it really is.)	**3.** Er meinte, der Mercedes **sei (wäre)** vielleicht der beste Wagen für ihn. (*is/was/would be*)
3. He felt the Mercedes *would* perhaps *be* the best car for him. (Notice that **sei** and **wäre** can have future meaning depending on the context.)	**4.** Er meinte, der Rolls Royce **sei** der beste Wagen **gewesen.** (*is being/has been/had been*)
4. He felt the Rolls Royce *had been* the best car.	**5.** Er meinte, der Rolls Royce **wäre** der beste Wagen **gewesen.** (*was being/would be/had been*)
5. He felt the Rolls Royce *had been* the best car.	**6.** Er meinte, der Rolls Royce **werde** der beste Wagen **sein.** (*will be/would be/is being*)
6. He felt the Rolls Royce *would be* the best car.	**7.** Er meinte, der Rolls Royce **würde** der beste Wagen **sein.** (*would be/will be/would have been*)
7. He felt the Rolls Royce *would be* the best car.	**8.** Er meinte, der Rolls Royce **wäre** wohl der beste Wagen **gewesen.** (*would be/had been/none*)
8. He felt the Rolls Royce *would* probably *have been* the best car. (Remember the future perfect may express past meaning.)	**9.** Ich fragte ihn, ob er Zeit für mich **habe.** (*has/would have*)
9. I asked him if he *would have* time for me.	**10.** Ich fragte ihn, ob er Zeit für mich **hätte.** (*would have/has*)
10. I asked him whether he *would have* time for me.	**11.** Ich fragte ihn, ob er gestern Zeit für sie **gehabt habe.** (*would have/had had*)

11. I asked him whether he *had had* time for her yesterday.	**12.** Ich fragte ihn, ob er gestern Zeit für mich **gehabt hätte,** wenn ich gekommen wäre. (*would have had/has had*)
12. I asked him whether he *would have had* time for me yesterday if I had come.	**13.** Ich fragte ihn, ob er morgen Zeit für mich **haben werde.** (*will have/would have*)
13. I asked him whether he *would have* time for me tomorrow.	**14.** Ich fragte ihn, ob er Zeit **haben würde.** (*would have/would have had*)
14. I asked him whether he *would have* time.	**15.** Ich fragte ihn, ob er bis morgen mittag genug Zeit **gehabt hätte,** um den Rolls Royce zu putzen. (*would have had to have/would have had*)
15. I asked him whether he *would have had* enough time by tomorrow noon to clean the Rolls Royce.	**16.** Sie sagte, das Haus **werde** eben **gebaut.** (*is being built/was built/was being built*)
16. She said the house *was* just *being built.*	**17.** Sie sagte, das Haus **würde** gerade **gebaut.** (*would be built/was being built/would have been built*)
17. She said the house *was* just *being built.*	**18.** Sie sagte, das Haus **sei** letztes Jahr **gebaut worden.** (*is being built/has been built/had been built*)
18. She said the house *had been built* last year.	**19.** Sie sagte, das Haus **wäre** letztes Jahr **gebaut worden.** (*is being built/had been built/was being built*)
19. She said the house *had been built* last year.	**20.** Sie sagte, das Haus **werde** nächstes Jahr **gebaut werden.** (*will be built/will have built/would be built*)
20. She said the house *would be built* next year.	**21.** Sie sagte, das Haus **würde** nicht vor dem Frühjahr **fertiggebaut sein.** (*would have built/would be finished*)
21. She said the house *would* not *be finished* (*completely built*) before spring.	**22.** **suchen** = *to look for* Sie schrieb, er **suche** den alten Hut. (*was looking for/looked for*)

22. She wrote that he *was looking for* the old hat.	**23.** Sie wünschte, er **fände** bald den alten Hut. (*would find/has found*)
23. She wished he *would* soon *find* the old hat.	**24.** Sie schrieb, er **habe** endlich seinen alten Hut **gefunden.** (*would have found/had found*)
24. She wrote that he *had* finally *found* his old hat.	**25.** Sie schrieb, er **hätte** endlich seinen alten Hut **gefunden.** (*had found/would have found*)
25. She wrote that he *had* finally *found* his old hat.	**26.** Sie schrieb, er **werde** den alten Hut wieder **verlieren.** (*would lose/is lost*)
26. She wrote that he *would lose* the old hat again.	**27.** Sie schrieb, er **würde** den alten Hut bestimmt wieder **verlieren.** (*would have lost/was lost/would lose*)
27. She wrote that he *would* surely *lose* the old hat again.	**28.** Sie schrieb, er **werde** wahrscheinlich den Hut inzwischen schon wieder **verloren haben.** (*will have lost/would have lost/has lost*)
28. She wrote that he probably *has* already *lost* the hat again in the meantime. (Notice the past meaning)	**29.** Sie schrieb, er **werde (würde)** wohl den Hut schon längst wieder **verloren haben.** (*would have lost/lost/will be lost*)
29. She wrote that he probably *lost* the hat again a long time ago.	

PROGRESS TEST

Choose the correct meaning of the indicated verbs.

1. Das Kind meinte, der König **habe** keine Kleider **an.**
   (a) did . . . have on (b) had . . . had on (c) has . . . on (d) would . . . have on
2. Der Wolf fragte Rotkäppchen, wohin sie **ginge.**
   (a) will go (b) goes (c) did go (d) was going

3. Anna fragte, ob Großmutter und Rotkäppchen wirklich von dem Wolf **verschlungen worden seien.**
   (a) have been devoured (b) would have been devoured (c) are being devoured
   (d) had been devoured
4. Klein-Bärchen schrie, jemand **habe** seine Suppe ganz **aufgegessen.**
   (a) has eaten up (b) had eaten up (c) could have eaten up (d) has to eat up
5. Rotkäppchen versprach, sie **werde** nie wieder Blumen **pflücken.**
   (a) will pick (b) are picked (c) would pick (d) were picked
6. Der Spiegel hatte der Königin gesagt, sie **sei** nicht die Schönste im ganzen Lande.
   (a) is (b) was (c) had (d) has been
7. Der Erzähler las, Schneewittchen **wäre** von den Zwergen vor der Königin **gewarnt worden.**
   (a) had been warned (b) was being warned (c) would have been warned (d) was warned
8. Aschenputtel sagte, sie **würde** so gerne zum großen Ball **hingehen.**
   (a) was going (b) would go (c) would have gone (d) will go
9. Die böse Königin hoffte, Schneewittchen **werde** von dem Jäger **getötet werden.**
   (a) was killed (b) will be killed (c) would be killed (d) would have been killed

Answer key: **1.** (a); **2.** (d); **3.** (d); **4.** (b); **5.** (c); **6.** (b); **7.** (a); **8.** (b); **9.** (c).

77. *Modals in indirect discourse—active and passive voice*

1. In active voice modals may be used as follows:

Inge sagte, daß sie jetzt *gehen müsse (müßte).*	*Inge said that she* ***had to go*** *now.*
Die Studenten erzählten, sie *haben* (*hätten*) gestern *rauchen dürfen.*	*The students related that they* ***had been allowed to smoke*** *yesterday.*
Er behauptete, er *werde* (*würde*) dafür kein Geld *sparen können.*	*He claimed he* ***would*** *not* ***be able to spare*** *any money for that.*

2. In passive voice modals may be used as follows:

Er fragte, ob das Buch *gelesen werden müsse* (*müßte*).	*He asked whether the book* ***had to be read.***
Sie sagte, das Lied *habe* (*hätte*) von ihm *gesungen werden sollen.*	*She said that the song* ***should have been sung*** *by him.*

The following frames will introduce you to the use of modals in active and passive voice in indirect discourse.

	1. Die drei kleinen Schweinchen dachten, der böse Wolf **könne (könnte)** sie nicht **verschlingen.** (*could swallow/could have swallowed*)

1. The three little pigs thought the bad wolf *could* not *swallow* them up.	**2.** Sie sagten, der Wolf **habe (hätte)** sie nicht **verschlingen können.**
2. They said the wolf *had* not *been able to swallow* them up.	**3.** Sie glaubten, der Wolf **werde (würde)** sie nicht **verschlingen können.** (*will be able to swallow/would be able to swallow*)
3. They thought the wolf *would* not *be able to swallow* them up.	**4.** Ich dachte, die drei Schweinchen **müßten** von dem Wolf **verschlungen werden.** (*must be swallowed/would have to be swallowed*)
4. I thought the three little pigs *would have to be swallowed* by the wolf.	**5.** Ich sagte, die drei Schweinchen **hätten** von dem Wolf **verschlungen werden sollen.** (*should have been eaten/shall have eaten*)
5. I said the three little pigs *should* (*ought to*) *have been eaten* by the wolf.	**6.** Er schrieb, der Prinz **wolle** durch das ganze Land **reiten,** um Aschenputtel zu finden. (*wants to ride/wanted to ride*)
6. He wrote that the prince *wanted to ride* through the whole country in order to find Cinderella.	**7.** Er schrieb, der Prinz **habe (hätte)** sie nicht **finden können.**
7. He wrote that the prince *had* not *been able to find* her.	**8.** Er glaubte, der Prinz **werde (würde)** sie nicht **finden können.** (*would be able to find/could have found*)
8. He believed that the prince *would* not *be able to find* her.	**9.** Der Prinz wollte wissen, ob Aschenputtel von ihm **gefunden werden könnte.** (*can be found/could be found*)
9. The prince wanted to know whether Cinderella *could be found* by him.	**10.** Er dachte, sie **hätte** von ihm **gefunden werden sollen.** (*shall be found/should have been found*)
10. He thought she *should have been found* by him.	

PROGRESS TEST

Choose the correct meaning of the indicated verbs.

1. Paul fragte, ob er wirklich in die Stadt **gehen müsse.**
   (a) has to go (b) had to go (c) must go (d) would go
2. Ich dachte, das Buch **könnte** von gelesen **werden.**
   (a) had been read (b) has been able to read (c) could be read (d) is able to read
3. Sie wunderte sich, warum man hier **nicht rauchen dürfe.**
   (a) may not smoke (b) cannot smoke (c) is not permitted to smoke (d) was not allowed to smoke
4. Er fragte, warum das Auto **habe (hätte) gewaschen werden müssen.**
   (a) had had to be washed (b) has had to be washed (c) would have to be washed (d) has to be washed
5. Schneewittchen fürchtete, sie **werde** den Weg zu den sieben Zwergen nicht mehr **finden können.**
   (a) has found (b) will be able to find (c) would be able to find (d) would have found

Answer key: **1.** (b); **2.** (c); **3.** (d); **4.** (a); **5.** (c).

READING PREPARATION

The following frames will introduce you to the vocabulary of the reading passage. Continue to circle all words you do not recognize and review them before going on to the reading passage. The passage consists of excerpts from Act I of ***Der Rosenkavalier****. All the excerpts deal with the nature and mystery of the passage of time. The characters mentioned in the excerpts are:* ***die Marschallin*** *(the field marshal's wife), a beautiful, mature woman whose beauty is just beginning to fade;* ***Baron von Ochs,*** *her "evil wretch" of a cousin, who is to wed a young pretty thing; and* ***Quin-quin,*** *her young lover and also a cousin, who eventually will wed the pretty young thing.*

	1. das Lesestück = *reading passage* Das Lesestück am Ende dieses Kapitels besteht aus drei Auszügen aus dem ersten Akt des *Rosenkavaliers.*
1. The reading passage at the end of this chapter consists of three excerpts from the first act of *Der Rosenkavalier.*	**2. komponieren** = *to compose, to write music* Vielleicht wissen Sie schon, daß der *Rosenkavalier* eine Oper ist, die von Richard Strauss **komponiert wurde.**
2. Perhaps you already know that *Der Rosenkavalier* is an opera (which was) *composed* by Richard Strauss.	**3. hervorragend** = *outstanding* Das Libretto ist aber von einem der hervorragendsten deutschen Dichter des zwanzigsten Jahrhunderts, Hugo von Hofmannsthal.

3. The libretto, however, was written by one of the most outstanding German poets of the twentieth century, Hugo von Hofmannsthal.	**4.** Und jetzt zum Text!
4. And now to the text!	**5.** **geheimnisvoll** = *mysterious* Das Thema ist „die Zeit" und was für ein geheimnisvolles Ding sie ist.
5. The theme is "time" and what a mysterious thing it is.	**6.** **besuchen** = *to visit* **der Besuch** = *visitor, visit* Als der Monolog beginnt, hat die Marschallin **eben** Besuch gehabt. (*even/just*)
6. As the monologue begins, the Marschallin has *just* had a visitor.	**7.** **der Ochs** = *ox* Es war der Baron von Ochs.
7. It was the Baron von Ochs.	**8.** Der Baron von Ochs, ein älterer, **schlechter** Kerl, will ein ganz junges und hübsches Mädchen heiraten. (*fine/evil*)
8. Baron von Ochs, an elderly *evil* fellow, wants to marry a very young and pretty girl.	**9.** **aufblasen** = *to blow up* **aufgeblasen** = *puffed up, inflated* Der Monolog fängt mit diesen Worten an: „Da geht er hin, der aufgeblasene, schlechte Kerl."
9. The monologue begins with these words: "There he goes, the puffed up, evil fellow."	**10.** **kriegen** = *to get* Der aufgeblasene, schlechte Kerl kriegt das hübsche, junge Ding.
10. The puffed up evil wretch gets the pretty young thing.	**11.** **der Binkel** = *leather bag* **einen Binkel Geld** = *a leather bag full of a lot of money* Nicht nur das Mädchen kriegt er, sondern einen Binkel Geld dazu, als **müßte** es so sein. (*must/had*)
11. He is getting not only the girl but in addition a purse full of money, as if it *had* to be so.	**12.** **müßts** = **müßte es** Der aufgeblasene, schlechte Kerl kriegt einen Binkel Geld dazu, als **müßts** so sein.

12. In addition, the puffed up evil wretch is getting a purse full of money, as if *it had* to be so.	**13.** **sich einbilden** = *to pride oneself, to flatter oneself, to imagine* **sich etwas vergeben** = *to compromise oneself about something* Er bildet sich ein, daß er sich etwas vergibt.
13. He prides himself (in thinking) that he is compromising his dignity (compromising himself).	**14.** **noch** = *moreover* Er bildet sich noch ein, daß ers (= er es) ist, der sich was vergibt.
14. Moreover, he prides himself in thinking that it is he who is lowering himself.	**15.** **sich erzürnen** = *to get angry* Die Marschallin fragt, warum sie sich darüber **erzürne.** (*should get angry/gets angry*)
15. The Marschallin asks why she *should get angry* about it.	**16.** **der Lauf** = *the way* Es ist **doch** der Lauf der Welt. (*still/after all*)
16. It is, *after all,* the way of the world.	**17.** **das Kloster** = *convent* (nuns), *monastery* (monks) Sie kommt frisch aus dem Kloster.
17. She comes fresh from the convent.	**18.** **das Mädel** = *girl* Sie **kann** sich auch an ein Mädel erinnern, . . . (*can/could*)
18. She *can* also remember a girl . . .	**19.** **die Ehe** = *marriage* **der Ehestand** = *married state, wedlock* . . . die frisch aus dem Kloster in den heiligen Ehestand **kommandiert worden ist.** (*had been ordered/was ordered*)
19. . . . who *was ordered,* fresh from the convent, into the holy state of matrimony. (Note that you would normally expect **ein Mädel, das . . . ,** not **ein Mädel, die . . .** for *a girl who . . .*)	**20.** Es ist der Lauf der Welt, daß ein Mädel in den heiligen Ehestand **kommandiert wordn (worden) ist.**
20. It is the way of the world that a girl *was ordered* into the holy state of matrimony.	**21.** Die Marschallin fragt, wo dieses Mädchen jetzt **sei.**

21. The Marschallin asks, where this girl *is* now. (When the introductory verb of an indirect statement is in the present tense you can translate the present tense subjunctive with the present indicative.)	**22.** **der Spiegel** = *mirror* Die Marschallin nimmt einen Handspiegel und fragt, wo sie (d.h. das Mädchen) jetzt sei.
22. The Marschallin takes a hand mirror and asks where she (i.e. the girl) is now.	**23.** **vergehen** = *to pass away* **vergangen** = *past* Sie **solle** den Schnee vom vergangenen Jahr **suchen.** (*is to seek/should seek*)
23. She *should seek* the snow from the previous year.	**24.** **Resi** = *nickname for Theresa, the Marschallin's middle name* Wo ist die kleine Resi jetzt? Ja, **such dir** den Schnee vom vergangenen Jahr.
24. Where is little Resi now? Might as well *look for* the snow of the previous year. (Well, *seek for yourself* the snow of the previous year.)	**25.** Aber wie **kann** das **sein,** daß ich die kleine Resi war . . .
25. But how *can* that *be,* that I was little Resi . . .	**26.** . . . und daß ich auch einmal die alte Frau **sein werd (= werde)!** (*would be/will be*)
26. . . . and that I *will* also one day *be* the old woman.	**27.** **der Fürst** = *prince* **die Fürstin** = *princess* Siehst du es, da geht sie, die alte Fürstin Resi.
27. Do you see (it), there she goes, the old Princess Resi.	**28.** **siehgst** = **siehst du** **s'** = **sie** Siehgst es, da geht s', die alte Fürstin Resi!
28. See, there she goes, the old Princess Resi!	**29.** Wie **könnte** denn das **geschehen?**
29. How *could* that *happen?*	**30.** Wie **macht** denn das der liebe Gott, wo sie doch immer die gleiche ist?
30. How *does* dear God *do* that, since (when) she is always the same person?	**31.** Und wenn ers (= er es) schon so machen muß . . .

31. And if He has to do it in this manner . . .	**32.** **dabei** = *at the same time* . . . warum laßt (= läßt) er mich denn zuschaun dabei?
32. . . . why does He let me look on at the same time? (The Marschallin leaves out the umlaut from time to time. This is typical for Southern German and Austrian dialects.)	**33.** **der Sinn** = *understanding* Sie fragte, warum **lasse (ließe)** Gott sie denn zuschaun (= zuschauen) dabei mit gar so klarem Sinn.
33. She asked why God *let* her look on at the same time with such a clear understanding.	**34.** **verstecken** = *to hide* Warum **versteckt** ers (= er es) nicht vor mir? (*does hide/did hide*)
34. Why *does* He not *hide* it from me?	**35.** **geheim** = *mysterious* (also: *secret, clandestine*) Das alles ist geheim, so viel geheim.
35. All that is mysterious, so very mysterious.	**36.** **ertragen** = *to endure* Der Mensch soll das ertragen, **dazu** ist er hier. (*for that purpose/there to*)
36. Man is to endure that, *for that purpose* he is here.	**37.** Und man ist dazu da, daß mans (= man es) ertragt (= erträgt).
37. And one is here to endure it. (Again the umlaut is missing in her speech.)	**38.** **der Unterschied** = *difference* Der ganze Unterschied liegt in dem „Wie" man das **Geheime** erträgt. (*mystery/mysterious*)
38. The whole difference lies in the "how" we endure the mysterious.	**39.** Und in dem „Wie" da liegt der ganze Unterschied.
39. And in the "how" there lies the whole difference.	**40.** In dem zweiten und dem dritten Auszug spricht die Marschallin mit Quin-quin.
40. In the second and in the third excerpts the Marschallin is speaking with Quin-quin.	**41.** **winden** = *to wind, to twist* **sich entwinden** = *to extricate oneself (from)* Die Marschallin entwindet sich Quin-quin.

41. The Marschallin extricates herself from Quin-quin (from his embrace).	**42.** Die Marschallin, sich ihm entwindend, sagt, daß Quin-quin ihr gut sein **solle.** (*shall/should/is*)
42. The Marschallin, disentangling herself from him, says that Quin-quin *should* be good to her.	**43.** **Er** = *you* (a more formal form of *you* than the **Sie** form) O **sei** Er gut, Quin-quin. (Here **sei** is the imperative and means ________.)
43. O *be* good, Quin-quin.	**44.** **zeitlich** = *temporal* **das Zeitliche** = ________
44. *the temporal* (*things*)	**45.** **spüren** = *to feel, to sense* Die Marschallin spürt das Zeitliche.
45. The Marschallin feels the temporal.	**46.** **recht** = *clear* Sie spürt die **Schwäche** von allem Zeitlichen recht bis in ihr Herz hinein. (*weakness/frailty*)
46. She feels the *frailty* of all temporal things clear to the bottom of her heart.	**47.** **mir ist zumute** = *I have a feeling* Es ist der Marschallin zumute . . .
47. The Marschallin has a feeling . . . (Note that **zumute** governs the dative case.)	**48.** Es ist ihr zumut (= zumute), als ob sie die Schwäche von allem Zeitlichen recht spüren **müsse,** bis in ihr Herz hinein. (*must/ought to*)
48. She has a feeling as if she *must* sense the frailty of all temporal things clear to the bottom of her heart.	**49.** Man **soll** nichts halten. (*should/is supposed to*)
49. One *is* not *supposed to* hold anything.	**50.** **packen** = *to grasp* Man kann nichts packen.
50. One can grasp nothing.	**51.** Man soll **weder** etwas halten **noch** etwas packen.
51. We are neither to hold anything nor to grasp anything.	**52.** **laufen** = *to run* **zerlaufen** = *to run into nothing, to melt away* Alles zerlauft (= zerläuft) zwischen den Fingern.

52. Everything escapes (runs into nothing) between our fingers.	**53.** **greifen** = *to reach* Alles, **wonach** wir greifen . . . (*for which/afterward*)
53. Everything *for which* we reach . . .	**54.** **lösen** = *to loosen* **auflösen** = *to dissolve* Alles löst sich auf, **wonach** wir greifen.
54. Everything *for which* we reach dissolves.	**55.** **dunstig** = *vaporous, misty, hazy* **der Dunst** = ________
55. *mist, vapor, haze*	**56.** **zergehen** = *to vanish, to melt, to dissolve* Alles zergeht **wie** Dunst. (*how/like*)
56. Everything vanishes *like* mist.	**57.** Alles zergeht wie Dunst und Traum.
57. Everything vanishes like mist and dream.	**58.** **die Sache** = *circumstance* Die Zeit **ändert** doch **nichts** an den Sachen. (*does not alter/does not suggest*)
58. Time *does not,* however, *alter* the circumstances. (Note that **ändern** plus **an** takes the dative.)	**59.** **im Grund(e)** = *fundamentally* Im Grund ändert die Zeit doch nichts an den Sachen.
59. Yet fundamentally time does not alter the circumstances.	**60.** **sonderbar** = *strange* Die Zeit, **die** ist ein sonderbares Ding. (*it/who*)
60. Time, *it* is a strange thing.	**61.** Sie sagte, daß die Zeit sonderbar **sei.**
61. She said that time *was* strange.	**62.** **hinleben** = *to live from day to day* Wenn man **so** hinlebt . . . (*so/like this*)
62. If one lives *like this* from day to day . . .	**63.** **rein** = *purely* **rein gar nichts** = *nothing at all, a mere nothing* Wenn man so hinlebt, ist sie rein gar nichts.

63. If one lives like this from day to day, it (= time) is a mere nothing.	**64.** **auf einmal** = *all of a sudden* Dann auf einmal spürt man nichts **als** die Zeit. (*as/than/but*)
64. Then all of a sudden one feels nothing else *but* time.	**65.** Aber dann auf einmal **würde** man nichts als sie **spüren.**
65. But then all of a sudden one *would feel* nothing else but it.	**66.** **drinnen** = *inside, within* Die Zeit ist nicht nur um uns herum, sie ist auch in uns drinnen.
66. Time is not only around us, it is also within us.	**67.** **rieseln** = *to trickle* Die Zeit rieselt in den Gesichtern.
67. Time trickles in our faces.	**68.** Nicht nur in den Gesichtern rieselt die Zeit, sondern auch im Spiegel rieselt sie.
68. Time not only trickles in our faces but also trickles in the mirror.	**69.** **die Schläfe** = *temple* (of the head) Die Zeit **fließt** in unseren Schläfen. (*flows/stops*)
69. Time *flows* in our temples.	**70.** Zwischen der Marschallin und Quin-quin fließt die Zeit.
70. Between the Marschallin and Quin-quin time flows.	**71.** Und zwischen mir und dir da fließt sie **wieder.** (*against/anew*)
71. And between me and you there it is flowing *anew* (*again*).	**72.** **lauten** = *to sound* **der Laut** = *sound* **laut** = *loud, noisy* **lautlos** = __________
72. *soundless, noiseless, silent*	**73.** Die Zeit ist so lautlos wie eine **Sanduhr.**
73. Time is as soundless as an *hour glass.*	**74.** **aufhalten** = *to stop, to detain* **unaufhaltsam** = *undetainable* Die Zeit ist unaufhaltsam.
74. Time cannot be stopped.	**75.** In den Schläfen fließt die Zeit unaufhaltsam.
75. Time flows incessantly in our temples.	**76.** **manchmal** = *sometimes, now and again* Manchmal, sagte die Marschallin, **habe** sie die Zeit unaufhaltsam **fließen hören.**

76. Sometimes, the Marschallin said, she *had heard* time *flowing* incessantly.	**77.** Manchmal **wäre** sie mitten in der Nacht **aufgestanden.**
77. Sometimes, she *had gotten up* in the middle of the night.	**78.** **stehenlassen** = *to stop* Sie läßt die Uhren alle stehen.
78. She stops all the clocks.	**79.** Manchmal hör (= höre) ich die Zeit unaufhaltsam fließen.
79. Sometimes I hear time flowing incessantly.	**80.** Manchmal steh (= stehe) ich auf und laß (= lasse) die Uhren alle stehen.
80. Often I get up and stop all the clocks.	**81.** **allein** = *yet, but, however* Allein man muß sich auch vor der Zeit nicht fürchten.
81. However, one must not be afraid even of time. (Note: **allein** is a coordinating conjunction when used initially in a sentence with normal word order.)	**82.** **das Geschöpf** = *creature, creation* Die Zeit ist auch ein Geschöpf des Vaters.
82. Time is also a creature of the Father.	**83.** Allein die Zeit ist ein Geschöpf **dessen, der** uns alle geschaffen hat. (*whose, who/of him, who*)
83. However, time is a creature *of Him Who* (has) created all of us.	

PROGRESS TEST

Choose the most nearly correct meaning for the following.

1. Man soll sich nicht erzürnen, denn es ist der Lauf der Welt, wenn ein Mädchen einen Mann ins Kloster kommandiert.
   (a) Men and women belong in either a monastery or a convent.
   (b) Such is the world, when a man is ordered by a girl to the monastery.
   (c) A girl has been sent to the convent and I should not worry about it as it is the way of the world.
   (d) One should not get angry when girls are sent to the convent.
2. Warum versteckt er es vor mir und läßt mich zugleich zuschauen dabei?
   (a) It seems there is a paradox here.
   (b) Why does he show me and at the same time place it before me?
   (c) Why does he hide from me while I look on?
   (d) Why does he let me hide from him while he looks on?

3. Alles außer Geld zerläuft, zergeht und löst sich auf bis in unser Herz hinein.
   (a) Only the heart conquers all.
   (b) Everything, even money, is conquered by the heart.
   (c) Money is the only permanent thing on this earth.
   (d) Our heart loves money above all else.

4. Das Zeitliche ist wie Dunst und Traum, und lebt in der Schwäche des Herzens fort.
   (a) The frailty of the heart is a temporal thing.
   (b) Temporal things can only exist in one's dreams.
   (c) Temporal things pass away like mist and dream.
   (d) The frailty of the heart is a permanent home for temporal things which are like dreams and mist.

5. Die unaufhaltsame Zeit ändert doch alles an den Sachen, da sie so sonderbar ist.
   (a) Time is a strange thing because it is incessant.
   (b) Time is strange because it incessantly alters circumstances.
   (c) The strangeness of time is responsible for the fact that incessant time alters circumstances.
   (d) Incessant time is a product of circumstances.

6. In **den Gesichtern** und **Schläfen** rieselt sie.
   (a) our faces . . . our sleep
   (b) our history . . . our sleep
   (c) our faces . . . our temples
   (d) our history . . . our temples

Answer key: **1.** (b); **2.** (a); **3.** (c); **4.** (d); **5.** (c); **6.** (c).

Review the vocabulary items you circled before going on to the reading passage.

Hugo von Hofmannsthal: Der Rosenkavalier

MARSCHALLIN
allein

Da geht er hin, der aufgeblasene, schlechte Kerl,
und kriegt das hübsche, junge Ding und einen Binkel Geld dazu,
als müßts so sein.
Und bildet sich noch ein, daß ers ist, der sich was vergibt.
Was erzürn ich mich denn? ist doch der Lauf der Welt.
Kann mich auch an ein Mädel erinnern,
die frisch aus dem Kloster ist in den heiligen Ehestand kommandiert wordn.

Nimmt den Handspiegel

Wo ist die jetzt? Ja, such dir den Schnee vom vergangenen Jahr.

Das sag ich so:
Aber wie kann das wirklich sein,
daß ich die kleine Resi war
und daß ich auch einmal die alte Frau sein werd! . . .
Die alte Frau, die alte Marschallin!
„Siehgst es, da geht s', die alte Fürstin Resi!"
Wie kann denn das geschehen?
Wie macht denn das der liebe Gott?
Wo ich doch immer die gleiche bin.
Und wenn ers schon so machen muß,
warum laßt er mich denn zuschaun dabei
mit gar so klarem Sinn? Warum versteckt ers nicht
vor mir?
Das alles ist geheim, so viel geheim.
Und man ist dazu da, daß mans ertragt.
Und in dem „Wie" da liegt der ganze Unterschied —

* * *

MARSCHALLIN
sich ihm entwindend

O sei Er gut, Quin-quin. Mir ist zumut,
daß ich die Schwäche von allem Zeitlichen recht spüren muß,
bis in mein Herz hinein:
wie man nichts halten soll,
wie man nichts packen kann,
wie alles zerlauft zwischen den Fingern,
alles sich auflöst, wonach wir greifen,
alles zergeht, wie Dunst und Traum.

* * *

Die Zeit im Grund, Quin-quin, die Zeit,
die ändert doch nichts an den Sachen.
Die Zeit, die ist ein sonderbares Ding.
Wenn man so hinlebt, ist sie rein gar nichts.
Aber dann auf einmal,
da spürt man nichts als sie:
sie ist um uns herum, sie ist auch in uns drinnen.
In den Gesichtern rieselt sie, im Spiegel da rieselt sie,
in meinen Schläfen fließt sie.
Und zwischen mir und dir da fließt sie wieder.
Lautlos, wie eine Sanduhr.
O Quin-quin!

Manchmal hör ich sie fließen unaufhaltsam.
Manchmal steh ich auf, mitten in der Nacht,
und laß die Uhren alle stehen.
. . .
Allein man muß sich auch vor ihr nicht fürchten.
Auch sie ist ein Geschöpf des Vaters,
der uns alle geschaffen hat.

Chapter Twenty-Four

78. *Additional uses of the subjunctive*

The subjunctive is used to express:
(a) possibility

Das *könnte* (*dürfte*) wahr sein.	*That **could** (**might**) be true.*

(b) uncertainty

Wie *wäre* es denn, wenn wir einen Spaziergang machten?	*How **would** it **be** if we were to take a walk?* (i.e. *How about a walk?*)

(c) conjecture

Er kommt morgen bestimmt, es sei denn, es *gäbe* kein schönes Wetter.	*He will certainly come tomorrow unless the weather **were** not good.*
Ob sie *geblieben wäre*?	*Do you think she **would have stayed?***

(d) anticipation, purpose

Sie gab ihm ihre Telefonnummer, damit er sie *anrufe*.	*She gave him her telephone number so that he **would call** her up.*

(e) doubt

Ich glaube nicht, daß sie Zeit *hätte*.	*I do not believe that she **would have** time.*

(f) concession

***Wäre* das Wetter n o c h so schön, ich gehe doch nicht schwimmen.**	*No matter how good the weather **is**, I will (still) not go swimming.*

Note that some of these uses are interrelated.

The following frames will give you additional examples for the above grammar explanation. Give the correct meaning of the indicated verbs as well as the meaning of the entire frame. Continue to circle all words you do not recognize and review them before going to the next section.

	1. **Wäre** es möglich, daß wir die letzten Menschen auf Erden sind? (*is*/*was*)
1. *Is* it (*could it be*) possible that we are the last people on earth?	**2.** **allerlei** = *all* (*sorts of*) Denn wie der Mensch allerlei lebendige Tiere **nennen würde,** so **sollten** sie **heißen.** (Bibel)
2. For however man *would name* all living animals, thus *should* they *be called.*	**3.** **bitten** = *to ask* **ums** = **um das** = *for the* Wo bittet unter euch ein Sohn den Vater ums Brot, der ihm einen Stein dafür **biete?** (Bibel) (*offer*/*would offer*)
3. Where among you does a son ask his father for bread, who *would offer* him a stone?	**4.** **dahin** = *to that place* Denn wer will ihn [den Menschen] dahin bringen, daß er **sehe,** was nach ihm geschehen wird? (Bibel) (*see*/*may see*/*saw*)
4. Who will bring him [man] to that place, that he *may see* what will take place after him?	**5.** **gewiß** = *certain* **der Verfasser** = *writer, author* Gewisse Bücher scheinen geschrieben zu sein, nicht damit man daraus **lerne,** sondern damit man **wisse,** daß der Verfasser etwas gewußt hat. (Goethe) (*may learn . . . may know*/*learned . . . knew*)
5. Certain books appear to be written not for the purpose that one *may learn* from them but so that one *may know* that the writer knew something.	**6.** Welche Regierung die beste **sei?** Diejenige, die uns lehrt, uns selbst zu regieren. (Goethe) (*is*/*was*)

6. Which government *is* the best? That which teaches us to govern ourselves. (In such rhetorical questions, indirect discourse is often inferred: You ask(ed) which government is . . . ? Therefore the subjunctive is used in German.)	**7.** **der Odem** = *spirit* **das Vieh** = *animal* Wer weiß, ob der Odem der Menschen aufwärts **fahre,** und der Odem des Viehes unterwärts unter die Erde **fahre?** (Bibel) (*goes/went*)
7. Who knows whether the spirit of man (men) *goes* upwards and the spirit of animals *goes* downwards beneath the earth?	**8.** Es ist nicht gut, daß der Mensch allein **sei.** (Bibel) (*should be/would be*)
8. It is not good that man *should be* alone.	**9.** Er kommt bestimmt, **es sei denn,** er hat keine Zeit.
9. He will certainly come, *unless* he has no time.	**10.** Ob das Hotel wohl **gebaut werden würde?** (*is being built/would be built*)
10. I wondered whether the hotel *would be built?*	**11.** Ob er ein kluger Mann **sei?** (*is/was*)
11. I wonder whether he *is* an intelligent man?	**12.** **das Erbe** = *legacy, inheritance* **erben** = *to inherit* **der Erbe, die Erbin** = *heir, heiress* Sie hat kein Geld, **es sei denn,** sie hätte es geerbt.
12. She has no money, *unless* she has inherited it.	**13.** **die Gehilfin** = (female) *helpmate* Aber für den Menschen ward (wurde) keine Gehilfin gefunden, die um ihn **wäre.** (Bibel)
13. But for man no helpmate was found who *would be* with him (around him).	**14.** Er brachte allerlei Tiere und allerlei Vögel zu dem Menschen, daß er **sähe,** wie er sie **nennte.** (Bibel)
14. He brought all kinds of animals and all kinds of birds to man, so that He *could see* how he *would name* them.	**15.** Sie glaubt nicht, daß er ins Kino **dürfe.** (*could/might/may*)
15. She does not believe that he *may* (*can*) go to the movies.	**16.** Inge glaubt nicht, daß Elke Sauerkraut **äße.** (*eats/would eat*)

16. Inge does not believe that Elke *would eat* sauerkraut.	**17.** **füttern** = *to feed* **Wäre** der Wolf noch so gefährlich, ich werde ihn doch füttern. (*no matter how . . .is/was*)
17. *No matter how* dangerous the wolf *is* (*might be*), I will still feed it.	**18.** **Hätte** er noch so viel Geld, ich werde ihn doch nicht heiraten.
18. No matter how much money he *has* (*might have*), I will not marry him.	

PROGRESS TEST

Choose the correct meaning for the indicated verbs.

1. **Wäre** es möglich, daß es heutzutage noch Menschenfresser gibt?
   (a) is (b) were (c) was (d) would have
2. Das **hätte** er **tun können!**
   (a) had done (b) could have done (c) has been able to do (d) could do
3. Sie können das nicht tun, **es sei denn,** sie fragen zuerst ihren Vater darüber.
   (a) but (b) it is for that reason (c) unless (d) because
4. Er liest das Buch, damit er etwas daraus **lerne.**
   (a) taught (b) will teach (c) learned (d) may learn
5. **Bliebe** er noch so lange da, sie will ihn doch nicht sehen.
   (a) no matter how . . . remains (b) remained (c) would remain (d) was remaining

Answer key: **1.** (a); **2.** (b); **3.** (c); **4.** (d); **5.** (a).

79. *Imperative forms*

The following forms express requests, commands, or wishes:
(a) the familiar singular (the **du** form)

Karl, *sing(e)* das Lied!	*Karl,* ***sing*** *the song!*
***Sei* ruhig, Hans!**	***Be*** *quiet, Hans!*
Sieh* mich *an!	***Look at*** *me!*

(b) the familiar plural (the **ihr** form)

***Sprecht* nicht so schnell, Kinder!**	***Don't speak*** *so quickly, children!*
***Seid* ruhig, Heinz und Inge!**	*Heinz and Inge,* ***be*** *quiet!*
Hört* doch *auf!	***Stop*** *it!*

Note that in the above forms the **du** and **ihr** are left out.

(c) the formal singular and plural (the **Sie** form)

***Fahren Sie* nicht zu schnell!**	*Don't **drive** too fast!*
***Seien Sie* ruhig, bitte!**	***Be** quiet, please!*
Halten Sie* das *fest!	***Hold** it **tight!***

(d) the present infinitive

***Einsteigen* bitte!**	***Get on (in),** please!*
Ruhig *bleiben!*	***Remain** quiet!*

(e) the past participle

Aufgepaßt!	*Watch out!*
Stillgestanden!	*Stand still!*

(f) a first or third person imperative in the subjunctive present tense

***Es lebe* die Freiheit!**	***May** freedom **live! Long live** freedom!*
Gehen wir!	***Let's go!***
***Besuchen wir* ihn morgen!**	***Let's visit** him tomorrow!*

Give the meaning of the indicated verbs.

	1. Du **liest** das Buch.
1. You *are reading* the book.	2. **Lies** das Buch!
2. *Read* the book!	3. **schauen** = *to look* **anschauen** = *to look at* Du **schaust** Paul **an.**
3. You *are looking at* Paul.	4. **Schau** Paul nicht so **an!**
4. *Don't look at* Paul so!	5. Ihr **schlaft** zuviel.
5. You *sleep* too much.	6. **Schlaft** nicht soviel!
6. *Don't sleep* so much!	7. **Fahrt** ihr morgen nach Hamburg **zurück?**
7. *Are* you *going to go back* to Hamburg tomorrow?	8. **Fahrt** morgen nach Hamburg **zurück!**
8. *Go back* to Hamburg tomorrow!	9. **Verstehen** Sie mich?

9. *Do* you *understand* me?	**10.** **Verstehen** Sie mich, bitte!
10. Please, *understand* me!	**11.** Sie **sind** ein dummer Kerl!
11. You *are* a stupid fellow!	**12.** **Seien** Sie nicht so dumm!
12. *Do*n't *be* so stupid!	**13.** **umsteigen** = *to transfer, to change* Sie müssen hier **umsteigen.**
13. You must *transfer* here (from one streetcar, bus, train, etc., to another).	**14.** **Umsteigen!**
14. *Change* (cars, trains, busses, etc.)!	**15.** **aussteigen** = *to climb out, to get out* Wollen wir hier **aussteigen?**
15. Do we want *to get out* here?	**16.** **Aussteigen,** bitte!
16. *Get out,* please!	**17.** Hilda **ist** um sechs Uhr **aufgestanden.**
17. Hilda *got up* at six o'clock.	**18.** **Aufgestanden!**
18. *Get up!*	**19.** **stillhalten** = *to keep quiet, to hold still* **den Mund halten** = *to hold one's tongue* Kann sie den Mund überhaupt nicht **halten?**
19. Can't she *hold* her tongue at all?	**20.** Jetzt aber **stillgehalten!**
20. Now *hold still!*	**21.** Der König **lebt** sehr lange, nicht wahr?
21. The king *is living* a very long time, isn't he?	**22.** Lang **lebe** der König!
22. Long *live* the king!	**23.** Gott **ist** mit uns.
23. God *is* with us.	**24.** Gott **sei** mit euch!
24. God *be* with you!	**25.** **der Heiland** = *savior* **Denke** nur niemand, daß man auf ihn als den Heiland gewartet habe. (Goethe)
25. *Let* no one *think* that one has waited for him as the savior!	**26.** Niemand **sage,** wenn er versucht wird, daß er von Gott versucht werde. (Bibel)

26. *Let* no one *say,* if he is tempted, that he is tempted by God.	**27.** Und Gott sprach: **Lasset** uns Menschen machen, ein Bild, das uns gleich sei. (Bibel)
27. And God spoke, *let* us make man, an image that is like ourselves.	**28.** **fruchtbar** = *fruitful* **sich mehren** = *to multiply, to increase* **Seid** fruchtbar und **mehret euch** und **füllet** die Erde. (Bibel)
28. *Be* fruitful and *multiply* and *fill* the earth.	**29.** **die Ameise** = *ant* **faul** = *lazy* **Gehe** hin zur Ameise, du Fauler; **siehe** ihre Weise **an** und **lerne.** (Bibel)
29. *Go* to the ant, thou sluggard; *look at* its way (of doing things) and *learn* (from it).	

PROGRESS TEST

Choose the correct meaning for the indicated verb.

1. **Sei** Er doch gut zu mir!
   (a) is (b) be
2. **Seid** ihr alle hier?
   (a) are (b) be
3. **Empfange** ihn mit offenen Armen!
   (a) receives (b) receive
4. Bitte, die Fenster **schließen!**
   (a) shut (b) are shutting
5. Jetzt aber langsam **gefahren!**
   (a) go (b) gone

Answer key: **1.** (b); **2.** (a); **3.** (b); **4.** (a); **5.** (a).

80. *The uses of* **werden**

1. The general uses and meanings of the verb **werden** in the indicative active and passive may be summarized as follows:

(a) **werden** + adjective or noun = *to become, to get*

Er *wird* Arzt.	*He **is becoming** (is going to be) a doctor.*
Sie *wurden* alt.	*They (you) **were getting** old.* *They (you) **got** old.*
Wie groß *ist* er *geworden?*	*How tall **has** he **gotten?***

(b) **werden** + infinitive(s) = future, or probability in the present

Wir *werden* ihn nächste Woche *sehen.*	*We **will see** him next week.*
Du *wirst* ihn nicht *kommen hören.*	*You **will** not **hear** him **come.***
Er *wird* wohl jetzt *schlafen.*	*He **is** probably **sleeping** now.*

(c) **werden** + perfect participle (perfect infinitive) = future perfect, or probability in the past

Bis morgen *werde* ich zehn Seiten *gelesen haben.*	***I will have read** ten pages by tomorrow.*
Sie *wird* das Buch wahrscheinlich schon *gelesen haben.*	*She **has** probably **read** the book already.*

(d) **werden** + past participle = passive: present or past

Was *wird gesagt?*	*What **is being said?***
Das Buch *wurde geschrieben.*	*The book **was being written.***

(e) **werden** + passive infinitive(s) = future passive

Das Auto *wird repariert werden.*	*The automobile **will be repaired.***
Das Auto *wird repariert werden müssen.*	*The automobile **will have to be repaired.***

(f) **worden** (*been*) = passive: in the perfect tenses

Das Schiff *ist gesehen worden.*	*The ship **has been seen** (**was seen**).*
Das Schiff *war gesehen worden.*	*The ship **had been seen.***
Das Schiff *muß gesehen worden sein.*	*One **must have seen** the ship* (i.e. *the ship **must have been seen***).

2. The general uses and meanings of the verb **werden** in the subjunctive active and passive may be summarized as follows:

(a) Subjunctive of **werden** + adjective or noun = *would become, would get, would have become, was getting*, etc.

Er sagte, er *werde* dick.	*He said he **would get** (**was getting**) fat.*
Er *würde* Arzt, wenn er genug Geld hätte.	*He **would become** a doctor if he had enough money.*

Er *wäre* dick *geworden*, wenn er immer Kartoffeln gegessen hätte. — *He **would have gotten** fat if he had always eaten potatoes.*

(b) **würden** + infinitive(s) = conditional: present or future meaning

Wir *würden gehen*, wenn wir Zeit hätten. — *We **would go** if we had the time.*

Sie sagte, sie *würde* es mir morgen *geben können*. — *She said she **would be able to give** it to me tomorrow.*

(c) **würden** + perfect participle (perfect infinitive) = conditional past

Er *würde* den Mantel (wohl) *gekauft haben*, hätte er das nötige Geld gehabt. — *He (probably) **would have bought** the coat, had he had the necessary money.*

(d) Subjunctive of **werden** + past participle = passive subjunctive: present or past

Er fragte, was für ein Unsinn hier getrieben werde. — *He asked what nonsense **was being done.***

(e) **worden** = passive subjunctive: present or past perfect

Sie fragte, wann das Haus *zerstört worden sei*. — *She asked when the house **had been destroyed.***

Wenn das Hotel nur *gebaut worden wäre!* — *If the hotel **had** only **been built!***

The following frames review only the general uses and meaning of **werden.** *If more detailed study is needed or desired, review those grammar sections which discuss the conjugation and meaning of verbs.*

	1. **schlank** = *thin* Er **wird** schlank, wenn er Zigaretten raucht.
1. He *will get* thin if he smokes cigarettes.	2. Er **wurde** wieder jung, als er das hübsche Mädchen sah.
2. When he saw the pretty girl he *became* young again.	3. **Wird** man schlank **bleiben,** wenn man immer Zigaretten raucht?
3. *Will* one *remain* thin if one always smokes cigarettes?	4. Ich **werde** dem Dummkopf immer **helfen müssen.**
4. I *will* always *have to help* that blockhead.	5. Wie dumm er **geworden ist!**
5. How stupid he *has become!*	6. Anna **wird** wohl zu Hause **geblieben sein.**

6. Anna probably *stayed* at home.	**7.** **Wird** sie das Auto schon **gekauft haben,** bevor ich sie warnen kann?
7. *Will* she already *have bought* the car, before I am able to warn her?	**8.** Der alten Frau **wurde geholfen.**
8. The old lady *was helped.*	**9.** **heute abend** = *this evening* Es **wird** heute abend **gesungen.**
9. There *will be singing* this evening.	**10.** Das Fenster **wird geöffnet werden müssen.**
10. The window *will have to be opened.*	**11.** Der Brief **hat geschrieben werden müssen.**
11. The letter *had to be written.*	**12.** Hier **ist** viel **getrunken worden.**
12. There *was* much *drinking done* here.	**13.** Man konnte sehen, daß hier viel **getrunken worden war.**
13. One could see that there *had been* much *drinking* here.	**14.** Mein Freund **würde** mir gerne **helfen,** wenn er nur wüßte, wie.
14. My friend *would* like *to help* me if he only knew how.	**15.** Sie wollte wissen, ob Berlin von den Bomben **zerstört worden sei.**
15. She wanted to know if Berlin *had been destroyed* by bombs.	**16.** **längst** = *long ago* Das Haus **hätte** längst **zerstört werden sollen.**
16. The house *should have been destroyed* long ago.	**17.** **genügen** = *to suffice* Spengler **würde** es immer wieder **sagen,** daß der Mensch ein Raubtier sei, aber einmal genügt.
17. Spengler *would say* again and again that man is a beast of prey, but once is enough.	**18.** **fehlen** = *to lack* **mir fehlt etwas** = *I am lacking something* Ich **könnte** meinen Freund **besuchen,** fehlte mir nicht die Zeit und das Geld dazu.
18. I *would be able to visit* my friend if I did not lack time and money (for it).	**19.** Wenn unser Haus nur nicht durch Feuer **zerstört worden wäre!**
19. If only our house *had* not *been destroyed* by fire!	

You will now be introduced to the vocabulary of the reading passage. Continue to circle all words you do not recognize and review them before proceeding to the passage itself.

	1. **x-mal** = *any number of times, at any moment* Unser letztes Lesestück stammt aus Rudolf Walter Leonhardts **X-mal Deutschland.**
1. Our final reading passage comes from Rudolf Walter Leonhardt's book: *X-mal Deutschland* (English title is: *This Germany*).	**2.** In seinem Buch versucht Leonhardt, das heutige Deutschland zu beschreiben.
2. Leonhardt tries to describe present day Germany in his book.	**3.** Leonhardt ist ein bekannter deutscher Schriftsteller, der schon **einige** Bücher über andere Länder geschrieben hat. (*some/own*)
3. Leonhardt is a well-known German writer who has already written *some* books about other countries.	**4.** Jetzt versucht er, als Deutscher über sein **eigenes** Land zu schreiben. (*several/own*)
4. Now, as a German, he is trying to write about his *own* country.	**5.** **unter anderem** = *among other things* Unter anderem beschreibt er seine **Unterhaltungen** mit Studenten aus anderen Ländern. (*conversations/fights*)
5. Among other things he describes his *conversations* with students from other countries.	**6.** **Eine** von ihnen fragte, ob er es eigentlich schön finde, Deutscher zu sein. (*a girl/a boy*)
6. *a girl:* the **-e** tells you. One of them asked whether he really liked to be a German.	**7.** Unser Lesestück ist ein Teil **seiner** Antwort auf diese Frage. (*his/of his*)
7. Our reading passage is a part *of his* answer to this question.	**8.** **gestehen** = *to confess* Leonhardt gesteht, daß er Deutschland und die Deutschen liebt, aber nicht nur **die** im Westen, sondern auch **die** im Osten. (*whom/the/those*)

8. Leonhardt confesses that he loves Germany and the Germans but not only *those* in the West but also *those* in the East.	**9.** **zuweilen** = *at times, now and then, occasionally* Leonhardt schreibt, diese Liebe **sei** zuweilen eine schmerzliche Liebe.
9. Leonhardt writes that this love *is* occasionally a painful love.	**10.** **trotz** = *in spite of* **der Trotz** = *defiance, obstinacy* Zuweilen ist sie eine schmerzliche Liebe, und es ist viel Trotz **dabei.** (*thereby/along with it*)
10. Now and then it is a painful love, and there is much defiance *along with it.*	**11.** Warum ist diese Liebe zuweilen schmerzlich, und warum ist viel Trotz dabei?
11. Why is this love at times painful, and why is there much defiance along with it?	**12.** **richten** = *to judge* **der Richter** = __________
12. *the judge*	**13.** Trotz den deutschen Politikern, Richtern und Parteifunktionären in der DDR . . .
13. In spite of the German politicians, judges, and party functionaries in the GDR (German Democratic Republic) . . . (Note that Leonhardt uses the dative case with **trotz.**)	**14.** Trotz den Parteifunktionären in der DDR, **deren** Haß gegen die Deutsche Bundesrepublik ein deutscher Haß ist . . .
14. In spite of the party functionaries in the GDR *whose* hate towards the German Federal Republic is a German hate . . .	**15.** Und trotz manchem, was in der Bundesrepublik hassenswert **sein möge . . .** (*may be/could be*)
15. And in spite of much that in the Federal Republic *may be* worthy of hate . . .	**16.** **verleugnen** = *to deny* Die deutsche **Vergangenheit** kann man nicht verleugnen. (*past/present/future*)
16. We cannot deny Germany's *past.*	**17.** Trotz der deutschen Vergangenheit, die wir ja nicht **einfach** verleugnen können . . . (*simple/simply*)
17. In spite of Germany's past, which we *simply* cannot deny . . .	**18.** **offenbar** = *obviously, evidently* Offenbar haben **manche** Deutsche nichts aus der Vergangenheit gelernt. (*many a/some*)

18. Evidently *some* Germans have learned nothing from the past.	**19.** Und trotz **den** Leuten, die aus der Vergangenheit offenbar nichts gelernt haben . . . (*the/those*)
19. And in spite of *those* people who evidently have learned nothing from the past . . .	**20.** Zuweilen gibt es Deutsche, die offenbar nichts aus der Vergangenheit gelernt haben.
20. Occasionally there are Germans who evidently have learned nothing from the past.	**21.** **gering** = *small, petty, inferior* **schätzen** = *to value, to esteem* **die Geringschätzung** = *contempt, disdain, scorn* **geringschätzen** = ________
21. *to despise, to scorn*	**22.** Manche können das **gar nicht** geringschätzen. (*not often/not at all*)
22. Some can*not* despise that *at all.*	**23.** Manche könnten das **gar nicht geringer schätzen.**
23. Some could *not despise* that *more.*	**24.** Es gibt Deutsche, die alles Deutsche **gar nicht geringer schätzen könnten . . .**
24. There are Germans who *could not despise more* all that is German . . .	**25.** **allgemein** = *general* **schön allgemein** = *rather general* . . . solange die **Geringschätzung** nur schön allgemein und abstrakt bleibt. (*contempt/appreciation*)
25. . . . as long as the *contempt* remains (only) rather general and abstract.	**26.** Ihr fragt, ob die Geringschätzung irgendeinen Wert **habe?**
26. You ask whether that contempt *has* any value?	**27.** Wie wollen die gleichen Deutschen ihre **eigene** kleine Welt sehen?
27. How do the same Germans want to see their *own* small world?	**28.** Rot, braun, grün, blau, orange, gelb und purpur sind Farben. (**Die Farbe** probably means ________.)
28. *color*	**29.** Wollen die gleichen Deutschen ihre eigene kleine Welt nicht anders als in den **allerfreundlichsten** Farben sehen? (*most hateful/most friendly*)

29. Do the same Germans want to see their own small world in none other than the *most friendly* colors?	**30.** Ihre eigene kleine Welt, die sie in den allerfreundlichsten Farben **sehen wollen,** . . .
30. Their own small world which they *want to see* in the most friendly colors . . .	**31.** . . . ist ihre Stadt, ihr **Beruf,** ihre Partei, sie selber. (*occupation/church*)
31. . . . is their city, their *occupation,* their party, and (they) themselves.	**32.** **der Kalte Krieg** = *the Cold War* **der Krieger** = *warrior* Wir Soldaten des Zweiten Weltkrieges haben **die Kalten Krieger** vermißt. (*the cold warriors/the Cold War warriors*)
32. We soldiers of the Second World War have missed *the Cold War warriors.* (Note **die kalten Krieger** = *the cold warriors*)	**33.** Wir haben die Kalten Krieger vermißt, als der Krieg heiß **wurde.**
33. We missed the Cold War warriors when the war *became* hot.	**34.** Schon beim letzten Male haben wir sie vermißt, als der Krieg heiß wurde.
34. We missed them already the last time when the war became hot.	**35.** **preisen** = *to praise, to extol, to glorify* Was preisen uns die deutschen Pseudo-Patrioten?
35. What do Germany's pseudo-patriots extol (to us)?	**36.** **äußerst** = *extreme* Sie preisen uns „äußerste **Härte**". (*severity/softness*)
36. They are extolling extreme frugality (*severity* in economic matters).	**37.** **wieder einmal** = *once again* Die deutschen Pseudo-Patrioten, die uns **öffentlich** wider einmal „äußerste Härte" preisen . . .
37. Germany's pseudo-patriots who once again *openly* praise extreme frugality (to us) . . .	**38.** **der Grundbesitz** = *real estate* . . . haben *privatissime* Grundbesitz in Irland. (*openly/secretively*)
38. . . . *secretly* have real estate in Ireland.	**39.** **das Bankkonto** = *bank account* **Die** haben *privatissime* Grundbesitz in Irland und ein Bankkonto in der Schweiz. (*who/they/she*)

39. *They* secretly have real estate in Ireland and a bank account in Switzerland.	**40.** Trotz den deutschen Pseudo-Patrioten, die uns öffentlich wieder einmal „äußerste Härte" preisen . . .
40. In spite of Germany's pseudo-patriots. who once again extol extreme frugality to us in public . . .	**41.** . . . **während** sie *privatissime* Grundbesitz in Irland und ein Bankkonto in der Schweiz haben. (*while/during*)
41. . . . *while* they secretly have real estate in Ireland and a bank account in Switzerland.	**42.** **die Vernunft** = *reason, common sense* **der Grund** = *argument, reason* **der Vernunftgrund** = ________
42. *argument based on reason, sensible reason*	**43.** **dennoch** = *yet* Für so viel Trotz und dennoch Liebe **gebe es** keine Vernunftgründe, meint Leonhardt.
43. Leonhardt feels, *there are* no sensible reasons for so much defiance and yet love.	**44.** Sind die Provinz-Europäer und die **Halbgroß-**Industriellen wirklich liebenswert? (*half-big/pseudo-big*)
44. Are the provincial European Germans and the *pseudo-big* industrialists truly likable?	**45.** Die Halbgroß-Industriellen sitzen in **irgendeinem** Schweizer Hotel.
45. The pseudo-big industrialists sit in *some* Swiss hotel *or other*.	**46.** **brüllen** = *to bellow, to roar* In irgendeinem Hotel **brüllen** sie „das Personal" **an.**
46. In some Swiss hotel or other they *bellow at* the personnel.	**47.** **greifen** = *to grasp, to catch* **begreifen** = *to understand, to comprehend* Sie können sich selber nur als Mittelpunkt begreifen und brüllen „das Personal" an.
47. They can only understand themselves as the focal point and they roar at the personnel.	**48.** Sie können „das Personal" nur als etwas Anzubrüllendes begreifen.
48. They can see the personnel only as something to bellow at.	**49.** If **Nachteil** = *disadvantage*, then **Vorteil** = ________
49. *advantage*	**50.** **wahrnehmen** = *to perceive, to notice, to observe* **einen Vorteil wahrnehmen** = ________

50. *to look after one's own interests*	**51. der Held** = *hero, champion* Die **Auto-Helden** nehmen jeden Vorteil wahr.
51. The *car supermen* look after their own interests every time.	**52. fahren** = *to drive* **die Bahn** = *the road, path* **wechseln** = *to change* **fahrbahnwechselnd** = ________
52. *weaving back and forth* (*changing from one driving lane to another*)	**53. der Rücken** = *back* **die Sicht** = *view* **die Rücksicht** = *consideration, respect, regard* **rücksichtslos** = ________
53. *inconsiderate, without regard*	**54. dauernd** = *continually* Die Auto-Helden, die dauernd fahrbahnwechselnd rücksichtslos jeden Vorteil wahrnehmen . . .
54. The car supermen, who continually weave back and forth and who inconsiderately look out for their own interests . . .	**55. großartig** = *great* Diese rücksichtslosen Auto-Helden **kommen sich dabei** großartig **vor.**
55. These inconsiderate car supermen *think they are* great (*think themselves* great).	**56. der Mut** = *courage, boldness* **mutig** = *courageous, brave* Sind die **Pseudo-Mutigen** wirklich liebenswert?
56. Are the *pseudo-brave* really likable?	**57. empor** = *up, upwards* **wachsen** = *to grow* **emporwachsen** = *to grow upwards* Die Pseudo-Mutigen wachsen empor.
57. The pseudo-brave grow upwards.	**58. überhöht** = *excessive* Sie wachsen zu überhöhter Arroganz empor.
58. They grow upwards to excessive heights of arrogance.	**59. ducken** = *to cringe, to cower, to duck* **geduckt** = *cringing, cowering* Aus geducker **Haltung** wachsen sie zu überhöhter Arroganz empor.
59. From a cringing *position* they grow to excessive heights of arrogance.	**60.** Sie wachsen zu überhöhter Arroganz empor, wo sie sicher sind . . .

60. They grow to excessive heights of arrogance where they are sure . . .	**61.** . . . daß ihnen niemand auf die Finger **klopfen** wird. (*rap/clop*)
61. . . . that nobody is going to *rap* their knuckles (will rap their fingers).	**62.** Die Freiheitsapostel halten sich für **unfehlbar.** (*fallible/infallible*)
62. The apostles of freedom consider themselves *infallible.*	**63.** Die **selbstgerechten** Freiheitsapostel, die sich für unfehlbar halten . . . (*self-deprecating/self-righteous*)
63. The *self-righteous* apostles of freedom, who consider themselves infallible . . .	**64. gönnen** = *to grant* Wollen die selbstgerechten Freiheitsapostel niemandem Freiheit gönnen?
64. Don't the self-righteous apostles of freedom want to grant anyone freedom?	**65.** Sie wollen niemandem die wichtigste **aller** menschlichen Freiheiten gönnen.
65. They do not want to grant anyone the most important *of all* human freedoms.	**66. sich irren** = *to err, to go astray* Die wichtigste Freiheit, die sie niemandem gönnen wollen, ist die Freiheit, sich zu irren.
66. The most important freedom, which they do not want to grant to anyone, is the freedom to err.	**67.** Sind denn diese Provinz-Europäer und Halbroß-Industriellen, diese Auto-Helden, Pseudo-Mutigen und Freiheitsapostel wirklich alle liebenswert?
67. Are all these provincial European Germans and pseudo-big industrialists, these car supermen, pseudo-brave, and apostles of freedom really likable?	**68.** Sind denn diese Politiker, Richter, Parteifunktionäre, Kalten Krieger und Pseudo-Patrioten wirklich alle liebenswert?
68. Are all these politicians, judges, party functionaries, cold war warriors, and pseudo-patriots really likable?	**69. je nun** = *well now, well really, well* Je nun . . .
69. Well now . . .	

PROGRESS TEST

Choose the closest approximation for the following.

1. Zuweilen wollen wir unsere Vergangenheit einfach verleugnen; offenbar liegt noch viel Trotz in unserer Seele.
  (a) We always want to lie about the past because we are rebellious souls at heart.
  (b) Defiant souls occasionally like to stir up the past.
  (c) There is apparently no defiance in our souls, only questions about the present state of affairs.
  (d) When we deny the past it is probably because we have rebellious souls.

2. Einige Deutsche schätzen alles Deutsche gering, solange die Geringschätzung schön allgemein und abstrakt bleibt.
  (a) Some Germans practice contempt only in generalities.
  (b) Germans are their own best critics.
  (c) All things German do not deserve our contempt.
  (d) Most Germans are very outspoken about those things they do not like.

3. Leute, die *privatissime* ein Bankkonto in der Schweiz und Grundbesitz in Irland haben, preisen immer noch „äußerste Härte".
  (a) One should still praise people for their extreme frugality even though they secretly have a bank account in Switzerland and real estate in Ireland.
  (b) Extreme frugality is a virtue which is still praised by those who secretly have a bank account and real estate.
  (c) Extreme frugality leads us to have secret bank accounts in Switzerland and secret real estate in Ireland.
  (d) People who secretly have a bank account in Switzerland and real estate in Ireland still consider themselves good examples of extreme frugality.

4. Geringer schätzen könnten wir diese schmerzliche Liebe, wenn Barbara hassenswert wäre.
  (a) Painful love causes despair.
  (b) We could despise Barbara more if only she were not so hateful.
  (c) We could look on this love with greater contempt if Barbara were a less likable person.
  (d) Love and hate may co-exist in the same individual.

5. Fahrbahnwechselnd brüllte der Auto-Held rücksichtslos alle anderen Fahrer an.
  (a) The car-superman bellows at other drivers because they are inconsiderate.
  (b) Inconsiderate drivers are those who bellow at others because they continuously weave back and forth.
  (c) All other drivers were inconsiderately yelled at by the car-superman.
  (d) Changing lanes inconsiderately, the car-superman bellowed at the other drivers.

6. Wir sollten den Pseudo-Mutigen ihre überhöhte Arroganz gönnen, denn sie irren sich genauso wie alle anderen Menschen.
  (a) The pseudo-brave are in danger of becoming arrogant.
  (b) The pseudo-courageous err just like everyone else and therefore we should grant them their excessive arrogance.
  (c) Although the pseudo-brave err as do all others, we shall grant them their excessive arrogance.

(d) Excessive arrogance is a virtue possessed only by those who do not grant the right to err.

Answer key: **1.** (d); **2.** (a); **3.** (b); **4.** (c); **5.** (c); **6.** (b).

Before proceeding to the reading passage, review those items which you have circled in the reading preparation frames.

R. Piper & Co. Verlag, München, 1964.

Rudolf Walter Leonhardt: X-mal Deutschland

Ja, ich liebe dieses Deutschland, das ganze Deutschland, und ich liebe die Deutschen, die in Dresden wie die in Hamburg. Das ist eine zuweilen schmerzliche Liebe, und es ist viel Trotz dabei: trotz den deutschen Politikern, Richtern, Parteifunktionären in der DDR, deren Haß gegen die Deutsche Bundesrepublik ein deutscher Haß ist — und trotz manchem, was in der Bundesrepublik hassenswert sein mag; trotz der deutschen Vergangenheit, die wir ja nicht einfach verleugnen können — und trotz den Leuten, die aus dieser Vergangenheit offenbar nichts gelernt haben; trotz den Deutschen, die alles Deutsche gar nicht geringer schätzen könnten, solange die Geringschätzung nur schön allgemein und abstrakt bleibt, und trotz den gleichen Deutschen, die ihre eigene kleine Welt (ihre Stadt, ihren Beruf, ihre Partei, sich selber) nicht anders als in den allerfreundlichsten Farben sehen wollen; trotz den Kalten Kriegern, die wir Soldaten des Zweiten Weltkrieges schon beim letzten Male vermißt haben, als der Krieg heiß wurde; trotz den deutschen Pseudo-Patrioten, die uns öffentlich wieder einmal „äußerste Härte" preisen, während sie *privatissime* Grundbesitz in Irland und ein Bankkonto in der Schweiz haben . . .

Und warum so viel Trotz? Und warum dennoch Liebe? Dafür gibt es keine Vernunftgründe . . .

Sind sie denn wirklich liebenswert: die Provinz-Europäer und Halbgroß-Industriellen, die in irgendeinem Schweizer Hotel sich selber nur als Mittelpunkt und „das Personal" nur als etwas Anzubrüllendes begreifen können? die Auto-Helden, die dauernd fahrbahnwechselnd rücksichtslos jeden Vorteil wahrnehmen und sich dabei großartig vorkommen? die Pseudo-Mutigen, die aus geduckter Haltung zu überhöhter Arroganz emporwachsen, wo sie sicher sind, daß ihnen niemand auf die Finger klopft? die selbstgerechten Freiheitsapostel, die sich selber für unfehlbar halten und die wichtigste aller menschlichen Freiheiten niemandem gönnen wollen: die Freiheit sich zu irren? Sind sie denn wirklich alle, alle liebenswert? Je nun . . .

Appendices

1. GLOSSARY OF GRAMMATICAL TERMS

Accusative case The form of the noun, pronoun, article, or adjective when used as a direct object and when used with certain prepositions, verbs and expressions:

Sie ißt *den roten Apfel.*	She eats *the red apple.*
Sie geht ohne *ihn.*	She goes without *him.*

Active voice *see* Voice.

Adjective A word that limits, qualifies, or describes a noun:

ein *großer* Hund	a *big* dog

Sometimes the definite and indefinite articles, the **der** and **ein** words and **alle, einige, mehrere, viele, wenige** are grouped under the term "limiting adjective." The term "descriptive adjective" would then necessarily encompass all other adjectives.

Adverb A word that modifies a verb, an adjective or another adverb:

Sie spricht *sehr schnell.*	She speaks *very quickly.*

Antecedent The word, phrase, or clause to which a pronoun refers:

Ich sah den *Mann.* Er war alt.	I saw the *man.* He was old.

Auxiliary verb A verb that helps to conjugate another verb **(haben, sein,** and **werden):**

Er *hatte* es getrunken.	He *had* drunk it.
Ich *bin* in die Stadt gegangen.	I *have* gone to town.
Sie *wird* bestimmt kommen.	She *will* certainly come.

Case The form of the noun, pronoun, article, or adjective that indicates its function or its relationship to other words in a given phrase or clause. There are four cases in German: the nominative, the genitive, the dative, and the accusative.

Clause A group of words that contains both a subject and predicate.

Conjugate To give the various tenses, numbers, persons, voices, moods of a verb. The present tense conjugation of the indicative mood of the verb *to see* is: *I see; you see; he, she, it sees; we see; you see; they see.*

Conjunction A word used to link together words or phrases:
Hans *and* Inge went to the opera, *but* they had forgotten their tickets.

Dative case The form of the noun, pronoun, or adjective when used as an indirect object and with certain prepositions, verbs, adjectives, and expressions:

Gehst du mit *ihm*?	Are you going with *him*?
Das ist *mir* schwer.	That is difficult for *me*.
Sie gibt *ihnen* das Buch.	She is giving *them* the book.

Decline To give the various forms of nouns, articles, pronouns and adjectives indicating gender, number and case. The noun **Mann** is declined.
der Mann, des Mannes, dem Manne, den Mann
die Männer, der Männer, den Männern, die Männer

Definite articles In German, the forms of **der, die, das;** in English *the*.

Dependent word order The word order used in dependent (subordinate) clauses. The verb with the personal ending is generally the last element:

Sie blieb zu Hause, weil sie eine kranke Mutter *hatte*.	She remained at home, because her mother was sick (because she *had* a sick mother).

Der words Words declined like the definite article: **dieser, jeder, jener, mancher, solcher, welcher.**

Gender Any set of categories into which words are divided and which determine agreement with modifiers, referents or grammatical forms. In German a noun may be masculine, feminine, or neuter:

***der* Mann** (m.), ***die* Frau** (f.), ***das* Kind** (n.)	the man, the woman, the child

Genitive case The form of a noun, pronoun, article, or adjective that indicates possession or relationship. Certain prepositions, verbs, adjectives, and expressions that do not necessarily indicate possession also take the genitive case.

Imperative A form of the verb expressing a command or request:

***Sprich* langsamer!**	*Speak* more slowly!

Indefinite article In German the forms of **ein, eine, ein;** in English *a* and *an*.

Indicative mood The mode of expression which deals with reality or fact:

Deutsch *ist* eine schwere Sprache.	German *is* a difficult language.

Infinitive The form of the verb that expresses the general meaning but does not identify the time or the performer of the action. In German the infinitive is identified by the endings **-en** or **-n**:

singen	*to sing*
erinnern	*to remind*

Irregular weak verb A verb that in the past tense and the past participle takes the vowel change of the strong verb and the endings of the weak verb:

bringen, brachte, gebracht	*to bring, brought, brought*

Modal auxiliaries Verbs that express attitudes of obligation, permission, ability, desire. The modals in German are: **dürfen, können, mögen, müssen, sollen, wollen.**

Mood The point of view from which the action is seen: statements of reality or fact (indicative); statements of unreality, of possibility, of doubt (subjunctive); statements of necessity (imperative).

Nominative case The case of the subject and predicate nouns, pronouns, articles, or adjectives:

Der *Student* da drüben ist *mein bester Freund.*	That *student* over there is *my best friend.*

Number The form of the noun, pronoun, adjective or verb which indicates how many persons or things are referred to:

Die alte Katze bleibt hier.	*The old cat remains* here.
Sie hat kein Geld.	*She has no money.*

Object The word that receives the action of a verb, either directly or indirectly:

Hans sieht seine *Frau.*	Hans sees his *wife* (direct object).
Nachher gibt er *ihr* einen Kuß.	Afterwards he gives *her* a kiss (indirect object).

The noun or pronoun that is affected by the preposition:

Ich gehe mit *ihm.*	I am going with *him.*
Er geht ohne *sie.*	He is going without *her.*

See also Genitive Case, Dative Case and Accusative Case.

Participle A form of the verb that may be used as a verb, as part of a compound tense, as an adjective or adverb. There are two, the present and the past:

(past) ***Gesagt, getan.***	No sooner *said* than *done.*
(past) **Hat Maria ihn schon *gesehen*?**	Has Maria *seen* him already?
(present) ***Singend* stand er da.**	He stood there *singing.*
(present) **Der *herlaufende* Mensch . . .**	The man *running* towards us . . .
(past) **Er kam *gelaufen.***	He came *running.*

Passive voice *See* Voice.

Person The form of the noun, pronoun, or verb that indicates whether the subject is the speaker, (first person), the person spoken to (second person), or the person of whom one is speaking (third person):

***ich* bin; *wir* sind** — *I* am, *we* are (first person)
***du* bist; *ihr* seid; *Sie* sind** — *you* are (second person)
***er, sie, es* ist; *sie* sind** — *he, she, it* is; *they* are (third person).

Preposition A word that relates a noun or pronoun in time, position, or direction to other elements in a clause.

Er geht *vor* die Klasse.	He goes *to* the front *of* the class.

Pronoun A word that stands in place of a noun:

Klaus hat seine Uhr vergessen. *Er* hat *sie* vergessen.	Klaus forgot his watch. *He* forgot *it*.

Relative pronoun A pronoun that joins two clauses:

Das Mädchen, mit *dem* er befreundet ist, ist hübsch.	The girl with *whom* he is friends is pretty.

An infinitive **stem** That part of an infinitive that remains after being shorn of its endings: **leben** (to live), **leb-.**

Strong verb A verb that changes its vowel when going from the present tense to the past tense:

er *findet*, er *fand*	he *finds*, he *found*

The past participle ends in **-(e)n; gefunden**—*found.*

Subjunctive mood The mode of expression that deals with conditions contrary to fact, unreality, wishes, doubts, possibilities, indirect discourse:

Wenn ich sie geliebt *hätte*, *hätte* ich sie geheiratet.	If I *had* loved her, I *would have* married her.
***Möchten* Sie ins Kino gehen?**	*Would* you like to go to the movies?

Tense The form of the verb that indicates the time of the action or state of being, such as past, present, or future.

Verb A word that expresses action or state or being:

Das Wetter *war* elend.	The weather *was* wretched.
Sie *haben* sich *erkältet*.	They *caught* (*have caught*) cold.

Voice The form of the verb that indicates whether the subject acts (active voice) or receives the action (passive voice):

Active: **Wolfgang *fängt* den Ball.**	Wolfgang *catches* the ball.
Passive: **Der Ball *wird* von Wolfgang *gefangen.***	The ball *is (being) caught* by Wolfgang.

Weak verb A verb that shows the change from present to past tense by its ending, rather than by a vowel change. In German a **-t-** is added to the stem:

er *sagt*, er *sag-t-e*	he *says,* he *said*

The past participle ends in **-t**: **gesagt.**

2. PRONUNCIATION GUIDE

The following guide to the pronunciation of German can only give you the approximate sounds of the language. Oral instruction in pronunciation should supplement what is presented here. In general, German is pronounced as it is spelled with no silent letters except *h* when it indicates that the preceding vowel is long. The accented syllable is generally the first syllable or the stem syllable (Deútschland, Váter, gewínnen).

Vowels—general rules of pronunciation

1. Vowels may be either long or short
2. They are long
   a. when doubled or followed by *h*
      Haar Ohr
   b. when either final in the word or at the end of an accented syllable
      du há-ben
   c. and generally when followed by a single consonant
      rot grün
3. They are short
   a. when followed by a double consonant
      küssen Mann
   b. when followed by two or more consonants
      sitzen Fenster

Specific rules of pronunciation:

a	Long as in *father*	**Vater, Saat, Bahn**
	Short as in *fun*	**Mann, Hand, Ball**
e	Long as in *gate* but without the final *ee* sound	**Schnee, stehen, geben**
	Short as in *bed*	**Bett, nennen, Fenster**
	Unaccented as in *sofa*	**Tage, Pflaume, gebe**
i	Long as in *spleen*	**Klima, Tiger, ihnen**
	Short as in *fist*	**ist, Mitte, Liste**
ie	Generally as the long *i*	**fliegen, sieben, die**

o	Long as in *no* but without the final *u* sound	**Boot**, **Rose**, **Lohn**
	Short as in *offer*	**oft**, **Gold**, **Gott**
u	Long as in *fool*	**Schuh**, **du**, **Hut**
	Short as in *push*	**und**, **Mutter**, **mußte**

The umlauted vowels (modified vowels)

ä	Long as in either *gate* or as in *their* (some Germans make no distinction)	**Väter**, **Mädchen**, **wähne**
	Short as in *bed* (i.e. it is identical to the short *e*)	**Männer**, **Säckchen**, **Kämme**
ö	There is no sound in English for either the long or short **ö**.	
	Long: round lips to pronounce *oh* but instead pronounce the long *a* as in *gate*.	**Öfen**, **Söhne**, **schön**
	Short: round lips to pronounce *oh* but instead pronounce the German short *e* as in *bed*.	**östlich**, **können**, **Hölle**
ü	There is no corresponding sound for either the long or short **ü**.	
	Long: round lips to pronounce the *oo* in *fool* but instead pronounce the *ee* as in *spleen*.	**kühl**, **Füßen**, **Bücher**
	Short: round lips to pronounce the *oo* in *fool* but instead pronounce the short *i* as in *fist*.	**küssen**, **Mütter**, **müßte**

ä, ö, ü, are occasionally written **ae, oe, ue**: **spaet**, **oeffnen**, **ueber** instead of **spät**, **öffnen**, **über**

The diphthongs

ei, ai, ey, ay are like the *i* in *mine*	**mein**, **Mai**, **Speyer**, **Mayer**
au is like the *ou* in *mouse*	**Maus**, **Haus**, **Laus**
eu, äu, are like the *oi* in *foil*	**neun**, **Feuer**, **Häuser**, **Fräulein**

The consonants—general rules of pronunciation

The following consonants and combinations of consonants are pronounced as they are in English: **f, h, k, m, n, p, t, ck, nk, ph.**

Special rules of pronunciation

b	when beginning a word or syllable is like the English *b*	**Ball**, **entbinden**
	when ending a word or syllable is like the English *p*	**Grab**, **abfallen**, **gibt**, **gebt**

c	when preceding **ä, e, i, y** is like *ts*	**C**äsar, **C**ello, **C**icero, **C**yrenius
	when preceding **a, o, u** is like the English *k*	**C**afe, **C**ousine, **C**uxhaven
ch	There are four different sounds:	
	a. the back **ch** or **ach** sound used after **a, o, u** and **au.** This sound is produced by arching the tongue against the rear part of the palate. The tip of the tongue rests below the teeth of the lower jaw.	a**ch**, do**ch**, Bu**ch**, Bau**ch**
	b. The front **ch** or **ich** sound follows all other vowels. It is pronounced like the *h* in *hew*.	i**ch**, Bü**ch**er, Be**ch**er, Ei**ch**e
	c. When beginning words of Greek origin or preceding the vowels **a** and **u** or consonants, it is pronounced like the English *k*.	**Ch**rist, **Ch**or, **Ch**arakter
	When preceding **i** or **e** however it takes the front **ch** sound.	**Ch**ina, **Ch**emie, **Ch**irurg
	d. When beginning words of French origin it is pronounced like the English *sh*.	**Ch**ef, **Ch**auffeur, **Ch**auvinist
chs	is like the English *ks* when *s* is part of the stem.	se**chs**, O**chs,** wa**chs**en
	When **s** is an ending the **ch** is pronounced according to the rules already given.	versu**ch**st, verflu**ch**st
d	when beginning a word or syllable is like the English *d*.	**d**umm, Bru**d**er
	when ending a word or syllable is like the English *t*.	Han**d**, Mä**d**chen
dt	is like the English *t*.	Sta**dt**, wan**dt**e
g	when beginning a word or syllable is like the English *g* in *girl*.	**G**arten, le**g**en, Mor**g**en
	when ending a word or syllable is like *k*. Often it is pronounced like a front or back **ch**.	Ta**g**, le**g**st
	The ending **-ig** is pronounced like the German **ich.**	Kön**ig**, fleiß**ig**, wen**ig**
	However, when an ending is added, **g** becomes as the *g* in *go*.	fleißi**g**er, weni**g**er
gn	Both letters are pronounced.	**Gn**om, **Gn**ostizismus

h	is silent when used to lengthen a vowel.	ste**h**en, i**h**nen
	When beginning a word or syllable, it is like the English *h*.	**h**aben, zu**h**ören, a**h**a
j	is like the English *y* in *yellow:*	**j**a, **J**ahr, **j**ung
J	is like the final consonant sound in *garage* when it introduces words of French origin.	**J**ournalist
kn	Both letters are pronounced.	**Kn**ie, **kn**oten
l	Pronounce this letter by placing the tip of the tongue against the upper teeth or the front edge of the upper gums and place the sound of the letter to the front of the mouth.	so**ll**en, **l**ang, Ba**ll**, ba**l**d, Stuh**l**
ng	is like the English *ng* in *singer* (and not like the *ng* in *finger*).	Si**ng**er, Fi**ng**er, E**ng**land
pf	Both letters are pronounced	**Pf**effer, A**pf**el
ps	Both letters are pronounced	**Ps**ychologie, **Ps**eudonym
qu	is like the English *kv*	**Qu**alität, **qu**alifizieren
r	is produced either by vibrating the tip of the tongue against the upper gum (the trilled **r**) or by vibrating the uvula (the guttural **r**). In other words the guttural **r** is a dry gargle which has a sound.	**r**ennen, g**r**aben, studie**r**en, füh**r**t Pfa**rr**er
	A final **r** has the following pronunciations:	
	There is a faint remnant of the trilled or guttural **r** in the ending **-r**.	**Jahr**, **klar**
	It is vocalized to a point where it is almost non-existent in the endings **-är**, **-er**, **-ir**, **-or**, **-ör**, **-ur**, **-ür**	**Bär**, Fing**er**, d**ir**, T**or**, st**ör**, Fl**ur**, T**ür**
s	when beginning a word or syllable before a vowel is like the English *z* in the English *zoo*.	**s**ieben, E**s**el, Kä**s**e, al**s**o
	In all other cases it is like the English *s* in *some*.	Hau**s**, Po**s**t, ha**s**t
	Before **p** and **t**, **s** is pronounced like the English *sh* when it begins a word or syllable.	**St**ein, ab**st**eigen, **Sp**iegel

ss, ß	are like the *ss* in the English *miss*. (**ss** is only used between two short vowels whenever a differentiation is made between **ss** and **ß**).	mü**ss**en, grü**ß**en, flie**ß**en, be**ss**er
th	is like the English *t*.	**Th**ron, **Th**eater, **Th**eorie
-tion	**t** is pronounced *ts*, the vowels are long	na**tion**al, Rota**tion**
tz	is like the English *ts* in *cats*.	Pla**tz**, se**tz**en
v	is like the English *f* in words of Germanic origin.	**v**on, **V**ater, bra**v**
	In words of foreign origin it is pronounced like the English *v*.	No**v**ember, E**v**angelium, **V**ase, Uni**v**ersität
w	is like the English *v*.	**W**ind, **w**ann, ge**w**esen
x	is pronounced like the English *ks* or final *x*.	Ma**x**, A**x**t, He**x**e
z	is pronounced like the English *ts* in *cats*.	**Z**eit, tan**z**en, kur**z**

The Glottal Stop

In addition to the sounds listed above the pronunciation of German words is characterized by an explosive quality. This results from closing the glottis (the space between the vocal cords) an instant before pronouncing a word or syllable which begins with an accented vowel.

ˊauf, ˊOhr, beˊeinflussen, ˊist, ˊüberˊaus

Accent

Rules for stressing the word already briefly mentioned above are as follows:

1. Simple German words are accented on the first syllable:

háben, Mútter, Kínder, lángsam

2. Compound nouns usually receive the accent on the first element:

Kránkenhaus, Ráumkapsel, Úntertasse

3. Separable prefixes are accented:

éinsteigen, ánfangen, vórgehen, wíedersehen

4. The inseparable prefixes **be-, emp-, ent-, er-, ge-, ver-, zer-** are unaccented:

bekómmen, entstéhen, empfínden, erréichen, gemácht, mißhándeln, verstéhen, zerbréchen

5. Words of non-Germanic origin usually receive the accent on the last syllable:

Studént, Universitä́t, Revolution

6. The suffix *-ei* receives the accent:

Metzgerei, Schlachterei, Schweinerei

3. NUMERALS

Cardinal numbers

0	null				
1	eins (ein-)	11	elf	21	einundzwanzig*
2	zwei	12	zwölf	22	zweiundzwanzig
3	drei	13	dreizehn	30	dreißig
4	vier	14	vierzehn	40	vierzig
5	fünf	15	fünfzehn	50	fünfzig
6	sechs	16	sechzehn	60	sechzig
7	sieben	17	siebzehn	70	siebzig
8	acht	18	achtzehn	80	achtzig
9	neun	19	neunzehn	90	neunzig
10	zehn	20	zwanzig	100	hundert

101 hunderteins
200 zweihundert
333 dreihundertdreiunddreißig
1000 tausend
2000 zweitausend
4444 viertausendvierhundertvierundvierzig
10 000 zehntausend
100 000 hunderttausend
1 000 000 eine Million
1 000 000 000 eine Milliarde
1 000 000 000 000 eine Billion

Ordinal numbers
The endings **-t** or **-st** added to cardinal numbers signify ordinal numbers.

first	**erst-**	seventh	**siebent-, siebt**
second	**zweit-**	eighth	**acht-**
third	**dritt-**	ninth	**neunt-**
fourth	**viert-**	tenth	**zehnt-**
fifth	**fünft-**	twentieth	**zwanzigst-**
sixth	**sechst-**	twenty-first	**einundzwanzigst-**

*Note that the unit digit precedes the tens digit.

thirtieth	**dreißigst-**	thousandth	**tausendst-**
hundredth	**hundertst-**	*etc.*	**usw.**

These numbers are used adjectivally and will take some kind of ending, generally an **-e** or **-en:**

das zweit**e** Kind   mit dem dritt**en** Bruder

Fractions

The endings **-tel** or **-stel** indicate a fraction:

$\frac{1}{2}$	halb, die Hälfte	$\frac{4}{25}$	vier Fünfundzwanzigstel
$\frac{3}{10}$	drei Zehntel	$1\frac{1}{2}$	anderthalb, eineinhalb
$\frac{15}{17}$	fünfzehn Siebzehntel	$2\frac{1}{2}$	zweieinhalb

General rules concerning numerals

1. Decimals are indicated by commas, not periods:

33,33 (German) = 33·33 (English)

2. A thin space is used where English uses the comma:

1 333,33 (German) = 1,333·33 (English)

3. Several numeral suffixes are:

German		English			
-ens	=	-ly	**zweitens**	=	secondly
			drittens	=	thirdly
-erlei	=	of . . . kind	**einerlei**	=	one of a kind
			dreierlei	=	three of a kind
-fach	=	-fold	**zweifach**	=	two-fold
			einfach	=	simple, simply (one-fold)
-mal	=	-ce, times	**einmal**	=	once
			zweimal	=	twice
			dreimal	=	thrice
			viermal	=	four times
			fünfundzwanzigmal	=	twenty-five times

4. EXERCISES IN GERMAN GRAMMAR

The following frames will check to see if you understand the grammar patterns and rules which have been presented in the text and the appendix. Enabling you to choose the grammatically correct form of a particular item is not considered to be a primary objective of this book. However, as there are national reading examinations in use which ask the student to supply correct grammatical forms, we feel that a section should be included to provide you with such practice. The vocabulary in the main is drawn from a number of the reading passages, with just enough unknown vocabulary to challenge you. Observe the context carefully as a means of helping you choose the correct answer.

Before you attempt to do these exercises, review the pertinent grammar sections. As you answer the questions, write your answer on a slip of paper which you can then check against the key. If you miss any answers, review the grammar section(s) until you feel you understand why you missed the problem.

Definite articles and *der* words: Choose the correct answer from the following:

1. Die Erkenntnis ________ Todes und ________ Auferstehung ist immer gegenwärtig.
(a) der . . . die (b) des . . . der (c) den . . . die (d) dem . . . der

2. Und dies nenne ich Diesseitigkeit, nämlich in ________ Fülle ________ Aufgaben, Fragen, Erfolge und Mißerfolge leben.
(a) den . . . der (b) die . . . den (c) der . . . die (d) der . . . der

3. Für ________ einzelnen Arbeiter war ________ nominelle Arbeitstag $11\frac{1}{2}$ Stunden.
(a) den . . . dem (b) der . . . der (c) der . . . den (d) den . . . der

4. Viele befinden sich in ________ Situation.
(a) dies (b) dieses (c) dieser (d) diesem

5. Ist ________ Proletarier in einer solchen Lage?
(a) jeder (b) jedes (c) jedem (d) jeden

6. Wenn alle Londoner Arbeiter in ________ Elend lebten . . .
(a) solchen (b) einem solchen (c) so ein (d) solcher

7. Wer mit ________ Weisen umgeht, der wird weise.
(a) den (b) des (c) die (d) denen

8. Wer aber ________ Narren (*fools*) Geselle (*companion*) ist, der wird Unglück haben. (*Bible*)
(a) die (b) des (c) den (d) der

9. Das Leiden gibt ________ Leidenden keine Rechte.
(a) des (b) der (c) das (d) dem

10. Dieser hört nicht auf mich, ________ tut alles.
(a) jenem (b) jener (c) jenen (d) jenes

Answer key: **1.** (b); **2.** (d); **3.** (d); **4.** (c); **5.** (a); **6.** (b); **7.** (a); **8.** (d); **9.** (d); **10.** (b).

Adjectives: Choose the correct form from the following:

1. Was ist ________ irgendein Laster?
(a) mehr schädlich (b) schädlicher als (c) schädlich wie (d) schädlicher

2. In ________ Jahren hat er mehr gelernt.
(a) dem letzten (b) den letzten (c) der letzten (d) des letzten

3. Die tiefe Diesseitigkeit ist ________ Zucht.
(a) voller (b) vollem (c) vollen (d) volle

4. Ich hatte ein Gespräch mit ________ Pfarrer.
(a) einen jungen französischen (b) ein junger französischer (c) eines jungen französischen (d) einem jungen französischen

5. Versucht er, ________ aus sich selbst zu machen?
(a) einem Kranken (b) eines Kranken (c) einen Kranken (d) ein Kranker

6. Das Christentum weist das Gebot als seinen ________ Anspruch vor.
(a) stolzesten (b) am stolzesten (c) stolzer (d) stolzester

7. Sie wohnte ________ Elende.
(a) das größte (b) großes (c) im größten (d) am größten

8. Nichts ist schwerer zu ertragen als eine Reihe von ________ Tagen. (Goethe)
(a) schönere (b) schönen (c) die schönsten (d) schöne

9. Bismarck besaß einen Sohn, dessen wahrlich ________ ________ Qualitäten er erstaunlich überschätzte.
(a) bescheidenes staatsmännisches (b) bescheidenen staatsmännischen (c) bescheidener staatsmännischer (d) bescheidene staatsmännische

10. Ein Lächeln ist oft ________. (A. de Saint-Exupéry)
(a) das Wesentliche (b) des Wesentlichen (c) dem Wesentlichen (d) den Wesentlichen

Answer key: **1.** (b); **2.** (b); **3.** (a); **4.** (d); **5.** (c); **6.** (a); **7.** (c); **8.** (b); **9.** (d); **10.** (a).

Possessive adjectives, *ein* and *kein*. Choose the form which fits the context of the sentence:

1. Sie führten mich vor ________ (*their*) Herrn.
(a) Ihren (b) ihren (c) euren (d) unseren

2. Wie bunt war ________ (*his*) Uniform!
(a) unsere (b) ihre (c) seine (d) deine

3. Der erste Satz ________ (*of our*) Menschenliebe ist, haße die Schwachen und Mißratenen.
(a) Ihrer (b) unserer (c) eurer (d) ihren

4. Wenn er der Sohn ________ Freundes ist . . .
(a) von meinem (b) von meiner (c) meinen (d) meines

5. Es war ________ sehr großes Werk auf dem Lande.
(a) ein (b) eines (c) eine (d) einer

6. Sie war die Witwe ________ alten Soldaten.
(a) eines (b) einem (c) ein (d) einen

7. Sie wohnte zusammen mit ________ neun Kindern.
(a) ihrer (b) Ihrem (c) ihren (d) eure

8. Geh nicht in die Stadt, denn ________ Mutter ist krank!
(a) seiner (b) eure (c) Ihre (d) deine

9. Die wirkliche Liebe beginnt, wo ________ Gegengabe mehr erwartet wird! (A. de Saint-Exupéry)
(a) keine (b) keinen (c) keinem (d) keiner

10. Wacht darüber, daß eure Herzen nicht leer sind, wenn mit der Leere ________ Herzen gerechnet wird. (Günther Eich)
(a) deiner (b) Ihrer (c) eurer (d) ihrer

Answer key: **1.** (b); **2.** (c); **3.** (b); **4.** (d); **5.** (a); **6.** (a); **7.** (c); **8.** (d); **9.** (a); **10.** (c).

Pronouns—personal, impersonal and reflexive. Choose the grammatically correct answer:

1. Zwei Soldaten kamen und ergriffen ________.
(a) ihr (b) mich (c) ihm (d) wir

2. Das hindert ________ nicht, dich zu fassen.
(a) uns (b) dir (c) er (d) ihr

3. Dann wirft ________ sich Gott ganz in die Arme.
(a) du (b) ihr (c) Sie (d) man

4. Du sollst den Nächsten lieben wie ________ selbst.
(a) sich (b) dich (c) Sie (d) euch

5. Es ist Unrecht an meinen Freunden, wenn ich den Fremden ________ gleichstelle.
(a) man (b) Ihrem (c) ihnen (d) du

6. Ich schlief mit einer kleinen Jacke über ________.
(a) sich (b) sie (c) mir (d) dich

7. Als der Polizeidiener zu ihr kam, fand ________ ________ in einem kleinen Zimmer.
(a) er sie (b) sie ihnen (c) ihn euch (d) ihr ihm

8. Man hält die Menschen gewöhnlich für gefährlicher als ________ sind. (Goethe)
(a) Sie (b) ihnen (c) sie (d) ihr

9. Statt ________ wird seine Schwester kommen.
(a) mein (b) meiner (c) meinem (d) mir

10. Das Buch darf nicht mehr von ________ gelesen werden.
(a) einen (b) eines (c) man (d) einem

11. Ich weiß wohl, daß zehn es besser haben, wo ________ so ganz und gar von der Gesellschaft mit Füßen getreten wird.
(a) ein (b) einem (c) einen (d) einer

12. ________ hätte einen dümmeren Sohn gehabt wie dieser!
(a) Kein (b) Keiner (c) Keinen (d) Keines

Answer key: **1.** (b); **2.** (a); **3.** (d); **4.** (b); **5.** (c); **6.** (c); **7.** (a); **8.** (c); **9.** (b); **10.** (d); **11.** (d); **12.** (b).

Relative and demonstrative pronouns. Choose the form which suits or completes the meaning of the sentence:

1. Das Mädchen, mit ________ Vater du ins Kino gehst . . .
(a) deren (b) dessen (c) denen (d) dem

2. Die Nation, ________ Bismarck hinterließ, war . . .
(a) die (b) das (c) dessen (d) der

3. Der Bruder, ________ wir nicht mehr kennen, wohnt in Berlin.
(a) der (b) dessen (c) dem (d) den

4. Das politische Erbe Bismarcks, ________ weiter auf die deutsche Nation arbeitete . . .
(a) dessen (b) welchem (c) welche (d) welches

5. Der große Staatsmann, von ________ das Volk alles erwartete . . .
(a) den (b) der (c) welchem (d) welches

6. Alles, ________ das Gefühl der Macht im Menschen erhöht . . .
(a) das (b) was (c) daß (d) der

7. Wahrscheinlich schlafen Leute besser, wenn sie ________ Ruheperiode genießen.
(a) demselben (b) derselben (c) dieselbe (d) derselbe

8. ________ konnte nicht so lange gearbeitet haben.
(a) Der (b) Dessen (c) Dem (d) Den

9. ________ hatte nur Lumpen, ________ zum Bette dienten.
(a) Dem . . . der (b) Die . . . die (c) Den . . . den (d) Denen . . . deren

10. Nur ________ verdient Macht, ________ sie täglich rechtfertigt.
(Dag Hammarskjöld)
(a) der . . . der (b) den . . . der (c) dem . . . den (d) den . . . den

11. Niemand ist mehr Sklave, als ________ sich für frei hält, ohne es zu sein. (Goethe)
(a) der (b) dessen (c) dem (d) den

12. Du bist zeitlebens für ________ verantwortlich, was du dir vertraut gemacht hast.
(Antoine de Saint-Exupéry)
(a) die (b) den (c) das (d) dem

Answer key: **1.** (b); **2.** (a); **3.** (d); **4.** (d); **5.** (c); **6.** (b); **7.** (c); **8.** (a); **9.** (b); **10.** (a); **11.** (a); **12.** (c).

Nouns—singular and plural forms. Choose the correct form from the possibilities given:

1. Was erhöht den ________ zur Macht im Menschen?
(a) Wille (b) Willen (c) Willens (d) Wollen

2. In historischen Zeiten war das Gebot der Nächstenliebe den ________ noch fremd.
(a) Mütter (b) Freundin (c) Mannes (d) Menschen

3. Die ________, die es jetzt gibt, sind nicht zu überwältigen.
(a) Schwierigkeiten (b) Glaube (c) Vätern (d) Fehlers

4. Ja, man muß seinen ________ verzeihen, aber nicht früher, als bis sie gehenkt worden sind.
(a) Feinden (b) Feinde (c) Feindes (d) Feind

5. Er arbeitete von morgens 6 Uhr bis 12 Uhr in die Nacht drei ________ durch.
(a) Nachts (b) Nacht (c) Nächte (d) Nächten

6. Die Federn waren fast über ihren nackten ________ gestreut.
(a) Körpern (b) Körper (c) Körpers (d) Köpfe

7. Der Polizeirichter erhielt von den ________ folgende Aufklärung.
(a) Polizeidieners (b) Polizeidienen (c) Polizeidienern (d) Polizeidiener

8. Gewissen ________ muß man ihre Idiotismen lassen. (Goethe)
(a) Geist (b) Geistes (c) Geister (d) Geistern

9. Frieden ist ________ jeder Gruppe zusammen mit ihrem Gegenüber. (Richard von Weizsäcker)
(a) Aufgabe (b) Aufgaben (c) Aufgeben (d) Aufgänge

10. Sie sind nur ________ mit ausgebrochenen Zähnen.
(a) Raubtier (b) Raubtiere (c) Raubtieren (d) Raubtieres

Answer key: **1.** (b); **2.** (d); **3.** (a); **4.** (a); **5.** (c); **6.** (b); **7.** (c); **8.** (d); **9.** (a); **10.** (b).

Prepositions. Choose the preposition which best suits the meaning and also which agrees grammatically with what follows it:

1. Was wollt ihr denn ________ (from) mir.
(a) nach (b) zu (c) von (d) bei

2. Das Militär hat Gewalt ________ (over) alles.
(a) auf (b) zwischen (c) an (d) über

3. Wenn er mich ________ (by) keinen eigenen Wert anziehen kann, wird es mir schwer, ihn zu lieben.
(a) mit (b) aus (c) durch (d) bei

4. ________ (during) eines ganzen Jahres arbeitete ich in einem Hochofen.
(a) Während (b) Gegen (c) Statt (d) Trotz

5. Sie lag tot ________ ihrem Sohn.
(a) ohne (b) außerhalb (c) jenseits (d) neben

6. Montag wurden zwei Knaben ________ das Polizeigericht gebracht.
(a) diesseits (b) vor (c) seit (d) gegenüber

7. ________ dem Tode ihres Mannes ist es ihr schlecht ergangen.
(a) Über (b) Außerhalb (c) Seit (d) Durch

8. ________ Geld ________ verdienen, mußte sie lange Jahre als Putzfrau arbeiten.
(a) Statt . . . zu (b) Um . . . zu (c) Bis . . . zu (d) In . . . zu

9. Jeder, ________ Ausnahme, ________ seine Schuld kann von gleichem Schicksal getroffen werden. (Which preposition will fill both blanks?)
(a) ohne (b) außer (c) seit (d) trotz

10. ________ allen Anstrengungen wird jeder von gleichem Schicksal getroffen.
(a) Durch (b) Gegen (c) Trotz (d) Ohne

11. Man sagt: „Er stirbt bald", wenn einer etwas ________ seine Art und Weise tut. (Goethe)
(a) bei (b) gegen (c) nach (d) mit

12. Unsere Leidenschaften sind wahre Phönixe. Wie der alte verbrennt, steigt der neue sogleich wieder ________ der Asche hervor. (Goethe)
(a) auf (b) während (c) hinter (d) aus

13. ________ der Angriffe, die sie weislich vermeiden, hassen sie andere.
(a) Aus (b) Hinter (c) Wegen (d) Unter

14. Er darf ________ mir bleiben.
(a) bei (b) ohne (c) seit (d) gegen

15. ________ der Sonne und dem Tier stand der Jäger.
(a) Über (b) Auf (c) An (d) Zwischen

Answer key: **1.** (c); **2.** (d); **3.** (c); **4.** (a); **5.** (d); **6.** (b); **7.** (c); **8.** (b); **9.** (a); **10.** (c); **11.** (b); **12.** (d); **13.** (c); **14.** (a); **15.** (d).

Verb forms. Choose the grammatically correct *indicative* form for each sentence from the following choices:

1. Der Offizier ________ und sagte: „Du bist ein Zivilist".
(a) lächelte (b) hast gelächelt (c) lächele (d) lächelten.

2. Was ist Glück? — Das Gefühl davon, daß ein Widerstand ________.
(a) überwinden werde (b) überwunden wird (c) überwunden werdet (d) überwunden worden sei

3. Ich glaube, daß Luther in dieser Diesseitigkeit ________.
(a) gelebt hattet (b) gelebt hat (c) geliebt hätte (d) gelobt werde

4. Ich __________ eines Gespräches, das ich damals in Frankreich hatte.
(a) werde sich erinnern (b) erinnert ihn (c) würde sie erinnern (d) erinnere mich

5. Wir __________ ganz einfach die Frage __________ . . .
(a) stellte . . . uns (b) wird uns . . . gestellt (c) hatten uns . . . gestellt (d) werdet . . . stellen

6. Ich glaube, daß er ein Heiliger __________.
(a) geworden ist (b) geworden sei (c) würde (d) wirst

7. Bonhoeffer __________ selbst ein heiliges Leben __________.
(a) versuchtet . . . zu führen (b) wird . . . zu führen versuchen
(c) müßt . . . führen (d) dürfte . . . führen

8. Etwa sechs bis sieben meiner Feinde __________.
(a) sollte aufgehängt worden sein (b) müssen aufgehängt werden
(c) wären aufgehängt worden (d) wollt aufgehängt werden

9. __________ deine Feinde!
(a) Kennt (b) Finde (c) Mögen Sie (d) Liebst

10. Nicht bis sie __________, werde ich ihnen verzeihen.
(a) gehenkt worden sind (b) erhängt sich selber
(c) gehenkt werden müsse (d) dich selbst erhängt hast

11. Ich __________ die ganze Nacht hier.
(a) möge (b) solltet (c) blieb (d) wußte

12. Das Loch __________ als Abtritt __________.
(a) sollt . . . benutzt werden (b) wurde . . . benutzt (c) muß . . . benutzen (d) sei . . . benutzt worden

13. Der halbgekochte Kuhfuß __________ vor das Polizeigericht __________.
(a) seien . . . gebracht worden (b) muß . . . gefressen werden
(c) hat . . . gebracht werden müssen (d) soll . . . gebraucht haben

14. __________ der Mensch immer ein Raubtier __________?
(a) Wollt . . . werden (b) Dürft . . . gewesen sein (c) Werde . . . gewesen (d) Ist . . . gewesen

15. Er __________ das nicht mehr __________.
(a) ist . . . gemocht worden (b) hätte . . . mögen sollen (c) hat . . . gemocht (d) werde . . . mögen

16. Doris __________ sehr arm sein.
(a) sollt (b) soll (c) solltet (d) solle

Answer key: **1.** (a); **2.** (b); **3.** (b); **4.** (d); **5.** (c); **6.** (a); **7.** (b); **8.** (b); **9.** (b); **10.** (a); **11.** (c); **12.** (b); **13.** (c); **14.** (d); **15.** (c); **16.** (b).

Verbs. Choose the grammatically correct subjunctive or conditional forms from the following choices:

1. Wenn der Junge das nur ________!
(a) hätte verstehen können (b) habet fressen gedurft
(c) müßte singen haben (d) verstanden wollen habe

2. Da sagte er, er ________ ein Heiliger ________.
(a) kann . . . wurden (b) könne . . . verstehen (c) möchte . . . werden (d) wird . . . geworden

3. Da dachte ich, ich ________.
(a) sein geglaubt worden (b) könnte glauben lernen
(c) hättet geglaubt (d) darf dem alten Pfarrer nicht glauben

4. Ja, wenn jener großartige Gebot ________.
(a) singen werdet (b) gesungen wurde (c) lauten würde (d) geläutet wird

5. Beschränkungen der Nachtarbeit ________ von wenig Wichtigkeit oder Interesse für uns.
(a) soll (b) mußte (c) wären (d) sei

6. Und wenn ich alle meine Habe den Armen ________ . . .
(a) gibt (b) gäbe (c) gebet (d) gäben

7. . . . und ________ meinen Leib brennen . . .
(a) ließe (b) läßt (c) ließ (d) ließt

8. . . . und ________ der Liebe nicht, so wäre mir's nichts nütze. (Bibel).
(a) hattest (b) haben (c) hatte (d) hätte

9. Wenn sie den Lustmörder ________ . . .
(a) hätten gerichtet hin (b) hingerichtet hätten
(c) hinrichten hätten müssen (d) werden hinrichten

10. Er sagte, es ________ dem jämmerlichsten Pazifisten nicht ________ . . .
(a) sei . . . gelungen (b) durfte . . . gelingen
(c) war . . . gelungen (d) hättet . . . gelingen dürfen

11. Ob er denn wirklich ________.
(a) hättet fahren müssen (b) geblieben war (c) schläft (d) singen müßte

12. ________ ruhig!
(a) Wird (b) Blieben Sie (c) Sei (d) Käme

13. ________ ich noch ein Glas Wasser, bitte?
(a) Dürfte (b) Mochte (c) Konnte (d)Muß

14. ________ er wirklich ________, wenn er das Geld gehabt hätte?
(a) Habe . . . geblieben (b) Hätte . . . fahren wollen
(c) Möge . . . gesungen (d) Will . . . gefahren sein

15. Sie fragte, ob sie nach Hause ________________.
(a) fliegen wollet (b) laufen mochte (c) schreiben konnte (d) gehen solle

Answer key: **1.** (a); **2.** (c); **3.** (b); **4.** (c); **5.** (c); **6.** (b); **7.** (a); **8.** (d); **9.** (b); **10.** (a); **11.** (d); **12.** (c); **13.** (a); **14.** (b); **15.** (d).

Vocabulary

General guidelines for use of the vocabulary.

1. When two endings follow a noun, the first ending is genitive, the second is plural:
   der **Mann, -es, ¨er** = der **Mann,** des **Mannes,** die **Männer**

2. One ending following a masculine or neuter noun indicates the genitive form:
   das **Leben, -s** = das **Leben,** des **Lebens**

3. After feminine nouns the ending given indicates the plural form:
   die **Frau, -en** = die **Frau,** der **Frau** (genitive), die **Frauen** (plural)

4. - given as the plural form indicates that the nominative singular and plural are identical:
   der **Wagen, -s, -** = der **Wagen,** des **Wagens,** die **Wagen**

5. Generally no endings will be given for adjectives and verbs used as nouns:
   der **Kranke,** das **Rauschen**

6. No endings following certain feminine nouns will indicate that there is no plural:
   die **Zufriedenheit**

7. The principal parts of strong verbs are given:
   gehen (geht), ging, ist gegangen

8. Verbs with separable prefixes are indicated with a centred period:
   ab·weisen

A

abends in the evening
aber but, however
abgelegen remote
abgesehen von apart from, without regard to
ab·halten (hält ab), hielt ab, hat abgehalten to hold, to give
der **Ablösungstermin, -s, -e** (work)shift
ablösungweise in relays
ab·magern to grow thin
ab·schaffen to abolish, to scrap
die **Abschaffung, -en** abolition, doing away with
ab·schneiden (schneidet ab), schnitt ab, hat abgeschnitten to cut off
die **Absicht, -en** intention
der **Abtritt, -(e)s, -e** lavatory
ab·weisen, (weist ab), wies ab, hat abgewiesen to reject
achtmal eight times
die **Achtung** respect
der **Affe, -n, -n** ape
afrikanisch African
ahnen to sense, to have a presentiment of
ähnlich similar to
die **Ahnung, -en** idea, presentiment
allbereits already
alle und jede all and every, any kind of
die **Allee, -n** drive, avenue
allein alone
aller, alle, alles all, everything
allerfreundlich most friendly

allgemein general
allmählich gradual(ly)
allzuoft all too often
allzusehr all too much, much too
die **Alpen** the Alps
als as, than, when
also thus, so, therefore, hence, consequently
alt old
das **Alter, -s** age
im Alter von at the age of
an at, on, from
in **Anbetracht** considering, in view of, in consideration of
ander different, other, else
der **Andere, -n, -n** other person
ändern to change
an·fangen, (fängt an), fing an, hat angefangen to begin
an·flehen to implore
angeblich alleged
sich an·gewöhnen to get accustomed
der **Angriff, -(e)s, -e** attack
die **Angst, ¨e** fear, anxiety
ängstlich anxious, uneasy, distressed, nervous, timid
der **Anlaß, -sses, Anlässe** cause, motive, reason
Anlaß geben to give rise to
die **Annäherung, -en** approach
die **Annahme, -n** assumption, acceptance
sich an·passen to adapt oneself
an·schauen to look at
sich an·schicken to prepare, to get ready
das **Anschwellen** the swelling up
an·sehen, (sieht an), sah an, hat angesehen to look at
das **Ansehen, -s** esteem
das **Anspruch, (e)s, ¨e** claim
die **Anstrengung, -en** exertion, struggle, effort
die **Antwort, -en** answer
antworten to answer
an·weisen, (weist an), wies an, hat angewiesen to direct, to order
an·wenden, (wendet an), wandte or **wendete an, hat angewandt** or **angewendet** to use, to employ
an·ziehen, (zieht an), zog an, hat angezogen to attract

arbeiten to work
arbeitend working
der **Arbeiter, -s, -** worker
der **Arbeitstag, -(e)s, -e** workday
der **Argwohn, -s** suspicion
der **Arm, -es, -e** arm
arm poor, needy, miserable
der **Arme** poor man, unfortunate person
die **Armenbüchse, -n** poor box
die **Armut** poverty
die **Art, -en** kind, sort, way, manner
der **Arzt, -es, ¨e** doctor
der **Astronom, -en, -en** astronomer
der **Atomkrieg, -(e)s, -e** atomic war
die **Atomwaffe, -n** atomic weapon
auch even, also
auch wenn even if
auf on, in, at, over
auf und ab back and forth
auf·bauen to build up
auf·blasen, (bläst auf), blies auf, hat aufgeblasen to inflate
auf·erlegen to impose upon
die **Auferstehung, -en** resurrection
auf·fassen to regard
die **Auffassung, -en** conception, comprehension, interpretation
auf·fordern to ask, to challenge
die **Aufgabe, -n** task, duty
der **Aufgeklärte, -n, -n** enlightened person
auf·hängen (hängt auf), hing auf, hat aufgehangen to hang
die **Aufklärung, -en** explanation, enlightenment, the Age of Enlightenment
auf·lösen to dissolve
die **Aufmerksamkeit, -en** attention, attentiveness
auf·reißen, (reißt auf), riß auf, hat aufgerissen to tear open
auf·stehen (steht auf), stand auf, ist aufgestanden to stand up, to get up
das **Aufstehen** getting up
auf·treiben (treibt auf), trieb auf, hat aufgetrieben to distend
die **Auftreibung, -en** swelling, distention
auf·treten, (tritt auf), trat auf, ist aufgetreten to appear, come forward
auf·wachen (aux. **sein**) to awake
das **Aufwachen** the waking up
sich auf·werfen, (wirft sich auf), warf sich auf,

hat sich aufgeworfen to set up
die **Aufzeichnung, -en** note, noting down
auf·ziehen (zieht auf), zog auf, hat aufgezogen to wind up (a watch)
das **Auge, -s, -n** eye
der **Augenblick, -(e)s, -e** moment
aus from, out of
das **Ausbleiben** absence, failure (to appear)
aus·brennen, (brennt aus), brannte aus, hat or **ist ausgebrannt** to burn out
der **Ausdruck, -(e)s, ⸚e** expression
der **Ausgang, -(e)s, ⸚** exit
ausgebrochen broken
ausgerottet exterminated, wiped out, destroyed
die **Ausnahme, -n** exception
aus·rotten to exterminate, to wipe out, to destroy
außer except, besides
äußeres exterior
außerirdisch extra-terrestial
sich äußern to express oneself
äußerst utmost, upmost
aus·tragen, (trägt aus), trug aus, hat ausgetragen to carry out, to carry on, to fight out
aus·üben to wield, to exercise

B

bald soon
das **Bankkonto, -s, -ten** or **-s** bank account
das **Bankwesen, -s, -** banking system
bauen to build
der **Bauernstand, -(e)s, ⸚e** peasantry
der **Baum, -(e)s, ⸚e** tree
der **Baustein, -s, -e** building stone, component
der **Bayer, -n, -n** Bavarian
die **Bayerischen Alpen** the Bavarian Alps
Bayern Bavaria
die **Beantwortung, -en** answer
bedecken to cover
bedeckt covered
das **Bedenken, -s, -** scruple, doubt
bedeuten to mean, to signify
die **Bedeutung, -en** meaning, significance
sich bedienen to make use of
bedingen to stipulate, to be conditioned by, to be conditional (dependent) on
die **Bedrohung, -en** threat
beeindrucken to impress
die **Beere, -n** berry
sich befinden (befindet sich), befand sich, hat sich befunden to be
befriedigen to satisfy
befriedigend gratifying, satisfying
beginnen (beginnt), begann, hat begonnen to begin, to start
das **Begreifen** understanding
der **Begriff, -(e)s, -e** concept
die **Begründung, -en** reason
behaften to burden
behaftet afflicted with, subject to
behaupten to maintain
bei on, at, by, in case of
beide both
beinahe almost
beiseite·schieben (schiebt beiseite), schob beiseite, hat beiseitegeschoben to push aside
das **Beispiel, -(e)s, -e** example
zum **Beispiel** for example
bei·tragen (trägt bei), trug bei, hat beigetragen to contribute
bejahen to affirm, to say yes to
bekämpfen to fight against
bekannt known
bekehren to convert
bekennen (bekennt), bekannte, hat bekannt to confess
bekommen (bekommt), bekam, hat bekommen to receive
beleidigen to insult
Belgien Belgium
sich bemühen to take trouble, to take pains, to strive
das **Bemühen** striving
benutzen to use, to utilize
benutzt utilized
die **Benutzung, -en** use
die **Beobachtung, -en** observation
bequem comfortable
der **Bequeme** comfortable one
der, das **Bereich, -(e)s, -e** sphere, scope, range, province
bereit ready
bereits already
der **Berg, -(e)s, -e** mountain
bergen (birgt), barg, hat geborgen to con-

tain, to shelter, to conceal, to harbor

der **Beruf, -(e)s, -e** profession

berufen (beruft), berief, hat berufen to call forth

beruhen to rest, to be based on

berühmt famous

besagen to mean

bescheiden modest

beschieden given

beschließen (beschließt), beschloß, hat beschlossen to decide, to resolve

beschränken to limit, to restrict

die **Beschränkung, -en** limitation

beschreiben (beschreibt), beschrieb, hat beschrieben to describe

die **Beschwerde, -n** complaint

besehen (besieht), besah, hat besehen to inspect

die **Besinnung, -en** reflection, consciousness

der **Besitz, -es, -e** possession

besitzen (besitzt), besaß, hat besessen to possess

besorgen to manage

die **Besorgnis, -se** anxiety, fear

besorgt = anxious

besser better

bessern to better

bestehen in, (besteht), bestand, hat bestanden to consist in, to lie in

bestimmt specific, definite, certain

bestürzen to dismay, to bewilder, to amaze

das **Bestürzende** dismaying thing

bestürzt dismayed, bewildered, confused

die **Bestürzung, -en** dismay, bewilderment, confusion

der **Besuch, -(e)s, -e** visit

besuchen to visit

betrachten to regard, to look upon, to consider

beträchtlich considerable

der **Betriebsame** busy person

die **Bettstelle, -n** bedstead

das **Bett(t)uch, -(e)s, ¨er** sheet

das **Bettzeug, -(e)s** bedding

sich beugen to submit oneself

beurteilen to judge, to criticize

die **Bevölkerung, -en** population

die **Bevölkerungszahl, -en** population figure

bevor before

der **Bevorzugte** the favored one

die **Bewahrung, -en** preservation

bewegen to move, to stir, to agitate

bewegend moving

die **Bewegungsfreiheit** freedom of movement

der **Beweis, -es, -e** proof, evidence

bewirtschaften to cultivate

bewohnen to live or reside in, to occupy

der **Bewohner, -s, -** inhabitant

bewohnt inhabited

bewußt conscious; known

das **Bewußtsein, -s** consciousness

bezahlen to pay

bezeichnen to denote, to stand for

bezeigen to show

die **Beziehung, -en** relationship, reference, connection

die **Bibel, -n** Bible

die **Bibelübersetzung, -en** Bible translation

der **Bienenstock, -(e)s, ¨e** beehive

bieten (bietet), bot, hat geboten to bid, to offer

das **Bild, -es, -er** picture

bilden to form

bildend forming

bis until, as far as, up to

das **Blatt, -es, ¨er** leaf, page

bleiben (bleibt), blieb, ist geblieben to stay, to remain

blicken to glance

bloß simply, only

die **Blume, -n** flower

das **Blut, -es** blood

der **Boden, -s, -** *or* ¨ territory, ground, floor

der **Bodensee, -s** Lake Constance

der **Bolschewist, -en, -en** Bolshevist

das **Böse** evil

brauchen to need

brav good

der **Brief, -s, -e** letter

bringen (bringt), brachte, hat gebracht to bring

das **Brot, -e** bread

der **Bruch, -s, ¨e** hernia

der **Bruder, -s, ¨** the brother

das **Bruttosozialprodukt, -(e)s, -e** gross national product

C

der **Chemiker, -s, -** chemist
der **Christ, -en, -en** Christian
das **Christentum, -s** Christianity
christlich Christian
Christus Christ
Credo quia absurdum. (Latin) I believe it because it is absurd

D

da here, there, since, then, because, in which, when, while, thereupon
dabei at the same time, thereby, close to it (them)
dabei sein to be present, to take part
dabei·sitzen (dabei sitzt), dabei saß, hat dabeigesessen to sit next to, close by
dadurch through it (that), in this way, by this means
dagegen on the other hand, against
daher thus
dahingegen on the other hand
damals at that time
damit with that
Dänemark Denmark
dann then
daran thereon, on it, at it
darauf on that, thereupon
darin in it, within
der **Darm, -(e)s, ⸚e** intestine
dar·stellen to represent
dartun (tut dar), tat dar, hat dargetan to show, to prove
darüber hinaus beyond it (that)
darum therefore
das which, that, the
das **Dasein, -s** existence
die **Daseinsgestaltung** (shaping of) existence
daß that
dauern to last
dauernd constant, continuous
davon by it, of it, from it
die **Decke, -n** cover
der **Deckschild, -(e)s, -e** cover
demgegenüber opposed to which, in relation to which
denkbar thinkable, possible
denken (denkt), dachte, hat gedacht to think
der **Denkende** the thinking person
denn for, because, then
dennoch nevertheless
derjenige, diejenige, dasjenige the one, he, she, that, that one, those, who, they
derselbe, dieselbe, dasselbe the same
deshalb therefore
deutsch German
der **Deutsche, -n, -n** the German
die **Deutung, -en** meaning, signification, interpretation
d.h. = das heißt i.e., that is
die **Diät, -en** diet
der **Dichter, -s, -** poet
die which, who, that, the
dienen to serve
der **Diener, -s, -** servant
der **Dienst, -es, -e** service
der **Dienstag, -(e)s, -e** Tuesday
dies, dieser, diese, dieses this, this one, the latter
diesseitig temporal
die **Diesseitigkeit** temporality, secular life, worldliness
das **Ding, -(e)s, e** thing
doch after all, since, but, nevertheless, though, still, yet, indeed
die **Donau** Danube
dort there
dortig in that town, of that place
drei three
drein = darein along, into that (it)
der **Dreißigjährige Krieg, -es** Thirty Years' War
dreizehn thirteen
dringlich urgent(ly), pressing(ly)
dritte third
drohen to threaten, to menace
die **Duldung** toleration
dunkel dark, somber
der **Dunst, -(e)s, ⸚e** vapor
durch through, by
durchaus absolutely
das **Durchgangsland, -(e)s, ⸚er** country through which others travel, land corridor

dürfen (darf), durfte, hat gedurft to be allowed

E

das **Ebenbild, -(e)s, -er** image
ebenfalls likewise
die **Eberesche, -n** mountain ash, rowan (tree)
die **Ecke, -n** corner
edel noble
die **Ehe, -n** marriage
ehemalig former
eher rather, before
der **Ehestand, -(e)s** married state
die **Ehre, -n** honor
ehrenwert honorable, respectable
die **Ehrfurcht** awe, deep respect, reverence
ehrlich honest(ly)
ehrwürdig respectable
eigen own
die **Eigensucht** selfishness
eigentlich actual(ly)
einander another
sich **ein·bilden** to imagine
der **Eine** one (person)
einer, eine, eines one (thing, person)
einfach simple, simply
der **Einfall, -(e)s, ⸚e** notion
ein·fallen (fällt ein), fiel ein, ist eingefallen to occur, to have an idea
ein·flößen to instil, to strike
der **Einfluß, -sses, ⸚sse** influence
eingeboren innate, inherent, native
der **Eingeborene** native
eingeklemmt strangulated, pinched
der **Eingriff, -(e)s, -e** intervention
die **Einheit, -en** unity
einig united
einige some
einmal once
einmalig unique
der **Einsatz, -es, ⸚e** employment, use
ein·setzen to employ, to put in
einstig former
ein·wenden (wendet ein), wandte ein or **wendete ein, hat eingewandt** or **eingewendet** to object
die **Einwirkung, -en** influence
der **Einwurf, -(e)s, ⸚e** objection
einzeln single, individual
einzig only, single, sole
das **Eisen, -s, -** iron
die **Eisenbahn, -en** railway
die **Eisengießerei, -en** iron foundry
eisern iron (adj.)
der **Eiserne Vorhang** Iron Curtain
das **Elend, -(e)s** misery
das **Elsaß** Alsace
empfinden (empfindet), empfand, hat empfunden to feel
enden to finish
eng narrow, tight, close, confined
engagiert to be employed
die **Enge, -n** closeness, narrowness, tightness
der **Engländer, -s, -** Englishman
entdecken to discover
entfesseln to release
entfliehen (entflieht), entfloh, ist entflohen to flee from, to escape
entgegen·sehen (sieht entgegen), sah entgegen, hat entgegengesehen to look forward to
enthalten (enthält), enthielt, hat enthalten to contain
entleeren to empty out
entreißen (entreißt), entriß, hat entrissen to tear away
entrüstet indignant, angry
entscheiden (entscheidet), entschied, hat entschieden to decide
die **Entscheidung, -en** decision
die **Entschließung, -en** resolution, determination
entsprechen (entspricht), entsprach, hat entsprochen to correspond to
entsprechend corresponding
entstehen (entsteht), entstand, ist entstanden to begin, to originate, to grow out of, to break out of
die **Enttäuschung, -en** disappointment
entweder . . . oder either . . . or
die **Entwicklung, -en** development
sich **entziehen (entzieht sich), entzog sich, hat sich entzogen** to avoid, to shun
das **Erbe, -s** legacy, heritage, inheritance
die **Erbschaft, -en** legacy, inheritance
die **Erde, -n** earth, ground

das **Ereignis, -ses, -se** event
erfahren (erfährt), erfuhr, hat erfahren to find out, to discover, to hear about
die **Erfahrung, -en** experience
der **Erfolg, -(e)s, -e** success, result
sich ergeben (ergibt sich), ergab sich, hat sich ergeben to submit
das **Ergebnis, -ses, -se** result
die **Ergebung, -en** submission
ergehen (ergeht), erging, ist ergangen to happen, to fare, to go
ergreifen (ergreift), ergriff, hat ergriffen to catch (seize, get, lay) hold of
erhalten (erhält), erhielt, hat erhalten to preserve, to maintain, to obtain, to receive
erhöhen to increase
sich erinnern to remember
erkennen (erkennt), erkannte, hat erkannt to recognize
die **Erkenntnis, -se** knowledge (of the truth), comprehension, perception
erklären to declare, to explain
die **Erklärung, -en** explanation, interpretation
erleben to experience
das **Erlebnis, -ses, -se** experience
der **Erlöser, -s, -** redeemer, deliverer
der **Erlöser, -s** (bib.) Savior, Redeemer
ernst serious
ernsthaft serious, grave
ernstlich serious
erregen to excite
erreichen to reach
erschaffen (erschafft), erschuf, hat erschaffen to create
erscheinen (erscheint), erschien, ist erschienen to appear
erst only, first, for the first time
erstaunen to astonish, to amaze
erstaunlich astonishing
erstaunt astonished
ertragen (erträgt), ertrug, hat ertragen to tolerate, to bear
erwachen (aux. **sein**) to awake
der **Erwachsene** adult
erwarten to await
die **Erwartung, -en** expectation
erzählen to tell, to relate
erzeugen to procreate, to breed, to generate, to produce
die **Erziehung** education
erzürnen to get angry
erzwingen (erzwingt), erzwang, hat erzwungen to determine, to force
das **Essen, -s, -** food, eating, meal, dinner, supper
das **Ethische** the ethical
etwa perhaps
etwas something, somewhat

F

die **Fahrt, -en** trip, journey, voyage, drive, ride
der **Fall, -(e)s, ⸚e** case
fallen (fällt), fiel, ist gefallen to fall
die **Farbe, -n** color
fassen to lay hold of, to comprehend, to understand
fast almost, all but
faul lazy
die **Faulheit** laziness
die **Feder, -n** feather
der **Fehler, -s, -** mistake
feiern to celebrate
feige cowardly
die **Feigheit** cowardliness
der **Feind, -(e)s, -e** enemy
die **Feindseligkeit, -en** hostility
das **Fenster, -s, -** window
fern far
ferner furthermore, farther
fest firm, fast, strong, firmly
fest·halten (hält fest), hielt fest, hat festgehalten to hold fast
fest·stehen (steht fest), stand fest, hat festgestanden to stand firm, to be certain
die **Feststellung, -en** ascertainment, observation
das **Feuer, -s, -** fire
finden (findet), fand, hat gefunden to find
die **Firma, -men** (pl.) firm, business
unter der Firma under the style (leadership) of
die **Fixsternsphäre, -n** fixed star, (sphere)
fleißig industrious
fliehen (flieht), floh, ist geflohen to flee

fließen (fließt), floß, ist geflossen to flow
die **Flur, -en** field
die **Folge, -n** succession, consequence, series, continuation; **als Folge** as a consequence
folgen (aux. **sein**) to follow; (aux. **haben**) to obey
folgend following
fördern to promote
forschen to search
fort gone
fort und fort over and over
fort·laufen (läuft fort), lief fort, ist fortgelaufen to run away, to continue on
fortlaufend continuous
fort·schaffen to carry off, to take away
fort·setzen to continue
fort·stäuben to fly away like dust
fortwährend incessantly
die **Frage, -n** question, problem
auf die Fragen Antwort geben to answer the questions
Frankreich France
der **Franzose, -n, -n** Frenchman
französisch French
die **Frau, -en** woman, wife
die **Freiheit** freedom
der **Freitag, -(e)s, -e** Friday
fremd strange, unfamiliar
der **Fremde, -n, -n** stranger
die **Freude, -n** joy
der **Freund, -(e)s, -e** friend
freundlich friendly, in a friendly way
der **Friede, -ns** peace
das **Friedensgerücht, -(e)s, -e** rumor of peace
friedlich peaceable
der **Friese, -n, -n** Frisian
frisch fresh
früh early
sich fügen to subordinate oneself
fühlen to feel, to perceive
führen to lead, to carry, to bring, to wage
führend leading
der **Führer, -s, -** leader
die **Fülle** fullness
fünf five
der **Fünfte** fifth one (male person)
fünfundvierzig forty-five
fünfzig fifty
der **Funke, -n, -n** spark
für for
die **Furcht** fear
furchtbar terrible, fearful, awful, frightful
fürchten to fear
die **Fürstin, -nen** princess
der **Fußboden, -s, ¨** floor

G

der **Gang, -(e)s, ¨e** walk
ganz complete, completely, whole, entire, entirely, totally, very, all
ganz und gar entirely
das **Ganze** the whole (**ein Ganzes** a whole), the whole thing
gar even
das **Gäßchen, -s, -** lane
die **Gasse, -n** street (narrow), alley
gebären (gebiert), gebar, hat geboren to give birth to, to produce
geben (gibt), gab, hat gegeben to give
es gibt there is (are)
es gab there was (were)
gebend giving
das **Gebiet, -(e)s, -e** field, area
gebieten (gebietet), gebot, hat geboten to tell, to order, to command
das **Gebirgsland, -(e)s, ¨er** mountainous country
geboren born
das **Gebot, -(e)s, -e** commandment
die **Geburt, -en** birth
der **Gedanke, -ns, -n** thought, idea
die **Gefahr, -en** danger
das **Gefängnis, -ses, -se** prison
gefaßt composed
das **Gefühl, -(e)s, -e** sentiment, feeling
gegen toward(s), against
gegeneinander contrary to, opposing one another, against
der **Gegensatz, -es, ¨e** contrast
gegenseitig mutual, reciprocal
der **Gegenstand, -(e)s, ¨e** subject
gegenüber towards
die **Gegenüberstellung, -en** confrontation
gegenwärtig present
der **Gegner, -s, -** opponent

geheim secret
das **Geheimnis, -ses, -se** secret, mystery
gehen (geht), ging, ist gegangen to go, to walk
gehören to belong
der **Geist, -es, -er** spirit
geistig spiritual
gelangen to reach
das **Geld, -es, -er** money
die **Gelegenheit, -en** opportunity, occasion
die Gelegenheit on the occasion of
gelingen (gelingt), gelang, ist gelungen to succeed
gelten (gilt), galt, hat gegolten to be considered
gemeinsam common, together
gemessen measured
gemessen am Weltkrieg compared to a world war
genau precisely, exactly
das **Genie, -s, -s** genius
genießen (genießt), genoß, hat genossen to enjoy
genügend sufficient
geordnet ordered
geraten (gerät), geriet, ist geraten to fall into
geraum roomy, spacious, ample
für geraume Zeit for a long time, for some time
der **Gerechte, -n, -n** the just individual, righteous man
die **Gerechtigkeit, -en** justice
gering slight, little
die **Geringschätzung, -en** disdain
der **Germane, -n, -n** Teuton
gern with pleasure, gladly, readily, willingly
gerührt full of emotion
gesamt entire, total
das **Geschäft, -(e)s, -e** business
geschehen (geschieht), geschah, ist geschehen to happen, to occur
gescheit shrewd, clever, intelligent
die **Geschichte, -n** history, story
geschickt skilled
das **Geschlecht, -(e)s, -er** generation
das **Geschöpf, -(e)s, -e** creature
das **Geschrei, -s** cry, cries, shouting, shouts
die **Gesellschaft, -en** society, company
das **Gesetz, -es, -e** law
das **Gesicht, -(e)s, -er** face
die **Gesinnung, -en** disposition, characteristic way of thinking, mental attitude
das **Gespenst, -es, -er** ghost, apparition, phantom, specter
die **Gestalt, -en** shape, figure
gestern yesterday
das **Gestirn, -(e)s, -e** star, constellation
gesund healthy
der **Gesunde, -n, -n** the healthy man
die **Gesundheit** health
gewähren to grant, to allow
die **Gewalt, -en** power
gewaltig gigantic, powerful
gewinnen (gewinnt), gewann, hat gewonnen to acquire, to gain
gewiß certainly
die **Gewißheit, -en** certainty
sich gewöhnen to accustom, to familiarize
gewöhnlich usual, ordinary
etwas Gewöhnliches something quite usual
gewohnt accustomed
gewünscht desired, wished
das **Giftgas, -es, -e** poison gas
der **Glaube, -ns** religious faith
glauben to believe, to think, to suppose
gleich like, equal, similar, same
gleich·achten to esteem alike
gleichmäßig uniform, similar, equal
gleich·stellen to place on the same level
die **Glocke, -n** bell
das **Glück, -(e)s** luck, happiness
glücklich happy
glücklichst luckiest, happiest, most advantageous, most fortunate
die **Gnade, -n** privilege, mercy
der **Gott, -es, ¨-er** god, deity, God
göttlich divine, godly
grau gray
grauenhaft horrible, dreadful, ghastly, hideous
grausam cruel, brutal, fierce
grausig gruesome, grisly, lurid, weird
greifen (greift), griff, hat gegriffen to grasp, to touch
der **Greis, -es, -e** old man
die **Grenze, -n** border
groß great, large, big

großartig splendid
Großbritannien Great Britain
die **Großen** the great nations
die **Großmacht, ¨-e** great power
der **Grund, -(e)s, ¨-e** basis
der **Grundbegriff, -(e)s, -e** fundamental concept
der **Grundbesitz, -es** landed property, real estate
die **Grundgegebenheit, -en** fundamental factor
die **Grundidee, -n** fundamental idea
die **Grundlage, -n** foundation, basis
gründlich thoroughly
das **Grundstück, -(e)s, -e** real property *or* estate
grüßen to greet
Grüß Gott! Good day (to you)!
günstig favorable
gut good, well
das **Gut, -(e)s, ¨-er** treasure, property, goods
das **Gute** the good

H

haben (hat), hatte, hat gehabt to have
die **Haft** arrest
das **Hagestolzenleben, -s** life of a bachelor
halb half
halt just
halten (hält), hielt, hat gehalten to hold
das **Hammerwerk, -(e)s, -e** iron works
die **Hand, ¨-e** hand
der **Handspiegel, -s, -** hand mirror
hängen (hängt), hing, hat gehangen to hang
die **Hansestadt, ¨-e** Hanseatic city
die **Härte** hardness
der **Haß, -sses** hatred
hassen to hate
hassenswert hateful
der **Haufen, -s, -** pile
häufig frequent
am häufigsten most frequently
das **Haupt, -(e)s, ¨-er** head
die **Hauptstadt, ¨-e** capital city
das **Hauptziel, -(e)s, -e** main objective
das **Haus, -es, ¨-er** home, house
die **Haustür(e), -en** front door
der **Heeresbericht, -s, -e** army communiqué
heilig holy
der **Heilige, -n, -n** saint
das **Heimatgefühl, -(e)s, -e** love for one's home
heim·kommen (kommt heim), kam heim, ist heimgekommen to come or return home
heimlich (adj.) secret, concealed, hidden; (adv.) secretly, furtively, stealthily
heiß hot
heißen (heißt), hieß, hat geheißen to name, to be called, to mean, to command
helfen (hilft), half, hat geholfen to help
herab down
heran·ziehen (zieht heran), zog heran, hat herangezogen to draw upon, to consult, to summon
herauf up
heraus·heben (hebt heraus), hob heraus, hat herausgehoben to lift out
der **Herbst, -es, -e** autumn
der **Herd, -(e)s, -e** stove
der **Herr, -n, -en** master, lord, God, Mister
die **Herrlichkeit, -en** grandeur
her·rühren to originate, to come from
die **Herstellung, -en** production, establishment, making, bringing about
herum about, on this account
das **Herz, -en, -en** heart
heulen to howl, to cry, to scream
heulend howling
heute today
heutig present day
hier here
hierhin here, this way
hierin herein, in this
hiervon out of this, from this
die **Hilfe, -n** help
der **Himmel, -s, -** sky, heaven, the heavens
himmlisch heavenly
hinaus·langen to reach out (beyond)
darüber hinaus·langen to reach beyond that (this)
das **Hinausschieben** postponement
hindern to hinder
hindurch through, over, throughout, all through
hin·geben (gibt hin), gab hin, hat hingegeben to give away

sich **hin·geben (gibt sich hin), gab sich hin, hat sich hingegeben** to devote, to submit, to execute
die **Hinsicht, -en** respect, view
hinter behind
der **Hintergedanke, -ns, -n** ulterior motive
hinterlassen (hinterläßt), hinterließ, hat hinterlassen to leave behind
das **Hinterstübchen, -s, -** small back room
der **Hinweis, -es, -e** reference, allusion, hint
hin·ziehen (zieht hin), zog hin, hat hingezogen to attract, to be drawn to
hinzu·fügen to add, to append, to join
historisch historic, historically
die **Hitze** heat
der **Hochofen, -s, ̈** blast furnace
höchst highest, greatest
hoffen to hope
die **Hoffnung, -en** hope
die **Hölle** hell
hören to hear
hübsch pretty
die **Humanität** humanity
der **Hund -(e)s, -e** dog
hundert hundred
die **Hütte, -n** cottage, hut

I

die **Idealforderung, -en** ideal standard
die **Idee, -n** idea
ihm (to) him
ihnen (to) them
ihr (to) her, you, her
ihre her, their, its
ihrerseits for their part, for her part
im in (the)
immer always, ever
immer noch still
immer wieder always, again and again
in into, in
indem in that, while, as, since
inmitten in the middle of, in the midst of
inner inner
innerlich within, inwardly, spiritually
das **Interesse, -s, -n** interest
irgend some, any
irgendein some, any, someone, anyone
irgendwann at some time or other
irgendwie in any way, somehow
irre·werden (wird irre), wurde irre, ist irregeworden to become disconcerted, confused, perplexed, lost
Italien Italy
italienisch Italian

J

ja yes, truly, even, of course
die **Jacke, -n** jacket
das **Jahr, -es, -e** year
die **Jahreszeit, -en** season
das **Jahrhundert, -s, -e** century
-jährig year old
jämmerlich wretched, deplorable, piteous, woeful
jammern to lament, to moan, to yammer, to whine, to mourn
jammernd moaning, lamenting
je ever
je nun why!, well (now)!
je . . . desto the . . . the
jeder, jede, jedes each, every
jedesmal every time, each time, always
jedoch however, yet, still
jeglich every, each
jemand someone, somebody
jener, jene, jenes that, the former
jetzt now, at present
Johannes der Täufer John the Baptist
das **Journal, -(e)s, -e** newspaper, magazine, journal, diary
jüdisch Jewish
Jugoslawien Yugoslavia
jung young
der **Junge, -n, -n** youth (boy)
der **Junggeselle, -n, -n** bachelor
der **Jüngling, -s, -e** youth, young man, lad, adolescent, youngster
die **Juristerei** law

K

der **Kaffeestrauch, -(e)s, ̈er** coffee bush
das **Kaffeetrinken** drinking of coffee
der **Kaiser, -s, -** emperor
die **Kaiserstadt, ̈e** imperial city

der **Kalte Krieg** Cold War
der **Kampf, -(e)s, ⸚e** struggle
kämpfen to fight, to struggle
kämpfend fighting, struggling
die **Kantine, -n** canteen
der **Käse, -s, -** cheese
die **Katastrophengefahr, -en** danger of catastrophe
kaum scarcely, hardly
kein, keine, kein no (one), none, no
kennen (kennt), kannte, hat gekannt to know
kennen·lernen to get to know
der **Kerl, -s, -e** fellow, chap, character
das **Kind, -(e)s, -er** child
der **Kirchenmann, -es, ⸚er** churchman
kirchlich ecclesiastical, churchly, clerical
klar clear
der **Klassenkampf, -(e)s, ⸚e** class struggle
klassisch classic(al)
kleben to stick, to paste, to glue
die **Kleidung** clothes, clothing, dress
klein small
im kleinen on a small scale
das **Kloster, -s, ⸚** monastery, convent
klug smart, intelligent, bright, clever
der **Knabe, -n, -n** boy, youth, lad
das **Kollegienlesen** giving of lectures
kommandieren to command, to order
die **Kommassation** reallocation of land
kommen (kommt), kam, ist gekommen to come
das **Kommende** (the) coming thing
der **Komponist, -en, -en** composer
der **König, -(e)s, -e** king
das **Königreich, -s, -e** kingdom
das **Konkubinat, -(e)s, -e** concubinage
können (kann), konnte, hat gekonnt to be able to, can
der **Kopf, -(e)s, ⸚e** head
der **Körper, -s, -** body
kostbar precious
die **Kraft, ⸚e** power, force, strength
kramen to rummage
krank sick
der **Kranke** invalid, sick person
die **Krankheit, -en** illness, disease
unter Krankheiten from diseases
der **Krieg, -(e)s, -e** war
kriegen to get
die **Kritik, -en** criticism
die **Krume, -n** crumb, speck
krumm crooked, bent, curved, twisted
der **Kuhfuß, -es, ⸚e** cow's foot
der **Kulturbereich, -(e)s, -e** cultural sphere
die **Kulturgesellschaft, -en** civilized society
der **Künstler, -s, -** artist, performer

L

lächeln to smile
der **Laden, -s, ⸚** shop, store
der **Laffe, -n, -n** fop
die **Lage, -n** position, condition, situation
die **Lampe, -n** lamp
das **Land, -(e)s, ⸚er** state, countryside, country, land
die **Landkarte, -n** map
die **Landstraße, -n** highway
lang long
langen to reach
lassen (läßt), ließ, hat gelassen to let, to leave, to cause
das **Laster, -s, -** vice, depravity, viciousness
der **Laszive** lascivious person, sensualist
das **Laub, -(e)s** foliage, leaves
der **Lauf, -(e)s, ⸚e** course, path
laufen (läuft), lief, ist gelaufen to run
lauschen to listen
lauten to say, to sound
lautlos soundless
lawinenartig resembling an avalanche
leben to live
das **Leben, -s** life, lifetime
auf Leben und Tod to the death
lebend living
lebendig living, alive, lively
das **Lebensgeheimnis, -ses, -se** mystery of life
die **Lebensgeschichte, -n** life history (story)
die **Lebensgier** desire to live
die **Lebensmittel** food (stuffs), groceries
der **Lebensraum, -s** living space, sphere of existence
das **Lebewesen, -s, -** living being, living creature
leer empty, void
die **Leere -n** emptiness, void(ness)
leergelassen left empty
legen to lay, to place

die **Legendenbildung, -en** formation of a legend
lehren to teach
der **Leib, -(e)s, -er** body
die **Leiche, -n** corpse, dead body
leicht easy
leiden (leidet), litt, hat gelitten to suffer
das **Leiden, -s, -** the suffering
die **Leidenschaft, -en** passion
leidenschaftslos apathetic, dispassionate, calm
leider unfortunately
leisten to accomplish
die **Leitung, -en** guidance, direction, control, leadership
lernen to learn
lesen (liest), las, hat gelesen to read
letzt last
leuchten to shine
die **Leute** (pl.) people
der **Liberalismus** liberalism
lieb dear, beloved
die **Liebe** love
lieben to love
liebenswert worthy of love
liegen (liegt), lag, hat gelegen to lie, to be situated, to be located
die **Lindenallee, -n** linden drive, linden avenue
die **Linie, -n** line
in erster Linie above all
das **Loch, -(e)s, ¨-er** hole
lokal local
los·lassen (läßt los), ließ los, hat losgelassen to let loose
der **Lumpen, -s, -** rag, tatter
die **Lust, ¨-e** enjoyment, desire, wish, lust
der **Lustmörder, -s, -** sex murderer

M

machen to make, to do
die **Macht, ¨-e** power, force, command, control
das **Machtinteresse, -s, -n** interest in power, desire for power
machtlos powerless
das **Mädel, -s, -** girl
die **Magie** magic
der **Magister** master (degree)
magyarisch Magyar
der **Majoritätsbeschluß, -sses, ¨-sse** resolution carried by a majority
das **Mal, -(e)s, -e** time, occasion
ein Mal once, one time
einige Male several times
man one, they, we, you, people, men
mancher, manche, manches many, many a; (pl.) some
manchmal sometimes
der **Mangel, -s, ¨** lack, defect, shortage
der **Mann, -es, ¨-er** man, male, husband
männlich male, masculine
das **Mannschaftsbordell, -s, -e** troop's brothel
das **Märchen, -s, -** fairy tale
das **Maß, -es, -e** degree, extent, measure, moderation, dimension
massenhaft abundant, numerous, wholesale
die **Maßnahme, -n** arrangement, measure
Maßnahmen treffen to take measures
die **Maßregel, -n** measure
der **Mathematiker, -s, -** mathematician
die **Mauer, -n** the wall
die **Medizin, -en** medicine
mehr more
mehrere several
die **Meile, -n** mile
meinen to be of the opinion, to mean, to suppose
meist most, mostly
melden to report
der **Mensch, -en, -en** human being, man, person
die **Menschenliebe** love of one's fellow man, philanthropy
das **Menschenrecht, -(e)s, -e** human right
das **Menschentum, -s** human race
die **Menschheit** humanity, man(kind), human race
menschlich human
messen (mißt), maß, hat gemessen to measure
die **Messestadt, ¨-e** trade fair city
mich me
die **Milch** milk
das **Militär, -s** military
minder less
der **Mißbrauch, -s, ¨-e** abuse, misuse

mißbräuchlich improper, wrong
der **Mißerfolg, -(e)s, -e** failure
die **Mißgeburt, -en** monstrosity, abortion, miscarriage
der **Mißratene, -n, -n** misfit
mit with
das **Mitleid, -(e)s** compassion, pity
mit-leiden (leidet mit), litt mit, hat mitgelitten to suffer with
mittags in the afternoon
die **Mitte** the middle
das **Mittel, -s, -** means
Mitteleuropa central Europe
der **Mittelpunkt, -(e)s, -e** center
das **Möbel, -s, -** (piece of) furniture
möchten would like (subjunctive)
das **Modell, -(e)s, -e** model
mögen (mag), mochte, hat gemocht to like to
möglich possible
die **Möglichkeit, -en** possibility, opportunity
der **Monat, -(e)s, -e** month
der **Mond, -(e)s, -e** moon
der **Montag, -(e)s, -e** Monday
die **Moral** morality, morals
moralinfrei free of moral hypocrisy
der **Mord, -(e)s, -e** murder
morgen tomorrow
der **Morgen, -s** morning
morgens in the morning
müde tired, weary, drowsy
die **Mühe, -n** trouble, pains, toil
München Munich
der **Mund -(e)s, ¨er** mouth
die **Mundart, -en** dialect
der **Musiker, -s, -** musician
müssen (muß), mußte, hat gemußt must, to have to
der **Mut, -(e)s** courage
die **Mutter, ¨** mother
die **Muttersprache** mother tongue
der **Mythos/Mythus, -, Mythen** myth

N

nach for, after, from, according to, toward
der **Nachbar, -s, -n** neighbor
das **Nachbarland, -(e)s, ¨er** neighboring country
nach·denken (denkt nach), dachte nach, hat nachgedacht to reflect, ponder
der **Nachfolger, -s, -** successor, follower
nach·forschen to investigate
nachmittags in the afternoon
nächst next
der **Nächste, -n, -n** neighbor, the next (person)
die **Nacht, ¨e** night
die **Nachtarbeit, -en** night work
die **Nachtmannschaft, -en** night shift
das **Nachtpersonal, -(e)s** night staff
die **Nachtzeit** night time
nach·weisen (weist nach), wies nach, hat nachgewiesen to point out, to prove
nackt naked
nah near, closely
die **Nahrung** food
der **Name, -ns, -n** name
nämlich namely, that is (to say), because
die **Nase, -n** nose
natürlich naturally
neben beside, next to
der **Neger, -s, -** negro
nehmen (nimmt), nahm, hat genommen to take
nennen (nennt), nannte, hat genannt to call, to name
neu new, recent, modern
neun nine
neunjährig nine year old
neunzehnjährig nineteen year old
nicht not
nichts nothing
  nichts anderes nothing else
nie never
die **Niederlande** the Netherlands
sich **niederlassen (läßt sich nieder), ließ sich nieder, hat sich niedergelassen** to settle down
niemand nobody, no one
das **Niveau, -s, -s** level
noch still, yet; nor (see **weder**)
  noch etwas one thing more, something else, anything else
das **Nomadenvolk, -(e)s, ¨er** nomadic people
nominell nominal

der **Norden, -s** north
nordöstlich northeastern
die **Nordsee** the North Sea
nötig necessary
die **Notsituation, -en** state of distress, state of emergency
notwendig necessary, necessarily, urgent
die **Nummer, -n** number
nun now, at present
nunmehr now, by this time
nur only, merely, but, just
nur noch still, only just, barely
der **Nutzen, -s** advantage, profit, benefit

O

die **Oberfläche, -n** surface
obig above (mentioned), former
obwohl although
oder or
offen open, unclosed, not shut
offenbar obvious, evident, apparent
öffentlich open(ly), (in) public
der **Offizier, -s, -e** officer
oft often, frequently, many times
Ogowe a river in Africa
ohne without
ohne alle und jede politische Erziehung without any kind of political education
ohne allen und jeden politischen Willen without any kind of political will
ökonomisch economic(al)
ordnen to arrange, to order, to organize
die **Ordnung, -en** order, putting in order, tidiness
der **Ostdeutsche, -n, -n** East German (person), inhabitant of East Germany
Ostdeutschland East Germany
der **Osten, -s** east
Österreich Austria
osteuropäisch East European
die **Ostsee** the Baltic Sea

P

packen to seize, to pack
die **Pappel, -n** poplar
die **Partei, -en** party, faction
Partei ergreifen to espouse a cause
der **Parteifunktionär, -s, -e** party official
der **Parteikampf, -(e)s, ¨-e** party struggle
der **Pazifismus** pacifism
die **Persönlichkeit, -en** individual
der **Pfaffe, -n, -n** parson, priest
der **Pfarrer, -s, -** pastor, clergyman, parson
das **Phänomen, -s, -e** phenomenon
die **Phantasie, -n** imagination, fancy, tale, fiction
der **Philosophengang, -es, ¨-e** philosopher's walk
plagen to plague, to pester, to bother, to worry, to torment
platt shallow, level, flat, even
der **Platz, -es, ¨-e** place, locality
Polen Poland
die **Politik** politics
der **Politiker, -s, -** politician
politisch political, politic
der **Polizeidiener, -s, -** policeman
das **Polizeigericht, -(e)s, -e** police court
der **Polizeirichter, -s, -** police magistrate
praktisch practical, pragmatic, practically
preisen (preist), pries, hat gepriesen to praise, to glorify
Preußen Prussia
preußisch Prussian
das **Prinzip, -s, -ien** principle
privatissime (Latin) most private
die **Produktionskosten** (pl.) costs of production
der **Professor, -s, -en** professor
die **Projektion, -en** projection
der **Proletarier, -s, -** proletarian
proportional in proportion, proportionately
die **Provinz, -en** province
das **Prozent, -(e)s, -e** percent
der **Punkt, -(e)s, -e** point

Q

die **Qual, -en** pain, torment, pang, agony
sich quälen to work oneself to death, to agonize
quer across

R

rasend furious, mad
die **Rasse, -n** race, breed, stock
die **Rassenhygiene** eugenics
die **Rassenmischung, -en** miscegenation
die **Rassenschande, -n** racial defilement
ratlos perplexed, helpless
die **Ratlosigkeit** perplexity
das **Raubtier, -(e)s, -e** beast of prey
der **Raum, -(e)s, ¨-e** space, area, expanse, room
der **Rausch, -es, ¨-e** intoxication, inebriation, ecstasy
das **Rauschen** rustle
recht right
das **Recht, -(e)s, -e** right
die **Rede, -n** speech, address, oration
reden to speak
regelmäßig regular, regularly, well regulated, orderly
der **Regen, -s** rain
die **Regierung, -en** government
das **Register, -s, -** record, register, list
reiben (reibt), rieb, hat gerieben to rub
das **Reich, -(e)s, -e** empire
der **Reiche, -n, -n** rich person
die **Reichsgesetzgebung, -en** legislation of the Reich
die **Reichstagsrede, -n** speech made before the Reichstag
die **Reihe, -n** series, row
rein pure, purely, clean
die **Reinerhaltung** preservation of purity
reinigen to cleanse
die **Relativitätstheorie** theory of relativity
der **Religionsphilosoph, -en, -en** religious philosopher
der **Renaissance-Stil, -(e)s** Renaissance style
retten to save, to rescue, to preserve, to deliver
die **Rettung, -en** deliverance, rescue, saving
richten to judge, to try, to sentence, to arrange, to set (right)
der **Richter, -s, -** judge
richtig true, right, real
rieseln to ripple, to murmur
der **Rock, -(e)s, ¨-e** coat, skirt
das **Rohr, -(e)s, -e** cane, pipe, reed, tube
die **Rolle, -n** role
die **Romanen** Neo-Latin people (Romance nations)
romanisch neo-Latin
Romaunsch Romansh, Romansch
der **Römer, -s, -** Roman (person)
die **Römerzeit** the time of the Romans
die **Rücksicht, -en** consideration, regard, respect
die **Ruhe** rest, quiet, peace, calm
die **Ruheperiode, -n** period of rest, lull, pause
ruhig calm, quiet, peaceful
rühren to move, to stir, to affect, to touch
Rumänien Rumania
Rußland Russia
die **Rüstung, -en** armor, armament, (military) equipment

S

die **Saat, -en** seed
die **Sache, -n** thing
Sachsen Saxony
die **Sage, -n** legend, fable, myth
sagen to tell, to say, to express
der **Same(n), -ns, -n** seed
sammeln to collect
der **Samstag, -(e)s, -e** Saturday
sämtlich all
die **Sanduhr, -en** hourglass
Sapere aude! (Latin) Dare to know!
der **Satz, -es, ¨-e** sentence, tenet
sauer sour
der **Schade(n), -ns, ¨-n** damage, harm, injury
schädigen to wrong, to prejudice
schädlich damaging, injurious, detrimental
schaffen, (schafft), schuf, hat geschaffen to bring, to pass, to create
die **Schande, -n** disgrace, defilement, shame
der **Scharfrichter, -s, -** executioner, hangman
schätzen to value, to estimate, to esteem
schauen to look, to see, to observe
scheinen (scheint), schien, hat geschienen to shine, to appear, to seem
die **Scheu** respect, shyness
das **Schicksal, -(e)s, -e** fate, destiny, fortune

schier very nearly, almost, sheer, utter
die **Schlächterei, -en** slaughter, butchery
die **Schlafbaracke, -n** sleeping quarters, dormitory
die **Schläfe, -n** temple
schlafen (schläft), schlief, hat geschlafen to sleep, to be asleep
schlecht bad, badly, poor, poorly
schlechthin simply
schließlich finally, in conclusion
schlucken to swallow, to gulp, to drink (down)
schlummern to slumber, to lie dormant
schmal narrow, slim, thin
der **Schmerz, -e(n)s, -en** pain, ache, sorrow, grief, anguish
schmerzlich painful, aching
die **Schmiede, -n** forge
der **Schnee, -s** snow
die **Schokolade, -n** chocolate
schon no doubt, surely, already, as early as
schön beautiful
die **Schönheit, -en** beauty
der **Schöpfer, -s, -** creator
schöpferisch creative, inventive, original
der **Schöpferwille, -ns** creative will
die **Schöpfung, -en** creation
der **Schrecken, -s, -** terror, fright, alarm, shock
schrecklich frightful, dreadful, terrible, awful
das **Schreiben** writing, letter
der **Schreiber, -s, -** scribe, writer (of a letter)
die **Schuld, -en** guilt, fault, blame
der **Schüler, s, -** pupil, schoolboy, student, disciple
die **Schürze, -n** apron
das **Schurzfell, -(e)s, -e** leather apron
der **Schutz, -es** protection, defence
schwach weak, feeble, frail
der **Schwache, -n, -n** weakling
die **Schwäche, -n** weakness, feebleness, frailty, infirmity
schwanken to waver, to wave to and fro, to totter
schwarz black, dark
der **Schwarze, -n, -n** negro, black man
der **Schweiß, -es** sweat, perspiration
die **Schweiz** Switzerland
schwer serious, difficult, hard, heavy
die **Schwermut** melancholy, sadness, dejection
der **Schwerpunkt, -(e)s, -e** emphasis, stress, focal point, center of gravity
schwerverständlich difficult to understand
schwierig difficult, hard, delicate, tough
die **Schwierigkeit, -en** difficulty
der **Schwindel, -s** humbug, swindle, fraud
sechs six
die **Seele, -n** soul
der **Seelsorger, -s, -** pastor
sehen (sieht), sah, hat gesehen to look, to view, to see
sehr very
sei es be it
sein (ist), war, ist gewesen to be
sein, seine, sein his, its
das **Sein, -s** being, existence, essence, true nature
die **Seinen** (pl.) his loved ones, his family
seinetwegen because of him
seit since
seitdem since then, from that time, ever after
selber myself, himself, yourself, themselves, etc.
selbst oneself, myself, yourself, etc.; even (adv.)
selbständig independent, self-reliant
selbstverschuldet self-imposed
selten seldom, rare, unusual
der **Sessel, -s, -** armchair, seat
setzen to place
sich himself, herself, itself, themselves, yourself, yourselves, oneself, each other
sicher sure, certain, secure, safe
sicherlich surely
sichern to secure, to steady, to fortify, to guarantee
sie she, her, it, they, them
sieben seven
der **Sinn, -es, -e** meaning, mind, sense, intellect
sitzen (sitzt), saß, hat gesessen to sit
der **Skandinavier, -s, -** Scandinavian (person)
der **Slawe, -n, -n** Slav (person)
slawisch Slavic
so so, thus, therefore, then

so ein, so eine such a
sogar even
sogenannt so-called, as it is called
sogleich immediately
der **Sohn, -(e)s, ⸚e** son
solange as long as
solch ein such a
der **Soldat, -en, -en** soldier
sollen (soll), sollte, hat gesollt to be obliged, to be supposed to
sonderbar strange, singular, peculiar, odd
sondern but
die **Sonne, -n** sun
sonstig other, former
die **Sorge, -n** care, grief, sorrow, anxiety
sorgen to care for, to take care of, to look after
soviel so much
der **Sozialethiker, -s, -** social moralist
der **Sozialismus** socialism
spalten to split, to divide
spärlich scanty, frugal, meager
spät late
spazieren (aux. **sein**) to walk (leisurely), to stroll
das **Spazierengehen** going for a walk
der **Spiegel, -s, -** mirror, reflector
spielen to play
die **Spitze, -n** head, point, top
die **Sprache, -n** language
sprachlich linguistic(ally)
sprechen (spricht), sprach, hat gesprochen to speak, to talk
der **Sprung, -(e)s, ⸚e** jump, leap, crack
spüren to feel, to notice
der **Staat, -(e)s, -en** the state, government
das **Staatsleben, -s** life of a state, political life
der **Staatsmann, -es, ⸚er** statesmen
staatsmännisch statesmanlike
die **Staatsordnung, -en** political system, political order
die **Stadt, ⸚e** town, city
der **Stahlfabrikant, -en, -en** steel manufacturer
der **Stamm, -(e)s, ⸚e** tribe, race, family
stammen to come from, to stem from, to be descended from
ständig constant, continuously
der **Standpunkt, -(e)s, -e** point of view
stark strong, stout
die **Stärke** strength, force, robustness
der **Stärkere, -n, -n** stronger one (person)
statt instead of
statt·finden (findet statt), fand statt, hat stattgefunden to take place
stehen (steht), stand, hat gestanden to stand, to remain standing, to be, to stop
stehlen (stiehlt), stahl, hat gestohlen to steal
steigern to raise, to heighten
stellen to set
sterben (stirbt), starb, ist gestorben to die
das **Sterben** dying
der **Stern, -(e)s, -e** star
still quiet, calm, motionless, peaceful
das **Stillschweigen, -s** silence
die **Stirne, -n** forehead
stocken to come to a standstill
stolz proud, haughty, disdainful
die **Straße, -n** street
die **Strecke, -n** way, distance, stretch, route
auf der Strecke by the wayside
streuen to strew
das **Strohdach, -(e)s, ⸚er** thatched roof
das **Stück, -(e)s, -e** piece, part, portion, fragment, play
die **Stunde, -n** hour
der **Sturm, -(e)s, ⸚e** storm
der **Sturz, -es, ⸚e** fall, tumble, collapse
suchen to search for, to look for, to seek
der **Süden, -s** south
südeuropäisch South European
südlich southern (to the south)
der **Südosten, -s** southeast
summen to buzz, to hum
der **Sünder, -s, -** sinner

T

der **Tag, -(e)s, -e** day
tagelang for days
die **Tagesarbeit, -en** day's work
die **Tageszeit, -en** time of day
das **Tag(e)werk, -(e)s** daily work, routine
das **Tal, -(e)s, ⸚er** valley
die **Taschenuhr, -en** pocket watch
die **Tat, -en** act, action, deed, achievement
tätig active, actively
tatsächlich in fact, as a matter of fact

das **Tausend, -s, -e** thousand
tausendjährig millenial
der **Teil, -(e)s, -e** part, piece, portion, section
zum Teil in part, partly
teilen to divide
teilweise in part, partial, partially
der **Teufel, -s, -** devil
der **Theolog(e), -en, -en** theologian, divine
theoretisch theoretical, theoretically
die **These, -n** thesis
tief deep, profound
die **Tiefe, -n** depth, deep, deep place, profoundness, profundity
tief unter dem Niveau far below the level
das **Tier, -(e)s, -e** animal, (dumb) creature, beast, brute
der **Tod, -(e)s, -e** death
der **Tor, -en, -en** fool, simpleton
tot dead
die **Totenschau, -en** coroner's inquest
tragen (trägt), trug, hat getragen to wear, to carry, to bear
der **Traum, -(e)s, ¨e** dream
treffen (trifft), traf, hat getroffen to strike, to hit, to meet
trennen to divide
treten (tritt), trat, ist (hat) getreten to enter, to step, to walk, to tread
das **Trommelfeuer, -s** ceaseless bombardment
der **Tropfen, -s, -** drop
trotz in spite of
der **Trotz, -es** spite, defiance, obstinacy
trotzdem nevertheless
trübe gloomy, dejected, sad, downcast, cloudy, overcast
die **Tschechoslowakei** Czechoslovakia
die **Tuberkel, -n** tubercle
die **Tüchtigkeit** efficiency, ability, proficiency
die **Tugend, -en** virtue, good quality
der **Tugendbold, -(e)s, -e** paragon of virtue
tun (tut), tat, hat getan to do, to perform
die **Tür(e), -en** door

U

über over
überdies besides, moreover
überflüssig superfluous
übergehen (übergeht), überging, hat übergangen to overlook, to omit, to skip
überhaupt in general, on the whole, altogether, at all
überhaupt nicht not at all
überlassen (überläßt), überließ, hat überlassen to give *or* to yield up, to leave, to abandon
die **Übermacht** supreme power, superiority, superior numbers
der **Übermut, -(e)s** pride, presumption, haughtiness, arrogance
übermütig presumptuous, haughty
übernehmen (übernimmt), übernahm, hat übernommen to take over, to take possession of
überschätzen to overestimate, to overrate
überschreiten (überschreitet), überschritt, hat überschritten to exceed, to overstep
übersehen (übersieht), übersah, hat übersehen to overlook
die **Übertreibung, -en** exaggeration, overstatement
überwachen to watch over, to supervise
überwinden (überwindet), überwand, hat überwunden to overcome
die **Überwindung, -en** overcoming, conquest
die **Uhr, -en** clock, watch, o'clock
das **Uhrwerk, -(e)s, -e** clockwork
um in order to, at, around, about
um·drehen to turn (around), to twist
umfassend extensive, comprehensive
umgeben (umgibt), umgab, hat umgeben to surround, to wall *or* fence in
umgekehrt vice versa, reversed
umgrenzt enclosed
umher·schauen to look around
umringen (umringt), umrang, hat umrungen to surround, to encircle, to enclose
umschließen (umschließt), umschloß, hat umschlossen to surround, to enclose
die **Umwelt** environment, the world around us, milieu
unanwendbar inapplicable, unusable
unaufhaltsam irresistible, unavoidable, unflagging
die **Unbefangenheit** ease, simplicity, naiveté
das **Unbehagen, -s** discomfort, uneasiness,

qualm
die **Unbill, -bilden** injustice, injury, insult, wrongs
und and
undurchgänglich impassable, blocked
unendlich infinite, endless, boundless
unergründlich unfathomable, inscrutable
unfähig incapable, unfit
unfaßbar inconceivable, incomprehensible
unfruchtbar unfruitful, barren, sterile, unproductive
Ungarn Hungary
ungefähr approximately, roughly, almost, about
der **Ungerechte, -n, -n** unjust *or* unfair person
das **Ungewisse** uncertainty, doubt
das **Ungeziefer, -s** vermin
unglaublich incredible, unbelievable
das **Unglück, -(e)s** accident, misfortune, ill luck, calamity
das **Universum, -s** universe
unmittelbar immediate, direct
unmöglich impossible
unmündig immature
die **Unmündigkeit** immaturity
das **Unrecht, -(e)s** injustice, wrong
unruhig restless, troubled
uns ourselves, us
unschwer easily, without difficulty, easy, not difficult
unser our
unsererseits for our part, as for us
der **Unstern, -(e)s** unlucky *or* evil star, misfortune, disaster, adverse fate
unteilbar indivisible
unter under, among
untereinander together, one (with) another, among one another, each other
unter·gehen (geht unter), ging unter, ist untergegangen to perish, to go down, to become extinct
unterhalten (unterhält), unterhielt, hat unterhalten to entertain, to amuse
unternehmen (unternimmt), unternahm, hat unternommen to undertake, to venture
das **Unterpfand, -(e)s** pledge, pawn, security
der **Unterschied, -(e)s, -e** difference, distinction
untersuchen to examine, to investigate
das **Unvermögen, -s** inability, incapacity
unwiderruflich irrevocable, irreversible, beyond recall
unwürdig unworthy
die **Ursache, -n** cause, reason, motive, occasion
die **Urtatsache, -n** original fact
der **Urwald, -(e)s, ⸚er** jungle, primeval *or* virgin forest
u.s.w. = und so weiter etc., and so forth

V

der **Vater, -s, ⸚** father
veneratio vitae reverence for life (Latin)
veranlassen to cause, to bring about, to induce
die **Verbindung, -en** union, combination, connection
verbrennen (verbrennt), verbrannte, hat verbrannt to burn up
verbringen (verbringt), verbrachte, hat verbracht to spend, to pass (one's time)
verdächtig suspect, suspicious
verdienen to earn
verdrießlich annoying, vexing, tiresome, troublesome
vereinfacht simplified
vereinigen to unite, to combine
sich verengern to narrow, to shrink
vergangen past, gone
die **Vergangenheit** past, past times
sich vergeben (vergibt sich), vergab sich, hat sich vergeben to compromise oneself
vergeblich (in) vain
vergessen (vergißt), vergaß, hat vergessen to forget
die **Vergessenheit** oblivion
der **Vergleich, -(e)s, -e** comparison, parallel
vergnügt pleased, delighted
das **Verhältnis, -ses, -se** relationship
verheerend devastating
verkaufen to sell
verkündigen to announce, to prophesy, to make known
die **Verlängerung, -en** prolongation, exten-

sion, lengthening
verleugnen to deny, to disavow, to renounce
die **Verlogenheit, -en** untruthfulness, mendacity
die **Vermehrung, -en** increase, multiplication
vermeiden (vermeidet), vermied, hat vermieden to avoid, to shun, to evade
vermissen to miss
das **Vermögen, -s, -** ability, power, means
vermuten to suppose, to suspect
vernichten to destroy, to annihilate
der **Vernichtungskrieg, -(e)s, -e** war of extermination
die **Vernunftgründe** (pl.) reasonable grounds
verpassen to miss, to lose by delay, to let slip
verpflichten to obligate, to oblige
die **Verpflichtung, -en** obligation, duty
versäumen to neglect, to miss, to leave undone
sich verschieben (verschiebt sich), verschob sich, hat sich verschoben to change, to shift
verschieden different, various, distinct
verschleiern to veil, to gloss over, to disguise
verschulden to be the cause of, to be guilty of
die **Versöhnung, -en** reconciliation
versprechen (verspricht), versprach, hat versprochen to promise
der **Verstand, -es** the faculty of reason, understanding, comprehension, discernment, intelligence
das **Verständnis, -ses** understanding, comprehension, appreciation, perception
verstecken to hide, to conceal
verstehen (versteht), verstand, hat verstanden to understand
die **Verstorbene** deceased one (fem.)
versuchen to try, to attempt, to tempt, to entice
versuchsweise by way of experiment, experimental
verteilen to distribute, to divide, to assign
der **Vertrag, -(e)s, ⸚e** treaty
das **Vertrauen, -s** confidence, trust
vervollständigen to complete, to supplement, to complement
verwerflich reprehensible, objectionable
verwüsten to devastate, to wreck, to ravage
verzehren to consume
verzeihen (verzeiht), verzieh, hat verziehen to forgive
verzichten to renounce, to abandon, to give up, to do without
die **Verzweiflung, -en** despair
viel much, many, a great deal
vielleicht perhaps
vielmehr rather
viert fourth
der **Vierte** fourth one (male person)
das **Vierundzwanzig-Stundensystem, -(e)s** twenty-four hour system
vierzehn fourteen
der **Viktualienhändler, -s, -** grocer
das **Volk, -(e)s, ⸚er** people, nation
völkisch national, popular, racial, ethnic, folkish
voll full, full of
vollbringen (vollbringt), vollbrachte, hat vollbracht to accomplish
vollends quite, altogether, entirely, wholly
die **Vollendung, -en** completion
vollführen to execute, to carry out
völlig fully
vollkommen perfect
vollständig complete
von of, from, about, by
vor before, in front of, for, from, in the presence of, ago
vor allem above all
vorbei over, completed
vorbei·wandeln to walk past
vorderhand for the time being, for the present
vor·dringen (dringt vor), drang vor, ist vorgedrungen to advance, to press forward, to make headway
vor·enthalten (enthält vor), enthielt vor, hat vorenthalten to withhold
vorhanden at hand, on hand, ready
das **Vorhandensein, -s** existence, presence
der **Vorhang, -(e)s, ⸚e** curtain
vorher beforehand, before, in advance
vorig last, previous

die **Vorliebe, -n** preference, liking
der **Vormund, -(e)s, -e & ⸚er** guardian, trustee
vornüber-sinken (sinkt vornüber), sank vornüber, ist vornübergesunken to sink forwards
das **Vorrecht, -(e)s, -e** privilege, prerogative, priority
der **Vorschuß, -sses, ⸚sse** (cash) advance
vor·sehen (sieht vor), sah vor, hat vorgesehen to provide for
die **Vorsehung** providence
die **Vorstellung, -en** presentation, performance, representation, notion, idea
vorüber over, past
vor·weisen (weist vor), wies vor, hat vorgewiesen to display, to show

W

wachen to be awake, to watch (over), to care (for)
wachsen (wächst), wuchs, ist gewachsen to grow, to expand
die **Waffe, -n** weapon
der **Waffenstillstand, -(e)s, ⸚e** armistice, cease-fire
wagen to dare
der **Wahlspruch, -(e)s, ⸚e** motto, device
wahr true, real, genuine
während during, while
der **Wahrer, -s, -** guardian (of peace)
wahrhaft true, veracious; (adv.) really
wahrlich truly, certainly
wahrscheinlich probable, probably
die **Währung, -en** currency
sich wälzen to roll around, to wallow
das **Walzwerk, -(e)s, -e** rolling-mill
wandeln (aux. **haben & sein**) to change, to walk, to wander
warten to wait
warum why
was what, whatever
was für what kind of
das **Wasser, -s, -** water
die **Wasserstoffbombe, -n** hydrogen bomb
der **Wechsel, -s, -** alternation, change, rotation
wechseln to vary
weder . . . noch neither . . . nor
der **Weg, -(e)s, -e** way, path, route
das **Weh, -(e)s** misery, woe, pain
sich wehren to resist, to defend oneself
weiblich female, womanly, feminine
die **Weiche** softness
weichen (weicht), wich, ist gewichen to give way, to yield
die **Weihe, -n** consecration, ordination, inauguration
weil because, since
weislich wisely, prudently
weiß white
die **Weißen** (pl.) the white races
weit wide, immense, far-reaching, distant, far
bei weitem by far
noch weiter still further
weiter·bringen (bringt weiter), brachte weiter, hat weitergebracht to bring further
weiter·gehen (geht weiter), ging weiter, ist weitergegangen to continue, to go on
welcher, welche, welches which, what, that
die **Welt, -en** world
das **Weltall, -s** universe
weltberühmt world-famous
weltbewegend earth shaking
der **Weltbrand, -es, ⸚e** universal conflagration
die **Weltgeschichte** world history
der **Weltkrieg, -(e)s, -e** world war
die **Weltliteratur** world literature
die **Weltraumaspiration, -en** space aspiration
die **Weltraumfahrt, -en** space travel
weltzermalmend world-crushing
wenig few, little
wenigstens at least
wenn when(ever), if
wer who, he who, whoever
werden (wird), wurde, ist geworden to become
werfen (wirft), warf, hat geworfen to throw
das **Werk, -(e)s, -e** factory, literary work, work
der **Wert, -(e)s, -e** worth, value
wertvoll valuable, precious
das **Wesen, -s, -** essence, creature

der **Westen, -s** west
westlich western, to the west
das **Wetter, -s, -** weather
wichtig important
die **Wichtigkeit** importance
widersprechen (widerspricht), widersprach, hat widersprochen to disagree, to contradict
der **Widerstand, -(e)s, ⸚e** resistance, obstacle
wie as, like, such, how
wieder again
die **Wiederherstellung** restoration, re-establishment, recovery
wiederholen to repeat
die **Wiedervereinigung, -en** reunification
die **Wiedervereinigungsfrage, -n** question of reunification
Wien Vienna
der **Wiener Vertrag** Vienna Treaty
der **Wille(n), -ns** will
der **Wille zum Leben** the "will-to-live"
winzig tiny
die **Wirkenskraft** actuating force
wirklich real, really, true, truly
wissen (weiß), wußte, hat gewußt to know
das **Wissen, -s** knowledge, learning
die **Wissenschaft, -en** science, learning, knowledge
der **Wissenschaftler, -s, -** scientist, man of science *or* learning
wissenschaftlich scientific, learned, scholarly
die **Witwe, -n** widow
wo where
die **Woche, -n** week
das **Wochenende, -s, -n** week-end
woher from where, how
wohl indeed, well, fit
wohnen to live, to dwell
der **Wohnraum, -s, ⸚e** dwelling space, living room
die **Wohnung, -en** apartment
die **Wolke, -n** cloud
wollen (will), wollte, hat gewollt to want, to will, to intend, to be about to
worin wherein, in which
das **Wort, -es, ⸚er** *or* **-e** word
die **Wundererzählung, -en** miraculous tale, legend
das **Wunderkind, -(e)s, -er** child wonder, prodigy
wunderschön beautiful
der **Wunsch, -es, ⸚e** wish
wünschen to wish, to desire, to long for
wurzellos without roots

X

x-mal ever so many times, over and over again, umpteen times

Z

der **Zahn, -(e)s, ⸚e** tooth
zehn ten
zeigen to show
die **Zeit, -en** time
das **Zeitalter, -s, -** age, era
zeitgenössisch contemporary
zeitlebens for life
zeitlich temporal, transient, secular
der **Zeitungsartikel, -s, -** newspaper article
die **Zeitungsnotiz, -en** newspaper item
das **Zentrum, -s, -tren** center
zerbeißen (zerbeißt), zerbiß, hat zerbissen to bite (to pieces)
zerfallen (zerfällt), zerfiel, ist zerfallen to fall to pieces
zergehen (zergeht), zerging, ist zergangen to disperse, to dissolve
zerlaufen (zerläuft), zerlief, ist zerlaufen to flow, to melt
zermalmen to crush, to bruise, to crunch
zerrinnen (zerrinnt), zerrann, ist zerronnen to melt away, to dissolve, to vanish
zerschneiden (zerschneidet), zerschnitt, hat zerschnitten to cut to pieces *or* through
zerstören to destroy, to demolish
zeugen to produce
ziehen (zieht), zog, hat gezogen to pull, to draw, to tug
das **Ziel, -(e)s, -e** goal, objective
ziemlich pretty, moderate, moderately, fairly, rather
das **Zimmer, -s, -** room
zitieren to summon, to call *or* conjure up, to quote

die **Zivilisation, -en** the civilization
der **Zivilist, -en, -en** civilian
zu too, to, into, at
die **Zucht** discipline, decency, manners, propriety
zueinander towards each other
der **Zufall, -(e)s, ⸚e** chance, accident, coincidence
zufrieden satisfied, content
die **Zufriedenheit** satisfaction, contentment
zu·fügen to add to
der **Zügel, -s, -** rein, bridle
zu·gestehen (gesteht zu), gestand zu, hat zugestanden to concede, to admit, to confess
zugleich simultaneously, also, at the same time
zugrunde gehen (geht zugrunde), ging zugrunde, ist zugrunde gegangen to go to destruction, to perish
zugunsten in favor of, for the benefit of
die **Zukunft** future
zumute sein to feel
zu·nehmen (nimmt zu), nahm zu, hat zugenommen to increase, to grow
zunehmend increasing, growing
sich **zurecht·finden (findet sich zurecht), fand sich zurecht, hat sich zurechtgefunden** to find one's way about
zurück·kehren to return
zurück·leiten to lead back
zurück·schreiben (schreibt zurück), schrieb zurück, hat zurückgeschrieben to write back
zusammen together
zusammen·brechen (bricht zusammen), brach zusammen, ist zusammengebrochen to break down, to collapse (under), to succumb
zusammen·fassen to concentrate, to summarize, to include
zusammen·halten (hält zusammen), hielt zusammen, hat zusammengehalten to hold together, to keep together
zusammen·hängen (hängt zusammen), hing zusammen, hat zusammengehangen to be connected with
zusammen·laufen (läuft zusammen), lief zusammen, ist zusammengelaufen to run together, to blend
die **Zusammenlegung, -en** the combining (of)
das **Zusammenrücken** the moving nearer, the coming together
zu·schauen to watch, to look on
zu·sehen (sieht zu), sah zu, hat zugesehen to look on, to watch
der **Zustand, -es, ⸚e** condition, state, position, situation
zustande bringen (bringt zustande), brachte zustande, hat zustande gebracht to bring about
zuverlässig reliable, certain, trustworthy
zuvor before, formerly
zuweilen at times, now and then, occasionally
zu·wenden (wendet zu), wandte zu or **wendete zu, hat zugewandt** or **zugewendet** to turn towards
zwanzig twenty
zwanzig Jahre vorher twenty years previously
zwar indeed, certainly
zwar . . . jedoch it is true . . . yet
und zwar namely
zwei two
der **Zweifel, -s, -** doubt, disbelief, hesitation
zweifeln to doubt, to have one's doubts about (a thing)
zweit second
der Zweite Weltkrieg the Second World War
zwischen between, among
zwölf twelve
zwölfstündig twelve hour

Index

Index prepared by Virginia M. Coombs.